FOUNDATIONS OF MENTAL HEALTH COUNSELING

Fourth Edition

FOUNDATIONS OF MENTAL HEALTH COUNSELING

Edited by

ARTIS J. PALMO, ED.D.

Bethlehem Counseling Associates, P.C.
Bethlehem, Pennsylvania

WILLIAM J. WEIKEL, PH.D.

Professor Emeritus and Private Practice
Morehead State University
Morehead, Kentucky

DAVID P. BORSOS, PH.D.

Assistant Professor of Psychology
Chestnut Hill College
Chestnut Hill, Pennsylvania

With a Foreword by

Edwin L. Herr, ED.D.

CHARLES C THOMAS • PUBLISHER, LTD.
Springfield • Illinois • U.S.A.

Published and Distributed Throughout the World by

CHARLES C THOMAS • PUBLISHER, LTD.
2600 South First Street
Springfield, Illinois 62794-9265

First Edition, 1986
Second Edition, 1996
Third Edition, 2006
Fourth Edition, 2011

ISBN 978-0-398-08635-0 (hard)
ISBN 978-0-398-08636-7 (paper)
ISBN 978-0-398-08637-4 (ebook)

Library of Congress Catalog Card Number: 2010042536

With THOMAS BOOKS *careful attention is given to all details of manufacturing and design. It is the Publisher's desire to present books that are satisfactory as to their physical qualities and artistic possibilities and appropriate for their particular use.* THOMAS BOOKS *will be true to those laws of quality that assure a good name and good will.*

Printed in the United States of America
MM-R-3

Library of Congress Cataloging in Publication Data

Foundations of mental health counseling / edited by Artis J. Palmo, William J. Weikel, David P. Borsos ; with a foreword by Edwin L. Herr. – 4th ed.
p. cm.
Includes biographical references and index.
ISBN 978-0-398-08635-0 (hard)–ISBN 978-0-398-08636-7 (pbk.)–ISBN 978-0-398-08637-4 (ebook)
1. Mental health counseling–Practice. 2. Mental health counseling. I. Palmo, Artis, J. II. Weikel, William J. III. Borsos, David P.
[DNLM: 1. Counseling–methods. 2. Mental Health. WM 55]

RC466.F68 2011
616.89'14–dc22 2010042536

CONTRIBUTORS

Dr. Casey Barrio Minton is Associate Professor of Counseling and Counseling Program Coordinator at the University of North Texas. A National Certified Counselor and Applied Suicide Intervention Skills Training (ASIST) Trainer, she specializes in crisis intervention, has experience working with adolescents and adults across mental health counseling settings, and has served as director of the Counseling & Human Development Center, a university-based mental health counseling training center. Dr. Minton is active on research teams regarding suicide and crisis, has published multiple journal articles regarding crisis and counselor preparation, and is co-author of a book regarding counselor preparation. She is an active member of state and national counseling associations, where she serves as President-Elect of Chi Sigma Iota (CSI) International, on the Executive Council for the Association for Assessment in Counseling and Education (AACE), and as co-chair of the AACE Task Force regarding CACREP Assessment and Evaluation Guidelines. Dr. Minton is an editorial review board member for *Counseling Outcome Research and Evaluation* and the *Journal of Professional Counseling*, and she serves as an ad hoc reviewer for *Counselor Education & Supervision.*

Dr. David P. Borsos is a licensed psychologist in Pennsylvania. He has treated a wide variety of clinical cases in his 25-year career. These include the "normal" outpatient mood and anxiety disorders, as well as some intense work with addictions and acting-out psychotics staying in community living arrangements. His professional interests these days revolve around integrating the various theories of counseling into a more unified field and teaching others how to do effective therapy.

To this end, Dr. Borsos teaches as an assistant professor in the Master's Program in Clinical and Counseling Psychology at Chestnut Hill College. Here he finds great pleasure in bringing new counselors into the field through such courses as Counseling Techniques, Theories, Psychopathology, Group Counseling, Supervision and other treatment-oriented courses. He also serves as the administrative coordinator for the program. Dr. Borsos looks forward to the day when all counselors and therapists are equally effective and efficient and when going to counseling is as accepted by the public as getting a flu shot.

Lisa A. Brenner, Ph.D. is a Board Certified Rehabilitation Psychologist, an Associate Professor of Psychiatry, Neurology, and Physical Medicine and Rehabilitation at the University of Colorado Denver, School of Medicine, and Director of Education for the VA VISN 19 Mental Illness Research Education and Clinical Center (MIRECC). Dr. Brenner is also the Director of Training for the MIRECC Psychology Post-Doctoral Fellowship program. Her primary area of research interest is traumatic brain injury (TBI) and comorbid psychiatric disorders. Dr. Brenner serves as Member at Large on two national boards: APA Division 22 and the VA Psychology Training Council. She is a member of the Colorado Brain Injury Advisory Board and has consulted with the Colorado Department of Human Services to improve care for persons with TBI receiving treatment in the community mental health system. Dr. Brenner is also a member of the research team at Craig Hospital. She is the Principal Investigator (PI) on grants entitled *Use of a TBI Screen in a Veteran Mental Health Population: Prevalence, Validation and Psychiatric Outcomes* (Colorado Brain Injury Trust Fund, Office of Behavioral Health and Housing) and *Executive Dysfunction and Suicide in Psychiatric Outpatients and Inpatients* (VA Merit Review), and a Co-PI on *A Longitudinal Study of Deployment-Related Mild TBI: Incidence, Natural History, and Predictors of Recovery in Soldiers Returning from OIF/OEF* (Congressionally Directed Medical Research Programs - Intramural TBI Investigator-Initiated Research Award) and *Health and Wellness Intervention for Individuals with TBI* (National Institute on Disability and Rehabilitation Research). Dr. Brenner has numerous peer-reviewed publications and recently co-authored a book chapter entitled "Deployment-Acquired TBI and Suicidality: Risk and Assessment."

JoLynn Carney, Ph.D. is Associate Professor of Counselor Education in the Department of Counseling Education, Counseling Psychology, and Rehabilitation Services at the Pennsylvania State University. She is a Licensed Professional Clinical Counselor who has experience working in community mental health agencies, private practice, and schools. She has been a trustee on a number of boards of directors that service at-risk youth, has served on state-counseling boards, works closely with local school districts, and is a recipient of several service awards from various professional groups. Dr. Carney is the current President-Elect of Chi Sigma Iota International, is chapter faculty advisor, and has served as Regional Chapter Facilitator for the North Atlantic Region. Her research and publishing focus on intervention/prevention aspects of youth violence and adolescent suicide.

Her scholarly work also includes wellness programming and counselor-training techniques. A significant focus is on the psychophysiological influence of chronic bullying on youth. She currently serves on editorial boards of nationally recognized counseling journals, publishes, and runs local, regional, and national trainings/workshops in her areas of expertise.

Stephen Feit, Ed.D., LCPC, NCC, ACS is a Professor of Counseling and past Chair of the Counseling Department at Idaho State University. His areas of interest include Supervision, Professional Identity, and Doctoral Student Career Development. Professionally, he has been President of the Association for Counselor Education and Supervision, a division of the American Counseling Association (ACA). He also is a past Chair of the ACA Ethics Committee. He currently is serving as the Interim Dean of the Kasiska College of Health Professions at Idaho State University.

Marc A. Grimmett, Ph.D. is an associate professor and coordinator for clinical mental health counseling in the counselor education program at North Carolina State University. He earned his doctorate in Counseling Psychology from the University of Georgia and is a Licensed Psychologist. Dr. Grimmett completed a postdoctoral fellowship at the University of South Carolina Counseling and Human Development Center, where his training focused on culturally competent counseling, marriage and family therapy, substance abuse counseling, and sexual abuse counseling. He has more than 10 years of professional mental health experience working in different settings, including university counseling, community mental health, and substance abuse treatment centers, as well as in-home counseling services and private practice. Dr. Grimmett's research focuses on multiculturalism, social justice, and the early career development of African American boys.

Dr. Peter Gutierrez is a clinical/research psychologist with the VA VISN 19's Mental Illness Research, Education, and Clinical Center and Associate Professor in the Department of Psychiatry at the University of Colorado Denver School of Medicine. A licensed psychologist in Colorado, he is an expert in adolescent and young adult suicide assessment, veteran suicide, and psychosocial interventions for suicidal veterans. He is the Principle Investigator on a grant-funded study investigating the impact of medication packaging changes on decreasing accidental and intentional overdoses in high-risk psychiatric patients. He is jointly directing a pending grant-funded military suicide research consortium. Dr. Gutierrez served on the U.S. Army Suicide Reduction and Prevention Research Strategic Planning

Workgroup, as the Soldier Identification and Case Management Expert Lead. He is a past President of the American Association of Suicidology and recipient of their Shneidman Award for outstanding research contributions in suicidology. He is co-author of the 2008 book *Adolescent Suicide: An Integrated Approach to the Assessment of Risk and Protective Factors.* Dr. Gutierrez is an associate editor of the premier journal in the field–*Suicide and Life-Threatening Behavior,* and he regularly reviews for numerous other journals. Previously, Dr. Gutierrez served on the Illinois Suicide Prevention Strategic Planning Task Force convened by the Illinois Department of Public Health. He ran the Adolescent Risk Project, a school-based suicide screening and assessment program at an urban high school for seven years.

Laura K. Harrawood, Ph.D., LCPC, LMFT, NCC has worked in numerous adjunct faculty positions while maintaining an active private practice. Her clinical work has focused on adult childhood survivors of abuse, mood disorders, grief and loss, as well as couple and family relational issues. Currently, she is Assistant Professor of Counseling at Idaho State University, where she teaches courses in the Mental Health Counseling program as well as the Marriage, Couple, and Family program. She is also active in the clinical supervision of Master's, Doctoral, and post-degree students. In addition, she is professionally involved in the Idaho Counseling Association and the Idaho Association for Counselor Education and Supervision.

Laurie Shepherd Johnson is Professor of Counseling and Director of the Graduate Programs in Counseling at Hofstra University in New York. Since 2001, she has also held the Sheelagh Murnaghan Visiting Professorship at Queens University in Belfast, Northern Ireland, where she has taught, consulted, and conducted research on systemic approaches to conflict resolution and reconciliation in this conflict traumatized society. Dr. Johnson also worked as a faculty associate for the United Nations University Institute on Conflict Resolution and Ethnicity studying ethnic conflict in war-torn states. As part of her research on dialogue and narrative approaches toward reconciliation and post-traumatic healing in conflict societies, she has been working most recently on a project with the Quaker Community in West Belfast that is aimed at promoting cross-community contacts between paramilitary families.

She pursued a Fulbright Scholarship to continue her work in Cyprus, another nation traumatized by conflict, starting in 2006. In summer 2004, she presented a workshop at the International Institute on Peace Education in Istanbul on "Creating Safe Places for Cross-Community Dialogue in Divided Societies" and she completed a comparative study of Northern Ireland and Cyprus, which was presented in Jerusalem in June 2005.

Dr. Johnson is certified in bereavement/thanatology and ARC Disaster Mental Health Services. She worked in disaster mental health relief efforts at Ground Zero and has provided bereavement support to the families and children bereaved by the 9/11 World Trade Center terrorist attacks since that time.

Don C. Locke is Distinguished Professor Emeritus of Counselor Education at North Carolina State University. He retired in 2007 following a 42-year career in education. His counselor education career focused on multicultural counseling with special attention to African Americans. He published six books and more than 100 articles during his career. He currently enjoys retirement in the mountains of Western North Carolina.

Dr. Susan C. McGroarty is Assistant Professor of Psychology at Chestnut Hill College. She has a B.A. and Ph.D. from the University of Pennsylvania. Susan's scholarly interests include Post-Traumatic Stress Disorder, diversity, health psychology, and therapist well-being. She has considerable clinical expertise working with children, adolescents and adults in a private practice setting, and she has also conferred with community groups and organizations on issues related to post-traumatic stress and diversity. She serves on the Diversity Committee of NJPA. She is a licensed psychologist and is a member of APA, NJPA, AFTA, and SPSSI.

Dr. Jane E. Myers is Professor of Counselor Education at the University of North Carolina at Greensboro, a National Certified Counselor, a National Certified Gerontological Counselor, and a Licensed Professional Counselor. She is a Fellow of the American Counseling Association and a Charter Fellow of the Chi Sigma Iota Academy of Leaders for Excellence. She is a past President of the American Counseling Association and two of its divisions, the Association for Assessment in Counseling and the Association for Adult Development and Aging, for which she was founding President. Dr. Myers also served as Chair of the Council for Accreditation of Counseling and Related Educational Programs (CACREP) and was the second President of Chi Sigma Iota. In 2003, she was selected for inclusion in *Leaders and Legacies in Counseling,* a book that chronicles the contributions of the 25 individuals selected as among the most significant leaders in the counseling profession over the last century.

Dr. Myers developed a model and curriculum resources for the infusion of gerontological counseling into counselor education, coauthored the national competencies for training gerontological counselors, and co-produced eight training videotapes in gerontological counseling. She has written and edited numerous publications, including 16 books and monographs, more than 125 refereed journal articles, and was noted twice, most recently in 2010, as being in the top 1% of contributors to the *Journal of Counseling & Development,* ACA's flagship journal. Her books include *Adult Children and Aging Parents, Empowerment for Later Life,* the co-authored *Handbook of Counseling, and Developmental Counseling and Therapy: Promoting Wellness Over the Lifespan,* co-authored with Allen and Mary Ivey and Tom Sweeney. She is co-author with Dr. Sweeney of one theoretical and two evidence-based models of wellness and assessment instruments based on these models.

Dr. Spencer Niles is Professor and Department Head for Counselor Education, Counseling Psychology, and Rehabilitation Services at the Pennsylvania State University. He is also Director of the Center for the Study of Career Development and Public Policy at Penn State. He also serves as Vice-President for International Development for Kuder, Inc. Dr. Niles is the recipient of the National Career Development Association's (NCDA) Eminent Career Award, a NCDA Fellow, an American Counseling Association (ACA) Fellow, ACA's David Brooks Distinguished Mentor Award, the ACA Extended Research Award, and the University of British Columbia Noted Scholar Award. He served as President for the National Career Development Association and Editor for *The Career Development Quarterly.* Currently, he is the Editor of the *Journal of Counseling & Development* and has authored or co-authored approximately 100 publications and delivered more than 100 presentations on career development theory and practice. He is an Honorary Member of the Japanese Career Development Association, Honorary Member of the Italian Association for Educational and Vocational Guidance, and a Lifetime Honorary Member of the Ohio Career Development Association.

Dean W. Owen, Jr. is currently a professor at Middle East Technical University in Ankara, Turkey, where he rejoined the faculty following a visiting professorship in 2007. He graduated from the University of Florida in 1977 with a Ph.D. in Counselor Education and holds undergraduate and graduate degrees in Psychology and Rehabilitation Counseling from the University of South Florida in Tampa. In 1977, he joined the graduate faculty of Morehead State University in Morehead, Kentucky where he served for 32 years before retiring and being granted emeritus status in June 2009. He is a licensed professional clinical counselor with more than 34 years of clinical experience. Educational and psychological testing has been one of his principle teaching areas throughout his career. Dr. Owen has extensive foreign teaching experience and twice served as a member of the European Faculty of Boston University. He is an active member of the European Branch of the American Counseling Association. His career has included teaching assignments in Germany, Belgium, England, Spain, Costa Rica, and Turkey.

Dr. Artis "Pete" Palmo is a Licensed Professional Counselor and Licensed Psychologist. He is CEO of Bethlehem Counseling Associates, P.C., a group private practice serving children, adolescents, and adults. He completed graduate training in Counseling at West Virginia University in 1971. He was a Professor of Counseling Psychology at Lehigh University for 17 years, followed by 22 years in private practice. He served various leadership positions in local, state, and national counseling organizations, including President of the Lehigh Valley Psychological Association, President of the Pennsylvania Counseling Association, and served on the boards of the American Counseling Association and the North Atlantic Region of the ACA. In addition, he was an active member of the American Mental Health Counselors Association from the early stages of the organization's development. He served on licensure committees for both Pennsylvania and nationally with ACA. Dr. Palmo has written numerous articles, chapters, and books on a variety of counseling topics. He enjoys writing, sports, and spending time with friends. Along with his wife, Linda, they have two grown children and four grandchildren. They spend their leisure time traveling and playing golf.

Linda A. Palmo, Ed.D. has been in private practice as a Counseling Psychologist since 1980. She completed her doctorate at Lehigh University in 1984. Her work experiences have included being an elementary school teacher and counselor, serving as a counselor for special needs students in the schools, counseling college students, serving as a psychologist for a general hospital and rehabilitation center, and working in a variety of general outpatient agencies. Dr. Palmo was one of the founders of Bethlehem Counseling Associates, P.C. in 1987. She has written articles and chapters on a variety of topics, including an emphasis on family dynamics. She has served as a lecturer at many local, state, and national meetings. She enjoys working with individuals, families, and couples, and she specializes in health psychology, family counseling, and improving client coping skills and self-awareness.

Alishea Rowley is a doctoral student in the counselor education program at North Carolina State University. She earned a Master's degree in counselor education from the University of Central Florida with concentrations in school counseling. Ms. Rowley has more than four years of professional counseling experience in a variety of settings, including work as a school counselor with a specific focus on reducing high school retention rates, individual therapy, family therapy, and in-home counseling services, as well as co-teaching experiences for Master's level counseling courses. Her research interests are African American single mothers and health disparities within the African American community.

Dr. Russell A. Sabella is currently Professor of Counseling in the College of Education, Florida Gulf Coast University, and President of Sabella & Associates. His concentration of research, training, consultation, and publication includes individual and group counseling, counseling technology and tech-literacy, comprehensive school counseling programs, peer helper programs and training, sexual harassment risk reduction, solution-focused brief counseling/consultation, and solution-focused leadership and organizational development.

Dr. Sabella is author of numerous articles published in journals, magazines, and newsletters. He is co-author of two books entitled *Confronting Sexual Harassment: Learning Activities for Teens* (Educational Media, 1995) and *Counseling in the 21st Century: Using Technology to Improve Practice* (American Counseling Association, 2004). He is also author of the popular *SchoolCounselor.com: A Friendly and Practical Guide to the World Wide Web* (2nd edition; Educational Media, 2003); *GuardingKids.com A Practical Guide to Keeping Kids Out of High-Tech Trouble* (Educational Media Corporation, 2008); and well known for his Technology Boot Camp for Counselor workshops conducted throughout the country. Dr. Sabella is past President (2003–2004) of the American School Counselor Association.

He has trained and consulted with thousands of school counselors, educators, parents, and organizational leaders throughout the country.

Mary B. Seay, Ph.D. is currently a middle school counselor with the Allentown School District in Allentown, Pennsylvania. She previously taught in the Department of Psychology for Lehigh University, Muhlenberg College, DeSales University, and Kutztown University. While at Kutztown University, Dr. Seay also taught counseling courses for the Master's Degree programs. Dr. Seay has published in a number of psychology journals. She also has given numerous workshops, paper presentations, and research papers at local and national conferences. Dr. Seay is a member of several professional associations such as the Eastern Psychological Association and the American School Counseling Association.

Thomas A. Seay, Ph.D. is Professor Emeritus of Counseling at Kutztown University in Pennsylvania, after having taught there for more than 30 years. In addition, he is currently Professor and Director of the Master of Social Sciences in Counselling Psychology program at Hong Kong Shue Yan University in Hong Kong, China. Previously, he taught at Austin Peay State University, Southern Illinois University, Allentown College (now DeSales University), Lehigh University, and Chestnut Hill College. He has taught courses in Germany and Austria. He was an invited lecturer to the Diplomatic Academy in Moscow, Russia, and to Hong Kong Shue Yan University, where he was an invited keynote speaker. Over the years he has given many presentations at professional conferences, and he has conducted numerous workshops in the United States, Europe, and Asia. Dr. Seay has numerous journal publications, including two recent publications in one of the Asian counseling journals. He has published several books and monograms. In addition, Dr. Seay is a licensed psychologist and until recently maintained a private practice specializing in family addictions and couples therapy. He is a National Certified Counselor and an Approved Clinical Supervisor with the National Board for Certified Counselors. Also, he is a Clinical Member of the American Association for Marriage and Family Therapy.

Dr. Seay is an Honored Board Member of the Asian Professional Counselling Association. In addition, he is a member of several other professional associations such as the American Counseling Association, Eastern Psychological Association, and the American Association for Marriage and Family Therapists.

Laura R. Shannonhouse is a doctoral student at the University of North Carolina at Greensboro and is a National Certified Counselor specializing in crisis intervention and disaster response. She has participated in culture-centered clinical outreach efforts within the United States (post-Katrina New Orleans and post-earthquake with Haitian communities in Florida), Southern Africa and Botswana (illness-related trauma), and Mexico (prolonged grief work). She has completed a two-year Gestalt Training program and volunteered at the Alachua County Crisis Center, both training and supervising other volunteers. Her experiences with disaster response naturally lend themselves to social justice concerns. Her interest and passion for advocacy and aging developed through her work with marginalized peoples and her desire to make a difference in some small way.

Natalie F. Spencer, MEd, LPC, NCC is a Counselor Education doctoral student at North Carolina State University. She earned her Master's Degree in School Counseling from The University of North Carolina at Chapel Hill, and she is a licensed professional counselor in the state of North Carolina. Ms. Spencer has more than five years of experience as a school counselor and therapist providing services to both children and adults. She has taught undergraduate and Master's-level courses as well as provided supervision to counselors in training. Ms. Spencer's research focuses on multicultural counseling, racial identity, and the academic achievement of gifted/talented African American adolescents.

Dr. Howard B. Smith recently retired as Interim Dean and Professor Emeritus in the College of Education and Counseling at South Dakota State University in Brookings, South Dakota. He is a Nationally Certified Counselor, a Certified Clinical Mental Health Counselor, and a Licensed Professional Counselor in the state of Louisiana. He has private practice experience and has served as Department Head of the Counseling and Human Resource Department at South Dakota State University and the Educational Leadership and Counseling Department at the University of Louisiana–Monroe. Before going back to South Dakota, he was the Associate Executive Director for Professional Affairs at the American Counseling Association (ACA). While at ACA, he also taught as adjunct professor at George Mason University in Fairfax, Virginia.

Dr. Smith has a distinguished career in leadership positions, having served as President of the American Mental Health Counselors Association, and he has chaired numerous Committees of the American Counseling Association. He has received numerous awards, including the prestigious Carl Perkins Award for outstanding service to the profession in the area of public policy. More recently, he and two colleagues received the Experienced Researcher of the Year Award of the British Association for Counseling and Psychotherapy for their work on the American Counseling Association's Practice Research Network. He has extensive experience in the area of Disaster Mental Health and has volunteered for the American Red Cross in response to more than 20 national disasters. He is widely published on a variety of counseling-related topics.

J. Michael Tyler, Ph.D. is Dean of Research at Baker College, Center for Graduate Studies. His research interests and publications cover a number of topics, including technology; small-group behavior; gay, lesbian, bisexual, and transgender issues in counseling and business; and ethics. He has worked in various community mental health and human service settings and worked for ten years as a counselor educator and faculty member in a department of psychology. He is the co-author of *Using Technology to Improve Counseling Practice: A Primer for the 21st Century,* published by the American Counseling Association. Recently, he has become involved in the application of mental health and psychology issues in business settings. In addition, he is increasingly focusing his attention on issues of assessment in business and educational settings.

David Van Doren, Ed.D., LPC, LPsy, CCMHC, MAC, NCC is Associate Professor of Counselor Education at the University of Wisconsin–Whitewater. Dr. Van Doren received his Ed.D. in Counselor Education at the University of Maine in 1981. He has been a counselor educator in Wisconsin for almost three decades. Dr. Van Doren maintains a private practice, which has included working with perpetrators of abuse, as well as others impacted by trauma. He has presented nationally and regionally on childhood maltreatment, the treatment of trauma, and intimate partner violence. Dr. Van Doren is a member of the American Counseling Association, American Mental Health Counselors Association, American Psychological Association, Association for Counselor Education and Supervision, Association for Specialists in Group Work, and International Society for the Study of Trauma and Dissociation.

Erika Wagner-Martin, MS is a counselor who has experience with a wide range of issues, including intimate partner violence, sexual assault and sexual abuse, post-trauma symptoms, anxiety and mood disorders, career exploration, substance abuse, and women's issues. Her clinical interests also include gender identity and sexual orientation, self-empowerment, and family and intimate relationships. Ms. Wagner-Martin received her Master's Degree in Community Counseling at the University of Wisconsin–Whitewater and also holds the National Certified Counselor Credential. Her approach to counseling is holistic, and she is committed to working with clients to honor their needs and build on their strengths in order to live more functional, healthy, and meaningful lives.

William J. Weikel, Ph.D. is Professor Emeritus at Morehead State University in Kentucky. He currently resides in Cape Coral, Florida, where he maintains a part-time consulting practice. He also occasionally teaches as an adjunct professor at Florida Gulf Coast University in the graduate counseling program. Dr. Weikel is an LPCC and has held numerous national certifications. He is a past President of AMHCA and the Kentucky Counseling Association and a past Chair of the Southern Region of ACA. In addition, he has chaired numerous committees in his more than 35-year career for ACA, AMHCA, and KCA. He was the founding editor of the *AMHCA Journal* (*JMHCA*) in 1979 and also editor of the *AMHCA News* (*Advocate*), *KCA Journal,* and *KCA News.* Dr. Weikel has authored or co-authored more than 50 professional articles, monographs, and books. When not involved in counseling activities, he is busy with his business, "Patriot Rare Coin and Currency," specializing in early U.S. coins and obsolete currency. He can be found at many national coin bourses as well as Florida shows.

Hyung Joon Yoon, SPHR is a Ph.D. candidate in Workforce Education and Development at Penn State. He is also an instructor at Penn State, and he teaches a career development course for students in Counselor Education and Workforce Education and Development. Mr. Yoon has developed and/or validated career assessment tools such as the Assessment of Human Agency (AHA) and the Career Flow Index (CFI). In addition, he has created self-actualization-oriented career development models, called Human Agency Based Individual Transformation (HABIT) and the Integrative Cognitive Information Processing (ICIP). He also has been involved in the development of the Hope Centered Career Development theory with Dr. Spencer Niles. He has presented his work at National Career Development Association (NCDA) and Academy of Human Resource Development (AHRD) conferences.

Dr. Palmo dedicates this edition to his wife, Linda, whose encouragement and support make these professional accomplishments possible. He also wants to dedicate this work to Dr. Harold "Doc" Whitmore, his mentor, and Mr. Jack Superka, his friend and colleague. Both of these men were outstanding professionals, committed friends, and wonderful sources of laughter. Although the two of them will not be able to understand this dedication, it is important for Dr. Palmo to honor their accomplishments and mourn the loss of their companionship.

Dr. Weikel dedicates his work on the latest edition of this book to AMHCA pioneers and friends for 35 years: Dr. Ed Beck, Dr. Bill Krieger, Dr. Pete Palmo, Dr. Gary Seiler, and Dr. Howard Smith, and to both Dr. David Brooks and Mr. Robert Rencken (deceased). Without these people and a handful more, there would be no book and no profession of mental health counseling. Dr. Weikel would also like to thank his wife, Vanessa, children, Bill and Amanda, and granddaughter, Kaitlyn, for their love and support.

Dr. Borsos dedicates his work to Ethan, his parents, and his grandparents. You know who you are.

FOREWORD

The importance of mental health counseling has grown, as has the array of mental health issues that arise in an uncertain and a fragile world. As chronicled in this book, mental health counseling has evolved and matured across the four editions that have been published. Each edition has included new terrain that needs to be described and its treatment explained. Among the expanded content addressed to currently important topics in mental health counseling are those focused on the effects of terrorism and trauma and individual recovery and treatment. Each day, as more military personnel are committed by the United States and its allies to conflicts in Iraq and Afghanistan, as well as the uncertainty military and civilian populations experience in the non-violent but stressful and abusive relationships among nations, the need for more mental health counselors increases.

Regardless of the impact on mental health of the conflicts present among nations around the world, this book is not primarily about terrorism or trauma. It is also about the widening range of mental health issues that are now within the scope of treatments provided by mental health counselors. They include intimate partner violence, substance abuse, career counseling, mental health and aging, multiculturalism, and cultural conflict.

As suggested earlier, mental health counseling has evolved over the four editions of this book and, in doing so, has "come of age." "Coming of age" means, as a central point, that mental health counselors have created, refined, and strengthened their professional identities. In doing so, they have differentiated themselves from other groups of mental health providers and focused on what they, as mental health counselors, can contribute to achieving mental health for those suffering from mental health problems.

The rise to professional maturity, to the "coming of age" as a profession, requires an understanding of the history of mental health counseling, the barriers it has surmounted as a profession, and the trends that have motivated its particular characteristics. More than half of the chapters in this book address the tools and constructs that undergird mental health counseling. They include the role of theory, assessment, research, ethics, and technology, and the preparation of mental health counselors. Each of these chapters addresses what is different in each of these bodies of knowledge, as well as their integration to create the professional identity of mental health counselors. This identity is forged and reinforced in the work settings and the private practices in which mental health counselors are primarily employed.

Foundations of Mental Health Counseling (Fourth Edition) provides a comprehensive view of this important profession. The content of the book brings together multiple sources of knowledge: historical perspectives, conceptual models, the settings and clientele served by mental health counselors, the mental health issues that are dominant, the interventions used, and the professional identity and credentialing of mental health counselors. This information, while of major importance to mental health counselors, can also be useful to other mental health providers as they ponder the field and the ways in which they can collaborate with mental health counselors.

Foundations of Mental Health Counseling (Fourth Edition) is a unique book. It includes an excellent group of authors from a variety of settings to demonstrate the need for, the range, and the complexity of mental health counseling. Edited books rarely have a unified and an integrated structure. However, this book is an exception. It is well edited, the authors write well and with authority, and they do so from a number of important vantage points. The various chapters probe, with insight and relevance, major contemporary issues facing mental health counselors today.

Clearly, mental health counseling has "come of age." Over the last 20 or so years, the profession has won important legislative and professional victories, including 50 state statutes providing licensure for professional counselors. The place of mental health counselors among mental health providers is secure, and all of the elements required to achieve professional identity and professional excellence are in place. Every mental health counselor will be enriched by this book's analyses of the legacies of the past, the present, and the future. I endorse it without reservation.

EDWIN L. HERR
Distinguished Profesor Emeritus
The Pennsylvania State University
University Park, Pennsylvania

PREFACE

It has been 25 years since the original edition of *Foundations of Mental Health Counseling* was published. During that time, there have been countless positive changes in the field of mental health, including counselor licensure in all 50 states and the recognition of licensed professional counselors by managed care organizations and insurance companies. The field of professional counseling has developed and grown beyond the authors' expectations, becoming the true "fifth core mental health provider" as described in the First Edition of the book.

The First Edition highlighted the new mental health counselor, the Second Edition focused on the push to put the profession to the forefront of mental health care, and the Third Edition celebrated the profession's accomplishments. The Fourth Edition focuses on an in-depth examination of the field of mental health counseling, demonstrating the depth and breadth of professional counseling, from theory to practice issues, technology to humor in everyday practice, professional identity to diversity and multiculturalism, and much, much more.

Once again, the latest edition has been totally revised to reflect the status of professional counseling at this time. We have added 12 new authors in this Fourth Edition, all of whom have contributed to providing an up-to-date text for the student starting a career in professional counseling. Roughly 93% of the book has been rewritten and updated, providing the most comprehensive book on professional counseling anywhere.

As a special note, in the Fourth Edition, we have expanded the highly acclaimed section entitled "The Professional Counselor in a World of Uncertainty." We added a highlight section covering the stress faced by our military personnel and the role that mental health professionals can play in assisting the combat veterans to reintegrate back into the community. Also in this section, we added a chapter on "Trauma Counseling," an important aspect of professional counselors' role in their work with clients. There are improved and expanded chapters on career counseling, ethics, partner violence, multiculturalism, counselor preparation, and technology. The editors have also expanded the final chapter of the book, "The Future of Professional Counseling," to include a more comprehensive examination of what the future may bring to bear on the profession.

Finally, the editors want to thank all of the professional authors who contributed to our latest efforts. Through the hard work and dedication of these authors, we have been able to develop a book that provides Master's- and Doctoral-level counseling students complete and accurate information regarding the field they have chosen to enter. We also thank the staff at Charles C Thomas for their input, patience, and guidance in the compilation of this book. As we have done with each of this book's editions, we thank those professional men and women who have nurtured, guided, and pulled the field of professional counseling to the highest level possible. We dedicate this Fourth Edition to all of those professionals who offered and gave so much to the field of counseling and now face the end of their careers. The three of us have been privileged to work with many of the professionals (several are authors in this Fourth Edition) who brought the field of counseling from infancy to adulthood–we thank all of them!

A.J.P.
A.J.W.
D.P.B.

CONTENTS

SECTION V–LICENSURE, CREDENTIALING, AND LEGISLATION RELATED TO MENTAL HEALTH COUNSELING

SECTION VI–ASSESSMENT, RESEARCH, ETHICS, CURRICULUM, AND TRENDS IN MENTAL HEALTH COUNSELING

FOUNDATIONS OF MENTAL HEALTH COUNSELING

Section I

MENTAL HEALTH COUNSELING IN A HISTORICAL PERSPECTIVE

Chapter 1

PROFESSIONAL COUNSELING COMES OF AGE: THE FIRST 35 YEARS

HOWARD B. SMITH AND WILLIAM J. WEIKEL

In Memory of and with Appreciation to David K. Brooks, Jr.

In an organized sense, mental health counseling is a young discipline. At the time of this writing, the profession is not quite age 35, but it remains a dynamic discipline, where there is still active debate about professional identity, role, function, and professional preparation. When the history of mental health counseling is written in a more definitive fashion than is possible in 2010, the past and present generation of activists and true believers may discover that their professional careers have paralleled most of the profession's significant milestones and that they have had a hand in shaping their own destinies and that of their profession. Practitioners in few other fields have been able to make this claim. These first 30+ years have been dominated by establishing an identity, credentials, and recognition for the profession. Although these three dominant tasks are not yet complete, it is impossible to know what will evolve in the next 35 years. Thus, the history of mental health counseling is still very much in the process of becoming.

Although the profession is rather young, mental health counseling did not emerge full blown in 1976 with no previous history. A number of antecedents led to the founding of the American Mental Health Counselors Association (AMHCA) in that year, and certainly there were many individuals who were practicing mental health counselors (MHCs) before they began to apply the title to themselves and their work. These antecedents do not form a traceable and purposeful historical path, but each may be considered an essential thread, without which the fabric of the profession would be less than whole.

HISTORICAL ANTECEDENTS

The beginnings of contemporary approaches to the treatment of mental and emotional disorders are usually traced to the late 18th century. Prior to that time, persons suffering from mental and emotional disorders were either confined in asylums with wretched conditions and no systematic treatment or lived as itinerant paupers, driven from town to town. Earlier still, mental illness had been viewed as a spiritual disorder resulting from demonic possession and curable only by exorcism or burning at the stake.

Moral Treatment

The event usually credited with bringing about a change in attitude toward mental illness was the appointment in 1793 of Philippe Pinel as director of the Bicetre, the largest mental hospital in Paris. The French Revolution was in full flower, and Pinel brought the principles of "liberty, equality, and fraternity" to his new task. One of his first acts was to release the inmates from their chains. To the surprise of his critics, Pinel's reforms worked. He forbade corporal punishment and used physical restraint only when his patients presented a danger to themselves or others. He introduced his methods to the Salpetriere, a hospital for women, when he was made director there in 1795. Pinel later wrote an influential book on institutionalized treatment, in which he developed a system for classifying various disorders and advocated the use of occupational therapy as an adjunct to treatment. He kept detailed statistics on the patient populations in his charge, and his claims of cure rates resulting from his methods are impressive even by contemporary standards (Murray, 1983).

At about the same time, William Tuke, a Quaker, founded the York Retreat in England. Although this was in many respects a utopian community, the Retreat focused on providing a restful, orderly environment in which those suffering from emotional disorders could return to normal functioning.

During the first half of the 19th century in the United States, a number of reformers, most notably Dorothea Dix, were successful in founding private asylums and state hospitals operated on humane principles similar to those advanced by Pinel and Tuke. These highly structured environments emphasized the removal of distressed persons from their families or other accustomed settings, manual labor, regular religious devotions, and systematic educational programs aimed at redirecting thought patterns and teaching self-control. This combination of what would be known today as milieu therapy and psychoeducational programming represented a significant alternative to both the medical and custodial models of treatment. Crucial to the success of these institutions was the role of the attendants as models of appropriate behavior (Sprafkin, 1977).

Following the Civil War, however, there was a dramatic change in patterns of institutionalized care. The state asylums were required to accept a broader range of patients, including alcoholics, the criminally insane, and apparently deranged immigrant paupers. The generation of antebellum reformers had done an inadequate job of choosing and training their successors. Thus, as they retired or died, new hospital superintendents were installed who were unfamiliar with the humanitarian ideals of their predecessors. Levels of funding declined from both public and private sources. Furthermore, the medical model of treatment reasserted itself as medicine became a more organized discipline. As Sprafkin (1977) points out, these factors combined to seal the doom of moral treatment approximately 75 years after it began.

During the next half century, conditions related to the care of the institutionalized mentally ill declined steadily. For all intents, state hospitals and most of the private asylums were little more than warehouses for society's castoffs. Once committed, patients rarely emerged to reenter anything resembling a normal life. A significant and most fortunate exception to this pattern was Clifford W. Beers, who had spent much of his youth and early adulthood in a series of institutions. In 1908, Beers published *A Mind That Found Itself,* an autobiographical account of his experiences in mental hospitals. The heightened public interest created by his book led Beers to found the National Committee for Mental Hygiene in 1909. This organization acted as an advocate for the humane treatment of the mentally ill and was the forerunner of the present National Mental Health Association. These groups have had a powerful, positive impact on public policy related to mental health issues for the last century.

Clifford Beers' early efforts in the area of mental health reform occurred during the Progressive Era, a period of American history characterized by intense activity in a variety of social concerns. Progressive reformers directed their energies toward economic justice by the passage of antitrust legislation and toward improving the lot of the urban poor by the founding of settlement houses, among other activities. Beer's ideas fell on fertile ground during this period.

Vocational Guidance

Youth unemployment was a major problem at the turn of the 20th century. Frank Parsons, another Progressive reformer, focused his energies in this area, working first at the Bread Winners Institute, which was operated by a settlement house, and later founding the Boston Vocational Bureau. Parsons was one of the first to be aware of the tremendous change in occupational choices presented by rapid industrialization coupled with the social dislocation created by the movement of entire families from failed farms to the burgeoning cities. This experience was particularly bewildering for older boys who had been accustomed to working on the farms and whose potential wages were needed for family support, but who found that they lacked both the skills and the needed orientation to an industrialized workplace (Whiteley, 1984).

The purpose of the Boston Vocational Bureau, founded in 1908, was to work with young men to match their interests and aptitudes with appropriate occupational choices. Parsons described his procedures in *Choosing a Vocation* (1909), a short and straightforward work that details a process of interviewing, rudimentary motor skills testing, and providing information about various occupations. Frank Parsons died shortly after founding the Vocational Bureau and before his book was published, but his efforts led to the first national conference on vocational guidance in 1910, sponsored by the Boston Chamber of Commerce (Whiteley, 1984). Later, in 1913, the National Vocational Guidance Association (NVGA) was founded to foster vocational guidance services in schools and to encourage the advancement of this new profession by providing a forum for the exchange of ideas among practitioners.

Moral treatment and vocational guidance are the two major historical antecedents of the mental health counseling movement. Moral treatment is crucial for its emphasis on the potential of disturbed persons for recovery and its early anticipation of psychoeducational methods as viable treatment modalities. Vocational guidance is important for its establishment of the role of the professional counselor, although much of that original role has changed and expanded in the years since. In the same sense that the Progressive Era's settlement houses gave birth to the profession of social work, the early vocational guidance programs often found in these same institutions were the incubator of modern mental health counseling.

ANTECEDENTS IN PROFESSIONAL PRACTICE

In addition to moral treatment and vocational guidance, there were a number of other antecedents necessary to the development of mental health counseling. Among these were advances in testing and assessment technologies, the emergence of nonmedical approaches to psychotherapy, research and theory building focused on normal human development, innovations in group counseling and psychotherapy, and the development of psychoeducational approaches to treatment. Each of these antecedents in professional practice is sketched briefly in this section.

Testing and Assessment

Prior to the early years of the 20th century, estimation of human abilities and aptitudes was based largely on speculation about the relationship between intelligence and heredity. Educational achievement of the time was more closely related to socioeconomic status than to intellectual ability, with the "sons of riches" (Green, 1985) almost always receiving a superior education regardless of their level of mental ability.

Two French psychologists, Alfred Benet and Theodore Simon, were commissioned by their government to study ways of detecting measurable differences between normal and retarded children so that placement into special education programs would be facilitated for those who needed such experiences. Their work resulted in a series of standardized tasks that could be performed by children of different mental ages. The concept of mental age led to the development of the intelligence quotient (IQ) as a standard measure of intellectual ability.

This was the beginning of widespread and sustained activity in testing and assessment that has continued throughout the years. Group intelligence tests emerged with the United States' entry into World War I and became a fixture in the public schools shortly thereafter. Tests of specific aptitudes were first developed for selection of streetcar motormen in 1912 and now measure everything from musical ability to clerical speed. Vocational interest measurement achieved statistical respectability and acquired greater utility through the work of E. K. Strong and G. Frederic Kuder.

Personality assessment is yet another area in which measurement specialists have been extremely active. The first objective personality test was developed by Edward Elliott in 1910. The publication of the Minnesota Multiphasic Personality Inventory (MMPI) by McKinley and Hathaway (1940) paved the way for the systematic application of standardized measures to the diagnosis of mental and emotional disorders. Another category of personality measures is projective instrumentation, the most prominent of which are the Rorschach inkblot test, first published in 1921, and the Thematic Apperception Test, initially developed in1938.

As pointed out by Brooks and Weikel (1996), advances have been made in clinical assessment as well. Despite the present sophistication of both objective and projective measures, mental health practitioners in several disciplines have found that such approaches are often insufficient to adequately diagnose a client's difficulties. The multiaxial scheme presented in the fourth edition of the *Diagnostic and Statistical Manual of Mental Disorders* (American Psychiatric Association, 1994) is widely used, as are a variety of behavioral assessment procedures.

Perhaps the most challenging assessment issue confronting mental health counselors and allied professionals involves evaluation of treatment outcomes. Demonstrated therapeutic effectiveness is being demanded by government funding sources, private insurance carriers, and managed care plans. Research that has been underway for nearly three decades continues to attempt to more accurately describe what happens in the process of behavior change and to measure its progress in both process and outcome dimensions. One of the most promising methods of gathering these data comes in the form of Practice Research Networks (PRNs). This method of data gathering, first initiated by the American Psychiatric Association in the early 1990s, is now being developed by virtually all mental health care provider professions. It provides a method of gathering information on predetermined data elements by practitioners and measuring the efficacy of treatment in terms of client outcomes directly from the clients themselves.

Nonmedical Approaches to Psychotherapy

Prior to World War II, psychotherapy was practiced almost exclusively by psychiatrists or nonphysician therapists who relied on medical models of treatment. *Counseling and Psychotherapy* (1942) was the first of several works in which Carl Rogers, a clinical psychologist by training, advocated client-centered therapy, now known as the person-centered approach. Rogers had no use for diagnostic labels or prescriptive methodologies. It was his conviction that individuals, regardless of how bizarre their symptoms might appear, have within themselves the resources for positive behavior change. He stressed that the conditions of the relationship between counselor and client are the primary medium through which such change occurs. It is difficult to imagine an approach to psychotherapy that is more at variance with the traditional medical model.

The various behavior therapies have been almost as influential as Rogers, although they differ considerably from his basic tenets. Based on principles of learning and conditioning, the behavior therapies view emotional disorder as the result of faulty learning. Because maladaptive behavior has been learned, it can be unlearned and replaced with new behaviors that are more advantageous to the individual. A more recent version is cognitive-behavioral therapy, which emphasizes the role of cognitions as mediators between stimulus and response.

The postwar era has witnessed the propagation of a number of other nonmedical approaches. Although none of these has had the widespread impact of the person-centered approach or the behavior therapies, each of them claims a substantial number of adherents. Among these are reality therapy, gestalt therapy, humanistic-existentialist therapies, transactional analysis, rational-emotive-behavioral therapy (a type of cognitive-behavioral therapy), family systems approaches, neurolinguistic programming, narrative therapy, and solution-focused brief therapy.

One powerful mitigating circumstance on all of these approaches has been the managed care phenomenon. The influence of managed care on these approaches has had at least two profound results because of the conflicting philosophies of mental health care and the managed care environment. Mental health care has the driving philosophy of doing whatever it takes for as long as it takes to affect some level of cure or positive growth in the client. Managed care, in contrast, is driven by its bottom line motive of minimum necessary care. They want the client to return to functioning and work as soon as possible. They do not reimburse for rapport building or what we might call "personal growth," only for the minimum necessary for a return to productivity. This has led to the growing popularity of the solution-focused and other brief therapies.

Theories of Normal Human Development

Increased research and theory building in the area of abnormal human behavior accompanied the emergence of psychology as a scientific discipline in the late 19th century. Normal development, with the exception of inquiry into sensation and perception, was not regarded as worthy of scientific study. Although Sigmund Freud (1905/1953, 1923/1961) posited the first comprehensive theory of human development, his interest was in psychopathology not normal behavior.

Jean Piaget (1896–1980) was a Swiss developmental psychologist whose work forms a foundation for much of what is currently accepted about normal human development. Most of Piaget's research was concentrated on the cognitive development of young children, but more recent investigators have applied some of his basic principles to other areas of human functioning as well as tracking developmental processes across the lifespan. Examples of this activity include Kohlberg's (1973) stages of moral development, Perry's (1970) formulations of intellectual and ethical development in college students, and Selman's (1976, 1977) studies of social perspective-taking in young children.

Closely related to the cognitive-developmental school is the work of Jane Loevinger (1976) in ego development. Focusing on the ego as the "master trait," Loevinger's research has resulted in the identification of 10 stages of ego development. According to Rodgers (1980), cognitive-developmental theorists (including Loevinger) focus on the "how" of human development, whereas psychosocial developmental theorists concern themselves with the "what." Erik Erikson was the best-known theorist of the psychosocial group.

For him, lifespan development consisted of eight developmental crises, each of which involves resolution of a crisis of polar opposite dimensions of an individual's life (Brooks & Weikel, 1996).

It should be apparent that there is much diversity of opinion among the various theorists as to what constitutes normal development. There are some common elements or themes that tend to tie the various schools together. Most of the theorists agree that the interaction between person and environment is critical to satisfactory development in virtually all dimensions. There is also general agreement about the presence of a motivating force or organizing structure at work within the individuals. With respect to the nature of the developmental process, most theorists agree that within normal individuals, development is relatively orderly, sequential, generally stage-related but not necessarily age-related, and cumulative, and it proceeds from simple to complex structures and/or operations (Brooks, 1984). These common themes allow the sketching of a rough model of normal human behavior that is descriptive of development at various points along the lifespan depending on which theory one is using as a referent. Practitioners may thus assess their clients according to multiple dimensions of functioning.

Group Counseling and Psychotherapy

Like several of the antecedents discussed thus far, the origins of group counseling and psychotherapy can also be traced to the early years of the 20th century. According to Gazda (1982), the earliest application of the group medium for treatment purposes was in 1905 when J. H. Pratt used group meetings to instruct tuberculosis patients in hygienic practices. Although Pratt originally began this practice to save time, he noticed that the effects of group interaction tended to increase the attention patients paid to his instructions. Another American pioneer was L. C. Marsh, who used a variety of group techniques to treat hospitalized schizophrenics. Marsh's motto, "By the crowd they have been broken; by the crowd they shall be healed" (quoted in Gazda, 1982, p. 9), summarized the beliefs of many pioneers in group counseling and psychotherapy.

It might be expected that the Viennese psychiatric schools would have contributed to the early development of therapeutic group work, and, indeed, this was the case. As early as 1921, Alfred Adler, who had previously broken with Freud and established his own system of psychotherapy, was conducting therapeutic interviews with children before audiences of his fellow therapists. Although he initiated this practice for purposes of training, Adler noticed differences in the progress made by his young clients in the presence of a group. He began to involve the group more in the interview process and developed what would today be known as multiple therapy (i.e., more than one therapist working with a client simultaneously). Adler's followers in the United States have modified his practices to incorporate family therapy into the group interview process (Brooks & Weikel, 1996).

Jacob Moreno was another Viennese therapist who began his work with groups of prostitutes. Immigrating to the United States in 1925, he was extremely influential in the development of modern group therapy, coining the term in 1932 (Gazda, 1982). Moreno is principally known for his work in psychodrama, "an extension of group psychotherapy in which there is not just verbalization but the situation is acted out in as realistic a setting as possible" (Moreno & Elefthery, 1982, p. 103). Although Moreno's name is synonymous with psychodrama, it was several years before he was given credit for his influence in the development of a number of other approaches to group work.

There are at present group applications for virtually every major system of individual counseling and psychotherapy. The range of therapeutic possibilities open to counselors and clients is thus expanded by the tremendous activity in the group work arena over the past 90 years and particularly those developments of the past four decades.

Mental health counseling has been especially influenced by developments in group counseling and psychotherapy because much of the research, theory building, and practice of the last 40 years have been done by individuals primarily identified with the counseling profession. The works of George Gazda, Merle Ohlsen, Walter Lifton, Don Dinkmeyer, and Gerald Corey are standard reading in virtually every graduate counseling program.

Psychoeducational Approaches to Treatment

As was shown to be the case with group counseling and psychotherapy, it is difficult to pinpoint the exact beginnings of psychoeducational approaches to treatment. Most writers agree that such approaches did not exist in the professional literature prior to the 1960s. Several commentators (Authier, Gustafson, Guerney, & Kasdorf, 1975; Gazda & Brooks, 1985) emphasize the impact of Carl Rogers and his associates (Rogers, Gendlin, Kiesler, & Truax, 1967) in specifying the conditions under which behavior change is most likely to occur. Authier et al. (1975) also recognize the role played by Skinner and his fellow behaviorists in providing the basis for the technology of psychoeducational approaches.

Regardless of their origins, psychoeducational approaches are different from other approaches to treatment in that they emphasize the client as learner rather than as patient and cast the role of the mental health professional as teacher rather than as healer. In other words, such approaches are the antithesis of the medical model. Often called "training-as-treatment," these approaches assume that the client is merely deficient in skills needed for effective living, rather than being sick and in need of a cure. The counselor's task, therefore, is to teach the necessary skills in a systematic way so that they can be applied not only to the presenting problem but generalized to other areas of the client's life as well.

An impressive array of skills training programs and packages has emerged in the past 40 years. Included among these have been programs in interpersonal communication skills (Carkhuff, 1969a, 1969b; Egan, 1982; Gazda, Asbury, Balzer, Childers, & Walters, 1984; Ivey & Authier, 1978), assertiveness training (Alberti & Emmons, 1970; Galassi & Galassi, 1977; Lange & Jakubowski, 1976), relaxation training (Bernstein & Borkovec, 1973; Benson, 1975), and rational thinking (Ellis & Harper, 1975). More recently, we have training for individuals who are first responders to disasters or crises using critical incident stress debriefing (Mitchell, 1983).

Professionals identifying themselves as mental health counselors were not involved in the development of all of these training programs, but the impact of these programs on the practice of mental health counseling has been profound. It would be difficult to find mental health counselors, except perhaps those of an orthodox psychoanalytic orientation, who did not use psychoeducational methods in their work with clients. This is not to say that these approaches constitute the major component of a mental health counselor's skills, but they have found favor in dealing with such client issues as stress management, low self-esteem, poor social interactions, or bothersome and counterproductive reactions to crisis situations. There is little doubt that the practice of mental health counseling would be difficult if psychoeducational skills training methodologies had not been developed.

LEGISLATION AND PUBLIC POLICY

So far, this chapter has traced historical and professional practice precursors that were necessary for the emergence of mental health counseling in the late 1970s. These antecedents were the result of both societal trends and movements and professional advances within the mental health disciplines. To have major impact, however, both societal phenomena and significant shifts in treatment must find expression in political actions. It is therefore safe to say that mental health counseling would probably not have developed at all had it not been for a series of legislative initiatives spanning more than half a century. It is almost equally certain that the future development of mental health counseling depends to a considerable extent on the outcome of future legislative decisions.

Legislation Affecting the Development of the Counseling Profession

Professional counseling received its initial legislative mandate in the Smith-Hughes Act of 1917. The National Vocational Guidance Association had been founded four years earlier, and youth unemployment was still a major social priority. The Smith-Hughes Act, like its predecessors the Morrill Acts of 1862 and 1890, represented a major federal excursion into education funding, a matter traditionally left to the states. Although the intent of Smith-Hughes was focused on funding vocational education program, a section of the law provided for vocational guidance programs in public schools. Vocational guidance was supported by at least three other vocational education acts prior to World War II. Among the key provisions of these acts was funding for vocational guidance leadership positions within state departments of education. Such funding was continued well into the 1970s. Following World War II, Congress enacted legislation providing for veterans' educational benefits that included funds for vocational guidance services. These benefits were later extended to veterans of the Korean conflict (Brooks & Weikel, 1996).

Federal legislative initiatives in support of vocational guidance were important for the future development of mental health counseling because such acts reinforced the professionalization of counseling and provided funds for the delivery of counseling services. The fact that counselors focused almost entirely on vocational issues during this time is less important than the emergence of counseling prior to 1950 as a unique human services profession.

The impact of counseling in educational settings was further enhanced by the passage of the National Defense Education Act (NDEA) of 1958. This act provided a major funding source for school-based counseling services and for university programs to train counselors. Passed in part as a reaction to the launching of the Sputnik satellite by the former Soviet Union, NDEA was designed to help the United States overcome what were perceived as serious educational deficiencies. Of particular concern was the relatively low number of youth expressing interest in careers in mathematics and the physical sciences. Remedies supported by NDEA included a testing program to identify students with math and science abilities. Test results were to be used to "counsel" promising students to enter these career fields. Other titles of the act provided support for vastly expanded secondary school guidance programs and for university-sponsored institutes to train new counselors to staff these programs. Many of the more than 600 graduate counselor education programs that are training mental health counselors today originated as a result of NDEA funding to train secondary school counselors.

The NDEA was renewed and amended in 1964, with new titles aimed at the support of counseling programs in elementary schools and community colleges. Funds for counseling socially and economically disadvantaged students, especially at the elementary school level, were provided by the Elementary and Secondary Education Act (ESEA) of 1965. The Emergency School Assistance Act (ESAA) of 1971 funded additional school counselors to assist in the desegregation of school districts. Later in that decade, the Education Amendments of 1976 (PL 94-142) strengthened the role of counseling in vocational education programs and authorized an administrative unit for counseling and guidance in the U.S. Office of Education. Although a few more recent federal initiatives have provided funding for school counseling programs, none of these can be construed as having an impact on the development of mental health counseling.

The importance of NDEA and subsequent federal education legislation to mental health counseling lies in the impact of these laws on counselor education programs and on the economics of supply and demand as it affected counseling positions. Encouraged by federal funding and supplemented by other funding sources, schools and colleges of education were turning out counselors at rates that showed little regard for the demands of the marketplace. Birthrates were declining by the late 1960s, a phenomenon that resulted in lower school enrollments. The drain on national resources created by the combination of federal spending on the Vietnam War and on the Great Society social initiatives (Lyndon Johnson's promise that the nation could afford both guns and butter) led to an economic recession in the early 1970s that took its toll on public school budgets. The combined effect of counselor oversupply and the reduced number of school counselor positions was predictable: Those counselors entering the field increasingly found positions in nonschool settings (Brooks & Weikel, 1996). A quiet revolution was begun, to which we return later.

In the more recent past, several pieces of federal legislation that have had an impact on mental health counselors serve as examples that mental health counseling is still active in shaping public policy. In 1996, the Mental Health Parity Act established minor federal requirements on the coverage of mental health services by most private sector health plans. The 1997 Balanced Budget Act included language prohibiting Medicaid and Medicare managed care programs from discriminating against providers on the basis of their type of license. Perhaps the legislation that had the greatest impact on practice was the 1998 Health Insurance Portability and Accountability Act (HIPAA), which led to the development of federal health information privacy standards affecting all health care delivery in the United States. Also in 1998, the Health Professions Education Partnership Act established Licensed Professional Counselor (LPC) eligibility for an array of federal health professional training and support programs. In 2000, the Department of Defense authorization act set up a TRICARE demonstration project allowing LPCs to practice independently under the TRICARE Programs. Finally, the Veterans Benefits Healthcare and Information Technology Act of 2006 seems to be opening the door for MHCs to practice within the Veterans Affairs (VA) system. Negotiations for this expansion are being held among the administration, ACA, AMHCA, NBCC, AAMFT, and others as this chapter is being written.

Legislation Affecting the Delivery of Mental Health Services

The National Committee for Mental Hygiene (NCMH), founded by Clifford Beers during the Progressive Era, was quite active in improving mental hygiene education and patient treatment prior to and immediately following World War I. The National Mental Health Association, the successor to NCMH, along with professional organizations representing a variety of mental health disciplines, has been a persuasive advocate for mental health legislation in the period since World War II. The National Mental Health Act was passed in 1946, authorizing the establishment of the National Institute of Mental Health (NIMH). The NIMH has in turn supported the training of psychiatrists, clinical and counseling psychologists, and psychiatric nurses.

The Joint Commission on Mental Illness was established by the National Mental Health Study Act of 1955. The findings of the commission provided the basis for congressional passage of the Community Mental Health Centers Act of 1963. This act provided federal funds to states to plan, construct, and staff community mental health centers and to develop multidisciplinary treatment teams of professionals and paraprofessionals. Funding extensions were passed in 1965, 1970, and 1975, each of which expanded services to a broader population.

The Carter Administration's commitment to improvement of mental health services was first manifested in the 1978 report of the President's Commission on Mental Health, chaired by First Lady Rosalynn Carter. The report revealed problems and inadequacies in the mental health services delivery system and emphasized the need for community-based services, including long- and short-term care, access to continuity of care, changes to meet the needs of special populations, and adequate financing. Also addressed was the tension among the mental health professions. The Mental Health Systems Act of 1980 was based on the commission's recommendations and emphasized "balanced services," with appropriate attention to both preventive and remedial programs. This legislation mandated new services for children, youth, the elderly, minority populations, and the chronically mentally ill. The act was repealed almost before the ink was dry as the result of severe federal budget cuts for social programs during the first year of the Reagan Administration.

Federal mental health legislation since 1963 has been important to the development of mental health counseling for two reasons. First, the gradual evolution of models for community-based care of persons formerly housed in state hospitals has had profound effects on these individuals and their families as well as society at large. These effects will be dealt with in more detail in the next section. Second, the emergence of the community mental health center has provided a rich environment in which the counseling profession could develop and expand from its previous history in educational settings. The "quiet revolution," referred to earlier, continued as graduates of counselor education programs found that their skills were effective with populations and in settings other than those for which they had originally been trained. They gradually realized that they had been limiting themselves in the application of their skills, rather than the skills they possessed being limiting factors.

These pioneer mental health counselors found, however, that there was much that they needed to know that was not covered by traditional counselor education curricula. They filled in the gaps in their knowledge base by additional coursework, in-service training, by consultation with and supervision from other mental health professionals on the center staffs, and ongoing clinical experience. The presence of counselors in community mental health centers had an interactive effect as well, as they shared their expertise with their colleagues, especially in areas involving consultation and community education. Still missing in the early 1970s, however, was a coherent professional identity for counselors working in the centers and other community settings (Brooks & Weikel, 1996). This deficit would not be remedied for several more years.

OTHER OUTCOMES OF FEDERAL MENTAL HEALTH LEGISLATION

It is clear that federal mental health legislative initiatives have had a profound impact on the development of mental health counseling as a profession. The establishment of community mental health centers in particular provided the entrée for counselors to move from primarily educational settings to community settings serving a much more varied population. It is also worthwhile to note that several other outcomes of mental health legislation since World War II. Among these are the development of community-based delivery systems, the impact of the NIMH, and the organized efforts of community mental health centers through the National Council of Community Behavioral Healthcare (NCCBH), formerly known as the National Council of Community Mental Health Centers.

Community-Based Delivery Systems

In the last 50 years, mental health services have begun to move toward community-based delivery systems on a large scale. The Joint Commission on Mental Illness established by the National Mental Health Study Act of 1955 realized that large state hospitals were becoming warehouses for the mentally ill, with little treatment taking place. It was as though the reforms instigated by Dix, Beers, and others had never happened. Another related phenomenon was that medical research was in the early stages of what has become a burgeoning psychopharmaceutical frontier. With the discovery of new psychotropic medications, many of the individuals who had been "written off," for lack of a better term, or warehoused by society could function at near normal if not normal capacity with the proper medication.

After the passage of the Community Mental Health Centers Act of 1963, the state hospitals gradually saw a decline in patient census. Halfway houses and group homes flourished as communities strained to find residences for thousands of released patients.

Various mental health programs, with strong support from the Kennedy, Johnson, and Nixon Administrations, also improved services for the mentally retarded. The 1970 funding extension mandated programs for children and adolescents, drug and alcohol abuse, and mental health consultation. Several additional programs were provided for by the 1975 amendments: follow-up care, transitional living arrangements, child and adolescent treatment, and follow-up, screening, and additional programs in alcohol and drug abuse.

The NIMH

The NIMH is the oldest institute in the Alcohol, Drug Abuse and Mental Health Administration (ADAMHA), into which the NIMH was incorporated by and act of Congress in 1974. The NIMH is 1 of 27 components of the National Institutes of Health (NIH), the federal government's principal biomedical and behavioral research agency. The NIH is part of the U.S. Department of Health and Human Services. The NIMH, the National Institute on Alcohol Abuse and Alcoholism, and the National Institute on Drug Abuse are charged with advancing scientific knowledge in these fields.

Studies conducted by the NIMH have shown that as many as one in five Americans suffer from mental or emotional problems. These range from anxiety and phobias to schizophrenia and other debilitating illnesses, with various types of depression accounting for the suffering of a significant portion of the population. The institute is devoted to the prevention and treatment of these illnesses through research, public education, and model treatment programs.

The NIMH supports a wide range of scientific studies in universities, hospitals, and other research centers to advance knowledge of the biological, genetic, and cognitive bases for behavior and effective new ways to treat and prevent mental illness. Examples include fundamental studies of brain chemistry and the role of molecular and cellular mechanisms in triggering mental illness, as well as the normal processes of memory, learning, and cognition. Behavioral studies span mental, emotional, and behavioral development and factors involved in dysfunctional behavior.

The NIMH also conducts and supports epidemiology research to collect national data on the incidence and prevalence of mental illness. These studies indicate the mental health status of various segments of the population.

In the area of prevention research, the NIMH supports studies to promote healthy behaviors and coping skills and studies of the most effective ways to help people who have undergone a life crisis, such as death in the family, or a catastrophic event, such as a flood, hurricane, or other natural or manmade disasters. A special focus of the institute's prevention studies are people considered at risk of developing mental or emotional problems, such as children of parents who are mentally ill or are separated or divorced. Studies are also supported in special areas, such as the mental health of minorities, antisocial and violent behavior, sexual assault, work and mental health, and the mental health of the elderly (DHHS Publication No. [ADM] 84-1320, 1984).

The National Council for Community Behavioral Healthcare

The National Council for Community Behavioral Healthcare (NCCBH) is the national organization that represents community mental health centers in government relations efforts and serves a networking and clearinghouse function to enable its constituent members to better communicate among themselves. The NCCBH is a nongovernmental body, but it is a direct result of federal legislative initiatives beginning with the Community Mental Health Centers Act of 1963.

Founded in 1970 as the National Council of Community Mental Health Centers, the NCCBH represents more than 1,600 agencies today and is the only trade association representing the providers of mental health, substance abuse, and developmental disability services. Through its sections and divisions, the organization also provides membership opportunities for individuals who share common interests in specialized areas of community mental health. The NCCBH conducts an annual national convention that provides opportunities for professional development and renewal as well as consideration of policy and government relations initiatives.

MENTAL HEALTH COUNSELING: THE IDENTITY EMERGES

At the beginning of this chapter, the major historical antecedents of moral treatment and vocational guidance were presented. Antecedents in professional practice, including testing and assessment, nonmedical approaches to psychotherapy, theories of normal human development, group counseling and psychotherapy, and psychoeducational approaches to treatment, were briefly sketched. These were followed by chronological accounts of legislative and public policy influences affecting the development of both the counseling profession and the delivery of mental health services. As important as all of these factors have been for the development of mental health counseling, none of them can be said to have been the causal factor of the dynamic profession that exists today. To be sure, all of them were necessary, but none is sufficient as an explanation. The heritage of mental health counseling cannot be traced so directly.

The "Quiet Revolution"

The date when the first counselor joined the staff of a community mental health center is not recorded. It is safe to say that the first cohort of counselors began working in the centers sometime in the mid-1960s. By then the decline in the number of school counselor openings and the expansion of counselor education curriculum to include areas that prepared counselors for settings other than schools added to the oversupply of counselor education graduates and created a ready supply of personnel for the centers.

The staffing patterns of most community mental health centers reflected the established professions of psychiatry, clinical and counseling psychology, social work, and nursing. Most counselors were initially hired as paraprofessionals because their preparation was not in one of the recognized disciplines. Their status and pay were correspondingly lower than that of their colleagues. A wide variety of job titles, such as psych tech, mental health specialist II, and psychiatric aide, was applied to the counselor's positions.

As new community-based programs were inaugurated in the late 1960s, counselors found positions in these as well. Youth services bureaus, drug and alcohol rehabilitation centers, women's centers, and shelters for runaway youth were but a few of the agencies that provided career options for counselors. In these settings also, the recognized professions held the principal posts, with counselors often relegated to paraprofessional status. This was due in large part to the lack of a clear identity of the professional counselor.

By the early 1970s, professional counselors were becoming well entrenched in mental health centers and other community settings. Pay and status did not always improve commensurate with their skills, but counselors were becoming frontline providers of mental health services. Many doctoral graduates of counselor education programs were unable to secure licensure as psychologists as many of their predecessors had done. They were also finding positions as counselor educators increasingly difficult to obtain. As a result, they began to set up private practices as professional counselors. They were gradually joined by more and more counselors with master's degree training, many of whom were veterans of community mental health centers. The "quiet revolution" was gathering momentum, but the identity of mental health counseling was yet to be affixed to its banners.

A New Professional Organization

The American Personnel and Guidance Association (APGA) was founded in 1952 when four professional counseling and guidance organizations merged into a single association structure that permitted them to retain their separate identities facilitating cooperative efforts. During the following 25 years, APGA grew to encompass 12 divisions accommodating counselors in school, college, rehabilitation, employment, and corrections settings. Divisions also represented special interests and skills, such as vocational counseling, measurement and evaluation, group work, religious and values issues, humanistic education, multicultural concerns, and counselor education and supervision (Brooks & Weikel, 1996).

In the early years, many counselors working in mental health and other community settings were APGA members, even though the association did not include a division that addressed their unique concerns. Calls for the formation of such a division began around 1975, setting in motion a series of events that led to the founding of the American Mental Health Counselors Association (AMHCA) as an independent organization in 1976 and its affiliation as APGA's 13th division in 1978 (Weikel, 1985).

AMHCA: Taking the Profession into the 21st Century

From its founding in 1976 until around 1990, it was virtually impossible to separate the development of mental health counseling as a profession from its organizational expression. The new association seemed an idea whose time had come, attracting members from a variety of mental health and other community settings, from rehabilitation and correction agencies, and from educational settings at all levels, elementary school through university. Growing to more than 10,000 members in less than ten years, AMHCA's membership was more diverse than any of its sister divisions, with the largest single group being private practitioners.

The association's agenda concentrated initially on issues related to professional identity and recognition. AMHCA's first major goal was to establish a national certification process for mental health counselors. The National Academy of Certified Clinical Mental Health Counselors was founded in 1979 to provide a vehicle through which the considerable skills of mental health counselors could be validated on a voluntary basis. Coupled with the national certification effort, AMHCA members threw their support behind the activities underway in a number of states to achieve passage of counselor licensure statutes.

During the 1980s, AMHCA leaders pressed NIMH officials and Congress for full recognition of mental health counselors and their involvement at all levels within the NIMH. Other early policy priorities included eligibility for clinical training funds and research into areas of concern to counselors. Professional counselors saw themselves as supporting the goals of the NIMH without receiving any direct benefit from the institute. Mental health counselors were successful in negotiating a seat on the NIMH Advisory Council.

Concurrently, AMHCA sought a greater voice within the National Council of Community Mental Health Centers (the predecessor to the NCCBH). The association was represented by its leaders at the NCCMHC conventions during most of the 1980s, but the relationship between the two groups has been less involved in recent years.

In the federal legislative arena, AMHCA supported legislation aimed at opening federally sponsored mental health programs to mental health counselors. Special targets during the 1980s were programs funded by Medicare and Medicaid and by the Older Americans Act. These initiatives were unsuccessful in achieving their immediate goals, but mental health counselors learned a great deal about legislative advocacy during this period. More recent efforts have met with mixed success.

Following on the heels of efforts to secure state licensure and national certification was a cluster of priorities that focused on achieving parity with the older mental health disciplines. Labeled "recognition and reimbursement" by AMHCA President David Brooks (1986–1987), these priorities encompassed: (a) third-party insurance reimbursement, (b) recognition by federal benefit systems such as the Office of Civilian Health and Medical Programs of the Uniformed Services (OCHAMPUS) and the Federal Employees Health Benefits Program (FEHBP), (c) official recognition in federal statutes as a core provider discipline of mental health services, and (d) inclusion by title in state personnel classification systems, among others. Partial recognition by OCHAMPUS was accomplished in 1987 after an intensive three-year effort, but even Certified Clinical Mental Health Counselors were not recognized as independent practitioners.

At the state level, mental health counselors achieved eligibility for health insurance reimbursement much more slowly. The first state to pass licensure legislation, which is the basic criterion for reimbursement, was Virginia in 1976. During the fall of 2009, California became the final state to pass a licensure law for counselors. It is interesting to note that the level of collaboration between AMHCA and ACA has remained fairly strong on the issue of licensure, with both associations contributing to the efforts of the State Branches through grants and/or technical assistance.

Also worthy of mention are the vendorship statutes that some states have passed or in others where the insurance code has been amended by rule for similar effects. At this writing, 20 states have such laws impacting mental health counselors. These laws either mandate that specific provider groups be reimbursed for their services or require insurers to offer the services of a provider when the services are covered by a health plan.

To date, considerable unevenness still exists in patterns of reimbursement eligibility. The advent of managed care, even with the failure of the health care reforms of the Clinton Administration, raised the possibility that the decades-long effort to achieve reimbursement eligibility would become a moot point. At the time of this writing, at the end of the George W. Bush Administration and the first year of the Obama Administration, the situation remains too fluid and too diverse to be able to make general and definitive statements about the status of mental health counselors in a managed care environment.

AMHCA and ACA: Impact and Change

Mental health counselors and their professional organization have had substantial impact on the larger counseling profession as well. Immediately after affiliation in 1978, AMHCA leaders sought to change the name of the APGA so that the word "Counseling" was included in the name of the parent body. They achieved partial success in 1983 when APGA changed its name to the American Association of Counseling and Development (AACD). Following the disaffiliation of its college student development division in 1991, AACD, at AMHCA's urging, changed its name once more, this time to the American Counseling Association (ACA), and it remains so today.

Tensions surrounding the name changes were mirrored in other policy differences among AMHCA members, other units within APGA/AACD/ACA, and the parent body itself. Setting priorities for the government relations agenda was one flashpoint. In the late 1970s and early 1980s, APGA (ACA) was more comfortable lobbying for issues and funding affecting school counselors with whom there was a much longer history and whose issues were understood more clearly. AMHCA leaders decided to hire their own lobbying firm to move forward their agenda, a less than popular move within APGA. By 1985, primarily because of success in educating the larger association about issues of concern to MHCs, AMHCA leaders returned to a strategy of operating inside the ACA government relations apparatus. This was due in no small part to AMHCA's recognition that an association of 50,000 members (i.e., ACA) was much more effective than any of its divisions alone in influencing public policy. There were other points of dispute that centered on ACA's internal governance, fiscal accountability, and general posture with respect to advocacy for mental health counselors.

Twice in the 1990s, relations between the elected leaders of AMHCA and the ACA governance structure reached the threshold of disaffiliation. In February 1994, the AMHCA Board of Directors voted by a narrow margin to disaffiliate from ACA and to put the matter to an every-member referendum for ratification. They were opposed by a cadre of past presidents and other leaders who raised questions about the haste and wisdom of such an action. In April 1994, the membership voted by more than 70% to remain under the ACA umbrella (Smith & Robinson, 1995). In the summer of 1995, the AMHCA Board took similar action, again with similar results.

Since that time, however, ACA and AMHCA have worked together on selected issues, not the least of which is the passage of licensure laws. At this writing, as was mentioned earlier, all states have now passed licensure laws for mental health counselors. There are seven states that still have "Title" licensure laws as opposed to "Practice" licensure laws. Practice laws are considered stronger because they prohibit the practice of professional counseling without obtaining a license where the Title laws only prohibit the use of the title "Licensed Professional Counselor." As more states have been successful in passing licensure laws, the resistance to mental health counselors from the sister professions has diminished somewhat. This sometimes amounts to a grudging acceptance of the mental health counseling profession. For the most part, however, mental health counselors, through both AMHCA and ACA, have taken the high road and attempted to form or join coalitions on federal and state legislation that benefit all mental health care providers. With the realization that it is much easier to kill a bill than to get one passed into law, their support has been accepted for the most part, and recognition by the sister professions and public policymakers is slowly becoming a reality.

Counselor education programs that are accredited by the Council for the Accreditation of Counseling and Related Educational Programs (CACREP) have taken notice that the specialty area of "Community Counseling" is being phased out and that CACREP will soon recognize only the more rigorous Clinical Mental Health Counseling track for accreditation. This track requires 60 semester credit hours, and there is emphasis on diagnosis and treatment planning. As an interesting side note, in a majority of states, the licensure laws require a 60 semester credit hour degree for licensure of mental health counselors who will be in independent practice. Although the battle is not finished, in retrospect, mental health counseling, as a profession, continues to make good progress toward full recognition as a provider.

SUMMARY

Descendents of a rich heritage extending back well before the 20th century, mental health counselors began their trek to professional identity and recognition in the late 1960s. Drawing from several historical and professional practice antecedents, this new profession rose during the 1970s to the front line of service delivery in a variety of settings but lacked a coherent identity until the AMHCA was founded in 1976. During the next decade, the AMHCA experienced unprecedented growth, reaching a membership high of more than 12,700 in 1989, and had emerged as an assertive and articulate voice for the identity and advancement of mental health counseling. Its impact within and outside the counseling profession has been felt in areas of training and credentialing and of increased consumer access to mental health services.

REFERENCES

Alberti, R. E., & Emmons, M. I. (1970). *Your perfect right.* San Luis Obispo, CA: Impact Publishers.

American Psychiatric Association. (1994). *Diagnostic and statistical manual of mental disorders* (4th ed.). Washington, DC: Author.

Authier, J., Gufstason, K., Guerney, B., & Kasdorf, J. (1975). The psychological practitioner as a teacher: A theoretical-historical and practical review. *Counseling Psychologist, 5,* 31–50.

Beers, C. W. (1908). *A mind that found itself.* Garden City, NY: Longmans, Green.

Benson, H. (1975). *The relaxation response.* New York: Avon Books.

Bernstein, D. A., & Borkovec, T. D. (1973). *Progressive relaxation training: A manual for the helping professions.* Champaign, IL: Research Press.

Brooks, D. K., Jr. (1984). *A life-skills taxonomy: Defining elements of effective functioning through the use of the Delphi Technique.* Unpublished doctoral dissertation. University of Georgia.

Brooks, D. K., & Weikel, W. J. (1996). Mental health counseling: The first twenty years. In W. J. Weikel & A. J. Palmo (Eds.), *Foundations of mental health counseling* (2nd ed., pp. 5–29). Springfield, IL: Charles C Thomas.

Carkhuff, R. R. (1969a). *Helping and human relations: Vol. 1. Selection and training.* New York: Holt, Rinehart & Winston.

Carkhuff, R. R. (1969b). *Helping and human relations: Vol. 2. Practice and research.* New York: Holt, Rinehart & Winston.

Egan, G. (1982). *The skilled helper: A model for systematic helping and interpersonal relating* (2nd. ed.). Monterey, CA: Brooks/Cole.

Ellis, A., & Harper, R. A. (1975). *A new guide to rational living.* Hollywood, CA: Wilshire Books.

Freud, S. (1953). Three essays on the theory of sexuality. In J. Strachey (Ed.), *The standard edition of the complete psychological works of Sigmund Freud* (Vol. 7). London: Hogarth Press. (Original work published 1905)

Freud, S. (1961). The infantile genital organization: An interpolation into the theory of sexuality. In J. Strachey (Ed.), *The standard edition of the complete psychological works of Sigmund Freud* (Vol. 19). London: Hogarth Press. (Original work published 1923)

Galassi, M. D., & Galassi, J. P. (1977). *Assert yourself!* New York: Human Services Press.

Gazda, G. M. (1982). Group psychotherapy and group counseling: Definition and heritage. In G. M. Gazda (Ed.), *Basic approaches to group psychotherapy and group counseling* (3rd ed., pp. 5–36). Springfield, IL: Charles C Thomas.

Gazda, G. M., Asbury, F. R., Balzer, F. J., Childers, W. C., & Walters, R. P. (1984). *Human relations development: A manual for educators* (3rd ed.). Boston: Allyn & Bacon.

Gazda, G. M., & Brooks, D. K., Jr. (1985). The development of the social/life-skills training movement. *Journal of Group Psychotherapy, Psychodrama and Sociometry, 38*(1), 1–10.

Green, T. F. (1985). The last forty years–The next forty years. *Nexus, 7*(2), 13–17.

Ivey, A. E., & Authier, J. (1978). *Microcounseling: Innovations in interviewing, counseling, psychotherapy, and psychoeducation* (2nd ed.). Springfield, IL: Charles C Thomas.

Kohlberg, L. (1973). Continuities in childhood and adult moral development revisited. In P. B. Baltes & K. W. Schaie (Eds.), *Life-span development psychology: Personality and socialization* (pp. 179–204). New York: Academic Press.

Lange, A. J., & Jakubowski, P. (1976). *Responsible assertive behavior: Cognitive/behavioral procedures for trainers.* Champaign, IL: Research Press.

Loevinger, J. (1976). *Ego development: Conceptions and theories.* San Francisco: Jossey-Bass.

McKinley, J. C., & Hathaway, S. R. (1940). A Multiple Personality Schedule (Minnesota): I. Construction of the schedule. *Journal of Psychology, 10,* 249–254.

Mitchell, J. T. (1983). When disaster strikes: The critical incident stress debriefing process. *Journal of Emergency Medical Services.*

Moreno, J. L., & Elefthery, D. G. (1982). An introduction to group psychodrama. In G. M. Gazda (Ed.), *Basic approaches to group psychotherapy and group counseling* (3rd ed., pp. 101–131). Springfield, IL: Charles C Thomas.

Murray, D. J. (1983). *A history of western psychology.* Englewood Cliffs, NJ: Prentice-Hall.

Parsons, F. (1909). *Choosing a vocation.* Boston: Houghton Mifflin.

Perry, W. G., Jr. (1970). *Forms of intellectual and ethical development in the college years: A scheme.* New York: Holt, Rinehart & Winston.

Rogers, C. R. (1942). *Counseling and psychotherapy.* Boston: Houghton Mifflin.

Rogers, C. R., Gnedlin, E. T., Kiesler, D., & Truax, C. B. (1967). *The therapeutic relationship and its impact.* Madison: University of Wisconsin Press.

Rodgers, R. F. (1980). Theories underlying student development. In D. G. Creamer (Ed.), *Student development and higher education: Theories, practices, and future directions* (pp. 10–95). Cincinnati: American College Personnel Association.

Selman, R. L. (1976). Social-cognitive understanding. In T. Lickona (Ed.), *Moral development and behavior.* New York: Holt, Rinehart & Winston.

Selman, R. L. (1977). A structural-development model of social cognition: Implications for intervention research. *Counseling Psychologist, 6*(4), 3–6.

Smith, H. B., & Robinson G. P. (1995). Mental health counseling: Past, present, and future. *Journal of Counseling and Development, 74,* 158–162.

Sprafkin, R. P. (1977). The rebirth of moral treatment. *Professional Psychology, 8*(2), 161–169.

Weikel, W. J. (1985). The American Mental Health Counselors Association. *Journal of Counseling and Development, 63,* 457–460.

Whiteley, J. M. (1984). A historical perspective on the development of counseling psychology as a profession. In S. D. Brown & R. W. Lent (Eds.), *Handbook of counseling psychology* (pp. 3–55). New York: Wiley.

Chapter 2

PROFESSIONAL IDENTITY: 25 YEARS LATER

ARTIS J. PALMO

Since the first edition of the text in 1986, much has changed for the professional counselor. Culminating years of lobbying and legislative work, counseling is now legally defined in all 50 states, Washington, DC., and Puerto Rico. Now, for the first time in the history of counseling, when seeking the definition of professional counseling, you simply find a copy of the appropriate counseling legislation for your state! With this information in mind, it is more important than ever to do an exploration of the history of the professional counselor.

As noted previously (Palmo, 2005), professional counseling began around 1900. According to Aubrey (1983), "the early pioneers of guidance and counseling (Jesse Davis, Frank Parsons, Eli Weaver) were quite adamant in wishing to prepare people to successfully cope with and master the social environment" (pp. 78–79). At this early time, guidance was the only function, with counseling being mentioned in the literature for the first time in 1931. From a historical standpoint, counseling as a professional function has been discussed for only the past 80 years! However, during the past 25 years, much more has been accomplished than in the previous 25.

Up until the past 25 years, the most important professional change for counseling occurred during the 1940s and 1950s. During this time, there was a dramatic shift from the "mechanistic-deterministic" philosophy of behaviorism and psychoanalysis to "self-determinism" of the humanistic philosophy espoused by Carl Rogers (Aubrey, 1977, 1983). Rogers' overall impact on the field of counseling, both philosophically and pragmatically, was tremendous. The birth of the field of counseling as a separate entity from guidance, psychology, and psychiatry can be traced directly to the work of Rogers. Although many varied techniques and theories of counseling exist today, the philosophical groundwork for the profession of counseling rests on the humanistic work of Rogers and his contemporaries. With Rogers' work, the guidance role has expanded to include a wide range of counseling functions as well.

Two other important historical events need to be mentioned in relation to the professional identity of the Professional Counselor (PC). First, the training of counselors took a giant step forward in 1958 (Aubrey, 1983) with the establishment of the National Defense Education Act (NDEA). This legislation was in direct response to Russia initiating the space race with the launching of Sputnik. Along with the emphasis on math and science education in the schools, the NDEA legislation resulted "in the preparation of thousands of counselors" (p. 79). The legislation promoted the rapid growth of counselor education programs throughout the country, which leads to the second point.

Following the decline of the NDEA programs in the 1960s, counselor education programs began a slow transition from the training of guidance counselors for the schools to the training of counselors who could function in a variety of mental health settings (see Chapter 9 on Work Settings) besides the schools. This shift in the professional direction of counseling was a tremendous divergence from the early roots of the guidance and counseling movement. Counselors began to function effectively in settings that were traditionally the exclusive propriety of the fields of psychology and medicine. By the late 1970s and early 1980s, the counseling professional could be found in such varied roles as "developing career education programs; . . . working to help chronic schizophrenics attain optimal vocational adjustment, and . . . dealing with adolescent developmental crises" (Goodyear, 1976, p. 513). The roles performed and work settings occupied by the budding professional counselors of the 1960s and 1970s were numerous.

Additionally, the American Counseling Association in conjunction with several divisions developed the accrediting arm of counseling. During the 1980s and into the 1990s, the Council for the Accreditation of Counseling and Related Educational Programs (CACREP) was developed to provide a set of comprehensive training standards (Council for the Accreditation of Counseling and Related Educational Programs, 1994). With an active accrediting body, the field of professional counseling blossomed.

In summary, the broad-based, developmental nature of professional counseling can be traced from the early vocational exploration of the 1900s, Rogers' self-theory of meeting individual needs in the 1940s and 1950s, the development of professionalism in the 1960s, the use of counseling methodologies with all types of clientele in the 1970s and 1980s, and the advent of fully accredited counselor education programs (Bradley, 1978). Having such a broad base, however, causes the profession to have a severe identity crisis, as Aubrey noted as far back as 1977, Sherrard and Fong again in 1991, and Bradley and Cox in 2001. Important questions arise as a result of the identity crisis. What type of clientele should be served? What counseling methodologies should be employed by the counselor? What is the goal of the profession of counseling?

The intent of this chapter is to answer the questions posed above as well as to provide the reader with a framework for professional counseling. Although counseling as a profession has generally suffered an identity problem, the true identity of the PC has been more completely defined only recently. With this in mind, the chapter explores the basic philosophical and theoretical premises that underlie the profession of counseling, which make the PC a distinct entity in the helping professions.

MENTAL HEALTH PROVIDERS

Development of the American Mental Health Counselors Association

The identified field of *professional counseling* can be traced directly to the development of the American Mental Health Counselors Association (AMHCA) during the late 1970s within the American Personnel and Guidance Association (later named the American Association for Counseling and Development and presently the American Counseling Association). AMHCA's development was the direct result of the dissatisfaction of many counselors with the existing professional groups and associations primarily oriented toward clinical and counseling psychology, psychiatry, social work, and guidance counseling. These early counseling professionals felt that their training and orientation did not fit the traditional, contemporary styles of existing professionals in the field of mental health. Rather than attempt to fit within the existing organizational structures, a group of counseling professionals initiated AMHCA with the expressed purpose of providing counselors working in the field of mental health a vehicle for the exchange of ideas, methods, and research.

The development of AMHCA parallels the development of the professional title, Mental Health Counselor, and now, the Licensed Professional Counselor (LPC). Through the efforts of the early AMHCA leaders, the title Mental Health Counselor became the accepted designation for those counseling professionals whose primary affiliation and theoretical basis is counseling and not psychology, psychiatry, or social work. Through the work of the founding AMHCA professionals, such as Steve Lindenberg, James

Messina, Nancy Spisso, Joyce Breasure, Gary Seiler, and Bill Weikel, tremendous strides were made in developing the concept of Mental Health Counselor that ultimately led to today's title of Professional Counselor.

As an aside, there are numerous variations of the titles (Lum, 2010) used in licensure laws throughout the country. Two thirds of the state counseling boards utilize the title Licensed Professional Counselor; however, there are some variations. For example, two frequently used titles are Licensed Clinical Professional Counselor and Licensed Mental Health Counselor. There are other titles, including Licensed Professional Mental Health Counselor, Licensed Professional Clinical Counselor, Licensed Clinical Mental Health Counselor, and Licensed Professional Counselor of Mental Health. The identity crisis for professional counseling is not over, but we inch ever closer to a unified identity and title.

It is important to note the development of AMHCA as a professional association when discussing the origin of the title of Mental Health Counselor. The contemporary title of Mental Health Counselor (MHC) found in some licensure laws is a direct result of AMHCA's tireless struggle to have mental health counseling legislatively recognized. Although the roots of the MHC, and the resultant identity problems, can be traced to the beginnings of the guidance movement, the title MHC was the antecedent to the more prevalent title of Professional Counselor used by state licensing boards. Therefore, the professional identity of the PC is grounded in the beliefs and philosophies of counseling's past as well as the recent developments of the past 20 years. The primary purpose of MHCs during the past 35 years has been to establish professional counseling as one of the core professions of mental health services along with psychiatrists, psychologists, social workers, and psychiatric nurses. In order to do this, PCs had to demonstrate why they belonged as well as how they differed from existing professionals in the field of mental health.

Professional Counselor

Prior to 1980, if one were to review the professional literature, the titles most frequently used to distinguish the professionals associated with community mental health are the community counselor, community psychologist, psychologist, psychiatrist, or social worker. Other than an article by Seiler and Messina (1979), it was unlikely that the reader could find literature that related directly to the issue of the professional identity of the MHC or PC and the role of the MHC or PC within community mental health (Lewis & Lewis, 1977). Not until the 1980s and 1990s does the literature regularly begin to discuss the issues surrounding the identity crisis being faced by PCs within the community mental health movement.

In 1981, Palmo developed a manuscript for the AMHCA Board of Directors, which described the role and function of the MHC. This manuscript was developed and approved for the purpose of ultimate inclusion in the *Dictionary of Occupational Titles* (1991) and the *Occupational Outlook Handbook* (1984). Eventually, in 1984, segments of the description were placed in the *Occupational Outlook Handbook,* establishing for the first time mental health counseling as one of the core providers of mental health services.

Previously, four groups of helping professionals were recognized and identified legislatively as being the core providers of mental health services. They included psychiatrists, psychologists, psychiatric nurses, and clinical social workers (Asher, 1979; Lindenberg, 1983; Randolph, Sturgis, & Alcorn, 1979). With the advent of licensure and certification throughout the United States, the core providers today primarily include psychiatrists, psychologists, clinical social workers, licensed professional counselors, and marriage and family counselors. Although there are significant overlaps between and among the roles and functions of the identified core providers and the PC, there are several important differences that must be discussed. First, the original definition of an MHC:

> Performs counseling/therapy with individuals, groups, couples, and families; collects, organizes, and analyzes data concerning client's mental, emotional, and/or behavioral problems or disorders; aids clients and their families to effectively adapt to the personal concerns presented; develops procedures to assist clients to adjust to possible environmental barriers that may impede self-understanding and personal growth. (Palmo, 1981)

This early definition of the MHC provided the necessary distinctions between counselors and the other core providers. Primarily, the PC has a concern for the environment surrounding the client (Hershenson & Strein, 1991). Although there is an emphasis on the identified client, the PC has a more global view of the client concern that includes family and other personal associations. As Hershenson and Strein relate, "Clients rarely spend more than a few hours each week in counseling; the bulk of their time is spent in other settings, such as home, work, and community" (p. 248). The concern for the environmental factors is a major aspect of the PC's approach to treating clients.

Another primary goal of counseling is the development of the client's self-understanding and promotion of his or her personal growth. Self-understanding and personal growth on the part of the client means continued self-direction and effective mental health for the individual. The definition also includes the following:

> Utilizes community agencies and institutions to develop mental health programs that are developmental and preventive in nature. Trained to provide a wide variety of therapeutic approaches to assist clients, which may include therapy, milieu therapy, and behavioral therapy. Employed in clinics, hospitals, drug centers, colleges, private agencies, related mental health programs, or private practice. Required to have knowledge and skills in client management, assessment, and diagnosis through a post-graduate program in mental health or community mental health counseling. (Palmo, 1981, p. 1)

The second aspect of the definition expresses more clearly the major distinguishing characteristics for counseling. A key characteristic is the emphasis on a developmental model of counseling and therapy within an overall prevention scheme, with a "focus on promoting healthy development of coping capacities and on using environmental forces to contribute to the goal of wellness. . ." (Hershenson & Strein, 1991, pp. 250–251). What this meant was that the counselor examines clients' concerns as part of the normal developmental issues and crises faced by most people as they progress through daily living experiences. The client is not viewed as "sick" but rather as an individual who must learn more effective coping mechanisms in order to function appropriately and gainfully within society (Hershenson & Strein, 1991; Lindenberg, 1983; Palmo, Shosh, & Weikel, 2001; Weikel & Palmo, 1989). It is important to stress that the developmental/preventative model does not deny that client concerns vary in severity, and, at times, the client suffering from more severe distress may be referred to the services of other professionals in the helping fields.

According to the *Occupational Outlook Handbook* (Counselors, 2010–2011), an MHC is defined as follows:

> *Mental health counselors* work with individuals, families, and groups to address and treat mental and emotional disorders and to promote mental health. They are trained in a variety of therapeutic techniques used to address issues such as depression, anxiety, addiction and substance abuse, suicidal impulses, stress, trauma, low self-esteem, and grief. They also help with job and career concerns, educational decisions, mental and emotional health issues, and relationship problems. In addition, they may be involved in community outreach, advocacy, and mediation activities. Some specialize in delivering mental health services for the elderly. Mental health counselors often work closely with other mental health specialists, such as psychiatrists, psychologists, clinical social workers, psychiatric nurses, and school counselors.

Prevention is an important role stressed by the PC. Prevention has been a defining characteristic to mental health counseling from the beginning of the movement (Kiselica & Look, 1993). As outlined by Goodyear as far back as

1976, prevention counselors "build on clients' strengths and teach clients the life skills necessary for problem mastery" (p. 513). This does not mean that the client may never face the need for direct counseling intervention, but rather the PC's role is one of mental health educator (Heller, 1993; Lange, 1983; McCollum, 1981; Myers, 1992; Shaw, 1986; Sperry, Carlson, & Lewis, 1993; Weissberg, Kumpfer, & Seligman, 2003; Westbrook et al., 1993). Mental health education means instructing the public regarding various methodologies that can be utilized to handle the everyday stressors of life.

In summary, an examination of the definition of counselor shows several important distinctive qualities for the counseling professional. First, there is an environmental/milieu approach to the client that stresses the client's adjustment to societal pressures, whether it be at home, school, work, or in the community. Second, there is a developmental/preventive (Biglan, Mrazek, Carnine, & Flay, 2003; Nation, Crusto, Wandersman, Kumpfer, Seybolt, Morrissey-Kane, & Davino, 2003; Weissberg, Kumpfer, & Seligman, 2003) model that underlies the orientation the PC utilizes in his or her work with individuals, groups, and families.

Before continuing the discussion of the PC's role definition, it is useful to define the role and function of the other major core providers–psychiatrists, psychologists, and social workers. To fully understand the role and function of the PC, it is important to be familiar with the definitions of the other mental health care professionals.

MENTAL HEALTH PROVIDERS

Psychiatry

A professional psychiatrist, according to the *Occupational Outlook Handbook* (Physicians and Surgeons, 2010–2011), is defined as follows:

> *Psychiatrists* are the primary mental health caregivers. They assess and treat mental illnesses through a combination of psychotherapy, psychoanalysis, hospitalization, and medication. Psychotherapy involves regular discussions with patients about their problems; the psychiatrist helps them find solutions through changes in their behavioral patterns, the exploration of their past experiences, or group and family therapy sessions. Psychoanalysis involves long-term psychotherapy and counseling for patients. In many cases, medications are administered to correct chemical imbalances that cause emotional problems.

Several key aspects to the role of the psychiatrist differ from all other mental health professionals. First, the psychiatrist utilizes the medical model in his or her interventions with a client or, as the model dictates, patient. The medical model assumes there is an illness or a sickness, with the best intervention for the patient being medicinal. Second, because the psychiatrist is a physician, he or she is the only mental health professional who can prescribe psychopharmacological drugs. Because many serious mental illnesses involve some form of organic problem, the use of drugs as a treatment of choice has become more and more popular.

Some movement has been made toward having psychologists trained in psychopharmacology in order to meet the documented need for additional assistance in medical management in some areas of the country (Tulkin & Stock, 2004; Wiggins & Wedding, 2004). As of this writing, New Mexico and Louisiana have passed legislation authorizing prescriptive privileges to psychologists trained in psychopharmacology (Holloway, 2004a, 2004b).

A third important role most often assumed by the psychiatrist is the director of a team of professionals working with patients. This means the psychiatrist is usually the most powerful professional in determining the direction of the therapy to be completed with the patient. Most frequently, in hospitals and other agencies, the psychiatrist has the final say regarding the methods to be utilized by the mental health care team.

As with other mental health professions, the field of psychiatry has had to make significant changes in its role and function. Because of the proliferation of mental health providers from other fields, psychiatry has taken a more consultative role in working with the other core providers of mental health services. PCs have taken effective and active roles in the private and public sector of community mental health, forcing the other professional groups to adapt their treatment approaches to better treat the clientele seeking assistance.

A brief case example demonstrates the consultative relationship that can exist between a PC and a psychiatrist:

> Bill was an LPC working in a private practice and treating Warren, a 17-year-old high school junior who was having severe socialization problems at home, school, and community. In addition to individual counseling with Warren, Bill did family counseling as well as maintaining a consultative relationship with Warren's school counselor. Warren's primary problems had subsided as a result of counseling, but he continued to have severe behavioral outbursts whenever he was faced with stressful situations. For example, one Saturday, Warren's girlfriend broke-up with him, creating a situation where Warren became angry and abusive with her and the family. This was just one example of his behavioral outbursts that had occurred recently. Since Bill was no longer sure that the problem was environmental/social, he referred Warren to the psychiatrist who headed the local hospital's adolescent psychiatric unit. Through physiological tests and psychometric examinations, the psychiatrist determined some organic abnormalities with Warren, and placed him on medication.

Warren was told to remain in counseling in addition to the medication. In the consultative role, the psychiatrist was able to assist Bill in treating this young boy and his family.

This case is a good example of how the professional fields can come together to treat someone, rather than to make arbitrary distinctions between mental health groups. As the world of community mental health changes, there are more and more collaborative efforts in the field. PCs have contributed a great deal to this collaborative effort over the past 25 years through their active involvement with all professional groups in the field.

Psychology

Utilizing the *Occupational Outlook Handbook* (Psychologists, 2010–2011) description, clinical psychologist is defined as follows:

> *Clinical psychologists*–who constitute the largest specialty–are concerned with the assessment, diagnosis, treatment, and prevention of mental disorders. While some clinical psychologists specialize in treating severe psychological disorders, such as schizophrenia and depression, many others may help people deal with personal issues, such as divorce or the death of a loved one. Often times, clinical psychologists provide an opportunity to talk and think about things that are confusing or worrying, offering different ways of interpreting and understanding problems and situations. They are trained to use a variety of approaches aimed at helping individuals, and the strategies used are generally determined by the specialty they work in.
>
> Clinical psychologists often interview patients and give diagnostic tests in their own private offices. They may provide individual, family, or group psychotherapy and may design and implement behavior modification programs. Some clinical psychologists work in hospitals where they collaborate with physicians and other specialists to develop and implement treatment and intervention programs that patients can understand and comply with. Other clinical psychologists work in universities and medical schools, where they train graduate students in the delivery of mental health and behavioral medicine services. A few work in physical rehabilitation settings, treating patients with spinal cord injuries, chronic pain or illness, stroke, arthritis, or neurological conditions. Others may work in community mental health centers, crisis counseling services, or drug rehabilitation centers, offering evaluation, therapy, remediation, and consultation.
>
> Areas of specialization within clinical psychology include health psychology, neuropsychology, geropsychology, and child psychology. *Health psychologists* study how biological, psychological, and social factors affect health and illness.

> They promote healthy living and disease prevention through counseling, and they focus on how patients adjust to illnesses and treatments and view their quality of life. *Neuropsychologists* study the relation between the brain and behavior. They often work in stroke and head injury programs. *Geropsychologists* deal with the special problems faced by the elderly. Work may include helping older persons cope with stresses that are common in late life, such as loss of loved ones, relocation, medical conditions, and increased care-giving demands. Clinical psychologists may further specialize in these fields by focusing their work in a number of niche areas including mental health, learning disabilities, emotional disturbances, or substance abuse. The emergence and growth of these, and other, specialties reflects the increasing participation of psychologists in direct services to special patient populations.
>
> Often, clinical psychologists consult with other medical personnel regarding the best treatment for patients, especially treatment that includes medication. Clinical psychologists generally are not permitted to prescribe medication to treat patients; only psychiatrists and other medical doctors may prescribe most medications. (See the statement on *physicians and surgeons* elsewhere in the *Handbook.*) However, two States–Louisiana and New Mexico–currently allow appropriately trained clinical psychologists to prescribe medication with some limitations.
>
> *Counseling psychologists* advise people on how to deal with problems of everyday living, including problems in the home, place of work, or community, to help improve their quality of life. They foster well-being by promoting good mental health and preventing mental, physical, and social disorders. They work in settings such as university or crisis counseling centers, hospitals, rehabilitation centers, and individual or group practices. (See also the statements on *counselors* and *social workers* elsewhere in the *Handbook.*)

There are several other aspects to the role and function of the clinical psychologist mentioned in the *Occupational Outlook Handbook* that are important. The clinical psychologist usually collaborates with a psychiatrist in diagnosis and treatment; frequently is responsible for the research that is conducted with patients; develops mental health programs for social, educational, and welfare agencies; and generally has a specialty such as the severely disturbed, criminals, delinquents, elderly, or other special group.

The field of psychology has many varied specialties, as can be noted by reading the list of professional divisions of the American Psychological Association. According to the *Occupational Outlook Handbook,* the listing of titles includes: Experimental, Developmental, Personality, Social, Counseling, Educational, School, Industrial, Community, and Health. Although there has been much confusion surrounding the title of psychologist over the years, with the academics and training requirements varying from state to state (Wayne, 1982), through a coordinated effort on the part of state psychological associations, there is a more consistent set of national standards defining the field of psychology.

For the purposes of the discussion in this chapter, the term *psychologist* will refer to clinical and counseling psychologists because those are the two most frequently used titles related to the treatment of clients in the mental health field. In addition, the professional definition most closely related to professional counseling is either clinical or counseling psychology.

There are many similarities between the role definitions for psychologists and counselors, but significant differences remain. The most important distinctions include the psychologist's emphasis on psychometrics and various forms of assessment. Generally speaking, projective and intellectual assessments are almost always done by the psychologist. The clinical psychologist frequently works with institutionalized persons or those with more severe problems, in conjunction with the psychiatrist. Evaluations and assessments by the psychologist are important to the diagnostic evaluation ultimately completed by the psychiatrist. Many therapeutic interventions are based on the assessments done by the psychologist, but psychopharmacological treatments are always assigned by the psychiatrist.

As with psychiatry, the field of psychology has made some drastic professional changes over the past 40 years. Private practice was originally the domain of the psychiatrist, but with modern society came many social changes demanding treatments beyond the psychopharmacological treatment of the psychiatrist. Many mental health professionals, including professional counselors and psychologists, began to offer the general community some alternative treatments, such as family counseling, school interventions, marriage counseling, and other forms of proactive counseling. In fact, many of the early participants in the MHC movement were psychologists, social workers, and psychiatrists who believed in a community mental health model based on wellness not illness, proactive treatments not reactive treatments, and collaboration not separatism.

Because there has been a broadening of the roles performed by psychologists, many are presently providing services in private practice settings. Being a licensed professional makes the private practice setting a viable alternative to the traditional role of assessment and treatment within an institutional setting. The key issue is licensure, along with acceptance by insurance carriers who often pay for part of the treatment. For the PC, licensure is a reality as well as being accepted/reimbursed by insurance carriers. In the area of private practice, psychologists have been widely accepted, along with psychiatrists, by the insurance industry, while LPCs are continuing to work in this important area.

In summary, utilizing various forms of assessments, the clinical psychologist is the primary nonmedical diagnostician of mental health care professionals. In addition, the broadening of the roles performed by psychologists have led them into all areas of psychology and counseling practice, including private practice. Historically, psychologists have worked closely with psychiatrists in the management of cases as well as being direct providers of service. Although they have made many changes in their approach to counseling and therapy, psychologists remain directed by the medical model because of the need for diagnosis and illness identification.

Social Work

The third core provider with legislative recognition (*Occupational Outlook Handbook,* Social Workers, 2010–2011) is the field of social work. No professional field has had the major growth in all areas of mental health care as social workers. From advancements in licensure to expanded roles in institutions to private practice, social workers have made great professional strides to reach acceptance in the community. Two titles are most frequently used when discussing social work–Clinical Social Worker or Licensed Clinical Social Worker. Like the LPC, both titles usually require two years of graduate study leading to a master's degree in social work with specialties in psychiatry or clinical practice.

The *Occupational Outlook Handbook* (Social Workers, 2010–2011) defines a social worker as follows:

> *Child, family, and school social workers* provide social services and assistance to improve the social and psychological functioning of children and their families. Workers in this field assess their client's needs and offer assistance to improve their situation. This often includes coordinating available services to assist a child or family. They may assist single parents in finding day care, arrange adoptions, or help find foster homes for neglected, abandoned, or abused children. These workers may specialize in working with a particular problem, population or setting, such as child protective services, adoption, homelessness, domestic violence, or foster care.
>
> In schools, social workers often serve as the link between students' families and the school, working with parents, guardians, teachers, and other school officials to ensure that students reach their academic and personal potential. They also assist students in dealing with stress or emotional problems. Many school social workers work directly with children with disabilities and their families. In addition, they address problems such as misbehavior, truancy, teenage pregnancy, and drug and alcohol problems and advise teachers on how to cope with difficult students. School social workers may teach workshops to entire classes on topics like conflict resolution.

> Child, family, and school social workers may be known as child welfare social workers, family services social workers, or child protective services social workers. These workers often work for individual and family services agencies, schools, or State or local governments.

Historically, the role of the social worker remained somewhat defined and stable through the 1970s and early 1980s. The professional social worker was generally the link between the client and the community, providing adjustment counseling and support for the client and his or her family. From the 1990s to the present, the role has been expanded to include long-term individual and family counseling through community agencies and institutions. In addition, as noted above, private practice has become a viable option for employment for many social workers.

The important distinction to make with social work is between bachelor's level and master's level. Bachelor's-level social workers are generally involved with an agency, an institution, or a hospital, assisting patients and their families in readjusting to the community from which they came. The master's-level social worker may be involved in these functions but is also trained to provide counseling services.

Psychiatric Nursing

Generally, the professional nurse associated with mental health care is usually employed in a hospital or an institution for the chronically ill. In this medical position, the professional nurse is a critical part of the mental health team headed by the psychiatrist or other medical staff (*Occupational Outlook Handbook,* Registered Nurses, 2010–2011). Once again, besides the psychiatrist, the psychiatric nurse is the only mental health professional with a medical background in addition to mental health training. The *Occupational Outlook Handbook* has only one line that defines psychiatric nurse:

> *Psychiatric-mental health nurses* treat patients with personality and mood disorders.

The psychiatric nurse has intensive training in working with severely emotionally disturbed individuals. They are the medically trained assistant to the psychiatrist entrusted with the responsibility for medical care, distribution of drugs, and offering some therapeutic interventions with individuals and groups of patients in institutional settings or community readjustment programs.

Because of the shift from the hospitalization of severe, long-term disturbed patients to less restricted community-based programs, psychiatric nurses are performing more of their functions in outpatient settings. As a core provider, psychiatric nurses have been accepted by insurance carriers for quite some time because of their advanced training and the necessity for a license to practice. However, nurses do not usually open private practices or compete in the open community mental health market; therefore, they are not often compared to PC because of their specific functions within treatment.

SUMMARY

The four previously defined core providers have some distinct individual characteristics but also many overlapping functions. Also, the PC has different as well as similar functions to the other core providers. The overlapping role for all five professional groups (Psychiatry, Psychology, Social Work, Nurse, and LPC) is counseling or therapy. Each professional group is involved in some level of counseling/therapy, although the orientation or model utilized may differ as well as the content and style of advanced training. For the reader's purpose, the following general definitions for each profession should be kept in mind for the remainder of the chapter:

1. **Psychiatrists** hold doctorates in medicine and are the only mental health professionals who can **administer drugs** (although the Veterans Administration Hospitals began a project to teach psychologists the use of psychopharmacological treatments);
2. **Clinical Psychologists** hold doctorates and are the professionals generally entrusted with the **assessment** of intellectual and personality functioning, in addition to providing counseling/therapy;
3. **Psychiatrists** and **Psychologists** are usually the mental health professionals **directing mental health care teams** in agencies, hospitals, and institutions;
4. **Social Workers** usually provide the link between the institutional services for clients/patients and the integration of the individual back into the social milieu; and
5. **Psychiatric Nurses** provide the **medical linkage** between the agency or institution and the client/patient after hospitalization.

The key to this chapter is to examine the role, function, and identity of the PC in comparison with other mental health care providers. Hopefully, the previous discussion has clarified the roles performed by each of the core providers, which permits an in-depth discussion of the specific professional characteristics of the counselor that makes mental health counseling a profession unto itself.

PC AS A PROFESSION

Back in 1979, Seiler and Messina stated, "Although mental health counselors have existed for many years, they have labored under the burden of being professionals without a distinct identity" (p. 3). This identity crisis for the PC is finally dissipating with the passage of licensure laws through the United States. Although there is overlap among the PC, psychologist, and social worker, distinct and unique characteristics remain for the PC. Several distinctions make professional counseling a separate profession (Hershenson & Strein, 1991; Palmo, Shosh, & Weikel, 2001; Sherrard & Fong, 1991; Weikel & Palmo, 1989).

One of the important questions that arises from this discussion is, "What is a profession?" As far back as 1979, Messina attempted to demonstrate that professional counseling was a profession by citing Peterson's long-accepted criteria for a profession: (a) defined objectives for the professional work; (b) techniques of the profession that can be taught to attain the objectives; (c) techniques are basically intellectual operations, and the techniques are applied according to the individual problems; (d) techniques are founded in principles of science, theology, or law and not readily accessible to the novice; (e) professionals are members of an organized society; and (f) the professional organization has altruistic goals, is not totally self-serving, and has a statement of professional ethics.

The field of professional counseling has all the necessary characteristics to be noted as a profession along with the other four core providers of mental health care. An examination of the most recent standards published by the Council for Accreditation of Counseling and Related Educational Programs (2009) for the counseling profession demonstrates that counselors have to meet the academic and professional training qualifications that make it a profession. The professional techniques are founded upon a sound body of knowledge, the goals of the profession have been clearly stated, training programs have an established set of standards, and the PC is associated with two primary professional groups (American Counseling Association [ACA] and AMHCA). ACA and AMHCA have existing professional groups that are responsible for the development of training standards (CACREP) as well as standards for professional certification (National Board of Certified Counselors [NBCC]).

The following discussion provides some specific philosophical and theoretical orientations that make professional counseling distinct from the other core mental health providers.

THE DISTINCTIVENESS OF THE COUNSELING PROFESSION

Counselor Use of Self

Probably the most important aspect of the theoretical and philosophical foundations of mental health counseling is the counselor's therapeutic use of his or her own experiences, reactions, and information in the counseling relationship. Although many variations and styles of counseling are used by today's PCs, historically, the field of counseling is founded on the works of Carl Rogers (Aubrey, 1977). Rogers' approach was based on field theory and founded in the client's present rather than the past, as previously emphasized by Freudian psychology (Hershenson & Strein, 1991; Meador & Rogers, 1973). Rogers' strong belief in the "dignity of the individual" (p. 121) permeates the philosophy and theory underlying the field of counseling.

The counseling relationship provides a permissive environment where a client can explore his/her own needs, desires, and goals (Hershenson & Strein, 1991; Palmo et al., 2001; Weikel & Palmo, 1989). More important for the PC, Rogers advocated that the counselor also be free in the counseling relationship to use his or her experiences in the sessions as feedback for the client. Thus, the concept of the active "use of self" on the part of the counselor became a critical part of the PC's role and function. This aspect of the role makes the PC a distinctly different professional from other mental health care providers.

Traditionally, other mental health providers have followed a more analytic therapeutic approach. The psychiatric/medical model has permeated the helping profession since the time of Freud. Using the work of Rogers as a foundation, professional counseling became the first helping profession that advocated the "use of self" as a necessary aspect of therapy that provides the groundwork for client improvement. The "use of self" is one professional characteristic that sets counseling apart from all other helping professionals.

Positive Approach to Mental Health

A second differentiating factor for the MHC is the belief that the individual has the capability to correct whatever problems he or she faces (Palmo et al., 2001; Weikel & Palmo, 1989). As Seiler and Messina (1979) stated in one of the original articles on mental health counseling, the model is based "on the client's strengths and on helping develop skills necessary for successfully dealing with life" (p. 5). The medical model is based on the premise that someone is sick, whereas the developmental preventive model emphasizes the need to focus on normality and wellness.

This leads to the second aspect of the positive approach to mental health–prevention. As noted earlier in the chapter and in the Highlight section on prevention, the primary professional responsibility and energy for the counselor is placed on the prevention of mental illness as well as assisting individuals and groups in crisis. The PC has to be "prepared . . . to work more on preventing onset (primary prevention) and less on the overwhelming task of working with already affected individual clients (secondary prevention)" (Hershenson & Strein, 1991, p. 250). Professional counseling remains dedicated to primary prevention within the total model.

The concept of prevention does not deny the existence of crises in each person's life. Rather, it is expected that everyone goes through a variety of crises, large and small, throughout a lifetime. Crises are a part of every individual's normal development. The community at large is more comfortable with the concepts of prevention, which views people in positive ways and does not label them as mentally ill. Therefore, the counseling philosophy of prevention as a major aspect of the model helps alleviate the stigma usually associated with mental health services.

Self-Development as a Continued Process

Normal development for any individual is fraught with many crises and problems. The problem for most individuals is not *How to avoid a crisis* but rather how to deal with a crisis once it is upon them. The PC's basic philosophy is founded on the belief that a person has the capability to handle the problems he or she faces and to continue to develop personally while attempting to "fix" the problem. Therefore, not all individuals should be labeled "sick" when they are having difficulty facing a certain problem situation. A person who is temporarily nonfunctional because of a problem may not be necessarily "sick," but in need of assistance to overcome his or her difficulties.

Although a certain percentage of individuals seeking mental health services may need consistent and continual care, a majority of the population needs help to get through crisis situations only. The effects of the crisis may last one month or one year, but eventually the person can function on his or her own. The counselor believes that an individual, who may be nonfunctional for a period of time, will more than likely return to functional in the future. Self-development is a process of personal "ups and downs" that continues throughout a person's life, with dysfunctional not necessarily meaning abnormal.

Counseling Relationship

Presented 25 years ago and relevant today, Boy and Pine (1979) masterfully wrote, "Counselors may be the last professionals in our society who are committed to meeting the needs of clients through the process of counseling" (p. 527). Although this statement is 25 years old, it remains true for PCs today! The counselor's role and function in prevention are quite important, but *mental health counseling is founded on the counseling process.* Of all the core providers, the PC remains the helping professional who is committed to the counseling relationship. Although the PC may function in a variety of settings and roles, his or her primary function is counseling (Bubenzer, Zimpfer, & Mahrle, 1990; Palmo, et al., 2001; Seligman & Whitely, 1983; Weikel & Taylor, 1979; Wilcoxon & Puleo, 1992; Zimpfer & DeTrude, 1990).

SUMMARY

Although professional counseling is a relatively new profession when compared with the other core providers of mental health services, it has now emerged and been recognized as an important part of the total health care system. The field of counseling is seen as continuing to grow in the future (Ginter, 2001; Palmo et al., 2001; Weikel & Palmo, 1989) because of the needs of the community at-large.

The need for counselors has been demonstrated through the rapid development of licensure across the states over the past 15 years. In addition, the acceptance of the LPC by the insurance industry has given professional counseling a major boost. The consistent work of the professional counselors over the past 20 years has ensured a bright future for the newest group of mental health care providers.

REFERENCES

Asher, J. K. (1979). The coming exclusion of counselors from the mental health care system. *American Mental Health Counselors Association Journal, 1,* 53–60.

Aubrey, R. F. (1977). Historical development of guidance and counseling and implications for the future. *Personnel and Guidance Journal, 55,* 288–295.

Aubrey, R. F. (1983). The odyssey of counseling and images of the future. *Personnel and Guidance Journal, 62,* 78–82.

Biglan, A., Mrazek, P. J., Carnine, D., & Flay, B. R. (2003). The integration of research practice in the prevention of youth problem behaviors. *American Psychologist, 58,* 433–440.

Boy, A. V., & Pine, G. J. (1979). Needed: A rededication to the counselor's primary commitment. *Personnel and Guidance Journal, 57,* 527–528.

Bradley, M. K. (1978). Counseling past and present: Is there a future? *Personnel and Guidance*

Journal, 57, 42–45.

Bradley, R. W., & Cox, J. A. (2001). Counseling: Evaluation of the profession. In D. C. Locke, J. E. Myers, & E. L. Herr (Eds.), *The handbook of counseling* (pp. 27–41). Thousand Oaks, CA: Sage.

Bubenzer, D. L., Zimpfer, D. G., & Mahrle, C. L. (1990). Standardized individual appraisal in agency and private practice: A survey. *Journal of Mental Health Counseling, 12,* 51–66.

Council for Accreditation of Counseling and Related Educational Programs. (1994). *CACREP accreditation standards and procedures manual.* Alexandria, VA: Author.

Council for Accreditation of Counseling and Related Educational Programs. (2009). *CACREP accreditation standards and procedures manual.* Alexandria, VA: Author.

Dictionary of occupational titles (4th ed.). (1991). Indianapolis, IN: JIST, Inc.

Ginter, E. J. (2001). Private practice: The professional counselor. In D. C. Locke, J. E. Myers, & E. L. Herr (Eds.), *The handbook of counseling* (pp. 355–372). Thousand Oaks, CA: Sage.

Goodyear, R. K. (1976). Counselors as community psychologists. *Personnel and Guidance Journal, 54,* 512–516.

Heller, K. (1993). Prevention activities for older adults: Social structures and personal competencies that maintain useful social roles. *Journal of Counseling and Development, 72,* 124–130.

Hershenson, D. B., & Strein, W. (1991). Toward a mentally healthy curriculum for mental health counselor education. *Journal of Mental Health Counseling, 13,* 247–252.

Holloway, J. D. (2004a, June). Louisiana grants psychologists prescriptive authority. *Monitor on Psychology, 35,* 20–21.

Holloway, J. D. (2004b, June). Gaining prescriptive knowledge. *Monitor on Psychology, 35,* 22–24.

Kiselica, M. S., & Look, C. T. (1993). Mental health counseling and prevention: Disparity between philosophy and practice? *Journal of Mental Health Counseling, 15,* 3–14.

Lange, S. (1983). The ten commandments for community mental health education. *Personnel and Guidance Journal, 62,* 41–42.

Lewis, J. A., & Lewis, M. D. (1977). *Community counseling: A human services approach.* New York: John Wiley & Sons.

Lindenberg, S. P. (1983). Professional renewal: Counseling at the crossroads. *Pennsylvania Journal of Counseling, 2,* 1–10.

Lum, C. L. (2010). Licensure & certification–state professional counselor licensure boards. Alexandria, VA: American Counseling Association.

McCollum, M. G. (1981). Recasting a role for mental health educators. *American Mental Health Counselors Association Journal, 3,* 37–47.

Meador, B. D., & Rogers, C. R. (1973). Client-centered therapy. In R. Corsini (Ed.), *Current psychotherapies* (pp. 119–165). Itasca, IL: Peacock.

Messina, J. J. (1979). Why establish a certification system for professional counselors? A rationale. *American Mental Health Counselors Association Journal, 1,* 9–22.

Myers, J. E. (1992). Wellness, prevention, development: The cornerstone of the profession. *Journal of Counseling and Development, 71,* 136–139.

Nation, M., Crusto, C., Wandersman, A., Kumpfer, K. L., Seybolt, D., Morrisey-Kane, E., & Devino, K. (2003). What works in prevention: Principles of effective prevention programs. *American Psychologist, 58,* 449–456.

Occupational outlook handbook. (1984, April). U.S. Department of Labor, Bulletin #2205. Washington, DC.

Occupational outlook handbook, 2010–2011 edition. Counselors. U.S. Department of Labor. Retrieved January 4, 2010, from http://bls.gov/oco/print/ocoso74.htm.

Occupational outlook handbook, 2010–2011 edition. Physicians and surgeons. U.S. Department of Labor. Retrieved January 4, 2010, from http://bls.gov/oco/print/ocoso74.htm.

Occupational outlook handbook, 2010–2011 edition. Psychologists. U.S. Department of Labor. January 4, 2010, from http://bls.gov/oco/print/ocoso74.htm.

Occupational outlook handbook, 2010–2011 edition. Registered Nurses. U.S. Department of Labor. Retrieved January 4, 2010, from http://bls.gov/oco/print/ocoso74.htm.

Occupational outlook handbook, 2010–2011 edition. Social Workers. U.S. Department of Labor. Retrieved January 4, 2010, from http://bls.gov/oco/print/ocoso74.htm.

Palmo, A. J. (1981). *Mental health counselor.* Unpublished manuscript developed for the American Mental Health Counselors Association Board of Directors, Washington, DC.

Palmo, A. J. (2005). Professional identity of the professional counselor. In A. J. Palmo, W. J. Weikel, & D. P. Borsos (Eds.), *Foundations of mental health counseling* (pp. 30–48). Springfield, IL: Charles C Thomas.

Palmo, A. J., Shosh, M. J., & Weikel, W. J. (2001). The independent practice of mental health counseling: Past, present, and Future. In D. C. Locke, J. E. Myers, & E. L. Herr (Eds.), *The handbook of counseling* (pp. 653–667). Thousand Oaks, CA: Sage.

Randolph, D. L., Sturgis, D. K., & Alcorn, J. D. (1979). A counseling community psychology master's program. *American Mental Health Counselors Association Journal, 1,* 69–72.

Seiler, G., & Messina, J. J. (1979). Toward professional identity: The dimensions of mental health counseling in perspective. *American Mental Health Counselors Association Journal, 1,* 3–8.

Seligman, L., & Whitely, N. (1983). AMHCA and VMHCA members in private practice in Virginia. *American Mental Health Counselors Association Journal, 5,* 179–183.

Shaw, M. C. (1986). The prevention of learning and interpersonal problems. *Journal of Counseling and Development, 64,* 624–627.

Sherrard, P. A. D., & Fong, M. L. (1991). Mental health counselor training: Which model shall prevail? *Journal of Mental Health Counseling, 13,* 204–210.

Sperry, L., Carlson, J., & Lewis, J. (1993). Health counseling strategies and interventions. *Journal of Mental Health Counseling, 15,* 15–25.

Tulkin, S. R., & Stock, W. (2004). A model for predoctoral psychopharmacology trainings: Shaping a new frontier in clinical psychology. *Professional Psychology: Research & Practice, 35,* 151–157.

Wayne, G. (1982). An examination of selected statutory licensing requirements for psychologists in the United States. *Personnel and Guidance Journal, 60,* 420–425.

Weikel, W. J., & Palmo, A. J. (1989). The evolution and practice of mental health counseling. *Journal of Mental Health Counseling, 11,* 7–25.

Weikel, W. J., & Taylor, S. S. (1979). AMHCA: Membership profile and journal preferences. *American Mental Health Counselors Association Journal, 1,* 89–94.

Weissberg, R. P., Kumpfer, K. L., & Seligman, M. E. P. (2003). Prevention that works for children and youth. *American Psychologist, 58,* 425–432.

Westbrook, F. D., Kandell, J. J., Kirkland, S. E., Phillips, P. E., Regan, A. M., Medvene, A., & Oslin, Y. D. (1993). University campus consultation: Opportunities and limitations. *Journal of Counseling and Development, 71,* 684–688.

Wiggins, J. G., & Wedding, D. (2004). Prescribing, professional identity, and costs. *Professional Psychology: Research & Practice, 35,* 148–150.

Wilcoxon, S. A., & Puleo, S. G. (1992). Professional-developmental needs of mental health counselors: Results of a national survey. *Journal of Mental Health Counseling, 14,* 187–1995.

Zimpfer, D. G., & DeTrude, J. C. (1990). Follow-up of doctoral graduates in counseling. *Journal of Counseling and Development, 69,* 51–56.

Section II

THEORY AND PRACTICE OF MENTAL HEALTH COUNSELING

Chapter 3

THE ROLE OF THEORY IN THE PRACTICE OF MENTAL HEALTH COUNSELING: HISTORY AND DEVELOPMENT

THOMAS A. SEAY AND MARY B. SEAY

Why has mental health counseling in its various incarnations survived for so long? The answer, of course, depends on many reasons too numerous to iterate here and most of which are addressed by other authors within these pages. Historically, the most practical reason lies in meeting a national need not served by other mental health professionals. Of equal historical importance, however, is the **PHILOSOPHY → THEORY → PRACTICE** (see Figure 3.1) paradigm (Seay, 1980a). In an age where most practitioners consider themselves practical (if not theoretical) eclectics in their approaches to counseling (Kendall, & Chambless, 1998; Lazarus, 1993; Lazarus, Beutler, & Norcross, 1992; Lazarus, 1993; Mahoney, 1991; Norcross, 1993), this paradigm is even more important to the continued existence of the profession than true previously. However, problems associated with eclecticism abound.

The underlying paradigm for therapeutic intervention, **PHILOSOPHY → THEORY → PRACTICE**, contributes in many important ways to the development of counseling as a vibrant profession. This philosophy to practice paradigm is the foundation for advancements in therapeutic intervention. Furthermore, it provides the cushion necessary for deviations from tradition to occur safely. Revolutionary changes (such as HMOs, HIPAA regulations, brief therapy, and family therapy) are occurring in the field of mental health, and further changes lie ahead. As teachers and practitioners, we must understand the meaning and significance of our profession's history in relation to future directions if we are to continue to provide quality services.

To ignore our history presages the eventuality of a fear expressed by Bergin (1997) that these changes are forcing therapists into little more than "cookie cutters" (p. 85). The many treatment manuals in existence that dictate to counselors how they should conduct their interventions with specific problems seem to bare fruit to Bergin's fear. The present chapter explores the history and development of counseling and psychotherapy, and more specifically the role of theory, as an influential force in the directions taken by mental health counselors (MHCs) as core providers of mental health services.

To understand fully the role of therapy in contemporary mental health, we must first look at its philosophical and historical roots. Only then does the phenomenon of mental health counseling make some sense. This chapter examines historical antecedents and current trends and developments to determine the role played by theory. What is required is an understanding of what brought about these changes, what the changes mean for the profession, and what impact they are likely to have on the future of counseling. However, first it is necessary to examine the legitimacy of the mental health counselor's role and skills.

Role Legitimacy

MHCs have joined the ranks of psychiatrists, psychologists, social workers, and psychiatric nurses as primary mental health care providers. However, are we legitimate primary caregivers? Acceptance has not been easy, nor have we fully won over significant power brokers in the mental health field. The primary reason is in the developmental history of the practice of mental health care.

Although the origins of mental health counseling are multifarious, three major trends have played an immediate and potent role in mental health counseling. Each deserves special attention. The first trend refers to the numerous changes in the methodology of psychotherapy used to treat society's mental health casualties. Such changes flow directly from the history and evolution of psychotherapy. The profession's history shows movement from model dependency, with a restricted range of strategies and techniques allotted each model, to an attitude of eclecticism. With eclecticism almost any strategy or technique is acceptable so long as it gives the appearance of working (e.g., evidence-based or empirically based therapy procedures) (Chambless & Hollon, 1998; Chambless & Ollendick, 2001; Roth & Fonagy, 1996). Even more recent attention seems to be focused on specific process dynamics and attributes such as the stage of change a client may have attained in his or her therapeutic process (Dolan, 2004; Freeman & Dolan, 2001; Prochaska, 1991; Prochaska & DiClemente, 1982) and the therapeutic interventions necessary within each stage. Some of these developments are occurring as a direct result of the managed care movement (Austad & Hoyt, 1992). Although it is still too early to know where such developments will lead, these trends will receive detailed attention throughout the remainder of the chapter.

The second development is of more recent origins and is found in the community mental health movement of the 1960s and 1970s. Returning society's casualties to the community for treatment was a revolutionary step toward recognizing the relationship among intrapsychic, interpersonal, and environmental sources of etiology and between etiology and treatment. The trend also provided an organizational model for mental health counseling, a psychoecology perspective (Seay, 1983).

The third trend grew from the guidance movement of the 1950s. Although it resulted in the production of counselors who worked primarily in educational settings, these counselors used methodology drawn almost entirely from models of psychotherapy. Consequently, it should come as no great surprise that the counselors would eventually turn their knowledge and skills toward a larger community of people in need. These three developments–changes in psychotherapy delivery, ecological psychology, and production of psychologically and educationally trained counselors–merged together to create a fifth core mental health provider–one who possesses the knowledge and skills necessary to work with society's casualties. Yes, we are legitimate.

Counseling and Psychotherapy: What's in a Name?

One of the perennial controversies within the health care professions is whether counseling can be considered the same as psychotherapy or whether the counseling profession represent different roles, skills, and methods (see e.g., Hackney & Cormier, 2001; Hill & Lambert, 2004; Neukrug, 1999; Patterson, 1974). Many leading authorities believe that the two represent distinctive approaches to helping people, and that the approaches differ in essential, identifiable ways. Other professionals hold that such a controversy is meaningless, and that any distinction serves the sole purpose of creating professional elitism.

It is indeed difficult to distinguish between the two on the basis of the type of client served, the theoretical underpinnings, the therapeutic processes, and the major strategies and techniques. Practitioners of counseling and psychotherapy work with the same people, use the same methodology, and work toward the same goals.

In the past, factors such as the type of therapy delivered, the degree of disturbance, the clinical work setting, and the type of training received (Patterson, 1974) were employed to distinguish between counseling and psychotherapy. Differentiation based on the type of therapy delivered follows the argument that counseling is emotionally expressive, supportive, and educative, whereas psychotherapy is depth-oriented, uncovering, and remediative.

Such a distinction creates problems. Persons employed as counselors encounter clients who begin to disclose deep levels of self. Thus, counselors either move or are "shoved" into an uncovering process. It is hard to imagine saying to a client, "Please stop, don't say anything further. My profession won't allow me to get into this much depth." Furthermore, uncovering is the first step in any therapeutic encounter. It is impossible to remain at a superficial level for any length of time. Remediation is also the desired outcome whether one is attempting vocational counseling or attempting therapeutically to intervene into the private world of a schizophrenic. To create such a distinction is unrealistic.

At one time, the work setting served as an adequate means of differentiating between counseling and psychotherapy. Historically, counselors were employed primarily in educational settings, whereas psychotherapists worked in clinics, mental health agencies, hospitals, and private practice. This is no longer true, as can be easily verified by examining current employment practices across the nation. Today, practitioners whose primary identification is with counseling and those who identify more with psychotherapy are employed in all major work settings and work side by side for the betterment of their common clientele.

Traditionally, the medical degree and the PhD in clinical psychology represented the necessary training to function as psychotherapists. Persons earning the EdD or PhD in counseling psychology were labeled counselors and were expected to work with clients other than mentally disturbed patients. Not only have these practitioners earned the right to practice psychotherapy, but over the past 25 years, people trained at the master's level (MA, MS, MSW, and MDiv) have moved toward and, in some instances, won recognition as legitimate practitioners in mental health. As the demand for services continues to increase and the supply of practitioners continues at levels inadequate to meet current mental health needs, the line of differentiation based on professional degree will continue to diminish. The master's-level practitioner will also continue to gain recognition as a mental health provider. Licensure for the master's-level counselor is already a reality across the nation. In part, the Managed Health Care movement, with its emphasis on minimal reimbursement of licensed practitioners and session limits, assists the impetus toward licensure and master's-level private practice.

None of the prior arguments suffices to distinguish between counseling and psychotherapy. In the latest edition of the well-respected *Bergin & Garfield's Handbook of Psychotherapy and Behavior Change,* Lambert, Bergin, and Garfield (2004) pay homage, albeit reluctantly, to this receding differentiation.

The professional community of mental health providers must now recognize at least five core providers in the treatment of society's casualties. The tasks of the future will be recognizing that these practitioners share common theoretical nets and a core of therapeutic intervention skills, and identifying the unique contribution each practitioner makes to overall caregiving. For example, psychiatry is unique in that practitioners dispense medication, not that they deliver psychotherapy that differs from that of the psychologist. Each core provider should and can provide something unique. The professional community must seek both that uniqueness and the core skills shared in common, rather than mire itself in inane debates over whose credentials are best or which practitioner is the rightful heir of therapeutic intervention. It would seem that our time is more valuable when spent providing services to clients.

Historical Perspective

Counseling is an artistic endeavor that uses scientific methodology to help people lead more effective lives. Counseling, growing as it has from the practice of psychotherapy, is now more than 100 years old. Much time and effort have been expended in developing the philosophies, theories, and practices of therapy. For such a young endeavor, compared with other sciences, it has been relatively successful (Lambert & Ogles, 2004; Smith, Glass, & Miller, 1980).

Counseling is a vibrant profession. Practitioners, over the last 40 years, have witnessed phenomenal changes. The plethora of strategies and techniques available today were either absent or enjoyed only restricted use in the 1960s. Research has grown into a more sophisticated endeavor, moving from questions such as "which approach is best" to "what are the components of effective therapy" to "which strategy works with which client under what specified set of circumstances." The next 10 to 20 years will witness even more changes. The rapidity and magnitude with which these changes are occurring present difficulties for the novice and the experienced counselor alike in gaining a firm grasp of the field.

To understand what is currently happening in the field of mental health counseling, it is necessary to understand how the field evolved into its present status. Numerous changes in the philosophical and theoretical foundations for intervention have led to innovations in processes and strategies. These, in turn, have resulted in major breakthroughs in the treatment of society's casualties.

Philosophical Foundation

A major strength of counseling/psychotherapy has been the internal consistency that binds a set of practices to a theoretical net and the net's underpinning philosophical foundation. That is, the foundation for the various counseling models is composed of a set of philosophical beliefs about human beings, which in turn guides the formation of theoretical propositions about human functioning. Based on these theoretical propositions, a set of practices designed to change aspects of human functioning evolves. To be a viable force, however, the movement from philosophical beliefs to counseling practices must be internally consistent. This consistency has enabled counseling to make its impact on society demonstrable and its legitimacy solidified. Figure 3.1 represents how this internal consistency may be viewed.

PHILOSOPHY → THEORY → PRACTICE

Figure 3.1. Internal Consistency as a Foundation for Counseling.

The philosophy to practice consistency enables practitioners to evaluate how well their theory predicts actual behavior in counseling, provides an explanation for how change occurs, and establishes expectations for what should be done to create change for clients. The theory builder develops certain philosophical assumptions about the nature of "humanness" and about the source of knowledge (epistemology) or how change occurs. These assumptions should lead directly to a set of theoretical propositions about human functioning. The theory of human functioning then dictates the nature of the counseling process and the intrasessional behaviors that are necessary to create change (Freeman & Dolan, 2001; Prochaska & Norcross, 2002).

Following this paradigm, some concepts are appropriate within a given model, whereas others are not. If a primary assumption concerning the source of knowledge holds that the human mind is analogous to a blank paper "written on" by environmental forces, then "wired-in" or inherited cognitive configurations for learning and such notions as memory traces and insight probably should not be postulated.

Seay (1980b; Braswell & Seay, 1984) traced the development of various counseling (psychotherapy) models from their philosophical foundations. As can be seen by examination of Figure 3.2, the lines of influence are not clear-cut. Current philosophical beliefs developed from the Greek traditions. Plato's world of representations of ideals resulted in contemporary phenomenology; and Aristolean thought is expressed in modern empirical philosophy.

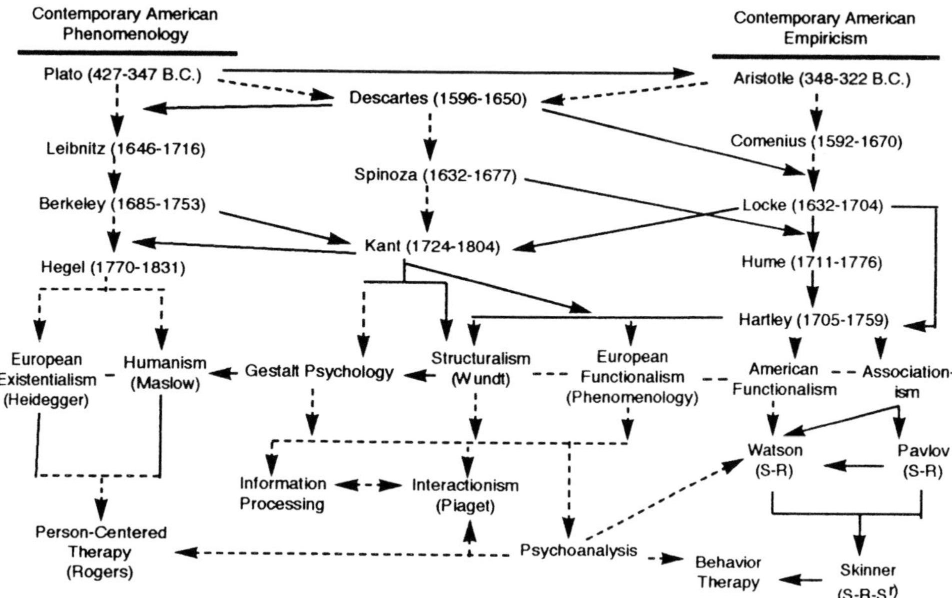

Figure 3.2. Philosophical-Ideological Foundations for Models of Knowledge and Therapy.

Contemporary phenomenology is best expressed through the work of Leibnitz in philosophy and by the humanistic or "third-force" movement in psychology. Leibnitz provided the defining characteristics of phenomenology when he proposed that the subjective world of the mind was the source of knowledge. The basic datum for phenomenologists is experience. Thus, knowledge or the source for client change resides in the perceptual awareness of the individual. Considerations of an external reality are useless because the only source of knowledge about reality is created through the subjective, interpretive system inherent to the perceiver's mind. Shlien (1970) states that "the phenomenologist is convinced that much goes on 'inside,' and that the behavioristic concept of the 'empty organism' is narrow, and largely spurious. Most of our experience and its meanings exist in 'private worlds'. . . " (p. 96).

Shlien (1970) captures the essential position of phenomenologists when he writes that "physiological indexes of internal states will have immense value for the study of experience, but heart rate, brain waves, pupil size, endocrine output, or whatever comes will only measure increases or decreases without meaning unless the identifying code is first given and then continually validated by the wise and willing knower" (p. 96). A thing is knowable only in so much as the perceiver values and invests value in the thing known. Leibnitz, in contrast to Locke, viewed people as actors on and creators of their environment (Allport, 1955).

The second source of influence on counseling was derived from the work of John Locke and others of the empiricist tradition. Locke's view represents the empiricist tradition in philosophy and associationism (behaviorism) in psychology. Locke's system maintained that human beings are passive recipients of environmental events and sensory experiences from an external environment. According to Rychlak (1969), "Locke believed that the contents of mind could only be those which come in from the outside" (p. 215). At birth, the child is a "blank paper" that is written on by environmental experiences. "The mind itself is passive, storing and combining such inputs in a pseudo-mathematical fashion, but never imposing structure onto the world of experience" (Rychlak, 1969, p. 215).

The world exists external to the perceiver, and examining the natural order of things derives knowledge. Nature follows a set of laws that enable scientists to understand it. Humans are simply an element of nature, and they emulate natural order. There is little need to look outside nature or the external environment for answers. Mental health and mental illness follow the same basic laws found in nature. Thus, knowledge and, consequently, change come from sources external to the perceiver. People react to their environment and their environment acts on them (Allport, 1955). People are not creators but only part of the natural order. Mind and brain are the same thing, and the brain is only a physical organ, albeit a complex organ designed to receive environmental stimuli.

The third major philosophical position is derived from the work of Kant. Kant's system represents an interactionist position, which holds that, although knowledge is subjective and knowable only within the interpretive realm of the perceiver, the stimuli for knowledge are found in an external reality. According to Rychlak (1969), "Kant viewed ideas as conceptions of reason which transcended experience" (p. 215). However, what is to be known is real. Nature and natural laws provide the stimuli for knowledge and are susceptible to scientific validation, but some things are known only because of the perceiver. "Man's mentality never senses reality directly, 'things in themselves' (noumena), but deals only with sensory representations (phenomena) mediated by the understanding" (Rychlak, 1969, p. 215). The subjective reality of the perceiver interacts with the objective reality of the environment to produce knowledge and, thereby, change. "What is vital to the Kantian conception is his view of mind as an organizing experience in a certain way" (Rychlak, 1969, p. 215). The mind organizes what it perceives and then transforms the newly organized perceptions into meaningful thoughts. Kant's interactionism is a separate and distinct line of thought.

Each of these major philosophical systems has resulted in a particular line of thought leading directly to a major "school" or "model" of counseling.

Leibnitzian philosophy provides the foundation for personology or what is now called humanistic psychology. In counseling, the primary model is Rogers' Person-Centered Psychotherapy. The Lockean tradition became the basis for Behavior Therapy and Behavioral Counseling. Kantian interactionism provides the foundation for Freud's psychoanalysis. Each of these three models became the major paradigm from which other models are derived (see Figure 3.3). As Corsini (2000) observed, "all psychotherapies are intended to change people: to make them think differently (cognition), to make them feel differently (affection), and to make them act differently (behavior)" (p. 6).

Stages of Theory Development

The practice of individual psychotherapy is now more than 90 years old. During this developmental period, only three primary models of psychotherapy evolved. Each of these three models developed from one of three primary philosophical systems.

Using a historical perspective to examine the development of counseling and psychotherapy, certain stage-related progressions can be discerned. These progressions are classified as stages in the development of counseling theory. As with all developmental stages, these are arbitrary impositions on the natural flow of development. However, such impositions aid in understanding the current state of the profession. Seay (1980b) identified five stages (Table 3.1) through which theory development has progressed. The complete stage model is as follows.

Table 3.1. Historical Overview of Stages of Theory Development

Stage	*Name*	*Examples*
1	Original Paradigm	Psychoanalysis, Client-Centered & Behavior Therapy
2	Paradigm Modification	Jung, Adler, Paterson, Bandura
3	Paradigm Specificity	Berne, Jourard, Genlin, Beck, Krumboltz
4	Paradigm Experimentation	Strupp, Mitchell & Aron, Ellis, Beutler, Wexler, Lazarus
5	Paradigm Consolidation	Potentially Lazarus, Seay, Beultler

Each of the stages is examined.

Figure 3.3 shows these developments and the interrelatedness of the various models that have been based on or derived from the original three paradigms (Stage 1: Original Paradigm).

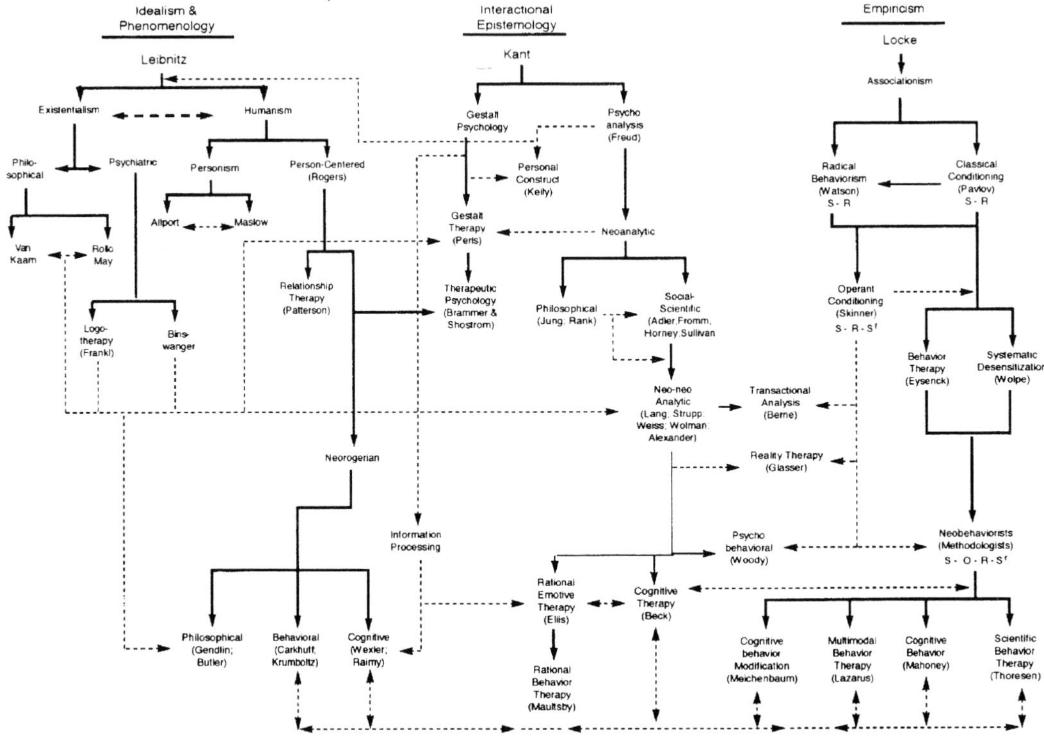

Figure 3.3. Interrelatedness Among Therapies Based on Epistemological Divergence and Lines of Influence.

Also, Rychlak (1965) examined psychotherapy from the perspective of the motives for engaging in psychotherapy. Interestingly, Rychlak's three motives correspond to what Seay (1980b) refers to as the three original paradigms of therapy. Rychlak identified the basic motives for psychotherapy as the scholarly motive, the ethical motive, and the curative motive.

Stage 1 developments resulted in the creation of an original paradigm. Each paradigm is based on a different source of knowledge or change (human modality) and has as its foundation a distinct philosophical system. The first paradigm to be developed was Freud's. Psychoanalysis, which became the prototype for counseling and psychotherapy, sought the source of knowledge in insight, a cognitive process. The goal of psychoanalysis was and still is the development of insight by therapists into their patients' intrapsychic dynamics and conflicts. Psychoanalysis explained how these conflicts arose and how Freud's "talking therapy" resolved them through insight–oriented techniques. The model had a high degree of internal consistency from its foundational philosophy to its set of prescribed practices. The underlying theme that held the model together was that knowledge (psychological change) came from cognitive activity (subjective) of natural events (objective). Psychoanalysis is an excellent translation of Kant's philosophy into real-world problems.

The first of Rychlak's (1965) motives, the scholarly motive, corresponds to the purpose of psychotherapy best represented by Freud. By examining intrapsychic dynamics using the psychoanalytic method, the analyst could learn about human nature and human motives. The therapist was essentially a scientific scholar. In fact, Freud thought the technique of free association as analogous to the scientist's microscope. The fact that Freud had no difficulty in seeing the applicability of the natural sciences to the study of mental activity is a direct demonstration of the power of Kantian philosophy–an external reality examined from the internal world of perceiver. Freud's emphasis influenced Seay's (1980b) designation of psychoanalysis as a cognitive paradigm.

Carl Rogers created the second original paradigm. Rogers focused on the subjective experiencing of people and on how change was created within these subjective experiences. Rogers' approach corresponds to Rychlak's second motive, the ethical motive. "Felt" levels of experiencing come from interpersonal relationships–relationships that either did or did not provide the necessary elements of growth. Rogers' model focuses on the interpersonal difficulties of clients. Thus, Rogers' Person-Centered Therapy represents an affective, interpersonal model or a phenomenological experiencing. Thus, Client-Centered Therapy is one theory that represents the phenomenological philosophy.

Rychlak's second motive emphasized the ethical consideration of helping people to grow and was primarily the focal point of Rogers. The basic reason for conducting psychotherapy is to help people grow. This task is accomplished through a subjective encounter with the patient. Rogers (1964) labeled this type of epistemology "interpersonal knowing or phenomenological knowledge." The primary analogy is experience. The therapist comes to know the patient's (client's) attitudes and emotions (the "felt" level of experiencing). Rychlak (1965) refers to this emphasis on felt experiencing as "the ethics of self-determination through congruent interpersonal relations" (p. 115).

Locke's philosophy provides the foundation for modern scientific inquiry. A scientific model of counseling and psychotherapy was a natural extension of the Lockean tradition. Behavior Therapy, the application of learning theory to human suffering, represents the third motive–the curative purpose. The therapeutic emphasis is to help people change their ineffective behaviors. This orientation is epitomized by the work of Wolpe (1973). The purpose for conducting therapy is to cure the patient. The appropriate analogy for therapy is the experimental design (Rychlak, 1965). Treatment is established as an experiment in the modification of behavior. Behavior is the focal point because it is an observable event. The experimental design calls for observation as the method used to derive basic data. In this sense, Behavior Therapy is consistent with the Lockean tradition (British Empiricism) with its emphasis on the observable, external reality. Human suffering is explained as learned associations. What was once learned could be unlearned or re-learned. True to Lockean philosophy, Behavior therapists see little need to postulate internal processes to account for psychological dysfunctions. Thus, Behavioral counseling completes the therapeutic triad corresponding to the triad of human modalities–cognition (Psychoanalysis), affect (Client-Centered Therapy), and behavior (Behavior Therapy). Each of these three basic models forms the tradition (cognitive, affective, and behavioral modalities) from which numerous other models were derived. Each of the three models represents a major shift of focus in both theory and practice. Each represented a paradigm shift from what was tradition at that time.

Beyond the Original Paradigm

The human mind thrives on inquiry. Not long after the development of each of these three paradigms, members of the professional community began to modify the original paradigms, thus ushering in the second stage of development–the Modification Stage. Stage 2 developments occurred when proponents of the original paradigm discovered a lack or an unfulfilled need in the original theory. For example, Jung tempered Freud's biosexual theory with a philosophical perspective, and Adler provided a social perspective. Both theorists gave psychoanalysis depth and breadth, but neither changed the paradigm's basic structure.

The third stage was classified by Seay as the Specificity Stage. During this stage, proponents of a particular paradigm adapted aspects of the original paradigm to their perceived needs. Thus, while leaving the basic structure of the parent paradigm intact (e.g., Berne's use of parent, child, and adult for Freud's superego, id, and ego), they developed approaches to counseling based on some specific aspect of the original. Within Stage 3 adaptations, the integrity of the original paradigm suffered few violations to its parameters.

Current Developments: Stage 4 Experimentation

Current Status

Counseling has undergone radical changes over the past 30 or 40 years. Also, the rules used to signify appropriate conduct in counseling have changed. As a result, it is difficult for practitioners to fathom the multitude of innovations and current practices as organized and following a specific path of development. Yet that is precisely what has happened.

Seay (1980b) indicated that a fourth stage, the Experimentation Stage, accounts for these changes. The fourth stage is used to reflect the current status of the profession. Theoreticians violated the parameters of the original paradigms by experimenting with theoretical structures, processes, and paradigm-linked techniques. Once such experimentation occurs when the counseling profession enters Stage 4: Experimentation, but the resulting changes and innovations to emerge thus far have already profoundly impacted the practice of counseling (Ellis & Dryden, 1987; Gurman & Messer, 2003; Lazarus, Beutler, & Norcross, 1992; Mahoney, 1991). For example, once previously radical behaviorists accept internal processing, such as cognitions, they violate the parameters of their basic paradigm. However, in doing so, behaviorists, as a group, move closer to the humanists. In the interim period, many of the "third force" humanists are beginning to conduct therapy by increasingly using relaxation techniques, homework assignments, and a wide array of other behavioral techniques. Also, some practitioners with a primary identification of psychoanalysis sound more like behaviorists than many current behaviorists. In addition, with the growing acceptance of family therapy, a Stage 4 development, as a viable methodology for treatment, the panorama of therapy is explicitly altered. We as practitioners have moved beyond being able to ignore any aspect of human functioning as fair game for therapeutic intervention, particularly the "felt level of experiencing" (Rychlak, 1978).

Stage 4, however, has yet to run its course. The experimental manipulation of paradigm parameters is only just beginning. Also, researchers are beginning to emphasize the scientific validation of strategies and techniques. Once paradigm parameters are breached, the philosophy to practice internal consistency that gave counseling its foundation falls apart. For example, the Lockean philosophy cannot provide a firm philosophical foundation for cognitive-behavior therapy. A cognitive-behavioral view implies an interactive involvement with the environment (non-S-R) and inherent (perhaps even deep) structures of cognitive organization. An affective-behavioral approach such as Robert Carkhuff's (1969) model is a reinterpretation of Rogers' Client-Centered Therapy and, as such, can no longer claim a Leibnitzian base. Thus, Stage 4 is a stage of models without internal consistency or foundational supports. Paradigm violation is Lazarus' (1976; Lazarus, Beutler, & Norcross, 1992) "technical eclecticism" in action. Note that the previous is not a criticism, just a statement of current status. Technical eclecticism is seen here as a necessary step toward Kuhn's (1970) "scientific paradigm" status and as a natural outcome of Stage 4 experimentation.

At some point in the future, this problem, because it is a problem, must be reconciled. The profession must have a means of anchoring its practices, in both theory and philosophy. Philosophy and theory underpin therapeutic practices whether practitioners acknowledge or ignore their existence.

Perhaps a new philosophy will evolve. Perhaps a combinatory alternative to current philosophical positions will be found (Seay, 1978). Although the future does not lend itself to accurate predictions, sufficient evidence is accruing that points to a fifth stage. As previously mentioned, practitioners are becoming more and more alike in their actual intrasessional behaviors and practices. In addition, theoretical efforts are assuming a combinatory flavor by adapting concepts drawn from diverse models. It is no longer unusual to talk of cognitive-behavioral or affective-behavioral approaches or even cognitive-behavioral-affective approaches. Speculating on the outcome of these changes, Seay called the fifth state possibility the Consolidation Stage. Stage 5 represents the evolution of a single paradigm for conducting counseling. Such a paradigm should be based on scientifically validated processes, strategies, and techniques. Once such a model is established, it becomes possible to build an appropriate theoretical net. From a well-defined theory, the underlying philosophical propositions can be ascertained, thereby reconstituting the philosophy to practice internal consistency. Finally, counseling and psychotherapy will enter Kuhn's (1970) scientific era. However, not for one minute does this possibility negate the artistry that will always be a part of counseling and psychotherapy, because each session is truly a unique encounter. However, saying that counseling/psychotherapy is an art form equally does not mean that scientific knowledge should be dismissed or taken lightly.

As previously mentioned, Stage 4 developments are having a significant impact on counseling. Part of this impact can be seen in the restraint exercised by theoreticians on further theoretical developments. None has expressed this better than Lazarus (1976), who calls for a "technical eclecticism" until the profession can grow into its own. Kuhn (1970) proposed that a true scientific discipline is one where only a single paradigm exists as the guiding model for the discipline. Counseling currently has no fewer than 250 such competing paradigms (Herink, 1980). Lazarus' call for a moratorium on theorizing is appropriate and timely. The effect of deemphasizing theory building is a granting of freedom from the shackles of model dependency. The price, however, is the desperate need for a scrupulously delimited research mosaic that can answer the myriad of therapeutic questions that must be answered if we are to move forward.

By deemphasizing theoretical dependency, the diminution of model dependency occurs and model boundaries are crossed. Counselors are free to create a mixture of models or what some identify as eclecticism (Norcross, 1986, Seay, 1978). Such mixture is easily demonstrated and more clearly conceptualized if the various models are loosely classified into one of three cat-

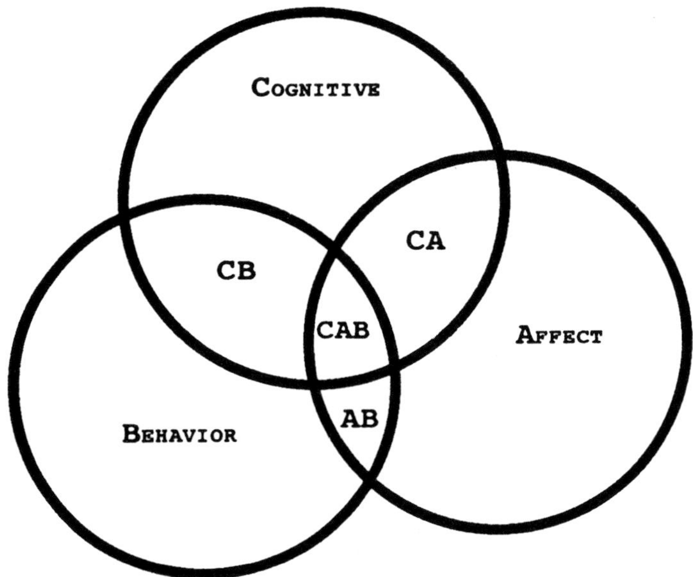

Figure 3.4. Diagram of the Interrelationships Among Cognition, Affect, and Behavior.

egories (Seay, 1978; 1980b). All approaches, where the primary focus for change is on thinking processes or mental structures (cognition) such as Freud's insight-oriented psychoanalysis and Beck's Cognitive Theory, can be grouped together as Cognitive approaches. Other approaches focus almost entirely on the "felt" level of experiencing, such as Rogers' Person-Centered Therapy. Rogers (1964) refers to this felt level of experiencing as phenomenological knowledge. These approaches can be classified as Affective. Finally, the behavioral approaches such as Wolpe's Behavior Therapy and the behavior modification movement (Meichenbaum, 1985) will be classified as Behavior because of the primary emphasis on changing current maladaptive behaviors. Using such a classification system, it becomes easy to diagram (see Figure 3.4) the changes that are occurring.

Where the area lines are uncrossed, pure models are represented. These models emphasize only a single modality such as cognition. Where the lines do cross, two or more human modalities become the point of focus for client change, where the first term (e.g., cognitive in the cognitive-behavior therapy model) is the modifier of the second term (e.g., behavior in the cognitive-behavior therapy model). Thus, counselors are crossing model lines to combine theoretical components, strategies, and processes from different models. The CB component refers to practices that combine the cognitive and behavioral modalities. Thus, the cognitive-behavior therapy movement of recent years (e.g., Meichenbaum, 1977, 1985) can be understood and explained from this perspective. The CB group emphasizes a modification of behavior, but they may accomplish the modification by enabling the client to restructure or otherwise change the way the client thinks first. CA refers to those theorists and practitioners who combine information-processing models of thinking with affective models (an approach consistent with the James theory of emotions) (see Hilgard, 1987) to form a cognitive-affective approach to counseling (Wexler, 1974). The AB designation accounts for approaches that combine the affective modality with the behavioral, such as Krumboltz and Thorensen (1969) and Carkhuff (1969). At this point, few approaches emphasize equally all three modalities (CAB). Lazarus' (1981) multimodal therapy approach stands as an exception. As research continues to identify appropriate tools and processes for counseling, all three modalities (CAB) can be expected to play a more prominent role. New strategies are being developed and will continue to be developed that are designed to address multiple modalities simultaneously. Hopefully, from these efforts a new model will emerge.

Practitioners, in crossing the boundaries of models, are forcing paradigm shifts to occur. As paradigm shifts occur, theoretically divergent practitioners are finding common ground in their practices. What the outcome of this movement will be is difficult to determine, but the profession may be moving toward a consolidation of paradigms (Seay, 1980b). If so, Kuhn's (1970) criterion for a scientific discipline may be achieved in the not-so-distant future. Once the scientific component of counseling has achieved a strengthening of practice, the remaining task becomes one of integrating the artistic encounter of counseling with its scientifically established practices.

Due to the crossing of paradigm boundaries, counselors can identify a multitude of strategies and techniques currently available for their use. In the past, counselors rigidly adhered to a particular model for knowledge concerning appropriate conduct for their counseling practices. Such adherence brought a measure of security and the ability to communicate with others professionals of like mind. However, within these models, practitioners were limited in their ability to utilize strategies and techniques (Seay, 1980b). In fact, practitioners were limited to only techniques identified for their model as being appropriate methods of accomplishing the goals of the model. The effect of model dependency is to force all clients who walk through the door to conform to the model parameters. Model dependency appears to have ended. Counselors are much more free to use a wider variety of techniques drawn from diverse models. A counselor who claims allegiance to one of the humanistic models of counseling can use systematic desensitization or cognitive restructuring without fear of accusations of incompetence (Raimy, 1975). By the same token, it is not at all unusual to find Behavior therapists engaging in cognitive restructuring or affective focusing (Lazarus, 1976, 1981; Mahoney, 1991). They too will no longer be viewed as incompetent or heretical.

Paradigm shifts and multidimensional strategies are not the only changes growing from Stage 4 experimentation. Practitioners are decidedly more eclectic in their approach to helping people. They seem more willing to use whatever they deem necessary to help their clients without fear of paradigm violations. Interestingly, eclecticism comes full circle. Hart (1986) points out that the origins of eclecticism lies not in the 20th century but in the 19th century, where William James in American and Pierre Janet in Paris were part of a group of practitioners who were decidedly eclectic in their approaches.

Obviously, problems result from a haphazard and unsystematic application of techniques. Eclecticism, to be a viable force in counseling, must be systematic, integrative, and process oriented (Seay, 1978). In lieu of philosophy and/or theory, practitioners must evolve some method of case conceptualization to anchor their practices. Examples of case conceptual methods can be found in Lazarus (1976) and Seay (1978). Another possibility is to function as if adhering to a particular model (e.g., Client-Centered Therapy) but still use a greatly expanded repertoire of strategies and techniques that make sense in light of the presenting client problem and the overall goal of intervention.

Additional Stage 4 Developments

Another major development that has occurred recently may eventually change the face of applied psychology. Community psychology, a relatively recent entry in the field of psychology, has already had a significant impact on professional practices (Seay, 1983). Community psychology, as the words imply, is the application of psychological principles to community elements, structures, and dynamics. The origins of community psychology are diverse, but its primary impact can be traced to the conditions within the mental health field in the early 1960s. Because of the recognition that major changes must occur in mental health delivery, John F. Kennedy, then president of the United States, signed into law a bill calling for the establishment of community mental health centers. These centers shifted the responsibility for providing mental health services from state-maintained hospitals to the community. Psychiatrists, psychologists, and social workers were quick to become involved in this new movement, but it has taken the counseling profession somewhat longer to move from a primary emphasis on school settings to the community.

In many areas of the country, counselors have now earned the right to take their place alongside other practitioners in community mental health delivery. In fact, in these authors' geographical location, counselors represent one of the largest, if not the largest, professional group. Thus, the community mental health movement has opened a new arena for professional employment. In so doing, however, the impetus has fallen back to colleges and universities to upgrade and update their training programs. Counselors whose training was geared toward schools have found themselves inadequately trained for the majority of a community's mental health needs. Counselors have found that working in the community necessitates using counseling skills more similar to those of psychiatrists, psychologists, and social workers than those derived from the old guidance movement of the 1950s and early 1960s. Where university programs have provided such a shift in emphasis, counselors are finding jobs even in light of a national economy that has fallen on hard times with unexpected budgetary restrictions, lower productivity, massive job losses, and severely reduced employee salaries and benefits (Herrick, Seay, & Seay 2004).

If no other claims can be made, at least the outcome of the community mental health movement has demonstrated the degree of importance of environment in the remediation of mental health problems.

Developments in Nontraditional Directions

Delivery Systems

There are many different ways to deliver counseling. However, only three basic types of therapy are readily identifiable: (a) individual, (b) group, and (c) family therapy. The distinguishing features of each type are their theoretical nets and their delivery rather than the processes or methodologies involved.

Individual Therapy: The individual form of counseling/psychotherapy refers to the processes and techniques for encountering the client in a one-to-one relationship. The focus of this relationship is on the client and the client's modes of experiencing. The methodology of individual psychotherapy is designed to identify and modify specific aspects of the client's intrapsychic (internal), interpersonal, behavioral, and/or environmental dysfunctions.

Group Therapy: The group approach still focuses on the individual but uses the natural force of group interaction as part of the therapeutic process. Group members become the primary ingredients of change as each person discloses "self." Each member contributes to the process by supporting and uncovering "self" with other members. The methodologies (e.g., psychoanalytic techniques) used in group therapy may not differ greatly from those used in individual therapy, but the mutual support and the direction that psychological change takes through the group effort will differ extensively.

Family Therapy: Family therapy is the newest form of therapy to appear on the professional scene. It differs from the other two types in that family, as an interlocking, interacting system, is the focal point for treatment rather than an individual who may be identified as the patient. The systemic interaction of the family provides the avenue for intervention and change. In fact, for many practitioners, the family is the client not the individual family members.

The dynamics of the therapeutic interaction differ extensively among the three types of delivery. The dynamics of family therapy acknowledge that the family comprises a powerful social institution, and that it has internal supports and motivational systems for change not found in other types of therapy. Family therapy utilizes such forces to impact the family structures and the family members' patterns of interaction.

Also as subclassifications of family therapy, marital therapy, divorce therapy, and sex therapy have gained recognition as legitimate approaches to specific dysfunctions within the family unit. Each of these approaches can be expected to continue to have an impact on the way mental health counseling is practiced. Family therapy already has changed how we practice group and individual therapy. The systems view of human dynamics has entered mainstream counseling and psychotherapy.

Innovative Models

Counseling models cross-paradigm boundaries by focusing on more than one modality. The three modalities are Cognition (C), Affect (A), and Behavior (B). Models or approaches classified as nontraditional are those models based on more than one of the basic three human modalities: cognition, affect, and behavior. Several additional nontraditional systems are described.

Humanistic Behaviorism (A)

Robert Carkhuff (1969) developed a model that follows three process stages: (a) the facilitation or relationship stage; (b) the self-development, self-understanding stage; and (c) the action stage. Carkhuff combined aspects of client-centered and behavior therapy to form the elements of this model.

Personal Science (CB)

Michael Mahoney (1977, 1991) developed a cognitive-behavioral approach to therapy. Personal Science, the title he used, indicates that the client performs his or her own scientific investigation into the nature of personal coping skills and monitors his or her own behavior. Mahoney employs an acronym, SCIENCE, to describe the therapy process involved. Specifically, Mahoney's stages are: (a) specify problem area (S); (b) collect data (C); (c) identify patterns or sources (I); (d) examine options (E); (e) narrow options and experiment (N); (f) compare data (C); and (g) extend, revise, or replace (E). This therapy process is a basic problem-solving sequence in which the therapist serves as a consultant and trains the client to use his or her own resources as a problem solver. By 1991, Mahoney had expanded his approach to resemble more of a CAB model of eclecticism.

Rational Behavior Therapy (CB)

Maultsby's (1977) RBT approach is derived from Ellis' (1973) Rational Emotive therapy. Unlike Ellis, however, Maultsby employs concerted and direct effort toward working with the client's emotionality. The context is still cognitive, but the techniques that he uses tend to follow a more affectively and behaviorally oriented therapy. Maultsby employs a five-step process (Emotional Re-education):

(1) intellectual insight (created through rational self-analysis);
(2) converting practice (behaving consistently with the newly gained insight);
(3) cognitive-emotive dissonance (focusing on the gap between what the client thinks and what he or she may feel that is caused by converting practice);
(4) emotional insight (feeling right or being consistent in feelings that correspond to the newly acquired rational thinking); and
(5) new personality trait (causing the new way of thinking and feeling to become as much a habitual and natural way of living as was the old, more irrational way).

Psychobehavioral Therapy (CB)

Woody (1971) has attempted to combine technique and theory from the psychoanalytic and behavioral approaches. To some extent, Woody is eclectic in that he is willing to use many of the insight techniques while relying on behavior modification techniques to enhance transfer of learning.

Cognitive Client-Centered Therapy (CA)

David Wexler (1974) outlined a theoretical modification in Client-Centered thinking that reemphasized the role of cognition in affective experiencing. Wexler draws extensively from Information-Processing Theory as the basis for his position on the role of cognition. He, like the cognitive behaviorists, places emphasis on cognitive control. Emotional experiencing cannot occur without thought occurring first.

Multimodal Behavior Therapy (CAB)

Arnold Lazarus (1976, 1981) proposed what is probably one of the most comprehensive methods of combining client conceptualization and therapy procedures developed to date. Lazarus emphasized that a client utilizes many human modalities in everyday living. Effective therapy capitalizes on this fact. Traditional approaches to therapy are usually modality limited (i.e., Psychoanalysis focuses on cognition, Rogerian therapists on affect, and Behavior therapists on behavior), whereas no approach fully utilizes all of the human modalities. Lazarus identified seven modalities, which are summarized by the acronym **BASIC ID**. The corresponding modalities are behavior, affect, sensory, imagery, cognition, interpersonal, and drugs. Lazarus' method of therapy was one of the first to identify and use essential problem themes. These themes were classified according to the **BASIC ID** category that best represented the item. Thus far, there is no theoretical base to guide the therapist in choosing useful techniques. Lazarus has emphasized that there is no therapy process involved in multimodal therapy. A theme is identified and a technique is applied.

Brief Counseling

With few exceptions, the various approaches to counseling had their origins in methodologies developed for individual treatment. However, in recent years, a dire need for brief, crisis intervention methodologies requiring short periods of time to produce meaningful results has come to the notice of the professional community.

Several reasons exist to explain why this development has occurred. One of the primary social changes supporting brief intervention is the growing public demand for mental health services and the corresponding shortage of professionals available to deliver services. More people require services than there are services available.

Also, technological and institutional changes are occurring at such a rapid pace that the human condition is one of accelerating difficulty in adequately coping (Toffler, 1980). Technological changes are out pacing social- and personal-value changes. The outcome is a gap between the values produced by technology (e.g., the meaning of one's life is brought about through the creative use of leisure time) and the values attributable to social conformance and social convention (e.g., the meaning in one's life is gained by the quality of one's life work). The times in which we live are difficult because they create mental health coping problems. The briefer methodologies offer a less costly process of remediation because of the limited time involved.

An additional, but seldom-mentioned, reason is that psychotherapy is a short-term process for most clients. A review of the literature (Garfield, 1978) on the average number of therapy sessions revealed that the typical client remains in therapy for only three to eight sessions. Garfield's findings are supported by the more recent literature review by Clarkin and Levy (2004). In addition, Clarkin and Levy (2004) found that few clients who truly need psychotherapeutic help actually seek it. Therefore, therapy, in general, is not the long-term venture that professionals have been led to believe. If the typical client is to benefit, the benefit must come in a relatively short period of time. Because these figures represent an average, many clients both require and stay in counseling/therapy for a longer period of time. After an extensive review of the literature, Lambert and Ogles (2004) concluded that about 75% of all patients improve after 50 sessions, and by limiting the number of sessions to 10 to 20 sessions, as some insurance carriers insist, patients lack the ability to maximize the potential benefit available to them.

Another impetus is worth mentioning. The Managed Health Care movement (Austad & Hoyt, 1992; Berman, 1992; Wooley, 1993), with its primary emphasis on containing excessively escalating mental health costs, is gaining ground. The movement may result in a complete change in the conduct of psychotherapy, or it may not last, losing ground to some other cost-containment method. However, the movement cannot be ignored whether it is best or not for our patients (Lambert & Ogles, 2004).

Butcher and Koss (1978) have listed several characteristics that seem common to most brief approaches: (a) the time factor (25 sessions or less); (b) limited goal setting; (c) focused interviewing (problem-centered); (d) present-centeredness; (e) active and directive intervention; (f) quick assessment (diagnostics); (g) flexibility (eclecticism) in the use of therapeutic tools; (h) prompt intervention; (i) inclusion of a ventilation process; (j) the therapeutic relationship (positive transference); and (k) careful selection of clients.

Of the several approaches to brief, crisis intervention, Small (1979) developed a six-step model that seems to offer promise as a methodology for conducting therapy. The first step is to identify and continually focus on the presenting problem. The second step is to take a personal history to assist in determining essential characteristics of the client's situation. The third step is to establish a therapeutic relationship with the client. This relationship is essentially the same as establishing positive transference and is accomplished in a short period of time, even one session. The fourth step is to devise a plan for intervention which includes strategies (and a wide variety of techniques) specific to the client and the client's situation. The fifth step is to resolve or otherwise work through the problem. This step includes reinforcing the client for transferring learning outside the specific therapy context. The final step is successful termination of therapy. Success includes leaving the client with positive transference feelings and positive attitudes toward returning if the need arises. This last step recognizes that therapy is not forever–that people's life situations change as they change and develop and as their milieu changes.

A more recent development, but still within the framework of Small's model, is Solution-Focused Therapy (SFT). The goal of SFT is to construct an atmosphere in which clients can generate specific solutions to their presenting problems (de Shazer, 1988; Lipchik, 1990). The fundamental assumptions of this approach hold that clients, in an atmosphere of acceptance and support, will generate possible positive solutions to their problems. The therapist functions as a co-facilitator, providing support and a nondefensive climate. The therapist assists the client through guided and scaled questions to clarify the problem and to examine situations when the problem is "better" or less intense. The therapist reinforces the existing strengths of clients and the positive and useful ways clients are currently reacting. Therapy focuses on clients' assessment of the problem. Clients are entreated to define clear and specific goals that lead to the generation of client-specific solutions. There is little focus on the roots of the problem or on the past in the therapy sessions, and SFT does not use diagnostic categories as a guide to strategies or treatment. Although originally SFT dealt primary with client's cognitions and behaviors, recent authors (e.g., Kiser, Piercy, & Figley, 1993) have focused more on the role of emotion in the therapeutic process.

Diagnostic and Assessment Procedures

When drastic changes in theory occur, the way opens for difficulties in the use of old methods and for the development of new methodologies. As shifts in theory occur, the focus centers more on the practices of counseling than was true of the past. Nowhere is this more apparent than with diagnosis and assessment. Psychological testing and assessment appears to have fallen into disfavor. In some circles, an anti-testing attitude seems to prevail. What impact Managed Health Care will have on this attitude remains to be seen. In addition, even if diagnosis is underplayed, assessment, whether formal or informal, must still occur.

Alternative methods are being explored, and new techniques are being developed. Traditional techniques of diagnosis include a medical exam, life history questionnaire, projective tests, and paper-and-pencil tests. Recent trends indicate that therapists are less inclined to use these measures, and they are less inclined to use the corresponding restrictive nomenclature, preferring instead to engage in alternative methods of diagnosis and assessment. Three such alternatives are present. These methods are derivations from current theoretical developments, and each is forcing a rethinking of current theoretical propositions.

Neuropsychological Assessment

One such alternative that has gained in popularity in recent years is neuropsychological assessment. Neuropsychology is the study of the relationship between brain and behavior. Neuropsychology acknowledges that human psychology is related to a physiological/neurological base (Diamond, 1978). Every human action is caused by some finite physiological or neurological change or causes some physiological/neurological change. Neuropsychology has three primary purposes: (a) diagnosis, (b) patient care, and (c) research (Lezak, 1976).

Behavioral Assessment

Behavioral assessment differs from traditional assessment procedures in two essential ways: (a) what is examined, and (b) what is done with the findings. The behavioral assessor looks at observable biological, physiological, and social behaviors to determine how each impacts adaptive functioning. The behavior assessor attempts to assess the degree to which a particular behavior (e.g., social relations skills) is present or absent. These behaviors are then related directly to desired outcomes.

Thematic Assessment

Assessment of major themes that occur in a person's life offers another way of understanding the client (Braswell & Seay, 1984; Seay, 1978). Usually assessment occurs as a natural part of the therapeutic process. Major themes emerge as clients talk about their problems. Thematic assessment attempts to translate findings into concrete statements about the various interrelated themes that tie together the client's life. These themes are usually interdependent, and assessment should be oriented toward understanding their interrelatedness. Actual assessment procedures can range anywhere from paper-and-pencil tests such as the Minnesota Multiphasic Personality Inventory (MMPI) to behavioral charting (e.g., frequency of disruptive anger) to process assessment techniques (e.g., cognitive imagery) to clinical interview techniques.

Methodological Innovations

While counseling methodology per se is not of concern in this chapter, how it relates to theoretical developments is. The major thesis of this chapter is that theory has and is undergoing radical changes. These changes are resulting in numerous innovative strategies and techniques. The methodology used by practitioners is no longer dependent on theoretical orientation for legitimacy. In short, the basis for conducting counseling has expanded considerably. Methodology refers to the processes, strategies, and techniques used in therapy to create client change (epistemological change). Although there are numerous methodological advances available, only a few will be presented here, along with several general references. In addition, because one of the major themes has been the examination of therapy in terms of three human modalities, consistency is maintained by subdividing the presentation of methodological innovations according to their use in the cognitive, affective, and behavioral modalities.

Cognitive Techniques

Of the three modalities, the greatest development in technique usage seems to have occurred in relation to cognition. All of these techniques are used to modify faulty thinking (irrational ideas, misconceptions, and automatic thoughts), instill decision making, and engage in reality testing (Seay, 1980c). Cognitive strategies include such techniques as advanced therapy organizers, bibliotherapy, blow-up, cognitive imagery, cognitive rehearsal, cognitive restructuring, cognitive self-talk, covert reinforcement, free association, graded task assignments, mastery and pleasuring, paradoxical intention, rational self-analysis, reality testing, distancing and centering, and repeated review. Several general references for cognitive techniques are available (Beck, 1976; Foreyt & Rathjen, 1978; Lazarus, 1981).

Affective Techniques

Affective strategies and techniques are designed to bring a "felt" experience into full cognitive awareness so that it can be fully experienced, understood, and diffused. The previous statement is true whether the attempt is to have the client reexperience a previously difficult "feeling" or to identify what is being experienced. The techniques in the affective domain include affective focusing, body awareness, catharsis, emotional reeducation, empathic responding, empty chair, evocative reflections, here and now focus, iconification of feeling, psychodrama, stress inoculation, ventilation, and warmth and acceptance. References for affective techniques include Gendlin (1978), Hart and Tomlinson (1970), Seay (1980c), and Wexler and Rice (1974).

Behavioral Techniques

Various behavioral techniques are designed to focus directly on the observable behaviors of the client and on the environmental contingencies supporting those behaviors. The behavioral techniques include assertiveness training, audiovisual feedback, aversive control, behavioral rehearsal, contracting, decision making, escalation, extinction, feedback, fixed role therapy, homework, hypnosis, minimal effective response, modeling, pain control, reinforcement, relaxation training, role reversal, self-control procedures, time out, systematic desensitization, and contingency management. Several general references for behavioral techniques include Foreyt and Rathjen (1978), Lazarus (1971), and Masters, Burish, Hollon, and Rimm (1979).

Future Directions

A Physiological Basis for Psychotherapy

Of increasing importance is the biopsychological approach to therapy, which assumes that psychological disorders are related to physiological, primarily brain dysfunctions. The assumptions underlying much of the current biopsychological research is that all human behavior can be accounted for by knowledge of the biological mechanisms involved (Uttal, 1978). By understanding these mechanisms, it is possible to understand human behavior.

Treatments altering brain chemistry (e.g., drug therapies) have been used since the 1950s and remain an important treatment approach today. However, alternate means of altering psychology, such as the use of exercise with depressed clients, increasingly demonstrate the intricate relationship of physiological and psychological processes. Future research can be counted on to further elaborate the role of biology in psychological processes.

Community Psychology is an Organizatoinal Model for Intervention

All societies experience psychological casualties. Casualties create a severe drain on a nation's economy, and they represent a terrible waste of human resources. Numerous intervention strategies and programs have been developed to provide therapeutic relief for psychological suffering and to counteract the losses suffered by society. These efforts, while producing limited successes, have proved to be expensive and less effective than originally expected (Rappaport, 1977; Sarason, 1974).

Traditional approaches treat the psychological casualty as victimizer-victim; that is, the victim is to blame for his or her own difficulties. Professional thinking has centered on intrapsychic conflicts, interpersonal (affective) deficits, or maladaptive behaviors (Seay, 1978, 1980b) as the sources for mental illness. Regardless of the external or interpersonal events affecting them, clients now carry these internalized processes as their own. Person-created difficulties such as internal conflicts, lack of love and caring, or inappropriate behaviors have resulted in the victim status. Because these conditions are internal, they must be treated by changing or otherwise modifying the person. Experience, however, has taught us that, although theories that focus on human dynamics do result in change, the change may be short-lived, lasting only until the return of the person to the original environment where conditions and natural support systems work against previously acquired changes. An example of this dynamic is turning a schizophrenic back to his or her schizophrenigenic family.

Alternatives to the human dynamics theories have been proposed and include the social reform/social action movement. Such reflections have led to attempts to change major structures within society. These efforts also have been less effective than desired. In many instances, they have been resisted by the very people for whom they were intended.

An alternative to traditional treatment models is emerging in the literature (Rappaport, 1977; Sarason, 1976). Rappaport (1977) refers to this alternative as the psychoecological perspective (theory). From this perspective, mental health, mental illness, and a host of psychosocial problems such as crime and delinquency are better understood by looking at the person-environment interactions. This theory provides a basis for incorporating and solidifying mental health practitioners and practices. Psychoecology, as applied to the community, refers to the psychological effects of the interaction between people and their environment.

The major premise presented here is that historically either the person or the society has been labeled as sick. Such views place severe limits on the type of treatment that can be provided. Professionals are encouraged instead to view the fit between person and community as being in accord, thereby representing healthy living or being in relative discord and representing mental and/or social illness (Rappaport, 1977).

Effective treatment, then, must impinge on the interaction between person and environment. To accomplish the necessary changes, psychoecological treatment requires the use of strategies designed to modify aspects of the person that contribute to the overall problem. The strategies must be designed to modify aspects of the environment that provide stress and otherwise hinder growth, and strategies designed for problems resulting from the interaction between person and environment.

Seay (1983) has indicated that almost everything in a client's environment, including the intrapsychic and interpersonal interactions, can become therapeutic. In fact, intervention should occur on a number of levels simultaneously. Psychotherapy (individual, group, or marriage/family) should be considered only one strategy among numerous possibilities when attempting to help a client modify his or her life functioning. What is necessary for the professional community at this time is an organizational model that brings together all of the different therapeutic intervention methodologies and community resources for comprehensive intervention. The professional community can no longer afford the limited intervention approaches so characteristic of our past history, where agencies and professionals isolated themselves away from each other and provided services from only their limited perspective, thereby effectively ignoring the contributions that could be made from other resources.

Seay (1983) presented an example of a theoretical and an organizational model for psychoecological delivery based on targets of delivery, sources of psychoecological effects, and services to be delivered. Seay's model identified the target areas for mental health delivery as Primary (direct preventive interventions), Secondary (remediative), and Tertiary (aftercare) Prevention. These areas are consistent with the recommendations of Caplan (1964).

The psychoecological environments or sources of intervention were: (a) residential, (b) community/society, (c) educational, (d) business and political, and (e) the private sector. Together these five areas constitute most of the major environments of clients.

Identified services required for the model were: (a) psychotherapy (including individual, group, and family), (b) consulting, (c) educational programming, (d) coordinating the various systems in operation, (e) environmental structuring/restructuring, (f) community networking, (g) advocacy, (h) referral, (i) professional training, (j) psychodiagnostics, (k) research and evaluation, and (l) funding.

The intent of this tripartite model is to bring all therapeutic intervention methods under one organizational model. Thus, counseling/psychotherapy, marital and family therapy, drug and alcohol therapy, environmental restructuring, funding, community health centers, and a host of other strategies are simply strategies in the larger intervention system of community mental health. Whether this model or some other similar model can accomplish its intended goal remains to be demonstrated. However, the idea offers great potential for organizing the mental health field. The model also provides the opportunity to bring the five core providers under one roof and on an equal status basis because each would provide unique aspects of the model.

Perhaps psychoecology can provide the necessary organization that is currently so lacking in the field. Certainly, the field needs an organizational net that will allow all of the various practices and practitioners to function in concert.

UNIFIED PARADIGM FOR MENTAL HEALTH COUNSELING

As practitioners use mixed models of therapy to guide their practices, the face of mental health counseling is forced to change. What are the short- and long-term effects of these changes? One such effort is the movement away from the Philosophy → Theory → Practice paradigm in favor a "technical eclecticism" that, to some extent, ignores philosophical and theoretical foundations. Abstinence from theory and philosophy frees the practitioner to use a wide variety of strategies and techniques. In examining the use of mixed models, it would seem that the diversity of therapeutic views is slowly becoming more similar. A single paradigm for therapeutic intervention may eventually emerge. Arguments against an emerging unified paradigm are based on the idea that existing models are drawn from irreconcilable philosophical positions. Although therapists may agree on practical theory procedures, they will never agree on a unified philosophical or theoretical base for those procedures. Using existing philosophies (Seay, 1980b), this argument is undoubtedly valid. Traditional philosophies are, in many instances, in direct opposition to one another. They all cannot be true. Nothing short of developing a new philosophy, one that can reconcile the different views of human behavior, increasingly has distinct possibilities. In the past, philosophical beliefs have evolved from day-to-day living and practices. Philosophy is the explanation of the abstract human being. Thus, by developing a scientific approach to conducting therapy, it may become possible to build a theory of human functioning around those practices. From theory, a philosophy becomes possible.

REFERENCES

Allport, G. (1955). *Becoming.* New Haven, CT: Yale University Press.

Austad, C. S., & Hoyt, M. F. (1992). The managed care movement and the future of psychotherapy. *Psychotherapy, 29,* 109–118.

Beck, A. (1976). *Cognitive therapy and emotional disorders.* New York: International Universities Press.

Bergin, A. E. (1997). Neglect of the therapist and the human dimensions of change: A commentary. *Clinical Psychology: Science and Practice, 4,* 83–89.

Berman, W. H. (1992). The practice of psychotherapy in managed health care. *Psychotherapy in Private Practice, 11,* 39–45.

Braswell, M., & Seay, T. A. (1984). *Approaches to counseling and psychotherapy.* Prospect Heights, IL: Waveland Press.

Butcher, J. N., & Koss, M. P. (1978). Research on brief and crisis-oriented psychotherapies. In S. L. Garfield & A. E. Bergin (Eds.), *Handbook of psychotherapy and behavior change* (2nd ed., pp. 725–768). New York, Wiley.

Caplan, G. (1964). *Principles of preventive psychiatry.* New York: Basic Books.

Carkhuff, R. R. (1969). *Helping and human relations* (Vol. 1). New York: Holt, Rinehart & Winston.

Chambless, D. L., & Hollen, S. D. (1998). Defining empirically supported therapies. *Journal of Consulting and Clinical Psychology, 66,* 7–18.

Chambless, D. L., & Ollendick, T. H. (2001). Empirically supported psychological interventions: Controversies and evidence. *Annual Review of Psychology, 52,* 685–716.

Clarkin, J. F., & Levy, K. N. (2004). The influence of client variables on psychotherapy. In M. J. Lambert (Ed.), *Bergin and Garfield's handbook of psychotherapy and behavior change* (5th ed., pp. 3–15). New York: John Wiley & Sons.

Corsini, R. J. (2000). Introduction. In R. J. Corsini & D. Wedding (Eds.), *Current psychotherapies* (6th ed., p. 6). New York: Thomason.

de Shazer, S. (1988). *Clues: Investigating solutions in brief therapy.* New York: Norton.

Diamond, S. J. (1978). *Introducing neuropsychology.* Springfield, IL: Charles C Thomas.

Dolan, M. J. (2004). *Assessment of the revised stage of change model.* Unpublished doctoral dissertation, Philadelphia College of Osteopathic Medicine, Philadelphia.

Ellis, A. (1973). *Humanistic psychotherapy: The rational-emotive approach.* New York: Julian Press.

Ellis, A., & Dryden, W. (1987). *The practice of rational emotive therapy.* New York: Springer.

Foreyt, J., & Rathjen, D. (1978). *Cognitive behavior therapy.* New York: Plenum.

Freeman, A., & Dolan, M. J. (2001). Revisiting Prochaska and DiClemente's stages of change therory: An expansion and specification to aid in treatment planning and outcome evaluation. *Cognitive and Behavioral Practice, 8,* 224–234.

Garfield, S. L. (1978). Research on client variables in psychotherapy. In S. L. Garfield & A. E. Bergin (Eds.), *Handbook of psychotherapy and behavior change* (2nd ed., pp. 191–232). New York: Wiley.

Gendlin, E. (1978). *Focusing.* New York: Everest House.

Gurman, A. S., & Messer, S. B. (2003). *Essential psychotherapies: Theory and practice* (2nd ed.). New York: The Guilford Press.

Hackney, H. L., & Cormier, L. S. (2001). *The professional counselor* (4th ed.). Boston: Allyn & Bacon.

Hart, J. (1986). Functional eclectic therapy. In J. C. Norcross (Ed.), *Handbook of eclectic psychotherapy* (pp. 201–225). New York: Brunner/Mazel.

Hart, J., & Tomlison, T. (1970). *New directions in client-centered therapy.* Boston: Houghton-Mifflin.

Herink, R. (1980). *The psychotherapy handbook.* New York: New American Library.

Herrick, M., Seay, M. A., & Seay, T. A. (2004). Graduate Counseling Preparatory Students Employment Survey. Presented to the Eastern Psychological Association meeting. Washington, DC.

Hilgard, E. R. (1987). *Psychology in America: A historical survey.* San Diego: Harcourt, Brace, Jovanovich.

Hill, C. E., & Lambert, M. J. (2004). Methodological issues in studying psychotherapy processes and outcomes. In M. J. Lambert (Ed.), *Bergin and Garfield's handbook of psychotherapy and behavior change* (5th ed., pp. 84–135). New York: John Wiley & Sons.

Kendall, P. C., & Chambless, D. L. (Eds.). (1998). Empirically supported psychological therapies. *Journal of Counseling and Clinical Psychology, 66,* 3–167.

Kiser, D. J., Piercy, F. P., & Lipchik, E. (1993). The integration of emotion in solution-focused therapy. *Journal of Marital and Family Therapy, 19,* 233–242.

Krumboltz, J., & Thorensen, C. (1969). *Behavioral counseling.* New York: Holt, Rinehart & Winston.

Kuhn, T. (1970). *The structure of scientific revolutions.* Chicago: The University of Chicago Press.

Lambert, M. J., Bergin, A. E., & Garfield, S. L. (2004). Introduction and historical overview. In M. J. Lambert (Ed.), *Bergin and Garfield's handbook of psychotherapy and behavior change* (5th ed., pp. 3–15). New York: John Wiley & Sons.

Lambert, M. J., & Ogles, B. M. (2004). The efficacy and effectiveness of psychotherapy, In M. J. Lambert (Ed.), *Bergin and Garfield's Handbook of Psychotherapy and behavior change* (5th ed.,

pp. 139–193). New York: John Wiley & Sons.
Lazarus, A. A. (1971). *Behavior therapy and beyond.* New York: McGraw-Hill.
Lazarus, A. A. (1976). *Multimodal behavior therapy.* New York: Springer.
Lazarus, A. A. (1981). *The practice of multimodal therapy.* New York: McGraw-Hill.
Lazarus, A. A. (1993). Tailoring the therapeutic relationship, or being an authentic chameleon. *Psychotherapy, 30,* 403–407.
Lazarus, A. A., Beutler, L. E., & Norcross, J. C. (1992). The future of technical eclecticism. *Psychotherapy, 29,* 11–20.
Lezak, M. D. (1976). *Neuropsychological assessment.* New York: Oxford University Press.
Lipchik, E. (1990). Brief solution-focused psychotherapy. In J. K. Zeig & W. M. Munion (Eds.), *What is psychotherapy?* San Francisco: Jossey-Bass.
Mahoney, M. J. (1977). Personal science: A cognitive learning therapy. In A. Ellis & R. Grieger (Eds.), *Handbook of rational-emotive therapy* (pp. 352–366). New York: Springer.
Mahoney, M. J. (1991). *Human change processes.* New York: Basic Books.
Masters, J. C., Burish, T. G., Hollon, S. D., & Rimm, D. C. (1987). *Behavior therapy.* Fort Worth, TX: Harcourt, Brace, Jovanovich.
Maultsby, M. C. (1977). Emotional re-education. In A. Ellis & R. Grieger (Eds.), *Handbook of rational-emotive therapy* (pp. 231–247). New York: Springer.
Meichenbaum, D. (1977). *Cognitive behavior modification.* New York: Plenum.
Meichenbaum, D. (1985). *Stress-inoculation training.* New York: Pergamon.
Neukrug, E. (1999). *The world of the counselor.* Pacific Grove, CA: Brooks/Cole.
Norcross, J. C. (1993). Tailoring relationship stances to client needs: An introduction. *Psychotherapy, 30,* 402–403.
Norcross, J. C. (Ed.). (1986). *Handbook of eclectic psychotherapy.* New York: Brunner/Mazel.
Patterson, C. H. (1974). *Relationship counseling and psychotherapy.* New York: Harper & Row.
Prochaska, J. O. (1991). Prescribing to the stages and levels of change. *Psychotherapy, 28,* 463–468.
Prochaska, J. O., & DiClemente, C. C. (1982). Transtheoretical therapy: Toward a more integrative model of change. *Psychotherapy: Theory, Research and Practice, 20,* 161–173.
Prochaska, J. O., & Norcross, J. C. (2002). Stages of changes. In J. C. Norcross (Ed.), *Psychotherapy relationships that work* (pp. 303–313). Oxford: Oxford University Press.
Raimy, V. (1975). *Misunderstandings of the self.* San Francisco: Jossey-Bass.
Rappaport, J. (1977). *Community psychology.* New York: Holt, Rinehart, & Winston.
Rogers, C. R. (1964). Toward a science of the person. In T. W. Wann (Ed.), *Behaviorism and phenomenology.* Chicago: The University of Chicago Press.
Roth, A., & Fonagy, P. (1996). *What works for whom?* New York: The Guilford Press.
Rychlak, J. F. (1965). The motives of psychotherapy. *Psychotherapy, 2,* 151–157.
Rychlak, J. F. (1969). Lockean vs. Kantian theoretical models and the "cause" of therapeutic change. *Psychotherapy: Theory, Research and Practice, 6,* 214–223.
Rychlak, J. F. (1978). The stream of consciousness: Implications for a humanistic psychological theory. In K. S. Pope & J. L. Singer (Eds.), *The stream of consciousness* (pp. 91–116). New York: Plenum.
Sarason, S. B. (1974). *The psychological sense of community.* San Francisco: Jossey-Bass.
Sarason, S. B. (1976). Community psychology, networks, and Mr. Everyman. *American Psychologist, 31,* 317–328.
Seay, T. A. (1978). *Systematic eclectic therapy.* Jonesboro, TN: Pilgrimage Press.
Seay, T. A. (1980a). Nontraditional psychotherapy. *Journal of Counseling and Psychotherapy, 3,* 1–5.
Seay, T. A. (1980b). Toward a single paradigm. *Journal of Counseling and Psychotherapy, 3,*

47–60.

Seay, T. A. (1980c). Recent innovations in counseling. *Pennsylvania Personnel and Guidance Journal, 7,* 29–39.

Seay, T. A. (1983). Psychoecological treatment as a model for community psychology. *Journal of Counseling and Psychotherapy, 5,* 1–12.

Shlien, J. (1970). Phenomenology and personality. In J. Hart & T. Tomlinson (Eds.), *New directions in client-centered therapy* (pp. 95–128). Boston: Houghton-Mifflin.

Small, L. (1979). *The brief psychotherapies* (rev. ed.). New York: Brunner/Mazel.

Smith, M. L., Glass, G., & Miller, T. I. (1980). *The benefits of psychotherapy.* Baltimore: Johns Hopkins University Press.

Toffler, A. (1980). *The third wave.* New York: William Morrow.

Uttal, W. R. (1978). *Psychobiology of the mind.* Hillsdale, NJ: Lawrence Erlbaum.

Wexler, D. (1974). A cognitive theory of experiencing self-actualization, and therapeutic process. In D. A. Wexler & L. N. Rice (Eds.), *Innovations in client-centered therapy.* New York: Wiley.

Wexler, D. A., & Rice, L. N. (Eds.). (1974). *Innovations in client-centered therapy.* New York: Wiley.

Wolpe, J. (1973). *The practice of behavior therapy.* New York: Pergamon Press.

Woody, R. H. (1971). *Psychobehavioral counseling and psychotherapy.* New York: Appleton-Century-Crofts.

Wooley, S. C. (1993). Managed care and mental health: The silencing of a profession. *International Journal of Eating Disorders, 14,* 387–401.

Chapter 4

INTEGRATING THEORIES INTO PRACTICE

DAVE BORSOS

INTRODUCTION

Counseling or psychotherapy is a fairly new "science." The idea of using words and human interaction to improve or cure various human maladies is revolutionary as a method of healing. Still now, 100 years after Freud got us started, many people still scoff at this idea or believe totally in better living through "psychochemistry."

One of the "problems" in our new science is that it has a splintered and fractured nature. There are many counseling theories available to us; all insist on their individual superiority and efficacy. The truth, in both practice and research, is that no one from Freud to Beck and back has proved itself to be the one best therapy or the one and only way to understand and help others through their psychological travails. Prochaska and Norcross (1994) have stated that, "no single definition of psychotherapy has won universal acceptance" (p. 5). As the American Psychological Association once quoted the dodo bird from *Alice in Wonderland,* "All have won and all will have prizes." Basically, there is some truth, effectiveness, and failure in all theories, methods, and individual schools of counseling.

However, our science has progressed to the point where we need no new theories that are just variations on existing themes. What we need now is a logical, effective way to bring it all together in a unified, integrated way. Our field's search for psychological truth has been like the story of the seven blind men all feeling different parts of the same elephant, convinced he has the whole picture of the beast. Each of our theories has been convinced of its "truth" in relation to the understanding and counseling of human problems.

"It's the unconscious . . . No! The early maternal bond . . . No! The existential angst." "No, it's the belief systems . . . the family system . . . the environment, the conditioned responses," as if we were so many lab rats or pigeons.

In reality, humans are all of the above and more. Their lives are all of the above as are their problems and pathologies. What we need now for our profession and our clients is a way to bring together 100 years of counseling and therapy theory. We need a confluence and integrating of ideas, not a dogmatic loyalty to one. We need to more accurately explain only two things: How do people get psychologically ill and how can we help them improve? We need an integrated model of psychotherapy. This chapter is an attempt to do just that.

The Relationship

Research has consistently and reliably demonstrated that the therapeutic relationship, the real, human bond between counselor and client, is the essential factor in successful counseling (Hubble, Duncan, & Miller, 1999; Prochaska & Norcross, 1994). People come to counseling to explore various aspects of the self, particularly those that are dysfunctional, pathological, or just hurting. They are confused, sad, anxious, and unable to help themselves. Their pain pushes them to make an ultimate leap of faith–a leap to you as a counselor or therapist. They make the tentative step to trust the most powerful and intimate parts of their lives to a perfect stranger. We have to be ready for it, ready to handle it all humanely and compassionately.

So you can see how our ability to form a safe, trusting environment is crucial for our clients and their willingness to reveal their hidden, hurting selves to us. They need to feel accepted for who they are in all of their self-perceived flaws and failures. They need to feel accepted not only by you as the professional but also by themselves as individuals. They've been hiding and fighting shameful, painful parts of the self for years. Therefore, they need you to help them to accept and feel safe with themselves and the growing exploration and critique of the self. If the counselor can accept them as they are, they can learn to as well. Certainly, this is easy to say yet difficult for most of us to do. Who has taught us the most about accepting others as they are and helping them do the same? Carl Rogers (1942, 1951, 1957, 1961) has taught us the most about forming and keeping that therapeutic relationship, which he saw as simply a human one.

His qualities of genuineness, empathy, unconditional positive regard, and a nonjudgmental attitude are key elements to forming that trusting relationship. As a client reveals some painful or shameful information about himself, he notices the counselor accepts it and does not criticize him for it. The counselor empathizes with the pain and, with a genuine warm and caring demeanor, encourages the person to continue. He or she usually does.

As the client grows in trust and feelings of safety, he or she reveals more to the counselor and to the self. This process enables us to proceed with the next part of the therapy–getting the facts of the person's life, hearing him or her tell the story more and more intimately and with greater detail. We are trying to collect data. We are mining the story of the individual's life in a framework of safety and trust to reveal the important details so we both can work with them.

Besides our empathetic counseling demeanor, we use other Rogerian-style interviewing techniques to keep the client talking. We use open-ended questions or statements to explore a story. We use "How?" and "What?" questions that require elaboration and revelation. "How did the fight with your wife begin?" or "What events led up to the fight?" will draw out more data than closed-questions such as "Did you fight about money?" or "Whose fault was it this time?"

Try to avoid "Why?" questions. They have a tendency to sound accusatory, attacking, or even parental and authoritarian. Note the difference in tone between "Why did you fight with your wife again?" and "What events led up the fight?" Say them both out loud. Can you hear the difference?

Other counseling, interviewing techniques in the Rogerian style include paraphrasing the content of a story, reflecting the emotional content, using encouragers like "I see" and "Please continue," summarizing, and focusing on an area of concern. The safer the client feels, the stronger the counseling bond will be. The stronger the bond, the more the client will risk exploring and revealing his life story to you. The more data that are revealed, the more you can work with the material and help a client change toward a healthier behavior.

Yet now comes the next phase of counseling, perhaps the hardest part. What do we do with all of those client data, with all the details of his or her trials and tribulations? For some clients, simply telling all in the empathetic environment is enough. Carl Rogers (1957) always thought that this was sufficient. Yet it usually is not enough for most clients. We need to work with the material of a person's life in some meaningful way. As Prochaska and Norcross (1994) stated, we must combine some kind of action with the growing insight and awareness of the client. We have to do something!

Our psychology libraries are bursting with theories on how to work effectively with all of the client's therapeutic material. Clinicians and theorists from Adler to Volpe, from Freud to Frank and all of the Perls of wisdom in between, are promoting their particular version of how people get psychologically ill and how to help them get well again. The balance of this chapter shows you how each one can be integrated with the others to help you be a more effective and versatile counselor. You will be able to help more people more often and not just the ones' who fit well into one particular theoretical orientation.

Understanding and Using Cognitions

While forming the treatment relationship and eliciting as much of the client's story as possible, the effective counselor must listen with the "third ear" for patterns in the client's material. We must listen for patterns of positives and negatives, strengths and weaknesses, and certainly for patterns of pain, pathology, and dysfunction. All of our modern theorists have simply decided to organize those particularly human patterns by a few main categories: cognitions, conditioned behaviors, unconscious processes, relationships, emotions, coping, and decision-making processes. Each theory emphasizes one or two over the others, yet the treatment experience has taught us that we are composed of all of these parts and more. Each has part of the elephant, but no one describes the whole being. The effective counselor should work with all of these components of our clients in a flexible but integrated way according to their individual needs and pathologies.

Albert Ellis (1973) and Aaron Beck (1972, 1976) are contemporary theorists who have accented the role of our thoughts, belief systems, and cognitions as the cause of pathology. The two most widely researched theories on all of counseling are Beck's Cognitive Therapy and Ellis' Rational-Emotive Therapy. The main premise of both is that how we think leads to how we feel and behave, whether functionally or dysfunctionally.

Cognitive approaches may nod a little to the role of parents, family of origin, culture, and other influences on the person's belief systems but insist the origins are irrelevant to understanding and changing them. For example, a person who continually believes that "I am worthless and unlovable" will therefore feel depressed and behave in a depressive manner by crying, isolating, or not eating. The cognitivists work at identifying and changing patterns of dysfunctional or irrational thoughts. They ask for proof of the dysfunctional belief, dispute it, and teach the client to replace it with a belief or thought that is more functional and believable. The client who believes himself worthless and unlovable will be asked to show the (nonexistent) proof of this belief and then taught to rethink his beliefs about the self in a more positive and functional way. "I am a loving and capable person who does have accomplishments in my life." These rethinking, cognitive approaches have been shown to be effective with a variety of problems: anxieties, addictions, mood disorders, and lately even with borderline personality disorders, to name a few (Ellis & Dryden, 1997). It must be noted, however, that a good therapeutic relationship has been shown to be crucial for successful cognitive work (Burns & Nolen-Hoeksema, 1992).

As an example, I had a client named Turner whose chief complaint was an extreme tension in his body, especially the jaw. He was irritable, his marriage was suffering, and his job was quite stressful. He was the only northern representative of a company located down south. He had to trouble-shoot, service, and handle the complaints about their equipment in a large tri-state area. His superiors kept putting him in no-win situations by demanding he go to fix unfixable problems, get the equipment to provide services that were not part of the normal equipment package, and keep everyone happy from the sales staff to the customers–even if he had to lie to do it.

Turner was also an obedient, hard-working perfectionist who believed he should be able to do all that his superiors demanded, on time, perfectly, and with a smile on his face. The impossible demands of the job ran directly into his beliefs of obedience, being a good worker and being perfect in all he did ("I should be able to please my bosses . . . and do it all perfectly"). The resulting collision of opposing mental forces squeezed him into a constant state of tension, which settled painfully into his jaw and his marriage.

After weeks of treatment, a breakthrough occurred when he truly realized that his cognitive patterns of "shoulds" and "musts" were hurting him. We successfully disputed these beliefs, especially in relation to his job's impossible demands. The tensions in his jaw and his life began to relax as he learned to rethink the harsh demands he put on himself. He started to believe it was okay to be imperfect, and make mistakes, and that he didn't always have to bow to the will of the authority figures in his life. He successfully completed treatment in three to four months relying on the cognitive approach to counseling.

When working with the people who come to you for help, you should be listening for some of these patterns of dysfunctional belief systems and cognitions. They often revolve around certain common and almost predictable absolutist beliefs like perfectionism, black-and-white thinking, overgeneralizing, needing to always be liked or loved, feeling worthless, looking through rose-colored glasses, blaming others for our own feelings, self-condemnation, personalizing everything, and catastrophizing, to name a few. You must help your clients detect their irrational beliefs, dispute or debate them, and substitute and practice more functional beliefs while learning to discriminate between rational thoughts ("I will work hard to get my assignment done but I am not a failure if I'm late") and irrational ones ("My life is ruined forever if the boss doesn't like this proposal") (Dryden, 1995).

Understanding and Using Behaviorism

Other theorists have proposed other ways to understand and conceptualize the patterns and pathologies of human life. Behaviorists such as Skinner,

Wolpe, Watson, and Pavlov have used animal and human studies to explain all human behavior, including psychopathology, as learned or conditioned. Therefore, they propose that all dysfunctional behaviors can be unlearned or extinguished through the behavioral principles of classical or operant conditioning.

The classical conditioning theories of Pavlov have shown that some behaviors can be learned or "conditioned" by pairing them with unconditioned stimuli like food. Watson and Rayner (1920) extended this experiment by conditioning a young boy to have a phobia of anything white and furry by pairing his startle response with white lab rats. This is, of course, an experiment we would not do today because of stronger ethical considerations for our subjects. Anyone who has ever developed a fear of driving after a car accident knows the power of unconditioned stimuli and their resultant conditioned responses.

These behavioral observations have led to counseling techniques such as relaxation exercises and systematic desensitization, which pairs relaxation responses with a phobic object. My client, Earl, was a construction worker in high-rise buildings. "Coincidentally," he developed a phobia of elevators. He literally spent months running up and down dozens of flights of steps to get to his work site in the upper reaches of buildings. Earl had the best cardiovascular fitness of all my clients, but was of course miserable as a result of his pathological fears. He responded best when I taught him relaxation exercises and paired them with trips to actual elevators nearby. He gradually learned to relax in their presence, sitting in them, then with the elevator moving, and then moving to higher and higher floors. He never really learned to "love" elevators, but he was able to return to a more normal work routine. No exploration of childhood trauma or analyzing patterns of dysfunctional beliefs was necessary. Counselors can successfully use such conditioning models of counseling to treat various anxieties, insomnia, pain management, and even the cravings of addictions.

Another behavioral technique is that of operant conditioning most associated with B. F. Skinner (1974). He proposed that all behaviors, including feelings, are learned and repeated because they are somehow reinforced or rewarded in the environment. Therefore, they can be unlearned or extinguished by removing the rewards or reinforcements.

Therefore, a client's pathology will only continue if it is somehow being reinforced by the world around him. The depressed wife may maintain her symptoms because it causes her husband to be more loving and considerate. The "problem child" acts out at home because it is the only way to get mom's undivided attention. Herbert develops anxiety at home because when he does he is rewarded with a reduction in responsibilities and workload.

Behaviorists using this model look for the patterns that reinforce pathological behaviors. They attempt to bring them to the attention of the client and introduce healthier patterns to accomplish the same goals of attention or work reduction. Every token economy and every contingency contract is based on the principles of operant conditioning. These ideas build systems (new patterns) of rewards and punishments to shape pathological behavior and develop healthier behaviors.

Another aspect of Behaviorism is Social Learning Theory as developed by Albert Bandura (1969, 1971). This idea proposes that behaviors are not just conditioned or reinforced, but that people also learn new behaviors by watching others and modeling their behaviors on that which seems somehow desirable. Children learn aggressive behaviors by watching it modeled in others or on television. Drug abuse is learned by watching peer group members model it with apparent pleasure. A client learns depression by watching a depressed parent live that way all of their life. The antidote, then, to pathological behavior is to watch a more functional behavior as modeled by the counselor, by another person in life, or perhaps even by a group member. Yet it is still only a single part of the view of the elephant.

So the behaviorists have taught us that all behaviors, functional or dysfunctional, are learned by interactions with others that condition or model patterns within us. Treatments include relaxation exercises, imagery, systematic desensitization, reinforcement contingencies, positive role modeling, and token economies.

The Cognitive and Behavioral Theorists Meet

In recent years, the cognitivists and behaviorists decided they really could work together without contradiction; they could join their disparate views of the elephant of counseling. Both looked at human patterns of thoughts and behaviors that were learned. Both saw their particular approach as psychoeducational, time-limited, and targeted at specific, measurable problems (Corey, 2001). Both saw their approach as more scientific, measurable, and observable than that grand-daddy of counseling theorists, Freud.

So, the Rational Emotive Therapy (RET) of Albert Ellis became Rational Emotive Behavior Therapy (REBT) and the Cognitive Therapy (CT) of Beck became Cognitive-Behavioral Therapy (CBT). This is a successful integration of counseling theories. New counselors are being trained to discover their clients' patterns of dysfunctional thoughts and behaviors while learning interventions from both approaches. During the past 20 years, many well-known theorists taught an integrated model of cognitive and behavioral therapy. It was demonstrated that a client could challenge his core, dysfunctional beliefs during a panic attack while practicing a relaxation exercise. In addition, a depressive, withdrawn person could challenge his thoughts of worthlessness while still learning assertiveness techniques to teach him new behaviors.

Arnold Lazarus (1976) also developed his model of integrating cognitive and behavioral approaches, which he calls Multimodal therapy. It emphasizes using various techniques based on his construct of the BASIC ID. This acronym stands for behavior, affect, sensations, imagery, cognitions, interpersonal relations, and drugs/biological factors. He suggests ways to assess the pathology in each of these areas of life as well as ways to intervene in them. Lazarus gives a little more attention to affect and emotion than others who have been mentioned. Yet, I always got the feeling he does it begrudgingly and prefers to emphasize behaviors and thought patterns while moving quickly through emotional content and client history. A main part of the whole elephant is still missing.

Understanding and Using Psychodynamic Theories and the Role of the Unconscious

However, this leaves the developing counselor with the long shadows of Freud and other psychodynamic theorists. These theories posit that much of human behavior is controlled or motivated by patterns of unconscious processes, unconscious conflicts, emotions, and introjects. They also say that the best way to help someone change his or her unhealthy behavior is by making these unconscious patterns more conscious, thereby allowing the client to "work them through" and reintegrate them into his or her personality rather than deny or suppress them (Freud, 1949, 1963). Working through is a process of developing insights into past problems, family of origin issues, and repressed memories or feelings and understanding how they still impact one's life in the present. This allows a release of unconscious conflict and the development of new patterns of feeling and acting that are more functional than the prior ones. Modern psychodyamic theories that look at a client's past are not just archeological expeditions that spend years mining old hurts but active approaches that help connect one's past events to current problems.

The effective counselor may be short-changing himself and his clients' chances of success if he relies exclusively on cognitive-behavioral approaches to treatment. Not every client requires in-depth counseling, but many do. The counselor should always inquire about parental relationships, family dynamics, emotions, unfinished business, unconscious processes, defense mechanisms, and the like.

There are far too many of these theorists to review in this short space. The evolving writings of Freud take up a large bookshelf on their own. His followers and contemporaries such as Abraham (1927), Sullivan (1953), and

Jung (1966) could take up another large room. Others have used Freud as a launching point to adapt, add to, or expand his ideas into many different and useful directions. These include people such as Fritz Perles and Gestalt Therapy (Perles, 1969, Zinker, 1978), Alfred Adler and his Individual Psychology (1958), the Object-Relations Theory, Self-Psychology, and Short-Term Dynamic Therapies of people like Davanloo (1978).

It may be impossible to master all of these various approaches to counseling, yet one does not really need to as an effective counselor. It is possible to look at the commonalities, the patterns of these theories, and apply them in an effective, efficient, and integrated way to your clients' problems. All of these theories require the client to become aware of and understand the events of his early life and how they impact his behavior today in the here and now. All of these theories look at unconscious processes, motivations, and the effects of early relationships on how we relate to ourselves and others. Each psychodynamic writer has a slightly different perspective on these processes, on their piece of the elephant. Let's look at some of the ideas that can be readily used with clients.

Freud (1949) originally proposed that pathology is a result of unconscious conflicts deep in the mind. These conflicts created anxiety that must be defended against through defense mechanisms and through the formation of symptoms such as a phobia or conversion disorder. The conflicts were seen to be between the natural drives or instincts found in the id and the inhibitions or learned restrictions of the super-ego or conscience. Our sense of self, our ego, was left with the task of managing these conflicting forces, sometimes successfully and oftentimes dysfunctionally.

He asserted two primary id instincts: eros and thanatos or the life and death instincts. The life instinct includes such processes as loving and connecting to others, preserving life, nurturing, caring, and sexuality. The death instinct includes our more destructive tendencies such as the fighting response, anger, hate, and/or aggression.

The opposing super-ego is constructed from the incorporated rules and regulations of our parents, family, religion, and culture. We all, of course, have such lists in our mind to help us know right from wrong and to guide us in making good decisions in our lives. We run into trouble when these rules are overly restrictive, punishing, or inhibitive.

When Freud listened carefully to his (mostly female) patients, he observed that their natural sexual urges were being inhibited by their overly proper, restrictive, and punishing consciences. Their internalized rules learned from their proper Victorian mothers consistently told them that "Nice girls don't have sexual urges . . . only bad women do." Yet of course their natural sexual urges existed and sought expression. He saw this battle between sexual expression and sexual repression as an unconscious conflict and the source of the hysterical paralysis and other anxieties of these clients. He also started to notice that talking through these conflicts led to insight, understanding, and emotional release, which led to symptom relief.

Today's counselor may not find many people with internal conflicts around sexual expression, but it will always be useful to look for other potential conflicts in your clients' lives of which they are unaware. Perhaps there is a great, suppressed anger toward an abusive father that is contributing to a depression. Perhaps there is an unmourned grief or sadness over a parental death or abandonment. Perhaps the client has never allowed herself to express the ambivalent, love-hate feelings she has for her stepdad.

I once had a client who, although depressed, could smile broadly while crying her eyes out. This was her inner conflict expressed widely across her face. She wanted badly to believe her family was perfect and good for her while avoiding the reality that she felt abandoned with her mom's death and her dad's subsequent emotional detachment from her. With some months' work, she was able to release, accept, and work through these conflicting emotions.

A useful technique instituted by Freud is that of free association (Freud, 1963; Kris, 1982). This simply encourages and allows the client to say anything and everything that comes into his or her mind without censorship, without holding anything back. It requires the person to express all inner thoughts, feelings, and memories without inhibition. Through this process, the individual is able to explore deeper and more hidden parts of the self that can illuminate unconscious processes and make them accessible to change. Although Freud never mentioned it, what can enable or encourage a person to explore and expose secret and possibly hurtful parts of the self? A secure and trusting relationship to a counselor whom is nonjudgmental, positively regarding, and empathetic. The safer a client feels, the better able he or she will be to explore unsafe, painful areas that need attention. So we see that the concepts of Rogers and the treatment relationship are compatible with classical Freudian approaches.

Later analytic traditions developed other useful ways to explain and examine unconscious patterns. The Object-Relations School (Horner, 1991) asserts that our early relationships with our primary caregivers are crucial in understanding human development. A growing infant/child takes in messages about the self and the world around him or her from those who are caring for him or her–usually the parents. If the messages are primarily those of safety, security, self-worth, nurturance, and caring, then the individual will grow with a positive and healthy self-image and a healthy, realistic approach to relationships with others. If the child grows up with predominating messages of being unloved, worthless, bad, or ashamed, he or she will grow up with a self-image that is negative and a view of others as dangerous, rejecting, hurtful, or untrustworthy. These views become part of the conscious and unconscious personality of the individual and influence the patterns of how he or she acts in the world, with others, and with the self (Mahler, 1968).

For example, it is easy to see how a person who has internalized lifelong messages of worthlessness and shame could develop depression or relationship problems. Or with another person, we can see how he may act out his inner hurtful, rejecting messages by trying to hurt others with violence, crime, or psychopathic behaviors. Perhaps an individual has developed a sense of self that requires the constant pleasing of authority figures to feel self-esteem. This person could live in a constant state of anxiety over needing to always do the right thing or fear being punished or demeaned. These lifelong messages also substantially overlap the cognitive therapy idea of irrational thoughts or negative schema. Striving to please authority figures to feel worthwhile is really the same as having an irrational belief that says, "I must always please those in charge or I am bad." So there is a certain conjunction of ideas from the cognitive and psychodynamic theories of counseling. Both are talking about inner parts of the personality that contribute to pathology. One calls it a belief system or schema, whereas another calls it an incorporated object relation. Both approaches seek to bring this pattern to the awareness of the client so it can be changed for the better. The techniques of change differ, but I believe one can effectively work from both models at the same time. The counselor can have a client challenge and restructure his or her thoughts while later in the session try to uncover the origin of those thoughts and early negative experiences.

A useful idea emerging from this approach is that our early relationships set up an inner pattern or template for relating to the world and ourselves. We act out these patterns in our relations to others. Therefore, we can learn a lot about an individual by having him or her talk about personal relations with others over the years and what made them work well or poorly. We may discover that a person who has a strong sense of rejection and worthlessness will constantly set up relationships to fail by rejecting the partner before he or she gets rejected. Another person may be struggling with an intense fear of being criticized as mom always did to her or him. These fears led the individual to rarely say anything that led people to criticize her or him as being aloof or snobby, thus depressing and isolating the person even more.

One client I treated spent 45 years of her life actively hating and rejecting the parents and stepparents whom had raised her. Unfortunately, this led her to be constantly rejecting the aspects of herself that were like them. She was depressed and self-defeating throughout her life because she never developed a sense of her real identity on which she could rely. She was always living "not" to be as they were but not knowing then who she was. She developed a false front of a self, an inauthentic self, that made her believe she was "heroic" in her struggles, above the petty needs of everyone else, and not in need of anyone to make her life more satisfying. Improvement only came for her when she became aware of her patterns of relating and began to accept the walled-off and hated parts of herself.

The object-relations ideas expand the original Freudian ideas of drive theory by making the urge or "instinct" to form relationships the main impetus to how we develop. The relationships we form will include loving and destructive aspects. But the unconscious processes and patterns we introject through our early developmental years become a crucial part of our mental health. Exposing, exploring, and reworking those patterns become the key to change, and that work must occur in a new, trusting, and nurturing relationship with a counselor. Not only can the client explore the repressed or denied parts of the self and change them, but he or she can also absorb new, healthier qualities from the counselor who is a constant, safe, and empathic person in the client's life.

These ideas certainly overlap the original Freudian concept of transference. The concept simply states that an individual will have a tendency to act toward others as they would have acted toward powerful figures in his or her past. This interaction takes place in the counseling setting also. A client will have a tendency to treat you in a manner that is reminiscent of how they treat other authority figures in life. Noticing that pattern and helping the client to realize it will greatly help them understand themselves and change his "automatic" transference reactions to others. So a counseling session can become a great incubator where a client will act out some of his or her characteristic patterns of development and relationship. The effective counselor can then guide the person toward insight and restructuring the unhealthy aspects of these patterns.

After some time counseling Cindy, I noticed she had a pattern of coming into the session and reporting on her life in a matter-of-fact way that sounded like she was reading from a book report. She would then sit back and wait for my approval of a job well done. Feeling that our relationship was strong enough to challenge her, I pointed out my observations that her revelations were report-like, detached, and emotionless. She immediately became angry and cried that she thought "that's what I wanted" and that I was "impossible to please." As we talked this through, she accused me of being like her mother, who wanted to know everything but was never happy with anything. This led to deeper and more personal revelations about her relationship with mother and its effects on her self-image as someone who could never measure up. Cindy had tried to feel better about herself over the years by using sexual promiscuity and generous doses of cocaine. Clearly, Cindy had transferred some of her thoughts and feelings about her mother onto the counselor, and we were able to use that process to help her gain increased insight into her unconscious or inner feelings about herself. Bringing something from the "inside" of a person to the "outside" where it can be handled is a potent tool for the counselor. It allows the client to rethink and refeel the issue, and it robs it of its power over the person; the negative influence is defused.

There is an important caution about the need for therapeutic insight and emotional release. Even Freud noticed that insight was rarely enough to change a person for good. Your client must use the knowledge gained in session outside in his or her daily life. The person must act on the insight; he or she must consciously behave and think differently in situations that were trouble before. So for Cindy, after the session above, she was encouraged to notice other places in her life where she behaved in a subservient, childlike manner and make conscious attempts to act more appropriately, more adult-like. She was to notice if her fear of "mom's" criticism emerged to inhibit her and remind herself that she was safe now and a competent adult who could act on her own judgments. We also identified some areas of life where this could happen: with mom still, at work, or with a new boyfriend. We then practiced some new healthier behaviors in the safety of the counseling office.

This is the "working through" of a person's issues in vivo. One can also see that the counselor is using cognitive rethinking techniques and behavioristic role-plays to help strengthen the changes that became apparent during a more psychodynamic session. The counselor can effectively use integrated approaches to promote positive changes in people. The effective counselor can "insert" techniques from other schools of thought as needed and as they fit with the client's current issues. The counselor is cautioned to use various techniques only if they are appropriate to a current issue. One must have a plan in mind for using techniques and should not just use them randomly or to "see what happens" or because you just had a training in some new idea. Integrating various counseling schools means we must do it in a sensible, planned way that fits with a client's needs and therapeutic goals.

When using psychodynamic or analytic ideas to explore someone's past, it is still crucial to note that we use the information, memories, and feelings to help illuminate the client's current life and problems. We are helping a person understand the causes and effects of their developmental history not to blame others but to facilitate change. People find it easier to change when they understand and "own" more of their personal story. There is always an internal consistency to a person's life story. Events occur in relationship with others during the vulnerable, early years and individuals react in characteristic ways that become reinforced and internalized more with time. This is a human process that we all go through. For most, the patterns are substantially (not perfectly) healthy and life-affirming. Our patterns become so ingrained and automatic that we are usually unaware of them unless they cause us trouble and we work them out in some positive way.

Again, the theme of this chapter is that we can understand our clients' patterns from cognitive, behavioral, and psychodynamic perspectives and effectively integrate the various approaches depending on the particular needs and story of a client's life. The counselor who is attuned to his or her client will be actively listening for the patterns, causes, effects, and internal consistencies in the story. Almost simultaneously, the counselor will be evaluating the best way to address the unhealthy aspects of the story. Will a cognitive restructuring suffice? Should I do a role-play? An empty chair technique so Cindy can express her anger at mom? Do I need to go more deeply into family of origin issues to help capture some lost parts of the self and flesh out the story more fully? The directions rely on the counselor's clinical judgment and experience. The approach of the counselor also depends on the client's reactions to what has been done so far. If the person's anxiety is not responding to continued relaxation exercises, then do something different and grounded in an accepted theory. One can investigate cognitions and insert a cognitive restructuring around a possible irrational belief that is causing the anxiety. If ineffective, one must look more deeply at possible unconscious conflicts or dysfunctional early relationships.

INTEGRATING THE THEORIES

As we have seen, the cognitive theorists have joined the behavioral to give us the beginnings of an integrated theory of counseling. This approach sees no contradiction in being able to conceptualize a person's problems from a behavior model as well as one that emphasizes cognitions. Yet this, I believe, still does not fully give us a picture of the elephant. It is time to blend these ideas with the deeper, psychodynamic theories. Wachtel (1977) began an elegant process of pointing out how the concepts of psychoanalysis and behaviorism actually overlap, except for the vocabulary. For example, he shows how the process of systematic desensitization is really similar to the process of a client continually free-associating to deeper memories and experiences of his anxiety (dynamic desensitization). He also noted that the changes from the analytic approach generalized more readily across other situations in a person's life and that it was always crucial to combine insight with some action.

This blending of ideas will give us an integrated view of individuals as composed of thoughts and behaviors as well as unconscious processes and feelings. All of these components are needed to understand psychopathology and help people change. This is not to say that all approaches are equally important all of the time. Different populations need different approaches. For example, children respond better to behavioral or family-centered approaches than anything deeply analytic. Many other people respond well to briefer cognitive or cognitive-behavioral approaches. However, for the many who do not, we need to integrate all the available counseling tools into our toolbox. We need to operate from an "integrated model of psychotherapy." Let's use a real-life case study to elaborate this idea.

Case Study

Nick comes to counseling as a 30-something, White, middle-class professional who works from home. He is happily married and has three young sons, ages 6, 9, and 11. Nick has also been suffering from panic attacks with agoraphobia for many years. They have been scary enough to put him into the emergency room a few times out of fear of a heart attack. They are upsetting his home life and interfering with his ability to venture out with his wife and kids. They are restricting his work opportunities because he can only work in positions where telecommuting is possible. He can drive short distances alone but needs a loved one with him for anything past a couple of miles. He had an unsuccessful counseling experience a year or two ago that mitigated his symptoms a little, but they are back now and stronger than ever.

Nick is constantly on guard to the world around him. He checks people for their reactions to him and adjusts himself according to what he feels they want. He fears any confrontation or even a whiff of conflict. He stifles his every reaction or emotion out of fear that someone will respond against him somehow. Nick would rather "stuff" his own legitimate emotions than risk any negative response from another. He consistently sees himself as in the wrong, weak, or otherwise flawed. Whatever it is, it's always his fault. It would be impossible to live like this without some constant anxiety.

His family history has its problems. He was raised in a home where his parents frequently fought and never modeled or gave much in the way of nurturing relationships. Anger and aggression were ubiquitous. After an ugly divorce, he was raised by his harsh mother whom he learned to fear greatly. She was demanding, overly critical, and quick to punish. She had far fewer times of fun or loving interactions with him. He learned to always strive to do perfectly for her, to jump quickly when called, and to monitor her moods carefully so he could act as she wanted to avoid any harsh punishment or rejection. He tried to constantly anticipate her unpredictable moods and actions to keep himself safe and unattacked. Nick discloses that he "always felt anxious around mom."

For the counselor, how one conceptualizes a case should lead you to your methods of intervention. Is this anxiety caused by a behaviorally learned conditioning process? Is it a result of some harsh, core belief systems? Or is it some unconscious conflict or harsh, punishing introject? The integrated counselor will use his or her knowledge of all these theories to consider the truth of all the above and orient an intervention that could include all the above in some integrated, systematic way. We try to see the totality of the person's life and not just predetermined parts of the life–the "elephant." Much of how we act may not emerge until we get more data about the client's story; the more we can gather, the more we will have to guide us in our work.

As stated earlier, the best way to learn the client's story is through an empathic, Rogerian-style relationship and interviewing techniques. As Nick talks, he feels safer; he trusts more and he reveals more and more about himself and things he even finds shameful or "weak." The treatment alliance not only allows him to disclose more but also prepares him to accept the directives of the counselor and to act on them.

After a few sessions, we have learned enough through some free association and Rogerian interviewing to begin to make some tentative interventions. There are some obvious irrational thoughts and dysfunctional belief systems contributing to Nick's symptoms. When intervening with a person, it is best to use a recent example of the problem with which to work. The more specific, the better. For Nick, we begin with the anxiety he endures around the parents of the kids he coaches in soccer. He keeps a running commentary in his head while trying to fathom *and control* their reactions to him. He is constantly fearful they may criticize or disapprove of something he does or says to the kids. He carefully sculpts his words to both parent and child to try to avoid or deflect any possibility of anger or criticism. His decisions on how to discipline the kids on the team or how to use them in games are constantly influenced by how he fears the parent will react. He tries to control their reactions by telling them what he thinks they want to hear. Despite these constant anxieties, to his credit, he plugs along in this volunteer position but feels miserable about it.

The dysfunctional thought patterns that emerge during our therapeutic dialogue as a cause of this anxiety are variations on the common themes of, "I can't let anyone be mad at me or dislike me" and "I'm just a screw-up anyway who deserves to be criticized." From an analytic/object relations point of view, we can easily see that he has internalized a sense of self from his relationship with his mother that is incompetent and deserving of criticism. His template of his relations with others also tells him that it is terrible to have anyone get mad at him because he expects the punishment will be harsh and fearful. These internalizations have produced the dysfunctional thought patterns mentioned above.

Nick was not totally aware of these thoughts and beliefs within him until they emerged in session. We intervene on a more cognitive level rather than a psychodynamic one because it is often quicker for the client. I point out the destructive beliefs and how they are operating in him to inhibit behavior and increase anxiety. He knows no other way to think about the situation. Together, we develop an alternative thought pattern that is more functional, healthier, and realistic. It allows him to rethink his beliefs in a fashion that says, "I am a capable person, and it's okay if everyone doesn't like me. I'll never see most of these parents again anyway." We practice these new patterns in session, and Nick goes home to practice them in real life.

Over a few weeks, Nick practices restructuring his thoughts in this situation, and other situations emerge in our dialogue that are similar in tension and in the patterns of dysfunctional thinking. He notices, for example, that he constantly looks for his wife's approval for anything he does. If it is not forthcoming, it immediately increases his persistent, hypervigilant anxiety. He learns to challenge the belief, "I need my wife to approve of me to be allowed to feel good about myself." The more he practices these restructured thoughts, the better he feels and the more automatic the new perspectives become.

Life is improving, but it is not great yet. During this work, he also starts having memories and feelings around mom and how these old feelings parallel the way he acts in his life to his wife, the soccer parents, and others. Ellis and Beck (both are "reformed" analysts) assert that understanding these historical connections do not matter, and perhaps for some they do not. But for Nick, and others like him, the ability to access those repressed memories and feelings helps him make sense of his life story and put more power and control into his ability to change thoughts, behaviors, and symptoms.

As we work on these issues, we tackle his anxiety about driving or going anywhere without a support. Relaxation exercises and imagery from the behavioral schools of counseling have shown their effectiveness for this kind of problem. I teach Nick some progressive muscle relaxation and help him pair the relaxed state with images of him driving to help reduce or eliminate the anxiety now paired with driving. This does help him somewhat over time but not enough to qualify as a success. In three months, Nick has made marked progress in his fears of others, his self-criticizing beliefs, his ability to see himself as a functional adult and father, and in reducing his overall anxiety. He has taken a couple of drives that he could not before, and he even managed one long weekend with the family at a favorite local vacation spot. The cognitive and behavioral techniques are certainly helping, but there is more. Something is standing in the way of a more complete return to normal life, and for this we explore further his family of origin and relations to his main caretakers. Simultaneously, we encourage him to keep practicing the new thoughts and relaxation techniques during times when he feels he needs to cope better with his daily demands. Successes build to other successes, but improvement is stalled out. He cannot yet drive in traffic, and he continues to fear any lengthy trips. At times he can manage nearby trips. He is still too harsh and critical to himself, and he fears he will not be able to handle it if his job is downsized and he has to work out of the home.

Within the safety of our treatment alliance, Nick free associates to his memories of the past and the relationship with both mom and dad. Various memories of harsh, criticizing treatment emerge, along with some of the strong emotions of fear, anger, and hate that occurred and were repressed. As a child, he lived in constant fear of anger or punishment, yet he was not allowed to express it anywhere. Expressing it risked the danger of more yelling or punishment. These hurtful feelings grew and were bottled up inside, where they seemed safe. Yet for Nick, they retained their strong emotional power and sought expression. Of course, his internalized super-ego would not allow the expression of any of this emotion. This set up a classic conflict in his unconscious between the necessary expression of strong aggressive feelings and the need to keep them bottled up. It was a persistent bottleneck of conflicting feelings he worked hard to avoid, repress, and not have to feel, although this constant struggle did contribute to his well of anxiety, which seemed never-ending to him. He feared being overwhelmed by these strong emotions as if he were still a child incapable of safely handling them.

Part of his vigilance about avoiding conflict with and disapproval from others was a projection of his inner fear of confronting his own emotions and conflicts and his super-ego's disapproval of him for daring to have such negative feelings about mom and dad. It gets tricky. But the process, or defense mechanism, for him was to avoid confronting others or getting mad himself because it could tap into and release this great repressed well of anger and hurt. Also, he must be vigilant about the disapproval of others because it could trigger the fear and hurt that was still within him over mom's disapproval and criticism. It was necessary for Nick to continually tap into that well of hurt, fear, and anger that he had been repressing for so long, release it in small doses, and start to own it as part of whom he was. This reduces the power of repressed feelings over an individual and allows them to more successfully work out other changes in their present lives.

There are a variety of ways to help a client unearth and release repressed emotions, but two points are crucial in this process. First, it must not simply be an intellectual acknowledgment of emotion. Many people can talk about feelings without really feeling the feelings. It must be truly felt and sincerely expressed, especially in the safe, accepting relationship with the counselor, who can validate and accept the feelings as true and legitimate. The counselor provides the safe "containing environment" where the feelings will not get out of control or overwhelm the client. Together, client and counselor can handle anything the client has been afraid to face alone.

Second, the feelings cannot be simply expressed by some screaming, crying, or pillow punching. During and after their expression, they must be talked through to the counselor and understood and accepted as part of the client's story–a cause or effect in the patterns of the client's life. This allows the rational, adult mind to gain control of the powerful, forbidden feelings and reintegrate them in an accessible, healthy manner as an accepted part of the self. Nick was eventually able to express and manage his deep feelings of hurt, anger, and rejection by both parents. No one has to like what happened, but one does have to accept it as part of one's life story. Acceptance of reality rather than resistance to it is power.

There are various methods for going after repressed or denied emotions when therapeutically necessary. One can use free association to various events and memories from a person's life. Dream interpretation may help, as could analysis of the transference onto the counselor. One could use the various, powerful "experiments" of Gestalt treatment like the "empty chair" technique, role-playing parts of the personality, or having the client talk about both sides of a "polarity" on a particular feeling, event, or issue. Part of Nick's counseling was to have him talk to his "mom" in an empty chair as if she were really there and feel free to really express everything to her that he had been afraid to for these many years. The effective counselor could have a person journal about a topic, write a letter to an important individual, or draw and talk about a picture of the family doing an activity. Some people with repressed feelings have an uncanny way of being angered or saddened by minor or inappropriate events, movies, and even songs or commercials that somehow touch a hidden feeling. If your client always cries over a certain song or emotes over a 30-second commercial about a lost puppy finding its family, there could be some real meaning in there. Ask him or her to talk through or free associate to the meanings of those stimuli. You may be shocked at what emerges. However you may get the client to express feelings, remember to have the person process the feelings, talk them through, as well as feel them through to ensure mastery of the affect.

Nick learned to express many of his old hurts and thereby accept them as part of his life story. He also learned to challenge and change the inner representations of himself as worthless and unlovable. He was able to replace these with newer, healthier thoughts of himself and his relation to the world. He continued to get better and more automatic at challenging his irrational cognitions, and he was able to use some relaxation and imagery exercises to help him cope with panic or anxiety whenever it arose. With many months of hard work, he was able to terminate counseling feeling rarely anxious, often in control of himself, and more mature and capable of running his own life without depending on others to "save" him. Other counselors in the past had tried one theoretical approach or another to help him, but he needed an overall, integrated approach to really get him to his goals of a more normal life.

SUMMARY

This chapter is an attempt to show the developing counselor how to use the main counseling theories in an integrated way in the service of our clients. You may have been taught that they are incompatible or that some are more "empirically validated" than others, but even the American Psychological Association (Stiles, Shapiro, & Elliot, 1986) has recognized the importance of all the approaches used above. The effective and ethical counselor who wants to increase his or her chances of really helping a desperately suffering client should be able to use many models of counseling in a rational, integrated way. The following is an outline of a recommended approach toward using an integrated model.

1. Use Rogerian techniques and demeanor to form and strengthen the therapeutic relationship. While doing this, you are drawing out the details of the client's life story.
2. Look for patterns in the story that could explain the presenting problems as well as possible strengths.
3. Use cognitive or rational-emotive interventions to help a client become aware of his or her destructive belief systems if they emerge as a pattern in the client's story. Teach the person to recognize and change these beliefs.
4. Maintain the empathic, nonjudgmental attitude while still asking about deeper layers of the client's life story. Listen with the "third ear" for other key issues or patterns, especially with family, sense of self, loss, trauma, other relational issues, coping skills, and normal emotional accessibility or expression.
5. Use behavioral techniques for symptom relief or to help develop new skills in the person as it seems clinically necessary. For example, teach relaxation for anxiety problems, practice assertiveness skills with people who need to learn to speak up for themselves, teach effective communication skills for those who need it, and teach anger management skills or other impulse control skills to those who need that. Some people may need help in learning to cope with stress. Others may need action plans to work toward goals and objectives such as finding a job or getting through school. Others may need reinforcement schedules built into their day to help them motivate toward changing. You will

probably find many people whose behaviors are inhibited by negative thinking and you will have to attack another negative belief system about things such as failure, acceptance, or being good enough as a person.

6. If a person is still having trouble changing or improving, keep listening for deeper issues relating to family of origin issues, possible trauma, pathological object relations with primary caregivers, unconscious conflicts around emotional expression or other taboo subjects like sex, aggression, or anything that may be individually important to that particular client.
7. Help clients become aware of unconscious or repressed issues that interfere with their lives and help them accept them, "own them," and be able to reintegrate them back into a healthier sense of self.
8. Teach them or help them develop better ways of looking at the forbidden issues and help them see their struggles as a normal part of the human experience that does not make them "sick" or "crazy" but just injured through certain causal patterns that you have identified. Remind them we are not seeking to blame others or have them fall into a victim mentality. We are just using a powerful process of understanding and action to facilitate change.
9. Try to be flexible to give a client what he or she may need at a particular moment. This may change from week to week with the same person. Perhaps today the client just needs to vent about a frustrating experience without being challenged on it. Perhaps on another day he or she will need to use the anxiety as a motivation to finally look at some self expectations honestly and not have the anxiety "relaxed" or medicated away. Always try to ask yourself, "What is going on with the person right now and how can I best intervene to help her or him at this moment?"
10. Keep evaluating what you are doing. If it ain't working, do something different. Try another perspective or theoretical approach to the issue. Reconceptualize the case from the point of view of a particular expert such as an Ellis, Rogers, Perls, or Freud. Avoid locking yourself into one way of thinking about a problem. People are usually more complicated than the one way you are thinking about.

Not every client will need a combination of approaches. Some will respond well to six or ten structured sessions of cognitive therapy. Others will legitimately need a couple years to storm through the various travails of their lives to feel whole again (Okun, 1990). Some are quicker to insight than others, and for some we are unsuccessful despite our best efforts. Keep savin' lives.

REFERENCES

Abraham, K. (1927). *Selected papers.* London: Hogarth Press.

Adler, A. (1958). *What life should mean to you.* New York: Capricorn.

Bandura, A. (Ed.). (1971). *Psychological modeling: Conflicting theories.* New York: Aldine-Atherton.

Bandura, A. (1969). *Principles of behavior modification.* New York: Holt, Rinehart, & Winston.

Beck, A. T. (1972). *Depression: Causes and treatment.* Philadelphia, PA: University of Pennsylvania Press.

Beck, A. T. (1976). *Cognitive therapy and emotional disorders.* New York: International Universities Press.

Burns, D., & Nolen-Hoeksema, S. (1992). Therapeutic empathy and recovery from depression in cognitive-behavioral therapy: A structural equation model. *Journal of Consulting and Clinical Psychology, 60,* 441–449.

Corey, G. (2001). *Theory and practice of counseling and psychotherapy* (6th ed.). Pacific Grove, CA: Brooks/Cole.

Davanloo, H. (1978). *Basic principles and techniques in short-term dynamic psychotherapy.* New York: Spectrum.

Dryden, W. (1995). *Rational-emotive behavior therapy: A reader.* London: Sage.

Ellis, A. (1973). *Humanistic psychotherapy: The rational-emotive approach.* New York: Julian Press.

Ellis, A., & Dryden, W. (1997). *The practice of rational-emotive therapy* (rev. ed.). New York: Springer.

Freud, S. (1949). *An outline of psychoanalysis.* New York: Norton.

Freud, S. (1963). *Therapy and techniques: Essays on dream interpretation, hypnosis, transference, free association and other techniques of psychoanalysis.* New York: Collier Books.

Horner, A. J. (1991). *Psychoanalytic object relations therapy.* Northvale, NJ: Jason Aronson.

Hubble, M., Duncan, B., & Miller, S. (1999). *The heart and soul of change: What works in psychotherapy.* Washington, DC: American Psychological Association.

Jung, K. G. (1966). *The practice of psychotherapy.* Princeton, NJ: Princeton University Press.

Kris, A. (1982). *Free association: Method and process.* New Haven, CT: Yale University Press.

Lazarus, A. A. (1976). *Multimodal behavior therapy.* New York: Springer.

Mahler, M. S. (1968). *On human symbiosis and the vicissitudes of individuation.* New York: International Universities Press.

Okun, B. (1990). *Seeking connections in psychotherapy.* San Francisco, CA: Jossey-Bass.

Perls, F. (1969). *In and out of the garbage pail.* Moab, UT: Real People Press.

Prochaska, J., & Norcross, J. (1994). *Systems of psychotherapy: A transtheoretical analysis.* Pacific Grove, CA: Brooks/Cole.

Rogers, C. (1942). *Counseling and psychotherapy.* Cambridge, MA: Riverside Press.

Rogers, C. (1951). *Client-centered therapy.* Boston, MA: Houghton-Mifflin.

Rogers, C. (1957). The necessary and sufficient conditions of therapeutic personality change. *Journal of Consulting Psychology, 21,* 95–103.

Rogers C. (1961). *On becoming a person.* Boston, MA: Houghton-Mifflin.

Skinner. B. F. (1974). *About behaviorism.* New York: Knopf.

Stiles, W. B., Shapiro, D. A., & Elliott, R. (1986). Are all psychotherapies equivalent? *American Psychologist, 41,* 165–180.

Sullivan, H. S. (1953). *Interpersonal theory of psychiatry.* New York: Norton.

Wachtel, P. L. (1977). *Psychoanalysis and behavior therapy: Toward an integration.* New York: Basic.

Watson, J. B. & Rayner, R. (1920). Conditioned emotional reactions. *Journal of Experimental Psychology, 3,* 1–14.

Zinker, J. (1978). *Creative process in gestalt therapy.* New York: Random House (Vintage).

Chapter 5

GERONTOLOGY: MENTAL HEALTH AND AGING

JANE E. MYERS AND LAURA A. SHANNONHOUSE

The number of older persons worldwide increased dramatically in the last century, notably in the last 50 years, in large part due to advances in medicine and health care. In the United States in 1900, only 4% of the total population was over 60 years of age compared with 12.8%, or more than one in eight persons over 65, in 2009 (Administration on Aging, 2009). By the year 2020, a further 36% increase in the older population is expected (Administration on Aging, 2009), at which time people over age 65 will comprise 19.3% of the population (Administration on Aging, 2009).

Estimates of the number of older persons with significant mental disorders range from 20% to 33% (American Association for Geriatric Psychiatry, 2004; Smyer & Qualls, 1999). These figures fail to include normative developmental issues such as adjustment to retirement and reduced income, grandparenthood, second careers, and coping with loss (death of a partner or friend, loss of health or mobility). When developmental issues are included, clearly the incidence of mental health needs among the older population increases. In this chapter, the challenges of later life that combine to make older persons a population at risk are considered. The mental health needs of this population and the current status of the mental health system as it relates to older individuals (including individual and systemic barriers to effective treatment) are discussed. Finally, the need for mental health counselors to receive specialty training in gerontological issues is addressed.

NORMAL AGING

One of the first challenges in working with older adults is to distinguish normal aging from pathological, disease-related processes that may occur. A useful rule of thumb is to view all age-related changes as gradual. Any sudden changes are not normal and require medical evaluation. The high incidence of co-morbid mental and physical problems in later life makse prevention, accurate assessment, and early intervention vital concerns (Birren & Schaie, 2001; Myers & Harper, 2004). Normative changes may be understood in terms of life transitions (which require coping with change and loss), similarities and differences between older and younger adults, and the life review process.

Life Transitions

Older persons experience a variety of transitions and changes at a time when their coping, physical, emotional, social, and material resources may be decreasing. Common transitions include adjusting to retirement and reduced income, entry into second (or third) careers, grandparenthood, the challenge of creating a leisure lifestyle, adjusting to declining health, and adjusting to widowhood and single living. Although any of these, or other life changes, can be for better or worse, older persons spontaneously cope and adapt, the majority doing so without seeking mental health care. However, older persons are more likely than persons of other ages to experience multiple, sequential losses. The grief process for any single loss becomes compounded, and a situation of bereavement overload is not uncommon as the capacity to cope can be significantly compromised (Smyer & Qualls, 1999). In these circumstances, an older individual may understandably become immobilized in his or her ability to cope with changing life circumstances.

Old age clearly is a time of change. Although continued growth in the later years and healthy aging have become increasingly common (Friedman, Martin, & Schoeni, 2002), helping professionals tend to focus on the dynamics of particular life situations or losses rather than on how to intervene to effectively work with older persons to reduce the negative impact of transition (Myers & Harper, 2004). Transition and loss may involve either environmental/extrinsic or intrinsic factors, or some combination of the two. The former include losses such as spouse, friends, and significant others, social and work roles, prestige, and income. The latter may include loss of physical strength and health, changes in personality or sexual abilities, and the loss of psychological resilience.

For both men and women, widowhood is the among the most severe of the transitions because it may result in severe depression and is a risk factor for dying. Unstructured groups have shown to reduce depression and increase feelings of support (Myers & Harper, 2004). Another transition is to that of a caregiver. There are an increasing number of older persons, particularly older women, who are experiencing caregiver burden, and studies have shown that social support is the strongest correlate to reducing burden (Myers & Harper, 2004). Grandparenthood is another developmental shift that sometimes involves raising grandchildren, mediating between parents and grandchildren, and the loss surrounding being denied access to grandchildren as adult children divorce and remarry (Myers & Harper, 2004).

Situational crises may arise for older persons as they are faced with a decreasing array of resources to meet an increasing array of needs. Most older persons can cope successfully with these changes. Certainly, all have the potential to react to the vicissitudes of aging in psychologically healthful and growthful ways. This is reflected in the fact that most older people are able to remain in community living environments. Only 4.1% lived in institutional settings in 2008 (Administration on Aging, 2009). Another 10% to 15% are largely homebound due to mental and/or physical disabilities, but they are able to continue living independently with some assistance. Unfortunately, the increased stresses of aging create adjustment problems that impact the mental health of some older adults.

Similarities and Differences Between Older and Younger Adults

Although older persons are more similar to persons of other ages than they are different, the unique challenges imposed by later life transitions and the need for coping with loss, often experienced in terms of multiple and overlapping losses, create unique needs for adjustment. Older persons experience an increased risk for depression in response to losses; in addition, co-morbidity of mental and physical health problems is common.

More than half of all older persons experience physical limitations due to age-related physical changes (Administration on Aging, 2009), with ethnic minority status and low socioeconomic status contributing to greater incidences of chronic activity limitations (Administration on Aging, 2009). Older adults experience substantial co-morbidity, such that the interaction between physical and mental health is an especially common and complicating factor in later life. Physical problems can lead to mental distress, mental distress can exacerbate physical symptoms, and the interaction between the two can lead to an exacerbation of clinical pathology (Birren & Schaie, 2001). Thus, unique challenges for differential diagnosis are present with the older population, and the need to determine whether problems are due to normative changes or concerns that can be remediated perpetually complicates treatment.

The Life Review Process

The brief review of transitions and losses described earlier underscores the fact that challenges faced by older persons are many and varied. Erikson (1963), the first and most prominent lifespan developmental theorist, postulated that older persons experience (and most resolve) the central psychosocial challenge of achieving integrity versus despair. Butler (1974) identified the normative process of life review, commonly observed in the telling of "stories" by persons in later life, as the process by which integrity is reached. Life review occurs with a purpose–that being an integration of life experiences and a sense that the life one lived is the best one could have lived. This is defined as a state of integrity. Older persons who look back on their lives with regret, realizing that they have little time left to make significant changes, may experience a state of depression characterized by despair. Early recollections (ERs) can be used in conjunction with life review. ERs are obtained by asking a client to relate his or her earliest memory of a single event and are used to explore the meaning they make of these childhood experiences. ERs create space to explore one's early memories, which gives direct insight into how one functions in daily life (Clark, 2002; Sweeney, 2009). This can be a useful alternative to the full life review process, because failing to achieve integrity can have negative consequences (Myers & Harper, 2004).

MENTAL HEALTH AND AGING

As noted earlier, as many as one third of older persons experience mental health problems that warrant professional intervention. This includes older people with clinically significant depression and those diagnosed with major affective disorder or bipolar depression. In Gatz and Smyer's review of epidemiological data, they note that around 20% of older adults met the criteria for mental disorder (cited in Birren & Schaie, 2001), which is lower than the prevalence of mental disorders in younger adults. Serious mental health concerns do not necessarily increase with increasing age as was once widely believed. In fact, future increases in the mental health issues of an older adult may well be the result of inherited disorders that were evident at a much younger age (Birren & Schaie, 2001).

The American Association for Geriatric Psychiatry (2004) reported that the most common mental health disorders, "in order of prevalence, are: anxiety, severe cognitive impairment, and mood disorders. Studies report, however, that mental disorders in older adults are underreported. The rate of suicide is highest among older adults compared to any other age group–and the suicide rate for persons 85 years and older is the highest of all–twice the overall national rate" (p. 1).

According to the American Association for Geriatric Psychiatry (AAGP), 11.4% of adults over age 55 were diagnosable with an anxiety disorder in 1994, which is a lower rate than is seen among younger persons. Such studies reveal that anxiety may be more common than depression among older individuals. However, given the complexities of diagnosis of both depression and anxiety in older persons (e.g., the difficulty of differential diagnosis of physical and emotional disorders), it is possible that depression is more prevalent than diagnoses indicate. For example, the AAGP reported that the prevalence of major depression declines with age but that depressive symptoms actually increase. This organization estimated that as many as one in five older adults living in the community and one in three living in primary care settings suffer from depression.

Significant cognitive impairment resulting from organic brain disorders is evident in increasing numbers of older persons as they age, and such impairment typically is part of a syndrome of co-occuring disorders. Alzheimer's disease, the most common cause of dementia in older people, affects as many as 1 in 10 persons over the age of 65, and as many as 50% of persons over the age of 85 are thought to have some form of dementia. The incidence of impairment is even higher among residents of long-term care facilities. Piacitelli (1992) noted that one half of older patients with Alzheimer's disease and one half of those with multi-infarct dementia are diagnosed concurrently with depression and psychosis.

Alcohol abuse has been difficult to study in the older population and is widely viewed as a hidden problem. However, a panel convened by the National Institutes of Health, Substance Abuse and Mental Health Administration, estimated that as many as 17% of older persons misuse or abuse prescription drugs or alcohol (Blow, 1998). Smyer and Qualls (1999) noted that accurate assessment of substance abuse among older persons is complicated by co-morbidity of dementia and other mental and physical disorders, including sleep disorders.

Older persons comprised 18% of all deaths by suicide in 2000 (National Institute of Mental Health, 2003), the highest rate of any age group in the U.S. (American Psychological Association, 2003). According to American Psychological Association (2003), "20% of older adults who commit suicide visited a physician within the prior 24 hours, 41% within the past week and 75% within the past month." Lethality is particularly strong among older persons, for whom the completion rate for suicide is 1:4 compared with 1:20 in the general population. These facts suggest that older persons who are depressed or emotionally distressed do not receive timely intervention. Moreover, outreach and case finding may be especially important with this population, because the lethality rate for suicide is so high.

THE MENTAL HEALTH SYSTEM AND OLDER ADULTS

Unfortunately, existing mental health services for older persons have not met the demand for care. Studies of service usage conducted over the past 25 years reveal a consistent pattern of underservice in both community mental health and private practice settings (Smyer & Qualls, 1999). The American Associatoin for Geratric Psychiatry (2004) reported that older adults comprise "only seven percent of all inpatient mental health services, six percent of community based mental health services, and nine percent of private psychiatric care," and the American Psychological Association (2003) estimated that 63% of older adults with mental disorders do not receive needed services.

Older persons who are homebound have little access to mental health services, and those residing in long-term care settings almost never receive mental health treatment. In contrast, most of the mental health care needed by older persons is provided through the general health sector, with as few as 3% of older adults receiving the services they need from mental health providers (American Association for Geriatric Psychiatry, 2004; American Psychological Association, 2003). In other words, physicians are the primary mental health care givers for older individuals, even though they are, as a group, poorly trained to recognize and treat emotional disorders. Further, physicians may be less likely to refer older patients than younger patients for needed mental health care.

Preventive care or early intervention is important for preventing or postponing hospital admissions and sustaining quality of life for older adults with mental health concerns. Older persons tend not to seek mental health care for their problems, but rather seek care from their primary physicians. This is due, in part, to the lack of a vocabulary for emotional issues in today's older persons. From another perspective, many people who are older today hold strong values of independence in resolving personal problems, as evidenced by clichés such as "You don't air your dirty laundry in public." It is also true that today's older persons were raised in a time when mental health services were available only to those with the most severe impairments, and the resultant negative stigma of receiving such services is great. As the baby boomers age, these values may change, as this population is known to be among the greatest consumers of popular psychology, self-help literature and are otherwise demanding of services to maintain a healthy and an engaged lifestyle.

Barriers to the provision of mental health services for older adults also exist among mental health care providers (Robb, Chen, & Haley, 2002). These barriers include the reluctance of mental health counselors to work with older clients due to factors such as lack of sufficient training in geriatric issues, bias against older clients, and third-party payment policies and other systemic factors, which prohibit providers from accepting older persons as clients. It has been almost 30 years since Cohen (1977) established that therapists may be reluctant to work with older clients due to unrecognized negative countertransference reactions, in that older clients may stimulate the therapist's fears of personal aging or the aging and death of parents. He further suggested that older clients may be perceived as rigid and unwilling or unable to change. The few years they may have remaining can serve as a disincentive to the therapist who feels that his or her time is being "wasted." These issues remain barriers to service delivery today.

Mental health counselors are subject to the same negative perceptions and stereotypes of older persons that are common in our society. Myths such as "old people are all sick, poor, angry, sad, lonely" tend to discourage counselors from working with older clients. Although global negative attitudes may not be as prevalent as once thought, specific biases–ageism–still may interfere with service to older clients. Misperceptions of organic brain syndrome prevalence and symptomology tend to discourage mental health providers from active involvement with many older persons.

The net result of the barriers to service delivery is that large numbers of older persons experience significant mental health problems due to lack of suitable preventive and remedial interventions. This is especially true for older individuals experiencing situational adjustment reactions. Although the clinical picture of geriatric mental illness is depressing, it also is an artifact of our current treatment system. The potential of older persons to respond to mental health interventions is excellent. The results of multiple studies reveal that psychotherapy is as effective with older persons as with people of any age group (see Myers & Harper, 2004; Roth & Fonagy, 1996, for reviews of relevant literature). With appropriate, accessible services, major mental illness among older people can be prevented, to a great extent, and treated where preventive efforts are unsuccessful or lacking. The resultant savings in both dollars and human resources are potentially tremendous.

TRAINING GERONTOLOGICAL MENTAL HEALTH COUNSELORS

As the older population increases, proportionate needs for mental health services may be projected to increase as well. If the mental health counseling profession is to respond effectively to the challenges presented by this age group, increasing numbers of gerontological mental health counselors, trained to identify and meet the needs of older people, will be required.

Over the past few decades, counselors have become increasingly aware of the need of older persons and have begun to direct resources toward meeting those needs. In 1975, only 6% of counselor education programs offered even an elective course in counseling older persons, but by 1988, the percentage had grown to 36%. In the early 1980s, courses in gerontological counseling were the third most frequent new course in counselor education, lagging behind courses in marriage, family, and substance abuse. Although a distant third in the 1980s, new courses in this area declined in the 1990s.

Another event that signified a waning interest in gerontological issues within the counseling profession was the suspension of the National Certified Gerontological Counseling (NCGC) specialty credential by the National Board for Certified Counselors (NBCC). Although the Council for Accreditation of Counseling and Related Educational Programs (CACREP) approved a gerontological counseling specialty in the early 1990s, to date only two counselor preparation programs have sought this specialty accreditation. The author coordinates the specialty track in one of those programs, and the dearth of interested students is a continuing concern.

Obviously, the need for increased gerontological training for mental health counselors is both appropriate and timely in response to dramatic increases in the numbers of older persons and documentation of significant developmental, preventive, and remedial mental health needs in this population. Still, the job market for geriatric mental health services remains largely within the purview of related professions, notably medicine (psychiatry), psychology, and social work. If gerontological mental health counselors are to obtain jobs commensurate with their training, active advocacy by the profession is required. The job market for gerontological mental health counselors is relatively new and may be expected to expand as counselors focus their efforts on the older population and document the success of mental health interventions.

REFERENCES

Administration on Aging. (2009). *A profile of older Americans.* Retrieved April 15, 2010, from http://www.aoa.gov/AoARoot/Aging_Statistics/Profile/2009/docs/2009profile_508.pdf

American Association for Geriatric Psychiatry. (2004). *Geriatrics and mental health–The facts.* Retrieved September 19, 2004, from http://www.aagpgpa.org/prof/facts_mh.asp

American Psychological Association. (2003). *Guidelines for psychological practice with older adults.* Retrieved April 15, 2010, from http://www.apa.org/practice/guidelines/older-adults.pdf

Birren, J., & Schaie, K. W. (Eds.). (2001). *Handbook of the psychology of aging* (5th ed.). San Diego, CA: Elsevier Academic Press.

Blow, F. C. (1998). *Substance abuse among older adults: Treatment improvement protocol series.* Rockville, MD: Substance Abuse and Mental Health Services Administration.

Butler, R. N. (1974). Successful aging and the role of the life review. *Journal of the American Geriatrics Society, 22,* 529–535.

Clark, A. J. (2002). *Early recollections: Theory and practice in counseling and psychotherapy.* New York: Brunner-Routledge.

Cohen, G. (1977). Mental health services and the elderly: Needs and options. In S. Steury & M. L. Black (Eds.), *Readings in psychotherapy with older people.* Rockville, MD: National Institutes of Mental Health.

Erikson, E. (1963). *Childhood and society.* New York: Norton.

Friedman, V. A., Martin, L. G., & Schoeni, R. F. (2002). Recent trends in disability and functioning among older adults in the United States: A systematic review. *JAMA, 288,* 3137–3146.

Myers, J. E., & Harper, M. (2004). Evidence-based effective practices with older adults: A review of the literature for counselors. *Journal of Counseling & Development, 82,* 207–218.

Piacitelli, J. D. (1992). *Beyond therapy: The role of mental health professionals in addressing the needs of the mentally ill elderly.* Paper presented at National Press Conference on Aging, Washington, DC.

Robb, C., Chen, H., & Haley, W. E. (2002). Ageism in mental health and health care: A critical review. *Journal of Clinical Geropsychology, 8*(1). Retrieved from http://www.springerlink.com/content/gx05765126721755/ April 22, 2010.

Roth, A., & Fonagy, P. (1996). *What works for whom? A critical review of psychotherapy research.* New York: Guilford Press.

Smyer, M. A., & Qualls, S. H. (1999). *Aging and mental health.* Malden, MA: Blackwell.

Sweeney, T. J. (2009). *Adlerian counseling and psychotherapy.* New York: Prentice-Hall.

Chapter 6

MULTICULTURALISM AND DIVERSITY IN COUNSELING

MARC A. GRIMMETT, DON C. LOCKE,
ALISHEA S. ROWLEY, AND NATALIE F. SPENCER

Everyone is pulling from what they know.
–JLMG, feminist, educator, and activist

In order to develop multicultural counseling awareness, knowledge, and skills and to work for social justice, it is necessary to intentionally explore unknown and unfamiliar personal and social spaces, to chance having your worldview, beliefs, values and behaviors challenged, and to experience truly uncomfortable feelings. To try to avoid or escape these fundamental processes in developing multicultural counseling competence is to believe that you can learn as much from preparing a microwavable dinner as you can from–loving recipes, carefully selected ingredients, appropriate utensils, and taking your time to really cook.

–MAG

SYSTEMS OF HUMAN DEVELOPMENT

Human beings are essentially the same genetically, biologically, and physiologically, yet each person is individually, socially, and culturally unique (Shreeve, 2006). The physical features of our individual human bodies are diverse in size, shape, color, and texture, as are our personalities and lived experiences with family, friends, school, work, and community. How we understand ourselves and other human beings, and make meaning of our experiences, develops through our continually evolving social relationships and cultural contexts (Comstock et al., 2008). Individuals are also intricately connected to history by their family, their communities, and the larger world that we all share. The Social Ecological Model (SEM; see Figure 6.1), adapted from Brofenbrenner's (1995) bioecological model, illustrates our individual uniqueness in dynamic relationship with living social, cultural, and historical systems. Our *life map* (i.e., our personal SEM) is the natural lens and structure for how we perceive, interpret, and understand information, as well as how we relate to other human beings. *Multicultural Counseling Competence* requires the ability to understand ourselves and our clients as cultural beings with diverse backgrounds living in dynamic contexts (Arredondo et al., 1996). In a multicultural counseling relationship, it cannot be taken for granted that the counselor and client have the same backgrounds and are operating from the same worldview (Gelso & Fretz, 2001). The worldview and actions of the client and the counselor stem from *their own* personal experiences and develop through continuous, multilevel, informational exchange and processing between the self systems of the counselor and client and their social ecosystems (Kunkler & Rigazio-DiGilio, 1994). Constant interaction between the individual and the elements of their environment leads to the creation, formulation, and development of thoughts, feelings, and behaviors associated with a personal sense of being in the world (Ivey, 2000). Mental health counselors in multicultural counseling relationships need to be aware that a culturally different client may think, feel, and act differently than they are accustomed because of historical, social, economical, political, and cultural variations in socialization and lived experiences.

Each system of the SEM, represented by the circles on Figure 6.1, is interconnected and interdependent, consisting of living parts that develop and change over time. Larger systems include smaller (i.e., sub) systems, all of which are defined by particular characteristics and components. The community system, for example, contains families and individuals. The *individual system* includes personal characteristics such as age, gender, race, ethnicity, sexual orientation, ability, disability, and occupation. *Family systems* are defined by traditions, expectations, roles, and rules (Bowen, 1994; Satir, 1967). Availability and access to schools, hospitals, employment settings, and related resources constitute *community systems. Institutional systems* are the regulatory structures and policies for services provided within the community. The educational, financial, and healthcare systems as a whole, rather than specific community entities (e.g., school, bank, or hospital) are considered institutions. *Oppression,* in such forms as sexism, racism, and heterosexism, operates within institutional and cultural systems to restrict, limit, or obstruct human rights and life pursuits (Freire, 1970). Human behaviors typically associated with these forms of oppression (e.g., devaluing another person because of a dimension of his or her identity) are demonstrated at the interpersonal level or within individual, family, and community systems; howev-

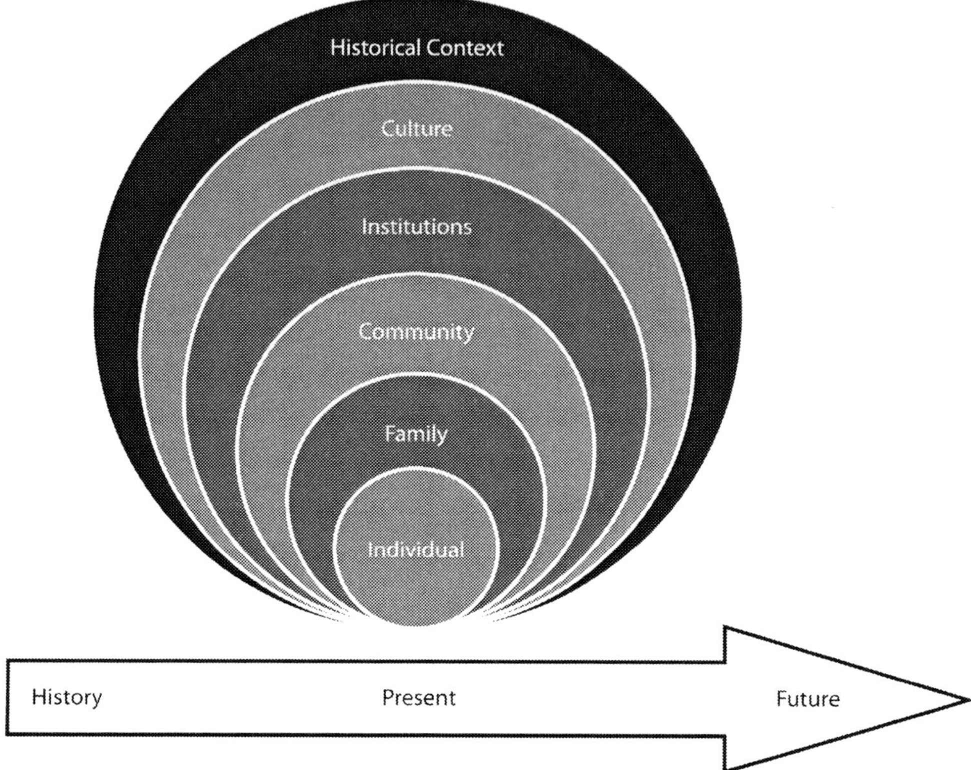

Figure 6.1. Social Ecological Model.

er, policies and practices that have historically and systematically advantaged particular social demographic groups (e.g., men) in the United States have an institutional and cultural foundation (e.g., all of the presidents of the United State have been men).

> If you examine the world that we live in it becomes very apparent that race affects every aspect of every day of everyone's life. The people who do not realize this are usually the privileged who are not oppressed by the social structure founded in white hegemony. If ever anyone questions the validity of this, the truth can be found in the disenfranchisement laws that prohibit convicted felons from voting. If you examine this public policy it does not take long to realize that minority imprisonment is high. Currently, the imprisonment of black males is at an all time high. While hard crime rates (murder, rape) remain stable/consistent, felon crimes due to drug possession and/ or distribution is at an all time high. Because of this Republicans have launched a "war on drugs." This war has stiffened street level drug tracking, penalizing, in many cases, black and/or Hispanic males between the ages of 20–29 and convicting

them of harsh felony offenses, taking away their freedom and stripping them of their right to vote FOREVER. Stripping them of the right to vote, eliminates their input into how power is distributed in the United States and who is given power. This disenfranchisement strips away a large minority vote which equates to the disenfranchisement that slaves, ex-slaves and blacks encountered as they fought to vote in order to change the power distribution that had previously consisted of the white vote, which legalized slavery and Jim Crow laws. Our current disenfranchisement laws are consistent with previous disenfranchisement laws, but cleverly masked by hyper media coverage that leads us to believe that minorities and minority neighborhoods are inundated with drugs and drug problems when in fact rich, educated whites compose the largest population of drug consumers.

–Counselor Education Student

- Describe, explain, and make meaning of oppression related to the legal and judicial systems of the United States.
- Imagine that the above journal entry expresses the beliefs of your client. Share and discuss your reactions, thoughts, and feelings to the content of the journal.
- Discuss how your belief system and worldview align with that of the client.

The larger cultural context encompasses and transcends each of the smaller subsystems (e.g., democracy, capitalism, patriarchy). At the same time, each subsystem and related components also have cultural characteristics (e.g., rural farming communities, urban developed cities). Cultural manifestations of oppression are often described, defined, and explained as ubiquitous, subtle, and invisible. Relative standards of beauty for women in the United States (e.g., thinness), for example, are presented consistently and comprehensively in all forms of media and therefore are cultural norms. Despite evidence that such standards of beauty are restrictive, artificial, unrealistic, and unhealthy, they continue to be perpetuated by powerful institutions (e.g., multinational media organizations), a form of cultural oppression (Hawkins, Richards, Granley, & Stein, 2004).

Definitions of *culture,* related to the SEM and relevant to understanding our clients, include the: (a) characteristic features of everyday existence shared by people in a place or time (e.g., Barack Obama was elected president of the United States in 2009; the oil spill in the Gulf of Mexico from the damaged British Petroleum drill–cultural system); (b) set of shared attitudes, values, goals, and practices that characterizes an institution or organization (e.g., the social networking culture of companies such as Facebook-institutional system); and (c) history, beliefs, values, traditions, behaviors, and customs of racial, ethnic, religious, or social groups (e.g., individuals who identify as Muslim or practice Islam-community, family, or individual systems).

The culture system, therefore, has many layers and requires the capacity to transmit cultural information to succeeding generations. Finally, *historical context* is depicted as the largest most inclusive system in the SEM. The arrow in Figure 6.1 illustrates that individuals, families, communities, institutions, and cultures all have histories.

Our ability to meaningfully and effectively work with clients and attend to their concerns requires that we also consider the historical, social, and cultural contexts from which they developed. Multicultural counseling incorporates a systems perspective by taking into account: (a) the person and his or her presenting concern, (b) the social environment relative to his or her presenting concern, and (c) the relationships between the person, his or her presenting concern, and the relevant social environment. Awareness of the systemic nature of client presenting issues highlights the systemic inequities present in various social systems. Multicultural counselors, equipped with systems understanding, design and employ interventions that promote positive social change in addition to healthy individual change. Inherent in multicultural counseling is a commitment to social justice.

Vera and Speight (2003) explain:

> social justice is at the heart of multiculturalism in that the existence of institutionalized racism, sexism, and homophobia is what accounts for the inequitable experiences of people of color, women, gay, lesbian, and bisexual people (among others) in the United States. Moreover, discrimination and prejudice are intimately connected to quality-of-life issues for these groups of people . . . [and] any multicultural movement that underemphasizes social justice is likely to do little to eradicate oppression and will maintain the status quo to the detriment of historically marginalized people. (pp. 254–255)

For that reason, the areas of social change are the places in society, such as homes (e.g., domestic violence, sexual assault, and child abuse), schools (e.g., discriminatory academic and suspension practices), and work (e.g., discriminatory hiring and promotion policies, culturally insensitive supervisors and colleagues) where injustices occur, adversely affecting the mental health and overall well-being of individuals living and operating in those systems. A systemic perspective rooted in a commitment to social justice combines personal-level interventions, such as teaching coping and empowerment skills, with being active at the societal level in an effort to eliminate some problems that clients experience at the source (Vera & Speight, 2003). Multicultural counselors must have the ability to function as a change agent at organizational, institutional, and societal levels when practices within institutions negatively affect a client's psychological welfare (Toporek & Reza, 2001).

> The neighborhood we visited . . . was more impoverished than any part of [the city] I had ever seen. In fact, I felt like I had been transported to a completely different town, different time, far away. . . . Don't get me wrong, I know what poor areas look like growing up [in my hometown], but I was startled to see such impoverishment. . . . Once we arrived at the home, we went inside to meet the family. As soon as we walked through the door, I was met with a strong odor. The house smelled terrible, it was the dirtiest and most unsanitary home that I have ever been in. The couch I sat on was stained and covered in dust, the walls were marked with grime and the floors were filthy. . . . I was just hoping that my allergies were not going to kill me in the next three hours. The friendly, welcoming grandmother wore dirty clothes and seemed unaffected by her living environment. . . . Combined there are six individuals who live in this small home. Not only does the grandmother take care of her granddaughter, she has two toddler grandsons (one of which who also receives Children's Developmental Service Agency services) to look after during the day. Her other daughter, who was not present, lives in the small duplex with her and has three children. . . . I thought about how these kids, though loved and enjoyed by their grandmother, were going to struggle in life . . . growing up in such an environment. . . . Belonging to a community with so few resources and to a home so impoverished (i.e., intellectually and physically), it is absolutely necessary that these children get the resources that they need.
>
> –School Psychology Doctoral Student who
> shadowed a social worker on a home visit

Describe and discuss the social justice issues presented in the above narrative.
Define and explain the systems of human development that are involved.
Discuss the role of advocacy in the work of mental health counselors.

Multicultural Counseling

The increasing diversity of the U.S. population requires that mental health professionals develop multicultural counseling competence to be effective and ethical in the services they provide (Arredondo, Tovar-Blank, & Parham, 2008; Essandoah, 1996). Multicultural counseling competence is certainly required for mental health counselors who often serve people who experience oppression and marginalization related to different aspects of their identity, such as race, ethnicity, sexual orientation, and immigration status (Chung, Bemak, Ortiz, & Sandoval-Perez, 2008). The Association for Multicultural Counseling and Development recognized the significant need for cultural sensitivity and understanding in counseling and created the Multicultural Counseling Competencies "to guide interpersonal counseling interactions with attention to culture, ethnicity, and race" (Sue, Arredondo, & McDavis, 1992, p. 64).

Multicultural counseling is historically rooted in social justice and parallels the civil rights movement of the 1950s and 1960s (Jackson, 1995). As societal issues of racism, discrimination, and segregation were being acknowledged to negatively influence the quality of life for people of color, so were the lack of attention, value, and inquiry given to the cultural backgrounds of clients being recognized to undermine the quality of mental health services provided to clients of color. Multiculturalism has since grown in professional appreciation as fundamental in counseling and applied psychology and vital to appropriate, ethical, and effective mental health practice (Pedersen, 1999). The practice of multicultural counseling requires universal and culture-specific knowledge and theoretical models (Fischer, Jome, & Atkinson, 1998). Given the vast cultural landscape of the increasingly more connected and porous global environment, cultural competence is best conceptualized and understood as an interactive process that mental health professionals engage in over the lifespan (Constantine, 2001; Paisley & Benshoff, 1996). As such, the preparation of multicultural mental health counselors requires a comprehensive, developmental, and longitudinal approach within training programs, departments, colleges, and institutions (Pack-Brown, Thomas, & Seymour, 2008; Reynolds, 1995).

Mental health counselors need multicultural counseling skills for appropriate interventions, advocacy, and effective use of culturally appropriate models (Sue et al., 1992). The American Mental Health Counselors Association (AMHCA) recognizes that multiculturalism is an essential component in effective and ethical mental health counseling practice. The American Mental Health Counselors Association (2010) makes the following statement on diversity in its code of ethics:

> Mental health counselors will actively attempt to understand the diverse cultural backgrounds of the clients with whom they work. This includes learning how the counselor's own cultural/ethical/racial/religious identity impacts his or her own values and beliefs about the counseling process. (Counselor Responsibility and Integrity, Competence, p. 9)

The still developing infusion of multiculturalism into the mental health field has created a broad and evolving conceptual and theoretical base. Subsequently, several related, yet distinct, definitions of multicultural counseling have arisen and can be briefly summarized in three general categories: (a) counseling approaches that integrate multicultural and culture-specific awareness, knowledge, and skills into counseling interactions (Sue et al., 1992); (b) counseling that occurs between counselors and clients from different cultural backgrounds (Fukuyama, 1990; Jackson, 1995; McFadden, 1999, Pedersen, 1991), and/or more specifically, (c) counseling that occurs between a counselor from one racial or ethnic group and a client from a different racial or ethnic group (Locke, 1990). Ultimately, multicultural counseling can morph, or take whichever form, necessarily to optimally fit the context and requirements of the specific counseling situation.

Given the complexity of multiculturalism, this chapter focuses more on the inclusive principles of multicultural counseling offered by Arredondo et al. (2008) to provide a conceptual base for the intentional inclusion of culture in mental health counseling. These principles are: (a) social justice and inclusion (vs. marginalization); (b) equity, pluralism, integration, and preservation (vs. assimilation); and (c) essentialness of cultural and contextual paradigms in the counseling profession. Multicultural counseling, regardless of the relative variation in definition, possesses characteristics that distinguish it from traditional, Euro-American counseling (Sue & Sue, 2003); it allows the culturally diverse client to fully come into being through an acceptance and appreciation of that client within his or her cultural context (Locke, 1998). The philosophical and theoretical foundations of multicultural counseling integrate systems, social justice, and prevention components, in addition to cultural awareness, knowledge, and skills (Lewis, Lewis, Daniels, & D'Andrea, 2003). A multicultural counseling perspective acknowledges that individuals exist in dynamic and complex social, cultural, economic, and political contexts (Robinson, 2005). Therefore, multicultural counselors are aware that challenges encountered and endured by clients involve some combination of continually interacting personal and environmental factors, over which clients have varying degrees of control. Multicultural counseling promotes the conceptual and practical expansion of traditional counselor roles (Lewis & Arnold, 1998). A multicultural counseling perspective acknowledges: (a) counseling is values based, (b) multiple dimensions of personal identity, and (c) worldview.

Counseling Is Values Based

Conventional models of health, wellness, and adaptive functioning, drawn on in the counseling field, reflect the Eurocentric values dominant or highly regarded in the culture of their origin, where clients were typically of European descent and from middle- to upper class segments of the population (Sue & Sue, 2003). Accordingly, traditional counseling theories tend to be individualistic, normative, intrapsychic, and remedial, with less focus on client systems, cultural context, environmental factors, and prevention (Lewis, Lewis, Daniels, & D'Andrea, 2003). Within the Eurocentric frame of reference are client expectations of openness, psychological-mindedness, insightfulness, and verbal, emotional, and behavioral expressiveness.

Multicultural counseling recognizes that all counseling approaches are culturally bound. Therefore, cultural consideration must be given to the appropriateness of interventions used with culturally diverse clients. Culturally competent counselors must understand that they bring to the counseling relationship a set of values, beliefs, attitudes, and opinions about the client and that some of their values, beliefs, attitudes, and opinions exist solely because the client is a member of a particular racial, ethnic, or distinct cultural group (e.g., stereotypes and prejudices) (Rollock & Gordon, 2000). To suggest that counseling is value-free is to support treating all clients alike (e.g., as if all clients were from White, middle-class, English-speaking, Protestant heterosexual backgrounds). Sue and Sue (2003) contend that such treatment reflects a primarily Eurocentric worldview, may represent cultural oppression, and may harm culturally different clients. Multicultural counseling requires counselors to consider the cultural background, values, and worldview of the culturally diverse clients and to work within the client's cultural context.

When [our professor] showed most of the counseling theorists are White men, I felt a kind of relief inside. Even though there are many articles [about] multicultural counseling pointing out this fact, I rarely had this kind of experience in a school setting in the U.S. It was a very encouraging experience to me. As an international [doctoral] student coming from different cultural backgrounds, I have always wrestled with the question: "How can I adapt Western counseling theories to clients with different cultural backgrounds?" Western psychotherapy comes from different worldviews and models of healing, which appear to be connected with individualism in Western theories. Even within my limited counseling experience with diverse populations, I have realized how family and community's involvements, the holistic understanding of mind and body, and spirituality . . . are important. I think that counseling theories are still a culturally encapsulated discipline confined to its national borders. Even in the context of globalization of counseling, I realize how easy it is for counselors and counselor educators to do a wholesale importation of mainstream counseling theories into other cultures. When I speak from a different cultural perspective, I sometimes feel burdened as I often seem to go against what mainstream theories talk about, or what the majority of Americans believe. But I think I am becoming increasingly ready to challenge cultural perspectives and to be challenged.

–Counselor Education Doctoral Student

Discuss the relative adaptability of European and U.S. originated counseling theories when working with culturally diverse clients.

What are the benefits and challenges of professional counselors whose country of origin is not the United States?

Discuss similarities and differences of cultural traditions across the world, as well as the practice of *counseling*.

At this point, it is important to acknowledge that multiculturalism is as much a personal, intentional, and active lifestyle as it is a professional counseling philosophy. Likewise, multicultural counseling is a theoretical framework that, through the counselor, can be overlaid onto and infused into traditional counseling interventions, rather than necessarily replacing them altogether. One goal of multicultural counseling is sustainable mental health for clients. Subsequently, the presenting issues of the client naturally encompass the various systems where they evolved and reside (e.g., family, school, work), rather than a singular focus on the individual client. Interventions prior to the multicultural movement within the field of counseling were primarily: (a) directed at the individual client (with the exception of the field of marriage and family therapy), (b) focused on creating healthy changes within the individual, and (c) designed to help the individual with a problem he or she was currently experiencing or to resolve some past conflict (Daniels, 2007).

Multiple Dimensions of Personal Identity

An important component of multicultural counseling competence is awareness of the interplay and influence of culture on the connection between counselors and clients. One way to understand the meaning and significance of culture for the client is to explore his or her multiple dimensions identity (Arredondo & Glauner, 1992). At any given point in our lives, we are sons, daughters, wives, husbands, partners, mothers, and fathers. We may also identify with specific cultures, ethnicities, regions, religions, and social groups or backgrounds. Identities related to race, ethnicity, gender, sexual orientation, religion, geographic region, language, class, and country of origin intentionally intersect, interact, and interconnect. For instance, if you are geographically from the northern, urban region of the United States you will identify with the nuances and traditions that comprise that region. Our responsibility as culturally competent counselors is to both appreciate and respect the multiple dimensions of our clients' identities and to help them work through challenges associated with identifying with particular groups. A multidimensional identity can also be beneficial and can help clients and counselors develop a better understanding about themselves, their culture, and their lives.

Salazar and Abrams (2005) point out that counselors must be aware that racial or ethnic identity development is not experienced the same by all individuals who identify with a particular racial or ethnic group, nor is identity development in sociocultural groups such as women, people with disabilities, members of the lesbian, gay, and bisexual communities, and transgendered individuals the same as racial and ethnic identity development. Each dimension of personal identity and its related sociocultural group has its own developmental processes and characteristics. In addition, "membership in a social or-cultural group defined by a particular racial, ethnic, gender, sexual, age, ability, or religious identity does not erase the reality of diversity among the individuals within that group" (Stewart, 2009, p. 256).

Brook, Garcia, and Fleming (2008) examined the effects of multiple identities on psychological well-being and found that recent research yielded conflicting conclusions. In other words, having multiple dimensions of identity is not necessarily associated with psychological well-being, particularly if a person identifies with groups that are marginalized (Rust, 1996). Additionally, when gender, race, class, and sexual orientation are examined separately, rather than as integrated identities of a whole person, the lives of people become compartmentalized into cultural categories instead of an accurate reflection of real life (Croteau, Talbot, Lance, & Evans, 2002; Harley, Jolivette, McCormick, & Tice, 2002; Moradi & Subich, 2003; Williams, 2005). Williams (2005) examined the strengths and limitations of two prominent culturally based counseling theories, Afrocentrism and feminism, utilizing a case study approach of an African-American female lesbian. For African-American women seeking therapy, it was suggested that therapists assist clients in recognizing the impact of racism, sexism, classism, and homophobia. Awareness of the multiple identities of clients means that counselors need to help clients develop a better understanding of themselves, their social environment, and how to navigate and work through challenges associated with marginalization and oppression.

Dimensions of Identity: Honoring the Whole Person

Carmen Maria is a 22-year-old, Cuban American woman living in Miami. Last year during the Fall semester of her senior year of college, she came out to her family and friends as a lesbian. Carmen Maria was raised in a traditional Cuban household and her family maintained strict religious views. Before she came out to her family her mom expressed that she wanted Carmen Maria to marry a "nice Cuban boy from a nice religious household." Frequently, Carmen Maria would over hear family members speak negatively about people who were gay or lesbian, as well as people that were not Cuban, which upset her. Carmen Maria's family does not discuss her sexual orientation and she feels shunned because she is a lesbian. She still loves her family and does not like feeling like an outsider. Carmen Maria has come to see you because she wants to introduce her family to her new girlfriend, Luisa. She has been dating Luisa for several months and she wants her family to acknowledge and respect their relationship.

What are the multiple dimensions of Carmen Maria's identity?
Describe, explain, and make meaning of the identity related conflicts experienced by Carmen Maria.
Briefly describe the multiple dimensions of your identity.
Explain how your identity may be helpful AND present challenges to you as Carmen Maria's counselor.

Worldview

A shared worldview by the counselor and client is an important factor in counseling relationships across cultural contexts. Gelso and Fretz (2001) outline five dimensions and provide related questions that illustrate differences in worldview often found between American ethnic minority clients and White American counselors. These dimensions include: (a) views about family (i.e., What is the relationship of self to the family? What is more important, the individual or the family?), (b) cooperation versus competition (i.e., Is the collective success of the group more valued than personal success of the individual?), (c) time orientation (i.e., Which is more important in time? The past, present, or future?), and (d) locus of control (i.e., How much can one control what happens in life?). All of these dimensions of worldview provide the counselor with useful reference points in therapy. A shared worldview between the counselor and client represents a mutual understanding regarding the nature of the client's distress. The counselor is able identify the client's difficulty and to provide an explanation consistent with the client's own understanding. From this common vantage point, the therapeutic contract can be established, operationalized, and modified.

> Something happened to me recently that caused me to look inward at just how open minded of a person I really am. My father married a woman from Venezuela a few weekends ago. I was surprised when I got there to see that my father's house had been completely redecorated into a place I no longer knew as, "My dad's house." There were now pictures of people I didn't know. There was new art on the walls. The rooms were all painted different colors, and everywhere I went smelled strongly of scented candles. I was taken aback by this new change, but that was nothing compared to what I experienced throughout the wedding celebration. My new step mother's family and friends far out-numbered those of my father's at the wedding. Most of her family and friends, including her, did not speak any English. This made communicating with my "new family" quite difficult. I immediately started feeling defensive. "They need to learn English so they can talk to us (my brother and me)." Their music is too loud!" "They drink too much . . . dance too much . . . talk too much. . . ." And the list went on. Before I knew it, I had decided "these people" weren't "my people." I couldn't believe I thought that! I'm one of the most

open minded people I know! At least that's what I thought. . . . What I learned after lots of self reflection, was that I had completely closed my mind and shut down out of fear. I know that celebrations are experienced differently for everyone, and now that includes people in my family . . . not just the ones I read about in our textbooks. It is so easy to say you accept everyone. It is so easy to say that you are open to other cultural traditions and ways of life. My tolerance and acceptance was tested that weekend and it surprised me. Luckily, I walked away from the experience learning more about myself and another culture. My awareness, acceptance and interest in another culture were broadened, and I feel that I grew as a person from having been a part of that wedding.

–Student Journal, Graduate Multicultural Counseling Course

Consider and discuss the possible identity, cultural background, cultural awareness, and worldview of this student. What role did these characteristics have in the student's experience of the wedding?
Discuss the therapeutic relationship and counseling process between a counselor, with initial beliefs, thoughts, and feelings similar to the student, working with clients similar to the stepmother.

Development of Cultural Competence

The *Multicultural and Diversity Awareness Continuum* (Figure 6.2) illustrates primary areas in the development of cultural competence and includes awareness of: (a) cultural self and cultural diversity, (b) oppression and marginalization, and (c) multicultural counseling competence in practice. This continuum is linear, developmental, and arranged so that the levels build on each other. The process from self-awareness to multicultural counseling competence is flexible because the counselor cannot achieve complete proficiency of any of the awareness levels. As stated earlier, cultural competence is best understood as a lifelong process. There is no definitive point to be reached by the counselor in any specific area before proceeding forward. At any point, the counselor needs to recycle (e.g., when referred a new client). However, it is important to proceed again to all subsequent levels on the continuum.

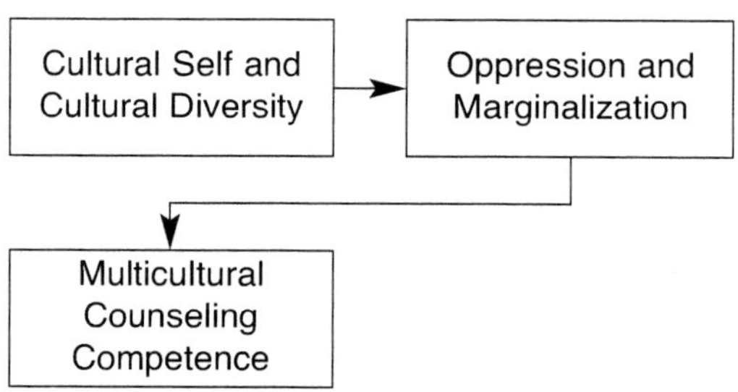

Figure 6.2. Multicultural and Diversity Awareness Continuum.

Cultural Self-Awareness and Cultural Diversity

Counselors often bring to the therapeutic relationship preconceived attitudes and ideas about culturally different clients (Fu, Chiu, Morris, & Young, 2007). These perceptions may be manifested in numerous ways during the counseling process. Consider *I Am A Cultural Being* below. Our responses to the statements in the exercise are indicators of our cultural identities and map the social context of our development. An active and reflective understanding of ourselves as cultural beings living in dynamic social-ecological systems ultimately helps us to better understand and help our clients. Closely related to the previous point is the recognition that sociocultural group membership is not totally responsible for all the behaviors of a client. Because culturally diverse persons must interact with the dominant culture, the degree to which an individual whose culture has been marginalized has acculturated to the dominant culture varies from individual to individual. This is the principle that necessitates the study of *within-group* differences among culturally diverse clients. To respond to all members of a particular culturally diverse population as if they share identical values, beliefs, attitudes, opinions, and worldviews is to stereotype and inhibits interpersonal learning. There is considerable evidence that members of specific sociocultural groups have heterogeneous talents, interests, and values (Locke, 1998).

I Am A Cultural Being

Your Background

Describe yourself in terms of basic demographics (e.g., age, gender, race, ethnicity, sexual orientation, ability/disability.) Where were you born? How many people are in your family? What generation in the United States do you represent? Where are your ancestors from? Do your consider your ancestors voluntary or involuntary immigrants to the United States?

What was the occupation of your parents when you were a child? How would you describe your family's economic class? Where did you go to school? Does your immediate or extended family practice ethnic or cultural customs that you or they value or with which they identify (e.g., foods, celebrations, traditions, social behaviors, manners, beliefs)? What customs do you prize most? Do your relatives speak your ethnic group language?

Your Group Awareness

Describe your earliest recollection of learning your gender, race, ethnicity, sexual orientation, ability/disability religion and/or spiritual practice? How did you learn to identify with these groups? Where there any groups of people that were devalued by your family? Did you have similar feelings? Did your family discuss culturally diverse groups of people? What was your parents' main advice to you about people from other cultural groups?

Your Social Awareness
Describe your earliest recollections of learning that people were "different." When do you first remember learning about prejudice? How do you recall feeling at that time? When was the first time you remember learning about racism, sexism, heterosexism, ableism, and other forms of oppression? How did you first come to understand oppression existed? What did you learn from this experience? When did you first know people who said things that you thought were prejudiced? When was the first time you recall seeing someone act in a way you thought was prejudiced, racist, sexist, homophobic, or discriminatory? Describe your feelings about that situation.
Your Encounter Experiences
How much cultural diversity did you have in your home town? What was the general perception surrounding people who were not White American or recent immigrants in your home town? Did your immediate family share these views? How were people who identified as gay, lesbian, bisexual, or transgendered perceived? When (if this is applicable) did your perceptions of any of these groups change? How would your parents respond, or have responded, if you announced plans to marry a member of a different ethnic group or religion, a person of the same sex, or a person with a disability? How do you think you would respond for your child?
Your Present Views
Describe significant relationships that you have with people from different cultures. What is most rewarding about these relationships? Least rewarding? What has been the major source of information which has shaped your perceptions of people from different cultures?
As a counseling professional, how do you think your cultural background and attitudes help you in working with culturally diverse clients? How will they hinder you in working with culturally diverse clients? Briefly discuss your feelings about describing yourself as a cultural being.

Oppression and Marginalization

Multicultural counseling competence requires counselors to develop an understanding for valued and devalued groups when working with clients in the United States (Comstock et al., 2008). *Valued groups* have characteristics that are considered, within social systems, to have worth, importance, and usefulness associated with power, respect, and resources. Common social demographic categories in the United States, such as age, race, ethnicity, gender, sexual orientation, disability, religion, educational attainment, occupation, financial net worth, and others, can be assessed by the relative dominant and subordinate position of the various groups of people within those categories. Put another way, social systems are historically, culturally, and fundamentally structured for certain social demographic groups to be more valued than others, therefore having more power than others. Tatum (1997) explains which the dominant group, that is the group that maintains the highest level of social, political, and economic power, in American society is seen as the norm for humanity. Some of the valued groups in the United States include people who are healthy, young, educated, wealthy, male, heterosexual, White American, English speaking, employed, and Christian. Identification with any of the valued groups in the United States is associated with sociocultural advantages, privileges, and benefits.

Devalued groups, conversely, are considered to have relatively less worth, importance, and usefulness, and therefore less power and resources. As a result, members of devalued groups experience marginalization due to the differentially oppressive structure of the social systems in which we live (Utsey, Ponterotto, & Porter, 2008). People who are sick, elderly, uneducated, female, gay, lesbian, bisexual, transgendered, non-White American, non-English speaking, non-native English speakers, unemployed, and non-Christian are members of some of the relatively less valued, less powerful groups in the United States. Although all human beings have inherent value, sociocultural systems assign value differentially based on social characteristics. Counselors and clients often identify as members of both valued and devalued groups. It is important, then, for culturally competent counselors to have an initial understanding of the complex identity dynamics that results from relative social valuation and related experiences of privilege and marginalization.

The Power of Identity: Social Dynamics

Lesbian	Christian	Masculine	Rich	Educated	Suburban
Rural	Feminine	Bisexual	Transgender	Heterosexual	Feminist
Republican	Democrat	Independent	Introvert	Urban	
Professional					
Athletic	Disabled	White	American	International	Muslim
Asian	Black	African-American	Latino	Latina	Hispanic
Middle-Class	Low SES	Conservative	Older	Woman	Man
Tech Savvy	Undocumented	Immigrant	English-Speaking	Bilingual	Thin
Overweight	Time Adherent	Time Flexible	Cognitive	Extrovert	Agnostic
Vegetarian	Spiritual	Emotional	Individualistic	Collectivistic	Religious

Circle the groups with which you identify. What are the advantages of identifying with these groups? What are the disadvantages? What groups have power in the cultural and institutional levels of the Social Ecological Model? What groups have less power? What groups are valued? What groups are devalued? What groups are marginalized? Describe, explain, and discuss the indicators of power, value, and marginalization? What other dimensions of your identity are not included in the above list? Evaluate your other identity dimensions.

Multicultural Counseling Competence in Practice

The final level on the continuum is the integration of the multicultural and diversity awareness process into the practice of counseling. A multicultural counseling framework is a tool that brings attention to certain cultural factors that may influence the counseling process and outcome. It needs to be interactive, interchangeable, and upgrade-able depending on the specific client, presenting issues, and current multicultural counseling research. At the same time, core structures make up the multicultural framework and include culturally distinctive: (a) communication styles, (b) beliefs about psychological problems, (c) strategies for coping with and resolving personal problems, (d) counseling expectations and behavior, (e) identity development and acculturation, and (f) worldviews (Locke, 1998). Fischer, Jome, and Atkinson (1998) identified and provided empirical support for several factors in the counseling literature that were common to producing a successful counseling experience and outcome in conventional psychotherapy and in culturally diverse healing methods. The four factors identified as having universal healing properties across cultural contexts were: (a) the therapeutic relationship, (b) a shared worldview between the client and counselor, (c) client expectations for positive change, (d) and interventions believed by both client and counselor to be a means for alleviating client distress. A multicultural counseling framework integrates counselor beliefs, cultural differences between the counselor and the client, and collaboration throughout the therapeutic process. Counselor cultural self-awareness and cultural knowledge provide the grounding for the client to be authentic in therapy, although he or she may be culturally different from his or her counselor. Development of a trusting counseling relationship creates a space of respect and care for the counselor and client to mutually decide on the goals, process, and interventions employed in therapy.

A counselor needs to be able to authentically model openness, patience, security, respect, understanding, flexibility, adaptability, and love. These characteristics are as important to demonstrate multicultural counseling competence as knowledge of current research and best practices. The development and progression of the multicultural counseling competence is dependent on the counselor intentionally building a sense of community with individuals from diverse cultural backgrounds. All community members need to be honored with respect to their individual historical, social, and cultural backgrounds. It is important in the first session to openly engage the client in building a structure for respect and understanding that will ultimately help the client and counselor connect with one another and form a therapeutic relationship. Making explicit the invitation for the active inclusion of the client's culture within the counseling process makes this connection possible.

"All aspects of your identity and your culture are welcome and honored and are fundamental to the counseling process. You contribute unique experiences and resources that are necessary for and valuable to creating an optimal therapeutic environment for your growth, development, health, wellness, and healing. The counseling relationship is, therefore, an intentional, working, partnership where you are expected to be actively and meaningfully involved in the direction, content, and process of our work together." The counselor creates a safe and supportive space for the client to cultivate his or her *voice.* Clients are encouraged to share their experiences and perspectives, as they feel comfortable and prepared. Some clients readily and freely share their point of view, whereas others are more pensive and reluctant. These likely styles are acknowledged at the outset, and all are to be respected. Over time in the counseling, however, it is hoped that all clients will eventually become empowered to affirm their own innate value and to validate their own experiences.

Counselors are interpersonal learners in the therapeutic relationship, allowing ourselves to be affected and impacted by their clients' stories and experiences. When we are able to truly feel and know our connection to our clients, a secure foundation is in place to support transformative personal change. The significance of intentional inclusion of culture in the counseling process is to create a structured opportunity for clients to candidly engage with the counselor along planes and dimensions ordinarily difficult to access in their individual everyday lives. In multicultural counseling, clients are encouraged to share about the different dimensions of their identity, culture, and worldview. A culturally competent counselor needs to have the knowledge, skills, and adaptability to welcome, engage, educate, challenge, and support client members of diverse communities while continually learning from the clients and the process.

REFERENCES

American Mental Health Counselors Association. (2010). *Code of ethics.* Retrieved June, 1, 2010, from http://www.amhca.org

Arredondo, P., & Glauner, T. (1992). *Personal dimensions of identity model.* Boston: Empowerment Workshops.

Arredondo, P., Toporek, R., Brown, S. P., Jones, J., Locke, D. C., Sanchez, J., & Sadler, H. (1996). Operationalization of the multicultural counseling competencies. *Journal of Multicultural Counseling and Development, 24,* 42–78.

Arredondo, P., Tovar-Blank, Z. G., & Parham, T. A. (2008). Challenges and promises of becoming a culturally competent counselor in a sociopolitical era of change and empowerment. *Journal of Counseling and Development, 86,* 261–268.

Bowen, M. (1994). *Family therapy in clinical practice.* New York: Jason Aronson.

Brofenbrenner, U. (1995). The bioecological model from a life course perspective: Reflections of a participant observer. In P. Moen, G. H. Elder, & K. Luscher (Eds.), *Examining lives in context: Perspectives on the ecology of human development* (pp. 599–647).

Brook, A. T., Garcia, J., & Fleming, M. (2008). The effects of multiple well identities on psychological well-being. *Personality and Social Psychology Bulletin, 34,* 1588–1600.

Chung, R. C., Bemak, F., Ortiz, D. P., & Sandoval-Perez, P. A. (2008). Promoting the mental health of immigrants: A multicultural/social justice perspective. *Journal of Counseling and Development, 86,* 310–317.

Comstock, D. L., Hammer, T. R., Strentzsch, J., Cannon, K., Parsons, J., & Salazar II, G. (2008). Relational-cultural theory: A framework for bridging relational, multicultural, and social justice competencies. *Journal of Counseling and Development, 86,* 279–287.

Constantine, M. G. (2001). New visions for defining and assessing multicultural competence. In J. G. Ponterotto, J. M. Casas, L. A. Suzuki, & C. M. Alexander (Eds.), *Handbook of multicultural counseling* (2nd ed., pp. 482–498). Thousand Oaks, CA: Sage.

Croteau, J. M., Talbot, D. M., Lance, T. S., & Evans, N. J. (2002). A qualitative study of the interplay between privilege and oppression. *Journal of Multicultural Counseling and Development, 30,* 239–258.

Daniels, J. (2007). The fourth force in counseling and therapy: Multicultural and feminist perspectives. In A. E. Ivey, M. D'Andrea, M. B. Ivery, & L. Simek-Morgan (Eds.), *Theories of counseling and psychotherapy: A multicultural perspective* (6th ed., pp. 319–358).

Essandoah, P. K. (1996). Multicultural counseling as the "Fourth Force": A call to arms. *The Counseling Psychologist, 24,* 126–137.

Fischer, A. R., Jome, L. M., & Atkinson, D. R. (1998). Reconceptualizing multicultural counseling [Electronic version]. *The Counseling Psychologist, 26,* 525–588.

Freire, P. (1970). *The pedagogy of the oppressed.* New York: Continuum.

Fu, J. H., Chiu, C., Morris, M. W., & Young, M. J. (2007). Spontaneous inferences from cultural cues: Varying responses from cultural insiders and outsiders. *Journal of Cross-Cultural Psychology, 38,* 58–75.

Gelso, C., & Fretz, B. (2001). *Counseling psychology* (2nd ed.). Belmont, CA: Wadsworth.

Harley, D. A., Jolivette, K., McCormack, K., & Tice, K. (2002). Race, class, and gender: A constellation of positionalities with implications for counseling. *Journal of Multicultural Counseling and Development, 30,* 216–238.

Hawkins, N., Richards, P. S., Granley, H. M., & Stein, D. M. (2004). The impact of exposure to the thin-ideal media image on women. *Eating Disorders: The Journal of Treatment and Prevention, 12*(1), 35–50.

Ivey, A. (2000). Development therapy: Theory into practice. North Amhert, MA: Microtraining Associates.

Jackson, M. L. (1995). Multicultural counseling: Historical perspectives. In J. G. Ponterotto, J. M. Casas, L. A. Suzuki, & C. M. Alexander (Eds.), *Handbook of multicultural counseling* (pp. 3-16). Thousand Oaks, CA: Sage.

Kunkler, K. P., & Rigazio-DiGilio, S. A. (1994). Systemic cognitive-developmental therapy: Organizing structured activities to facilitate family development. *Simulation & Gaming, 25,* 75–87.

Lewis, J. A., & Arnold, M. S. (1998). From multiculturalism to social action. In C. C. Lee & G. R. Waltz (Eds.), *Social action: A mandate for counselors* (pp. 51–66). Alexandria, VA: American Counseling Association.

Lewis, J. A., Lewis, M. D., Daniels, J. A., & D'Andrea, M. J. (2003). *Community counseling: Empowerment strategies for a diverse society* (3rd ed.). Pacific Grove, CA: Brooks/Cole.

Locke, D. C. (1990). A not so provincial view of multicultural counseling. *Counselor Education*

and Supervision, 30, 18–25.
Locke, D. C. (1998). *Increasing multicultural understanding: A comprehensive model* (2nd ed.). Newbury Park, CA: Sage.
McFadden, J. (Ed.). (1999). *Transcultural counseling* (2nd ed.). Alexandria, VA: American Counseling Association.
Moradi, B., & Subich, L. M. (2003). A concomitant examination of the relations of perceived racist and sexist events to psychological distress for African American women. *The Counseling Psychologist, 31,* 451–469.
Negy, C., Shreve, T. L., Jensen, B. J., & Uddin, N. (2003). Ethnic identity, self-esteem, and ethnocentrism: A study of social identity versus multicultural theory of development. *Cultural Diversity and Ethnic Minority Psychology, 9*(4), 333–344.
Pack-Brown, S. P., Thomas, T. L., & Seymour, J. M. (2008). Infusing professional ethics into counselor education programs: A multicultural/social justice perspective. *Journal of Counseling and Development, 86,* 296–302.
Paisley, P. O., & Benshoff, J. M. (1996). Applying developmental principles to practice: Training issues for the professional development of school counselors. *Elementary School Guidance and Counseling, 30*(3), 163–170.
Pedersen, P. (1999). *Multiculturalism as a fourth force.* Philadelphia: Brunner/Mazel.
Pedersen, P. B. (1991). Multiculturalism as a generic approach to counseling. *Journal of Counseling and Development, 70,* 6–12.
Reynolds, A. L., (1995). Challenges and strategies for teaching multicultural counseling courses. In J. G. Ponterotto, J. M . Casas, L. A. Suzuki, & C. M. Alexander (Eds.), *Handbook of multicultural counseling* (pp. 312–329). Thousand Oaks, CA: Sage.
Robinson, T. L. (2005). *The convergence of race, ethnicity, and gender: Multiple identities in counseling* (2nd ed.). Upper Saddle River, NJ: Pearson Education, Inc.
Rollock, D., & Gordon, E. W. (2000). Racism and mental health in the 21st century: Perspectives and parameters. *American Journal of Orthopsychiatry, 70,* 5–13.
Rust, P. (1996). The impact of multiple marginalizations. In E. Disch (Ed)., *Reconstructing gender: A multicultural anthology* (pp. 289–296).
Salazar, C. F., & Abrams, L. P. (2005). Conceptualizing identity development in members of marginalized groups. *Journal of Professional Counseling: Practice, Theory, & Research, 33,* 47–59.
Satir, V. (1967). *Conjoint family therapy.* Palo Alto, CA: Science and Behavior Books.
Shreeve, J. (2006, March). The greatest journey. *National Geographic,* pp. 61–69.
Stewart, D. L.(2009). Perceptions of multiple identities among black college students. *Journal of College Student Development, 50,* 253–270.
Sue, D. W., Arredondo, P., & McDavis, R. J. (1992). Multicultural counseling competencies and standards: A call to the profession. *Journal of Multicultural Counseling and Development, 20,* 64–68.
Sue, D. W., & Sue, D. (2003). *Counseling the culturally diverse: Theory and practice* (4th ed.). New York: Wiley.
Tatum, B. D. (1997). *Why are all the Black kids sitting together in the cafeteria?* New York: Basic Books.
Toporek, R. L., & Reza, J. V. (2001). Context as a critical dimension of multicultural counseling: Articulating personal, professional, and institutional competence. *Journal of Multicultural Counseling and Development, 29,* 13–30.
Utsey, S. O., Ponterotto, J. G., & Porter, J. S. (2008). Prejudice and racism, year 2008–Still going strong: Research on reducing prejudice with recommended methodological advances. *Journal of Counseling and Development, 86,* 339–347.
Vera, E. M., & Speight, S. L. (2003). Multicultural competence, social justice, and counseling

psychology: Expanding our roles. *The Counseling Psychologist, 31,* 253–272.
Williams, C. B. (2005). Counseling African American women: Multiple identities–multiple constraints. *Journal of Counseling & Development, 83,* 278–283.

Chapter 7

CAREER COUNSELING: CURRENT CHALLENGES AND OPPORTUNITIES FOR MENTAL HEALTH PRACTITIONERS

SPENCER G. NILES AND HYUNG JOON YOON

Mental health counselors often discard the notion that career counseling will be an essential element of their counseling work. Yet few things capture more attention for adolescents and adults than their career decisions. Freud himself noted that work and love are central to the human experience and that making effective decisions in these two life domains is critical to experiencing a satisfying life. When career situations go awry, negative psychological and physical consequences often occur. Increases in unemployment correlate significantly with increases in substance abuse, referrals to mental health centers, physical ailments (e.g., coronary heart disease), child abuse, and partner abuse (Herr, 1989). Thus, coping effectively with career development tasks becomes important for experiencing positive mental health. In addition, mental health counselors in all professional settings will continue to encounter clients attempting to successfully cope with career concerns.

Thus, in this chapter, we identify the career development challenges most workers experience in the current context and highlight the changing demographics at work. We then identify the implications of these factors for mental health counselors, discuss the roles and scope of practice in which career counselors engage, and, finally, provide a brief overview of approaches that counselors can use as they attempt to help their clients resolve career issues.

CAREER DEVELOPMENT CHALLENGES IN THE CURRENT CONTEXT

Central to understanding the career development challenges that most workers encounter is acknowledging that career development tasks reflect societal situations impacting workers, work conditions, and opportunities for work. Career development tasks vary as the cultural, historical, political, and economic contexts change. For example, career development tasks in a developing nation tend to reflect the most pressing economic, social, and political needs of that country, whereas career development tasks in more developed countries are less entwined with national needs. Likewise, career development tasks in the current context within the United States differ from the career development tasks U.S. workers experienced 100 years ago.

The current work context in America presents multiple challenges for adults engaged in work as well as young people preparing for it. Calling attention to these changes, authors use such dramatic phrases as "the career has died" and "work has ended" (Bridges, 1994; Rifkin, 1995). Although such declarations are not to be taken literally, they are to be taken seriously. The "career is dead" authors alert mental health practitioners to the fact that understanding how work is changing is essential information for responding effectively to the career concerns currently confronting adults in contemporary society.

Niles, Herr, and Hartung (2002) note that high levels of global unemployment, corporate downsizing, and a jobless economic recovery are indicators that reveal the way work is changing. High unemployment rates translate into a myriad of economic, social, physical, and psychological maladies (Niles, Herr, & Hartung, 2002). Reports of these events appear daily in various news media and include behaviors such as homicides, suicides, and high levels of depression.

Technological advances also point to important changes in how business is conducted as small companies compete globally via the information highway and computers perform tasks once assigned to workers. Near workerless factories now exist as computers replace workers in occupations ranging from tollbooth collectors to engineers. U.S. workers now compete with workers from around the globe as they seek to fill a limited number of occupational vacancies. Many workers, especially those who value job security, struggle to adjust to this new reality.

Contemporary workers also struggle to balance their various life role commitments as predictions concerning ways in which technology would create a leisure society have proved to be inaccurate. Rather than creating more leisure time, advances in technology have made it easier (and often necessary) to work more hours. Americans take fewer vacation days per year than workers in other industrialized countries (Mercer, 2009). Unfortunately, technology can change work, but it cannot change the fact that days still occur in 24-hour cycles and more of those hours are being filled by work activity.

Niles, Herr, and Hartung (2002) noted that these shifts have led to changes in the "rules of the game" relative to work. The implied social contract in which employees demonstrate loyalty to employers and employers display commitment to their employees has disappeared. "On demand workers" replace long-term employees (Rifkin, 1995). Employers hire contingent workers to complete a particular project and, once the project is completed, so is their employment. Corporate downsizing results in flattened organizational structures and fewer career ladders to climb. As adults attempt to smooth the career turbulence they experience, they realize that old solutions for increasing job security (e.g., being competent and working harder) often have little impact on new situations. Workers who have lost their jobs via corporate downsizing are now less willing to sacrifice everything for their careers when the organizations for which they work are so willing to sacrifice them (Niles & Harris-Bowlsbey, 2009). Those who have been "sacrificed" are often left feeling betrayed, anxious about competing, and insecure about the future. Given these shifts, it is not surprising that many people express concerns related to low career self-efficacy, anxiety due to ambiguous career paths and a lack of job security, confusion over how to obtain training to update their skills, and frustration related to conflicting life role demands (Anderson & Niles, 1995).

Obviously, these changes in the nature of work are not benign. They have important implications for current and future workers. Many jobless workers must cope with economic and family responsibilities without adequate financial resources. High unemployment rates persist and offer little hope for the future. Thus, the ripple effects and the costs of unemployment become substantial to the individual, the family, and society. These are the career concerns with which clients often struggle within the course of career counseling. They demonstrate that there are few things more personal than a career choice. Accordingly, addressing career concerns adequately requires mental health counselors to interweave career counseling interventions with more general mental health counseling strategies. The likelihood that mental health counselors will encounter clients with career concerns is great.

To become more aware of the career issues that clients are likely to present in counseling, it is also important to understand the demographic changes occurring in the workforce.

Changing Cultural Demographics at Work

During the past four decades, the United States has been awash in cultural pluralism. According to the U.S. Census Bureau (2008), people of color represent 26% of the U.S. population, and it is predicted that by the year 2050, people of color will represent more than half (54%) of the population. The influx of new immigrants into the United States will also continue in large numbers. Between 703,542 to 1,266,129 immigrants per year obtained legal permanent resident status in the United States between 2000 and 2009 (U.S. Department of Homeland Security, 2009). In some regions of the United States, persons of color are nearly equal in number to Whites. Hispanics have already surpassed African Americans and are expected to continue to remain the largest minority group in the United States within the next four decades (U.S. Census Bureau, 2008).

Changing demographics, multiple worldviews, and cultural plurality influence the career development intervention process. Whereas the workforce now more closely reflects the cultural pluralism existing within society, there is ample evidence to suggest that women, people of color, persons with disabilities, gay men, lesbian women, and transgendered persons continue to encounter tremendous obstacles in their career development. For example, according to the 2000 U.S. Census, 14.3% of African Americans 25 years of age or older possess a college degree and 72.3% completed high school. By comparison, 26.1% of Whites 25 years of age or older possess a college degree and 83.6% have completed high school. The unemployment rate for African Americans has been above 7.3% each year since 1972 and was an average 2.2 times the rate for Whites in the last five decades (U.S. Bureau of Labor Statistics, 2010b). Whites and Asians tend to be employed in managerial and professional specialty occupations (occupations that tend to have job security, decent salaries, and due processes in hiring and firing). Only 27% of African Americans and 18% of Hispanics are employed in such occupations, compared with 48% of Asians and 37% of all Whites (U.S. Bureau of Labor Statistics, 2009). According to Herr, Cramer, and Niles (2004), "more than half of the employed Hispanic women are either clerical workers or non-transport operatives (dress-makers, assemblers, machine operators, and so on)" (p. 277).

Additional statistical data provide evidence that occupational and economic disparities exist according to gender and ethnic background. For example, men are still 18.7 times more likely than women to be in higher prestige occupations in science, math, or technology (Farmer, Rotella, Anderson, & Wardrop, 1998). African-American and Hispanic families earn approximately 65% and 75%, respectively, of the income of White, non-Hispanic families. When compared with Asian families, the ratios become 51% and 59%, respectively. In terms of health insurance coverage, 31.7% of

American Indians and Alaska Natives and 32.3% of Hispanics are not insured, whereas 10.7% of all Whites and 16.6% of Asians are not insured (CeNavas-Walt, Proctor, & Smith, 2009).

Despite legislation aimed at protecting their rights (e.g., Public Law 93-112, the Rehabilitation Act of 1973; Public Law 94-142, the Education for All Handicapped Children Act of 1975; Public Law 95-602, the Rehabilitation, Comprehensive Services, and Developmental Disabilities Amendment of 1978; Public Law 101-476, the Education of the Handicapped Amendments of 1990; Public Law 101-336, the Americans with Disabilities Act of 1990), Americans with disabilities have fared no better. According to Bureau of Labor Statistics (2010a), of the 26.5 million people with disabilities who are age 16 years and over, 22.3% are in the civilian labor force and 14.7% are unemployed. Over the 10 years, almost no progress has been made; therefore, still "nearly half of those with a work disability are outside the work structure" (Isaacson & Brown, 1997, p. 313). The number of Americans reporting some type of disability now approaches 50 million according to the U.S. Census (2000). Postsecondary school employment outcomes for many young people are of concern, to put it mildly. According to the National Council on Disability (2000), 350,000 people between the ages of 18 and 25 receive social security income support (and, therefore, are not employed). Widen the age range to include all adult persons with disabilities and the data are no more positive. Two-thirds of working age people with disabilities are unemployed, even though the majority of those persons wish to work (Fabian & Liesener, 2005).

Gay, lesbian, and bisexual individuals also experience discriminatory treatment in the labor force. Twenty years ago, Goleman (1990) suggested that the negative bias toward this group is often more intense than that directed toward any other group. Fourteen years later, Herr, Cramer, and Niles (2004) noted that gay, lesbian, and bisexual persons are essentially barred from certain occupations and find vertical mobility blocked simply because of their sexual orientation. Despite this obvious discrimination, career development theorists and practitioners have been slow to respond to the issues of bias toward gay, lesbian, and bisexual individuals (Chung, 2003; Pope & Barret, 2002).

These statistics reveal that many women, people of color, persons with disabilities, and gay/lesbian/bisexual individuals regularly experience discriminatory practices in hiring and promoting, insufficient financial resources, and a lack of role models and mentors. Thus, traditional career interventions may not be appropriate for assisting members of diverse groups in their career development. Career development interventions in contemporary society must be reconceptualized to more adequately meet the career development needs of the members of an increasingly diverse society.

Career Counselors' Roles and Scope of Practice

Stereotypical views of career counseling reflect assumptions that include the perspective that career counseling simply involves the administration and intrepretation of standardized test batteries. Many consider career counseling to be a rather mechanistic and routinized activity in which the counselor "tests and tells" the client which occupational options provide the greatest probability for success. Despite notions that career counseling is "less sophisticated" than other counseling specialties, the knowledge and skills required for providing effective career counseling encompass and exceed those required in more general counseling. For example, the career counseling competencies identified by the National Career Development Association (2003) indicate that career counselors need knowledge and skills in career development theory; individual and group counseling; individual/group assessment; career information/resources; program promotion, management, and implementation; career coaching/consultation; multicultural counseling; supervision; ethical/legal issues; and using technology effectively in the career intervention process. These skills are in addition to the requisite skills for effective counseling practice.

Moreover, the topics related to career development interventions are exciting and challenging. Essentially, career practitioners seek to help their clients increase their life satisfaction. Career counselors help people consider how they will develop and use their talents as they live their lives. Career counselors in the 21st century seek to empower people to construct meaning out of their unique life experiences and then translate that derived meaning into appropriate occupational and other life-role choices. Translating life experiences into career choices requires people to possess a relatively high level of self-awareness (Niles & Harris-Bowlsbey, 2009). Accordingly, career counselors strive to provide interventions to help their clients clarify and articulate their self-concepts. These interventions can include formal, standardized assessments as well as informal, nonstandardized assessment activities that actively and creatively engage clients in the career intervention process (Amundson, 1998). Because the former type of assessments often contain cultural limitations, the latter assessment category (nonstandardized) can often be of greater use for persons from diverse backgrounds. Sorting through career concerns and engaging in career planning are complex processes. Therefore, competent career counseling practice also requires counselors to be skilled at developing effective working alliances with their clients (Anderson & Niles, 2000). Career counselors meet their clients at the intersection of what has been and what might be in their clients' lives. When career counselors work collaboratively and innovatively with their clients to construct a clear career direction, both the client and counselor experience the intervention process as exciting and positive.

Career decision making is rarely a simple task. Therefore, good career counseling is never mechanistic and routine. When we consider the fact that decisions about work are made within cultural, familial, and life contexts that intertwine with other life roles and responsibilities, the complex and often stressful nature of career decision making becomes clear. What might seem on the surface to be a relatively straightforward process of making a decision about work can quickly become overwhelming, frustrating, and complicated when important factors such as family expectations, limited occupational opportunities, financial limitations, and multiple life-role commitments are considered.

Given the complexity of career decision making, there should be little surprise that many clients seeking career counseling experience substantial levels of psychological distress (Niles & Anderson, 1993). Obviously, career counselors must address their clients' distress as they also help their clients clarify their values, skills, life-role salience, interests, and motivation. When clients also experience low self-esteem, weak self-efficacy, and little hope that the future can be more satisfying than the past, the counselor's task becomes even more challenging. Clients coping with such issues require more assistance in resolving their career dilemmas than a test battery can provide. Given this fact, it is not surprising that career counseling clients describe the support and the experience of an effective therapeutic alliance with their career counselors as one of the most helpful aspects of their career counseling experience (Anderson & Niles, 2000). Obviously, skills found to be essential counseling skills (e.g., establishing rapport, reflective listening, expressing empathic understanding) are also essential career counseling skills.

Working collaboratively and effectively with clients also requires career counseling practitioners to possess multicultural competencies at an advanced level (Leong, 1995). For instance, clients operating from a collectivistic orientation engage in the career planning process in important ways that differ from clients operating from an individualistic orientation. Working with the client's cultural context is essential to providing effective career assistance. For example, Kim, Li, and Liang (2002) found that career counselors focusing on the expression of emotion were perceived as having greater cross-cultural competence than counselors focusing on the expression of cognition when working with Asian American college students with high adherence to Asian values. Leong (2002) found acculturation to be positively related to job satisfaction and negatively related to occupational stress and strain. Gomez et al. (2001) found that Latina career development is strongly influenced by sociopolitical, cultural, contextual, and personal variables. Specifically, factors such as socioeconomic status, family, cultural identity, and the existence of a support network all helped to shape the course of career development for the Latinas participating in the Gomez et al. study. The client's constellation of cultural/contextual variables clearly matters in the career intervention process. Thus, similar to general counseling interventions, the career development intervention process is a dynamic, complex, and challenging one that requires career counselors to draw on multicultural counseling skills to effectively help their clients move forward in their career development (and, like general counseling, all career counseling is multicultural counseling).

Indications are that the career development process will become more, rather than less, complex in the near future. The current work context requires workers to demonstrate an extensive set of skills, behaviors, and attitudes to manage their careers effectively. Among other things, effective career self-management today requires the ability to (a) continuously learn new skills, (b) cope with change and tolerate ambiguity, (c) acquire and use occupational information effectively, (d) interact competently with diverse coworkers, (e) adjust quickly to changing work demands, and (f) use technology effectively (Niles & Harris-Bowlsbey, 2009). To help people acquire these competencies, career development interventions must be holistic, comprehensive, and systematic. Moreover, because career development is an essential aspect of human development, career practitioners must be skilled at helping their clients cope with their career concerns within a developmental context. Because children, adolescents, and adults are presented with career development tasks, professional counselors must be skilled at providing career interventions and understanding the career development process regardless of their work setting (Niles & Pate, 1989).

It is clear that the need for providing systematic assistance to individuals attempting to deal more effectively with the influence of work in their lives is tremendous. The young, the elderly, the unemployed, the underemployed, the displaced homemaker, the displaced worker, and members of diverse racial, ethnic, and socioeconomic groups are each confronted with work-related issues that have significant implications for their lives. How well they are able to cope with these issues may well be the difference between living a life that is meaningful and productive and one that is largely void of meaning and satisfaction.

Effective Approaches to Coping With Career Concerns

Professional counselors provide career assistance to their clients in a number of ways. For example, counselors in high school, postsecondary, and community settings can teach clients the types of skills (e.g., self-assessment, job search, and career information acquisition) that are necessary for effective career planning and career decision making. Professional counselors in all settings can also help their students/clients to realize that decisions about work influence their total life. Correspondingly, counselors can help clients develop realistic expectations for what work can provide in terms of personal satisfaction. When work is lacking in personal satisfaction, meaningful participation in other life roles helps offset this lack of satisfaction. Given the extreme emphasis we place on intra-individual variables in career development, a major task confronting counselors involves helping people to realize that self-worth is not defined by one's work situation. Self-worth relates more to how one lives rather than where one works. These are important lessons, especially in traditional Western cultures, that professional counselors in school, postsecondary, and community settings can teach and reinforce in their clients.

Definitions Influence Interventions

Career development interventions are shaped, in part, by how we define our terms. A major issue within the area of career development interventions is the misuse of terminology among career practitioners as well as clients. For example, it is not uncommon for professional counselors to use the terms *career* and *work* interchangeably. It is also not unusual to hear professionals talk about "doing career development" as if career development were an intervention rather than the object of an intervention. Similarly, counselors often confuse the terms *career guidance* and *career counseling.* This lack of precision confuses practitioners, students, clients and, policymakers, and therefore is a barrier to advancing the efficacy of, and legislatative support for, career development interventions. When language lacks precision, the implication is that terminology does not matter. Words have power, however, in that career counselors are "engaged in a verbal profession in which words and symbols frequently become the content of the interactions they have with clients" (Herr, 1997, p. 241). Thus, the need exists for greater clarity and specificity with regard to the key terms related to career development interventions. Such specificity enhances the credibility of the counseling profession and provides a common ground for devising, implementing, and evaluating career development interventions.

CAREER. Rather than limiting the definition of career to work, Niles and Harris-Bowlsbey (2009) advocate viewing career as a lifestyle concept. Super's (1976) view of *career* as the course of events constituting a life, and Herr, Cramer, and Niles' (2004) notion of career as the total constellation of roles played over the course of a lifetime provide more wholistic definitions of *career.* Broader definitions highlight the multiple life roles that people play and acknowledge differences across people regarding life-role salience generally and provide flexibility regarding the areas in one's life where work is located. For example, broad definitions of career apply to those locating work in the life role of homemaker or in volunteer activities.

CAREER DEVELOPMENT. Career development refers to the lifelong psychological and behavioral processes as well as contextual influences shaping one's career over the lifespan. As such, career development involves the person's creation of a career pattern, decision-making style, integration of life roles, values expression, and life-role self-concepts (Niles & Harris-Bowlsbey, 2009). Professional counselors intervene to foster positive career development in their clients. Thus, career development is the object of interventions rather than an intervention.

CAREER DEVELOPMENT INTERVENTIONS. Career development interventions, defined broadly, involve any activities that empower people to cope effectively with career development tasks (Spokane, 1991). For example, activities that help people develop self-awareness, develop occupational awareness, learn decision-making skills, acquire job-search skills, adjust to occupational choices after they have been implemented, and cope with job stress can each be labeled as career development interventions. Specifically, these activities include individual and group career counseling, career development programs, career education, computer-assisted career development programs, and computer information delivery systems, as well as other forms of delivering career information to clients.

CAREER COUNSELING. Career counseling involves a formal relationship in which a professional counselor assists a client, or group of clients, to cope more effectively with career concerns (e.g., making a career choice, coping with career transitions, coping with job-related stress, or job searching). Typically, career counselors seek to establish rapport with their clients, assess their clients' career concerns, establish goals for the career counseling relationship, intervene in ways that help clients cope more effectively with career concerns, evaluate clients' progress, and, depending on clients' progress, either offer additional interventions or terminate career counseling (Niles & Harris-Bowlsbey, 2009).

Although career counselors provide the most comprehensive career interventions to clients and have the highest level of relevant training, other career practitioners exist and offer a variety of services to clients. Although their scope of practice is more limited and, in most cases, their training is less extensive, they provide useful career-related services.

Global Career Development Facilitators

In an effort to enhance the training of paraprofessionals engaged in providing career services, the leading professional association focused on career development, the National Career Development Association (NCDA), developed the Career Development Facilitator (CDF) curriculum based on a project funded by the National Occupational Information Coordinating Committee (NOICC) in 1992. A CDF is a career development practitioner who has successfully completed the CDF curriculum (Splete & Hoppin, 2000). The CDFs who satisfy prior work experience requirements in addition to completing the CDF training can acquire the Global Career Development Facilitator (GCDF) certification, which is awarded by the Center for Credentialing and Education (CCE). The GCDF credential is recognized nationally and internationally. So far, GCDF training has been offered across the United States and internationally in 13 countries such as Bulgaria, Canada, China, Germany, Japan, Romania, Turkey, South Korea, Macedonia, and New Zealand (Center for Credentialing and Education, 2010). The GCDF credential is one of the fastest-growing credentials within the career development field.

The CDF curriculum covers a wide variety of topics. It includes 120 hours of training, which can be either a 100% classroom or a hybrid (both classroom and online) format. The curriculum provides in-depth, standard knowledge and skills around such 12 CDF competencies as helping skills, labor market information and resources, assessment, diverse populations, ethical and legal issues, career development models, employability skills, training clients and peers, program management and implementation, promotion and public relations, technology, and consultation. Those with GCDF certification may work as a career group facilitator, career resource center coordinator, career development case manager, career coach, employment/placement specialist, job search trainer, workforce development staff person, or labor market information resource person. Because of the quality of the CDF curriculum and professional recognition of GCDF, a growing number of people, including professional counselors, are taking the course. As of 2010, more than 18,000 individuals have completed the curriculum and became GCDFs (for more information, see http://www.ncda .org).

Due to the increasing need to provide career services to students, South Carolina now mandates the CDF curriculum and the GCDF certification for middle school or high school career specialists as well as school counselors. These practitioners must also abide by the Code of Ethics of the CDF (South Carolina Guidance and Counseling Writing Team, 2008). School counselors supervise these career specialists. Duties of the career specialists in the South Carolina school system include coordinating and presenting career development workshops, assisting school counselors, offering information on career and technology programs, supporting students in career exploration, assisting with administration of career assessments, and coordinating diverse career development resources for parents and students.

Career Coaches

Another area related to career development practice is career coaching. Over the past 10 years, the coaching industry has grown rapidly. The term *coach* originated from the concept of a sports coach; however, the use of the term has been expanded to the business world. There are many different types of coaches, such as an executive coach, a leadership coach, a career coach, a life coach, a financial coach, and a relationship coach. The primary professional association for coaches is the International Coach Federation (ICF; http://www.coachfederation.org), which was established in 1995 and has 17,000 members worldwide as of 2010. In 2008, the ICF established a code of ethics for professional coaches. The ICF is the most dominant professional organization in the coaching industry; however, not all coaches are member of the ICF. Because the title "career coach" is not protected by licensure laws, anyone can use this label without undergoing any training or certification process. There are, however, formalized training programs for career coaches. Coaching training hours vary from 30 hours for a single workshop to two years for a master's degree. Recently, some universities, such as University of Sydney and University of Texas at Dallas, began offering a professional coaching program. The content of career coach training includes basic listening skills, learning how to provide effective feedback, using career assessments, teaching career decision-making skills, resume writing skills, interview skills, and salary negotiation skills (Bench, 2008).

There are similarities and differences among the work performed by those with the GCDF credential, career coaches, and professional counselors. Some of the similarities are the use of active listening, the emphasis of establishing an effective working relationship between the career practitioner and the client, and maintaining confidentiality. In addition, all career practitioners must have knowledge about career development processes and occupational information.

There are also, however, important differences among these career practitioners. For example, career counselors are the only career practitioners trained to use counseling techniques. In many states, they are also the only career practitioners eligible to use certain standardized career assessments. In essence, career counselors provide the highest level of service to their clients. Career coaches and GCDF practitioners are trained to help clients develop job search skills, make career decisions, and effectively manage work-related concerns.

Early Approaches to Career Development Interventions

The definitions of the terms described above have evolved over the decades. Early approaches to career development interventions reflected an emphasis on helping clients acquire career-related self-information, providing them with occupational information, and advising them as to which occupational choices seemed to offer a reasonable chance for experiencing occupational success. This was the approach articulated by Frank Parsons (1909) in the early 1900s. An engineer by training and a social reformer by personal commitment, Parsons merged his training and commitment to outline a systematic process of occupational decision making, which he referred to as "true reasoning." Zytowski (2001) noted that Parsons delivered a lecture in 1906, titled "The Ideal City," to the Economic Club of Boston. In this lecture, Parsons discussed the need for young people to receive assistance in the choice of a vocation. The lecture generated interest and requests by recent high school graduates for personal meetings with Parsons. From these activities, Parsons generated his systematic approach to vocational guidance. This approach was described in detail in Parsons' (1909) book, *Choosing a Vocation.* In his book, published one year after his death, Parsons discussed various principles and techniques that he found useful in helping the adolescents with whom he worked, first at the Breadwinners' College at the Civic Service House, a settlement house in Boston, and then at the Boston Vocation Bureau.

Parsons helped young people achieve the goal of "choosing a vocation." Parsons advocated activities such as reading biographies, observing workers in their settings, and reading existing occupational descriptions. These techniques were incorporated into the "Parsonian approach," which consisted of three steps or requirements for helping someone make an occupational choice. These requirements were:

- Develop a clear understanding of yourself, and your aptitudes, abilities, interests, resources, limitations, and other qualities.
- Develop knowledge of the requirements and conditions of success, advantages and disadvantages, compensation, opportunities, and prospects in different lines of work.
- Use "true reasoning" on the relations of these two groups of facts. (Parsons, 1909, p. 5)

Parsons developed his model against a background of social (e.g., rapid urbanization, child labor, immigration), economic (e.g., the rise of industrialism and the growing division of labor), and scientific (e.g., the emergence of human and behavioral sciences) changes occurring in the United States. These changes resulted in the need to place workers in jobs requiring specific skills and aptitudes, to help young people develop career plans, and to protect young people from child abuse in the labor force. Parsons' approach also fit nicely with the dominant scientific thinking of the 20th century, which emphasized positivism and objective methodology. That is, the Parsonian model encouraged practitioners to objectify interests, values, and abilities through the use of standardized assessment to guide people in identifying where they fit within the occupational structure.

The three requirements of the Parsonian approach formed the basic elements of what is now labeled as the *actuarial* or *trait-and-factor* approach to career counseling. These elements are essentially self-knowledge, occupational knowledge, and decision-making skills. The trait-and-factor approach emphasizes the identification of a person's relevant traits or characteristics usually through the use of standardized tests or inventories. The same approach is used in describing occupational factors or requirements (i.e., occupations are profiled according to the degree to which they require certain traits such as aptitudes). Then the individual's profile of traits is matched with the factors or requirements of specific occupations. The goal of this type of matching is to identify the degree of fit between the person and an occupation. It is also the goal that Frank Parsons had in mind when he sought to help others find a vocation and not merely hunt for a job (Parsons, 1909).

More Recent Approaches to Career Development Interventions

It is important to note that career counseling theories have evolved significantly beyond traditional trait-and-factor approaches. The work of John Holland, Donald Super, John Krumboltz, Linda Gottfredson, Robert Lent, Steven Brown, James Sampson, Robert Reardon, Janet Lenz, Mark Savickas, and others represents important advances in the evolution of career development theory and practice. These theories embrace developmental perspectives, cognitive approaches, and person-environment interactions in addressing career development. There is also a growing recognition of the important ways in which context influences career development. Many theorists address the ways in which contextual factors can affect cognitive processes that, in turn, influence choice behavior.

Many theories today also incorporate an orientation to the client's subjective career experience. More specifically, these theories emphasize the client's attempts at making meaning out of life experiences and then translating that meaning into a career direction. Such theories tend to rely on informal assessment strategies and the counseling process to empower clients as they move forward in their careers. Many of these approaches reflect a postmodern epistemology and incorporate narrative traditions into their intervention strategies. An in-depth coverage of these theories is beyond the scope of this chapter. However, we recommend that readers become familiar with the work of the theorists mentioned earlier. The theories represent a rich tapestry of important statements that guide the work of career counselors.

Career Counseling, Mental Health Counseling, and Social Action

As theories have evolved and expanded the conceptual as well as practical repertoire of career counselors, some have advocated that those providing career counseling expand their practice to include more systemic and proactive interventions to help current and potential clients cope with their career concerns more effectively. Herr and Niles (1998) contend that incorporating social action strategies in the career intervention process is one way in which career practitioners can respond more effectively to the career obstacles confronting many clients in contemporary society. Lee (1989) agrees, stating that career counselors must act as "career development advocates for disenfranchised clients by actively challenging long-standing traditions that stand in the way of equity in the workplace" (p. 219).

Career counseling for social action requires counselors to provide multifaceted career interventions and to expand their roles beyond traditional, individual career counseling practice. Career counseling for social action integrates the roles of facilitator and clinical mental health counselor into the career counseling process. More specifically, career counseling for social action begins with career counselors possessing the multicultural competencies (i.e., knowledge, skills, and attitudes) necessary for understanding how the environments their clients occupy interact to influence the interpretations and meanings clients attach to work and occupational opportunities. Blustein and Noumair (1996) note the importance of understanding how contextual factors (e.g., history, family, economics, and culture) interact with clients' intrapersonal experiences to shape their life-role identities. Acquiring this understanding serves as the foundation for identifying social action strategies aimed at facilitating client career development.

Career counseling strategies address contextual factors by drawing on community resources to provide clients access to information and opportunities (e.g., employment offices, "one-stop career shops," support groups). Learning about career resources available in the community facilitates appropriate referrals and increases the probability that clients will receive the services they need. Therefore, career counselors engaging in social action also play the role of facilitator by providing information, referrals, and encouragement to clients (Enright, Conyers, & Szymanski, 1996). Playing this role effectively requires career counselors to maintain files of useful resources, including names of potential mentors representing diverse backgrounds (e.g., African American, Asian American, individuals with disabilities, gay and lesbian men and women), information on accommodations for disabled individuals with different functional limitations, names of employers willing to provide opportunities for job shadowing and internship experiences, and names of individuals willing to participate in informational interviewing experiences (Enright et al., 1996).

Having a thorough knowledge of career resources available in the community also allows counselors to identify areas where services are lacking. In these instances, counselors once again take on a strong advocacy role and seek to rectify service deficiencies in their communities (Lee, 1989).

Advocacy is also important when clients' career concerns are the result of external factors, such as large-scale downsizing. In these instances, counselors concerned with social action address not only the career concerns of individual clients but also the career concerns of the community at-large (Cahill & Martland, 1996). This also is accomplished by integrating individual career counseling skills with community counseling skills. Integrating career counseling and community counseling strategies is especially critical in rural communities where economic restructuring can threaten the existence of the community. Cahill and Martland argue that community career counseling builds on the strength of individual career counseling and offers assistance to people in their struggle to maintain their communities as they create opportunities for career development. Thus, in addition to individual career counseling skills, counselors need skills in facilitating group problem solving, consensus building, and an understanding of the socioeconomic development process to help clients advance their careers in contemporary society. Essentially, career counselors who instill hope in their clients and empower them to manage their careers are multiculturally competent, act as facilitators of information and referrals, advocate for their clients when employment practices and community traditions stand in the way of equity in the workplace, and integrate individual career counseling skills with community counseling skills to assist people in their struggle to maintain their communities and create opportunities for career development. This combination of skills expands traditional approaches to career counseling and equips counselors for effective social action aimed at facilitating career development in clients.

CONCLUSION

There are numerous points of intersection between career counseling and mental health counseling. In fact, due to the prominence of career issues in the current economy, one could argue that, to be an effective mental health counselor, one must also be a competent career counselor and vice versa. Evolutionary shifts in the nature of work and demographic changes in work create opportunities for mental health counselors to be of greater assistance to their clients as they cope with their career concerns. More recent approaches to career counseling rely on many skills and perspectives commonly used in mental health counseling. Adapting an epistemology that interprets *career* choice and development to mean *human* development through a constellation of work and non-work life roles holds great promise for contemporary career counseling practice and for society (Cook, 1994; Richardson, 1993; Savickas, 2000; Super & Sverko, 1995). The movement toward human development and away from more narrowly defined notions of career development is reflected in more recent approaches to career counseling. Mental health counselors who are prepared to address their clients' career concerns and who understand how these concerns relate to mental health issues will be poised to offer comprehensive mental health services to clients seeking to live more fulfilling and satisfying lives.

REFERENCES

Amundson, N. E. (1998). *Active engagement: Enhancing the career counselling process.* Richmond, BC: Ergon Communications.

Anderson, W. P., & Niles, S. G. (1995). Career and personal concerns expressed by career counseling clients. *The Career Development Quarterly, 43,* 240–245.

Anderson, W. P., Jr., & Niles, S. G. (2000). Important events in career counseling: Client and counselor descriptions. *The Career Development Quarterly, 48,* 251–263.

Bench, M. A. (2008). *Career coaching: An insider's guide* (2nd ed.). Havasu City, AZ: High Flight Press.

Blustein, D. L., & Noumair, D. A. (1996). Self and identity in career development: Implications for theory and practice. *Journal of Counseling and Development, 74,* 433–441.

Bridges, W. (1994). *Job shift.* Reading, MA: Addison-Wesley.

Cahill, M., & Martland, S. (1996). Community career counseling for rural transition. *Canadian Journal of Counseling, 30,* 155–164.

CeNavas-Walt, C., Proctor, B. D., & Smith, J. C. (2009). *Income, poverty, and health insurance coverage in the United States: 2008* (No. P60-236). Current population reports. Washington, DC: U.S. Census Bureau. Retrieved from http://www.census.gov/prod/2009pubs/p60-236.pdf

Center for Credentialing and Education. (2010, Spring). History of the GCDF competencies and credential. *The global career development facilitator connection.* Retrieved from http://www.cce-global.org/extras/cce-global/pdfs/gcdfnewsletterspring10.pdf

Chung, Y. B. (2003). Career counseling with lesbian, gay, bisexual, and transgendered persons: The next decade. *The Career Development Quarterly, 52,* 78–86.

Cook, E. P. (1994). Role salience and multiple roles: A gender perspective. *The Career Development Quarterly, 43,* 85–95.

Enright, M. S., Conyers, L. M., & Szymanski, E. M. (1996). Career and career-related educational concerns of college students with disabilities. *Journal of Counseling & Development, 75,* 103–114.

Fabian, E. S., & Liesener, J. J. (2005). Promoting the career potential of youth with disabilities. In S. D. Brown & R. W. Lent (Eds.), *Career development and counseling: Putting them and research to work* (pp. 551–572). Hoboken, NJ: Wiley & Sons.

Farmer, H., Rotella, S., Anderson, C., & Wardrop, J. (1998). Gender differences in science, math, and technology careers: Prestige level and Holland interest type. *Journal of Vocational Behavior, 53,* 73–96.

Goleman, D. (1990). Homophobia: Scientists find clues to its roots. *The New York Times,* pp. C1, C11.

Gomez, M. J., Fassinger, R. E., Prosser, J., Cooke, K., Mejia, B., & Luna, J. (2001). Voces abriendo caminos (Voices forging paths): A qualitative study of the career development of notable Latinas. *Journal of Counseling Psychology, 48,* 286–300.

Herr, E. L. (1989). Career development and mental health. *Journal of Career Development, 16,* 5–18.

Herr, E. L. (1997). Super's life-span, life-space approach and its outlook for refinement. *The Career Development Quarterly, 45,* 238–246.

Herr, E. L., Cramer, S. H., & Niles, S. G. (2004). *Career guidance and counseling through the lifespan: Systematic approaches* (6th ed.). Boston, MA: Allyn & Bacon.

Herr, E. L., & Niles, S. G. (1998). Career: A source of hope and empowerment in a time of despair. In C. Lee & G. Walz (Eds.), *Social action: A mandate for counselors* (pp. 117–136). Greensboro, NC: ERIC/CASS.

Isaacson, L. E., & Brown, D. (1997). *Career information, career counseling, and career development* (6th ed.). Boston: Allyn & Bacon.

Kim, B. S. K., Li, L. C., & Liang, C. T. H. (2002). Effects of Asian American client adherence to Asian cultural values, session goal, and counselor emphasis of client expression on career counseling process. *Journal of Counseling Psychology, 49,* 3–13.

Lee, C. C. (1989). Needed: A career development advocate. *The Career Development Quarterly, 37,* 218–220.

Leong. F. T. L. (1995). *Career development and vocational behavior of racial and ethnic minorities.* Mahwah, NJ: Lawrence Erlbaum Associates.

Leong. F. T. L. (2002). Challenges for career counseling in Asia: Variations in cultural accommodations. *The Career Development Quarterly, 50,* 277–284.

Mercer. (2009, October 13). *Employee statutory and public holiday entitlements: Global comparisons.* Retrieved from http://www.mercer.com/summary.htm?siteLanguage=100&idContent=1360620#22

National Career Development Association. (2003). *Career counseling competencies.* Tulsa, OK: Author.

National Council on Disability. (2000). *Transition and post-school outcomes for youth with disabilities: Closing the gaps to post-secondary education and employment.* Retrieved from http://www.ncd.gov/newsroom/publications/2000/transition_11-01-00.htm#2

Niles, S. G., & Anderson, W. (1993). Career development and adjustment: The relation between concerns and stress. *Journal of Employment Counseling, 30,* 79–87.

Niles, S. G., & Harris-Bowlsbey, J. (2009). *Career development interventions in the 21st century* (3rd ed.). Upper Saddle River, NJ: Pearson.

Niles, S. G., Herr, E. L., & Hartung, P. J. (2002). Adult career concerns in contemporary society. In S. G. Niles (Ed.), *Adult career development* (3rd ed., pp. 3–20). Tulsa, OK: National Career Development Association.

Niles, S. G., & Pate, R. H., Jr. (1989). Competency and training issues related to the integration of career counseling and mental health counseling. *Journal of Career Development, 16,* 63–71.

Parsons, F. (1909). *Choosing a vocation.* Boston: Houghton-Mifflin.

Pope, M., & Barret, R. (2002). Providing career counseling services to gay and lesbian clients. In S. Niles (Ed.), *Adult career development: Concepts, models, and practices* (3rd ed., pp. 215–232). Tulsa, OK: National Career Development Association.

Richardson, M. (1993). Work in people's lives: A location for counseling psychologists. *Journal of Counseling Psychology, 40,* 425–433.

Rifkin, J. (1995). *The end of work.* New York: Putnam.

Savickas, M. L. (2000). Renovating the psychology of careers for the 21st century. In A. Collin & R. Young (Eds.), *The future of career* (pp. 53–68). Cambridge, England: Cambridge University Press.

South Carolina Guidance and Counseling Writing Team. (2008). *The South Carolina comprehensive developmental guidance and counseling program model.* Columbia, SC: South Carolina Department of Education. Retrieved from http://www.ed.sc.gov/agency/Innovation-and-Support/Youth-Services/Guidance/documents/Ann-4-SCCDGCPM06-23-08Final.pdf

Splete, H. H., & Hoppin, J. M. (2000). The emergence of career development facilitators. *Journal of Employment Counseling, 48,* 340–347.

Spokane, A. R. (1991). *Career interventions.* Upper Saddle River, NJ: Prentice Hall.

Super, D. E. (1976). *Career education and the meaning of work.* Monographs on career education. Washington, DC: The Office of Career Education, U.S. Office of Education.

Super, D. E., & Sverko, B. (Eds.). (1995). *Life roles, values, and careers: International findings of the work importance study.* San Francisco: Jossey-Bass.

U.S. Bureau of Labor Statistics. (2009). *Labor force characteristics by race and ethnicity, 2008.* Retrieved from http://www.bls.gov/cps/cpsrace2008.pdf

U.S. Bureau of Labor Statistics. (2010a). *The employment situation: May 2010.* Retrieved from http://www.bls.gov/news.release/pdf/empsit.pdf

U.S. Bureau of Labor Statistics. (2010b). *Labor force statistics from the current population survey.* Retrieved from http://data.bls.gov/cgi-bin/surveymost?ln

U.S. Census Bureau. (2000). *Profiles of general demographic characteristics: National summary.* Retrieved from http://www.census.gov

U.S. Census Bureau. (2008). *2008 national population projections.* Retrieved from http://www.census.gov/population/www/projections/2008projections.html

U.S. Department of Homeland Security. (2009). *2009 yearbook of immigration statistics.* Retrieved from http://www.dhs.gov/files/statistics/publications/LPR09.shtm

Zytowski, D. G. (2001). Frank Parsons and the progressive movement. *The Career Development Quarterly, 50,* 57–65.

Chapter 8

COUNSELING AND THE USE OF HUMOR

DAVID P. BORSOS

INTRODUCTION

A disgruntled mother and father walk up to a famous therapist at his book signing. "Son, if we knew you were going to write a book about us," they complain, "we would have treated you better." This old joke may produce mild laughter or solemn groans from a group of actual counselors. Yet it serves to introduce us to an important topic in the counselor experience, a topic that is rarely mentioned in graduate school and never taught–the use of humor in the counseling session. Is it ever appropriate? If so, when and how? Is it harmful? Helpful? Or even professional? There has been some research on the effective use of humor in the counseling setting and some warnings about it. It is, after all, a common human trait and a normal part of life. Can't it also be a normal part of therapeutic life? This chapter explores some of the positive and negative effects of using humor in counseling, as well as some of the positive, physical effects of humor and laughter. But first, how do we define humor?

Definitions of Humor

Definitions of humor are as abundant as laughter itself. Most, however, can be categorized into three generally accepted areas: incongruity, release, and superiority. Although the three often overlap, they are briefly discussed as separate areas of understanding.

Incongruity: A high-class call girl is sent to visit an 85-year-old man on his birthday. "Your friends asked me to come by and give you some super sex for your birthday," she offers. The man thinks a moment and drawls, "At my age, I'll take the soup."

This story illustrates the incongruity definition of humor. Humor occurs when the listener builds up one set of expectations in a communication only to have the reply, the "punch line," be discrepant or incongruous from these expectations (Holland, 1982). In other words, humor occurs when two incompatible, yet internally consistent, themes are juxtaposed in the same sequence of events. The humor of this story obviously turns on the divergent interpretations of the sound of the word, *super* (soup or). The incongruity of the remark must also be resolved for the listener to find it humorous (McGhee, 1979; McGhee & Goldstein, 1983). The humor of this story would be lost on someone who did not understand the potential double meanings of the sound of the word.

The reader can, no doubt, recall many humorous gags, stories, or scenes that turn on the unexpected incongruity of the situation. Many examples are so common that they are fairly clichéd: the grandmother driving the sports car, the child on a sitcom outsmarting the dad, or a family pet slyly doing some activity that only a human should be able to do.

Release: During the latter days of the Civil War, the White general of an all-Black regiment noticed that one soldier seemed to follow him everywhere. Finally, the general remarked on this apparent devotion and said, "Well, my son, you have stood by me well in these battles."

"Yes, sir," said the soldier, "My momma told me to stick to the White generals and I'd never get hurt."

The humor of this story springs from the undercurrents of racial relationships that have and still do exist in this country. The story is a veiled attack on White privilege as seen through the eyes of a Black man. It is a release of aggression, yet one that is disguised as "humorous" and thereby more acceptable to the target than a direct criticism of racial differences and benefits (Grieg, 1923).

The release definition of humor sees it as a safety valve for the release of repressed emotion or tension–especially aggressive or sexual ones (Freud, 1960; Gruner, 1978). It also allows the expression of taboo thoughts (Fisher & Fisher, 1981) and the release of pent-up physical tension (Berlyne, 1972). Anyone who has ever laughed heartily at the end of a tense roller-coaster ride knows the experience of humor as a release of bodily tension. Sarcasm, put-down humor, and a biting wit are forms of aggression being released in a disguised and (sometimes) more acceptable fashion. Feminists have looked at the use of humor to attack some of the male dominance in society or to enhance gender equity (Case & Lippard, 2009). "If they can send a man to the moon, why not just send all of them?" Pornographic jokes are obvious forms of humor that allow the release of some sexual impulses or allow one to remark on a taboo topic with some safety.

Superiority: Blondes and various nationalities, ethnicities, religions, and professions (even therapists) have been the butt of many jokes. "How many blondes does . . .What's the difference between a lawyer and . . . A priest and a rabbi walk into a bar. . . ." Perhaps you've wondered what it says on the bottom of the ethnic's soda bottle? "Open other end."

As we laugh at this, we wonder how the ethnic could be so stupid. We are secure in our knowledge that we could never be so bone-headed. We find humor in our belief that we are definitely better or more superior to the person who is the butt of the joke. Ridicule or disparagement of another with the sudden, attendant feelings of being above them is the essence of the superiority definition of humor (Gruner, 1978).

To understand this form of humor, we need to know whom is disparaged, how, and why. The target may be vague: eggheads, beauty queens, "dumb" athletes, or as specific as the current president of the United States, if we dislike him or her. This definition is usually traced to Hobbes' derision theory of humor. He said we laugh at a "sudden eminence" in ourselves in comparison to the observed fault or folly in another or in our former selves (Hobbes, 1968). If you've ever laughed at any slapstick humor, such as an actor slipping on a banana peel or bumping his head on a low door frame, then you've enjoyed the guilty pleasures of the superiority aspects of humor (Goldstein & McGhee, 1972).

Correlates of Humor

A fuller understanding of humor requires the addition of three correlates of effective humor. These aspects of humor are generally seen as necessary but not sufficient for the perception of humor. These are: suddenness, optimal arousal levels, and a play frame.

Suddenness: The resolution of incongruity, the release of tension, or the realization of superiority must occur suddenly or surprisingly for humor to occur. The build-up to the joke must not take too long, and the resolution must be understood immediately for the humor to work well (McGhee, 1979). Few people really find humor in remarks that are not new or if they can anticipate the conclusion. Humor that must be explained afterward is also a sure-fire failure.

Optimal Arousal: Each humorous stimulus causes some increase of arousal in the subject. It may be intellectual, emotional, or physical arousal. Yet for the humor to be effective, it must be at some moderate level of arousal (McGhee, 1979). A stimulus that is not stimulating will be tossed off as childish or inconsequential. This is why adults usually will not find humor in childish jokes, situations, or some puns; they are just not very provoking.

"What did one wall say to another?" "Meet you at the corner."
"Why is six afraid of seven?" "Because seven eight nine."
"Why did the chicken cross the road?" You get the idea.

Humor that is perceived as too tense or arousing can be perceived as painful or fear-provoking (Berlyne, 1972). A child may not laugh at daddy's silly mask because he perceives a more scary arousal than playful. A "dirty" joke may arouse more disgust than fun for some people, or humor in areas about which people are sensitive can arouse more hurt than fun. For example, the wife of an alcoholic is not going to be optimally aroused by jokes about drinking.

Play Frame: Finally, the audience must know the stimulus is meant to be funny and accepts it that way. It must contain certain cues or clues that the situation is meant to be in a "play-frame" (Holland, 1982), a fantasy mode (McGhee, 1979), or somehow safe and nonthreatening (Rothbart, 1977). Facial expression, tone of voice, context, or prior experience may all signal the playful intent of the humorist. These signals let us know that the remarks or events are not to be taken seriously. We won't laugh at the man slipping on the banana peel if we think he is really getting hurt.

The American Association of Therapeutic Humor (2010) seeks to "study, practice and promote healthy humor and laughter." To that end, they have used the definitions of humor and expanded them to define therapeutic humor itself. It is defined as "any intervention that promotes health and wellness by stimulating a playful discovery, expression or appreciation of the absurdity or incongruity of life situations. This intervention may enhance health or be used as a complimentary treatment of illness to facilitate healing or coping, whether physical, emotional, cognitive, social or spiritual."

Physical Effects

Humor and laughter have been shown to have positive effects on the body. Kisner (1994) has demonstrated that it can alleviate or moderate pain in cancer patients who are dying. Others have shown an increase in endorphin levels (Levinthal, 1988) or improvements in the immune system (Bennett, 1998) for those involved in humorous activities.

Berk (2010) categorizes some areas of physical improvements that are associated with humor and laughter. They can "reduce tension . . . enhance memory . . . increase pain tolerance . . . increase energy . . . enhance creative thinking . . . exercise respiratory muscles." Sultanoff (2004) also concludes that humor does, indeed, reduce the level of hormones released during stress responses. It also increases the levels of imunoglobin A, a disease-fighting antibody. He also finds that it improves pain tolerance as well as heart rate and circulation.

Laughter has been shown to lower blood pressure in stroke victims (Ananova, 2004). In an experiment, two groups of matched stroke patients were given the same rehabilitation regimen, but one was given a "laughing technique" component. The control group had no change in blood pressure, whereas the "laughter" group had a significant drop in pressure. Miller (2010) at the University of Maryland Medical Center demonstrated that laughter improved blood flow in patients by expanding the endothelium, the inner lining of the blood vessels. When the same participants were shown a film that caused mental distress, it caused the blood vessels to contract, thereby restricting blood flow.

One of the more famous examples of the healing power of humor came to us from Norman Cousins (1979). While he was recovering from a serious illness his doctors thought was unchangeable, he prescribed himself a daily regimen of humorous books, tapes, movies, and other works. Cousins credits much of his unlikely recovery to his use of humor and laughter to stimulate his ailing body.

Psychotherapeutic Benefits

As we know from Carl Rogers (1951) and others (Hubble, Duncan, & Miller, 2001), the therapeutic relationship is a crucial part of any counseling situation. A careful use of therapeutic humor has been shown to improve the client–counselor relationship (Haig, 1986, 1988) and the levels of trust in that process (Buckman, 1994). Zall (1994) believes that a shared humor in counseling implies an enjoyment of the relationship, and Sultanoff (2004) points out that it improves a counselor's ability to connect with people.

McGhee (1979) calls the relationship-enhancing effects of humor the "lubricant" effects that initiate and facilitate social interaction. It can open up dialogue and signal a friendly intent on the counselor's part, showing him or her to be nonthreatening. It is a low-risk offering to the client that seeks a reply or some reciprocity (Coser, 1959). Buckman (1994) points out that a humorous person is seen to be more trustworthy than a serious one. A study from the medical field discovered that patient satisfaction correlated highly with the physician's sense of humor (Zolnierek-Haskarl et al, 2009).

One explanation for the relationship-enhancing effects of humor is that it implies a commonality between the two people sharing the humor (Coser, 1959). It presupposes some shared worldview between client and counselor. Even Freud (1960) saw humor as indicative of some conformity between patient and counselor. In an interesting experiment, Murstein and Brust (1985) tested 30 romantically involved couples on two factors: their attractiveness to their partners and their individual humor interests. They found a strong correlation between shared humor interests and a couple's attractiveness to each other. The research seems to show that an effective use of humor can enhance the client-counselor relationship.

The counselor may also use humor to reduce client tension in appropriate circumstances (Buckman, 1994). It helps bring a softer touch to areas of client sensitivity (Zwerling, 1955), allowing a client to approach a painful area of life with less anxiety. It becomes a comfortable way to approach an uncomfortable zone. Tallmer and Richman (1994) point out the effective use of humor as a way to point out troubled areas and help the ego overcome the resultant stress.

Of course, one of our earlier definitions of humor included its tension-releasing functions as a crucial aspect of humor. Tension can be developed in the telling of a story or in the actions or words that are shared in a social, humorous setting. It seems only logical that the tension developed in a treatment setting between a client and counselor, or a client and some aspect of himself, can be relieved with a judicious use of appropriate humor. It has been shown to reduce stress in a variety of settings, both clinical and non-clinical (Apte, 1985). Obrdlik (1942) found citizens using humor to cope with the Nazi occupation of a small Czech town. Coser (1959) found that hospital patients used humor to relieve the tensions of their inpatient stays. He also found that humor gave them some sense of mastery over a painful situation where they had little real control. Minden (1994) also found that humor helped patients master their painful environment. She took a group of veterans hospitalized with major depression and taught them to use humor as a coping device. She found a significant decrease in symptoms after just six sessions. Certainly, our clients may use or appreciate humor as one way to get some sense of control over their own tensions and anxieties.

Along with releasing tension, the therapeutic use of humor allows a client a manageable way to release aggression, anger, or any other feelings that may be taboo or repressed. It can help a client break through resistance to difficult feelings (Buckman, 1994), allowing appropriate expression, not repression (Bergler, 1957). Albert Ellis (1977) has been a strong proponent of using humor to help clients express taboo or harsh feelings. He feels it takes away the power of these feelings to harm or inhibit an individual. Ellis (1987) even developed a series of humorous songs that help a client make light of forbidden feelings, thereby reducing their impact on the individual. Freud (1960) spoke at length about the benefits of humor to the ego as a way of expressing taboo feelings of sex or aggression.

Effective use of therapeutic humor has also allowed clients to gain a new perspective on an issue, to step back from it, accept it, and work on it from a new angle (Berk, 2010). Dana (1994) promotes it as a way to help clients avoid overseriousness around an issue. A classic example of the use of therapeutic humor to encourage a client to adopt a new and healthier perspective on things is that of paradoxical intention first proposed by Frankl (1960). Paradoxical intention pushes a client to exaggerate a problem or symptom to such an extreme that it provokes absurdity and laughter, and therefore a new perspective. A person complaining of insomnia may be directed to stay awake no matter what happens. An anxious person may be ordered to exaggerate and extend their anxieties to areas of life that are anxiety-free.

Sultanoff (2004) points out another benefit of humor in counseling–a humorous feeling may replace a more negative one. One cannot feel simultaneously sad and humorous, angry and gleeful, and so on. Therefore, he states, a humorous interaction may serve to pull someone out of a more negative mood. This idea has been supported by Strick et al. (2009), who found that the cognitive distraction of humor can prevent negative thoughts or feelings. A person needs to shift attention from the negative ideas to the intellectual work needed to resolve the incongruity of the humorous remark, thereby reducing the depressed or anxious feelings.

Interestingly, brain research has shown that, when presented with a humorous story or puzzle, brain areas involved in resolving problems are activated right before those reward areas involved in the pleasure (Goel & Dolan, 2001). This shows that attention is first paid to resolving the incongruity, and then to the positive emotions released by the humor.

Martin (2007) lists four types of humor that may be observed in a counseling setting: affiliative, self-enhancing, aggressive, and self-defeating. These types categorize humor by its purpose: to join with others (affiliative), to esteem oneself (self-enhancing), to attack others (aggressive), or to put oneself down or show poor self-worth (self-defeating).

Kuiper and McHale (2009) have shown that those who predominantly use self-defeating humor show greater levels of depression and social supports that harm well-being. Esteeming or affiliative humor was seen to increase positive social bonds, reduce negative self-images, and reduce depression.

If the observant counselor hears various kinds of self-defeating humor, he or she may use that as a symptom of the client's overall low sense of self-worth. Honest affiliative humor may be a sign of trying to reach out to the therapist. Aggressive humor may be healthy in a repressed client who needs to express more anger or a bad sign in someone who is stuck in his anger and knows nothing else but sarcasm and aggressive humor. As with most topics in counseling, we must be aware of our client and the context of any topic that arises. Certainly, the careful counselor will avoid aggressive or self-defeating humor aimed at the client and make judicious use of affiliative and self-enhancing humor.

Possible Harmful Effects

There are many ways a therapeutic use of humor could backfire on a counselor and cause more harm than help. Brooks (1994) warns that a counselor should only use humor if he or she understands how the client will understand or respond to it. Of course, the best way to ensure this is not to use humor until a strong treatment relationship is established. The client may misunderstand the humor and see it as ridicule, punishing, or hurtful rather than helpful (Buckman, 1994). Some people are particularly sensitive to being laughed at and see all laughter as threatening or bullying. They are unable to distinguish fun or playful laughter from purposefully hurtful humor (Fuhr, Proyer, & Ruch, 2009). These clients often come from shame-based early family relationships or have suffered from past traumatic bullying. The authors have coined the term *gelotophobia* for the particular fear of being laughed at.

Humor should not be used to relieve the counselor's tensions. Satisfying the helper's needs in session is almost always counterproductive for the client (Buckman, 1994). Brooks (1994) advises against using humor if you dislike the client or are having any kind of countertransference problem with him or her. The client will pick up the therapist's negativity and feel a violation of the relationship. Sarcasm, put-downs, cheap-shots, or anything that may sound like veiled hostility should be avoided (Buckman, 1994). Saper (1987) says that humor should always be used for some conscious therapeutic benefit for the client or it will interfere with treatment. This could include tension relief, rapport-building, ice-breaking, therapeutic detachment, and the like.

Another potential problem with humor in therapy is that the client could be using it as a defense mechanism (albeit an attractive one) or to avoid some pathology or topic (Marcus, 1990). There are times when a client's use of humor should be challenged and discussed as such a defense and not accepted as healthy or appropriate. The author once had a client who consistently joked about the various troubles in her life. Every story would be followed by a smiling guffaw and a hearty knee-slap. This happened whether she was talking about a neighbor's squeaky door or her husband abandoning her and moving to another state. It became clear that her persistent use of humor was a defense against facing her deep hurts and anger at him as well as other people in her life. It was also her way of avoiding any conflict in life even when necessary. The repression of these feelings was directly causing the anxiety and depression that led her to treatment in the first place.

A study of humor interactions by hospital patients shows other possible problems with its use. Patients used humor as a way of trying to please the clinician or to look like the "good patient" being compliant or ingratiating

(McCreadie & Wiggins, 2009). This should alert the clinician to possible transference behaviors or defensive styles by the patient. The participants also used humor to bring up personal concerns in a deferential or subservient manner. They were trying to connect to the clinician in a way that minimized them being "trouble" to anyone.

Humor should be avoided in a client's crisis situations. The person is too overwhelmed by the strong feelings of the moment to appreciate any possible advantages of its use. One must develop some detachment from the crisis where a play frame is possible and there are no more bad surprises. A person tends to blend the self into the situation and would feel that any humor, even at the event itself, is an attack aimed at the individual. Humor here is contraindicated and insensitive (Sultanoff, 2004). Although after some time has passed, humor can help cope with the results of a crisis. There was a sign seen at the Midwest property of a person whose home had recently been destroyed by a tornado. It said, "Home for sale–some assembly required!"

The psychoanalyst, Lawrence Kubie (1971), expressed some of the strongest warnings against the use of humor in any counseling situation. He insists it may mask therapist hostility and divert the client from the counseling task. The client may start to wonder whether the counselor is being funny or serious with some remarks. The counselor may lose objectivity in the client's eyes or be seen as just narcissistically showing off his or her wit. The humor may be interpreted as mocking or misunderstanding the client's suffering and harm the relationship.

RECOMMENDATIONS ON USING HUMOR IN COUNSELING

Most humor researchers see humor as a normal part of the human experience and a useful aspect of treatment if used carefully and with purpose (Kuhlman, 1984). As Franzini (2001) points out, therapeutic humor should be used for the client's benefit, and the counselor should be consistently self-monitoring to ensure that he or she is not using it for the counselor's pleasures or purposes. A counselor should be sensitive to client issues, be verbally quick, and have some sense of comic timing (Brooks, 1994). As we have seen in our humor definitions, the fun of the humor should be gotten suddenly. If there is poor timing in a remark delivered too late or too soon, it is likely to sound unfunny and inhibit the work or at least make the counselor look out of touch with the client feelings (Salameh, 1987). He also points out that the best use of therapeutic humor is that which arises spontaneously from the dialogue or the treatment setting and not that which is prepared. The artificiality of prepared jokes or stories will most likely insult or put off the client (Franzini, 2001).

Humor should only be used when the relationship is established and we have some idea of the client's reactions. Another good barometer of when to use humor is after a client uses it with you (Sultanoff, 2004). For example, while walking through the complicated hallways to the author's office, some clients will gripe, "Gee, I feel like a rat in a maze. Do I get some cheese at the end?" This cues me to the client's mood, and I feel safe remarking back, "No, but perhaps we should drop some bread crumbs to help us find our way out." We then share a small, but mutual laugh, and I believe the client has some sense of bonding and tension release on this first visit to the counselor. Importantly, too, the bonding may occur because the humorous offering of the client is accepted and responded to on an equivalent level by the counselor. Ignoring a client's humor or responding in a serious manner may be off-putting and may even make the counselor look aloof or not accepting of the individual.

As mentioned earlier, humor should not be used in the immediacy of a crisis or defensively by the client or counselor. It should be well timed like any other counselor intervention (Buckman, 1994). In fact, Fenichel (1945) believed that if a client laughs at a therapeutic interpretation, it shows us the accuracy of the remark. To be most useful, a humorous intervention should display a relevance to a client's situations, conflicts, or personality (Franzini, 2001). Franzini has actually proposed actual humor training for counselors. He believes that this most human skill can be taught didactically just as other skills are. Components of his training program include modeling techniques by supervisors, learning humor techniques, and learning to be sensitive to a client's humor.

Prerost (1985) proposed specific humor techniques for use in sessions. This involves inducing a client into a state of relaxation while imagining scenes of personal trouble or tension. He then guides the client into introducing some humor into the imagined scene, developing laughter and incongruity. He reports that this helps clients resolve some of their issues with a new perspective and new coping skills. Salameh (1987) has begun to develop a training program called Humor Immersion Training, which involves learning to use incongruity, exaggeration, reversals, and wordplay in the counseling setting.

Sultanoff (2004) also believes one can increase one's sense of and use of humor. He suggests immersing oneself in humorous stimuli such as books, movies, and tapes. He also encourages the counselor to observe the world with new perspectives, such as exaggeration or silliness. Using humorous props such as bubbles or clown noses are recommended to open up one's sensitivity to humor. Planning and practicing humor is also encouraged by him. Sultanoff reports collecting humorous articles and jokes and practicing them in a way to increase his ability to use humor appropriately.

O'Connell (1981) has developed a humor-oriented technique he calls humordrama. He uses a psychodrama format to help introduce humor as a coping skill into a client's issues. The client talks or plays out a situation while a double from the group tries to stimulate humor through exaggeration, wordplay, understatements, and the like.

It seems clear that the judicious use of humor can be a useful tool in the work we do with clients. As with most tools, it can help or hurt if used improperly or carelessly. The author believes this human trait should be developed by the aspiring counselor as an aid in relationship building, client coping abilities, tension release, and other benefits discussed earlier. It should flow naturally from the dialogue and should seem a natural part of the counselor's personality and style. Certainly, counseling and therapy are serious endeavors for our clients and for us. Yet there are good times to bring a little humor or joy into a client's life. They deserve it.

REFERENCES

American Association of Therapeutic Humor. (2010). *Official definition of therapeutic humor.* Retrieved February 26, 2010, from http://www.aath.org/

Ananova. (2004 March). *Laughter really is the best therapy.* Retrieved October 2, 2004, from http://crystalinks.com/laughter2.html.

Apte, M. L. (1985). *Humor and laughter: An anthropological approach.* Ithaca, NY: Cornell University Press.

Bennett, M. P. (1998). The effect of mirthful laughter on stress and natural killer cell cytotoxicity. *Dissertation Abstracts International: Section B: Science and Engineering, 58*(7-B), 3553.

Bergler, E. (1957). *Laughter and sense of humor.* New York: Intercontinental Medical Books.

Berk, R. (2010). *What everyone should know about humor and laughter.* Retrieved March 2, 2010, from http://www.aath.org/documents/aath-whatwe knowrevised.pdf

Berlyne, D. (1972). Humor and its kin. In J. H. Goldstein & P. E. McGhee (Eds.), *The psychology of humor* (pp. 220–232). New York: Academic Press.

Brooks, R. (1994). Humor in psychotherapy: An invaluable technique with adolescents. In E. S. Buckman (Ed.), *The handbook of humor: Clinical applications in psychotherapy* (pp. 53–74). Malabar, FL: Krieger Publications.

Buckman, E. S. (1994). *The handbook of humor: Clinical applications in psychotherapy.* Malabar, FL: Krieger Publications.

Case, C. E., & Lippard, C. D. (2009). Humorous assaults on patriarchal ideology. *Sociological Inquiry, 79,* 240–255.

Coser, R. L. (1959). Some functions of laughter: A study of humor in a hospital setting. *Human Relations, 12,* 171–182.

Cousins, N. (1979). *The anatomy of an illness.* New York: Norton.

Dana, R. S. (1994). Humor as a diagnostic tool in child and adolescent groups. In E. S. Buckman (Ed.), *The handbook of humor: Clinical applications in psychotherapy* (pp. 41–52). Malabar, FL: Krieger Publications.

Ellis, A. (1977). Fun as psychotherapy. *Rational Living, 12,* 2–6.

Ellis, A. (1987). The use of rational, humorous songs in psychotherapy. In W. F. Fry & W. A.

Salameh (Eds.), *Handbook of humor and psychotherapy: Advances in the clinical use of humor* (pp. 265–285). Sarasota, FL: Professional Resource Exchange.

Fenichel, O. (1945). *The psychoanalytic theory of neurosis.* New York: Norton.

Fisher, S., & Fisher, R. L. (1981). *Pretend the world is funny and forever: A psychological analysis of comedians, clowns, and actors.* Hillsdale, NJ: Erlbaum.

Frankl, V. (1960). Paradoxical intention: A logotherapy technique. *American Journal of Psychotherapy, 14,* 520–535.

Franzini, L. R. (2001). Humor in therapy: The case for training therapists in its uses and risks. *Journal of General Psychology, 128,* 170–193.

Freud, S. (1960). *Jokes and their relation to the unconscious.* New York: Norton.

Fuhr, M., Proyer, R. T., & Ruch, W. (2009). Assessing the fear of being laughed at (gelotophobia): First evaluation of the Danish GELOPH <15>. *Nordic Psychology, 61,* 62–73.

Goel, V., & Dolan, R. J. (2001). The functional anatomy of humor: Segregating cognitive and affective components. *Motivation and Emotion, 24,* 237–258.

Goldstein, J. H., & McGhee, P. E. (Eds.). (1972). *The psychology of humor.* New York: Academic Press.

Greig, J. Y. (1923). *The psychology of laughter and comedy.* New York: Dodd-Mead.

Gruner, R. (1978). *Understanding laughter: The workings of wit and humor.* Chicago, IL: Nelson-Hall.

Haig, R. A. (1986). Therapeutic uses of humor. *American Journal of Psychotherapy, 7,* 113–116.

Haig, R. A. (1988). *The anatomy of humor: Biopsychosocial and therapeutic perspectives.* Springfield, IL: Charles C Thomas.

Hobbes, T. (1968). *The Leviathan.* Harmondsworth, England: Penguin Books. (Originally published 1651)

Holland, N. N. (1982). *Laughing: A psychology of humor.* Ithaca, NY: Cornell University Press.

Hubble, M. A., Duncan, B. L., & Miller, S. D. (2001). *The heart and soul of change: What works in psychotherapy.* Washington, DC: American Psychological Association.

Kisner, B. (1994). The use of humor in the treatment of people with cancer. In E. S. Buckman (Ed.), *The handbook of humor: Clinical applications in psychotherapy* (pp. 133–154). Malabar, FL: Krieger Publications.

Kubie, L. S. (1971). The destructive potential of humor in psychotherapy. *American Journal of Psychotherapy, 127,* 861–866.

Kuhlman, T. L. (1984). *Humor and psychotherapy.* Homewood, IL: Dow Jones-Irwin.

Kuiper, N., & McHale, N. (2009). Humor styles as mediators between self-evaluative standards and psychological well-being. *Journal of Psychology: Interdisciplinary and Applied, 143,* 359–376.

Levinthal, C. F. (1988). *Messengers of paradise: Opiates and brain chemistry.* New York: Anchor Press.

Marcus, N. N. (1990). Treating those who fail to take themselves seriously: Pathological aspects of humor. *American Journal of Psychotherapy, 44,* 423–432.

Martin, R. (2007). *The psychology of humor: An integrative approach.* Burlington, MA: Elsevier Academic Press.

McCreadie, M., & Wiggins, S. (2009). Reconciling the good patient persona with problematic and non-problematic humor: A grounded theory. *International Journal of Nursing Studies, 46,* 1079–1091.

McGhee, P. E. (1979). *Humor: Its origin and development.* San Francisco, CA: Freeman Company.

McGhee, P. E., & Goldstein, J. H. (Eds.). (1983). *Handbook of humor research* (Vol. 1). New York:

Springer.

Miller, M. (2010). *University of Maryland School of Medicine study shows laughter helps blood vessels function better.* Retrieved March 1, 2010, from http://www.umm.edu/news/release/laughter2.html

Minden, P. (1994). Humor: A corrective emotional experience. In E. S. Buckman (Ed.), *The handbook of humor: Clinical applications in psychotherapy* (pp. 123–132). Malabar, FL: Krieger Publications.

Murstein, B., & Brust, R. (1985). Humor and interpersonal attraction. *Journal of Personality Assessment, 49,* 637–640.

Obrdlik, J. (1942). Gallows humor: A sociological phenomenon. *American Journal of Sociology, 47,* 709–716.

O'Connell, W. E. (1981). Natural high therapy. In R. Corsini (Ed.), *Innovative psychotherapies* (pp. 554–568). New York: Wiley.

Prerost, F. J. (1985). A procedure using imagery and humor in psychotherapy: Case application with longitudinal assessment. *Journal of Mental Imagery, 9,* 67–76.

Rogers, C. (1951). *Client-centered therapy.* New York: Houghton-Mifflin.

Rothbart, M. (1977). Psychological approaches to the study of humor. In A. Chapman & C. Foot (Eds.), *It's a funny thing, humor* (pp. 123–142). New York: Pergamon Press.

Salameh, W. A. (1987). Humor in integrative, short-term psychotherapy (ISTP). In W. F. Fry & W. A. Salameh (Eds.), *Handbook of humor and psychotherapy: Advances in the clinical use of humor* (pp. 195–240). Sarasota, FL: Professional Resource Exchange.

Saper, B. (1987). Humor in psychotherapy: Is it good or bad for the client? *Professional Psychology: Research and Practice, 18,* 360–367.

Strick, M., Holland, R., van Baaren, R. B., & van Knippenberg, A. (2009). Finding comfort in a joke: Consolatory effects of humor through cognitive distortion. *Emotion, 9,* 574–578.

Sultanoff, S. M. (2004). *What is humor?* Retrieved October 2, 2004, from http://aath.org/art_sultanoff01.html.

Tallmer, M., & Richman, J. (1994). Jokes psychoanalysts tell. In H. S. Strean (Ed.), *The use of humor in psychotherapy* (pp 179–188). Northvale, NJ: Aronson.

Zall, D. S. (1994). "Ya, get it?" Children, humor and psychotherapy. In E. S. Buckman (Ed.), *The handbook of humor: Clinical applications in psychotherapy* (pp. 25–40). Malabar, FL: Krieger Publications.

Zolnierek-Haskarl, K. B., Dimatteo, M. R., Mondala, M. M., Zhang, Z., Martin, L. R., & Messiha, A. H. (2009). Development and validation of the physician-patient humor rating scale. *Journal of Health Psychology, 14,* 1163–1173.

Zwerling, I. (1955). The favorite joke in diagnostic and therapeutic interviewing. *Psychoanalytic Quarterly, 24,* 104–114.

Section III

EXPANDING EMPLOYMENT OPPORTUNITIES FOR THE PROFESSIONAL MENTAL HEALTH COUNSELOR

Chapter 9

WORK SETTINGS FOR THE PROFESSIONAL COUNSELOR

ARTIS J. PALMO

Now, more than any other time in the 100-year history of counseling has the profession of counseling become such a major force in providing mental health services and consultation throughout all aspects of society. Forty years ago, you would find the vast majority of counselors working in school settings, with precious few employed in community clinics, hospitals, rehabilitation centers, or businesses. Today, in addition to educational settings, professional counselors can be found working in private practice, employee assistance programs, hospitals, outpatient clinics, criminal justice systems, and nursing homes. With the advent of licensure for the 50 states and insurance reimbursement for services offered, professional counselors are no longer limited in their choice of a career direction. According to the Bureau of Labor Statistics (2010), the field of counseling is expected to show continued growth over the next 10 years!

The purpose of this chapter is to review some of the available professional placements for counselors. The chapter discusses counseling careers in a variety of settings, including educational, medical, community mental health, business and industry, and private practice. Please keep in mind that the choice of a direction for a career in counseling is only limited by your individual imagination. Professional Counselors (PCs) have been able to actively and positively compete for mental health counseling positions with social workers, psychologists, and nurses. Because of increased academic demands in counselor education training programs and professional counselor licensure, the Professional Counselor/Mental Health Counselor (PC/MHC) has become much in demand by a variety of employers.

EDUCATIONAL SETTINGS

Elementary and Secondary Schools

Traditionally, counseling positions in elementary and secondary schools have been filled by certified school counselors. Most states require counselors involved in the school to be certified by the individual state's department of education. However, over the past 20 years, more and more special programs have been developed to meet the needs of problematic children and youth who may be at risk for not completing school, drug and alcohol problems, pregnancy, and a myriad of other concerns. To meet these "noneducational" needs of the students at risk, many states have taken aggressive steps to develop special programs to reduce the impact of poor home situations, criminal activity, and drug use on academics.

PCs have been employed by elementary and secondary schools to offer numerous services to special needs and at-risk students, including:

- Weekly counseling to assist students with identifying the issues that have been negatively affecting their ability to adjust to the pressures and demands of home, community, and school.
- Group counseling with children and adolescents to teach skills in socialization, appropriate school behavior, managing family difficulties, developing effective problem-solving skills, or combating negative thought processes that inhibit their productivity at school.
- Consultation with teachers, principals, guidance counselors, and other professionals involved with the child to increase the possibilities that the child can be successful in life.
- Crisis intervention services with children and adolescents who have difficulties meeting the behavioral expectations of the school, threaten suicide, become abusive to other students or are abused themselves, and any other severe behavioral concern affecting the educational functioning of the student.
- Consultation and family counseling with parents of at-risk students. Interventions can be direct counseling services to the student and family or referral to appropriate agencies and assistance to meet specific needs presented by the student.

Whereas school counselors' responsibilities have been to evaluate students' academic abilities, career interests, college selection, and general social development (Bureau of Labor Statistics, 2010), Licensed Professional Counselors (LPCs) have been employed to provide other critical services. An interesting example of the use of LPCs in the schools can be seen with the New Jersey Department of Human Services programs entitled School Based Youth Services begun in 1987. The Phillipsburg School Based Youth Services Program (New Jersey Department of Human Services, 1988) brochure states that the mission of the program "is to assure that teens are both physically and emotionally prepared to take full advantage of their educational opportunities and experiences. . . ."

The LPCs employed in the Phillipsburg School Based Youth Services Program (PSBYS) offer services in adolescent pregnancy prevention, employment, General Educational Development (GED) Testing, individual counseling, group counseling, support groups, and classroom instruction covering mental health issues. The PCs are seen as adjuncts to the school counselors and are expected to be able to provide a broader range of services, including therapy with individuals, families, and groups. The importance of the program to the school system has grown and the expectations have broadened (Horn, personal communication, January 10, 2010).

Colleges and Universities

PCs are employed in a number of major areas in colleges and universities. First, and most obvious, some colleges have an array of mental health professionals who work in the college counseling center, including PCs. The LPC in the college counseling center provides various services, including individual and group counseling, consultation/liaison with faculty, and advisement to various social groups on campus. Generally, the clients seeking services through the counseling center are self-referrals. In recent times, there has been a significant increase in the demand for counseling services through the college counseling centers, creating a situation where some colleges limit the number of visits a student can make for services during a semester. If the student has a significant psychological problem that would create too much of a demand for the time of the center staff, that individual is referred to an outside, private mental health professional or agency.

Both Benton, Robertson, Tseng, Newton, and Benton (2003) and Sharkin (2004) noted that the severity of client problems and the frequency of crises in the college population make it imperative that counseling center staff be highly trained to handle emergencies and referral. In some instances, the student demand for services through the college counseling center can no longer be met because of reduced budgets, reduced staff, and increased severity of student problems.

The second primary setting for PCs on college campuses is through the career and placement centers. Counselors in career centers offer such services as résumé preparation, interest and aptitude assessment, career counseling/advisement, and job placement. Frequently, the most active center on campus is the career placement center. It has been the experience of the editors that in many instances counselor training programs have not given trainees a thorough understanding of career development and vocational counseling. It is clear that the field of career development and vocational counseling is going to expand over the next 20 years (Bureau of Labor Statistics, 2010). As an aside, students in the field of counseling need to gain as much training and experience as possible in career and vocational counseling. Regardless of the setting, PCs are constantly faced with individuals in need of career assistance. Whether it is the recovering alcoholic, confused college student, or dissatisfied housewife, the LPC needs to be adequately skilled and knowledgeable to assist clients during career crises (see Chapter 7 for more information).

A third area where PCs have been utilized on campuses is through proactive drug and alcohol programs. Because addiction issues have become a high-profile problem on many campuses, there has been a more active attempt by college administrators to increase the availability of counseling and educational programming for students. From drug and alcohol (D & A) counseling through prevention programming, counselors have taken an active role in servicing students on campuses who have addiction issues.

Student Assistance Programming

PCs have taken a more active role in the development, operation, and evaluation of programs aimed at reducing the number of students at risk for academic failure, substance abuse problems, suicide, behavioral problems, and any other issue that inhibits normal development. In the 1980s, Pennsylvania (Pennsylvania Department of Education, 1987) began Student Assistance Programs (SAPs) throughout the schools to assist in identifying students who were having difficulty reaching normal developmental milestones because of "at-risk" behaviors. The success demonstrated by these programs has been the result of the use of multidisciplinary teams of professionals to assess, intervene, and refer students and families to appropriate individuals and groups who have the capacity to most effectively assist the student. PCs have been a major component of the SAP teams in the schools. These are exciting positions that promote the interaction of PCs with school personnel, community agencies, and the medical community.

SAPs have become a mainstay of the prevention programming in most schools because of the systematic approach utilized to identify at-risk students of all ages from K through 12. Referrals to the SAP can be made by anyone in the school system, including teachers, counselors, other students, or administrators. Every aspect of the program is handled in a confidential manner, and the students' well-being is the directing force behind all interventions.

MEDICAL SETTINGS

As noted by Seligman and Ceo (1996) and Snyder and Lopez (2002), the medical setting offers the professional counselor the opportunity to be a part of an exciting multidisciplinary treatment team. Treatment teams can include a wide variety of professionals, including physicians, nurses, physical and occupational therapists, dietitians, psychologists, and rehabilitation specialists of many kinds. In assessing the potential roles for the PC within the medical setting, the opportunities are limitless. As noted by Johnson and Radcliffe (2008), the field of mental health is replete with investigations that show the success of counseling interventions on the improvement of medically related problems. This section examines some of the roles performed by PCs in the medical setting.

Rehabilitation

One clear area of growth for counseling will be rehabilitation (Bureau of Labor Statistics, 2010). With the population continuing to age, the growth potential for counselors in the area of rehabilitation is outstanding. The rehabilitation counselor's role is to assist individuals in managing the effects of their disability on their personal, occupational, social, and psychological well-being. Rehabilitation counselors are specifically trained to evaluate the strengths and limitations of individuals, provide personal and occupational counseling, collect information on training programs, and assist with long-range life planning. The counselors who are involved in rehabilitation settings generally are Certified Rehabilitation Counselors (CRCs), a special designation for those counseling professionals who have completed graduate programs in rehabilitation counseling.

Hospice and Grief Counseling

One of the major shifts during the past 30 years has been the advent of hospice centers and hospice care. The growth of hospice care programs has been phenomenal and will continue to grow (Larson & Hoyt, 2007; Nydegger, 2008). PCs have had a tremendous impact on the growth of services for individuals and families dealing with crises, illness, and death. The role of the PC within hospice care is to assist the patient and his or her family during the time prior to death and those close to the patient after death. Counselors assist patients by having them deal with the issues of death and dying as well as aiding them in handling pragmatic issues such as living wills, financial concerns, family of origin issues, and much, much more. Most important, the PC gives the hospice patient the opportunity to deal with the end of their life with dignity and caring.

As the population ages, there will be more and more of a need for professionals who specialize in caring for seriously ill and dying patients. PCs have been active over the years in developing hospice/grief programs, and the future for growth in this exciting and challenging field is quite bright.

Eldercare

With the population rapidly aging, counselors who specialize in treatment, assessment, and consultation with the elderly are finding a wealth of opportunities for employment. From nursing homes to outpatient rehabilitation settings to in-home care, mental health counselors are finding a wealth of opportunities to work with the elderly as a part of a treatment team or as individual practitioners. The counselor who works with the elderly must possess certain important professional skills, including:

- Training in the assessment of the cognitive abilities and emotional status of the elderly patient.
- Ability to effectively interact and counsel with the older individual.
- Training and ability in grief and bereavement counseling.
- Knowledge of medical problems that can afflict the elderly and the effect of the medical problems and medications on the individual's daily functioning.
- Training and ability to offer family counseling to the extended families of the elderly patient.
- Extensive knowledge of the services and facilities that are available for treating and serving the elderly patient.
- Understanding of laws that may affect the treatment process for the elderly.
- Professionals' referral sources for the elderly patient and their family, including lawyers, medical doctors, financial advisors, insurance specialists, and community support services.

Treating the elderly is a wonderfully rewarding experience for the PC. Counseling an elderly patient through times of change in lifestyle can prove to be an enlightening and satisfying experience. There is much to be learned from the elderly, and having the opportunity to establish an intimate and warm relationship can lead the person to new levels of personal comfort in his or her life. Within the process of assisting the elderly, the PC is provided with a great deal of personal growth and professional satisfaction.

Other Related Health Fields

Besides the professional areas noted earlier, the Bureau of Labor Statistics (2010) cites several other areas of interest for counselors interested in working in the medical field. For example, one of the newer areas is genetic counseling, where the counselor assists individuals and families affected by birth defects or inherited conditions. Other PCs provide services to doctors and dentists treating highly anxious patients. At times, certain dental patients are so "dental phobic" that they are unable to receive the necessary treatment. Counselors with skills in relaxation training, hypnosis, or biofeedback can find many opportunities for employment within the medical field.

COMMUNITY MENTAL HEALTH

Within the general community, there are numerous groups, facilities, and associations offering services to residents. Community centers vary in their purpose and goals depending on the population they serve. There are numerous opportunities for employment for the professional counselor, including some of the following areas:

- Treating adults and children who are victims of abuse, including the elderly.
- Assessment and treatment of individuals suffering from addiction.
- Interviewing, assessing, and counseling couples and families in the process of adopting children.
- Adult treatment centers for the chronically mentally ill or the mentally retarded.
- Treatment centers for the aging and elderly.
- AIDS treatment and support services, as well as other specialized groups that offer counseling and support for an array of concerns and issues.
- Family and children community service centers that offer counseling, conflict resolution, and educational services for couples, families, and children.
- Employment counseling, placement, and testing service for individuals seeking to find work.

As you can see, there are numerous opportunities within most communities for counselors seeking employment. A perusal of the blue pages of any phone book will demonstrate the breadth of the opportunities available for PCs.

Criminal Justice System

According to the Bureau of Labor Statistics (2010), one of the areas of growth for counseling will be the treatment of adolescents and adults who have been incarcerated or are about to be incarcerated. More and more states have moved away from incarceration to the utilization of mental health treatment programs for individuals who are charged with drug and alcohol-related crimes as well as other less serious crimes. With the jails so overpopulated with individuals charged with drug offenses, there has been a significant move toward alternative treatment approaches rather than immediate incarceration. There are positions available with addiction centers established for the expressed purpose of treating the criminal population.

In addition to the formal addiction and crime treatment centers, counselors with a criminal justice background have been employed as probation officers, juvenile offender officers, and other positions within the criminal justice system. As noted, with the ever-expanding criminal population, a PC with the interest and skills for treating the prison population will always be able to find employment. It can be a demanding and stressful field for the PC, but a field that offers the opportunity for many personal rewards.

Private Practice

When discussing community mental health, one would be remiss to not mention private practice (see Chapter 10, for a complete description of private practice). With counselor licensure and insurance reimbursement a reality in most venues, the PC has the opportunity to work in his chosen field as an independent professional. Private practice is professionally and personally demanding; however, it is one of the most rewarding positions for a skilled professional practitioner.

BUSINESS AND INDUSTRY

Since the 1940s, counselors have made consistent progress in establishing themselves within business and industry (Shosh, 1996). According to Shosh, approximately 85% of the Fortune 500 companies offer Employee Assistance Programs (EAPs). EAPs are an outgrowth of the early counseling programs at the Hawthorne Plant of Western Electric in Chicago, Illinois, and the Prudential Insurance Company in Newark, New Jersey, in the 1940s. In addition, Alcoholics Anonymous (AA) became involved with business and industry in an attempt to help troubled, alcoholic workers prior to being terminated from their position. EAPs are a direct descendant of AA programs and the early employee research and interventions done at Western Electric and Prudential.

Although EAPs began as tools to assist impaired workers, primarily with alcohol problems, by the 1970s and 1980s, the program began to focus on a broader range of worker concerns. EAP counselors were trained in mental health assessment as well as worker performance enhancement. Shosh (1996) pointed out that the EAP counselor became the individual assigned to assist employees, supervisors, and managers in evaluating work performance and making determination regarding the most effective way to assist an individual to be a more productive employee. The emphasis on productivity has made the EAP an ideal approach for assisting companies in handling "problem" employees.

Within business and industry, the PC can perform numerous functions. Organizations expend tremendous amounts of time, energy, and resources during the hiring process. Therefore, whenever an employee has a difficulty, the organizations generally understand that it is more cost effective to keep an employee than replace an employee. With that idea in mind, counselors within business and industry perform a broad array of professional tasks, including:

- Direct counseling services to the employee for a plethora of issues, including job performance, job dissatisfaction, drug and alcohol problems, family concerns affecting work, retirement, and many other related concerns.
- Training and education seminars on a variety of topics to assist the employee with work, personal, and family functioning, all with the expressed purpose of making workers more satisfied with their present position.
- Consultation with supervisors, managers, other employees, and outside resources in an attempt to assist workers in becoming successful employees.
- Managing crises that occur at a work site that affect the mental health of the workers, such as workplace accidents or deaths, violence in the workplace, sexual harassment, and sudden workplace changes such as layoffs.

It is apparent from the prior list of functions that the counselor in business and industry has some exciting opportunities to be involved in a dynamic position. Although the focus of counseling in a business setting is making employees as productive as possible, the counselor has to have a wide range of skills and talents to meet the challenge. Frequently, the troubled employee is having difficulty with his or her personal life that then affects his or her productivity at work. Being able to assist an individual or a group of employees to manage their personal and professional life more effectively is both stimulating and challenging!

Counselors as Coaches

One of the rapidly growing areas of the counseling profession is being a personal coach. Although the skills and behaviors are similar to and sometimes indistinguishable from counseling, coaching has been an attempt to move away from licenses, insurance, and the stigma of counseling/therapy. Personal coaches advise individuals on decisions that they face in their personal and professional lives. They can do the advisement during face-to-face sessions or over the phone or via e-mail. Because a personal coach is not subject to professional licensing boards or professional associations, there is freedom from the restrictions that at times hamper licensed professionals.

The chapter author has a client who was recently released from his high-level position at a major company over artistic differences between himself and the new owners of the business. In addition to the typical items included in severance packages, such as one year of his present salary, insurance benefits, and stock options, he was given a set amount of money for hiring a personal coach. The coach was to advise him over the year regarding his future work, personals life issues, and anything that was affecting his progress toward a new position. According to Hart, Blattner, and Leipsic (2001), the coach's orientation is one of "prospective, focusing on goals, untapped potential, and critical success factors in a whole person"(p. 230). The coach worked on overlapping issues with my client's therapy, but the coach's focus was maximizing the fulfillment of his life goals and work.

For more information on coaching as a career choice, review some of the readings listed in the reference section of this chapter (Berglas, 2002; Diedrich & Kilburg, 2001; Hart, Blattner, & Leipsic, 2001; Hudson, 1999; Kilburg, 1996a, 1996b).

SUMMARY

One of the most important considerations to be made by graduate students when beginning a graduate program in counseling is the direction they would like to take with their career once their program is completed. From their first courses in professional counseling, graduate students need to be making plans for their future in the profession. The selection of appropriate graduate courses is paramount. Being exposed to a broad array of counseling coursework enables budding PCs to determine the direction of their career.

By taking courses in family counseling, couples counseling, children, adolescents, addictions, elderly, and rehabilitation, graduate students determine not only what they like about the profession but also what they do not care to do with their career. Not everyone in the profession is able to work with couples, facilitate groups, or do play therapy. However, the best way to determine whether you are able to adequately counsel children or couples is to be exposed to these modalities during training. Try to enroll in a broad array of courses in order to be exposed to as many aspects of the profession as possible.

Finally, there is nothing as important as practicum and internship experiences during graduate training. Being directly exposed to the treatment process, where a variety of modalities are utilized to assist individuals, couples, families, and groups with their mental health concerns, is the best way to determine your skills, interests, and abilities in the field of counseling. The students who gain the most from their training programs are the ones who take every opportunity to expose themselves to various professional and learning situations. To make the most of your graduate training, experience all that you can in your formal coursework, practica, internships, and volunteer placements. Keep an open mind to new experiences because you may find that you have effective skills and talents to serve a wide variety of client populations.

REFERENCES

Benton, S. A., Robertson, J. M., Tseng, W. C., Newton, F. B., & Benton, S. L. (2003). Changes in counseling center client problems across 13 years. *Professional Psychology: Research and Practice, 34,* 66–72.

Berglas, S. (2002, June). The very real dangers of executive coaching. *The Harvard Business Review,* pp. 87–92.

Bureau of Labor Statistics. (2010). U.S. Department of Labor. *Occupational Outlook Handbook, 2004-05 Edition.* Counselors. Retrieve May 29, 2004, from http://www.bis.gov./oco /ocos067.htm

Diedrich, R. C., & Kilburg, R. R. (2001). Foreword: Further consideration of executive coaching as an emerging competency. *Consulting Psychology Journal: Practice and Research, 53,* 203–204.

Hart, V., Blattner, J., & Leipsic, S. (2001). Coaching versus therapy: A perspective. *Consulting Psychology Journal: Practice and Research, 53,* 229–237.

Hudson, F. M. (1999). *The handbook of coaching.* San Francisco: Jossey-Bass.

Johnson, N. B., & Radcliffe, A. M. (2008). The increasing role of psychology health research and interventions and a vision of the future. *Professional Psychology: Research and Practice, 39,* 652–657.

Kilburg, R. (1996a). Executive coaching as an emerging competency in the practice of consulting. *Consulting Psychology Journal: Practice and Research, 48,* 59–60.

Kilburg, R. (1996b). Toward a conceptual understanding and definition of executive coaching.

Consulting Psychology Journal: Practice and Research, 48, 134–144.

Larson, D. G., & Hoyt, W. T. (2007). What has become of grief counseling? An evaluation of the empirical foundations of the new pessimism. *Professional Psychology: Research and Practice, 38,* 347–355.

New Jersey Department of Human Services. (1988). *Phillipsburg school based youth services program.* Phillipsburg, NJ: Author.

Nydegger, R. (2008). Psychologists and hospice: Where we are and where we can be. *Professional Psychologist: Research and Practice, 39,* 339–363.

Pennsylvania Department of Education. (1987). *Achieving success with more students: Addressing the problem of students at risk, K–12.* Harrisburg, PA: Author.

Seligman, L., & Ceo, M. N. (1996). Multidisciplinary mental health treatment teams. In W. J. Weikel & A. J. Palmo (Eds.), *Foundations of mental health counseling* (2nd ed., pp. 163-182). Springfield, IL: Charles C Thomas.

Sharkin, B. S. (2004). Assessing changes in categories but not severity of counseling center clients' problems across 13 years: Comment on Benton, Robertson, Tseng, Newton, & Benton (2003). *Professional Psychology: Research and Practice, 35,* 313–315.

Shosh, M. (1996). Counseling in business and industry. In W. J. Weikel & A. J. Palmo (Eds.), *Foundations of mental health counseling* (2nd ed., pp. 232-241). Springfield, Il: Charles C Thomas.

Snyder, C. R., & Lopez, S. J. (2002). *Handbook of positive psychology.* New York: Oxford University Press.

Chapter 10

COUNSELORS IN PRIVATE PRACTICE

ARTIS J. PALMO AND LINDA A. PALMO

As the mental health field continues to grow and change, private practice has become more and more the occupational choice for many Professional Counselors (PCs). Palmo, Shosh, and Weikel (2001) reported that large groups of counselors have chosen private practice. The generic definition of private practice is seen as providing direct mental health services to the general public for a fee. There are problems with this simplistic definition. First, "What are the direct mental health services provided to the public?" Second, "How are these mental health services rendered to the public?" The purpose of this chapter is to discuss:

(1) the broad array of services that actually comprise private practice;
(2) pragmatic issues in delivering services to the public;
(3) the advantages and disadvantages of private practice;
(4) financial concerns and reimbursement; and
(5) professional issues related to the operation of a successful and ethical private practice.

IMPORTANT CHARACTERISTICS OF THE PRIVATE PRACTITIONER

As in all career choices, the first step in determining whether private practice is appropriate for the PC is to take time to reflect on the personal characteristics desired for a successful private practitioner. After assessing the successful practitioner's personal characteristics, the PC then compares those desired characteristics with his or her own personal characteristics as a counselor. An accurate understanding of the personal and professional demands of the private practice work setting is essential for the potential success of a counselor in this career area.

First, a strong commitment to the choice of private practice is the most important aspect of operating a successful mental health counseling practice. Regardless of whether the PC decides to enter full-time or part-time practice, he or she must be willing to devote significant time and energy to the initiation and development of the practice. When trying to determine the amount of time needed to devote to a private practice, the "rule of thumb" from our experience is that for every hour you spend with a client, you will spend another additional hour managing varying aspects related to the case. For example, you may need to complete case notes, have a phone consult with the client's physician, or complete the billing requirements in order to be reimbursed. In addition to direct services to the client, the business of private practice requires marketing, program development, and courting insurance companies and managed care organizations (MCOs).

If you desire to carry a weekly caseload of 10 clients, you will most likely spend 20 hours per week in private practice. If you desire to carry a weekly caseload of 25 clients per week, you may spend up to 50 hours per week! The time demands placed on the neophyte private practitioner can be overwhelming and, in some instances, devastating. It has been the authors' experience that many professionals choose private practice without fully understanding the commitment needed to succeed. Therefore, before entering private practice, the PC must be realistic about the time and energy commitment that accompanies the establishment of a private practice.

Second, one of the most important personal characteristics for the private practitioner is the ability to develop a structure and boundaries for his or her practice. The private practitioner must discard myths such as "You can make your own hours," "You don't have to answer to anyone," and "You can be your own boss." Certainly these myths have some semblance of reality. However, in truth, the private practitioner must develop an organized system for the delivery of client services, including set hours, answering to client demands, managing ethical dilemmas, and struggling to maintain an appropriate balance between work time and personal time. Although there may be no administrative superior to dictate hours, vacation, or meetings, the successful private practitioner may work harder with longer hours than those required by an agency or institutional setting.

Finally, the PC desiring to enter private practice needs a high level of competence, patience, and self-confidence. Unlike other salaried positions in the field of mental health, the financial stability of the private practice practitioner is directly related to the number of clients seen each week. If your practice is located in the Northeast and is budgeted on the basis of serving

25 clients per week, and you are faced with winter storms in January and February that reduce your caseload to 12 clients per week, what do you do to overcome the devastating financial losses? Also, clients are constantly evaluating your ability to help them reach their goals. If they are not satisfied, they will leave your practice, challenging your level of self-confidence and competence. With this example, the importance of patience and self-confidence becomes obvious.

Potential private practitioners must be confident in their own abilities to effectively serve the public through their counseling and consultation skills while having the patience to develop an effective referral base in the community. Keep in mind that the hours away from direct counseling services are extremely important to the practice's growth. The PC must also have the confidence and patience to believe he or she will recover from the snags and setbacks he or she may encounter in private practice. Although private practice can eliminate administrative superiors, it increases the professional's dependency on the general public as consumers of services. Beginning a private practice is a professionally challenging task as well as a financially frightening proposition. To overcome the challenges involved, the PC must have the patience, flexibility, competence, and self-confidence to withstand the pressures and demands of private practice.

COMPONENTS OF PRIVATE PRACTICE

The mental health services provided by private practitioners can be as individually unique as the private practitioner. As PCs develop practice goals, they need to consider four general components of private practice: (a) counseling services, (b) consultation services, (c) supervision, and (d) community involvement. Each PC needs to integrate these components and define the general and specific areas of practice that are of most interest and meet the professional's level of ability.

COUNSELING SERVICES

Counseling services are the basic component to any private practice. Regardless of the services provided in a varied practice, counseling usually is the primary focus of the activities and the skill that generates the most consistent revenue in the practice. The counselor can offer individual, group, family, and/or marriage counseling depending on his or her training and experience. It is possible to specialize in unique services such as career counseling, adolescent or child counseling, rehabilitation counseling, or drug and alcohol counseling. But as mentioned earlier, a broad array of counseling skills is needed to keep the practice functioning in addition to a specialty area focus.

The key to providing counseling services is to know one's own counseling specialties/skills and to recognize the potential needs of the population to be served. First, a private practitioner may gain expertise in a counseling specialty by academic or experiential training. In either case, it is the responsibility of the counselor to recognize and develop the counseling services he or she can offer as a private practitioner as well as market these specialties to potential consumers. Second, surveying the community needs prior to establishing a practice is a must for the aspiring private practitioner. Talk about your plans with ministers, social agencies, school counselors, private practitioners, medical doctors, and employers before beginning the practice in order to gain some insight into the needs of community.

Third, the counselor needs to be realistic about whether or not there is a sufficient client base to support a practice in his or her areas of interest/expertise or whether the interest/expertise areas will need to be expanded. For example, one PC wanted to have a practice that specialized in eating disorders of women, a specialty the counselor had developed while working at an in-patient hospital setting for eating disorders. However, the counselor quickly learned that maintaining these clients in an outpatient setting was much more difficult than in the hospital setting. For this particular professional, a rethinking about practice goals and professional skills was in order. Professional development of a variety of treatment modalities and counseling specialties is a key to success in private practice. The specialty area is only one part of the counselor's practice, but maintaining a broad variety of clientele will maintain the practice.

CONSULTATION SERVICES

A second major component of private practice services is consultation. There are typically two types of consultation services that can be incorporated into a private practice: (a) unpaid consultation with professionals from other types of mental health settings, and (b) paid consultation with other groups, agencies, businesses, or institutions. In the first type of consultation, the PC is seeking further information by a free exchange of data and impressions with other professionals involved with one of the practitioner's clients. Of course, this exchange is always done with the appropriate releases of information. The consultation process is a important aspect of a successful practice because the process links the PC with a broad range of other professionals who may be able to offer services for your clientele and vice versa. The sustenance of a growing private practice depends partially on the ability of the professional to benefit from interaction with others in the mental health community.

The second type of consultation, establishing paid consultative relationships with other organizations that desire and need your expertise, can offer some exciting and fulfilling alternatives for the PC in private practice. Specific consulting relationships can be developed with schools, agencies, industries, hospitals, or other professionals needing your services. For example, one PC was hired as a counseling consultant to offer individual and group counseling for students at a small private school. The school could not afford to hire a full-time counselor, so the PC was hired to do 12 hours of counseling per week. Another counselor was hired to offer parenting classes at a community center for parents desiring assistance with handling prekindergarten children. One private practitioner, with a specialty in the elderly, was hired to offer group counseling at a nursing home. These examples are but a few of the multitude of consulting opportunities available to the ambitious and creative professional in private practice.

In addition to the areas mentioned, employee assistance programs (EAPs) utilize aspects of both counseling and consultation. As noted in Chapter 9, "Work Settings for the Professional Counselor," EAPs are expanding, offering professional counselors an exciting employment opportunity. Importantly, EAPs can be a crucial aspect of a private practice if the practitioner effectively markets the services needed by business and industry.

Bethlehem Counseling Associates, P.C. (BCA), the authors' private practice, provides EAP services in several different programs. First, the practice has a capitated contract with a company located in the area to provide EAP services for all employees. With the capitated contract, BCA is paid a predetermined fee (e.g., $24.00 per employee per year) for each employee and is contracted to service all employees as often as needed. Typically, BCA services between 6% and 10% of the employees per year. Second, BCA is a representative for numerous national and international EAP companies (NEAS, Dorris, Lytle) servicing large corporations throughout the country and the world. In this instance, BCA provides the EAP services for employees working at local plants or businesses in the area. Finally, BCA has contracts with various managed care organizations (MCOs) to provide EAP services for their subscribers. Being active in providing EAP services has given the professionals in the private practice new opportunities to market other counseling, consultation, and psychoeducational programs to the companies and their employees. The exposure gained with the EAP services has significantly increased the client referrals to the practice.

SUPERVISION

A third component to private practice is supervision. Being able to give and receive supervision can enhance the viability of a practice. Supervision is a means for every professional mental health care provider to increase their expertise as well as earn additional credentials for providing specific services in the mental health field. In addition, no matter what level of training has been reached, every professional counselor needs a clearly defined system of checks and balances. Therefore, seeking the clinical advice and direction of another professional regarding certain cases being carried in the practice is a necessity on an ethical, a professional, and a personal level.

Supervision can play a major role in private practice for a PC in a number of ways. One, the demands placed on private practitioners by professional boards, insurance carriers, and MCOs dictate the need for supervision between and among professionals. In our offices, a group of 17 mental health professionals from various fields meet in peer supervision groups and one-on-one supervision to discuss cases and review treatment plans. In this way, each of us is meeting our own professional needs as well as meeting the requirements of our certificates and/or licenses. Another form of peer group supervision done by solo practitioners has been to form a group among solo practitioners from one geographical area. This has worked for many of our own professional acquaintances.

The second form of supervision within a private practice can be the supervision by a PC of another counselor's work for financial remuneration. Most newly degreed counselors are required to have professional supervision of their caseload to be licensed to practice independently. Also, if a PC has a specialized area of expertise, he or she may be able to market this expertise to others in supervision groups or individual supervision. The sharing of professional techniques and insights is rewarding and expands the domain of private practice to a broader definition of mental health services. Supervision can be professionally stimulating, an opportunity to meet with others, and a way to avoid professional isolation within the practice.

A final note on structured supervision within a private practice needs to be mentioned. Most MCOs require LPCs to be licensed for two or three years before they are accepted on the MCO panel as providers. However, at BCA, we were able to have our newly licensed employees and independent contractors accepted on MCO panels because we have a structured individual and group supervision program for EVERY professional in the practice. Every professional meets individually and in a group for case presentations and discussions. When BCA presented this information to the provider relations departments of several MCOs, they were more than willing to offer panel memberships to LPCs, MSWs, and psychologists who did not meet the two- to three-year postlicensure requirements.

The important message about supervision is quite simple–every professional mental health care provider needs ongoing individual and group supervision to be an effective and ethical practitioner.

COMMUNITY INVOLVEMENT

The final component of the private practice services is community involvement and public relations. Because the general public is the consumer of mental health services, the private practitioner will benefit from developing a visible and definitive image within the community. Community involvement can sometimes mean delivering free services for local groups and organizations, such as the PTA, Diabetes Support Group, Singles Group at the local church, or a bereavement seminar. There is a great benefit gained from taking the opportunity to present and educate the public to the necessity and importance of mental health services. In short, the community service and public relations work done by counselors on a voluntary basis will promote respect for each individual counselor and the mental health field in general, as well as develop a broad-based referral network.

Community service is an important professional component and obligation for all PCs, whether in private practice or another setting. To meet the requirements of the professional code of ethics and the definition of a profession as outlined in Chapter 3, professional counselors should devote some part of their professional life to giving something back to the community. Although this is at times a difficult task for the private practitioner, community service is a necessity for all practitioners.

In summary, the four general components to private practice services can be individually organized and translated by each PC. It is obvious that part of the autonomy of private practice is the individual's choice of services to be offered. A private practitioner can simply offer counseling services or broaden his or her scope to incorporate a variety of mental health services. The definition of private practice need only be limited by the skills and confidence of the professional. But one of the fears that may inhibit a PC from developing a private practice is the "fear of being in business." The pragmatics of a private practice can be handled as effectively as any other life problem. Simply pinpoint the issues to be faced in a privately owned business and begin to make choices. Viewing the pragmatics of private practice as business choices diffuses anxiety and enhances the freedom to change directions as one's career develops.

PRIVATE PRACTICE WORK SETTINGS

There are three different private practice work styles for PCs: incorporated groups, expense sharing groups, and sole proprietors. Each private practice style has unique characteristics that can meet the particular needs of any PC. The choice of a particular type of work setting can depend on personal goals, professional goals, and/or simply taking advantage of an opportunity.

In contrasting the incorporated groups, expense sharing groups, and sole proprietors, the differences focus on the structure of the private practice. Incorporated groups may include a diverse group of mental health providers such as psychologists, psychiatrists, social workers, and PCs or simply a group of PCs. More than likely in today's mental health market, the incorporated group is a broadly defined group of mental health professionals rather than a singular professional group. The group is bound by a legal document that makes each group member a legal partner in the business. The nature of the legal document creates a dependency between partners for the success or failure of the business. All moneys earned are given to the corporation. Each partner earns a weekly or monthly "draw" (salary) depending on his or her contribution of time, status, or initial investment. The legal document also clearly defines the procedures for leaving the business. Leaving a practice, moving a practice, or incorporating a practice can be a challenging event. Each practitioner needs to be familiar with the regulations and requirements of making major changes in a private practice. Some suggested readings are provided in the reference section of this chapter (Hall & Boucher, 2003; Jonason, DeMers, Vaughn, & Reaves, 2003; Kim & VandeCreek, 2003; Koocher, 2003; Manosevitz & Hays, 2003; McGee, 2003; Stout, Levant, Reed, & Murphy, 2001).

BCA is a professional corporation owned and operated by the authors. We have had a group private practice since 1985, and we incorporated in 1997. Our initial goal was to develop a group practice where experienced mental health professionals worked directly with new clinicians seeking supervision and an introduction into private practice. This arrangement worked quite well until shifts occurred with client insurance coverage. At first, licensed psychologists were permitted to sign for supervisees (submitted for insurance reimbursement), but that changed around the mid-1990s with the advent of MCOs. Shortly after the initiation of MCO contracts, every practitioner was required to be licensed and an approved provider on the MCO's panel.

Shortly after the shift to MCOs occurred, we incorporated BCA. The practice was expanded to include 15 additional independent contractors, including LPCs, LCSWs, and psychologists. The independent contractors varied in the amount of time they were available to the practice, with some doing two evenings a week to others doing four days and two evenings a week. Each of the contractors sought to be involved with BCA because of the structure and operation of the group–central billing services, consistent referrals, supervision, and rotating coverage for weekends and holidays. The key component for the individuals in the group is the number of referrals that are available to keep their caseload completely full. BCA pulls referrals from the community in general but also from the insurance companies and MCOs, where we are listed as a preferred provider group. All of our contractors are licensed and approved providers on most every panel at BCA.

In expense sharing groups, there may also be a diverse group of mental health professionals or simply a group of PCs, but there is no legal document that binds the group together as a corporation. Each individual makes his or her own salary and functions as a sole proprietor, but the group shares office expenses or consulting fees for other professionals. Within this structure, the group may eventually become incorporated or an individual may leave and develop his or her own private practice as a sole proprietor. The expense sharing groups usually have contracts (Stout, Levant, Reed, & Murphy, 2001) defining the specific financial and business responsibilities each professional shares as part of the group. In this way, there are no misunderstandings of each professional's responsibilities to the group.

Finally, sole proprietors usually work alone in their private practice and develop consulting relationships with other mental health providers. Although the colleagues of a sole proprietorship are not physically present in the office, the sole proprietor is dependent on a network of mental health providers within the community. Sole proprietors earn their own salary and pay their own expenses. One of the interesting transitions that has taken place over the past few years has been the development of mental health groups comprised of sole proprietors who have chosen to function as a group for generating and maintaining clients but not losing their autonomy or having to leave their individual offices. These groups are sometimes referred to as "groups without walls" (*Psychotherapy Finances,* Ed. John Klein, Ridgewood Financial Institute, Inc., 1425 U.S. Highway 1, Ste. 286, Juno Beach, FL 33408). Changes in managed care and preferred provider networks have forced private practitioners to examine new and creative professional arrangements to survive in the field of mental health.

As the PC considers the possibility of establishing a private practice, a complete knowledge of various business and professional relationships is a necessity. Therefore, the authors suggest that the reader attend various workshops sponsored by the American Counseling Association, the American Mental Health Counselors Association, or any local affiliate associations. In addition, there have been books published by both organizations that speak to the establishment of a private practice. Read as much as you can, talk to other professionals in private practice, and seek the advice of professional financial advisors.

Remember, the initiation of a private practice can be a frightening undertaking; therefore, seek as much advice as possible. In addition, private practice is a relatively new career for the majority of PCs. A review of the past 30 years of the *ACA Journal* will show that the articles related directly to private practice began to appear on a regular basis during the past 20 years. For PCs, they will need to have much patience and self-confidence as they approach the building of a private practice and not lose focus on the importance of personal integrity for themselves or their clients.

NETWORKING WITHIN MENTAL HEALTH

The "aloneness" factor can be a major surprise for the PC in private practice. If one's previous work setting was an agency or educational setting, the lack of continuous daily contact with other professional colleagues can change solitude to loneliness. Although there are no distractions, there is also no immediate outlet for the intense demands of continuous counseling cases. If a PC chooses to work as a sole proprietor in private practice, it is important to recognize the need for professional associations and outlets through local, state, and national counseling organizations. The purpose of establishing a professional network of mental health colleagues is to continue personal growth, avoid professional loneliness, and limit professional burnout.

The concept of working in a group setting of PCs has several distinct advantages. First, several PCs working in a group can offer support and encouragement to each other. The group can also provide opportunities for professional growth through discussion of cases and assisting with difficult cases (i.e., co-therapy or psychological evaluation). The ability to conceptualize professional cases and improve counseling skills can only come with continued discussion of cases with other professionals.

Second, PCs can join a group with other mental health providers who have complementary skills. For example, within a group of three PCs, one may have a specialty in child counseling, one in marriage counseling, and the third in vocational assessments. By joining together in private practice, they can offer a broader range of services to the public as well as learn from each other's area of expertise.

Third, the PC in private practice is dependent on other mental health providers for consultation and referral. It is advantageous to be able to offer a range of mental health services within one private practice setting. For example, a private practice may consist of a psychiatrist, PC, and psychologist. If the PC has a client in need of a psychiatric or psychological evaluation, this can be completed within the group practice. Without the resources of these colleagues within the practice, the PC would have to refer the client to other agencies or individuals to attain these specialized services. In addition to the consulting role of the psychiatrist and psychologist, they can also serve as a referral source for the PC and vice versa.

Although there are several advantages to working in a group setting, there is also a risk involved. The association with colleagues within a group practice can have legal and financial ramifications. Being business partners or simply business associates calls for a high level of trust. Before entering or initiating a group practice, an attorney and accountant should clarify the legal and financial responsibilities of each group member. In this way, later misunderstandings can be avoided. Having a well-written document outlining the association among practitioners is a must.

One final note about networking needs to be made. Whether you become involved in a formal group practice or group without walls, it is important for the individuals to set specific times and days for meetings, consultations, and/or supervision. Frequently, colleagues in the same office only have contact between counseling sessions or on a haphazard basis, leaving many decisions to hurried moments in between appointments. Professionals dedicated to networking have to commit to setting aside time for meetings, supervisions, and general conversation.

PRAGMATIC NEEDS OF THE PRIVATE PRACTITIONER

Beginning a Private Practice

Relatively few essential items are needed to initiate a private practice office. Unlike other professions, such as dentistry, the PC may need to make a relatively small financial investment in acquiring the supplies and services necessary to initiate a practice. The essentials for the PC in practice are office space, office equipment, computer, phone service, answering service/machine, FAX, office supplies, and liability insurance.

The PC has two choices in selecting appropriate office space: renting or purchasing a professional setting. Most neophyte private practitioners choose to begin practice on a part-time basis and consequently rent office space. In a part-time practice, it is most efficient to rent office space for the time it will be used. If the part-time practitioner chooses to rent office space from an established mental health provider, the benefits can be numerous. The PC can gain not only office space, but also the use of office equipment, established phone service, and the professional "mentoring" of the more established mental health provider. Renting office space from an established practitioner is also applicable for a PC entering private practice on a full-time basis. Some practitioners we know have actually rented space in physicians' offices or with a group of attorneys.

The other approach for selecting office space in private practice is to purchase an office building or office space. This can be accomplished by an individual or group of professionals. There are several important considerations in determining whether to rent or purchase office space that need to be discussed. First, what are the financial resources available to the PC? Private practice is a business, and success is dependent on income being greater than expenses. A PC needs to determine how much he or she is willing to spend for office space and then decide whether to buy. Second, what are the short- and long-term professional goals of the PC? Some PCs have no desire for a full-time private practice, whereas others begin part time with an expressed desire to become full time. Professional goals are imperative in determining the financial investment in acquiring office space. Third, what professional mental health support systems can be facilitated in this office space? Some PCs may desire to work with the mentoring of an established practitioner, whereas others desire more autonomy. The location of office space makes a statement about the PC's professional identity in the mental health community and with individual clients. By identifying the PC's individual needs, the choices regarding office location and the option to rent or purchase office space can become quite clear.

Finally, many neophyte practitioners are tempted to establish a private practice within their homes to reduce financial expenses. It takes great self-control to maintain the home as a personal part of the PC's life when the private practice demands professional time in the home. The ramifications of practice in the home impact on every member of the PC's family. The PC must consider the many types of clients he or she will serve and question, "Would I want these individuals to know where I live and have access to my personal home?" The disadvantages of establishing office space in a home are the increase in the feelings of being "trapped" by the practice, the additional feelings of "loneliness" from the mental health community, and the decreased ability to set professional "boundaries" with clients. These disadvantages need careful consideration before selecting this approach to private practice.

Depending on the approach to securing office space, a PC may need to make decisions about acquiring office equipment and phone/communication systems. In the beginning, a less sophisticated office may be necessary, but as the practice grows, the needs can change drastically. The usual needs for a private practitioner include a desk, several chairs and/or a sofa, pictures, tables, lamps, and framed diplomas/certificates. This equipment can also be rented or purchased depending on financial resources and professional goals. Office supply stores or furniture outlets can assist the neophyte in cutting costs. In acquiring office equipment, the PC should strive for professionalism and comfort. The ambience of the office will set the tone for the client-counselor relationship. The office equipment reflects the PC's identity as a professional. It is important for the PC to be comfortable within the setting he or she creates, as well as creating a comfortable environment for the clients.

One of the most important pieces of equipment a PC will purchase is the phone and the answering services to accompany the phone. The authors suggest the practitioner secure a professional answering service to handle crises and emergencies, along with an answering machine to manage day-to-day questions and client scheduling changes. An automated answering service/system can be effective in handling office questions, such as whether the counselor's office is going to be open if there is a snow storm. Be aware that the initial investment in a phone and answering system is high, but they are real necessities for a smoothly functioning office.

When using an answering machine, the practitioner has to be sure that clients having an emergency receive the appropriate attention. Some of our professional colleagues leave a message on their answering machines for clients indicating one or all of the following: "If this is an emergency and I cannot be reached: (a) call my associate Mr. Frank B. at 555-5555; (b) call Crisis Intervention at 555-5555 for immediate assistance; and/or (c) go to the nearest emergency room at the hospital." It is important that the client have an avenue for receiving assistance in case of a crisis; therefore, the answering system needs to provide as much information and help as possible.

Office supplies are the necessary materials to be utilized on a day-to-day basis in the office. These materials include: professional cards and stationery, files for record-keeping, intake forms for clients, receipts for services rendered, and any other materials needed in a professional office. These types of materials are a necessity for public relations, billings, and keeping information in appropriate forms at the office. As a beginning, the practitioner should have business cards, stationery, and envelopes, intake forms, file folders, and billing forms. Office supplies are an absolute necessity for the business and professional demands of a private practice. An effective office software package for the computer can make the day-to-day operation of the practice much easier. Client and counselor schedules, record keeping, billing, and general statistics regarding the practice are much easier to maintain with an effective computer software package.

As part of today's legalistic society, the PC must secure professional liability insurance for his or her professional security and employment. Liability insurance not only protects against the possibility of errors of commission or omission but also is a requirement of many preferred provider and managed care groups that will seek your business. Information regarding various types of liability insurance can be obtained from either ACA or APA. In addition, depending on whether the office is in the PC's home or another building, the PC should be sure he or she is covered for any accidental injuries that could occur on the premises, such as someone falling and hurting him or herself. Because the office eventually becomes a large investment, insurance coverage is necessary to protect against loss of furniture, equipment, and other office materials.

Finally, the amount of money needed to initiate a private practice can vary greatly depending on the needs and desires of the individual PC. Some professionals begin with a significant amount of financial backing, (e.g., $10,000), while others begin with only several hundred dollars. The PC must decide how much of a financial risk he or she is willing to take in investing in the pragmatics of initiating a private practice. Financial expenses range from renting office space and equipment to purchasing an office building and equipment. Determining the amount of money to be spent can only be done after a clear set of professional goals has been written. Success is dictated by the professionalism of the PC, not the financial resources available to the PC. Private practitioners are in business to provide services to the general public. The office atmosphere is the "icing on the cake."

Attorney and Accountant

Over the tenure of a private practice, the two most important professional advisors for the practitioner (in addition to colleagues) are an effective attorney and an accountant. As early as possible, the practitioner needs to secure the services of both. Being in private practice means being in business, and it is the PC's responsibility to protect his or her professional interests, both legally and financially. Private practice is not only doing cases, but also the operation of a business, hopefully, a successful business.

An attorney can serve important roles for the PC. As professionals, PCs are susceptible to the demands of consumers; therefore, to be an effective professional, the PC must be able to determine what is best for consumers within the ethical guidelines of mental health counseling. Frequently, the process of determining what is best for the client/consumer involves the interpretation of legal as well as ethical guidelines. Having an effective attorney who is familiar with mental health laws will provide the PC with the security to provide services that meet the highest ethical standards as well as ethical guidelines. Having an effective attorney will provide the PC with the security to provide services that meet the highest ethical standards as well as meeting legal necessities. With the initiation of Health Insurance Portability and Accountability Act (HIPAA) regulations in 2004, it is more important than ever to have a legal advisor available to assist with difficult questions regarding confidentiality of treatment records. See the suggested readings sections at the end of the chapter for some resources regarding the impact of HIPAA regulations.

In addition, the attorney can provide the necessary advice, determine guidelines, and produce legal documents for the business aspects of the practice. It is necessary to have written agreements before entering any cooperative arrangements with other professionals. To do this most efficaciously, the PC should enroll the services of an attorney.

Finally, with the tremendous growth in family law caused by the increase in divorce and disintegration of the family, attorneys have sought the counseling services of PCs to handle the resulting personal problems faced by their clients. More and more, a strong relationship between attorneys and counselors is developing because of the needs of children and divorcing adults. Maintaining an effective consultative relationship with an attorney(s) is an important aspect of private practice for counseling professionals. From providing child custody evaluations to handling divorce mediation/counseling to counseling abused spouses, the PC will find that full involvement with the legal community is an important aspect of the practice.

Regarding the financial protection of the business, the PC will need to purchase the services of an accountant. The accountant/business advisor can assist the practitioner in business arrangements with other professionals or agencies, develop an effective accounting/billing system for the practice, handle the paperwork required by the Internal Revenue Service (IRS), provide advisement for financial investments, determine retirement plans, and on and on. Because most PCs do not have a business and finance background, securing the services of a financial advisor is a necessity.

In addition to financial advisement, the accountant can assist the PC in determining realistic business goals for each upcoming year. For example, the accountant can assist the PC in determining an appropriate goal for amount of income to be earned in the coming year. Projecting income on a yearly basis assists in the planning of future activities of the practice. The projections can help determine the amount of time to spend with direct counseling services to clients versus consultation versus other professional activities.

If a PC does not have ready access to an accountant or the financial resources to secure such services, local banking institutions employ advisors that can be of tremendous assistance. The bank can provide similar types of advisements regarding investments and future financial planning. The new private practitioner must quickly realize that the practice is a business and take the necessary steps to protect and enhance the business components. As the IRS states, if a business does not make money in three years, it becomes a hobby. An accountant or a financial advisor assists the PC to develop a business rather than a hobby.

Complications

Finally, to understand more completely the necessity for maintaining professional contacts (networking) with other mental health professionals, an attorney, and a business advisor, a brief case study is presented to demonstrate the types of problems that can arise in a practice that necessitates the securing of advice from allied professionals:

> A PC in private practice was faced with a clear-cut case of child abuse. As a result, the parents of the child were reported to the county office of child abuse. The problems that arose for the PC as a result of the case were numerous. First, shortly after reporting the abuse, the parents withdrew from the counseling, but the child wanted to remain in counseling with the PC. Second, the parents had their attorney file papers against the PC for reporting the abuse. Third, the county children's services demanded significant amounts of time from the practitioner in order to appropriately pursue the abuse charges and provide services for the family. Fourth, the family was referred to another counselor suggested by the agency, but the child refused to attend.

There is obviously much more to this case than is presented in one paragraph, but the brief description of the difficulties provides the necessary information to demonstrate the need for assistance from other professionals. In cases such as this, the private practitioner needed advice regarding the best possible ethical, legal, and financial avenues to follow. The PC utilized two other counseling professionals for advice in addition to consults with the children's agency. Because the case involved abuse, the PC consulted an attorney to determine her rights legally as well as to obtain advice regarding the necessary services to be provided under the ethical guidelines of the profession.

For the private practitioner involved in a case such as this, another factor soon enters into the picture–finances. First, much of the time spent on the case was not based on receiving fees. Second, the child chose to remain in counseling with this practitioner without the emotional or financial support of the parents. Because of the nature of the case, the child could not ethically be referred to another counselor for fear of further psychological damage. Third, the agency began demanding more time from the practitioner by requesting written reports and attendance at legal hearings. As you can see, the case also began to infringe on the financial aspects of the practice. If the practitioner were to have several cases such as this at one time, the drain of the financial resources of the practitioner would be outstanding.

The moral to the case that is presented is simple. To operate an effective private practice, PCs must do adequate planning and surround themselves with a set of advisors who will assist them in determining ethical practices, understanding legal requirements, and establishing a well-functioning "business" practice. If a PC is considering a part-time practice as an adjunct to a full-time job, they should remember this case. We have been associated with several part-time practitioners who have faced such circumstances and found them to have a major dilemma on their hands. The demands of abuse cases did not fit with the demands of their full-time jobs, which made them vulnerable, legally and ethically. Anyone who is considering part-time practice needs to keep in mind that some cases can be very difficult and quite time consuming.

As an aside, it should be noted that the private practitioner may spend inordinate amounts of time taking care of the business aspects of the practice. At those times, when the authors are involved in managing business issues, such as records transfers or subpoenas for attorneys, the practice's attorney will remind him or her that "this is the price of doing business." Sometimes there is no way to financially cover or recover money and time spent handling business issues.

Referral Sources

The most common error made by the PC initiating a practice is to neglect the building of an effective referral base. Although the financial investment in the practice is important, it is not the most important aspect of establishing a private practice. If the practice is to grow, the PC must allocate the time and resources for the development of a strong referral system.

Sources of referral in the community are numerous. They include schools, private and public agencies, churches, businesses, industries, other mental health professionals, hospitals, doctors, and rehabilitation centers. Gaining access to these agencies and individuals is not always easy; therefore, the planning of methods to gain entry into their offices is a must.

Entry can be accomplished by various means. PCs can send publications about their practice to the directors of the organizations or to established professionals such as doctors, lawyers, school counselors, and judges. In addition, the PC can direct letters to the heads of various organizations (churches, agencies, hospitals) requesting to meet with them. Obviously, it is important to attend these meetings as well prepared as possible regarding those services you can provide the individual or organization. It has been the authors' experience that the best access to many of these organizations is through volunteering your services for special programs that you can present. Churches, community agencies, and schools are often willing to invite a counseling professional to present on topics such as stress, family issues, drugs, parenting, wellness, and other contemporary topics.

Throughout the initiation of a practice, the PC must always remember that the investment in referral building is an investment in the practice. Doing the work with referral sources sets the stage for the beginning of a successful practice in the community. Although it has not been true 100% of the time, most free or nominal fee presentations we have done have created new referrals in the practice. If at all possible, we attempt to make ourselves available for presentations that will add to the referral base for the practice.

Most important, the private practitioner must remember that every phone call placed to someone in the client's milieu is a major aspect of building a referral base. In counseling a child, a phone call for consultation with the child's teacher or counselor can be the beginning of the development of an active referral source for the practice. Consulting with a client's primary care physician can provide a valuable entrance into another source of referrals. Effective client care provides many opportunities to build your practice through contact with other professionals and organizations.

Finally, in keeping up with the growth of the Internet over the past 10 years, practitioners would significantly increase their visibility in the community by establishing a website. One of the most important decisions that we made at BCA was establishing www.bethlehemcounselingassociates.com. The website provides potential clients with information about BCA, biographies of the clinical staff, all of the necessary intake forms to be completed prior to a first session, answers questions about insurance, and much more. We have increased referrals since establishing a website as more and more people seeking counseling assistance use the web for information and not the Yellow Pages.

Goal Setting

Probably one of the most important activities that a private practitioner can do for him or herself is to plan, on a yearly basis, the goals for the practice. The planning of goals should be in certain specific areas, including: (a) professional goals, (b) financial goals, (c) skill development, and (d) personal/family goals.

Professional goals include establishing guidelines for the types of activities you will attempt to accomplish over the period of a year. These can include: (a) the number of cases you would like to carry during an average week or month, (b) the types of cases (individual, couples, families, and groups) you want to be carrying, (c) the extent and type of consulting or training you would like to provide, and (d) the amount of supervision you want to do with other professionals. Each of these aspects of practice needs to be defined within the PC's skills, desires, and professional aspirations.

In conjunction with the establishment of professional goals, the PC will also need to set certain parameters for the financial growth of the practice. The number of cases carried, the types of consulting opportunities available, and any other activities to be attempted must be put within the context of the financial aspects of the practice. For example, to meet the professional goal of increasing consulting for the year, the PC may have to do more voluntary types of activities (such as a parenting program for a local agency). At the same time, the practitioner may need to increase the number of counseling sessions per week to meet established financial goals. The point to be made is that the setting of one professional goal may mean the alteration of other previously established goals.

Third, the PC in private practice needs to establish a direction for his or her own skill development. To continue to grow professionally, the year's activities for training will need to be carefully planned in terms of time away from the practice and the financial investment. The greatest difficulty for the practitioner is the professional loneliness factor. To combat the loneliness, the PC needs to plan both training and professional organizational involvement along with an effective schedule of personal activities to remain a truly effective professional.

Finally, the PC must establish separate personal goals for him or herself to remain a well-rounded individual and professional. As counselors continually recommend to their clients, "Take care of yourself!", the practitioner must insist on establishing a personal life plan for the year. This means setting guidelines and boundaries for the amount of time spent on the practice each week, the planning of vacations, involvement with the family, and other personal needs. The effective PC in private practice is the individual who not only attends to the "business" but also attends to his or her own personal life. Modeling "wellness" is an important goal for the practitioner, because the clients watch closely the activities of the counselor.

UNDERSTANDING MENTAL HEALTH INSURANCE

Understanding mental health insurance coverage and payment systems is one of the most important aspects of maintaining a productive and financially successful practice. Funding for psychological and counseling services can vary from simply being paid your established fee for a counseling session to complex insurance reimbursement processes to retrieve full or partial reimbursement. The direct payment of a fee for services provided is the simplest of the payment methods. After fee for service, there are three types of basic insurance plans: Indemnity Plans, Preferred Provider Organizations (PPOs), and Health Maintenance Organizations (HMOs).

Indemnity Plan

Indemnity plans allow for the insurance payment to go directly to the client or the responsible party for the client. Responsible party refers to the person responsible for payment when a client receives counseling services. In most cases, the client is the responsible party. However, with children who receive counseling services, the parent is the responsible party. The client or responsible party pays in full for the mental health services provided. Following the session, the provider gives the client a receipt that can be submitted to the insurance carrier. Once the responsible party submits the receipt, the insurer then reimburses them.

With Indemnity Plans, there is often a deductible amount that must be paid by the client or responsible party before reimbursement is offered. Indemnity Plans reimburse on a Standard Fee (the fee charged by the practitioner) for services, allow clients to choose their own counselor, and allow the counselor to determine the number of session necessary to complete treatment.

Preferred Provider Organizations (PPOs)

PPO plans establish formal contracts with a group of counselors who are given the designation of being "in-network" providers. The PPO contracts establish the fees that an in-network provider can charge for services rendered. The fees are paid directly to the provider and not the responsible party. The cost to the client may include a deductible and/or co-pay. If the client or responsible party selects an out-of-network provider, the plan may be the same as an Indemnity Plan.

Health Maintenance Organizations (HMOs)

HMO plans operate in a similar manner to PPO plans; however, HMO plans have three unique characteristics. First, HMO plans require that the primary care physician (PCP) through the insurer precertify all mental health services prior to the client receiving services. Second, HMO plans require that the in-network counselor submit a treatment plan to a designated reviewer at the insurance company. The insurer then determines the necessity for services based on the treatment plans. Third, there is no benefit provided to the client or responsible party if an out-of-network counselor is chosen. Like PPO plans, HMO contracts set the fees for in-network providers, and the fees are only paid to the provider of services. HMO plans seldom have a deductible but almost always have the client pay a co-pay. HMO plans generally have lower premiums than Indemnity and PPO plans.

Insurance and Managed Care for the Counselor

The past decade has brought about major changes for the PC. Not only has there been the onset of licensure, but also the insurance companies are willing to include licensed professional counselors on their provider panels. Ten years ago, the professional associations were battling to have counselors included among the mental health providers receiving insurance reimbursement. Today, reimbursement by insurers, whether PPOs or HMOs, is a reality. The PC in private practice will have to explore and research all of the aspects of being a provider for various insurers. Being accepted on the provider panels for varied insurers is critical for most private practitioners. When beginning a practice, the neophyte has to do a thorough review of the insurers accepting new LPCs on their panels.

KEEPING IT TOGETHER

The mental health of a PC in practice is central to the ability to deliver effective mental health services to clients. It is impossible to help clients "get it together" if the PC cannot "keep it together." The PC in private practice needs to establish limits between personal and professional time to provide for his or her own needs. This is far easier said than done in a full-time practice. The amount of bonding and nurturing inherent in a positive client-counselor relationship can threaten personal development. So much time can be given to others that there is little time remaining for oneself. The inability to limit professional time can cause both personal and professional failures.

To have the level of energy necessary to work with many people on intense and demanding life problems, a PC must have moments out of the limelight. The "pleasure factor" in adult life is particularly important to the PC in private practice. It is extremely difficult for the neophyte private practitioner to see how much personal "playtime" can be lost when initiating a practice. A PC must be a master at identifying his or her own needs for time, space, and nurturing. Because of this, these authors believe that each PC, at some point in his or her life, should consider therapy for him or herself. Sitting in the client's seat can deter burnout, foster appropriate limit setting, and enhance personal growth and awareness.

The topics in this chapter cover many issues important for the PC considering a private practice. Creativity will generate referral sources, while skill and fortitude will sustain the practice. Financial resources can be an advantage but are certainly not a necessity. Self-awareness is a necessity. When the PC becomes stressed, clients and colleagues sense the hesitancy and the practice falls off. The number of PCs entering the world of private practice is growing. Within the arena of private practice, the rewards can be numerous, the stimulation evident, and the satisfaction immeasurable. With knowledge, motivation, dedication, and confidence, the PC can take his or her rightful place among the ranks of mental health providers in private practice.

REFERENCES

Hall, J. E., & Boucher, A. P. (2003). Professional mobility for psychologists: Multiple choices, multiple opportunities. *Professional Psychology: Research and Practice, 34,* 463–467.

Jonason, K. R., DeMers, S. T., Vaughn, T. J., & Reaves, R. P. (2003). Professional mobility for psychologists is rapidly becoming a reality. *Professional Psychology: Research and Practice, 34,* 468–473.

Kim, E., & VandeCreek, L. (2003). Facilitating mobility for psychologists: Comparisons with and lessons from other health care professions. *Professional Psychology: Research and Practice, 34,* 480–488.

Koocher, G. P. (2003). Ethical and legal issues in professional practice transitions. *Professional Psychology: Research and Practice, 34,* 383–387.

Manosevitz, M., & Hays, K. F. (2003). Relocating your psychotherapy practice: Packing and unpacking. *Professional Psychology: Research and Practice, 34,* 375–382.

McGee, T. F. (2003). Observations on the retirement of professional psychologists. *Professional Psychology: Research and Practice, 34,* 388–395.

Palmo, A. J., Shosh, M. J., & Weikel, W. J. (2001). The independent practice of mental health counseling: Past, present, and future. In D. C. Locke, J. E. Myers, & E. L. Herr (Eds.), *The handbook of counseling* (pp. 653–667). Thousand Oaks, CA: Sage.

Stout, C. E., Levant, R. F., Reed, G. M., & Murphy, M. J. (2001). Contracts: A primer for psychologists. *Professional Psychology: Research and Practice, 32,* 88–91.

Suggested Reading

Psychotherapy Finances, Ed. John Klein, Ridgewood Financial Institute, Inc., 1425 U.S. Highway 1, Ste. 286, Juno Beach, FL 33408.

Health Insurance Portability and Accountability Act websites:
www.hhs.gov/ocr/hipaa/privacy.html
www.hhs.gov/ocr/hipaa

Chapter 11

MENTAL HEALTH COUNSELORS ADDRESSING INTIMATE PARTNER VIOLENCE

DAVID VAN DOREN AND ERIKA WAGNER-MARTIN

"All the problems that come to therapy today can be subsumed under the category of the violence that people inflict on one another. This violence may be overt as in physical punishment or sexual assault, or it may be covert as in neglect or emotional abuse" (Madanes, 1995, p. 17).

Violence impacts everyone. Although some mental health disorders may have biological determinants, it is clear that the continuum of abuse creates and/or exacerbates these disorders. Mental health counselors need to become aware of the impact of violence and develop skills to address the trauma and enhance nonaggressive conflict resolution.

THE EPIDEMIC OF INTIMATE PARTNER VIOLENCE

At least one in four women experiences violence within an intimate partner relationship during her lifetime, and 85% of victims of intimate partner violence are women (Family Violence Prevention Fund, 2010; National Coalition Against Domestic Violence, 2007). "[Intimate partner violence] is the leading cause of death for African-American women aged 15 to 45 and the seventh leading cause of premature death for U.S. women overall. Intimate partner homicides make up 40 to 50 percent of all murders of women in the United States" (Campbell et al., 2003). Women experience two million injuries from intimate partner violence each year, and more than three women are murdered by their male intimate partners each day (Family

Violence Prevention Fund, 2010). These statistics indicate that intimate partner violence (IPV) is an epidemic that disproportionately victimizes women; they also highlight the broader social problem of gender inequality in Western society (Chavis & Hill, 2009).

It is important to acknowledge that women also commit violent acts and may need individual or group counseling to address this issue. When gender is compared, the number of acts of violence is fairly equal. Women's violence is often a reaction to men's violence (Grauwiler & Mills, 2004). Women are 7 to14 times more likely to suffer severe physical harm from an assault by an intimate partner (U.S. Preventive Services Task Force, 2004). "Violence by an intimate partner accounts for 21% of violence against women and 2% of violence against men" (Greenfield et al., 1998, p. v). An examination of research indicates that women are less likely to have a history of IPV offenses and nonviolent crimes and, if arrested, more likely to report that they had been injured or victimized by their partner at the time of their arrest (Busch & Rosenberg 2004). Women are as likely as men to have used drugs or alcohol prior to violent acts and to have used severe violence. Women are less likely to create fear and terror in their victims. Unlike the women in their study, men were able to severely injure their partners with their hands alone. "Women are more likely to report using violence to defend themselves against direct assault, to escape attack, or to retaliate for past abuse. Males were more likely to report that they used violence to dominate, control, or punish their partner" (Busch & Rosenberg, 2004, p. 51). Some women may need counseling to address their issues with anger and violence. Although women may not create as much physical damage as men, verbal and emotional abuses are significant aspects of the abuse continuum and create long-lasting damage. All abuse is destructive and warrants our attention. Counseling male abusers will limit the destruction and decrease overall violence.

IPV does not discriminate in terms of who is victimized. IPV is an epidemic that transcends race, ethnicity, age, ability, socioeconomic status, and education level. Women who possess multiple oppressed identities (e.g., African-American, poor, mentally ill, disabled, lesbian, and/or immigrant) sometimes face additional challenges when victimized (Chavis & Hill, 2009). Violence occurs at the same rate in same-sex relationships as in heterosexual relationships, although it is often reported less due to added safety concerns and the stigma of being gay or lesbian (Maine Coalition to End Domestic Violence, 2010). The biopsychosocial impact of IPV experienced by victims in any type of relationship is similar. For the purposes of this chapter and given that women are victims of IPV at a much higher rate than men, suggested interventions for mental health professionals will be framed in the context of treating female victims. The term IPV is used instead of *domestic violence* to be inclusive of couples that are unmarried or do not live together. The terms IPV and *abuse* are used synonymously.

Impact of Abuse

It is estimated that IPV costs the U.S. economy approximately $4.1 billion per year for physical and mental health care costs (Centers for Disease Control and Prevention, 2003). Abuse creates both "short- and long-term problems, including physical injury, psychological symptoms, economic costs, and death" (National Research Council, 1996, p. 74). Intimate partners who are being abused spend more time off from work and suffer more stress and depression than partners not being abused (National Research Council, 1996).

Violence is not limited to the intimate partner; children in the home are also physically or emotionally abused. A wealth of literature examines the impact of child abuse. When compared with neglected or sexually abused children, physically abused children are more likely to be arrested for a violent crime (Widom, 1992). Widom reports that there are long-term consequences of childhood victimization: mental health concerns (depression and suicide attempts), educational problems, health and safety issues, alcohol and drug problems, and occupational difficulties. The impact on a child's life is major even when they are not directly abused. "Many studies demonstrate the deleterious effects of witnessing abuse/violence between adults in the home. Children exposed to interparental violence fare poorer than the average unexposed child" (Zink, Kamine, Musk, Sill, Field, & Putnam, 2004, p. 256). Children who witness violence develop long-term physical and mental health problems, including alcohol and substance abuse, become victims of abuse, and perpetrate abuse (Felitti et al., 1998). A review of the literature related to the children of abused women suggests that these children experience lower self-esteem and increased symptoms of attention deficit/hyperactivity and obsessive-compulsive disorder. They also demonstrate more suicidal gestures, impaired social interaction and problem-solving skills, and increased aggressiveness and oppositional behavior (Feldman, 1997). Witnessing one's parents' violent interactions triples the likelihood of a child being diagnosed with a conduct disorder (Meltzer et al., 2009). Children exposed to maternal IPV were more likely to have borderline to clinical scores on externalizing behavior (aggressive, delinquent) and total behavioral problems (Kernic, Wolf, Holt, McKnight, Huebner, & Rivara, 2003). Experiencing child abuse has been identified as a predictor of IPV (Kwong, Bartholomew, Henderson, & Trinka, 2003). Males who have observed parents attack each other are three times more likely to assault their wives (Straus & Gelles, 1990). Witnessing a father's violence toward a mother can have a significant influence on the child's development of IPV in relationships as an adult (Wang, Home, Holdford, & Henning, 2008). Observing both parents violently attacking each other is a strong predictor of the child's future participation with IPV (Kwong et al., 2003). Silverman and Williamson (1997) found that children who witnessed abuse were more likely to believe battering to be justified. Shifting these cognitions becomes a critical aspect in addressing men who batter.

Studies suggest that approximately 40% of abused children go on to abuse their partner (Dutton, 1995). Being physically abused has been seen as an even stronger predictor of later development of IPV, than witnessing parents' IPV (Kwong et al., 2003; Wang et al., 2008). The fact that the majority of physically abused children do not become abusers suggests that many children are resilient and survive a negative situation without developing the same symptoms. These children may not grow up to batter their partners, but they may develop other symptoms and/or disorders.

With IPV, both parties contribute to the escalation of abuse (Grauwiler & Mills, 2004). An increased exposure to adverse and/or abusive experiences in childhood was associated with greater use of disengagement coping strategies (denial, avoidance, social withdrawal, and self-criticism) among undergraduate women in response to stressful events (Leitenberg, Gibson, & Novy, 2004).

Disengagement strategies can increase negative interaction in the dyad, as problems are not effectively addressed and distance between partners increases. Cumulative exposure to violence increases the likelihood of using disengagement coping strategies (Leitenberg et al., 2004). Research suggests that individuals who have not experienced abuse develop significantly more intimacy than those who have experienced abuse (Ducharme, Koverla, & Battle, 1997). Males often seek validation in relationships and fear abandonment (Wexler, 2000). The reaction to the use of disengagement is often defensiveness and anger.

Intimate relationships develop when both individuals have developed a positive sense of self. The experience of IPV in childhood and/or adulthood has a negative impact on the development of a positive sense of self. Lifetime abuse is associated with elevated levels of anxiety and depression for women. Women who experienced childhood abuse appear to be more likely to report adult partner abuse (Ramos, Carlson, & McNutt, 2004). In addition, higher levels of parental abuse are associated with greater likelihood of a diagnosis of lifetime alcohol dependence for women (Downs, Capshew, & Rindels, 2004). Higher levels of psychological aggression have been significantly associated with a higher likelihood of alcohol dependence for White women (Caetano, Field, & Nelson, 2003) and non-White women (Downs, et al., 2004).

Mental health counselors must be prepared to address the counseling needs of both victims and perpetrators. Mental health counselors address the needs of abuse victims when they come to counseling settings with mood disorders, anxiety disorders, posttraumatic stress disorder, and so on. (Madanes, 1995). Mental health counselors can also play a significant role in addressing violence in our society by treating perpetrators of interpersonal violence. Violent behaviors are passed from generation to generation. From this perspective, as individuals learn healthy nonviolent ways to resolve conflict, a healthier model can be passed down for generations to come.

PORTRAIT OF A VICTIM

Effects of the Cycle of Violence

IPV encompasses a continuum and variety of abusive behaviors, including verbal, sexual, economic, social, and physical abuse. More often than not, multiple types of abusive behaviors occur simultaneously and cyclically. The cycle of violence consists of the tension-building phase, the acute incident of abuse phase, and the contrition or honeymoon phase. During the tension-building phase, the victim might feel like she is walking on eggshells and that an incident of abuse is inevitable due to the pattern of signals she perceives in her partner/abuser. In the second phase, the acute incident of abuse can range from verbal insults to serious physical battery and/or sexual assault. During the third phase, most commonly referred to as the honeymoon phase, the abuser typically expresses remorse for his abusive behaviors and attempts to regain the victim's love and affection (Dutton, 1995; Walker, 2000). The frequency and duration of each phase differs in each relationship. The time between acute incidents of abuse tends to decrease and the intensity of the abusive behaviors tends to increase over the course of the relationship. Typically, because of the complex array of emotions it evokes (i.e., fear, terror, love, hope), the cycle of violence leaves the victim feeling confused, crazy, disoriented, and stuck (Bancroft, 2002; Dutton, 1995; Evans, 2010; Herman, 1997). The honeymoon phase, especially, leads to the idealization of the abuser, the denial of abuse, and the suppression of anger and other emotions (Walker, 2000). Over time, abusive relationships can become so all-consuming that the victim feels disempowered and loses her sense of self (Herman, 1997).

Isolation and Why Women Stay

The impact of IPV manifests physically, psychologically, emotionally, financially, and socially in the life of the victim. Isolation from friends, family members, and other interpersonal relationships is common, many times imposed by the abuser as a tactic to maintain power and control over the victim (Bancroft, 2002). The stigma of IPV, known to create feelings of shame, guilt, and embarrassment, prevents victims from seeking help. Such stigma varies depending on the victim's cultural background and/or religious beliefs. Safety concerns are another main reason victims do not seek help. It is important for mental health professionals to recognize isolation as a common effect of IPV and not to question her reasons for staying in the relationship. There are many complex reasons women that stay, including economic dependence, fear, shame/embarrassment, pressures from clergy and society, to protect her children, to keep the family together, positive feelings toward her partner, having nowhere to go, low self-esteem, and a history of past abuse that distorts the victim's view of healthy relationships (Women's Center, 2009). A woman's decision to stay in her relationship should be respected, especially in light of findings that a woman's risk of being murdered by her partner/abuser increases substantially if and when she leaves the relationship (Campbell et al., 2003; Liang, Goodman, Tummala-Narra, & Weintraub, 2005). Telling a victim of IPV that she should leave her relationship disempowers her further and undermines any therapeutic work to help her feel empowered within her relationship and in general. Connecting victims to informal (e.g., friends and family) and formal (e.g., police, social workers, crisis hotline workers, mental health professionals, clergy, and domestic violence advocates) support "improve[s] battered women's mental health, willingness and ability to seek help . . . and subsequent capacity to stay safe" (Liang et al., 2005, p. 27).

Abuse-Related Trauma

"Trauma can change the way a person develops, emotionally and psychologically. This is because traumatic events can disrupt your emotions, memory, consciousness and sense of self. Trauma can affect your relationships and your attachment to others. It can change the way your brain and body work" (Haskell, 2004, p. 1).

The impact of abuse-related trauma varies from person to person. Trauma specialists characterize the range of impact as existing on a continuum from simple or "little t" trauma to complex or "Big T" trauma (Haskell, 2004; Shapiro & Forrest, 2004). When counseling victims of IPV, what matters most is the individual's subjective experience of trauma (Liang et al., 2005). Haskell (2004) identifies traumatic stress response patterns among victims of abuse-related trauma to guide mental health professionals in recognizing signs of IPV. The victim may be on guard, may have trouble trusting others, may experience depression and/or feelings of despair, may feel alone, may have trouble expressing and regulating emotions, and may have trouble calming and taking care of herself.

Signs and Symptoms of IPV for Helping Professionals

The effects of abuse present in a wide array of symptoms, including but not limited to: anxiety, hyperarousal, depression, eating disorders, sleep disturbance, agitation, relationship difficulties, dissociation, flashbacks, substance abuse, and self-harming behaviors (Dejonghe, Bogat, Levendowsky, & von Eye, 2008; Haskell, 2001; Pico-Alfonso et al., 2006). In addition to psychological effects, some victims of IPV report somatic symptoms such as fatigue, muscle aches, low energy, rapid heart rate, gastrointestinal upset, and difficulty breathing (Briere & Scott, 2006; Levine, 1997). In settings that utilize the medical model of assessment and diagnosis (i.e., the American Psychiatric Association's *Diagnostic and Statistical Manual of Mental Disorders*), these symptoms mirror a number of psychiatric diagnoses, including post-traumatic stress disorder (PTSD), depression, anxiety, bipolar disorder, substance abuse/dependence, schizophrenia, and borderline personality disorder, depending on the history of abuse. Although mental illness is sometimes due to organic causes, mental health professionals should conduct a thorough, holistic assessment to rule out abuse-related trauma and, more important, to make an appropriate diagnosis and treatment plan.

A report published by the Centers for Disease Control and Prevention (2008) found that "Women who have experienced domestic violence are 80 percent more likely to have a stroke, 70 percent more likely to have heart disease, 60 percent more likely to have asthma and 70 percent more likely to drink heavily than women who have not experienced intimate partner violence." Physical symptoms should be taken seriously regardless of their cause, and mental health professionals have a responsibility to address these concerns as they relate to the client's mental health and wellness and to refer the client to her physician when appropriate.

Other signs that could point to IPV are employment status, involvement in social groups and relationships outside of the intimate partnership, economic independence and knowledge of finances, and feelings of autonomy and independence. An abuser may prohibit his partner from working, making decisions about money, or maintaining friendships as tactics to maintain power and control in the relationship.

Suggested approaches to screening an individual to find out whether they are in an abusive relationship include: assess the individual alone so that her ability to share is not hindered by family members who do not have the partner's best interests in mind; look for signs and symptoms holistically; ask direct questions in a nonjudgmental, nonthreatening tone (e.g., "Would it be okay if I ask you a question? Do you feel safe at home?"); and provide referrals to resources that specialize in helping victims of IPV (Mick, 2006). The Partner Violence Screen (Ebell, 2004) has been implemented in physicians' offices across the country. This is a brief screening measure that utilizes three questions:

> Have you been hit, kicked, or punched in the past year? Do you feel safe in your current relationship? Is there a partner from a previous relationship who is making you feel unsafe now? (p. 2422)

A response of yes to any of these questions would be seen as an indication of IPV.

A specific screening tool, the Danger Assessment Tool, has been developed by Campbell et al. (2003) and may also enhance screening for IPV. Growing awareness of IPV has led to this attempt to intervene. Individuals may often express symptoms of depression or anxiety without mentioning their present circumstances of violence. Specific assessment of IPV may supplement your present assessment and increase the identification.

TREATMENT APPROACHES

Reframing Stigma

When counseling victims of IPV, mental health professionals must bear in mind the stigma attached to IPV in our society. "Women who have experienced abuse . . . should not be stigmatized. Instead, it is important to recognize that the effects and symptoms of abuse-related trauma are themselves normal responses. They are ways of coping with the harm inflicted by abuse" (Haskell, 2001, p. 2). When working with victims of IPV, it is helpful to think of diagnoses as a way to describe a set of symptoms rather than a finite disorder. Likewise, it is helpful to view the signs and symptoms of abuse-related trauma as coping mechanisms. Doing so circumvents restigmatizing and, therefore, retraumatizing the victim by labeling her with a disorder. Through effective, trauma-focused therapy, the victim will begin to reframe her negative symptoms into unhealthy coping mechanisms and, eventually, learn new, healthier ways to cope with the effects of the abuse.

Stages of Healing

Healing from the effects of IPV is not a linear event. When victims seek help, their needs are unique from the needs of others and from their own needs at a different point in their process. It is important to be flexible in these situations; the phrase "meet the client where she's at" holds especially true when working with victims of IPV. Moreover, support services should be woman- (or person-) focused rather than service-focused and able to address her long-range needs for support, not merely crisis intervention needs (Liang et al., 2005). Depending on her situation, she might need help connecting to a protective shelter, community resources such as the food pantry or clothes closet, legal services, an employment agency, or mental health services. In many cases, the victim will need to address survival and safety needs before she is able to repair her self-esteem, restore her sense of self, or create the abuse-free life she deserves.

Useful Therapeutic Interventions

Individual and group counseling serve victims of IPV well for different reasons. Individual counseling provides space for the client to process deeper aspects of abuse-related trauma, whereas group counseling provides social connection within an egalitarian setting and a chance to see that IPV impacts a wide range of individuals. Group counseling helps the victim feel less isolated. Whether in individual or group counseling, a strengths-based approach to safety planning, identifying social supports, providing information about available resources, and providing education about abuse (namely, abusive behaviors, power and control, and the cycle of violence) are of primary importance (Tower, 2007).

There are a number of useful therapeutic models that can be used to help victims of IPV. These include dialectical behavior therapy (DBT), cognitive-behavior therapy (CBT), narrative therapy, eye-movement desensitization and reprocessing (EMDR), cognitive trauma therapy for battered women (CTT-BW), and the trauma therapy model. Iverson, Shenk, and Fruzzetti (2009) found that a 12-week DBT group counseling experience with emphases on self-esteem, mindfulness, and self-care resulted in decreased depressive symptoms, hopelessness, and mental distress. Another model, cognitive trauma therapy for battered women (CTT-BW), utilizes psycho-education about PTSD, stress management, assertiveness skills development, and education about abuse and how to identify abusers to effectively reduce symptoms of PTSD, alleviate guilt and depression, and increase self-esteem (Kubaney et al., 2004). Shapiro and Forrest (2004) report that in a study of rape survivors diagnosed with PTSD, 84% of the survivors had no symptoms of PTSD after only three sessions of EMDR therapy.

The trauma therapy model, which integrates many of the techniques of DBT, CBT, and CTT-BW, is implemented in three stages: (a) stabilizing and managing responses to traumatic stress, (b) processing and grieving traumatic memories; and (c) reconnecting with the world. The principles for the mental health professional to follow when using this model are to develop a relationship of collaboration with the client, understand signs and symptoms as normal responses to traumatic stress, recognize the severity of the trauma, and recognize social inequality (Haskell, 2004). Rasmussen, Hughes, and Murray (2008) found that motivational interviewing is particularly effective when counseling women in shelter settings, and Tower (2007) found that counseling victims of IPV from a feminist perspective pays heed to the unique dynamics of IPV within the broader sociocultural context of power differentials between numerous social groups (i.e., male over female, White over non-White, heterosexual over same-sex, wealthy over poor, etc.).

A multimodal approach is the most effective when counseling victims of IPV because it allows the mental health professional to meet the client's needs at any point in her personal process of healing or, in the group format, to meet the needs of multiple clients at once (Briere & Jordan, 2004). Regardless of the specific model or interventions, crucial themes for mental health professionals to incorporate while working with victims of IPV include safety planning, power and control, the cycle of violence, types of abuse, the effects of abuse, assertiveness, self-care, communication, self-esteem, expressing emotions, anger management, and available support resources (Briere & Scott, 2006; Haskell, 2001, 2004; National Coalition Against Domestic Violence, 2007; The Women's Center, 2009). In addition, it is important to prioritize treatment goals to address more immediate issues such as suicidal ideation, substance abuse, and social functioning (when using the group format) and to recognize that abuse can be intergenerational and, therefore, might play a more influential role in the victim's ability to overcome denial and seek help (Seamans, Rubin, & Stabb, 2007).

Finally, it is imperative that professionals counseling victims of IPV recognize the dangers of couples therapy when abusive behaviors are present in the relationship. "Couples therapy is designed to tackle issues that are mutual. It can be effective for overcoming barriers to communication, for untangling the childhood issues that each partner brings to a relationship, or for building intimacy. But you can't accomplish any of these goals in the context of abuse. There can be no positive communication when one person does not respect the other and strives to avoid equality," as is the case when the abuser behaves to maintain power and control in the relationship (Bancroft, 2002, p. 351).

From Victim to Survivor to Person

The journey for any victim of IPV is a long and complicated one. Mental health professionals are wise to remember to meet her where she's at in her process, to reframe negative symptoms as normal coping mechanisms, to help her explore healthier ways to cope, to be respectful and nonjudgmental, and to believe, accept, and honor the impact of abuse-related trauma on her life and her sense of self as she describes it. Ultimately, the goal is for the victim of IPV to feel empowered to live a fulfilling, abuse-free life, moving from Victim, to Survivor, to Person in the process.

CHARACTERISTICS OF MALE ABUSERS

It is important to understand some of the characteristics of men who abuse women. Silverman and Williamson (1997) identified abusers as individuals who have witnessed IPV in their family of origin, have had abusive male peers, have had a peer group that supports abuse, and have a sense of entitlement and an absence of nonsexual female peer intimacy. These individuals believe that battering is justified and that batterers are not responsible for their violence. "Greater than 25% did not disagree with the practice of beating a woman believed to be unfaithful; almost 10% did not disagree with the practice of beating a woman who consistently refuses to have sex with her male partner" (Silverman & Williamson, 1997, p. 161).

A childhood history of physical abuse is significantly related to intimate partner abuse as an adult. As chronicity of abuse increases during childhood, so does the potential to be abusive as an adult (Milner, Robertson, & Rogers, 1990). Some males abusers may suffer from delayed-onset PTSD developed from their experience of abuse as children (Van der Kolk, 1988). Browne and Saunders (1997) suggest that early trauma may lead to PTSD, depression, low self-esteem, and personality disorders. They found that two thirds of abusive men had depressive affect in the clinical range.

Childhood abandonment often leads to adult rage (Leibman, 1992). Dutton (1998, 2007) suggests that abusive males often experience three co-occurring socialization conditions in their family of origin: direct physical and emotional abuse by parents, rejection and shaming by fathers, and an insecure attachment to mothers. Anger is an aspect of attachment, and when experienced it is both blamed and projected onto the attachment object. Assaultive men have jealousy and abandonment issues. Although they try to remain cool and detached, they have a strong emotional dependence on their partners (Dutton, 1998, 2007).

Children need recognition and validation from parental figures (Shapiro, 1995). Often over time this sense of pride becomes incorporated into one's self-worth. This enables us as adults to have a sense of competence and worth. However, if significant adults provide put downs, insults, or a lack of responsiveness, the child continues to long for this recognition from others into adulthood, having developed little sense of worth. Bowlby (1988) stressed the importance of a secure attachment and the recognition that attachment issues developed in early childhood impact our lives until a secure base enables the individual to explore and develop a healthy attachment. An anxious or avoidant attachment leads to relationship problems due to neediness and a demand for an external recognition of one's worth. The individual seeks validation from a partner while defending himself from being hurt and/or abandoned. When lacking validation, men often attempt to use power and control to demand the recognition and validation they seek. However, this leads to greater distance and less validation, which then leads to greater self-doubt and increased defensiveness in an ongoing negative spiral. When compared with individuals who had an insecure attachment, secure attachments in childhood lead in adulthood to a more positive sense of self, more ability to express emotion, and greater intimacy and autonomy (Searle & Meara, 1999). Brown (2004) indicates that an aspect of this insecurity is the individual's development of shame. The experience of shame is a precursor to violence or other forms of abuse. Providing a secure base to explore their family of origin concerns and shame or other painful feelings will need to be a component of treatment for men who batter.

"Violent men have more insecure, preoccupied, and disorganized attachments, more dependency on and preoccupation with their wives and more jealousy and less trust in their marriage" (Holtzworth-Munroe, Stuart, & Hutchinson, 1997, p. 314). Their needs for nurturance and preoccupation with their romantic partner are similar, but happily married men do not simultaneously experience discomfort with closeness that is experienced by violent men. "Men appear to feel generally powerless, threatened, and out of control in intimate conflict" (Dutton, 2007, p. 52). In this intimate relationship, a threat to their sense of self leads to an inner state of discomfort and often less acceptable emotions of fear, guilt, sadness, or hurt. This is quickly translated into anger, a more acceptable masculine emotion. Abusive men find it less stressful to be angry than anxious (Dutton, 1998, 2007). Anger is able to shift the sense of powerlessness to a sense of omnipotence. Aggression/anger externalizes blame and aggressiveness takes action, which is designed to change these circumstances (Dutton, 1998, 2007).

Walker (1984) identified a battering cycle, which is fueled by the internal struggle for intimacy and the fear of it. The first step of the cycle is the building of tension, which occurs as the internal (unacceptable) feelings are beginning to emerge. As these feelings escalate and a sense of powerlessness emerges, they are shifted to anger/aggression (Stage 2 in the cycle), which leads to an increased sense of power and control. The aggression enhances the feeling of power, but the resulting loss of relationship leads to a sense of emptiness and feelings of guilt and/or shame (Stage 3, the contrition phase of Walker's model). This cycle continues and may escalate in intensity. Although understanding this cycle is helpful for clinicians and abusers, it is important to note that IPV does not always follow this pattern.

Most abusers blame the victim, ascribe the aggression to external factors, and minimize the severity of the abuse (Dutton, 1998). "Domestically violent men appear to distort the causes and consequences of their violent behavior by attributing it more often to external rather than internal factors and more transient, unstable states, rather than permanent, stable ones" (Feldman, 1997, p. 319). Husbands tend to display low internal and high external attributional styles, whereas women tend to display high internal styles (Shields & Hanneke, 1983). This leads to men blaming and women often accepting the blame. In almost all situations, both individuals can benefit by examining their own behavior. Every time that violence is successful in eliminating or reducing stress, or addressing the circumstances that produced the stress, violence becomes more entrenched. Intermittent reinforcement is most resistant to extinction, so this reward serves to strengthen the use of violence to address life's stressors (Dutton, 1998, 2007).

Types of Abusers

Most research suggests that abusers are not a homogenous group. Walker (1995) identified three types of abusers: (a) those whom batter at home, motivated by power and control needs; (b) those who have serious psychological problems; and (c) those who have committed other crimes as well as assaults and who could well be diagnosed with antisocial personality disorder. Holtzworth-Munroe and Stuart (1994) identified three similar subtypes: those who are abusive and aggressive within the family only, those who display dysphoric and/or borderline symptoms, and those who are generally violent/antisocial. Research appears to support that some abusers are high in borderline or antisocial personality symptoms (Else, Wonderlich, Beatty, Christie, & Staton, 1993). However, Gondolf (2003) states that only 25% of abusers were found to have mental health disorders and less than half showed evidence of personality disorder. This seems inconsistent with Dutton's (1998, 2007), research which more clearly supports the three subtypes identified by Holtzworth-Munroe and Stuart (1994).

Physical abuse is seldom the beginning point of the abusive cycle. Verbal and emotional abuse generally precedes physical abuse. However, without intervention, the pattern of conflict increases. Objects may be thrown and intimidation used for power and control. Power, control, intimacy, and autonomy issues lead to expressions of violence, followed in many cases by remorse. The antisocial group does not demonstrate remorse and is more likely to use instrumental violence to maintain dominance and power (Douglas, 1991). Although dominance and control are more evident at the extreme, they are apparent throughout the cycle of abuse and in each subtype of abusers.

Treatment for Males Who Perpetrate Abuse

Because there are different types of abusers, assessment becomes an important first step of treatment (Bern, 1990). Differing diagnostic symptoms may require differing treatment components to address violence. The abuser who has alcohol abuse/dependence issues and/or has a borderline personality may require more intensive treatment. Substance abuse problems may necessitate formal intervention. Individuals with anxiety and mood disorders may require psychiatric consultation and medication. "Men who have experienced (vicariously or directly) extreme and chronic levels of violence in the family-of-origin may require interventions not unlike those for post traumatic stress disorder" (Hamberger & Hastings, 1991, p. 145). Persistence in treatment is enhanced when the perpetrator has minimal risk of an alcohol disorder and negative cognitions related to partner abuse (Duplantis, Romans, & Bear, 2008).

Specific substance abuse/dependence issues may need to be addressed. It is important to challenge the assumption that alcohol is the cause of violence while also recognizing its role in the process (Conner & Ackerley, 1994). Alcohol is often identified as a common feature of intimate partner violence (Costa & Holliday, 1993). "Alcohol and violence are linked via pharmacological effects on behavior, through expectations, that heavy drinking and violence go together in certain situations, and through patterns of binge drinking and fighting that sometimes develop in adolescence" (Roth, 1994, p. 1). Duplantis et al. (2008) identified alcohol abuse as a predictor of increased treatment dropouts. However, blaming the alcohol by both victim and perpetrator decreases the acceptance of personal responsibility for the violence.

Treatment for abusers needs to be multifaceted in order to address the factors affecting the risk of violence–no single strategy works (Roth, 1994). Often psycho-educational and cognitive behavioral groups are utilized to treat abusive men. However, an integrative approach to treatment may be more effective and would include psychodynamic elements that explore the family of origin issues, which underlie the present behavior (Bern, 1990; Browne & Saunders, 1997). Treatment needs to challenge attitudes, beliefs, and the cognitive structures that lead to reflexive anger responses (Douglas, 1991). These cognitive issues include the shifting from external attribution to taking personal responsibility for behavior (internal attribution). Anger management, conflict resolution skills, communication skills, and substance-related training need to be included as well. It is essential that this be done in a supportive, nonthreatening manner. Confrontation leads to increased defensiveness and less change.

Anger management is a label for the group experience, which is more attractive and palatable for the group members. The group must proceed well beyond the focus on anger and include the issues of power and control that are central to intimate partner abuse. Focusing solely on anger may avoid the underlying struggles relevant to the abuser's striving for power and control. Inadvertently, anger management groups, which fail to address these underlying dynamics, may enhance the skills of the controller. For example, a group member may justify his abusive behavior in his report that he utilized "I" messages learned from group but his partner still didn't do what he desired. Development of personal responsibility for behavior is one aspect of addressing power and control, which enables attitudes and behavior to change. More challenging is the recognition and acceptance that a man can only control his own behavior.

Feldman (1997) points out the need to strengthen the attention given to early exposure and victimization in a program for adult males. When clients recognize their own role as victims in childhood and understand the rules, assumptions, and attributions developed in association with these early experiences, the level of empathy toward those whom they have victimized is enhanced. Attention to poor self-esteem, poor self-efficacy, poor social support networks, and the intergenerational nature of abuse and violence enable appropriate expression of emotion and promote shifts in attitudes and behaviors.

Understanding the attachment issues related to IPV suggests that an essential part of the treatment process includes acknowledging the internal pain that is a significant aspect of the great majority of batterers. With a motivational approach (Miller & Rollnick, 2002), the counselor facilitates understanding of this cognitive, emotional, behavioral struggle. The defiant, angry abuser will often claim that he should not be getting counseling, but his partner belongs in counseling. The counselor can reflect the strong desire of the client to be closer to his partner while helping him examine the impact of the behavior that led to this referral for treatment. The impact is most often a distancing in the relationship, the opposite direction that was desired by the client. Reflection can help the client to increase awareness of the frustrating and emotionally unsatisfying interactions experienced and acknowledge a personal desire to change. Initially this change may be externalized. However, a motivational approach will slowly shift the focus to self. When a counselor attempts to compel the client to assess responsibility for his behavior, the client frequently becomes defensive, resulting in decreased responsibility for the offensive behavior. Counselors need to acknowledge their own inability to control others' behavior, which may serve as good modeling.

Wexler (2000) acknowledges the defensiveness of clients who are abusive and warns to avoid criticism and aggressive confrontation, because this will often lead to increased defensiveness. Dutton (1998) points out that treatments focused on confronting the individual tend to increase shame, which increases the use of rationalizations, externalizations of blame, and anger. Approaches that enhance the group members' sense of self are more appropriate and are less likely to be facilitated by individuals who have not sufficiently addressed their own childhood pains.

Harris (2006) suggests that conjoint therapy can enhance communication and conflict resolution skills for the couple. Stith, Rosen, and McCollum's (2003) research suggests that couples counseling can decrease recidivism and increase marital satisfaction. Grauwiler and Mills (2004) suggest that a couples approach might be useful, because there is a collaborative nature of violence, and both parties contribute to the escalation of conflict. As mentioned previously, there certainly are potential dangers in conjoint therapy, and safety should be the highest priority. Ensuring no current violence is occurring is vital (Harris, 2006). Although it is important to acknowledge that both parties have some responsibility for the escalation, it is critical that the focus shift to personal responsibility in all aspects of one's own behavior. Accepting the mutual responsibility is only appropriate when it can be accepted as mutual rather than blaming. When most abusers enter treatment, responsibility assumption is not apparent, and efforts to maintain power and control are evident. In that case, trying to provide couples counseling is at best unproductive and at worst could increase abuse. Couples therapy can be an effective intervention after individual work has occurred and when safety is not an issue.

Group counseling is viewed as the preferred choice for treatment of abusers. The group format enhances learning by providing support, practicing new skills, and learning vicariously as others discuss their own personal issues. Individual sessions are often helpful initially to assess the client and orient him to the group format and may serve to supplement group in cases of significant levels of psychopathology.

The leadership of IPV groups is critical. There are some positive aspects of utilizing male group facilitators for a male IPV group. The interactions between group leaders can serve as positive models for the awareness and communication of feelings. Male and female co-leaders certainly can enhance these benefits because they can also model positive communication with the opposite gender. Browne and Saunders (1997) stressed that a close working relationship between the male and female co-leaders is necessary for effective treatment. It is critical that the co-leader relationship be an equal one so that models of power and control are not reinforced. Group leaders who have experienced abuse must examine their past history and its impact. Most men are referred to groups through the criminal justice system, and those who are forced to participate may consider these groups punitive. It is important that those who facilitate these groups do not utilize them to punish or exhibit their own power and control issues. If information is provided in a punitive, hierarchical format, the model reinforces the desire for power and control, rather than shifting the perspective to mutuality.

Manuals have been developed that provide useful outlines, assignments, and worksheets for individuals who are beginning IPV groups (Fall, Howard, & Ford, 1999; Wexler, 2000). An ideal group size is six to eight members, which is large enough for learning through interactions with group members but small enough to provide opportunities to examine each person's individual issues. If a group becomes too large, it becomes difficult to address the psychological needs of individual group members. Groups typically meet for two hours a week for a period of at least 16 weeks (Dutton, 1998; Hanusa, 1997; Fall et al., 1999, Wexler, 2000). Duration of treatment needs to be long enough and interactive enough to facilitate discussion related to anger and abusive activities that are occurring. Most group members begin group with a defensive posture and a determination to not display anger. Initial groups require ongoing gentle shifting to focus on their own attitudes, feelings, and behaviors, rather than their partners.

Group members can be helped to recognize anger as a normal emotion that does not necessitate an abusive response, which is an enlightening experience. As group members become comfortable examining their feelings, thoughts, and behaviors, they begin to share their anger and slowly come to recognize the hurt, sadness, embarrassment, and shame behind their anger. The group can begin to examine the continuum of abusive behaviors and help each other explore their specific abusive behaviors. Together they learn to identify healthier ways to interact and examine their goals for relationships. Group members can learn and practice new ways of communicating, owning thoughts and feelings, rather than telling others about their behavior. Clients can examine conflicts and discuss and practice healthy negotiation skills. Much time is used to explore family of origin and examine the feelings connected to childhood and the attitudes and behaviors developed through their childhood experiences (Dutton, 1998; Hanusa, 1997; Fall et al., 1999, Wexler, 2000). This enhances the development of empathy, which is also directly addressed through education and practice. Examination of empathy culminates with a writing task, where the client expresses his understanding of another's experience of violence.

This document (Dutton, 1998, 2007; Hanusa, 1997; Fall et al., 1999; Wexler, 2000) focuses on the event, that led to referral to the group and is written from the perspective of the victim and presented to the group. Group members help each other to identify the feelings and thoughts, which might have been a part of that experience, to enable more accurate empathy for a rewriting of the document. As the group nears an end, each group member clarifies what he has learned in a relapse prevention essay stating how he can apply what he has learned in the future. The relapse prevention plans examine warnings in terms of thoughts, feelings, and behaviors, which might lead to abusive behaviors. Each member can identify his anger and violence potential by the words that are used, internal thoughts, and physical signs, and he can utilize these to take some time to cool down and address the feelings in more productive ways.

Assessing Group Success

Success of group treatment becomes difficult to determine. One aspect that is of concern is what criteria are used to measure success. Cognitive-behavioral formats have been associated with reduced violence. Follow-up a year later showed continued decrease in physical violence, but threats of violence had returned (Faulkner, Stoltenberg, Cogen, Nolder, & Shooter, 1992). Even with reduced violence or no violent behavior, maltreatment in the form of terror, intimidation, and verbal and emotional abuse may continue. Edelson and Tolman (1992) suggest that studies which use zero violence at follow-up as the determinant of success and the most inclusive definitions of violence provide a more accurate indication of success rates. Studies reviewed by Edelson and Tolman reported successful outcomes from 53% to 85%. This would appear to be positive results when compared with research on personal change (Prochaska, DiClemente, & Norcross, 1992). Babcock's (2004) meta-analytic review of IPV treatment results indicated small treatment effects and minimal impact on reducing recidivism. Wexler (2000) notes some optimism for success with groups, which utilizes an integrative model.

FEMALE PERPETRATORS OF IPV

So far this chapter has discussed male abusers and female victims. Since the inception of the 1994 Violence Against Women Act and its zero tolerance of violence in intimate partner relationships, it is worth noting that the number of women arrested for IPV has increased (Grauwiler & Mills, 2004; Tower, 2007). Most women arrested for IPV, however, are not the primary aggressor in the relationship (Seamans, Rubin, & Stabb, 2007). According to Tower (2007),

> [W]omen's use of violence may be characterized by self-defense, false charges by their manipulative batterer, as well as use of violence, within the context of a long abuse history; hence, women's use of violence is qualitatively different from acts committed by batterers. Differences appear in women's and men's motivation, context, and consequences of violence in domestic relationships.

Most identified female perpetrators of IPV show marked differences in self-perception in the group counseling setting; whereas male abusers tend to devalue their partners, female perpetrators of IPV tend to devalue themselves (Schroffel, 2004).

Table 11.1. Outline of a 20-Week IPV Group

Week	*Topics/Exercises*
1	Participation agreement. Personal violence statements
2	Time out, basic anger principles, stress management skills
3	What you can and can't control? Conflict issue: emotions, actions Basic communication–"I" messages Assertive requests/refusals
4	Examining values–movie and reaction
5	Continuum of abuse–power wheel
6	Family of origin work: How did dad/mom show their feelings? Parenting style
7	Impact of abuse on their own lives. Detection of other prevalent emotions
8	Punishment/discipline
9	Praise–respect
10	Self-talk, examine scripts (Dutton, 1998, pp. 174–175)
11	Abuse cycle–communication
12	Empathy–listening, reflecting
13	Assertiveness
14	Consolidation of communication skills
15	Revisiting, rewriting power wheel
16	Intimacy
17	Empathy exercise
18	Continue empathy work
19	Relapse prevention plan
20	What did you learn? Sharing relapse prevention plan. What continues to be a problem? And how can you address it?

(Dutton, 1998, 2007; Fall, Howard, & Ford, 1999; Hanusa, 1997)

Whether females arrive for treatment as perpetrators or victims, the concepts and interventions deemed most effective are the same. Themes to be addressed include safety, power and control, the dynamics of abuse, anger management, communication skills, effects of violence on children, healthy coping, and self-care. "[T]he goal of a battered women's group is to promote safety and empowerment . . . [while] the goal of a violent-reactive women's group is to develop nonviolent resistance strategies and promote safety and empowerment" (Tower, 2007, p. 48). Again, most women identified as perpetrators of IPV do not have a history of being the primary aggressor; rather, they have a history of being abused. Regardless of what brings them to treatment, it is important to teach nonviolent alternative responses within their relationships.

CONCLUSION

Further research is needed to continue refining treatment and enhancing success rates. Violence continues to have an impact on all of our lives. Mental health counselors can play a significant role in reducing the violence and enabling the next generation to have healthier models for expression of feelings and resolving conflict.

REFERENCES

Babcock, J. (2004). Does batterers' treatment work? A meta-analytic review of domestic violence treatment. *Clinical Psychology Review, 23,* 1023–1053.

Bancroft, L. (2002). *Why does he do that? Inside the minds of angry & controlling men.* New York: Berkley Books.

Bern, E. (1990). Training in clinical work with physically abusive men. *The Journal of Training & Practice in Professional Psychology, 4,* 20–32.

Bowlby, J. (1988). *A secure base: Parent-child attachment and healthy human development.* New York: Basic Books.

Briere, J. B., & Jordan, C. E. (2004). Violence against women: Outcome complexity and implications for assessment and treatment. *Journal of Interpersonal Violence, 19*(11), 1252–1276.

Briere, J. B., & Scott, C. (2006). *Principles of trauma therapy: A guide to symptoms, evaluation, and treatment.* Thousand Oaks, CA: Sage Publications.

Brown, J. (2004). Shame and domestic violence: Treatment perspectives for perpetrators from self psychology and affect theory. *Sexual and Relationship Therapy, 19,* 39–56.

Browne, K., & Saunders, D. (1997). Process-psychodynamic groups for men who batter: A brief treatment model. *Families in Society: The Journal of Contemporary Human Services, 78,* 265–271.

Busch, A., & Rosenberg, M. (2004). Comparing women and men arrested for domestic violence: A preliminary report. *Journal of Family Violence, 19,* 49–57.

Caetano, R., Field, C., & Nelson, S. (2003). Association between childhood physical abuse, exposure to parental violence and alcohol problems in adulthood. *Journal of Interpersonal Violence, 18,* 240–257.

Campbell, J. C., Webster, D., Koziol-McLain, J., Block, C. R., Campbell, D., Curry, M. A., Gary, F., McFarlane, J., Sachs, C., Sharps, P., Ulrich, Y., & Wilt, S. A. (2003). Assessing risk factors for intimate partner homicide. *NIJ Journal, 250.* Retrieved January 26, 2010, from http://www.ncjrs.gov/pdffiles1/jr000250e.pdf

Centers for Disease Control and Prevention, National Center for Injury Prevention and Control. (2003). *Costs of intimate partner violence against women in the United States.* Atlanta, GA. Author. Retrieved August 24, 2004, from http://www.cdc.gov/ncipc/pub-res/ipv_cost/ipv.htm

Centers for Disease Control and Prevention. (2008). *Morbidity and Mortality Weekly Report, 57*(5), 113-117. Retrieved January 26, 2010, from http://www.cdc.gov/mmwr/preview/mmwrhtml/mm5705a1.htm

Chavis, A., & Hill, M. (2009). Integrating multiple intersecting identities: A multicultural conceptualization of the power and control wheel. *Women & Therapy, 32,* 121–149.

Conner, K., & Ackerly, G. (1994). Alcohol-related battering: Developing treatment strategies. *Journal of Family Violence, 9,* 143–155.

Costa, L., & Holliday, D. (1993). Considerations for the treatment of marital violence. *Journal of Mental Health Counseling, 15,* 26–36.

DeJonghe, E. S., Bogat, G. A., Levendosky, A. A., & von Eye, A. (2008). Women survivors of intimate partner violence and post-traumatic stress disorder: Prediction and prevention. *Journal of Postgraduate Medicine, 54*(4), 294–300.

Douglas, H. (1991). Assessing violent couples. *Families in Society: The Journal of Contemporary Human Services, 72*(9), 525–535.

Downs, W., Capshew, T., & Rindels, B. (2004). Relationships between adult women's alcohol problems and their childhood experiences of parental violence and psychological aggression. *Journal of Studies on Alcohol, 65,* 336–344.

Ducharme, J., Koverla, C., & Battle, P. (1997). Intimacy development: The influence of abuse and gender. *Journal of Interpersonal Violence, 12,* 590–599.

Duplantis, D. A., Romans, J. S. C., & Bear, T. M. (2008). Persistence in domestic violence treatment and self-esteem, locus of control, risk of alcoholism, level of abuse, and beliefs about abuse. *Journal of Aggression, Maltreatment & Trauma, 13*(1), 1–18.

Dutton, D. (1995). *The batterer: A psychological profile.* New York: Basic Books.

Dutton, D. (1998). *The abusive personality: Violence and control in intimate relationships.* New York: Guilford Press.

Dutton, D. (2007). *The abusive personality: Violence and control in intimate relationships* (2nd ed.). New York: Guilford Press.

Ebell, M. (2004). Routine screening for depression, alcohol problems, and domestic violence. *American Family Physician, 69,* 2421–2422.

Edelson, J., & Tolman, R. (1992). *Intervention for men who batter.* Newbury Park, CA: Sage Publications.

Else, L., Wonderlich, S., Beatty, W., Christie, D., & Staton, R. (1993). Personality characteristics of men who physically abuse women. *Hospital and Community Psychiatry, 44,* 54–58.

Evans, P. (2010). *The verbally abusive relationship: How to recognize it and how to respond* (3rd ed.). Holbrook, MA: Adams Media Corporation.

Fall, K. A., Howard, S., & Ford, J. E. (1999). *Alternatives to domestic violence: A homework manual for battering intervention groups.* Philadelphia, PA: Taylor & Francis.

Family Violence Prevention Fund. (2010). *Action center. Get the facts: The facts on domestic, dating, and sexual violence.* Retrieved January 26, 2010, from website http://www.endabuse.org

/content/http://www.endabuse.org/content/action_center/detail/754

Faulkner, K., Stoltenberg, C., Cogen, R., Nolder, M., & Shooter, E. (1992). Cognitive-behavioral group treatment for male spouse abusers. *Journal of Family Violence 7,* 37–55.

Feldman, C. (1997). Childhood precursors of adult inter partner violence. *Clinical Psychology: Science and Practice, 4,* 307-334.

Felitti, V., Anda, R., Nordenberg, D., Williamson, D., Spitz, A., Edwards, V., Koss, M., & Marks, J. (1998). Relationship of childhood abuse and household dysfunction to many of the leading causes of death in adults. *American Journal of Preventive Medicine 14,* 245–258.

Gondolf, E. (2003). MCMI results for batterers: Gondolf replies to Dutton's response. *Journal of Family Violence, 18,* 387–389.

Grauwiler, P., & Mills, L. (2004). Moving beyond the criminal justice paradigm: A radical justice approach to intimate abuse. *Journal of Sociology and Social Welfare, 31,* 49–69.

Greenfield, L. M., Craven, D., Klaus, P., Perkins, C., Ringel, C., Warchol, G., Maston, C., & Fox, J. (1998). *Violence by intimates: Analysis of data on crimes by current or former spouses, boyfriends, and girlfriends.* Washington, DC: U.S. Department of Justice, NCJ-167237.

Hamberger, L., & Hastings, J. (1991). Personality correlates of men who batter and nonviolent men: Some continuities and discontinuities. *Journal of Family Violence, 6,* 131–147.

Hanusa, D. (1997, November 7). *From power to empowerment: Working with domestic violence abusers and victims.* Paper presented at the Wisconsin Counseling Association annual convention. Madison, WI.

Harris, G. E. (2006). Conjoint therapy and domestic violence: Treating the individuals and the relationship. *Counseling Psychology Quarterly, 19*(4), 373–379.

Haskell, L. (2001). *Bridging responses: A frontline worker's guide to supporting women who have post-traumatic stress.* Toronto, ON: Centre for Addiction and Mental Health.

Haskell, L. (2004). *Women, abuse and trauma therapy.* Toronto, ON: Centre for Addiction and Mental Health.

Herman, J. (1997). *Trauma and recovery: The aftermath of violence–from domestic abuse to political terror.* New York: Basic Books.

Holtzworth-Munroe, A., & Stuart, G. (1994). Typologies of male batterers: Three subtypes and the differences among them. *Psychological Bulletin, 116,* 476–497.

Holtzworth-Munroe, A., Stuart, G., & Hutchinson G. (1997). Violent versus nonviolent husbands: Differences in attachment patterns, dependency, and jealousy. *Journal of Family Psychology, 11,* 314–331.

Iverson, K. M., Shenk, C., & Fruzzetti, A. E. (2009). Dialectical behavior therapy for women victims of domestic abuse: A pilot study. *Professional Psychology: Research and Practice, 40*(3), 242–248.

Kernic, M., Wolf, M., Holt, V., McKnight, B., Huebner, C., & Rivara, F. (2003). Behavioral problems among children whose mothers are abused by an intimate partner. *Child Abuse & Neglect, 27,* 1231–1246.

Kubaney, E. S., Hill, E. E., Owens, J. A., Iannce-Spencer, C., McCaig, M. A., Tremayne, K. J., & Williams, P. L. (2004). Cognitive trauma therapy for battered women with PTSD (CTT-BW). *Journal of Consulting and Clinical Psychology, 72*(1), 3–18.

Kwong, M., Bartholomew, K., Henderson, A. J. Z., & Trinke, S. J. (2003). The intergenerational transmission of relationship violence. *Journal of Family Psychology, 17,* 288–301.

Leibman, F. (1992). Childhood abandonment/adult rage: The root of violent criminal acts. *American Journal of Forensic Psychology, 10,* 57–64.

Leitenberg, H., Gibson, L., & Novy, P. (2004). Individual differences among undergraduate women in methods of coping with stressful events: The impact of cumulative childhood stressors and abuse. *Child Abuse & Neglect, 28,* 181–192.

Levine, P. A. (2007). *Waking the tiger: Healing trauma.* Berkeley, CA: North Atlantic Books.

Liang, B., Goodman, L., Tummala-Narra, P., & Weintraub, S. (2005). A theoretical framework for understanding help-seeking processes among survivors of intimate partner violence. *American Journal of Community Psychology, 36*(1/2), 71–84.

Madanes, C. (1995). *The violence of men: New techniques for working with abusive families: A therapy of social action.* San Francisco: Jossey-Bass.

Maine Coalition to End Domestic Violence. (2010). *GLBTQ relationships.* Retrieved January 25, 2010, from http://74.125.93.104/search?q=cache:4dh2_w7UQCcJ:www.mcedv.org/affect/glbtq.htm+same+sex+domestic+violence+department+justice&cd=10&hl=en&ct=clnk&gl=us

Meltzer, H., Doos, L., Vostanis, P., Ford, T., & Goodman, R. (2009). The mental health of children who witness domestic violence. *Child & Family Social Work, 14*(4), 491–501.

Mick, J. (2006). Identifying signs and symptoms of intimate partner violence in an oncology setting. *Clinical Journal of Oncology Nursing, 10*(4), 509–514.

Miller, W., & Rollnick, S. (2002). *Motivational interviewing: Preparing people for change* (2nd ed.). New York: Guilford Press.

Milner, J., Robertson, K., & Rogers, D. (1990). Childhood history of abuse and adult child abuse potential. *Journal of Family Violence, 5,* 15–34.

National Research Council. (1996). *Understanding violence against women.* Washington, DC: National Academy Press.

National Coalition Against Domestic Violence. (2007). Public Policy Office. *Domestic violence facts.* Retrieved January 26, 2010, from http://www.ncadv.org/files/DomesticViolenceFactSheet(National).pdf

Pico-Alfonso, M. A., Garcia-Linares, M. I., Celda-Navarro, N., Blasco-Ros, C., Echeburua, E., & Martinez, M. (2006). The impact of physical, psychological, and sexual intimate male partner violence on women's mental health: Depressive symptoms, posttraumatic stress disorder, state anxiety, and suicide. *Journal of Women's Health, 15*(5), 599–611.

Prochaska, J., DiClemente, C., & Norcross, J. (1992). In search of how people change: Applications to the addictive behaviors. *American Psychologist, 47,* 1102–1114.

Ramos, B., Carlson, B., & McNutt, L. (2004). Lifetime abuse, mental health, and African-American women. *Journal of Family Violence, 19,* 153–164.

Rasmussen, L. A., Hughes, M. J., & Murray, C. A. (2008). Applying motivational interviewing in a domestic violence shelter: A pilot study evaluating the training of shelter staff. *Journal of Aggression, Maltreatment & Trauma, 17*(3), 296–317.

Roth, J. (1994). Psychoactive substances and violence. *National Institute of Justice: Research in Brief,* 1–8.

Schroffel, A. (2004). Characteristics of female perpetrators of domestic violence in group therapy. *Smith College Studies in Social Work, 74*(3), 505–524.

Seamans, C. L., Rubin, L. J., & Stabb, S. D. (2007). Women domestic violence offenders: Lessons of violence and survival *Journal of Trauma & Dissociation, 8*(2), 47–68.

Searle, B., & Meara, N. (1999). Affective dimensions of attachment styles: Exploring self-reported attachment style, gender, and emotional experience among college students. *Journal of Counseling Psychology, 46,* 147–158.

Shapiro, F., & Forrest, M. S. (2004). *EMDR: The breakthrough eye-movement therapy for overcoming anxiety, stress, and trauma.* New York: Basic Books.

Shapiro, S. (1995). *Talking with patients: A self psychological view.* Northvale, NJ: Aronson.

Shields, N., & Hanneke, C. (1983). Attribution processes in violent relationships: Perceptions of violent husbands and their wives. *Journal of Applied Social Psychology, 13,* 515–527.

Silverman, J., & Williamson, G. (1997). Social ecology and entitlements involved in battering by heterosexual college males: Contributions of family and peers. *Violence and Victims, 12,* 147–164.

Stith, S. M., Rosen, K. H., & McCollum, E. E. (2003). Effectiveness of couples treatment for spouse abuse. *Journal of Marital and Family Therapy, 29,* 407–426.

Straus, M., & Gelles, R. (1990). *Physical violence in American families: Risk factors and adaptations to violence in 8,145 families.* New Brunswick, NJ: Transaction Publishers.

Tower, L. E. (2007). Group work with a new population: Women in domestic relationships responding to violence with violence. *Women & Therapy, 30*(1/2), 35–60.

U.S. Preventive Services Task Force. (2004). Screening for family and intimate partner violence: Recommendation statement. *Annals of Internal Medicine, 14,* 382–386.

Van der Kolk, B. (1988). Trauma in men: Effects on family life. In M. B. Straus (Ed.), *Abuse and victimization across the life span* (pp. 170–187). Baltimore, MD: Johns Hopkins University Press.

Walker, L. (1984). *The battered woman syndrome.* New York: Springer-Verlag.

Walker, L. (1995). Current perspectives on men who batter women–implications for intervention and treatment to stop violence against women: Comment on Gottman et al. *Journal of Family Psychology, 9,* 264–271.

Walker, L. E. (2000). *The battered woman syndrome* (2nd ed.). New York: Springer.

Wang, M., Home, S. G., Holdford, R., & Henning, K. R. (2008). Family of origin violence predictors of IPV by two types of male offenders. *Journal of Aggression, Maltreatment & Trauma, 17*(2), 156–174.

Wexler, D. (2000). *Domestic violence 2000: An integrated skills program for men. Group leader's manual.* New York: W. W. Norton.

Widom, C. (1992). The cycle of violence. *National Institute of Justice: Research in Brief,* 1–6.

The Women's Center. (2009). *Advocacy training manual.* Waukesha, WI: Author.

Zink, T., Kamine, D., Musk, L., Sill, M., Field, V., & Putnam, F. (2004, June). What are providers' reporting requirements for children who witness domestic violence? *Clinical Pediatrics,* pp. 449–460.

Chapter 12

SUBSTANCE ABUSE AND THE EFFECTIVE COUNSELOR

David P. Borsos

SCOPE OF ADDICTIONS

Substance abuse and dependency are common, pandemic issues that any well-trained counselor will encounter during his or her career. Surveys from the Substance Abuse and Mental Health Services Administration (SAHMSA) counted about 7.3% of the population over the age of 12 as drug dependent in 2008. The same studies show that 23.3% of those over 12 years old have been binge drinking in the 30 days prior to the study and about 7% are alcohol dependent or abusive (Substance Abuse and Mental Health Services Administration, 2009).

About 25% of the population has used marijuana at least once, and about 2% of the adult population are addicted to some illegal drug (Doweiko, 1999). Alcohol is complicit in 25% of successful suicides and 56% of domestic abuse cases. Chemical abuse is involved in 25%–30% of all emergency room visits, and four out of five minors arrested for crimes are drug or alcohol involved. It is also estimated that 22 to 34 million children grow up in alcoholic households and suffer accordingly (Doweiko, 1999). Children who do grow up in these environments have a ten times greater chance of developing their own problems with drugs and drinking.

A Brief History of the "High"

It seems as if America has been in a "war against drugs" or a "battle against the bottle" forever. The legal war against drugs actually began with the passage of the Harrison Narcotic Act in 1914. This was the federal government's first attempt to regulate or ban the use of drugs, especially those that were used for nefarious purposes, like fun. Previously, people could use whatever chemicals were available. Now these substances were illegal or only available within the scope of a medical practice. Drug use promptly went up (Brecher et al., 1972). It is true that cola drinks and other soda pop had small amounts of cocaine in them to give the drinker a little boost. The amount of cocaine was minimal and not like the potentially lethal doses of cocaine that are today found on the streets of most cities. The strength of the cocaine was more similar to a strong dose of caffeine that we now have in many soft drinks.

Around the same time, various "temperance societies" were crusading for a ban on the use of "demon rum" or any alcohol product. The religious and moral fervor of the times saw this substance as evil and a curse on civilized society. These groups succeeded with the passage of the 18th amendment to the constitution in 1919, which banned the sale, manufacture, and transportation of all alcohol products in America. Alcohol use promptly went up while the now unregulated beverage became less pure and more adulterated (Brecher et al., 1972). Many nondrinkers are reported to have taken up drinking socially in a quiet defiance of a government that had become overcontrolling of their behaviors. Normal adults did not want to be told what they could or couldn't do with their socializing. The banning of alcohol had other unintended consequences as well. Primarily, there was the rise of organized crime syndicates that would gladly risk breaking the law by providing people with alcohol, especially in secret clubs called "speakeasies." This grand national experiment in social and moral change was abandoned in 1933 with the passage of the 21st amendment canceling the 18th. It was the first and only time in history that an amendment to the American constitution was revoked or repealed.

Illegal drug use accelerated during the "counter-culture" years of the 1960s. Illegal drugs had never gone away, of course. They had remained in use in the backrooms of certain clubs and saloons. Drugs such as marijuana had remained the preserve of some musicians, actors, residents of poor neighborhoods, and others on the fringes of society. Yet during this tumultuous decade, the use of illegal drugs spread first to college campuses, then to high schools, to the workplace, the military, and gradually to every neighborhood and school. Military veterans were coming home from the war in Vietnam with heroin addictions. Some unfortunate souls were getting life sentences for possession of marijuana in states such as Texas and New York. Newer, stronger, and more dangerous drugs, such as "crack" cocaine and "ecstasy," were developed and sold over the past 40 years. They have become cheaper and accessible to anyone who is looking for the "high." In fact, it is estimated that anyone in America is only one or two phone calls away from accessing any illegal drug.

As drugs moved into the mainstream of society, the selection expanded dramatically. In the mid-1960s, marijuana was readily available. A few other unintended gifts from the pharmaceutical industry, such as Valium, barbiturates, and methamphetamine, were being abused by the bored, the daring, or the rebellious. Cocaine was an expensive powder for the rich, famous and wealthy only. Narcotics such as heroin had to be injected through a complicated process and were generally seen as being the province of "hard-core" addicts.

But, how the illegal pharmacopeia has expanded its wares. Brand-new drugs such as ecstacy, ropinhol, and oxycontin are readily available. A more lethal and cheaper version of cocaine has been developed and successfully marketed as "crack" cocaine. "Moderate" users now consider it acceptable to snort or smoke more potent, noninjectable versions of heroin. Even some legitimate drugs such as Quaaludes have come and gone because its abuse potential outweighed its medical value.

Despite enormous amounts of taxpayer money, school programming on drug prevention, DARE and "Just Say No" programs, increased law enforcement, and interdiction, the drug abuse and addiction problem has worsened since the 1960s. Drug and alcohol abuse has increased with larger and more easily accessible amounts available. Children and teens start at younger ages. Many parents who were raised in the 1960s now bring their drug habits with them into middle age and are sometimes sharing these habits with their own children. These are some of the many reasons that the well-prepared counselor can expect a substance abuse problem to walk into his or her door at any time. Substance abuse may exist in your client, his spouse or parent, a child, or some other family member. We'd better be ready.

STAGES OF DRUG AND ALCOHOL ABUSE

Many people reading this right now have used alcohol and/or other drugs, perhaps even often and to excess. We may all know friends and family members who have done the same and still lead happy and productive lives. Clearly all use, although illegal, is not abuse or addiction. Not everyone who uses illegal drugs or alcohol develops a diagnosable disorder or pathology. It is crucial for the effective counselor to be able to assess the difference between casual and caustic use as well as between the pathological and the experimental. To help us do this, we can divide drug/alcohol use up into five stages that exist on an overlapping continuum (Doweiko, 1999; Schaeffer, 1987).

Abstinence

Many people refrain from any and all use of psychoactive substances, including alcohol. They are not interested in the feelings of being high or the potential dangers of drug or alcohol use. The occasional glass of Christmas wine is enough adventure for those choosing abstinence. These people obviously will not be seeking counseling for their own substance abuse issues. However, many abstinent people are recovering addicts who must adopt the abstinent lifestyle to keep themselves safe, sober, and sane. Often our role as a counselor is to help these people maintain their abstinence.

Experimental Use

A person may move from an abstinent state to one of curiosity and experimentation. Experimentation usually happens during adolescence or even early adulthood. Sometimes this is referred to as "being introduced to the drug." The individual uses the chemical when it is around but does not actively pursue it and has no regular usage. The person may try marijuana a few times when offered it at a party or take an LSD "trip" once just to see what it is like. But for many at this stage, the usage remains infrequent, experimental, done under specific social contexts, and does not worsen. Well-known examples of this are former President Clinton, who admitted to trying marijuana in college during the 1960s or President Obama, who admitted to some youthful drug experimentation. It seems to be such a common occurrence that most people readily admit to trying drugs in their "youth" without fear of troubles. Although we have seen that, for some individuals, youth can go on a long time. Generally, these people will not show up in the counselor's office unless caught by an authority during one of their activities.

Social Use

After the initial experimenting, some individuals move up to a more regular, social use of drugs and alcohol. Here, the person regularly uses the chemical and in a sense "seeks" the high for fun and sociability. He or she is no longer just "trying out" something but actively pursuing it. At this point, the chemical is not yet a problem. The person can take it or leave it and would have no trouble stopping its use if necessary. For example, a person could easily quit using for a job interview or for a blood test to join a sports team. These individuals would generally not enter counseling unless forced by a parent or other adult authority.

Abuse

At the point of abuse, the chemical has evolved into a real problem for the user but not yet an actual, physical addiction. It is harming the person's life in some way: school, home, work, social relationships, or marriage. Using and getting high is taking more and more time and starting to interfere with the smooth functioning of life. Perhaps there is a drunk driving arrest or a bad fight with a spouse. Friends may start to avoid the person or ask him to "cut down a little." The substance is starting to take control. This person, if willing, is a prime candidate for counseling.

Chemical Dependency/Addiction

Here is where Johnny has finally hit bottom. There is a physical or psychological dependency on the chemical. Tolerance and withdrawal symptoms have developed. The drug is now in control of his or her life. Most of the day is spent in pursuing the high that now feels necessary and the only way to feel "normal" again. Careers and schooling are lost. Marriages dissolve and medical problems may develop. Death is even more likely from an overdose, accident, or a related medical problem such as cirrhosis of the liver or a cocaine-induced heart attack.

The pain and despair at this stage can often put the person at a high risk for suicidal behavior. He or she can also be at risk for an "accidental" suicide by performing reckless and dangerous behaviors. The author knew a client who, while in an alcoholic black-out, became determined to jump off every pier along the Jersey shore no matter what the water level was below him. He survived.

It is crucial for the effective counselor to assess the client's stage of use or abuse. Effective assessment guides the level of treatment, if any, that is necessary. For example, one does not want to put a 16-year-old into rehab if he's only been drunk twice in his life and this time he got caught by mom. A girl experimenting with "pot" at the prom will not need extensive treatment–no matter what the principal thinks.

Yet her friend who is passed out in the limo undiscovered by anyone may be in real need of alcoholism counseling or rehabilitation. Here are some guidelines a counselor could use to determine what interventions may be necessary depending on the stage of use of the client:

Stage 1: Abstinence. No treatment is needed unless the person is in recovery.

Stage 2: Experimental. Possible drug and alcohol education classes or groups.

Stage 3: Regular Use. An educational group, some counseling on alternatives to use, skill building around coping skills, and resisting peer pressures.

Stage 4: Abuse. Intensive out-patient program or at least weekly out-patient counseling sessions, support or 12-step groups.

Stage 5: Dependency. Inpatient rehab, long-term, residential treatment. Some may benefit from intensive out-patient with involvement in groups such as Alcoholics Anonymous (AA) or Narcotics Anonymous (NA).

MODELS OF ADDICTION

Explanations of the causes and treatments of substance abuse and addiction are not yet completely agreed on. As with many issues in counseling and psychology, there are a variety of theories and interventions. However, a few main models are generally accepted as fruitful and have some supporting research.

The Disease Model

The Disease Model, as promoted by the medical community and self-help traditions such as AA, is probably the predominant model of addiction today. It states that alcoholism and other addictions are diseases unto themselves, like any other disease. They have physical, psychological, and spiritual causes and are not caused by any other underlying pathology, unconscious conflict, or life event. It is a disease because it is chronic, and progressive and will lead to death if unchecked. It is never cured, only persistently managed, much like diabetes. "Once an alcoholic (or addict), always an alcoholic," this model says. A biologic or genetic cause or predisposition is presumed, although the evidence for this is as yet inconclusive.

Because the addiction is a disease unto itself, any other associated problems are a result of the disease and not vice versa (Thombs, 1999). There is a strong emphasis on the unproven genetic transmission of the disease. However, others note that this family transmission may be a result of learning, role modeling, or other family dynamics and pathology influencing the developing addict.

There are studies supportive of the genetic/disease model of addictions. An early study by Goodwin, Schulsinger, Hermansen, Guze, and Winokur (1973) compared the rates of alcoholism of Danish children who were adopted out of alcoholic households with those who were adopted out of nonalcoholic ones. He found significant differences in the number of alcoholics that developed from each group.

The alcoholic households spawned addiction in 18% of the kids, whereas the nonalcoholic ones led to a rate of 5%. Critics point out that his definition of addiction and problem drinking is problematic and also ask why the kids from nonalcoholic households still were addicted at a 5% rate if it is genetic.

Twin studies on the genetics of addiction have been inconclusive as well, except to point out some possible contribution but not an exclusive one. Concordance rates for male, monozygotic twins varied from 60%–80% with the variance being 30%–70%. But for female, monozygotic twins concordance varied from 30%–50% but the proportion of the variance accounted for by genetics in the female twins was exactly 0% (McGue, Dickens, & Svikis, 1992). Another study of female alcoholics (Kendler, Heath, Neale, Kessler, & Eaves, 1992) found that genetics contributed 40%–50% of the variance in predicting the development of alcoholism. During this study, the researchers controlled for family, social, and environmental factors.

E. M. Jellinek was the early pioneer in getting the American Medical Association to recognize alcoholism as a disease in 1956. Previously, doctors and society as a whole had simply considered it a moral or character issue. He was the first to see the disease traits of loss of control, progression, and lethality in alcoholism. Dr. Jellinek proposed four stages of the disease: prealcoholic, prodromal, crucial, and chronic. He hypothesized that alcoholics metabolize the chemical differently than others and that alcoholism was a disease that affected all areas of life: social, emotional, economic, and physical (Dowieko, 1999).

The loss of control is an important part of the disease model (Thombs, 1999). It is stated that unstoppable urges and cravings produce virtually unstoppable drinking behaviors. This process is started by the first drink, which begets the next and the next until the person is drunk or unconscious. There are a number of experiments contradicting the loss of control idea. Fingarette (1988) asserts that the amount of alcohol drunk by an alcoholic can be managed by systems of rewards and costs. Researchers got alcoholics to stop drinking by paying them not to drink. Others got alcoholics to moderate their consumption by threatening to remove them from a pleasing environment.

Thombs (1999) points out that alcoholics and addicts are prone to "mature out" (p. 67) of their addictions especially if they have prosocial supports and are not involved in any criminal activities. Marriage and entry into the workforce are also correlated with a reduction in drinking by prior alcoholics. This, of course, raises questions about the loss of control supposition and the automatic progressiveness of the disease.

The Psychoanalytic Model

Freud's analytic theories have been quite ambitious in their explanations of life since he first started writing in the 1890s. He began by working with conversion disorders (then called hysterias), sexual issues, and mood disorders. The analytic tradition and its branches surged into the treatment of schizophrenias (Rosen, 1962), major depression (Jacobson, 1971), personality disorders (Masterson, 1972), family problems (Scharff & Scharff, 1991), and all other varieties of human misery. As with all models, there are a variety of successes and helpful ideas here.

The analytic model presents unconscious conflicts as the chief cause of psychological and behavioral problems. This assumes an unconscious part of the mind, called the id, steaming with instincts burning to be satisfied. The instincts in question are two: libido and aggression, the life and death instincts, or eros and thanatos as the classically trained Freud called them. The superego is both conscious and unconscious. It is that part of the mind we call the conscience or the internalized rules of parents and society. The superego often works in opposition to the satisfaction of the id instincts. The ego is that conscious part of the mind we know as self. It must interact with the environment and balance the demands of the id and superego.

Emotional and behavioral problems are the result of unconscious conflicts and repressions among the ego, superego, id, and environment. An aggressive urge may be stirring to be released while the superego attempts to hold it back as taboo or unacceptable. The resulting conflict is felt in the ego as anxiety, which at times must be assimilated by some defense mechanism like denial, projection, or sublimation. So the id-based desire to hit back at a father who disappointed us is resisted by the superego's constraints against hitting. To handle this conflict and defend against the forbidden anger, the individual may project the anger onto another. "I'm not mad; he is." He may deny that it even exists while it seethes within him or he may use many of the other defenses against forbidden impulses. Symptoms and behaviors are seen as the compromise formulations used to cope with the unconscious conflicts.

In this theory, substance abuse is proposed as one way to deal with these anxious, unconscious conflicts. Using a mind-altering chemical dampens or removes the anxiety and other pain associated with the conflict, at least temporarily. Therefore, the abuse of alcohol or other drugs is seen as a symptom of some other inner problem of the individual and not as a prime disorder as proposed by the medical model.

The analytic model also leads us to the idea of using chemicals to mask or avoid painful, conscious emotions as well (Khantzian & Brehm, 1992; Murphy & Khantzian, 1995). Rather than feel anxiety, drink or smoke pot.

Rather than feel depressed, simply snort some cocaine or another stimulant. Rather than face the disappointments of my life, drink or do drugs so it doesn't matter. This is the concept of self-medication that is widely supported in addictions. Drugs and alcohol are used to numb away horrible feelings indefinitely (Horney, 1964). Of course, legal, prescription drugs can be used the same way at times.

Other important, theoretical branches that grew from psychoanalytic roots are Ego-Psychology (Hartmann, 1939) and Object-Relations (Horney, 1964; Klein, 1948). Ego Psychology posits that pathology can be caused by some deficit or weakness in the ego rather than by unconscious conflict. The pain and dysfunctions of these structural deficits could push someone into using substances to cope with or compensate for these deficits. The afflicted individual could also develop a whole, false, or inauthentic self to compensate for the original, flawed self. Ego-Psychology, then, requires the individual to identify and strengthen the weaknesses of the self through therapy rather than drink or do drugs to cope with these deficits or facades of the self.

The Object-Relations tradition sees individual development as based on seeking secure attachment and relations with others, especially parental caregivers. The individual absorbs or incorporates messages from the caregivers into the psyche and gradually develops an internalized image of self and the world around him or her from these messages. This may result in a relation to self that is relatively healthy or one that is pathological in its mistrust, shame, self-criticism, and sense of inferiority. It may also result in a way of relating to the world that is pathological and dysfunctional. If our earliest messages were that the world is negative, harsh, or undependable, we will form a template in our minds that will drive us to react to the world and others as if they are always negative or mistrustful (Pine, 1990). Substance abuse can be hypothesized to be one way to deal with that internalized negativity about self and with the failed relationships an individual creates around him or her.

Miller and Downs (1995) found a strong connection between early physical or sexual abuse and the development of an addiction. They hypothesize that the life-long emotional fallout of the abuse remains a potent force in the individual. He or she must then find a way to cope with the ongoing emotional turmoil. One way of coping could be the discovery of mind-numbing chemicals of abuse. Bradshaw (1986) has shown a relationship between any kind of severely dysfunctional relationships in the family and a later addiction. Overt abuse is not necessary. Any pattern of emotional pain between parent and child that occurs over time can lead a person to relieve their psychic pain through the abuse of chemicals (Khantzian & Mack, 1983). All of these examples can support the self-medication hypothesis.

Conditioning and Learning Theory Models

Conditioning theories of behavior from Pavlov to Skinner posit that all behaviors are learned and can be unlearned. This includes the behavior of substance abuse. Classical or Pavlovian conditioning simply states that a behavior can be conditioned to occur by associating it with an unconditioned stimulus and its unconditioned response. His dogs salivated at the sound of a bell because the bell had been paired with the unconditioned stimulus, a meat powder, which elicited the unconditioned response of salivation. Salivating to a bell without the powder was then a conditioned response to the conditioned stimulus of the bell.

Addicts and alcoholics can feel the urge to drink or do drugs if they find themselves in a situation that has been paired with the euphoria of the substance. So a man passing a corner where he used to buy cocaine can be stimulated to "salivate for" or have an urge for cocaine. Many people associate drinking with certain events or situations and feel the strong urge to drink in these situations. Weekends, a celebration, a sporting event, and being with certain people can all be associated with drinking or drugging and elicit that response in the individual. This trend has led to the AA/NA philosophy of avoiding people, places, and things associated with the addictive substance.

Operant conditioning states that a behavior will be more likely to occur if it is followed by some kind of reinforcement. There are positive and negative reinforcers to behaviors. A positive reinforcer is one that is felt as pleasurable to the subject and will increase the rate of the reinforced behavior. A negative reinforcer also increases the rate of a behavior by removing a noxious or an unpleasant feeling or situation. A negative reinforcer increases any behavior that removes a "negative" stimulus. A typical example of a negative reinforcer in alcoholism or drug addiction is the relief from withdrawal sickness. A person feels very ill from the lack of an addicted substance. Drinking alcohol or using heroin relieves the noxious, unpleasant feelings of the withdrawal. Therefore, this increases the probability of the addict/alcoholic using more of his substance. The using behavior is reinforced by the removal of the negative situation.

Relief from other unpleasant emotional states could also serve as a negative reinforcer. If I can relieve my work stress with a few cocktails, then I am more likely to do so whenever I feel stressed. Feelings of anger at his parents' yelling went away when the teenager smoked pot, increasing the possibility of doing it again in a similar spot. Positive reinforcers in substance abuse are generally seen to be things like euphoria or other drug-induced, pleasant feelings and social variables such as peer approval or acceptance. Punishments are another factor affecting behavior and generally reduces behavior, at least for a time (Thombs, 1999). Thombs states that behaviorists see the initiation of substance use as a combination of availability, a lack of reinforcers for alternate behaviors, and a lack of punishers for experimenting with substances. Therefore, addictive behaviors can be "extinguished" by eliminating reinforcers for them, reinforcing other alternative behaviors, and perhaps punishing the addictive behavior.

Albert Bandura (1977) proposes his social learning theory to explain behavior. He states that we are both actors and acted on in our environment and that we have the power to change it as much as it may change us; there is a reciprocal determinism between person and environment and person again. This is in contrast to the powerlessness of conditioning and analytic models , which theorize humans as passive victims of the unconscious or of reinforcement schedules. People can learn behaviors by watching others "model" that behavior. I learn to smoke marijuana by watching my older friend. Or people learn or inhibit a behavior based on watching a model be rewarded or punished for the behavior. My friend is admired by the peer group for getting high; or perhaps I see him get arrested for carrying an illegal substance. In either case, I adjust my drug-using behavior accordingly.

Social learning theory also explains that people can "self-regulate" their behaviors. They act according to an internal set of standards and can maintain behaviors independent of external rewards or punishments. If a discrepancy grows between one's behaviors and his or her set of standards, then the individual is inclined to change the behavior, the standards or perhaps both (Abrams & Niaura, 1987). If my internal standards say it is okay to drink because "everyone does," then it is far easier to develop a drinking habit than if I have a standard that says "Drinking is for losers like my alcoholic father."

ASSESSMENT

The assessment of chemical abuse or dependency is not an exact science. There are no concrete physical tests to use, no blood counts, MRIs or brain wave activities. Diagnostic tools for these problems generally revolve around a clinical interview and various structured questionnaires. It is highly recommended that the effective clinician have a face-to-face interview along with a structured questionnaire to get the most accurate assessment possible. Also, it is crucial to gather data on the client's history from other resources such as a spouse, parent, friend, coworker, and/or teacher. These people know your client better than you do and can provide important information, context, or background on the client's patterns of use or abuse.

Reliance on any one source of information can lead to many inaccuracies and a poorer chance of making the correct assessment. Also, we must understand someone's substance use in the context of his or her life. Drinking a six-pack of beer a day may be an unhealthy, high-calorie pastime for one person and a severe addiction for another depending on other factors affected by the drinking. Most structured surveys and questionnaires examine the same kinds of data. Basically, is the chemical harming the person's life in any way? How badly? Is there compulsive, impulsive, and excessive use? Is there a chronic loss of control of the substance?

The Clinical Interview

The counselor is probably familiar with the components of a good clinical interview or biopsychosocial evaluation, so we will not go through those elements in detail for this chapter. Let's look at the elements of a clinical interview for a drug and alcohol assessment, many of which will overlap other mental health interviews. A clinical interviewer is always poised to gather as much relevant data as he or she can about the important issues of a person's life so he or she can flesh out who the client is and how the individual got to this particular trouble spot in life.

Dowieko (1999) and Senay (1992) provide us with the elements necessary for the interview:

1. The reason for the referral. What happened? How?
2. A careful history of drug and alcohol use including substances used, age of first use, frequency and amounts of use, changes in use (especially if it has been worsening with time).
3. Longest periods of sobriety. What ended them?
4. Do you always use to the point of intoxication?
5. Are there legal issues related to use (DUIs, arrests)?
6. Is there a military history related to use?
7. Family history. Are there addictions in either side of the family? Are there other psychological dysfunctions in the family?
8. Is there a psychiatric history with the client?
9. What is the educational and work history? Are there drug or alcohol abuse related problems in these areas?
10. What is the medical history, especially related to substance use?
11. Is there a history of prior treatments? What happened with them?
12. Are there any tests showing the presence of drugs or alcohol in the body?

As you can see, the effective interview covers most of the areas of a client's life. While speaking, the counselor should be working on establishing rapport, a therapeutic relationship, and some sense of trust with the individual. This requires an empathetic and nonjudgmental attitude by the counselor.

The immediate benefit of this demeanor is to ensure more open and honest answers to your questions. Many clients in this situation have a tendency to lie, minimize, deflect, or otherwise shade the truth of many of their answers. Drug and alcohol abusers are notorious for this. This is also why information from others who know the client is valuable. One can cross-check a client's answer to the information gathered elsewhere. "I'm a little confused. You said you have never let your drinking interfere with work, but your boss said you have called out three times with hangovers. Can you explain this discrepancy to me?"

Assessment Tools: The MAST and the DAST

One of the structured assessment tools for this problem is the Michigan Alcohol Screening Test (MAST) (Selzer, 1971). It is a long-standing and respected instrument for evaluating alcoholism. It is composed of 25 yes-or-no questions, each one weighted with a value of points depending on the severity of the topic in the question. Five total points can categorize an alcoholic. It is quick and easy to administer, and the author states it is accurate to the .05 level of confidence. Questions ask about things such as the ability to successfully stop drinking and the habit of drinking in the morning.

Some studies (Jacobson, 1989) suggest that the five-point cut-off results in too many false positives and proposes using ten points as the cut-off for addictive drinking. This debate highlights the importance of using an assessment tool in the context of a clinical interview and a good therapeutic relationship. The Drug Abuse Screening Test (DAST) (Skinner, 1982), is a similar survey evaluating the drug use of a client and its impact on life.

Addiction Severity Index

The Addiction Severity Index (ASI) is another reliable and validated assessment tool for addictions. It evaluates the ways a person's substance use affects his or her life in many areas: medical, legal, family, social relations, employment, psychological, and psychiatric states. The test covers 180 items in a semi-structured interview format developed by McClellan, Luborsky, O'Brien, and Woody (1980).

The DSM-IV-TR

The American Psychiatric Association (2000) publishes its *Diagnostic and Statistical Manual of Mental Disorders* (4th ed., text revision) (2000) with generally accepted criteria to diagnose all psychiatric and psychological problems. This comprehensive manual, the *DSM-IV-TR,* is now in its fourth edition, not counting intermediate revisions. It contains an extensive chapter on diagnosing substance abuse and dependency. It lists a variety of criteria for substance abuse and another, stricter set of criteria to describe substance dependency.

The criteria for substance abuse is defined as "A maladaptive pattern of substance use leading to clinically significant impairment or distress . . ." (*DSM-IV-TR,* p. 182). The distress should display one or more of the following symptoms in the past 12 months: failure to fulfill a major life role or obligation, using when it is dangerous, related legal problems, or continued use despite recurring relational problems.

The criteria for dependency is also defined as a pattern of use that leads to significant problems in life. However, the criteria are stricter and include any three or more of these issues occurring within the past year: tolerance, withdrawal symptoms, using more than intended, failed efforts to reduce use, large amounts of time spent in pursuing the high, important activities in person's life reduced or abandoned, and continued use despite knowledge of ongoing physical or mental problems caused by the substance. One of the interesting things to note about these descriptions is that it does not necessarily require the client to have the physical symptoms of tolerance and withdrawal. They become only two of the total possible seven descriptors. So, it is technically possible for your client to be diagnosed as an addict or substance dependent person without manifesting any tolerance or withdrawal symptoms if he or she has three of the other four criteria in place. This could occur, for example, with inhalant abuse or abuse of other drugs that are not seen as addicting, such as some hallucinogens (LSD). It would also include clients who abuse a lot of drugs but have not developed the physical criteria. As you can see, the criteria for drug and alcohol abuse and dependency fit well into the five-stage use/abuse/dependency continuum discussed earlier. Stages 4 and 5 easily overlap the *DSM-IV-TR* criteria for abuse and dependency.

The SASSI

One of the ongoing problems with trying to accurately assess the substance abuse issues of our clients is their frequent lack of honest cooperation. Addicts and other users/abusers are notorious in the treatment world for trying to hide, deny, or minimize their patterns of use and their effects on life. There can be a variety of reasons for this. Perhaps the person is not yet being honest with him or herself about the use. Often people are afraid of being labeled, getting into more trouble, or getting "shipped off" to rehab against their will. There is the natural tendency to want to present the best image of the self to the counseling professional or anyone else involved in the process, such as a spouse or boss. Substance abusers are often ambivalent about their desire to actually quit using. Admitting to the extent of the problem leads to the obvious conclusion that it must be halted, regardless of whether the client really wants to stop. Many clients are willing to partially admit to some use and related problems but want to retain some information to themselves so they can maintain a rationale for using but "just cutting down a little."

Miller and Lazowski (1999) recently developed an inventory to address this problem, The Substance Abuse Subtle Screening Inventory (SASSI). This inventory aims to evaluate substance dependency when the client is being dishonest, secretive, or minimizing. There are two separate questionnaires: one normed on adolescents and one on adults. The questionnaires ask a series of questions that are not obviously related to substance use. There is a structured protocol in scoring the answers across various categories. Certain patterns of answering these questions have been correlated to the patterns displayed by admitted addicts or alcoholics. An easy-to-follow decision tree helps guide the counselor to a diagnosis of dependency or no diagnosis. The inventory only indicates a dependency not an abuse diagnosis, although the author suggests it can be used to approximate abuse as well.

The author claims a good accuracy rate with about 5% false positives. It is the only test I am aware of that tries to assess dependency in a client who is being secretive or evasive in responding.

SUBSTANCE ABUSE TREATMENT

It is commonly agreed that anyone who is abusing substances must try to remain abstinent and sober for any treatment to be effective. But the irony remains that these people also need some kind of treatment to help them stay sober and abstinent. The counselor must remain patient and tolerant of clients who have a difficult time staying away from drugs or drinking. Relapse into use is an ongoing part of any treatment protocol. Under no circumstances should the counselor try to treat a client who comes to the session under the influence of some chemical. No productive work can be done with a drug-affected mind. The emotions or thoughts that emerge will be chemically affected, and the ability to process and remember information will be impaired. One can politely but firmly ask the person to reschedule and explain why. One should also ensure that the client can leave and arrive home safely–no drunk driving, for example.

The best way, right now, to initiate someone into a sober lifestyle is to refer him to a local 12-step, fellowship meeting such as Alcoholics Anonymous (AA), Narcotics Anonymous (NA), or Cocaine Anonymous (CA). Attendance at these meetings is an important adjunct to successful counseling. But the meetings are not therapy and never claim to be. They are a crucial step in helping maintain a person's sobriety so that other treatments can be effective.

Participation in these meetings begins and maintains a variety of helpful processes for the recovering addict or alcoholic. Going to meetings serves as a substitute behavior when a person feels the urge to use. The recommendation is to attend meetings daily when early in recovery and to use them to cope with cravings, boredom, down time, and any other idleness that may lead to relapse. Attendance at meetings also involves the client in a social and accepting group of like-minded individuals who are looking to help each other in their common goals of sobriety. Everyone at a meeting is in similar trouble; everyone has lost some control over his or her life due to substances. Everyone there is trying to maintain his or her sober lifestyle and help others do the same.

Sober living is acceptable here, as opposed to many other settings in the client's life. Sobriety is reinforced and rewarded by the norms of the group. Members offer each other strategies and coping skills to stay straight. People get to vent about their particular frustration in a safe and supportive environment. Attendees are also encouraged to get a "sponsor" who is a mentor/friend with a longer period of sobriety. The sponsor is a personal contact to rely on during times of struggle or confusion. He or she may also serve as a positive role model for a successful life without drugs or drinking.

Many of the "curative factors" of group psychotherapy (Yalom & Leszcz, 2005) are evident in 12-step groups and do aid in recovery. Altruism is a strong factor evident in meetings. Members gladly give to and help each other, and in the process they help themselves. Altruism improves one's sense of self-efficacy by showing an individual that he or she does have value to others and can be productive. It strengthens the supportive bonds of members and helps by requiring someone to come out of his world and enter the world of another. In this way, it can decrease self-centeredness, narcissism, isolation, and unproductive attention seeking.

Group cohesion is another curative factor common to these groups. As members share, they get to know and trust each other; they work together and grow closer and more cohesive. This bonding can increase self-esteem and serve as a strong support for each member's struggle to stay sober. Interpersonal learning/input occurs as members take in new ideas from each other. Imitation also occurs as newer members seek to improve themselves by imitating the successful behaviors of older members.

The group curative factor of universality is a strong component of AA/NA meetings. The group member realizes that he or she is not alone with a problem. There is a commonality and unity of problems among all the members of the group. People so often feel isolated and ashamed as they struggle with the unmanageability of an addiction. Fellowship groups first ask their members to admit to this unmanageability, the out-of-control nature of the addiction. With this admission, the new member joins the "universe" of this fellowship and is no longer alone. Finally, the instillation of hope is an important part of these meetings. People see success where they have had none. People see others get their addictions under control, and hope for their own recovery is increased.

AA/NA meetings also introduce members to their famous "12-step" program for adopting a sober lifestyle. These steps require individuals to admit their "powerlessness" over the substance and then turn their recovery over to a "higher power," which could be God, the group, or some other positive force outside the self. There are steps of self-examination and insight, followed by plans of action to redress one's problems and past injuries to others (Alcoholics Anonymous, 1955). All along, the group is there to assist with these crucial and difficult steps.

Members also learn useful mind-sets, rules, or philosophies to maintain sobriety. Ideas like "One day at a time" remind the person to work on sober living now and not agonize about possible future troubles. Another "rule" is to avoid "people, places, and things" that are associated with using substances. These are the strong "triggers" that may cue off a bout of drugging or drinking in the addict. Members must avoid the places where they used and the people with whom they used. Even things associated with using, such as certain kinds of music or clothing, are to be avoided. There is no room for buying music in a "head shop" or stopping at the bar "just for cigarettes." People are urged to trash t-shirts with beer logos or pictures of pot leaves on them. Music that conjures up images of getting high or drunk is to be avoided. There are many other useful pieces of information from these groups that the effective counselor should investigate through the various publications they offer.

Although fellowship meetings are important in beginning and maintaining a drug–or alcohol-free lifestyle, they are not counseling or therapy. Most people in recovery will need professional counseling for various issues occurring before, during, or after their addiction. Varieties of counseling techniques have been developed, borrowed, or adapted from the many counseling theories available to us.

Behavioral theories of counseling have given us many useful techniques to use with recovering individuals. The urge to drink or do drugs is very powerful in most of these clients. They need an alternative way of handling these urges without backsliding (Marlatt & Gordon, 1985). Relaxation and imagery exercises are effective tools to help manage these cravings and temptations to use. Teach individuals to practice relaxation techniques or imagine themselves at the beach rather than cope with anxiety or a craving by using.

The principles of classical and operant conditioning can be used in treatment. A common problem for many recovering people is that of "euphoric recall" (Margolis & Zweben, 1998). With this, the client consistently remembers the fun and excitement associated with using, and this stimulates further desires to continue using. The counselor must help the client pair the negative consequences of the substance-abusing behavior to the addiction. The client must learn to remember the arrests, hangovers, arguments, and lost money and jobs that resulted from using rather than any positives associated to it. The author once had a 40-year-old cocaine addict, Pete, carry an ad from the phone book with him to remind him of negative consequences. It was an ad for a divorce lawyer, which he kept near a picture of his wife whom he loved and did not want to lose.

Recovering people have a desperate need to develop alternative behaviors as part of their life changes. They complain of boredom and a lack of fun activities to replace the drugs and drinking. It is crucial that the counselor help with that process. The Relapse Prevention Card is a wallet-sized card the client carries with him or her always. On one side of the card is a list of alternative activities developed just for that person. On the other is a list of important phone numbers the individual may need to call when tempted to relapse. It may include obvious actions such as "call your sponsor" and more personal ones such as "tell your wife what you're feeling" or "go meditate." It is important that the recovering addict/alcoholic does not try to do it all alone or keep things to him or herself.

Journaling the thoughts, feelings, weaknesses, and strengths of each day is another useful tool for the client. He or she may get many demons out in the open, where they can be dealt with in session or with other trusted individuals.

People who have had a lifelong addiction, especially one that started in their youth, are often deficient in many of the life skills that healthier people take for granted. You may need to help your client learn assertiveness skills (Alberti & Emmons, 1978) or refusal skills. They will need to practice and absorb communication and relationship skills. This could include expressing your needs clearly, actively listening to others, empathetic responses, using "I" statements, and the like. Job interviewing skills or good parenting skills are other areas your clients may be deficient in because of their lifelong addictive behaviors.

There are some studies that show success for operant styles of behavioral intervention. Researchers have used various reward systems and token economies to reinforce abstinence (Mehr, 1988). Higgins et al. (1991) found reinforcement and reward approaches that could overcome cravings to use cocaine. The addictions counselor could custom-make a reward system that the client would follow as an aid to staying clean. For example, the author once had a client agree not to use his drug of choice, and for every successful week, he could purchase a special item that he always wanted but could not afford when using. He was also required to keep his wife informed of his actions.

This intervention is also called contingency management or contracting at times (Thombs, 1999). With this, the client agrees to certain functional behaviors, and the counselor works out a system of rewards and punishments within his or her daily life to help shape client behavior and cooperation. This process often requires the help of parents, spouses, bosses, and others involved with the client. The usual requirements of a reward system are needed, especially that the rewards are close in time to the behavior and the rewards are meaningful to the client.

Cognitive theories have contributed some effective techniques to use with this population. Cognitive therapy for addicts follows the same basic techniques as cognitive therapy for other disorders. Beck and Liese (1998) point to dysfunctional thoughts and belief systems as important to understanding and treating addictions. Dysfunctional core beliefs lead to automatic negative thoughts about the self and the world, which can then lead to painful emotional states and drugging behaviors to cope with the thoughts and feelings. They point out the importance of being aware of this relapse chain in a personal way for each client. An intervention can be planned at any point in the sequence.

For example, "Pete," the 40-year-old cocaine addict, carried with him a constant belief that he was incompetent and unlovable. These beliefs often led to self-defeating, automatic thoughts such as, "I'll never be successful in anything" or "My wife will probably leave me no matter what I do." This thinking often led to debilitating feelings of abandonment, loneliness, anger, and hurt, which led to thoughts of using cocaine, which cued off using behaviors to cope with the whole cycle. Of course, a destructive side-effect of this process was a self-fulfilling prophecy: "See I am bad, a failure and unlovable because I used and that proves it!" Breaking the downward spiral of this thinking pattern is an important part of the job for the effective counselor.

Cognitive therapy attempts to intervene in these core beliefs and automatic thoughts by challenging their accuracy and substituting a healthier line of thought. For example, Pete could stop his negative thoughts of being unlovable and counter it with an idea such as, "I am a lovable and capable person, after all my wife loves me and shows it by supporting me."

Another way that automatic thoughts affect the addict is by becoming the first thing a person thinks of when in a dysphoric state: "I feel sad so I should get high . . . the stress of work is too strong so I need a drink." We should help clients become aware of these processes and help them rethink the outcomes in a more functional way. "I feel sad, so I should talk to someone or journal. . . . With work stresses being so tough right now I should unwind with a long walk or some relaxation exercises." Anticipating trouble spots and having alternative thoughts and behaviors ready are important parts of a successful intervention (Beck, Wright, Newmann, & Liese, 1993).

Psychodynamic and psychoanalytic traditions have developed some useful interventions for us (Dodes & Khantzian, 1998). The self-medication hypothesis leads to the need to have clients learn to identify and work through various taboo feelings in the safety of the counselor's office (Khantzian, 1985; Luborsky, 1984). This could also involve connecting with the genesis of these feelings in the client's family of origin through free association, dream interpretation, or other memory techniques.

The chemical is often observed to be a substitute for a missing and longed-for relationship with an internalized object (Krystal & Raskin, 1970; Wurmser, 1974). Early attachment problems between parent and child could be getting acted out through substance abuse. Perhaps the addict as a child incorporated an unhealthy self-image and impaired ability to relate to others as part of his or her personality structure. The drug of choice can easily become the relationship of choice because it is easy, nondemanding or noncritical, is always available, always soothing, and always feels good. Treatment centers have an increasing awareness of these relational deficits while taking in the healthier aspects of the relationship with the therapist. The client is also encouraged to reach out and relate to newer and less toxic kinds of people.

Eileen is a 35-year-old alcoholic raised by a harsh, demanding father and an abusive, schizophrenic mother. Her internalized images of self were distressingly negative and hopeless while her ability to relate to others was based on suspicion, mistrust, sexual acting-out, and emotional disconnection. Her best relationship had developed with the soothing effects of alcohol. In treatment, Eileen gradually became aware of her internalized object-relations and learned to accept and love herself within the stable, consistent, and nonexploitive treatment alliance.

Deeper, psychodynamic treatment is often indicated for clients who continually relapse despite strong motivation to abstain. If fellowship groups and behavioral and cognitive approaches have not worked, then it may be time to explore the other aspects of the psyche, unconscious motivations, and family-of-origin issues (Dodes & Khantzian, 1998). Many counselors and treatment agencies do not cover this part of their clients' lives, much to their detriment. This author has worked with many struggling addicts and alcoholics with long and extensive treatment failures. One commonality of these unfortunates is that no one ever asked about or knew how to work with the issues discussed here.

A recent development in addictions treatment is Motivational Interviewing, sometimes called Motivational Enhancement Therapy (Miller &

Rollnick, 2002). The approach has been described as a more directed, Rogerian style of counseling. The therapist consistently tries to structure the dialogue around motivating the client to see the problems in his or her behavior and motivating the need to change it. The main components of the approach are an empathetic relationship, rolling with client resistance rather than fighting it, developing discrepancy between what the client is doing and what he or she says he or she wants to do, or what his or her goals are, accepting and working to resolve ambivalence and promoting self-efficacy.

The authors describe it as an overall philosophy or interviewing style and not a set of techniques per se. It is an approach centered in the here and now and not the past. It attempts to enter the client's worldview and encourage him or her to make his or her own case for changing.

The government recently funded a large study to determine which interventions might be best for treating alcoholism (Project MATCH, 1998). It evaluated thousands of participants across many sites and compared the effectiveness of motivational enhancement therapy, cognitive-behavioral skills training, and a supportive therapy based on the 12-step model. In trying to control for counselor variations, all therapists used manualized versions of each treatment. Many clients benefited from all three approaches, yet no one method proved itself superior to the others. The good news was that treatment works; however, the other news is that the effective counselor should be familiar with varied approaches and be flexible and skilled enough to use them. One size does not fit all when it comes to addictions treatment.

The National Institute of Drug Abuse (2009) recently published 13 overarching principles of treatment that are recommended no matter what theoretical approach is taken with a client. Some of these principles include the idea that no one treatment is effective for everyone, so the clinician must be able to take a flexible approach. Treatment must address the various needs of the individual, such as family or work issues, and that treatment must change to adapt to the changing needs of the client. We must recognize that recovery takes time and that relapse is common. Some strong evidence demonstrates that lasting improvement usually takes three or four treatment episodes over a number of years. Many researchers compare the treatment and stabilization of addictive disorders to those of medical issues such as diabetes, asthma, or hypertension. Professionals can treat these disorders in a way that allows an individual to maintain a healthy and productive life without ever actually "curing" the illness (White, Boyle, & Loveland, 2003).

Interestingly, the National Institute of Drug Abuse (NIDA) report also states that involuntary treatment can be effective. Getting an unwilling person into therapy can help engage the individual to want to change. This helps explain the rise of drug courts that only work on cases involving drug or alcohol violations. Arrestees are given the choice of jail or drug treatment. Legal ramifications are used as leverage to try to get someone to treatment. The effective counselor should also look to other "leverages" to encourage a reluctant client into treatment. These may include family members, coaches, schools, bosses, or anyone else with some strong connection to the drug or alcohol abuser.

PHARMACOTHERAPY: DRUG-FIGHTING DRUGS

It may seem counterintuitive to use legal medications to fight dependency on illegal or abused chemicals. Yet there are a number of drugs that have proven themselves effective in aiding clients to maintain their sobriety from some drugs of abuse. Opioid addicts are able to access methadone or buprenorphine to help stay clean from heroin, morphine, or other narcotics. These drugs are taken daily in controlled, medical settings to stave off the severe symptoms of narcotics withdrawal. Clients use these medications instead of illegal ones. People on buprenorphine or methadone maintenance, with some adjunctive counseling, are able to maintain stable lives, families, and work settings (National Institute of Drug Abuse, 2009).

There are also a few drugs that help in the treatment of alcoholism and abuse. Disulfuram (Antabuse) is used daily by those trying not to drink alcohol. It makes a drinker very ill and nauseous if he or she drinks while taking the drug. It serves as a negative reinforcement in an overall treatment scheme. Antabuse works by interfering with the metabolism of alcohol in the body. This causes a buildup of acetaldehyde, a by-product of alcohol metabolism leading to the adverse effects mentioned. Acamprosate (Campral) reduces the symptoms of alcohol withdrawal and helps clients maintain sobriety by reducing urges to drink. Naltrexone latches onto receptors in the brain that block the euphoric effects of the chemical (Daley & Marlatt, 2005).

Newer medications are proving useful to reduce the urges for and block the effects of cocaine abuse. These are disulfiram, topiramate, propranolol, and baclofen (O'Brien, 2005).

SUMMARY

This chapter has attempted to introduce the counselor and counseling student to a major overview of the substance abuse field. A brief history was given as well as models of addiction, assessment tools, and treatment strategies. The interested counselor should pursue further training in assessing and treating these issues before working in this population. The well-trained counselor will find that he or she has many of the necessary skills to work with these people but will need some specialized training and knowledge to be truly effective and competent. I heartily recommend you seek out this training and work with this population. Change is hard, but the damage from the failure to change is far harder for these individuals. Breaking the cycle of addiction will not only help the man or woman in front of you but the many generations to follow.

REFERENCES

Abrams, D. B., & Niaura, L. S. (1987). Social learning theory. In H. T. Blane & K. E. Leonard (Eds.), *Psychological theories of drinking and alcoholism* (pp. 106–163). New York: Guilford.

Alberti, R., & Emmons, M. (1978). *Your perfect right: A guide to assertive behavior.* San Luis Obispo, CA: Impact Publications.

Alcoholics Anonymous. (1955). New York: AA World Services Inc.

American Psychiatric Association. (2000). *Diagnostic and statistical manual* (4th ed.-tr). Washington, DC: Author.

Bandura, A. (1977). *Social learning theory.* Englewood Cliffs, NJ: Prentice-Hall.

Beck, A. T., Wright, F. D., Newmann, C. F., & Liese, B. S. (1993). *Cognitive therapy of substance abuse.* New York: Guilford.

Beck, J., & Liese, B. (1998). Cognitive therapy. In R. Frances & S. Miller (Eds.), *Clinical textbook of addictive disorders* (2nd ed., pp. 547–573). New York: Guilford.

Bradshaw, J. (1986). *Bradshaw on: The family.* New York: Bantam Books.

Brecher, E., and the editors of Consumer Reports. (1972). *Licit and illicit drugs.* Boston: Little, Brown.

Daley, D. C., & Marlatt, G. A. (2005). Relapse prevention. In J. H. Lowinson, P. Ruiz, R. B. Millman, & G. J. Langrod (Eds.), *Substance abuse: A comprehensive textbook* (4th ed., pp. 772–785). Philadelphia: Lippincott Williams & Wilkins.

Dodes, L., & Khantzian E. (1998). Individual psychodynamic psychotherapy. In R. Frances & S. Miller (Eds.), *Clinical textbook of addictive disorders* (2nd ed., pp. 479–495). New York: Guilford.

Doweiko, H. (1999). *Concepts of chemical dependency.* Pacific Grove, CA: Brooks-Cole.

Fingarette, H. (1988). *Heavy drinking: The myth of alcoholism as a disease.* Berkeley, CA: University of California Press.

Goodwin, D. W., Schulsinger, F., Hermansen, L., Guze, S. B., & Winokur, G. (1973). Alcohol problems in adoptees raised apart from biological parents. *Archives of General Psychiatry, 28,* 238–243.

Hartmann, H. (1939). *Ego psychology and the problem of adaption.* New York: International Universities Press.

Higgins, S. T., Delaney, D. D., Budney, A. J., Bickel, W.K., Hughes, J. R., Foerg, F., & Fenwick, J. W. (1991). A behavioral approach to achieving initial cocaine abstinence. *American Journal of Psychiatry, 148,* 1218–1224.

Horney, K. (1964). *The neurotic personality of our time.* New York: W. W. Norton.

Jacobson, E. (1971). *Depression: Comparative studies of normal, neurotic and psychotic conditions.* New York: International Universities Press.

Jacobson, G. R. (1989). A comprehensive approach to pretreatment evaluation: Detection, assessment and diagnosis of alcoholism. In R. K. Hester & W. R. Miller (Eds.), *Handbook of alcoholism treatment approaches: Effective alternatives* (pp. 17–53). Boston: Allyn & Bacon.

Kendler, K. S., Heath, A. C., Neale, M. C., Kessler, R. C., & Eaves, L. J. (1992). A population-based twin study of alcoholism in women. *Journal of the American Medical Association, 268,* 1877–1882.

Khantzian, E. J. (1985). The self-medication hypothesis of eating disorders: Focus on heroin and cocaine dependence. *American Journal of Psychiatry, 142,* 1259–1264.

Khantzian, E. J., & Brehm, N. M. (1992). A psychodynamic perspective. In J. Lowinson, P. Ruiz, R. Millman, & J. Langrod (Eds.), *Substance abuse: A comprehensive textbook* (2nd ed., pp. 106–117). Baltimore, MD: Williams & Wilkins.

Khantzian, E. J., & Mack, J. (1983). Self-preservation and care of the self. *Psychoanalytic Study of the Child, 38,* 209–232.

Klein, M. (1948). *Contributions to psychoanalysis.* London: Hogarth.

Krystal, H., & Raskin, H. (1970). *Drug dependence: Aspects of ego function.* Detroit, MI: Wayne State University Press.

Luborsky, L. (1984). *Principles of psychoanalytic psychotherapy: A manual for supportive-expressive (se) treatment.* New York: Basic Books.

Margolis, R., & Zweben, J. (1998). *Treating patients with alcohol and other drug problems: An integrated approach.* Washington, DC: American Psychological Association.

Marlatt, G. A., & Gordon, J. R. (Eds.). (1985). *Relapse prevention: Maintenance strategies in the treatment of addictive behaviors.* New York: Guilford.

Masterson, J. F. (1972). *Treatment of the borderline adolescent: A developmental approach.* New York: Wiley & Sons.

McClellan, A. T., Luborsky, L., O'Brien, C. P., & Woody, G. E. (1980). An improved evaluation instrument for substance abuse patients: The addiction severity index. *Journal of Nervous and Mental Diseases, 168,* 26–33.

McGue, M., Dickens, R. W., & Svikis, D. S. (1992). Sex and age effects on the inheritance of alcohol problems: A twin study. *Journal of Abnormal Psychology, 101,* 3–17.

Mehr, J. (1988). *Human services: Concepts and intervention strategies.* Boston: Allyn & Bacon.

Miller, B. A., & Downs, W. R. (1995). Violent victimization among women with alcohol problems. In M. Galanter (Ed.), *Recent developments in alcoholism* (Vol. 12, pp. 120–139). New York: Plenum Press.

Miller, F., & Lazowski, L. (1999). *The SASSI-3 manual.* Springville, IN: The SASSI Institute.

Miller, W., & Rollnick, S. (2002). *Motivational interviewing: Preparing people for change* (2nd ed.), New York: Guilford.

Murphy, S., & Khantzian, E. J. (1995). Addiction as a self-medication disorder: Application of ego psychology to the treatment of substance abuse. In A.M. Washton (Ed.), *Psychotherapy and substance abuse* (pp. 215–243). New York: Guilford.

National Institute of Drug Abuse. (2009). *Principles of drug addiction treatment: A research based guide.* Rockville, MD: U.S. Department of Health and Human Services.

O'Brien, C. (2005). Anticraving medications for relapse prevention: A possible new class of psychoactive medications. *American Journal of Psychiatry, 162*(8), 1423–1431.

Pine, F. (1990). *Drive, ego, object and self: A synthesis for clinical work.* New York: Basic Books.

Project MATCH. (1998). Matching alcoholism treatments to client heterogeneity: Project MATCH three-year drinking outcomes. *Alcoholism: Clinical and Experimental Research, 22*(6), 1300–1311.

Rosen, J. (1962). *Direct psychoanalytic psychiatry.* New York: Grune & Stratton.

Schaeffer, D. (1987). *Choices and consequences: What to do when a teenager uses alcohol and drugs.* Minneapolis: Johnson Institute.

Scharff, D., & Scharff J. (1991). *Object relations family therapy.* Northvale, NJ: Aronson.

Selzer, M. (1971). The Michigan alcohol screening test: The quest for a new diagnostic instrument. *American Journal of Psychiatry, 127,* 1653–1658.

Senay, E. (1992). Diagnostic interview and mental status exam. In J. Lowinson (Ed.), *Substance abuse: A comprehensive textbook* (2nd ed., pp. 416–424). Baltimore: Williams & Wilkins.

Skinner, H. A. (1982). The drug abuse screening test. *Addictive Behaviors, 7,* 363–371.

Substance Abuse and Mental Health Services Administration. (2009). *Results from the 2008 national survey on drug abuse and health: National findings.* Retrieved January 29, 2010, from http://oas.sahmsa.gov/nsduh/2k8nsduh/2K8results.cfm.

Thombs, D. (1999). *Introduction to addictive behaviors* (2nd ed.). New York: Guilford.

White, W., Boyle, M., & Loveland, D. (2003). Recovery management: Transcending the limitations of addiction treatment. *Behavioral Health Management, 23*(3): 38–44.

Wurmser, L. (1974). Psychoanalytic considerations of the etiology of compulsive drug use. *Journal of the American Psychoanalytic Association, 22,* 820–843.

Yalom, I. D., & Leczcz, M. (2005). *The theory and practice of group psychotherapy* (5th ed.). New York: Basic Books.

Section IV

THE PROFESSIONAL COUNSELOR IN A WORLD OF UNCERTAINTY

Chapter 13

TERRORISM: COUNSELOR'S ROLE IN RECOVERY AND TREATMENT

LAURIE JOHNSON

The nation, if not the world, was forever changed on Tuesday, September 11, 2001, when more than 3,000 people were killed and thousands more injured as a result of terrorist attacks on the World Trade Center (WTC) and the Pentagon. On that day, the "assumptive world" (Parkes, 1975) of vast numbers of Americans was shattered. A person's "assumptive world," what is believed to be true and constant about the world based on prior experience, provides the basis for psychological equilibrium. A traumatic event that shatters those assumptions violates the foundations that make the world safe and predictable and disrupts one's sense of control and efficacy (Janoff-Bulman, 1992). When one's fundamental assumptions are broken, intense feelings of vulnerability, helplessness, and low self-esteem and efficacy can ensue (Solomon, 2002). Loss of the assumptive world can mean loss of belief in the benevolence and meaningfulness of the world. For many, the terrorist attacks destroyed these illusions forever.

TERRORISM: HUMAN VERSUS NATURAL DISASTER

Disasters, whether by natural cause or human design, generate some form of post-traumatic stress reaction on the part of those who experience them. Each person experiences a disaster in unique ways and develops different meaning from and reactions to the experience. Although it is not overly productive to compare types of disaster experiences, research has noted some distinctions between the psychological effects of natural disasters (e.g., earthquakes, floods) and human-made disasters (e.g., terrorist acts, mass killings), which help to explain the psychological impact that 9/11, as a disaster of human design, generated in this country.

"All other things being equal, human made disasters are believed to have more serious consequences than natural disasters for survivors' mental health" (National Institute of Mental Health, 2002, p. 23). Those who experience mass violence are far more likely to be severely impaired psychologically than those who experience either natural or technological disasters (Norris et al., 2002). Research has noted higher incidence rates of post-disaster post-traumatic stress disorder (PTSD) for human-made disasters (Young, Ford, Ruzek, Friedman, & Gusman, 1998). Moreover, disasters involving social or political unrest have been found to generate a quicker onset of post-traumatic symptomology with greater intensity levels manifested by shock, rage, and grief reactions (Aguilera & Panchon, 1995). The notion of "intentionality" helps to explain the differential in emotional impact when comparing natural versus human-made disasters. Experiencing disasters that are intentionally caused, such as those generated by terrorist acts, can produce severe lasting psychological effects (Rubonis & Bickman, 1991). Part of the unique psychological fallout that a victim of terrorism experiences stems from having to confront the motives, logic, and psychological makeup of the terrorist (Duffy, 1988), in addition to the ongoing threat of recurrence. These distinctions suggest that a specialized knowledge and appreciation of the mental health implications of working with victims of mass violence and terrorism is in order. Although much of what we know about the psychological impact of disasters still applies, there is value in considering this area of work specifically. Given the increasing threat of terrorism and violence in this world, it is important for counselors to be poised to assume greater readiness to respond to these mental health needs.

Mental Health Effects of Terrorism

Terrorism is a uniquely human phenomenon; it is strategically designed by humans to engender feelings of terror in other humans for human (typically political) purposes (Cooper, 1976; Gidron, 2002). Although many would readily recognize terrorism's goal as seeking death and destruction of life and property for political purposes, the experts remind us that the underlying goal of terrorism is to generate psychological damage by inducing "a state of psychological uncertainty, personal vulnerability, and fear, that is, terror" (Everly & Mitchell, 2001, p. 134). The trauma that people experience as a result of terrorist attacks is uniquely shaped by the recognition that the destruction of life and property was intentional and symbolic. Because of this symbolic intentionality, the given terrorist act represents not an end in itself but rather a means to an end and therefore can reoccur at another unpredictable setting and time (Everly, 2000).

The psychological impact of terrorism goes beyond its physical impact in many ways because of the sense of victimization it engenders. Janoff-Bulman (1983) suggested that victimization works to shatter three basic assumptions held by most people: the belief in personal invulnerability; the perception of the world as meaningful, comprehensible, and controllable; and the view of self as able and in control. As a victim, the individual becomes preoccupied with the fear of recurrence. The terrorism victim begins to doubt the notion that one can prevent misfortune by engaging in sufficiently cautious behaviors. Self-images of being weak, helpless, needy, and frightened emerge, and a "sense of profound and enduring peril" is inflicted on the self (Kauffman, 2002, p. 206).

A terrorist act, because it is not confined to any specific geographic location or time, persists as a threat and can produce debilitating anxiety and phobic reactions (Abueg, Woods, & Watson, 2000; Lanza, 1986). Given its insidious nature, the impact of terrorism is such that even those who do not directly experience the terrorist act can suffer vicarious traumatization (Everly, 2000). This was observed after the 1995 Oklahoma City bombing of the Alfred Murrah Federal Building, where children not directly involved (but exposed through media) were found particularly affected in long-term ways (Pfefferbaum, Seale et al., 2000). This sense of vicarious trauma heightens the need for mental health support services.

Studies conducted in the aftermath of 9/11 found that the incidence of PTSD was significant across the population. Symptoms of depression and anxiety and involvement in self-harmful behaviors (e.g., alcohol and substance abuse) were widely observed (Pyszczynski, Solomon, & Greenberg, 2003). Several weeks after the 9/11 terrorist attacks, Galea and colleagues (2002) conducted a study of adults living in Manhattan in order to assess the incidence and correlates of posttraumatic stress and depression in this population. It was found that about 20% of the residents in the neighborhoods close to the WTC experienced PTSD. These authors concluded that substantial psychological morbidity may occur in the aftermath of terrorist attacks and, furthermore, that the ongoing threat of terrorist attacks may affect the severity and duration of these psychological symptoms. A contributing factor was exposure to the widespread, continual, and graphic media coverage of the attacks (Schlenger et al., 2002).

Victims of a terrorist act who see it as uncontrollable may react more strongly to future acts (even when milder or of less severity) than those who perceive it as controllable (Gidron, 2002). This finding supports the notion that individual differences in "cognitive appraisal" and coping style play a major role in influencing the psychological impact that exposure to stressors (in this case, terrorism) will have on individuals (Lazarus & Folkman, 1984). Those who are closer to the terrorist disaster site, injured themselves, and/or know one or more people who are injured or die are most likely to manifest severe symptomology and to develop PTSD (Pfefferbaum, Call, & Sconzo, 1999). A prior history of psychiatric disorders or trauma will increase the risk for PTSD, intrusive thoughts, and symptoms of avoidance and arousal (Abueg et al., 2000). Proximity to the site of violence has deleterious effects (Bat-Zion & Levy-Shiff, 1993), as was seen in the varying levels of psychological impact experienced by people living closer to the areas of attack on 9/11. Almost three years later, this differential was still observed in the levels of traumatic stress symptomology that persisted in people living closer to New York City and Washington, DC (Pyszczynski et al., 2003). Oftentimes posttraumatic symptoms do not occur until months following the crisis event. This was documented by Banuach and colleagues (2002), who found stress related problems initially emerging in NYC fire department rescue workers up to 11 months following the WTC disaster, after they had worked repeatedly at the site and had attended numerous funerals and memorial services during that time.

> In the days and weeks following the 9/11 terrorist attacks on the WTC, I worked as part of two mental health disaster support teams that were assembled within the first 24 hours after the planes struck the towers. I worked both with the American Red Cross Disaster Mental Health Services and also as part of a locally assembled team of mental health professionals in my hometown in Nassau County (within a 30-mile radius of Ground Zero) which had suffered dozens of deaths among its residents. I worked mainly with civilian survivors (those who had escaped from the buildings and were traumatized by the terror they had experienced) as well as with some rescue workers who were virtually "dragged" by their spouses to get help in the hopes of having them stop the round-the-clock devotion to rescue and body recovery efforts. These rescue workers presented as clearly exhausted and suffering from post-traumatic stress; in some cases they bordered on the irrational, demanding to be let back to their rescue work, despite having no sleep or rest for days. Other notable response patterns also emerged in this group. The first and most evident was the need for those who had been part of the disaster to reach out for human contact, a need to be close to others, especially family. For the civilian survivors, a second common response was outrage, alternately mixed with fear and anxiety, directed toward the terrorists as well as toward those who they identified as responsible for the number of "needless" losses experienced that day (e.g., security personnel and managers who told people to go back to their desks and await further instructions). In those first few days, I observed a wide range of behaviors including grief, helplessness, phobic reactions, guilt (survivor guilt was considerable for those who "ran for their life"), anger, and confusion. What was most striking was the sense of ongoing threat apparent in these individuals, as though they were "waiting for the next shoe to fall."

In describing the phases involved in working with survivors in the aftermath of the September 11, 2001, terrorist attacks, Neria, Suh, and Marshall (2004, p. 211) cite the work of Duffy (1988), which posited that most human-made disasters will go through a number of stages of recovery. Among these are the "heroic stage," characterized by altruistic actions directed toward saving lives and property; the "honeymoon period," characterized by solidarity and expectations of massive assistance; the "disillusionment" phase, in which people become disillusioned over delays in expected assistance; and the "reconstruction" period, during which victims assume a role in, and responsibility for, their own recovery. Many saw these stages unfold in the aftermath of the 9/11 disaster.

The psychological devastation of the September 11th terrorist attacks may not be known for years (Everly & Mitchell, 2001). These tragic events, in addition to the subsequent anthrax scares, the American Airlines crash in Queens, New York, only weeks later, and the ongoing posting of terrorist alerts and security warnings have "combined to create a nationwide mortality salience induction that is unparalleled in American history" (Pyszczynski et al., 2003, p. 94). Beyond the immediate emotional impact of these events, the ongoing threat of terrorism that now holds sway in the United States has contributed to a chronic psychological stress reaction that continues to takes its toll on the mental health of vast numbers of citizens, many of whom had no direct connection to the disaster.

The Role of the Mental Health Counselor

What happens in the immediate aftermath of a traumatic event may well determine the long-term mental health outcomes of those affected by the trauma (Auger, Seymour, & Roberts, 2004). In times of mass disaster, the role of the mental health professional changes from that played out in conventional practice. Clinical roles will vary from setting to setting and will change according to the stage of the disaster: the emergency phase, the early post-impact phase, and the restoration phase (Young et al., 1998). The initial work, sometimes referred to as "psychological first aid," takes on a crisis intervention orientation, where the focus is on ensuring safety; assessing level of need/triage; stabilizing survivors, the bereaved, and rescue workers; connecting them to support systems; and providing psychoeducational support and referral for additional care when needed. The basic principles followed by disaster mental health professionals in early emergency response include: protect, direct, connect, triage, acute care, and consultation/referral (Young et al., 1998).

As time goes on, disaster mental health services shift from crisis intervention mode to providing ongoing psychological support to individuals, families, and community groups in the forms of counseling, consultation, and referral. Emergency mental health practitioners provide therapeutic assistance to those affected but do not provide them with psychotherapy. Provision of emergency mental health services begins immediately on acknowledgment of the disaster and can continue as long as two years or more afterward.

Everly and Mitchell (2001) defined a three-phase framework for addressing disasters (i.e., the pre-attack phase, the acute event management phase, and the reconstruction phase) that included the following recommendations: establish crisis intervention services and facilities in affected areas; provide pre-incident resiliency training as well as ongoing psychological support to emergency response personnel; provide ongoing factual information to all affected people, including age-appropriate information to children to promote coping strategies; facilitate communications, calm fears, and reestablish sense of safety; reestablish normal schedules as soon as possible; and avoid premature psychological exploration, which can be counterproductive and interfere with natural recovery mechanisms.

To help people adjust to a world in which the basic assumptions of safety, predictability, and permanence no longer hold, counselors need to specifically promote strategies that will (a) provide social support and caring; (b) provide meaning (in tragedy) and understanding (of the world and our place in it), including working toward a reevaluation of priorities in one's life and a greater appreciation of life; and (c) provide opportunities for heroism and self-esteem building so that people can feel good about themselves by doing good deeds and contributing to society/others (Pyszczynski et al., 2003, p. 134).

In providing mental health interventions in human-made catastrophes, where the focus is on helping to reconstruct meaning, it is important to take into account local customs and values, including respect for the victim's faith and need for spiritual regeneration. An intervention framework that incorporates strategies from cognitive, behavioral, psychodynamic, and existential approaches has been recommended by Parson (1995). Under this model, the mental health worker can integrate both traditional and nontraditional (including indigenous self-help) forms of intervention and promote a sense of belonging, worth, and empowerment on the part of the survivor/bereaved as a means of helping to restore shattered meaning.

To help survivors come to terms with their shattered assumptions, psychological interventions need to focus on promoting a sense of coping, redefining the sense of victimization and vulnerability, and reestablishing a less malevolent or threatening worldview (Janoff-Bulman, 1983). Healing after violence and disaster requires "meaning management," where shattered, distorted meaning systems can be restructured (Parson, 1995). In substantiating this notion, Parson cites Meichenbaum's (1995) tenet that victims "do not merely respond to events in and of themselves, but . . . respond to their interpretation of events and to their perceived implications of these events" (p. 103). For the survivor of a terrorist act to successfully restructure these meanings in adaptive ways, and thereby avert long-term or chronic PTSD, depression, or anxiety, some form of healing intervention is useful.

Mental Health Interventions

Over the past two decades, a growing international body of research has added to our understanding of the psychological effects of terrorism and the strategies effective in treatment (e.g., Bat-Zion & Levy-Shiff, 1993; Curran, 1988; de Dunayevich & Puget, 1989; de Jong, 2002; Gillespie, Duffy, Hackman, & Clark, 2002; Lanza, 1986; Reilly, 2002; Shalif & Leibler, 2002). For the most part, the principles and practice protocols that have been used to help people deal with the aftermath of terrorism in this country have been derived directly from the general trauma and disaster knowledge base. However, it is important to recognize the nuances of working with those affected by terrorism and mass violence in order to determine the most appropriate interventions in these cases. When responding to a human-made terrorist disaster, where mass casualties have been experienced, basic assumptions about the world have been shattered, and ongoing threat remains, the psychological intervention principles that typically define working with trauma, disaster, and bereavement need to be differentially applied with regard to the additional context that terrorism brings to the trauma situation. As always, the guiding consideration should be, "what treatment, by whom, is the most effective for this individual with that specific problem, and under this set of circumstances?" (Paul, 1967).

Although a large range of interventions has been identified as effective in treating trauma and loss, the skilled practitioner will address cases (and groups) independently and modify treatment according to individual needs and vulnerabilities. In making intervention decisions, it is critical to take into account contextual, cultural, developmental, and personality variables. The stage of the disaster will also help to determine intervention strategy. Table 13.1 presents the guidelines proposed by the National Institute of Mental Health (2002) that were made available through the public domain for early psychological interventions according to disaster phase. In addressing the needs of those directly affected by the September 11th terrorist attacks, intervention strategies were largely shaped according to the person's identity as (civilian) survivor, bereaved, or rescue worker. Beyond these categories, further subgroupings were established for children, sometimes according to age; some survivor groupings were defined by work place/employer affiliation;

Table 13.1. Timing of Early Interventions for Survivors/Victims (National Institute of Mental Health, 2002)

Phase	Pre-Incident	Impact (0-48 hours)	Rescue (0-1 week)	Recovery (1-4 weeks)	Return to Life (2 weeks–2 years)
Goals	Preparation, improve coping	Survival, communication	Adjustment	Appraisal/planning	Reintegration
Behavior	Preparation vs. denial	Flight/fight, freeze, surrender, etc.	Resilience vs. exhaustion	Grief, reappraisal, intrusive memories, narrative formation	Adjustment vs. phobias, PTSD, avoidance, depression, etc.
Role of All Helpers	Prepare, train, gain knowledge	Rescue, protect	Orient, provide for needs	Respond with sensitivity	Continue assistance
Role of Mental Health Professionals	**Prepare** Train Gain knowledge Collaborate Inform and influence policy Set structures for rapid assistance	**Basic Needs** Establish safety/security/survival Ensure food and shelter Facilitate communication with family, friends, and community Assess the environment for ongoing threat/toxin	**Needs Assessment** Assess current status, how well needs are being addressed Recovery environment What additional interventions are needed for • Group • Population • Individual **Triage** Clinical assessment Refer when indicated Identify vulnerable, high-risk individuals and groups Emergency hospitalization or out-patient treatment	**Monitor the Recovery Environment** Observe and listen to those most affected Monitor the environment for toxins Monitor past and ongoing threats Monitor services that are being provided	**Treatment** Reduce or ameliorate symptoms or improve functioning via • individual, family, group psychotherapy • Pharmacotherapy • Short- or long-term hospitalization

Table 13.1–*Continued*

		Psychological First Aid Support and "presence" for those who are more distressed Keep families together and facilitate reunion with loved ones Provide information and education (i.e., services), foster communication Protect survivors from further harm Reduce physiological arousal **Monitoring the Impact on Environment** Observe and listen to those most affected Monitor the environment for stressors **Technical Assistance, Consultation, and Training** Improve capacity of organizations and caregivers to provide what is needed to reestablish community structure, foster family recovery/resilience, and safeguard the community Provide to • relevant organizations • other caregivers and responders • leaders	**Outreach and Information Dissemination** Make contact with and identify people who have not requested services (i.e., "therapy by walking around") Inform people about different services, coping, recovery process, etc. (e.g., by using established community structures, fliers, websites) **Fostering Resilience and Recovery** Social interactions Coping skills training Education about stress response, traumatic reminders, coping normal vs. abnormal functioning, risk factors, services Group and family support Foster natural social support Look after the bereaved Operational debriefings, when this is standing procedure in responder organizations Spiritual support		

and some interventions for the bereaved were grouped according to relationship to the deceased, such as spouse, teenage child, and so on.

In the following pages, research findings and practice protocols are interwoven with personal accounts and observations drawn from my work during the weeks and months following September 11, 2001. This interplay is intended to provide a personalized sense of what mental health response might involve when working with individuals affected by massive casualties stemming from terrorist violence.

Early Post-Disaster Interventions

During the immediate post-impact stage (i.e., between 24 and 48 hours after the event), qualified disaster mental health workers will primarily engage in psychological first aid, where the needs of survivors/bereaved are assessed, information is provided, and referral guidance is offered. At this point, counselors work to "protect, direct, connect, and triage" the survivors, the bereaved, and rescue personnel. As part of an integrated Critical Incident Stress Management (CISM) system of interventions designed to decrease the adverse psychological reactions stemming from crisis events, the small-group interventions of defusing and psychological debriefing are offered to disaster survivors and rescue workers (Mitchell, 1988). Defusings are brief and typically one hour, whereas psychological debriefings are longer (1 to 2 hours) and should be successively offered. Defusings can be considered "brief conversations" that aim to offer survivors the opportunity to receive support, reassurance, and information, whereas debriefings are structured processes that help survivors understand and manage their intense emotions, identify effective coping strategies, and receive support from peers (Young et al., 1998).

Psycho-educational debriefings can help survivors normalize their trauma experience while benefiting from psycho-educational support and guidance regarding standard post-traumatic stress reactions. Communal debriefings can help survivors destigmatize and depathologize trauma symptoms and help to correct inaccurate beliefs and cognitive distortions (Abueg et al., 2000). Practitioners, however, need to avoid offering any group-based interventions without pre- and/or post-intervention evaluation (Neria, Solomon, & Ginzburg, 2000; Neria, Suh, & Marshall , 2004). Mental health workers need skills in triage assessment to decipher between participants' intense emotions that would be common and those reflecting acute symptomology (e.g., suicidal ideation, substance abuse, severe dissociation), which would require referral for treatment. It is also important to note that psychological debriefing is considered inappropriate as an intervention for acutely bereaved individuals (National Center for Post Traumatic Stress Disorder, 2002).

A number of studies conducted on the use of psychological debriefings after 9/11 supported the efficacy of this modality in helping participants feel and communicate better (Cournos, 2002; Herman, Kaplan, & LeMelle, 2002). Although brief psychological debriefing has been widely used as group treatment for disaster and trauma survivors after it was adopted as the intervention of choice by the American Red Cross and the Federal Emergency Management Agency (FEMA) (Neria, Suh, & Marshall, 2004), cautions as to its use have been raised in recent years (Litz, Gray, Bryant, & Adler, 2002; National Center for Post Traumatic Stress Disorder, 2002; Neria, Solomon, & Ginzburg, 2000). Some research has questioned its efficacy and suggests that, as an intervention procedure, debriefing might actually increase the risk of PTSD (Mayou, Ehlers, & Hobbs, 2000). The use of psychological debriefing in cases of mass disaster remains a controversial consideration.

Later Phase Treatment: Cognitive-Behavioral Interventions

Cognitive-behavioral intervention strategies have been found effective in addressing the psychological impact of human-made trauma where people's basic assumptions about the world have been shattered (Cooper & Clum, 1989; Foa et al., 1999; Tarrier et al., 1999). Furthermore, cognitive-behavioral strategies have been successfully applied to address the mental health effects of terrorism in settings around the world (de Jong, 2002; Gillespie et al., 2002; Kleinman, 1989; Ofman & Mastria, 1995; Shalif & Leibler, 2002).

Cognitive-behaviorally based strategies were widely used in the treatment interventions that sought to address the stress and anxiety symptoms associated with 9/11 and its aftermath. One intervention strategy that counselors widely employed was to educate survivors in the use of relaxation as a method to allay anxiety and stress reactions. A significant value of this procedure is that individuals can follow it on their own, once properly instructed in its application, and benefit from its ability to diminish symptoms of stress and anxiety without requiring professional help. In addition to the standard precautions in using this methodology (e.g., checking the person's physical condition), counselors need to be wary of recommending relaxation techniques to surviving or bereaved individuals for whom the fear of overwhelming intrusive reexperiencing might be a concern. Counselors are advised not to teach deep relaxation methods that involve the potential for trance-like dissociation (e.g., guided imagery, autogenics) to survivors for whom intrusive reexperiencing is problematic. In these cases, the use of more present-focused and concrete methods (e.g., breathing exercises) will allow the person both enhanced sense of control and increased physical relaxation (Young et al., 1998).

To help address the shattered assumptions and self-defeating thoughts that can prevail in the aftermath of terrorist acts, cognitive-behavioral procedures that involve identifying and modifying thoughts and beliefs that cause distress can be helpful. In the later stages of intervention, such methods might include cognitive restructuring (Ellis, Gordon, Neenan, & Palmer, 1997), reframing, bibliotherapy, and homework strategies (Dattilio & Freeman, 2000). As the later intervention phase progresses, mental health professionals can employ cognitive-behavioral methods that have been found particularly effective in working to address stress and coping. For example, Stress Inoculation Training (SIT) helps individuals achieve mastery over stress by teaching coping skills and providing opportunity for rehearsal and practice.

Exposure Strategies

Based on cognitive-behavioral principles, exposure strategies have been widely documented as effective in later phase treatment of trauma symptoms (Dattilio & Freeman, 2000; de Jong, 2002; Silver & Rogers, 2002), but caution needs to be taken in recognizing the need for specialized training in these procedures (National Institute of Mental Health, 2002). During the reconstructive post-disaster phase, well-planned interventions that encourage the survivor/bereaved to reexpose the self (either through imaginal or in vivo methods) to the traumatic or feared event, object, or venue can be effective in desensitizing the person to the traumatic stimulus. Parson (1995) notes, for example, that taking a pilgrimage to the site of the disaster can be therapeutic for survivors and bereaved who seek answers and relief from personal suffering. Even individuals less directly involved in the 9/11 disaster found benefit from making personal pilgrimages to the WTC site as a means of bridging personal and political traumas (Conran, 2002).

One of the interventions that has gained increased credibility in the effective treatment of trauma over the past decade is Eye Movement Desensitization and Reprocessing (EMDR) (Shapiro, 1995), which was developed as a treatment protocol for PTSD with Vietnam War veterans. This multiphase intervention combines cognitive-restructuring and exposure-based procedures to assist victims to detoxify the power of painful memory (Parson, 1995).

In reviewing research conducted on EMDR across the globe, Silver and Rogers (2002) conclude that this procedure can be successfully applied in the treatment of war and terrorism trauma and recommend its integration into the therapeutic process. These authors, both trained trauma specialists, have been instrumental in organizing a worldwide cadre of clinicians who apply EMDR in regions traumatized by war and violence through the EMDR Humanitarian Assistance Program (www.emdrhap.org).

While acknowledging its use as a trauma treatment in the case of mass violence, the National Institute of Mental Health (2002) concludes, however, that it is no more effective than any of the other trauma intervention strategies being used in contemporary practice.

Bereavement Issues and Interventions

Counting both direct and indirect losses, it has been estimated that 6 million individuals in the United States were bereaved as a result of the terrorist attacks of September 11, 2001 (Schlenger et al., 2002). Bereavement over the massive casualties was traumatic and, in some ways, uniquely manifested.

> One major difference in counseling the bereaved of 9/11 was the public scale of the grieving that occurred. In this national disaster, customary privacy norms were almost impossible to invoke. For the bereaved of 9/11, the mourning was a very public mourning . . . for some, this was facilitative and, for others, it was obstructive to their grieving. For example, there were widows of firefighters and police whose decisions regarding the funeral and burial services of their life partner were determined almost entirely by department protocol and expectations who later came to resent the loss of personal touch in these services. The media seemed to be everywhere and entered the most private of spaces; grievers somehow had to be on their "best behavior." A sense of celebrity seemed to color things in difficult ways for the bereaved of 9/11. Certain individuals were made into instantaneous "heroes" by virtue of their situation of death, while others were not. Identity and status considerations seemed to play a role. "Disenfranchised grief" was imposed by a public that was not able to accept or recognize "the other" (such as in the case of unmarried lovers or ex-spouses of deceased rescue personnel now deemed heroes). A sense of what I would call "valuated grief" emerged, where comparisons of the supposed value of the loss were openly considered.

Grieving in the Wake of 9/11

For those who lost a loved one on 9/11, the intensity of common grief reactions was dramatically heightened, and the grieving process was extended and complicated. After the terrorist attacks, when assumptions of the world's meaningfulness were broken, many of the bereaved felt doubly victimized. Besides losing their loved one, they no longer felt the security of a larger backdrop they could rely on to catch them in their personal loss. In this regard, their loss was compounded.

Complicated grief is distinguished from "normal" or uncomplicated grief primarily by the presence of unremitting distress that interferes with functioning and persists for months or years following the loss (Gray, Prigerson, & Litz, 2004, p. 69). Complications in the grieving process emerged in the early weeks after the WTC disaster when, for many, the human remains of their loved one had not (yet) been found. In many of these cases, the living parent faced unique dilemmas, such as deciding what to tell the children whose parent was not (yet) found, at what point memorial services should be planned, and how to signify the burial with no body. Given the overwhelmingly public nature of this tragedy, many of the bereaved felt that control over the mourning rituals had been taken from them. In many cases, resentment emerged in the comparisons that were made regarding the status of the deceased (e.g., civilian vs. public servant). Compensation issues further complicated grieving in these families when decisions were being made in relation to accepting or denying payment from the September 11th Victim Compensation Fund in the months after the disaster; this decision (which meant foregoing the chance to sue airlines and security companies for alleged negligence) became politicized and created schism within the group despite the overall sense of community that emerged in the families of the 9/11 deceased.

With the death of a loved one, both the mourner's "global assumptions" (about the self, others, life, or the world in general) and "specific assumptions" (about the loved one's continued interactive presence and the expectations the mourner had for that person) are impacted (Rando, 1993, p. 51). Alternatives of despair or hope depend on how the survivor copes, as does the new set of basic beliefs that emerges from that coping (Corr, 2002, p. 132). Finding meaning in tragedy greatly facilitates the individual's ability to cope (Pennebaker, 1989). Interventions that center on meaning-making, where the focus is on "a rebuilding of trust and the reconstruction of a viable, assumptive world" (Janoff-Bulman, 1992, p. 69), will be most facilitative. With this in mind, mental health workers should avoid speaking to the bereaved about "recovery," or "getting back to normal," or "closure," which imply a return to the prior state or to a simple endpoint. Rather, the focus should be on an ongoing process of reinterpreting and integrating past, present, and future challenges in ways that promote healthy living (Corr, 2002, p. 137).

Constructivist Interventions

Interventions that come from the constructivist and narrative approaches, which focus on meaning reconstruction and "storying" (Neimeyer, 2001), can be particularly facilitative in addressing shattered assumptions that occur after human-made disaster. These strategies can help the bereaved find "significance in the experience of suffering, and transformation in the midst of tragedy" (Neimeyer et al., 2002, p. 44).

Rituals and Expressive Strategies

Rituals and other expressive strategies offer powerful meaning-making opportunities for the bereaved. Specifically, rituals help to transform suffering into meaning through allegorical reflection and activity (Johnson, 2003). Formal and informal rituals and commemorations allow the powerful emotions associated with traumatic loss experienced as a result of mass violence to be directed into activities that unify survivors with each other, the deceased, their community, and even the larger universe. Rituals can be particularly facilitative in the mourning process for survivors whose loved ones are killed as the result of a terrorist act because they help to offer the hope that compassion, love, and goodness are larger than evil; that humanitarian values ultimately triumph over hate (Young et al., 1998). In a time of massive loss, such as with the 9/11 terrorist attacks, rituals can facilitate healing across communities, in addition to providing opportunities for meaning-making on the part of the individual.

As such, the use of rituals was widely promoted by helping professionals in working with the 9/11 bereaved. For months after the disaster, funeral services and memorials were designed in ways that would speak to the unique meaning of the persons who died and the roles they played in life. Counselors supported family members in establishing rituals that would reflect the meaning and spirit of the loved one who died. Communities established memorials, renamed street signs, and instituted community events to memorialize their dead neighbors and, in so doing, helped to reconstruct meaning in their own lives.

Those who can derive meaning from crisis or suffering are better able to heal and grow. After 9/11, the bereaved individuals who were able to make meaning out of these tragic events (whether spiritually based or not) appeared to have better coping capacity than those who could derive no sense of meaning at all from the experience. In terms of mental health support, helping the bereaved to tell their stories and author the biographies of their loved one can be highly therapeutic.

> Over the past two years, I have volunteered as a healing circle leader for a bereavement camp program that runs bereavement support weekends for children and teens who lost a family member on 9/11. The goal of these circles is to provide safe and nurturing space for bereaved children to talk about their loss, their loved one, and what that person/loss means to them. I can think of no better illustration of the healing effects that come from making-meaning out of a tragedy than to share the account of one of the teenage members in a group I led about a year ago, who, in reference to his loss of his fireman father, said, "My father's father, my pop, was a fireman too . . . he died fighting a fire where he saved this lady's life from a burning building but went back in for more people and never came out. . . . My father

always told me that story every time he took me to the firehouse. My father went into the WTC to save lives and never came out, but I know he made it possible for others to get out. I think my father was meant to die in the WTC saving lives, just like his father did. I bet they are both up in heaven putting out fires right now . . . if they have fires up there anyway (smiling)."

Terrorism and Children: Mental Health Impact and Interventions

For children, stress reactions to traumatic events can include depression, anxiety, conduct problems, regression, and dissociative reactions (Clark & Miller, 1998). Furthermore, disaster trauma can compound co-morbid conditions in children and set the stage for embedding anxieties in the long-term (Bolton, O'Ryan, Udwin, Boyle, & Yule, 2000). The developmental age of the child influences how that child will react to the disaster. In young children, for example, common post-trauma reactions include helplessness, generalized fear, heightened arousal, nightmares, or sleep disturbances. School-age children might be more likely to demonstrate repetitive traumatic play, aggressive behavior, school avoidance, close attention to parents' anxieties, and preoccupation with danger. Adolescents' post-trauma reactions more commonly include rebellion, depression or social withdrawal, reckless risk-taking, efforts to distance oneself from feelings, and action-oriented responses to trauma (Pynoos & Nader, 1993).

The need for children to receive counseling after a terrorist attack has been documented in various research studies. Stuber and colleagues (2002) conducted a study with 112 parents living within six miles of Ground Zero shortly after the 9/11 terrorist attacks, which found that 22% of the children in the sample were reported to have received some form of counseling, mostly delivered in schools by teachers or school psychologists. This study was significant in finding a strong positive correlation between the parents' level of post-traumatic stress and their children's receipt of counseling. Bat-Zion and Levy-Shiff (1993) also found that parents serve as mediating factors in the post-trauma reactions of their children; negative parental expressions are associated with increased levels of distress feelings and positive parental attitudes are associated with increased coping efforts on the part of their children. In a telephone study conducted with more than 400 parents throughout Manhattan four months after 9/11, Fairbrother and colleagues (2004) found a substantial disparity between apparent need for and receipt of mental health services for children after the terrorist attacks. These findings underscore the need for intensified efforts to identify, refer, and treat children in need after events of mass violence.

To cope effectively with the traumatic effects of terrorist attacks, children need (a) close affectional bonds with a caring adult; (b) explanations that provide an age-appropriate understanding of the meaning and implications of the events that have transpired since 9/11, an understanding that enables them to still view the world as basically safe, meaningful, and fair; and (c) opportunities to do things that enable them to feel good about themselves and to perhaps feel they are contributing to solving the problem we are all facing (Pyszczynski et al., 2003). Mental health intervention strategies should aim to meet these needs. Part of this includes providing children the opportunity to talk about these events and to have age-appropriate explanations given to them by caring adults. Telling children the truth (in age-appropriate terms), but not more than they need to know, is usually the best practice in times of crisis.

In counseling youth for post-traumatic stress symptoms, use of cognitive-based rather than affective-based approaches is considered most effective. Rather than probing children who have experienced a traumatic event on their feelings, the counselor is better off helping them to tell their stories in progressive steps using fact-based information rather than feelings (Lovre, 2001). In treating for post-traumatic stress, it is important to recognize that younger children do not have the verbal or cognitive abilities needed to express the affect attached to traumatic events (Yule, Perrin, & Smith, 2001) Non-talk intervention methods become vital in addressing post-traumatic stress reactions in young or nonverbal children after disasters.

Research has demonstrated that play serves as a form of expression and reduction of anxiety in children (Saylor, 1991). In the months following the attacks on the WTC and the Pentagon, common observations included children engaged in traumatic repetitive play (e.g., playing with blocks portraying tall buildings and having toy planes [or other objects] crash into them and knock them down). Child's play, even that which might appear distressing to the adult eye, should be an encouraged intervention activity in times of crisis. In such cases, the child can be encouraged to role play the rescue personnel who helped to save lives in the tragedy as a way to promote a sense of meaning out of the tragedy. Of course, if a child seems obsessed with violent thoughts or images for more than a few days, further mental health assessment and intervention would be indicated (Retrieved April, 19, 2004, from www.nasponline.org/NEAT/children_war.html).

Play therapy has been found effective when employed with young children in crisis (Cerio, 1994). Similarly, creative arts therapy is an intervention strategy that promotes meaning-making for children in times of crisis. After the 9/11 terrorist attacks, creative arts therapists provided interventions for children and families who had been directly impacted by the terrorist attacks at both the WTC and Pentagon sites (Gonzalez-Dolginko, 2002; Howie, Burch, Conrad, & Shambaugh, 2002). Through the use of art materials and a safe environment, creative arts interventions can help to create a transitional space in which affected children can begin to creatively experience and, therefore, comprehend their world in a new way (Howie et al., 2002).

For practitioners working with children, schools, and parents in times clouded by the augur of terrorist threats, understanding how to foster a sense of safety and coping skills as a means of promoting resilience on the part of young people is critical (Cicchetti & Toth, 1997). As part of this, mental health specialists have been increasingly called on to serve as consultants to schools and parent groups for guidance on how to address the fears and anxious behaviors of children in these times (Pfefferbaum, Call, & Sconzo, 1999). Today more than ever, it is critical for parents and those who work with young people to understand how to recognize post-traumatic stress reactions as manifested in children at different ages and knowing how to take appropriate action in these cases.

Consultation Resources

Although counselors are not expected to possess expertise across all areas, they have an ethical responsibility to provide basic guidance and referral information to assist clients in accessing expert sources of assistance. Helpful resources to utilize in consulting with families, parents, schools, and community groups include the following:

- The American Academy of Pediatrics has prepared a Family Readiness Kit to help families prepare to handle a terrorist event, which includes determining a family disaster plan that specifies emergency contacts and the identification of rally points and disaster supplies (http://www.aap.org/family/frk/frkit29.htm). Additionally, information and resources related to the psychosocial aspects of addressing the needs of children in the aftermath of terrorism and disaster can be accessed at (www.aap.org/terrorism/topics/psychosocial_aspects.html)
- The American Red Cross (ARC) developed a set of guidelines for families to prepare for a terrorist attack. The contemporary practitioner will recognize the value that a sense of preparation for the unexpected can offer the individual to help offset the anxiety of nonspecific threat and sense of helplessness that cloud these troubled times. Counselors can refer their clients to ARC's four-step preparation plan as a means of helping to ease the anticipatory anxiety that has been wrought by ongoing terrorist threats (http://www.redcross.org/services/disaster/0,1082,0_589_,00.html).
- The National Association of School Psychologists (NASP) produced a handout titled "A National Tragedy, Helping Children Cope: Tips for Parents and Teachers" that can be downloaded from its website (www

.nasponline.org/NEAT/terrorism.html) for distribution to families and schools. This document outlines guidelines for parents, adults, and schools in steps that can be taken to help children effectively cope with terrorist attacks.

- The National Center for Children Exposed to Violence (NCCEV), which is part of Yale University's Child Studies Center, has produced helpful resources, guidelines, and publications that specifically address mental health response to children affected by terrorism, highlighting the distinctions between human-made and natural disaster response. Many of these resources, including guidelines for parents and teachers on talking to children about war and terrorism, can be found online: www.nccev.org/violence/children_terrorism.htm)
- The National Advisory Committee on Children and Terrorism (NACCT) produced a document in June 2003 that includes recommendations to the Secretary of Health and Human Services on matters related to terrorism and its impact on children. The importance of early intervention in promoting post-disaster resilience on the part of children and families is emphasized, as is the call to be sensitive to the different needs and vulnerabilities of children at different ages and from diverse cultural communities. This document can be accessed online (www.bt.cdc.gov/children/PDF/working/Recommend.pdf).
- The National Mental Health Association (NMHA) has online materials that address coping with disaster and loss resulting from war and terrorism (http:// www.nmha.org/reassurance.cfm).

The Need for Training and Supervision

Studies conducted after 9/11 bore out the need for mental health workers to be better trained in crisis intervention and response to trauma (Auger, Seymour, & Roberts, 2004). Counselors need to know the differences between disaster and nondisaster mental health services. Similarly important is the need for mental health responders to be prepared and supervised to prioritize their own self-care as a means of ensuring effective and ethical practice during this type of disaster (Kaul, 2002).

When I think about those early days and weeks after 9/11, I am dramatically reminded of the absolutely unique circumstances we all found ourselves in as counselors quickly mobilized to address the psychological needs of the survivors and rescue workers we encountered each day. Although great humanity and a helping spirit were shown in the days immediately following September 11th in the New York metropolitan area, it was often in the context of a great deal of confusion and inefficiency within and between helping agencies and personnel. In those weeks, there were myriad sites where disaster mental health services were

> being offered, including those sponsored by the American Red Cross and the Federal Emergency Management Agency, not to mention those provided by hospitals, churches, and community counseling centers. Good intentions and general competence notwithstanding, not all of the counselors involved in these efforts were well trained in disaster mental health services and early intervention procedures. As a Counselor Educator working in these extraordinary circumstances, I became very aware of the significant need for training in crisis intervention and disaster mental health services in the preparation of mental health counselors for contemporary practice.

As part of its disaster relief services, the American Red Cross (ARC) has established a formal disaster mental health service comprised of mental health professionals who have been trained specifically to address the first-order psychological needs of those affected by disasters. This certification training is considered mandatory for practitioners who wish to be qualified to engage in the provision of mental health services in disasters. As the threat of terrorism has become a greater reality, it is critically important that a body of trained mental health workers are prepared and ready to respond when and if the need arises. Mental health counselors interested in acquiring this training and certification are encouraged to contact their state or local branch of the American Red Cross (www.redcross.org).

Counselor Self-Care Issues

When a "crisis" event has a long-term impact or there is no immediate closure, such as in the aftermath of 9/11, the responding caregivers are at risk of burnout or "vicarious traumatization" or "compassion fatigue" (Figley, 1995), all of which can occur as a result of continued commitment to the helping role and involvement in stories of pain and suffering day after day. Burnout is characterized by symptoms such as sleep disturbances, overwhelming fatigue, somatic conditions such as headaches or backaches, irritability, mental confusion, cynicism, depression, and intense vulnerability. Counselors need to monitor these reactions and take care of their physical and emotional needs. Failure to do so can diminish their ability to function and potentially lead to more serious stress reactions, such as secondary traumatic stress disorder (STSD). As such, proactive support and good supervision for mental health workers are necessary to avoid the potential for becoming ineffective in working with disaster victims. Well-intended individuals who lack the requisite skills run the risk of adding to the crisis (retrieved June 2, 2004 from www.nasponline.org/NEAT/caregivers_general.html).

Mental health counselors need to be especially alert to the emergence of countertransference when dealing with the victims of mass violence (Gion, 2002). There are two forms of countertransference reactions that mental health practitioners can experience as a result of listening to survivors' pain, suffering, and traumatic circumstances when working with trauma victims (Wilson & Lindy, 1995). In "underresponsive" countertransference, the mental health practitioner may dissociate from the speaker, experience a numbing response, minimize the seriousness of the survivor's experience, or become overly clinical with the client. This is when the counselor seemingly "shuts down" and becomes underresponsive. In "overresponsive" countertransference, the counselor overidentifies on a personal level with the victim's trauma and can become psychodynamically enmeshed with the client. The potential for these types of reactions in disaster response work underscores the need for ongoing clinical supervision of the mental health worker. Given these implications, Harbert (2000) notes the need to better focus on the effects of countertransference in the graduate training curricula for helping professionals who will be working with trauma victims.

Counselors who work over the long-term with survivors of human-made disasters can become pessimistic and question the meaningfulness of a world in which such horror takes place. As with their clients, counselors can engage in self-care strategies that promote meaning-making and call on one's sense of spirituality to make sense of a world in which basic assumptions of safety and constancy no longer seem to apply. Basic strategies such as getting the proper rest, taking time away from the work scene (physically and mentally), physical exercise, relaxation, calling on social supports especially family, and enjoying the arts and recreation all can help to restore lost energy and reconstruct meaning for the counselor.

REFERENCES

Abueg, F. R., Woods, G. W., & Watson, D. S. (2000). Disaster trauma. In F. M. Dattillio & A. Freeman (Eds.), *Cognitive-behavioral strategies in crisis intervention* (2nd ed., pp. 243–272). New York: Guilford Press).

Aguilera, D. M., & Panchon, L. A., (1995). The American Psychological Association–California Psychological Association Disaster Response Training Project: Lessons from the past, guidelines for the future. *Professional Psychology: Research and Practice, 26,* 550–557.

Auger, R. W., Seymour, J. W., & Roberts, W. B. (2004). Responding to terror: The impact of September 11 on K–12 schools and schools' responses. *Professional School Counseling, 7,* 222–230.

Banauch, G., McLaughlin, M., Hirschhorn, R., Corrigan, M., Kelly, K., & Prezant, D. (2002). Injuries and illness among New York City Fire Department rescue workers after responding to the World Trade Center attacks. *JAMA: Journal of the American Medical Association, 288,* 1581–1584.

Bat-Zion, N., & Levy-Shiff, R. (1993). Children in war: Stress and coping reactions under threat of scud missile attacks and the effects of proximity. In L. A. Leavitt & N. A. Fox (Eds.), *The psychological effects of war and violence on children* (pp. 143–161). Hillsdale, NJ:

Lawrence Erlbaum Associates.

Bolton, D., O'Ryan, D., Udwin, O., Boyle, S., & Yule, W. (2000). The long-term psychological effects of a disaster experienced in adolescence: general psycholpathology. *Journal of Child Psychology and Psychiatry, 41,* 513–523.

Cerio, J. D. (1994). Play therapy: A brief primer for school counselors. *Journal for the Professional Counselor, 9,* 73–80.

Cicchetti, D., & Toth, S. (1997). *Developmental perspectives on trauma: Theory, research, and intervention.* Rochester, NY: University of Rochester Press.

Clark , D., & Miller, T. (1998). Stress response and adaptation in children: Theoretical models. In T. Miller (Ed.), *Children of trauma: Stressful life events and their effects on children and adolescents* (pp. 3–27). Madison, CT: International University Press.

Conran, T. (2002). Solemn witness: A pilgrimage to Ground Zero at the World Trade Center. *Journal of Systemic Therapies Special Issue: Reflections in the aftermath of September 11, 21,* 39–47.

Cooper, H. H. A. (1976). The terrorist and the victim. *Victimology: An International Journal, 1,* 229–239.

Cooper, N. A., & Clum, G. A. (1989). Imaginal flooding as a supplementary treatment for PTSD in combat veterans: A controlled study. *Behavior Therapy, 54,* 81–87.

Corr, C. A. (2002). Coping with challenges to assumptive worlds. In J. Kauffman (Ed.), *Loss of the assumptive world* (pp. 127–138). New York: Brunner-Routledge.

Cournos, F. (2002). Psychoeducational debriefings after the September 11. *Disaster Psychiatric Services, 53,* 479.

Curran, P. S. (1988). Psychiatric aspects of terrorist violence: Northern Ireland 1969–1987. *British Journal of Psychiatry, 153,* 470–475.

Dattilio, F. M., & Freeman, A. (Eds.). (2000). *Cognitive-behavioral strategies in crisis intervention.* New York: Guilford Press.

de Dunayevich, J. B., & Puget, J. (1989). State terrorism and psychoanalysis. *International Journal of Mental Health, 18,* 98–112

de Jong, J. (Ed.). (2002). *Trauma, war, and violence: Public mental health in socio-cultural context.* New York: Kluwer Academic/Plenum Publishers.

Duffy, J. C. (1988). The Porter lecture: Common psychological themes in societies' reaction to terrorism and disasters. *Military Medicine, 153,* 387–390.

Ellis, A., Gordon, J., Neenan, M., & Palmer, S. (1997). *Stress counseling.* New York: Springer

Everly, G. S. (2000). Crisis Management Briefings: Large group crisis intervention in response to terrorism, disasters, and violence. International *Journal of Emergency Mental Health, 2,* 53–57.

Everly, G. S., & Mitchell, J. T. (2001). America under attack: The "10 Commandments" of responding to mass terrorist attacks. International *Journal of Emergency Mental Health, 3,* 133–135.

Fairbrother, G., Stuber, J., Galea, S., Pfefferbaum, B., & Fleischman, A. R. (2004). Unmet need for counseling services by children in New York City after the September 11th attacks on the World Trade Center: Implications for pediatricians. *Pediatrics, 113,* 1367–1374.

Figley, C. R. (Ed.). (1995). *Compassion fatigue: Coping with secondary traumatic stress in those who treat the traumatized.* New York: Brunner-Mazel.

Foa, E. B., Dancu, C. V., Hembree, E. A., Jaycox, L. H., Meadows, E. A., & Street, G. P. (1999). A comparison of exposure therapy, stress inoculation training, and their combination for reducing posttraumatic stress disorder in female assault victims. *Journal of Consulting and Clinical Psychology, 67,* 194–200.

Galea, S., Ahern, J., Resnick, H., Kilpatrick, D., Bucuvalas, M., Gold, J., & Vlahov, D. (2002). Psychological sequelae of the September 11 terrorist attacks in New York City. *New England*

Journal of Medicine, 346, 982–987.

Gidron, Y. (2002). Posttraumatic stress disorder after terrorist attacks: A review. *Journal of Nervous & Mental Disease, 190,* 118–121.

Gillespie, K., Duffy, M., Hackmann, A., & Clark, D. M. (2002). Community-based cognitive therapy in the treatment of post-traumatic stress disorder following the Omagh bomb. *Behaviour Research & Therapy, 40,* 345–357.

Gion, M. K. (2002). It really hurts to listen: Psychotherapy in the aftermath of September 11. *Psychiatric Services, 53,* 561–562.

Gonzalez-Dolginko, B. (2002). In the shadows of terror: A community neighboring the World Trade Center disaster uses art therapy to process trauma. *Art Therapy, 19,* 120–122.

Gray, M. J., Prigerson, H. G., & Litz, B. T. (2004). Conceptual and definitional issues in complicated grief. In B. T. Litz (Ed.), *Early intervention for trauma and traumatic loss* (pp. 65–84). New York: Guilford Press.

Harbert, K. R. (2000). Critical Incident stress Debriefing. In F. M. Dattillio & A. Freeman (Eds.), *Cognitive-behavioral strategies in crisis intervention* (2nd ed., pp. 385–408). New York: Guilford Press.

Herman, R., Kaplan, M., & LeMelle, S. (2002). Psychoeducational debriefings after the September 11 disaster. *Psychiatric Services, 53,* 479.

Howie, P., Burch, B., Conrad, S., & Shambaugh, S. (2002). Releasing trapped images: Children grapple with the reality of the September 11 attacks. *Art Therapy, 19,* 100–105.

Janoff-Bulan, R. (1983). A theoretical perspective for understanding reactions to victimization. *Journal of Social Issues, 39,* 1–17.

Janoff-Bulman, R. (1992). *Shattered assumptions: Toward a new psychology of trauma.* New York: Free Press.

Johnson, L. S. (2003). Facilitating spiritual meaning-making for the individual with a diagnosis of terminal illness. *Counseling and Values, 47,* 230–240.

Kauffman, J. (2002). Safety and the assumptive world: A theory of traumatic loss. In J. Kauffman (Ed.), *Loss of the assumptive world* (pp. 205–211). New York: Brunner-Routledge.

Kaul, R. E. (2002). A social worker's account of 31 days responding to the Pentagon disaster: Crisis intervention training and self-care practices. *Brief Treatment & Crisis Intervention Special Issue: Crisis response, debriefing, and intervention in the aftermath of September 11, 2001,* 2, 33–37.

Kleinman, S. B. (1989). A terrorist hijacking: Victims' experiences initially and 9 years later. *Journal of Traumatic Stress, 2,* 49–58.

Lanza, M. L. (1986). Victims of international terrorism. *Issues in Mental Health Nursing, 8,* 95–107.

Lazarus, R. S., & Folkman, S. (1984). *Stress, appraisal and coping.* New York: Springer.

Litz, B. T., Gray, M. J., Bryant, R. A., & Adler, A. B. (2002). Early intervention for trauma: Current status and future directions. *Clinical Psychology: Science and Practice, 9,* 112–134.

Lovre, C. (2001) Grief vs. trauma: What's the difference? ASCA School Counselor, 39, 18-19.

Mayou, R. A., Ehlers, A., & Hobbs, M. (2000). Psychological debriefing for road traffic accident victims: Three year follow up of a randomized controlled trial. *British Journal of Psychiatry, 176,* 589–593.

Meichenbaum, D. (1995). *A clinical handbook/practical therapist manual for assessing and treating adults with post-traumatic stress disorder (PTSD).* Waterloo, Ontario, Canada: Institute Press.

Mitchell, J. (1988). The history, status and future of critical incident stress debriefings. *Journal of the Emergency Medical Services, 13,* 47–52.

National Center for Post Traumatic Stress Disorder. (2002). *Mental health interventions for disasters.* Retrieved June 20, 2004, from www.ncptsd.org/fascts/disasters/fs_treatment_disaster.html

National Institute of Mental Health. (2002). *Mental health and mass violence: Evidence-based early psychological interventions for victims/survivors of mass violence. A workshop to reach consensus on best practices.* [NIH Publication No. 02-5138.] Washington, DC: U.S. Government Printing Office.

Neimeyer, R. A. (Ed.). (2001). *Meaning reconstruction and the meaning of loss.* Washington, DC: American Psychological Association.

Neimeyer, R. A., Botella, L., Herrero, O., Pacheco, M., Figueras, S., & Werner-Wildner, L. A. (2002). The meaning of your absence: Traumatic loss and narrative reconstruction. In J. Kauffman (Ed.), *Loss of the assumptive world* (pp. 31–47). New York: Brunner-Routledge.

Neria, Y., Solomon, Z., & Ginzburg, K. (2000). Posttraumatic and bereavement reactions among POWs following release from captivity: The interplay of trauma and loss. In R. Malkinson, S. S. Rubin, & E. Witztum (Eds.), *Traumaic and non-traumatic loss and bereavement: Clinical theory and practice* (pp. 91–111). Madison, CT: Psychosocial Press.

Neria, Y., Suh, E. J., & Marshall, R. D. (2004). The professional response to the aftermath of September 11, 2001 in New York City. In B. T. Litz (Ed.), *Early intervention for trauma and traumatic loss* (pp. 201–215.). New York: Guilford Press.

Norris, F. N., Friedman, M. J., Watson, P. J., Byrne, C. M., Diaz, E., & Kaniasty, K. (2002). 60,000 disaster victims speak: Part I. An empirical review of the empirical literature, 1981–2001. *Psychiatry, 65,* 207–239.

Ofman, P. S., & Mastria, M. A. (1995). Mental health response to terrorism: The World Trade Center bombing. *Journal of Mental Health Counseling, 17,* 312–321.

Parkes, C. M. (1975). What becomes of redundant world models? A contribution to the study of adaptation to change. *British Journal of Medical Psychology, 48,* 131–137.

Parson, E. R. (1995). Mass traumatic terror in Oklahoma City and the phase of adaptational coping: Part II. Integration of cognitive, behavioral., dynamic, existential and pharmacologic interventions. *Journal of Contemporary Psychotherapy, 25,* 267–308.

Paul, G. L. (1967). Outcome research in psychotherapy. *Journal of Consulting Psychology, 31,* 109–188.

Pennebaker, J. W. (1989). Confession, inhibition and disease. In L. Berkowitz (Ed.), *Advances in experimental social psychology* (Vol. 22, pp. 211–244). San Diego, CA: Academic Press.

Pfefferbaum, B., Gurwitch, R., McDonald, N., Sconzo, G., Messenbaugh, A., & Schultz, R. (2000). Posttraumatic stress among children after the death of a friend or acquaintance in a terrorist bombing. *Psychiatric Services, 51,* 386–388.

Pfefferbaum, B., Nixon, S., Tucker, P., Moore, V., Gurwitch, R., Pynoos, R., & Geis, H. (1999). Posttraumatic stress responses in bereaved children after the Oklahoma City bombing. *Journal of the American Academy of Child and Adolescent Psychiatry, 38,* 1372–1379.

Pfefferbaum, B., Call, J. A., & Sconzo, G. M. (1999). Mental health services for children in the first two years after the 1995 Oklahoma City terrorist bombing. *Psychiatric Services, 50,* 956–958.

Pfefferbaum, B., Seale, T. W., McDonald, N. B., Brandt, E. N., Rainwater, S. M., Maynard, B. T., Meierhoefer, B., & Miller, P. D. (2000). Posttraumatic stress two years after the Oklahoma City bombing in youths geographically distant from the explosion. *Psychiatry: Interpersonal & Biological Processes, 63,* 358–370.

Pynoos, R., & Nader, K. (1993). Issues in the treatment of posttraumatic stress in children and adolescents. In J. P. Wilson & B. Raphael (Eds.), *International handbook of traumatic stress syndromes* (pp. 535–549). New York: Plenum.

Pyszczynski, T., Solomon, S., & Greenberg, J. (2003). *In the wake of 9/11: The psychology of terror.* Washington DC: American Psychological Association.

Rando, T. (1993). *Treatment of complicated mourning.* Chicago, IL: Research Press.

Reilly, I. (2002). Trauma and family therapy: Reflections on September 11 from Northern Ireland. *Journal of Systemic Therapies Special Issue: Reflections in the aftermath of September 11, 21,* 71–80.

Rubonis, A. V., & Bickman, L. (1991). Psychological impairment in the wake of disaster: The disaster-psychopathology relationship. *Psychological Bulletin, 109,* 384–399.

Saylor, C. F. (1991). Preschooler post-disaster play: Observations of a clinician, researcher and mother. *Disaster and Trauma Currents, 1,* 5–8.

Schlenger, W. E., Caddell, J. M., Ebert, L., Jordan, B. K., Rourke, K., Wilson, D. et al. (2002). Psychological reactions to terrorist attacks. *Journal of the American Medical Association, 288,* 581–588.

Shalif, Y., & Leibler, M. (2002). Working with people experiencing terrorist attacks in Israel: A narrative perspective. *Journal of Systemic Therapies Special Issue: Reflections in the aftermath of September 11, 21,* 60–70.

Shapiro, F. (1995). *Eye movement desensitization and reprocessing: Basic principles, protocols, and procedure.* New York: The Guilford Press.

Silver, S. M., & Rogers, S. (2002). *Light in the heart of darkness: EMDR and the treatment of war and terrorism survivors.* New York: W. W. Norton.

Solomon, R. M. (2002). Treatment of violated assumptive worlds with EMDR. In J. Kauffman (Ed.), *Loss of the assumptive world: A theory of traumatic loss* (pp. 117–126). New York: Brunner-Routledge.

Stuber, J., Fairbrother, G., Galea, S., Pfefferbaum, B., Wilson-Genderson, M., & Vlahov, D. (2002). Determinants of counseling for children in Manhattan after the September 11th attacks. *Psychiatric Services, 53,* 815–822.

Tarrier, N., Pilgrim, H., Sommerfield, C., Faragher, B., Reynolds, M., Graham, E., & Barrowclough, C. (1999). A randomized controlled trial of cognitive therapy and imaginal exposure in the treatment of chronic posttraumatic stress disorder. *Journal of Consulting & Clinical Psychology, 67,* 13–18.

Wilson, J., & Lindy, J. (1995). Empathic strain and countertransference. In J. Wilson & J. Lindy (Eds.), *Countertransference in the treatment of PTSD* (pp. 227–254). New York: Guilford Press.

Young, B. H, Ford, J. D., Ruzek, J. I., Friedman, M. J., & Gusman, F. D. (1998). *Disaster mental health services: A guidebook for clinicians and administrators.* Menlo Park, CA: Department of Veteran Affairs the National Center for Post-Traumatic Stress Disorder.

Yule, W., Perrin, S., & Smith, P. (2001). Traumatic events and post-traumatic stress disorder. In W. Silverman & P. Treffers (Eds.), *Anxiety disorders in children and adolescents: Research, assessment, and intervention* (pp. 212–234). Cambridge, England: Cambridge University Press.

Highlight Section

HELPING MILITARY PERSONNEL/VETERANS AND FAMILIES MANAGE STRESS REACTIONS AND NAVIGATE REINTEGRATION

PETER M. GUTIERREZ AND LISA A. BRENNER*

Available evidence indicates that the mental health needs of those who have served or are serving in Iraq and Afghanistan are significant (Lineberry, Bostwick, & Rundell, 2006; Milliken, Auchterlonie, & Hoge, 2007; Seal et al., 2008). Based on existing literature (Lineberry, Ramaswamy, Bostwick, & Rundell, 2006), we expect that the physical and psychological challenges faced by some individuals will require intervention, and that the type of care needed will evolve over time. Moreover, challenges associated with deployment are often also experienced by family members (e.g., spouses, children) (Eaton et al., 2008; Lincoln, Swift, & Shorteno-Fraser, 2008). Meeting the needs of military personnel/veterans and their families can be facilitated through community, Department of Defense (DoD), and Department of Veterans Affairs (VA) partnerships.

Hoge and colleagues (2006) studied a group of soldiers who had served in Iraq and found that 65% of individuals had a history of combat experience. Such exposure has been found to be associated with physical injuries, psychological wounds, or both (Gondusky & Reiter, 2005; Hoge et al., 2004). The RAND Corporation (Tanielian & Jaycox, 2008) applied prevalence estimates for post-traumtic stress disorder (PTSD) (5% to 15% of persons deployed) and depression (2% to 10% of persons deployed) to the 1.64 million service members who had been deployed at the time of the study. The

*Adapted from Gutierrez, P. M., & Brenner, L. A. (2009). Introduction to the special section: Helping military personnel and Veterans from Operation Enduring Freedom and Operation Iraqi Freedom (OEF/OIF) manage stress reactions. *Journal of Mental Health Counseling, 31*(2), 95–100.

resulting estimates of individuals with PTSD and depression were 75,000 to 225,000 and 30,000 to 50,000, respectively. Work by Terrio et al. (2009) suggested that 22.8% of soldiers in one Brigade Combat Team had a history of probable traumatic brain injury (TBI), with 7.5% of these individuals continuing to endorse sequelae at post-deployment. A follow-up study by Brenner, Ivins, and colleagues (2009) indicated that a combination of mild TBI and PTSD was more strongly associated with symptom prevalence (headache, dizziness, balance problems, irritability, and memory problems) than either condition alone. We do not yet know the potential long-term impact of psychological and/or physical symptoms on psychosocial functioning. Moreover, there are challenges associated with employing evidence-based assessment and/or treatment strategies when conditions are co-occurring (e.g., TBI and PTSD) (Brenner, Vanderploeg, & Terrio, 2009).

As individuals return from deployments and re-deployments to Iraq and Afghanistan, clinicians are seeing clients at differing points in their process of community re-integration. At the same time, the onset of symptoms and recovery appears to vary between individuals. Work by Corso et al. (2009) highlight that many individuals are exhibiting symptoms but do not meet the full diagnostic criteria for PTSD. Findings from the Millennium Cohort Study suggest that the onset of PTSD is often delayed as much as 10 months post-deployment (Smith, 2007). Providing early evidence-based interventions (Edward, 2005; Foa et al., 2005; Resick, Nishith, Weaver, Astin, & Feuer, 2002; Southwick, Vythilingam, & Charney, 2005; Wagner, Zatzick, Ghesquiere, & Jurkovich, 2007) may change the trajectory of recovery and ultimately facilitate function and re-integration.

It is helpful for clinicians to remember that some PTSD symptoms, such as hyper-vigilance, are adaptive while military personnel are in theater. Out of necessity, the long-term adoption of such strategies may have been reinforced across multiple deployments. Upon returning home, these same strategies (symptoms) can impede re-integration with the civilian community. Recently returned service members may need the assistance of an understanding clinician to make these connections and determine how best to adapt their coping strategies.

Doyle and Peterson (2005) contend that programs aimed at improving the process of re-entry and re-integration will normalize the experiences of returning military personnel. For active duty service members, these processes may be facilitated by military community support; however, for reservists and guardsman, "reintegration largely is shouldered by the communities from when they came" (Doyle & Peterson, 2005, p. 367). This reality serves as both a challenge and an opportunity for community-based providers. Doyle and Peterson also suggest that successful re-entry is enhanced when families are included in the process.

Military marriages face significant obstacles even without deployments, such as moves and separations, loss of friends and jobs secondary to reassignment, and parental absence (Gambardella, 2008). Eaton and colleagues (2008) found that military spouses screened positive for major depression or anxiety disorders at rates similar to those seen among military personnel returning from combat. Deployment-related stresses are also felt by the children of military personnel. Lincoln et al. (2008) suggested that, although most children are resilient to the effects of deployment, those with pre-existing psychological conditions (e.g., anxiety and depression) may be particularly vulnerable. Chartrand, Frank, White, and Shope (2008) found that children between the ages of three and five with a deployed parent experience more internalizing and externalizing symptoms than their peers who do not have a deployed parent. These findings held even after statistically controlling for the respondent parent's stress and depressive symptoms. The spouses studied by Eaton and colleges (2008) were much more likely to seek care for mental health-related complaints than their partners. Such care is often "outsourced" to civilian care providers (Eaton et al., 2008), thereby highlighting the need for community, Department of Defense, and Veterans Administration collaborations.

Clinicians are encouraged to explore evidence-based interventions aimed at decreasing stress-related symptoms. For example, exposure-based therapies have been shown to be effective for individuals with combat-specific PTSD (Black & Keane, 1982; Fairbank & Keane, 1982; Keane & Kaloupek, 1982; Resick & Schnicke, 1992). More recently, Orsillo and Batten (2005) have argued that Acceptance and Commitment Therapy (ACT; Hayes, Strosahl, & Wilson, 1999) could be particularly useful in reducing avoidance of unpleasant emotions and facilitating exposure and positive changes in clients' lives. A more difficult task may be helping returning military personnel establish and maintain healthy relationships with those outside the military/veteran community (Brenner et al., 2008). We therefore recommend couples or family therapy (e.g., Sherman, Zanotti, & Jones, 2005), possibly supplemented by targeted social skills training (e.g., Turner, Beidel, & Frueh, 2005) as supportive elements, particularly during transition periods. Community providers are also encouraged to learn about evidence-based psychotherapy dissemination, which is occurring with the VA (Karlin, 2009). Current national initiatives include training VA mental health clinicians in the delivery of evidence-based psychotherapies for PTSD (Cognitive Processing Therapy [Resick et al., 2002], Prolonged Exposure [Foa et al., 2005]), depression (Cognitive Behavioral Therapy [Beck, Rush, Shaw, & Emery, 1979]), and Acceptance and Commitment Therapy [Hayes et al., 1999]), and serious mental illness (Social Skills Training [Department of Veterans Affairs, 2010]).

Becoming familiar with the relevant areas of the treatment literature discussed so far is important for clinicians likely to be working with military and veteran clients. However, there are other steps that community mental health providers can take to enhance their ability to work with returning military personnel and their family members. Clinicians need to be aware of common factors (e.g., military culture, multiple deployments, combat experiences) and client worldviews, which may or may not differentiate these military personnel/veterans from members of the general population (Ridley, Chih, & Olivera, 2000). The importance of appreciating the military as a unique culture cannot be overstated. Clinicians are encouraged to increase their familiarity with military structures, history, and values. A review of Battlemind training (Walter Reed Army Institute of Research, 2007) may help to facilitate this process when working with returning army personnel. Although these educational materials were developed by the DoD to aid war fighters' transitions back home after deployments, they may also serve as a starting point for clinicians to become oriented to current army culture. Topics covered in Battlemind may also be used to facilitate discussions regarding re-integration.

The Department of VA (http://www.va.gov) and local VA hospitals are also a source for information and services. Community mental health counselors are encouraged to become familiar with national and local resources and acquire knowledge regarding how to help clients' access services (e.g., benefits, health care). Providing clients with information regarding VA health care options and benefits communicates both knowledge regarding the military/para-military culture and a willingness to augment existing care strategies. Conversely, VA and DoD clinicians are encouraged to become familiar with national and local non-military-related mental health and social services, engage with community providers, and encourage collaborative care. These approaches should reinforce the notion that all members of the mental health community are working toward a common goal. Helping military personnel/veterans establish and maintain the best possible trajectory toward recovery will take increased effort and creativity on the part of all involved. Clinicians in the community, DoD, and VA share the responsibility of working together and learning from each other to meet the needs of returning military personnel, veterans, and their families.

REFERENCES

Beck, A. T., Rush, A. J., Shaw, B. F., & Emery, G. (1979). *Cognitive therapy of depression.* New York: Guilford Press.

Black, J. L., & Keane, T. M. (1982). Implosive therapy in the treatment of combat related fears in a World War II veteran. *Journal of Behavior Therapy and Experimental Psychiatry, 13,* 163–165.

Brenner, L. A., Gutierrez, P. M., Cornette, M. M., Betthauser, L. M., Bahraini, B., & Staves, P. J. (2008). A qualitative study of potential suicide risk factors in returning combat veterans. *Journal of Mental Health Counseling, 30,* 211–225.

Brenner, L. A., Ivins, B. J., Schwab, K., Warden, D., Nelson, L. A., Jaffee, M., & Terrio, H. (2009). Traumatic brain injury, posttraumatic stress disorder, and postconcussive symptom reporting among troops returning from Iraq. *Journal of Head Trauma Rehabilitation* [PUBMED ID: 20042982].

Brenner, L. A., Vanderploeg, R. D., & Terrio, H. (2009). Assessment and diagnosis of mild traumatic brain injury, posttraumatic stress disorder, and other polytrauma conditions: Burden of adversity hypothesis. *Rehabilitation Psychology, 54*(3), 239–246.

Chartrand, M. M., Frank, D. A., White, L. F., & Shope, T. R. (2008). Effect of parents' wartime deployment on the behavior of young children in military families. *Archives of Pediatric and Adolescent Medicine, 162,* 1009–1014.

Corso, K. A., Bryan, C. J., Morrow, C. E., Appolonio, K. K., Dodendorf, D. M., & Baker, M. T. (2009). Managing posttraumatic stress disorder symptoms in active-duty military personnel in primary care settings. *Journal of Mental Health Counseling, 31,* 119–137.

Department of Veterans Affairs. (2010). VA social skills training program. Retrieved from http://www.mirecc.va.gov/visn5/training/social_skills.asp

Doyle, M. E., & Peterson, K. A. (2005). Re-entry and reintegration: Returning home after combat. *Psychiatric Quarterly, 76,* 361–370.

Eaton, K. E., Hoge, C. W., Messer, S. C., Whitt, A. A., Cabrera, O. A., McGurk, D., & Castro, C. A. (2008). Prevalence of mental health problems, treatment need, and barriers to care among primary care-seeking spouses of military service members involved in Iraq and Afghanistan deployments. *Military Medicine, 173,* 1051–1056.

Edward, K. (2005). Resilience: A protector from depression. *American Psychiatric Nurses Association Journal,* 11, 241.

Fairbank, J. A., & Keane, T. M. (1982). Flooding for combat-related stress disorders: Assessment of anxiety reduction across traumatic memories. *Behavior Therapy, 13,* 499–510.

Foa, E. B., Hembree, E. A., Cahill, S. P., Rauch, S. A., Riggs, D. S., Feeny, N. C., & Yadin, E. (2005). Randomized trial of prolonged exposure for posttraumatic stress disorder with and without cognitive restructuring: Outcome at academic and community clinics. *Journal of Consulting and Clinical Psychology, 73,* 953–964.

Gambardella, L. C. (2008). Role-exit theory and marital discord following extended military deployment. *Perspectives in Psychiatric Care, 44,* 169–174.

Gondusky, J. S., & Reiter, M. P. (2005). Protecting military convoys in Iraq: an examination of battle injuries sustained by a mechanized battalion during Operation Iraqi Freedom II. *Military Medicine, 170*(6), 546–549.

Hayes, S. C., Strosahl, K. D., & Wilson, K. G. (1999). *Acceptance and commitment therapy: An experiential approach to behavior change.* New York: Guilford Press.

Hoge, C. W., Auchterloine, J. L., & Milliken, C. S. (2006). Mental health problems, use of mental health services, and attrition from military service after returning from deployment to Iraq or Afghanistan. *Journal of the American Medical Association, 295,* 1023–1032.

Hoge, C. W., Castro, C. A., Messer, S. C., McGurk, D., Cotting, D. I., & Koffman, R. L. (2004). Combat duty in Iraq and Afghanistan, mental health problems, and barriers to care. *New England Journal of Medicine, 351*(1), 13–22.

Karlin, B. (2009). VCAO Update: Psychotherapy and psychogeriatrics. Retrieved from http://www.avapl.org/pub/2009%20Conference/Presentations/AVAPL%202009%20-

%20Karlin.pdf

Keane, T. M., & Kaloupek, D. G. (1982). Imaginal flooding in the treatment of posttraumatic stress disorder. *Journal of Consulting and Clinical Psychology, 50,* 138–140.

Lincoln, A., Swift, E., & Shorteno-Fraser, M. (2008). Psychological adjustment and treatment of children and families with parents deployed in military combat. *Journal of Clinical Psychology, 64,* 984–992.

Lineberry, T. W., Bostwick, J. M., & Rundell, J. R. (2006). U.S. troops returning home: Are you prepared? *Current Psychiatry, 5*(1), 13–22.

Lineberry, T. W., Ramaswamy, S., Bostwick, J. M., & Rundell, J. R. (2006). Traumatized troops: How to treat combat-related PTSD. *Current Psychiatry, 5*(5), 39–52.

Milliken, C. S., Auchterlonie, J. L., & Hoge, C. W. (2007). Longitudinal assessment of mental health problems among active and reserve component soldiers returning from the Iraq war. *Journal of the American Medical Association, 298,* 2141–2148.

Orsillo, S. M., & Batten, S. V. (2005). Acceptance and commitment therapy in the treatment of posttraumatic stress disorder. *Behavior Modification, 29,* 95–129.

Resick, P. A., Nishith, P., Weaver, T.L., Astin, M.C., & Feuer, C.A. (2002). A comparison of cognitive-processing therapy with prolonged exposure and a waiting condition for the treatment of chronic posttraumatic stress disorder in female rape victims. *Journal of Consulting and Clinical Psychology, 70,* 867–879.

Resick, P. A., & Schnicke, M. K. (1992). Cognitive processing therapy for sexual assault victims. *Journal of Consulting and Clinical Psychology, 60,* 748–756.

Ridley, C. R., Chih, D. W., & Olivera, R. J. (2000). Training in cultural schemas: An antidote to unintentional racism in clinical practice. *American Journal of Orthopsychiatry, 70,* 65–72.

Seal, K. H., Bertenthal, D., Maguen, S., Gima, K., Chu, A., & Marmar, C. R. (2008). Getting beyond "Don't Ask; Don't Tell": An evaluation of US Veterans Administration postdeployment mental health screening of veterans returning from Iraq and Afghanistan. *American Journal of Public Health, 98,* 714–720.

Sherman, M. D., Zanotti, D. K., & Jones, D. E. (2005). Key elements in couples therapy with veterans with combat-related posttraumatic stress disorder. *Professional Psychology: Research and Practice, 36,* 626–633.

Smith, T. C. (2007, August). *Millennium Cohort Study Team. PTSD: New onset and persistent symptoms after deployment and combat exposures in the millennium cohort.* Paper presented at the 10th annual Force Health Protection Conference, Louisville, KY.

Southwick, S. M., Vythilingam, M., & Charney, D. S. (2005). The psychobiology of depression and resilience to stress: Implications for prevention and treatment. *Annual Review of Clinical Psychology, 1,* 255–291.

Tanielian, T., & Jaycox, L. H. (Eds.). (2008). *Invisible wounds of war: Psychological and cognitive injuries, their consequences, and services to assist recovery* (RAND Corporation monograph series). Santa Monica, CA: Center for Military Policy Research.

Terrio, H., Brenner, L. A., Ivins, B. J., Cho, J. M., Helmick, K., Schwab, K., & Warden, D. (2009). Traumatic brain injury screening: Preliminary findings in a US Army brigade combat team. *Journal of Head Trauma Rehabilitation, 24,* 14–23.

Turner, S. M., Beidel, D. C., & Frueh, B. (2005). Multicomponent behavioral treatment for chronic combat-related posttraumatic stress disorder: Trauma management therapy. *Behavior Modification, 29,* 39–69.

Wagner, A. W., Zatzick, D. F., Ghesquiere, A., & Jurkovich, G. J. (2007). Behavioral activation as an early intervention for posttraumatic stress disorder and depression among physically injured trauma survivors. *Cognitive and Behavioral Practice, 14,* 341–349.

Walter Reed Army Institute of Research U.S. Army Medical Research and Material

Command. (2007). *Battlemind training II: Continuing the transition home.* Retrieved April 2, 2008, from http://www.battlemind.org/Battlemind/Soldier/Post-Deployment%2036%20Months%20PDHRA/Battlemind%20Training%20II%20Brochure%2013%20SEP%2006.pd

Chapter 14

TRAUMA COUNSELING

Susan C. McGroarty

OVERVIEW

Caring for trauma survivors can be challenging but rewarding work. Trauma can wreak havoc on people's lives, and skilled counselors help their clients forge a new beginning. Understanding trauma's impact, risk and resilience factors, cultural considerations, and the application of a stage-based model are the foundations for developing special expertise in this area.

Since the time of Hippocrates, healers have been instructed, "First do no harm." This caution is especially applicable to therapists providing treatment to trauma survivors. Often at a low point in their lives, these clients are particularly vulnerable and challenge us to do our best to relieve their suffering. The nature of the work can be debilitating to the therapist, and there is even some suggestion that "trauma work" can impact our personal relationships (Giordano, 2010). Dimidjian and Hollon (2010) remind us of the importance of choosing interventions and treatments designed to safely and effectively address the psychological aftermath of trauma. In the context of trauma counseling, Hippocrates' saying applies to the therapist in caring for their client and in caring for themselves!

To effectively treat trauma survivors, it is important to have some background understanding of psychological trauma. In this section, we discuss types of trauma and the risk of experiencing them.

TYPES OF TRAUMA

The evening news documents large-scale catastrophic traumatic events such as natural disasters, violence, terrorism, and earthquakes. Other events that are commonly considered "traumatic" include the experience of abuse, car accidents, and medical challenges. It is impossible to create a comprehensive list of events that can induce a traumatic reaction because many experts believe that trauma is in the perception of the survivor. A case example illustrates this point. Joan was in a minor car accident. She hit a light post and the air bag deployed. A white cloud engulfed her, and powder from the airbag swirled all around her. Joan believed she was dying and going to heaven. Although she did not sustain serious physical injuries in the accident and no one else was hurt, Joan incurred a serious case of post-traumatic stress disorder (PTSD) from what essentially could be described as a minor car accident. Her belief that she was dying created the intense fear that can precipitate PTSD.

RISK AND RESILIENCE

The case of Joan illustrates an important aspect of psychological trauma, the morbidity or risk of incurring a trauma reaction. It is important to remember that most people who are exposed to a trauma will NOT become traumatized (Yehuda, 2004). There are several critical factors to assess when evaluating level of risk: nature of trauma, degree of exposure, previous trauma, multiple risk factors, impact and coping factors (Brewin, Andrews, & Valentine, 2000, p. 748). Ozer, Best, Lipsey, and Weiss (2003) suggest that risk factors can be categorized into three groups: "(a) historical or static person characteristics such as family psychiatric history, intelligence, childhood adversity and other previous trauma; (b) trauma severity; and (c) social support and life stress" (p. 54).

The nature of the trauma is often a predominant risk factor. It is well documented in the literature (Voges & Romney, 2003) that man-made disasters (war, terrorism, torture, crime) are more traumatogenic than natural disasters (tsunamis, hurricanes, earthquakes). Although there are significant individual differences, the level of exposure to the trauma and severity are common predictors. A meta-analysis conducted by Brewin, Andrews, and Valentine (2000) found that other factors that predispose people to trauma reactions include previous psychological trauma, additional life stressors, female gender, low socioeconomic stress, multiple traumas, and lack of social/community support. Finally, Voges and Romney remind us of the interactional and kindling impact of multiple risk factors. The more traumatogenic events people are exposed to, the more likely they are to develop a trauma reaction. Survivors of Hurricane Katrina often endured multiple stressors and losses: the hurricane, loss of home, loss of work, separation from community supports, and institutional oppression. These factors combined to significantly increase the trauma morbidity (chance of developing trauma symptoms) for Katrina survivors.

The work of Ehring, Ehlers, and Glucksman (2008) in risk and resilience emphasizes the importance of understanding the personal meaning of the event to the survivor (Joan thought she was dying). Massad and Hulsey (2006) remind us that when something terrible happens, it is natural for people to try to understand why it happened. The authors outline the following factors in the attribution of causation: "Locus (me/outside of me); stability (fixed/unpredictable); controllability; generalizability" (Massad & Hulsey, 2006, p. 202). Internal locus of control, persistence of negative events, and global attributions are associated with a higher level of risk of mental health disorders (Gray & Lombardo, 2004; Levy, Slade, & Radasinghe, 2009).

Cognitive perspective has also been investigated as a risk factor for developing PTSD. Petersen et al. (2008) found that a pessimistic explanatory style (Bad things always happen to ME) is associated with increased mental health risk. Leikas, Lindeman, Roininen, and Lähteenmäki (2009) exhort us to consider the role of the cognitive/emotional style of avoidance in assessing trauma risk. People who do their best to try not to think about the event are often at the greatest risk for developing symptoms.

Finally, physiological responses may also account for risk. The role of the sympathetic, parasympathetic, and adrenergic systems in protecting and defending the brain and the nervous system is an exciting area for future study (Ozer et al., 2003). Resilience factors can often counteract even significant risk factors. Brewin, Andrews, and Valentine (2000) identify the following protective elements: age (not too young, not too old), gender (men are generally less vulnerable to PTSD), and social (family/community) support.

The role of social support and individual difference in risk and resilience emphasize the importance of incorporating multicultural and diversity factors in trauma therapy. Andermann (2002) cautions us about making assumptions and the importance social construction in views of trauma. What is traumatic for me may not be for you!

Risk and Resilience: Multiculturalism and Diversity

To fully understand who is the most susceptible, it is important to consider the multicultural and diversity aspects of the trauma-exposed individual. Factors such as the identification of what constitutes a trauma, the decision to discuss an event, expression of emotions, presentation of symptoms, and resources for help are all culturally mediated. For example, in some cultures, trauma presents as vague, undifferentiated somatic symptoms. Levy, Slade, and Ranasinghe (2009) studied the impact of belief in karma and the after effects of the 2006 tsunami. These authors found that belief in karma was associated with more significant symptoms.

Multicultural factors are frequently associated with risk. Groups that are oppressed and marginalized are often more vulnerable to adverse psychological consequences. For these reasons, it is important to understand your clients' multicultural background in order to treat them most effectively.

TRAUMA ASSESSMENT

There are many options for formal assessment of trauma symptoms. The National Center for PTSD publishes a comprehensive overview of instruments. The PTSD checklist (PCL-C: civilian, PCL-M: military, and PCL-S: specific) are typically available from the Center (see the Resources section).

Clinical assessment of trauma should focus on the typical material covered in an intake as well as trauma-specific symptoms. Reacting to triggers, dissociation, and nightmares are common problems. It is also important to ascertain safety and risk factors. In addition to the potential for suicide and other violent acts, trauma survivors often expose themselves to danger when re-experiencing some aspect of their trauma. For example, Donna, an incest survivor, re-experienced her childhood sexual abuse by prostituting herself. Many trauma survivors often engage in self-injury of para-suicidal behaviors such as "cutting." Depending on the client, self-injury can range from an attempt to prevent a more serious suicide attempt or a dissociative pain experience. Donna told me, "When I cut and see that blood oozing down my arm, I feel peace." When interviewing a client, it is often helpful to have a family member or other informant provide information.

A medical evaluation is almost always indicated. It is well documented in the literature that trauma impacts the body as well as the mind (van der Kolk, 1994). Researchers such as van der Kolk (1994), Shore (2002) and Scaer (2007) describe the physiological effects of trauma. Cognitive problems such as difficulty with memory and concentration and physical problems (such as thyroid dysfunction) resulting from over-activation of the nervous system are not uncommon. Medications are often useful in alleviating trauma symptoms.

TRAUMA DIAGNOSIS

The *Diagnostic and Statistical Manual of Mental Disorders* (4th ed., text revision) (*DSM-IV-TR*) (American Psychiatric Association, 2000) offers several options for diagnosing psychological trauma. Acute Stress Disorder (ASD) is typically diagnosed within a month of the event and requires symptoms consistent with dissociative tendencies. PTSD describes a persistent constellation of symptoms in the following categories: arousal, re-experiencing, and avoidance. It can be diagnosed shortly after the event or as "delayed onset." Diagnosis of both ASD and PTSD utilize the same initial criterion:

> A. The person has been exposed to a traumatic event in which both of the following were present: the person experienced, witnessed, or was confronted with an event or events that involved actual or threatened death or serious injury, or a threat to the physical integrity of self or others (2) the person's response involved intense fear, helplessness, or horror. (p. 457)

Complex trauma (Herman, 1992) is diagnosed when a client has been exposed to multiple traumas or has been suffering from severe, un-remitting symptoms for years. Complex trauma is also called Disorders of Extreme Stress Not Otherwise Specified (DESNOS). Neither DESNOS nor complex trauma has a current *DSM-IV-TR* equivalent. Many clinicians use the *DSM-IV-TR* category Anxiety Disorder Not Otherwise Specified.

When assessing trauma, it is also important to consider other co-morbid conditions such as Major Depression, another Anxiety Disorder, and Substance Use Disorders. Depending on intra-personal and cultural variables, some people who experience a traumatic event might be more susceptible to a Mood Disorder than to PTSD. Although not included in the present version of the *DSM-IV-TR,* trauma scholars are increasingly interested in cultural trauma. Cultural trauma occurs when a group of people have been oppressed and "refers to a dramatic loss of identity and meaning, a tear in the social fabric, affecting a group of people that has achieved some degree of cohesion" (Eyerman, 2002, p. 2).

EFFECTIVE TRAUMA TREATMENT

So what constitutes effective trauma therapy? This chapter delineates experts' consensus of good trauma therapy. There are essentially two broad components: care of the client and care of the therapist. Your care plan will vary depending on the time since the traumatogenic event, the symptomss and your role.

INITIAL STAGES

In the initial aftermath of a devastating event, counselors typically provide psychological first aid. This early stage intervention model focuses on providing comfort, support, and resources to the survivor. Bison et al. (2009) found that encouraging people to talk about the trauma too soon can create or exacerbate trauma reactions in otherwise psychologically healthy people. Other research corroborates this finding (Brymer et al., 2006). To address this concern, they developed the Psychological First Aid Field Operations Guide (PFA). The PFA incorporates research-based response strategies that facilitate adaptive coping and are applicable to people across the developmental spectrum (Vernberg et al., 2008). The authors identify the integration of multiculturalism as a strength of the PFA.

PFA intervention strategies are divided into eight modules (Vernberg et al., 2008). The core principles are based on (a) promoting sense of safety, (b) promoting calming, (c) promoting sense of self- and community efficacy, (d) promoting connectedness, and (e) instilling hope. Counselors responding to a disaster (such as the earthquake in Haiti) might find themselves helping people locate family members, finding clean water, or arranging transportation to religious services. In providing care, it is important to recognize the limits of the Western perspective of mental health and incorporate indigenous healing customs and traditions (Aina, 2009).

TREATMENT CONSIDERATIONS

Phase-based models are the most widely used approaches to individual trauma therapy. In 1992, Judith Herman revolutionized trauma care with the introduction of the tri-phasic model. The three phases of this model are "Safety and Stabilization, Remembrance and Mourning, and Reconnection" (Herman, 1992, p. 132).

Therapy of the traumatized client should not solely focus on the trauma. Presentation of trauma symptoms is complex and variable and usually impacts relationships. The nature of the trauma, developmental stage of the survivor, as well as factors such as culture and gender can mediate the expression of symptoms and course of treatment. For this reason, it is important to consider two caveats when treating trauma survivors. Trauma work should be part of psychotherapy and not treated as isolated symptoms. Treatment should also be formulated to meet the needs of the individual. The most common trauma therapies are integrative, which means they incorporate techniques from several different schools conceptualized to deliver stage-based trauma therapy. The standard of care is to use a stage-based model.

Let's review a few models. Herman's (1992) model is widely used. It consists of the following phases: Stage 1: Safety; Stage 2: Remembrance and Mourning; Stage 3: Reconnection. Briere (2002) has also formulated a phase approach to trauma treatment that integrates psychodynamic, cognitive-behavioral, and humanistic principles (Dass-Brailsford, 2007). His stages include: Stage 1: Safety and Support; Stage 2: Therapeutic Feedback; and Stage 3: Working Through.

In describing the meta-model or consensus model for treating manifold presentations of PTSD, Courtois (2008) describes the following stages:

> Stage 1: Pre-treatment issues, treatment frame, alliance-building, safety, affect regulation, stabilization, skill-building, education, self-care, and support. (p. 93)
> Stage 2: Deconditioning, mourning, resolution, and integration of the trauma. (p. 95)
> Stage 3: Self- and relational development, enhanced daily living. (p. 95)

This chapter mirrors Herman's model. It is important to remember that the stages aren't invariant: Just because you address affect regulation in Safety doesn't mean you won't revisit it in Remembrance & Mourning.

STAGE 1: SAFETY & STABILIZATION

Safety

In the initial stages of trauma therapy, it is vital to help our clients feel safe. Safety may have to account for threats from external factors (people, situations) or an internalized threat to the self. Many trauma survivors experience periods where they think about or actually engage in self-harm. As mentioned earlier, these behaviors can range from either unconscious or conscious dangerous re-enactments to self-injury (cutting) or suicidal gestures. Working with a client in this stage can be quite anxiety provoking for the therapist. Tools, documentation, and ongoing supervision can help minimize the risk to the clinician.

Some common tools used to establish safety include forming a strong working alliance, environmental manipulation, and the use of assessment tools to gauge level of risk. Helping the client develop a "first aid kit" can help minimize the incidence and severity of self-injury.

The literature is replete with documentation of the importance of a strong working alliance (Horvath & Symonds, 1991; Martin, Garske, & Davis, 2000), leading many to conclude that it is an essential aspect of therapy

(Norcross, 2002). Recently, Barber et al. (2009) found that the impact of a positive alliance prevails even after the client has finished treatment. The importance of considering multicultural factors when tending to the alliance cannot be overemphasized (Vasquez, 2007).

Environmental manipulation is defined as helping the client or their caregivers to change a dysfunctional element of their environment. Examples of such interventions include helping an abused partner find a shelter or helping a traumatized client find a new route to work that doesn't pass the site of the trauma.

Suicidal clients are particularly worrisome for the clinician. Tools such as the Beck Depression Inventory and the Beck Hopelessness Scale can help ascertain level of risk. The resources section of this chapter identifies several excellent web-based resources for managing suicide risk.

Self-injury is another common problem among trauma survivors. In a *Frontline* video (Frontline & Dallaire, 2003) detailing the factors that led up to the genocide in Rwanda, UN General Romeo Dallaire, part of a UN delegation, details his struggle with self-injury and PTSD. After his deployment ended, "I'd just drink and then I'd cut myself." Many clients find it helpful to assemble a self-injury first aid kit. Depending on the client, the kit can contain music, art supplies, inspirational reading, markers, rubber bands, and other items to distract and soothe.

Substance abuse is another safety consideration. Many trauma survivors struggle with co-morbid addictions. Seeking Safety developed by Najavitis (2002) is instrumental in working with addicted survivors. Unraveling the relationship between triggers and substance use is instrumental in helping clients address both problems. Other survivors could benefit from attending 12-step meetings and following a 12-step model of treatment.

Once safety is established, it is also important to address what Linehan (1993) terms therapy-interfering behaviors. Many clients, but especially trauma survivors, are ambivalent about treatment. Directly addressing therapy-interfering behaviors (lateness, missed appointments) in a compassionate but firm manner can enhance clients' commitment to treatment.

Psycho-education is another integral first-stage tool. Helping clients realize that they aren't "crazy," and that their trauma symptoms are actually a normal reaction to an abnormal situation, can significantly reduce clients' anxieties and cement a commitment to treatment. Cohen, Mannarino, and Deblinger (2006), the developers of Trauma-Focused Cognitive Behavioral Therapy (TF-CBT), present an excellent model of providing psycho-education to children and families. It could easily be adapted for work with adults (see "Resources").

Managing Emotions

Another important task in the Safety and Stability stage is helping clients deal with the emotional disruptions precipitated by the trauma.

Leslie Greenberg (2008) emphasizes the transforming nature of emotions. This discussion is particularly relevant to work with trauma survivors. Trauma typically precipitates significant emotional disruption; it can shatter the survivor's universe. Some people will present with symptoms of emotional dysregulation, whereas others will present with emotional over-regulation. Emotional dysregulation is illustrated in the case of Tom. After surviving a motor vehicle accident, in which the other driver and his passengers were killed, Tom experienced severe emotional outbursts. He lost his temper easily, had crying spells, and suffered from frequent panic attacks. Over-regulation is exemplified in the case of Kwame. Kwame, 14, fled to the United States after his village in the Sudan was raided. He watched as his father was murdered and mother and sisters were raped. Now settled in the United States for several years, Kwame presents in counseling because his girlfriend complains he sometimes seems cold and without feelings. As a result of the trauma, Kwame over-regulates his emotions.

The close proximity between the brain's emotion center (the limbic system) and the memory system (hippocampus) is frequently cited as a central factor in the development of PTSD. One of the most basic functions of emotions is to signal us of important dangers in our environment. It is hypothesized that the reason emotions are so close to memory is because it is adaptive to remember what is dangerous (children usually only need to touch a hot stove once before learning to be careful). This signaling function of emotions usually propels us to either fight or flight. Clients may experience symptoms of hyper-arousal (fear, anger, physiological arousal, anxiety) or hypo-arousal (traumatic dissociation). Scaer (2007) compares dissociation with an animal playing dead to escape a threat. The organism feels the threat is overwhelming, and the only way to (emotionally) survive is to use the mind to escape from the experience or to convince the predator that they are dead and there is no need for further attack. Scaer theorized that the brain mechanism that switches off this arousal system is impaired in survivors who develop PTSD. In summary, emotional difficulties are a central aspect of the trauma response.

Emotional responses are quite complex. Not only is there the emotional response produced in the limbic system, but Cameron and Jago (2008) point out that there is an emotional response to the experience of emotions. These authors suggest that most people experience some process of evaluating the acceptability of a given emotion. If an emotion is deemed to be "negative" or "unacceptable" (p. 216), a secondary emotional response (usually anxiety or negative self-criticism) is evoked. Thus, we potentially have a situation of "clouds on clouds," where one troublesome response evokes an even more distressing response (e.g., I am so mad at myself: I should be over these panic attacks). Techniques such as radical acceptance and mindfulness have been shown to be helpful in interrupting this negative cycle (Davidson, 2010).

Many empirically supported therapies for trauma center around helping people change their thoughts about the trauma and its aftermath. Linehan (1993) points out a limitation with this approach. In her work with people with complex trauma and Borderline Personality Disorder, Linehan noticed that survivors frequently terminated therapy pre-maturely. She hypothesized that survivors of complex trauma feel invalidated by a counselor's attempt to help them change their thoughts. In developing Dialectical Behavior Therapy, Linehan incorporated principles of radical acceptance of emotions to reduce the risk of the client feeling their thoughts and feelings are dismissed by their counselor.

Hayes (2004) also recognizes the importance of acceptance of emotions. Hayes postulates that most symptoms of psychological distress stem from attempts to avoid painful emotions. Acceptance and Commitment Therapy, another empirically supported approach to trauma therapy, incorporates the concept of radical acceptance in its design.

So what is radical acceptance? On one level, interventions oriented from this perspective are designed to help clients accept the unacceptable. Consider the Serenity Prayer (Alcoholics Anonymous History, n.d.), which is at the heart of many 12-step addiction recovery programs:

> Grant me the serenity
> To accept the things I cannot change,
> The courage to change the things I can,
> The wisdom to know the difference.

This simple prayer summarizes the principles of radical acceptance. It seems especially relevant to trauma work. One reason for this stems from the work of Hayes Wilson, Gifford, Follette, and Strosahl (1996). Their work postulates that mental health symptoms are the result of avoidance of emotions. G. Everly (personal communication, 2004) talks about the traumatagenic cognition at the heart of many survivors' pain. He gives the example of a police officer who watched helplessly as his partner was viciously attacked. "I should have done something," was the theme of many of the officer's trauma ruminations. This rumination reflects the importance of radical acceptance and helping the trauma survivor accept the unacceptable.

Mindfulness is a technique popularized by Linehan (1993) that helps clients with radical acceptance. It has its origin in the Buddhist tradition. It can be defined as "An openhearted, moment-to-moment, nonjudgmental awareness" (Kabat-Zinn, 2005, p. 24) and is thought of as a way of relating to oneself and the world that can be enhanced through training and practice (Erisman & Roemer, 2010, p. 72). Williams (2010) distinguishes from everyday "doing" mode to mindfulness-based "being mode." "Mindfulness training aims to cultivate an alternative ("being") mode through meditation practices that teach people how to pay open-hearted attention to objects in the exterior and interior world as they unfold, moment by moment. Attention is paid not only to the objects themselves but to our reactions to them" (p. 2). As part of trauma therapy, Kwame is learning to observe and notice what he is feeling, without judging or trying to change it.

No matter what your theoretical orientation, helping our clients manage their emotions is an integral aspect of trauma psychotherapy. Mindfulness techniques and radical acceptance are important tools to help our clients accept their thoughts, feelings, and experiences.

Managing Arousal

Related to helping our clients manage their affect is the specific skill of strategies for dealing with anxiety. Anxiety and hyperarousal are, by definition, an integral aspect of PTSD. Many trauma survivors find relaxation techniques such as focused, deep breathing and muscle/tension release exercises helpful tools to manage their anxiety. Basic stress management techniques are useful in helping people manage complicated lives exacerbated by traumatic stress symptoms.

Dissociation is often described as hypoarousal. Dissociative symptoms can range from momentary "spacing out" to the severe (and rare) case of Dissociative Identity Disorder. It is important to identify and aggressively treat dissociative symptoms. Untreated, this manifestation of trauma can lead to increased reliance on dissociative coping and marked dysfunction.

The first step in treating dissociation is to rule out health-related and substance abuse explanations. The fact that some medical conditions can look like dissociation underlines the importance of encouraging survivors to consult with their personal physician.

Grounding techniques help clients stay focused in the "here and now" instead of the "then and there." Some examples of grounding techniques include softly calling the person's name and calling his or her attention to the present state (sitting in the office with your feet firmly planted on the ground). In most cases, it is not recommended to touch a dissociating person to "pull them out of it." It can startle or frighten the client or become integrated into his or her traumatic, dissociative experience.

Triggers

Dealing with triggers is another important aspect in the initial stages of trauma therapy. Triggers are as unique as the individual. People, places, smells, and sounds can all cause survivors to momentarily feel like they are re-experiencing some aspect of the trauma. Usually, identifying triggers is an important first step in helping people manage this distressing symptom. Once identified, environmental manipulation, relaxation techniques, cognitive reframing, and affirmations (I am safe) are instrumental in helping the client experience a sense of control. For many people, medication is a useful adjunct in dealing with triggers.

John, a combat veteran, found that any red substance (ketchup, paint) could trigger a panic attack. Relaxation techniques paired with self-talk and medication helped him navigate those triggers common to everyday living.

Sleep

Re-experiencing symptoms coupled with heightened arousal often result in disrupted sleep. Waking up with panic attacks, nightmares, and primary and secondary insomnia are common complaints. Poor sleep can create a secondary cycle of symptoms if people are exhausted and trying to manage symptoms. Therefore, it is important to exercise vigilance in assessing sleep in trauma survivors. Psycho-education, relaxation techniques, and addressing day avoidance often result in more restful sleep. Sleep hygiene techniques (see "Resources") are useful tools. Some survivors benefit from instruction and practice in "lucid dreaming." After being raped, Judi's sleep was characterized by horrific nightmares. In session, she recounted the dreams and then created different endings that were more soothing to her. As she was falling asleep, Judi would recount the dreams and their new endings.

Memory

One of the hottest controversies in trauma psychology is that of recovered memory of childhood sexual abuse. Can people "forget" something so distressing? Freyd (1996) presents a paradigm for understanding this phenomenon in her conceptualization of betrayal trauma. Children's need for attachment and safety, coupled with a perpetrator's instructions "This didn't happen," can create a paradigm for forgetting. Other theorists argue that it is especially unlikely for anyone to forget a tragic event (McNally, 2003). The controversy rages on.

What is generally agreed on is that memory problems are an intrinsic aspect of PTSD. The nature of trauma can create problems with attention and concentration as well as impair recall of aspects of the traumatic event(s). Traumatic recall is typically fragmented, episodic, sensory, and highly emotionally charged. Some researchers have found that other clients can distressingly recall every detail (Jelinek et al., 2009). Until the client is stabilized, it is important not to push the him or her to remember because this can precipitate marked decompensation and/or can create "false memories."

Empirically Supported Treatments for PTSD

There is not a consensus among experts on a single model for treatment of PTSD. The International Society for Traumatic Stress Studies publishes guidelines for the effective treatment of trauma (Foa, Keane, & Friedman, 2000). Some commonly researched treatments include Cognitive Behavioral Therapy (CBT) with Direct Therapeutic Exposure (Foa, Hembree, & Rothbaum, 2007) and Eye Movement Densensitization and Reprocessing (EMDR).

It is important to remember that there is little research on the efficacy of these treatments for diverse populations. Given this paucity of research, it is important to consider cultural adaptations to existing treatments in order to enhance their utility with diverse survivors (Sue et al., 2006). The following case illustrates an example of a cultural adaptation of an empirically supported treatment. Maria, a Mexican immigrant, sought treatment for PTSD symptoms after a serious motor vehicle accident. She struggled with significant hyperarousal symptoms. In respect for the Latino principal of *famililiasm,* the therapist decided to include her mother and partner in some of the treatment sessions.

Trauma-Focused Cognitive-Behavior Therapy (TF-CBT). Developed by Esther Deblinger, Judith Cohen, and Anthony Marrino, TF-CBT is a comprehensive, empirically supported treatment (Deblinger, Cohen, & Marrino, n.d). It was originally developed to treat child survivors of sexual abuse, but its multi-faceted approach can be adapted to adults. The components of this approach include psycho-education, stress management, affect expression and modulation, cognitive coping, creating the trauma narrative, behavior management, and parent-child sessions (Cohen et al., 2006).

Cognitive Behavior Therapy. The traditional techniques of Cognitive Behavior Therapy (Beck, Rush, & Emery, 1979) are often helpful tools in working with clients with PTSD. Thought records, identifying distortions, cognitive restructuring, and identifying and challenging core beliefs are all empirically supported.

Direct Therapeutic Exposure (DTE). Initially discussed by Boudewyns (1983), DTE is a behavioral approach that integrates systematic desensitization and exposure treatments. It involves teaching relaxation skills, constructing a fear hierarchy, and then either real or imaginal exposure to the feared items. Rape survivors create narratives of their trauma as if it were happening now. The narratives are recorded, and clients are instructed to listen to them repeatedly. Repetition and re-conditioning to the feared stimulus usually result in significant symptom reduction (Foa, et al., 2007).

Eye Movement Desensitization and Reprocessing (EMDR). EMDR was developed by Francine Shapiro (1995) and is a psychotherapy approach using dichotic stimulation (either bi-lateral eye stimulation or tactile stimulation) to help clients reprocess their trauma. This treatment is considered an efficacious option for PTSD (Chambless et al., 1998; Chemtob, Tolin, van der Kolk, & Pitman, 2001).

Psychodynamic Therapy. There is scant research on the efficacy of psychodynamic therapies in the treatment of PTSD. However, the emphasis on the relationship and attachments would intuitively have an important role in the treatment of survivors. Supportive therapy (Misch, 2000) would be indicated in the initial stages of therapy. As stability replaces symptoms, the use of expressive and insight-oriented techniques may help clients heal from the deleterious impacts of trauma.

STAGE 2: REMEMBRANCE AND MOURNING

Introduction

Not all clients are capable of navigating the challenges of this stage of trauma therapy. Yves, 73, had endured multiple traumas in his life. He grew up in occupied Poland and at the age of five, was placed in an internment camp. He never saw his parents again. His career was in intelligence gathering in remote and dangerous places. He suffered from severe diabetes and hypertension. These multiple, complex problems resulted in debilitating symptoms of PTSD and depression. When I met Yves, he had significant suicidal ideation, and exhibited passive suicidal behavior by neglecting to take his diabetes and heart medications and abused alcohol. In the course of working together, Yves recommitted to living, decreased his alcohol abuse, and learned to manage his psychiatric symptoms. We attempted remembrance and mourning several times, followed by a dramatic return of suicidal ideations and binge drinking. Yves and I decided to focus therapy on maintaining his gains and addressing some deficits in his interpersonal relationships. We never reached the stage of developing a trauma narrative, but nevertheless the significant therapeutic gains helped alleviate his suffering and provided him with hope for the future.

Trauma Narrative

The importance of the human experience of story-telling dates to antiquity. When trauma happens, humans seem to have an inherent need to make sense of it, to talk about it. Effective trauma therapies harness this inborn need in the narrative aspects of trauma therapy. We help clients re-experience their story in a way that leads to freedom not continued re-enactment. Traumatic memories are often encoded differently than other types of memories. Often survivors have a piecemeal, fragmented recollection of the events (van der Kolk et al., 1996). Sensory memories such as smell are often the most salient. The disjointed nature of these memories may play a role in the brain's need to re-enact and re-experience the trauma. Therefore, helping survivors embed these disjointed fragments within the context of the trauma narrative can lead to the significant reduction of PTSD symptoms (Crossley, 2000).

Herman aptly named the process of developing a trauma narrative that incorporates affect as "Remembrance and Mourning." The focus of this stage is to help clients tell their story in a way that connects affect to the experience, diminishes suffering, and aids understanding of the trauma.

Personal Experiences

In my work with trauma survivors, I have found the Internet to be a useful adjunct. Jim, a combat veteran of a chaotic series of battles, had debilitating PTSD. After a year of work on Safety and Stabilization, we agreed to try some exposure techniques to help him manage the trauma. We first enlisted his support system, medical professionals, and Jim made sure there were no impending deadlines at work. In session, he worked on developing a first-person, real-time retelling of the battle. At home, Jim did an Internet search and found pictures of the equipment used in that particular skirmish. He illustrated his narrative with relevant war images. His partner, well prepared for this stage, listened and watched as he spent time re-telling his story. After about a week of daily exposure, Jim told me he was getting bored with himself. At the end of the exposure period, Jim felt differently about the battle. He had developed a more realistic appraisal of his roles and abilities, and, though incredibly sad, he was no longer tortured by guilt and recriminations. At this point, Jim was ready for the third stage of trauma work.

STAGE 3: RECONNECTION

What is the meaning of suffering? Why do bad things happen to "good" people? These questions are the typical domain of philosophers, artists, and world religions (Tedeschi & Calhoun, 1995). They are eternal questions for which no centrally agreed on meaning can be discerned. Traumatic events and the suffering they bring can change people's worldview. In the first stages of therapy, we attempt to alleviate this suffering with techniques and narratives. In this stage, we help people as they struggle with the question, "Why me?"

Tedeschi and Calhoun (1994) point out a central irony of traumatic experiences. Survivors are simultaneously more vulnerable due to their awareness that bad things DO happen and can feel more resilient: "I am more vulnerable, but stronger" (p. 1). Post-traumatic growth is defined as "the experience of positive change that occurs as a result of the struggle with highly challenging life circumstances. It is manifested in a variety of ways, including a richer appreciation for life, more meaningful interpersonal relationships, an increased sense of personal strength, and a richer existential and spiritual life" (Tedeschi & Calhoun, 2004, p. 1). This new sense of vitality and meaning does not imply an end to suffering but arms the survivor with a deeper appreciation for the "little things" in life.

This discussion of post-traumatic growth may remind you of our earlier discussion of resilience. So are post-traumatic growth and resilience variations on the same theme? Research investigating this intriguing question suggests that they are different and unrelated constructs. As you may recall, resilience protects people from developing PTSD; post-traumatic growth is associated with vulnerability to PTSD (Levine et al., 2009). Variables associates with post-traumatic growth include an optimistic temperament and minority status (Park & Hegelson, 2006). In a meta-analysis of benefit finding after negative life-events, Hegelson, Reynolds, and Tomich (2006) found that female gender, youth, and religiosity, as well as increased severity of the life-stressor, is associated with greater post-traumatic growth. Helping clients to develop anniversary commemorations, write letters (either sent or unsent), seek forgiveness, and plan and practice rituals may help augment post-traumatic growth (Anonymous, 2007).

The process of facilitating post-traumatic growth is an exhilarating and sustaining element for the trauma therapist. As you may surmise, there are significant clinical and personal challenges to the therapist. In fact, vicarious traumatization of the therapist is a significant risk for those who work with this population.

VICARIOUS TRAUMA

Also known as compassion fatigue, vicarious trauma (VT) describes the risk (and reality) of the trauma counselor developing symptoms as a direct result of providing therapy to trauma survivors. Pearlman and Saakvitne (1995) describe it as the "transformation in the inner experience of the therapist that comes about as a result of empathic engagement with clients' trauma material" (p. 31). Harrison and Westwood (2009) investigated factors that protect the therapist from developing VT. These authors found that therapists who had a strong social network, practiced mindfulness techniques, and were comfortable with complex and ambiguous situations were less vulnerable to this very real threat. These authors also cite ongoing supervision, personal psychotherapy, a balanced caseload, coping mechanisms, and stress management as protective factors.

In summary, burnout or compassion fatigue is a real risk to the trauma counselor. Although we may not realize it, bearing witness to suffering can be personally challenging. It is important to recognize this risk and take appropriate steps to minimize its impact. In my own practice, I find I need to take breaks from working with trauma clients to maintain my personal equilibrium. Working with child survivors can be particularly exhausting.

These caveats underscore the complexity of this type of work. Ongoing training, a commitment to a balanced life, and attention to my caseload have helped me in my 20 years as a traumatologist. Some of my most rewarding moments as a therapist transpired in the context of trauma therapy. Helping a survivor regain his or her sense of hope and reconnect with living is a truly incredible experience.

REFERENCES

Aina, O. (2009). "Psychotherapy by environmental manipulation" and the observed symbolic rites on prayer mountains in Nigeria. *Mental Health, Religion & Culture, 9,* 1–13.

Alcoholics Anonymous History. (n.d.). *The origin of our serenity prayer.* Retrieved from http://www.aahistory.com/prayer.html

American Psychiatric Association. (2000). *Diagnostic and statistical manual of mental disorders* (4th ed., text revision). Washington, DC: Author.

Andermann, L. F. (2002). Cultural aspects of trauma. *Canadian Psychological Bulletin.* Retrieved from http://ww1.cpa-apc.org:8080/Publications/Archives/Bulletin/2002/august/andermannEn.asp

Anonymous. (2007). The impact that changed my life. *Professional Psychology: Research and Practice, 38,* 561–570.

Barber, J., Connolley, M. B., Crits-Cristoph, P., Gladis, L., & Siqueland, L. (2002). Alliance predicts patients' outcome beyond in-treatment change in symptoms. *Personality Disorders: Theory, Research and Treatment, 5,* 80–89.

Beck, A., Rush, J., & Emery, G. (1979). *Cognitive therapy of depression.* New York: Guilford.

Bison, J., McFarlane, A., Rose, S., Ruzak, J. I., & Watson, P. (2009). Psychological debriefing for adults. In E. B. Foa, T. M. Keane, & M. J. Friedman (Eds.), *Effective treatments for PTSD: Practice guidelines from the International Society for Traumatic Stress Studies* (2nd ed., pp. 83–105). New York: Guilford Press.

Boudewyns, P. A. (1983). *Flooding and implosive therapy: Direct therapeutic exposure in clinical practice.* New York: Robert H. Shipley.

Brewin, C. R., Andrews, B., & Valentine, J. D. (2000). Meta-analysis of risk factors for posttraumatic stress disorder in trauma-exposed adults. *Journal of Consulting and Clinical Psychology, 68,* 748–766.

Briere, J. (2002). Treating adult survivors of severe childhood abuse and neglect: Further development of an integrative model. In J. E. B. Myers, L. Berliner, J. Briere, C. T. Hendrix, C. Jenny, & T. Reid (Eds.), *The APSAC handbook on child maltreatment* (2nd ed., pp. 175–203). Newbury Park, CA: Sage.

Brymer, M., Layne, C., Jacobs, A., Pynoos, R., Ruzek, J., & Steinberg, A. (2006). *Psychological first aid field operations guide* (2nd ed.). Los Angeles: National Child Traumatic Stress Network and National Center for PTSD. Retrieved from http://ncptsd.va.gov/ncmain/ncdocs/manuals/nc_manual_psyfirstaid.html

Cameron, L., & Jago, L. (2008). Emotion regulation interventions: A common-sense model approach. *British Journal of Health Psychology, 13,* 215–221.

Chambless, D. L., Baker, M. J., Baucom, D. H., Beutler, L. E., Calhoun, K. S., Crits-Cristoph, P., & Woody, S. R. (1998). Update on empirically validated therapies. *The Clinical Psychologist, 51,* 3–16.

Chemtob, D. I., Tolin, D. F., van der Kolk, B. K., & Pitman, B. K. (2001). Eye movement desensitization and reprocessing. In E. B. Foa, T. M. Keane, & M. J. Friedman (Eds.), *Effective treatments for PTSD: Practice guidelines from the International Society for Traumatic Stress Studies* (pp. 139–155). New York: Guilford Press.

Cohen, J. A., Mannarino, A. P., & Deblinger, E. (2006). *Treating trauma and traumatic grief in children and adolescents.* New York: Guilford Press.

Courtois, C. A. (2008). Complex trauma, complex reactions: Assessment and treatment. *Psychological Trauma: Theory, Research and Practice, 5,* 81–100.

Crossley, M. L. (2000). Narrative psychology, trauma, and the study of self/identity. *Theory & Psychology, 10,* 527–546.

Dass-Brailsford, P. (2007). Models of trauma treatment. In *A practical approach to treating trauma: Empowering interventions* (pp. 51–69). Thousand Oaks, CA: Sage.

Davidson, R. (2010). Empirical explorations of mindfulness: Conceptual and methodological conundrums. *Emotion, 10,* 8–11.

Deblinger, E., Cohen, J., & Mannarino, A. (n.d.). *Trauma-focused cognitive-behavior therapy.* Retrieved from http://tfcbt.musc.edu/.

Dimidjian, S., & Hollon, S. D. (2010). How would we know if psychotherapy were harmful? *American Psychologist, 65,* 21–33.

Ehring, T., Ehlers, A., & Glucksman, E. (2008). Do cognitive models help in predicting the severity of posttraumatic stress disorder, phobia, and depression after motor vehicle accidents? A prospective longitudinal study. *Journal of Consulting and Clinical Psychology, 76,* 219–230.

Erisman, S. M., & Roemer, L. (2010). A preliminary investigation of the effects experimentally induced mindfulness on emotional responding to film clips. *Emotion, 10,* 72–82.

Eyerman, R. (2002). *Cultural trauma: Slavery and the formation of African-American identity.* Cambridge: Cambridge University Press.

Foa, E. B., Hembree, E., & Rothbaum, B. O. (2007). *Prolonged exposure therapy for PTSD: Emotional processing of traumatic experiences: Therapist guide.* New York: Oxford University Press.

Foa, E. B., Keane, T. M., & Friedman, M. J. (2000). *Effective treatments for PTSD: Practice guidelines from the international society for traumatic stress studies.* New York: Guilford Press.

Freyd, J. (1996). *Betrayal trauma: The logic of forgetting childhood abuse.* Cambridge, MA: Harvard University Press.

Frontline (Interviewer) & Dallaire, R. (Interviewee). (2003). *Ghosts of Rwanda* [Interview transcript]. Retrieved February 11, 2010, from http://www.pbs.org/wgbh/pages/frontline/shows/ghosts/interviews/dallaire.html

Giordano, T. (2010). *Interpersonal relationships of therapists who work with adult survivors of child abuse.* Unpublished raw data.

Gray, M. J., & Lombardo, T. W. (2004). Life event attributions as a potential source of vulnerability following exposure to a traumatic event. *Journal of Loss & Trauma, 9,* 59–72.

Greenberg, L. (2008). Emotion and cognition in psychotherapy: The transforming power of affect. *Canadian Psychology, 49,* 49–59.

Harrison, R. L., & Westwood, M. J. (2009). Preventing vicarious traumatization of mental health therapists: Identifying protective practices. *Psychotherapy: Theory, Research, Practice, Training, 46,* 203–219.

Hayes, S. C. (2004). Acceptance and commitment therapy, relational frame theory, and the third wave of behavior therapy. *Behavior Therapy, 35,* 639–665.

Hayes, S. C., Wilson, K. W., Gifford, E. V., Follette, V. M., & Strosahl, K. (1996). Emotional avoidance and behavioral disorders: A functional dimensional approach to diagnosis and treatment. *Journal of Consulting and Clinical Psychology, 64,* 1152–1168.

Hegelson, V. S., Reynolds, K. A., & Tomich, P. L. (2006). A meta-analytic review of benefit finding and growth. *Journal of Consulting & Clinical Psychology, 74,* 794–816.

Herman, J. L. (1992). *Trauma and recovery.* New York: Basic Books.

Hippocrates. *The Hippocratic Oath.* (2002). (Michael North, Trans.). Retrieved from http://www.nlm.nih.gov/hmd/greek/greek_oath.html

Horvath, A. O., & Symonds, B. D. (1991). Relation between working alliance and outcome in psychotherapy: A meta-analysis. *Journal of Counseling Psychology, 38,* 139–149.

Jelinek, L., Randjbar, S., Seifert, D., Kellner, M., & Moritz, S. (2009). The organization of autobiographical and nonautobiographical memory in posttraumatic stress disorder (PTSD). *Journal of Abnormal Psychology, 118,* 288–298.

Kabat-Zinn, J. (2005). *Full catastrophe living: Using the wisdom of your body and mind to face stress, pain and illness.* New York: Bantam.

Leikas, S., Lindeman, M., Roininen, K., & Lähteenmäki, L. (2009). Avoidance motivation, risk perception and emotional processing. *European Journal of Personality, 23,* 125–147.

Levine, S., Laufer, A., Stein, E., Hamama-Raz, Y., & Solomon, Z. (2009). Examining the relationship between resilience and posttraumatic growth. *Journal of Traumatic Stress, 22,* 282–286.

Levy, B. R., Slade, M. D., & Ranasinghe, P. (2009). Causal thinking after a tsunami wave: Karma beliefs, pessimistic explanatory style and health among Sri Lankan survivors. *Journal of Religious Health, 48,* 38–45.

Linehan, M. (1993). *Skills training manual for treating borderline personality disorder.* New York: Guilford Press.

Martin, D. J., Garske, J. P., & Davis, M. K. (2000). Relation of the therapeutic alliance with outcome and other variables: A meta-analytic review. *Journal of Consulting and Clinical Psychology, 68,* 438–450.

Massad, P. M., & Hulsey, T. L. (2006). Causal attributions in post traumatic stress disorder: Implications for clinical research and practice. *Psychotherapy: Theory, Research, Practice, Training, 43,* 201–215.

McNally, R. (2003). Progress and controversy in the study of posttraumatic stress disorder. *Annual Review of Psychology, 54,* 229.

Misch, D. A. (2000). Basic strategies of dynamic supportive psychotherapy. *Journal of Psychotherapy Practice, 9,* 173–189.

Najavits, L. (2002). *Seeking safety: A treatment manual for ptsd and substance use.* New York: Guilford Press.

Norcross, J. C. (2002). *Psychotherapy relationships that work: Therapist contributions and responsiveness to patients.* New York: Oxford University Press.

Ozer, E., Best, S. R., Lipsey, T. L., & Weiss, D. R. (2003). Predictors of posttraumatic stress disorder and symptoms in adults: A meta-analysis. *Psychological Bulletin, 129,* 52–73.

Park, C., & Hegelson, V. (2006). Introduction to the special section: Growth following highly stressful life events–current status and future directions. *Journal of Consulting & Clinical Psychology, 74,* 791–796.

Pearlman, L. A., & Saakvitne, K. W. (1995). Treating therapists with vicarious traumatization and secondary traumatic stress disorders. In C. R. Figley (Ed.), *Compassion fatigue: Coping with secondary traumatic stress disorder in those who treat the traumatized* (pp. 150–177). Levittown, PA: Brunner/Mazel.

Scaer, R. (2007). *The body bears the burden: Trauma, dissociation and disease.* Binghamton, NY: Hayworth Medical Press.

Shore, A. (2002). Dysregulation of the right brain: A fundamental mechanism of traumatic attachment and the psychopathogenesis of posttraumatic stress disorder. *Australian and New Zealand Journal of Psychiatry, 36,* 9–30.

Shapiro, F. (1995). *Eye movement desensitization and reprocessing: Basic principles, protocols, and procedures.* New York: Guilford Press.

Sue, S., Zane, N., Levant, R. F., Silverstein, L. B., Brown, L., Olkin, R., & Taliaferro, G. (2006). How well do evidence-based versus treatment as usual satisfactorily address the various dimensions of diversity? In J. C. Norcross, L. E. Buetler, & R. Levant (Eds.), *Evidence-based practices in mental health* (pp. 329–374). Washington, DC: American Psychological Association.

Tedeschi, R., & Calhoun, L. (1994). Posttraumatic growth: A new perspective on psychotraumatology. *Psychiatric Times, 21,* 1–2.

Tedeschi, R., & Calhoun, L. (1995). *Trauma and transformation: Growing in the aftermath of suffering.* Thousand Oaks, CA: Sage.

Tedeschi, R., & Calhoun, L. (2004). Posttraumatic growth: Conceptual foundations and empirical evidence. *Psychological Inquiry, 15,* 1–18.

van der Kolk, B. (1994). The body keeps score: Memory and the evolving psychobiology of post traumatic stress. *Harvard Review of Psychology, 1,* 253–265.

van der Kolk, B., McFarlane, A., & Weisaeth, L. (1996). *Traumatic stress: The effects of overwhelming experience on mind, body and society.* New York: Guilford Press.

Vasquez, M. (2007). Culture differences and the therapeutic alliance: An evidence based analysis. *American Psychologist, 62,* 878–885.

Vernberg E. M., Steinberg, A. M., Jacobs, A. K., Brymer, M. J., Watson, P. J., Osofsky, J. D., & Ruzek, J. I. (2008). Innovations in disaster mental health: Psychological first aid. *Professional Psychology: Research and Practice, 39,* 381–388

Voges, M., & Romney, D. M. (2003). Risk and resiliency factors in post traumatic stress disorder. *Annals of Hospital Psychiatry, 2,* D4.

Williams, J. M. G. (2010). Mindfulness and psychological process. *Emotion, 10,* 1–7.

Yehuda, R. (2004). Risk and resilience in post traumatic stress disorder. *Journal of Clinical Psychiatry, (65 Supp),* 29–36.

Resources

There are many helpful resources for clinicians eager to supplement their knowledge of traumatic stress

National Center for PTSD
http://ncptsd.va.gov/ncmain/ncdocs/assmnts/ptsd_checklist_pcl.html

David Baldwin's Trauma Pages
http://www.trauma-pages.com/

National Child Traumatic Stress Network
http://www.nctsnet.org/nccts/nav.do?pid=hom_main

Sidran Foundation
http://www.sidran.org/

International Society for Traumatic Stress Studies
http://www.istss.org/

International Society for the Study of Trauma and Dissociation
http://www.isst-d.org/education/faq-dissociation.htm

National Institute for Health and Clinical Excellence (NICE) PTSD Guidelines
http://www.nice.org.uk/CG26

John Briere's Web Page
http://www.johnbriere.com/articles.htm

Suicide Risk Assessment
http://kspope.com/suicide/

Suicide Risk Assessment Booklet
http://spinner.cofc.edu/Betterthingstodo/Peer_Educator/suicide.pdf?referrer=webcluster&

Trauma-focused cognitive-behavioral therapy (TF-CBT)
http://tfcbt.musc.edu/

Section V

LICENSURE, CREDENTIALING, AND LEGISLATION RELATED TO MENTAL HEALTH COUNSELING

Chapter 15

THE IMPACT OF CREDENTIALING ON MENTAL HEALTH COUNSELING

HOWARD B. SMITH, WILLIAM J. WEIKEL, AND DAVID K. BROOKS, JR.*

"California Licenses Professional Counselors"–that headline was the culmination of a battle that has lasted more than 33 years. In the last edition of this book, we noted that Hawaii had become the 48th state to give legislative recognition to counselors. Then, in 2007, Nevada finally passed licensure. California came on board with strong votes in both houses in September 2009. That battle has finally ended a remarkable accomplishment when one considers that the first law was enacted in Virginia in 1976. The last 34 years have seen an incredible effort by the counseling profession, and most notably by the American Counseling Association (ACA) and the American Mental Health Counselors Association (AMHCA), to champion counselor licensing. It is hard to imagine that, in such a short period, the profession has emerged from the fog of what Brooks (1996) called a "legal limbo" to universal legislative recognition.

Licensure, however, is but one important aspect of credentialing. Credentialing is the process by which a profession:

*This revised chapter is dedicated to the memory of David K. Brooks, Jr., who died in 1996. David was the author of the chapter by this title in the 1996 edition of this book. He was a husband, father, Professor at Kent State University in Ohio, a past president of AMHCA, and past chair of the ACA Licensure Committee. Howard B. Smith has recently retired as Dean, College of Education and Counseling, South Dakota State University, and has worked as a consultant with ACA and other organizations. Howard too is a past AMHCA president. Bill Weikel is Professor Emeritus at Morehead State University (KY) and an Adjunct Professor at Florida Gulf Coast University, as well as a consultant working primarily in disability issues. He is also a past president of AMHCA.

1. Defines itself in terms of a body of scientific knowledge,
2. Identifies societal needs to which its services are directed,
3. Describes skills and competencies that address the identified needs,
4. Establishes standards for professional preparation and training,
5. Accredits training programs that meet the standards,
6. Endorses individuals demonstrating requisite professional skills as being competent to practice the profession through national certification, and
7. Maintains a professional Code of Ethics by which it monitors its own members relative to professional conduct, competency, and continuous professional development. (Modified from the American Personnel and Guidance Association Licensure Committee Brochure, 1983; McFadden & Brooks, 1983)

In plain English, credentialing is the process by which a profession demonstrates that its practitioners are capable of doing what they profess to do! The credentialing process can be best thought of as a system that involves three independent and interrelated components: standards, accreditation, and endorsement.

A CREDENTIALING SYSTEM

The credentialing system depends on and interacts with elements that are external to the system. We must assume a body of scientific knowledge to serve as a base for the counseling profession. We must assume societal needs to which those counseling services are directed and the existence of governmental and non-governmental institutions that have an interest in regulating the profession. These elements will be dealt with only tangentially in this chapter as we begin with an overview of professional standards for training and practice.

Standards of Professional Practice

The development of standards for professional practice is a task almost always undertaken by professional associations. As a general rule, the profession itself has been in existence for some time prior to the promulgation of standards. The impetus for standards development is usually the result of increasing activity among the ranks of the profession and a concomitant desire to define the limits to which professional activity extends.

Standards for professional preparation usually begin with a statement of the profession's knowledge base, followed by guidelines detailing how this knowledge base is to be imparted to those seeking the skills and competencies necessary for entry into the profession. Criteria for evaluating how well the skills are learned are frequently included as well. There may also be segments of the document that point to the development of procedures for accrediting preparation programs.

Standards for ethical practice tend to be based on broad philosophical principles related to the public good. Ethical standards are based on the assumption that the practitioner has received adequate professional preparation. It is further assumed that he or she will attempt no professional activity for which he or she cannot demonstrate professional competence as defined in those standards (i.e., academic coursework, supervised clinical experience, and certification by the appropriate body). There are usually specific guidelines related to the profession, such as guidelines for testing, the use of human and animal subjects in research, and so forth. Also included are specific forbidden acts, such as sexual relations with clients or any other type of relationship that has the potential to harm the client intentionally or unintentionally. Most ethical codes specify procedures for investigating and disciplining those members who violate the standards.

Accreditation or Program Approval

The purpose of the accreditation or program approval component of a credentialing system is to ensure that practitioners to-be receive appropriate preservice, professional preparation. Accreditation activities may be carried out by agencies of a state or federal government, by regional accrediting bodies, by professional associations, or by independent boards. These groups' purpose is to ensure minimal quality control in preparation programs.

Accreditation is always based on standards, but not always on standards that are relevant to a particular program. For example, regional accreditation of a university by groups such as the Southern Association of Colleges and Schools or the North Central Association of Colleges and Schools is based on the university's overall budget, physical plant, faculty-student ratio, library holdings, and other general areas of the university. However, there is little or no attention paid to whether any particular program, such as counseling, adheres to professional standards. Likewise, a school of education might be accredited by the National Council for the Accreditation of Teacher Education (NCATE) with total disregard for the standards offered by the Council for Accreditation of Counseling and Related Educational programs (CACREP). Thus, statements of accreditation should be viewed skeptically by asking "of what program?" and "by whose standards?"

Although accreditation standards usually apply to academic programs housed in university departments, this is not solely the case. Off-campus facilities such as satellite programs, internship sites in hospitals, community mental health centers, and clinics may also be subject to accreditation by various bodies.

Licensure and Professional Certification

The endorsement component of a credentialing system ensures that individual practitioners meet specific minimal standards for professional competency. The two major types of endorsement are licensure and professional certification. Stated slightly differently, licensure is a "practice" credential and certification can be seen as a "professional" credential, in most instances.

Licensure is statutory (i.e., by law) endorsement from a state or federal governmental agency. A licensing board, established by the act of a state legislature, is usually empowered to regulate both the use of the professional title and the scope of practice of members of a particular occupational or professional group. Based on the preparation standards set forth by professional organizations, the licensing boards adopt standards for education and supervised experience. Individuals who meet these standards are eligible to sit for a standardized written examination and in some jurisdictions an oral examination. Those who pass are issued a license to practice in that state. Most boards require evidence of continuing professional education for license renewal along with the appropriate fees.

State licensure boards are charged by law with overseeing the practice of the profession that they regulate. In implementing this mandate, they adopt codes of ethics based on those of the relevant professional organization. When charges of unethical conduct are lodged against practitioners under their jurisdiction, they investigate the charges and take appropriate action. This may involve suspension or revocation of the license as well as other penalties and punishments. Clients who feel that they have been wronged also have options under civil law, where they may seek monetary restitution for damages.

State boards are also responsible for investigating and, if necessary, prosecuting individuals who practice a regulated profession without a license. The underlying principle governing their activity is that the public must be protected against unscrupulous practitioners regardless of whether they are licensed. Unfortunately, some believe that this principle has often been ignored in practice. It is not that the individual board members are incapable or unwilling to work to protect the public, it is just that board appointees are most often members of the profession. As members of the profession, they will have internalized those goals and values of the profession and continue to hold the values associated with that profession (Shimberg, 2000). The action of professional boards in some jurisdictions has had at least the appearance of serving the profession rather than the public. The inclusion of "public" non-professional members on boards is one way to minimize this criticism and ensure that the board follows its mission.

Statutory certification and registration are less stringent forms of professional endorsement sometimes adopted by state governments. These procedures establish minimal educational and experiential requirements and usually require satisfactory performance on an examination, but they typically only restrict the use of a professional title.

Professional certification is an endorsement process administered by boards established by professional organizations. The mechanics of professional certification are similar to those of licensure, except that the procedure is voluntary rather than mandatory. Members of a profession seeking certification must demonstrate that they have met prescribed educational and supervised experience requirements, pass an examination, and pursue continuing professional education in order to keep their certificates current. Advantages of professional certification over licensure are that certification does not require the lengthy process of passing a state law, that the profession maintains more control over the credential, and that standards are frequently higher than is the case with licensure. Disadvantages include the inability of the certification board to enforce or impose legal sanctions of unethical conduct, inability to control the actions of those engaged in similar pursuits who are not certified, and the lack of legal recognition for the profession.

Having set forth a general framework of credentialing, it is appropriate to take a brief look at the historical developments in the counseling profession's ongoing efforts to achieve fully credentialed status.

HISTORICAL DEVELOPMENTS IN COUNSELOR CREDENTIALING

Almost all activities in the area of counselor credentialing have come from policies and actions taken by the American Counseling Association (formerly the American Personnel and Guidance Association [APGA]) and its various divisions, as well as from the American Mental Health Counselors Association and the state branches and affiliates of these organizations.

Standards

The counseling profession first began to address standards for preparation and practice in the late 1950s. After several years of committee work, APGA adopted its first Ethical Standards in 1961. These guidelines have been revised several times since then, often to account for changes in settings where counselors practice, especially in the private sector. The ACA Ethical Standards are the basis for several other ethical statements, including those of many state counselor licensure boards and several professional certification bodies. Without such adoptions by other groups, the ACA Standards would have no enforcement mechanism, save penalties determined by the ACA Ethics Committee, the most extreme of which is expulsion from the association.

Preparation standards also received initial attention by the profession in the late 1950s and early 1960s. The Association for Counselor Education and Supervision (ACES) led the way with the publication of training standards for secondary school counselors in 1964. Other standards followed, and in 1973 the ACES membership adopted the Standards for Preparation of Counselors and Other Personnel Services Specialists. Anticipating the need for preparation programs to provide experiences outside of educational settings, this document specified the need for counselor education programs to include "environmental and specialized studies."

Later, in 1977, ACES adopted standards for preparation at the doctoral level. At that time, however, there was no mechanism or procedure for evaluating programs to determine their degree of compliance with the standards at either the master's or doctoral levels. At about the same time, the American Mental Health Counselors Association was drafting standards that applied specifically to the preparation of mental health counselors. These early standards were eventually passed over to ACES for continued development.

Accreditation

ACES completed most of the early work in accreditation. Their accreditation committee developed a procedures manual and conducted five regional workshops in 1978 to train site visitors to conduct evaluations of counselor education programs. By the next year, five institutions were involved in a pilot program approval study. Modifications were made to the procedures, but at the same time there was pressure to make the approval of counseling programs the domain of the larger profession. Working together, APGA, ACES, ASCA, AMHCA, and others explored the development of a structure that would independently accredit counselor education programs. Accordingly, the CACREP was established by APGA in 1981 as an independent, legally incorporated accreditation body. CACREP assumed all accreditation duties of ACES and other bodies. By 2010, 235 universities had counselor education programs accredited by CACREP. Counting the various specialties, at present there are 669 master's-level programs accredited at these 235 universities and 55 doctoral programs (CACREP staff, personal communication, February 2010). In addition, numerous other programs are in the process of seeking accreditation or revamping their programs in an attempt to qualify for this prestigious honor. Several programs boast that their program is modeled after the CACREP model, and several state licensure laws require that an applicant be a graduate of a CACREP-approved program or the equivalent.

Endorsement

The counseling profession's attempt to put endorsement procedures into effect began around 1970. Prior to that time, most master's graduates were employed in public schools, where certification was a subcomponent of the same procedure of state departments of education that certified classroom teachers. Many doctoral graduates in counseling were being licensed as psychologists by state psychology licensing boards. At the beginning of the 1970s, three unrelated elements combined to focus attention and to direct action toward putting new endorsement structures for professional counselors into effect. The first of these was that many of the state psychology licensing boards, who a few years earlier had been accepting doctoral-level counselor education graduates as candidates for psychology licensure, were now refusing such persons to sit for the examination. The principal reason for this guild-oriented behavior was the expectation that national health insurance eligibility would require stricter professional standards than the boards could demonstrate were within the control of the discipline of psychology. There were also some internal pressures from psychologists relating to the pressures of supply and demand. As the private practice option became more available to clinical psychologists, there was some demand that the number of potential practitioners be controlled. Those persons most directly affected by this and the fact that there was also a shrinking demand for university-level counselor educators were new doctoral graduates from counselor education programs.

The second element affecting the interest of the profession in new endorsement structures also related to manpower supply and demand. The previous decade had been a period of tremendous growth in school counseling positions, but with budget cutbacks and declining enrollment in the 1970s, increasing numbers of school counseling graduates were finding positions in the schools increasingly difficult to obtain. These persons began finding employment in a variety of settings, such as the relatively newly opened mental health centers, as well as hospitals and clinics. Added to these recent graduates were counselors previously employed in school settings who were seeking new challenges in community settings. The effect was twofold: The identity of the mental health counselor began to emerge, and an increasingly larger pool of professionals trained as counselors and identifying with the counseling profession were becoming employed in settings for which no credentialing options were available.

The third element leading to a concern about credentialing arose within the profession. This can best be described as a new awareness of professional identity. In school settings, counselors increasingly saw themselves as different from teachers and administrators. In community settings, counselors were aware of the differences between themselves and their colleagues in psychology and social work. The effect of market demands on counselor educators caused them to realize that they were preparing individuals to assume new roles and responsibilities that were different enough from those of the previous decade that a new mental health profession was emerging. To meet the new demands, counselor educators were forced to change their focus to accommodate these needs. The composite effect of all of the transition was a sense of pride in the profession and a need to define what the profession was about in new and unique terms. The exclusion of doctoral graduates in counseling from psychology licensure, the new settings in which master's-level practitioners were working, and the growing sense of professional identity spurred APGA (1974) to establish a Special Commission on Counselor Licensure.

Licensure

The old APGA Licensure Committee was given an array of difficult tasks. They were to:

1. Develop and disseminate model legislation,
2. Establish procedures for state and regional workshops on licensure,
3. Initiate and maintain dialogue with professions related to counseling (e.g., psychology, psychiatry, social work, marriage and family therapists),
4. Testify on federal legislation having implications for individuals trained in counselor education programs,
5. Identify for members non-legislative activities having implications for the counseling profession,
6. Encourage cooperative efforts between the various divisions, affiliates, and branches of APGA, and
7. Identify possible discrimination against qualified members by boards of related professions as well as other tasks.

Thirty-six years have passed since the original tasks to this Commission, and many of the original goals have been met with stunning success, while others remain works in progress.

Virginia was the first state to achieve passage of a licensure law in 1976, following an earlier lawsuit in which the Virginia Board of Psychologists charged John I. Weldon, a counselor and APGA member, with practicing psychology without a license. This lawsuit galvanized the Virginia Counselors Association (then VPGA) into action to seek a licensure law. Arkansas and Alabama followed suite with licensure laws in 1979. By 1985, 13 more states had attained licensure, and by October 2009 the goal of licensure for all 50 states and the District of Columbia had been met.

The stated purpose of all counselor licensure laws is to protect the public by regulating the practice of professional counseling. To implement this mandate, most but not all states establish licensing boards that vary in size and composition. These boards exist to license or certify counselors, but in some states they are multi-task boards that cover more than one profession. In each state, enabling legislation or rules of the board establishes a minimum educational requirement as well as experience necessary for licensure application. These requirements vary from state to state, but all states also require passage of a written examination and in some jurisdictions an oral examination as well.

There is also some variance in title, with most states using "Licensed Professional Counselor," but others using terms such as "Licensed Clinical Mental Health Counselor." Some states provide for both generic and clinical levels of licensure. All of the laws provide for penalties to be imposed by the boards for ethical violations. They also provide for exemptions for members of related professional groups that also provide counseling services such as psychologists or members of the clergy. Most of the laws are private practice acts, exempting professionals in public and private practice agencies from the requirements of the law. All of the laws contain provisions for the renewal of the license as well as continuing education requirements, with the average number of contact hours being 20 each year.

Professional Certification

There are at present at least one generic and five specialty certification procedures that pertain to professional counselors and operate on a national or international basis, plus many smaller, highly specific types of certifying bodies. The oldest of these is administered by the Commission on Rehabilitation Counselor Certification (CRCC) and was founded in 1973 by representatives of seven professional rehabilitation associations. The CRCC administered its first nationalc examination in 1976 and has certified almost 30,000 CRCs since then. It maintains information on approximately 15,000 active certificants (Commission on Rehabilitation Counselor Certification, 2004).

The National Academy of Certified Clinical Mental Health Counselors (NACCMHC) was established by AMHCA in 1979 and administered its first national examination to 50 prospective certificants that year. The process was rigorous with no "grandfathering," and a clinical work sample was required. Because the Academy always maintained extremely high standards for this voluntary credential, the numbers never grew beyond 2,000 certificants. In the late 1990s, the Academy became a part of the National Board for Certified Counselors as a specialty certification.

The National Board of Certified Counselors (NBCC) was founded by APGA in 1982 to provide a generic counseling certificate. Like CACREP, NBCC became a separate, independent, and legally incorporated body distinct from APGA (now ACA). In 1983, more than 2,200 counselors took the first NBCC national examination. As of 2010, NBCC notes on its website that about 42,000 individuals are now National Certified Counselors (NCCs). Today, NBCC offers certifications such as the CCMHC noted above, as well as the National Certified School Counselor (NCSC) credential and the Master Addictions Counselor (MAC) certificate. The National Certification Examination (NCE) or variants of that test are used by the majority of the states, Guam, and the District of Columbia for licensure. You can log onto their website at www.NBCC.org.

As mentioned previously, there are both advantages and disadvantages to having the dual credentialing of licensure and certification. Licensure provides a legal definition for the profession in a given state and ensures licensed professionals in that state or jurisdiction the right to practice. It also entails legal sanctions, such as suspension, revocation, fines, and imprisonment, for violating the law. Greater public protection from unscrupulous practitioners is thereby assured. Professional certification boards can and usually do set higher standards for credentialing than is the case with licensing boards because they are much less subject to political repercussions. Certification is also easier to institute because it is done within the profession and does not involve the grindingly slow legislative process.

Is one type of endorsement preferable to the other? Yes . . . and no! Yes, as licensure is required to practice, and no because two credentials can work in concert to ensure quality mental health care to the public. The combination of legal sanctions and public protection afforded by state licensure, together with the higher standards of professional certification, provide a credentialing structure unequaled by any other mental health profession.

THE ROLE OF AMHCA IN CREDENTIALING

AMHCA was founded about the same time that Virginia counselors were seeking licensure in 1976, and the association was not actively involved in the licensure movement until the enactment of the Florida law in 1981.

However, several of the early AMHCA members and leaders were also active advocates of state licensure and were attracted to the then fledgling association because of the identity it provided to mental health counselors and its proactive stance for the new profession. AMHCA began providing "war chest" grants to states seeking legislative recognition in 1980 and has been active in the fight for licensure in virtually every state since 1981. AMHCA also "graduated" several of its leaders to prominent positions within ACA, which indirectly aided the licensure effort. The recognition of mental health counselors by third-party insurers provided further impetus for the AMHCA movement. It is appropriate that AMHCA was in the forefront of many of these activities, because the goals for counselor credentialing are perhaps more crucial for mental health counselors who typically operate in the public sector than for any other counseling specialty.

In addition to its political leadership at the state level, during the 1980s, AMHCA moved the credentialing agenda to the congressional agenda. The AMHCA National Legislative/Government Relations Committee caused several bills to be introduced to grant federal recognition to CCMHCs and licensed professional counselors as core service providers under the Medicare provisions of the Social Security Act and other federal programs. In 1984, AMHCA initiated efforts for recognition of mental health counselors as eligible service providers under programs administered by TRICARE, formerly the Office of Civilian Health and Medical Programs of the Uniformed Services (OCHAMPUS). That recognition was finally extended in 1987. However, the recognition given was only partial recognition and did not allow for CCMHCs to provide independent practice, but rather CCMHCs were required to have a "fully recognized" provider, such as an MSW, psychologist, or psychiatrist, sign off on the work they did. ACA and AMHCA are currently working with Congress and the Department of Defense to establish independent practice recognition under TRICARE that would put Licensed Professional Counselors on a par with other "fully recognized" providers. In point of fact, as of this writing, the Institutes of Medicine (IOM)/TRICARE study (2/12/10) has unequivocally recommended independent practice authority for professional counselors under the TRICARE programs.

The credentialing activities of the past decades that accompanied the growth and evolution of the counseling profession have changed the face of the health care delivery system in the United States. The degree of collaboration with other core mental health professions also continues to evolve. As MHCs gained recognition by Managed Care Organizations (MCOs), Preferred Provider Organizations (PPOs), and other third-party payers through the 1980s and 1990s, they often presented a threat to those other professions that were earlier to arrive on the treatment scene chronologically. These turf battles wax and wane and should eventually disappear as the counseling profession is fully assimilated into the "fold" of core professions.

THE FUTURE OF COUNSELOR CREDENTIALING

Mental health counseling (Smith & Robinson, 1995) is a profession and an ideal whose time has come. Full legislative recognition of counselors by all 50 states and the district was a major accomplishment. Counselor education programs have been changed and dramatically strengthened by CACREP's stringent mental health counseling standards and by the increasingly clinical emphasis of many state licensure laws. But battles remain. The emergence of managed care as a force in the insurance-supported mental health services has dramatically changed the landscape in terms of eligible service provider status, but MHCs are continually taking steps that will position them to compete in this market. Ongoing attempts to have counselors employed as staff members in Veterans Affairs health centers following the 2006 passage of P.L. 109-461 are within reach, and counselors should soon be on a par with licensed clinical social workers in these centers (*The Advocate,* October 2009). The credentialing activities of the last 35 years have changed the face of the counseling profession in ways that would have been unimaginable only a few years earlier. While parity with other non-medical providers remains to be universally achieved, the changes wrought by mental health counselors' licensure and other credentialing initiatives have literally created a new counseling profession, one that is poised for significant growth and influence in the years to come.

REFERENCES

American Association for Counseling and Development Licensure Committee. (1983). Suggested legislative language for counselor licensure laws. In J. McFadden & D. K. Brooks, Jr. (Eds.), *Counselor licensure action packet* (pp. 55–77). Alexandria, VA: AACD Press.

American Personnel and Guidance Association. (1974). *Licensure in the helping professions.* Minutes of the APGA Board of Directors Meeting. Washington, DC: Author.

Association for Counselor Education and Supervision. (1973). *Standards for the preparation of counselors and other personnel services specialists.* Washington, DC: American Personnel and Guidance Association.

Brooks, D. K., Jr. (1996). The impact of credentialing on mental health counseling. In W. J. Weikel and A. J. Palmo (Eds.), *Foundations of mental health counseling* (2nd ed., pp. 259–275). Springfield, IL: Charles C Thomas.

Commission on Rehabilitation Counselor Certification. (2004). Retrieved at http://www.crc certification.com/

McFadden, J., & Brooks, D. K., Jr. (Eds.). (1983). *Counselor licensure action packet.* Alexandria,

VA: AACD Press.

National Board of Certified Counselors. (2010). Retrieved at http://www.nbcc.org/

Shimberg, B. (2000). The role that licensure plays in society. In L. Smith & C. G. Schoon (Eds.), *The licensure and certification mission: Legal, social and political foundations* (pp. 145–163). New York: Forbes Custom Publishing.

Smith, H. B., & Robinson, G. P. (1995). Mental health counseling: Past, present, and future. *Journal of Counseling and Development, 74,* 158–162.

The Advocate. (October, 2009). Alexandria, VA: American Mental Health Counselors Association.

Highlight Section

THE MENTAL HEALTH COUNSELOR AS POLITICAL ACTIVIST

William J. Weikel and Howard B. Smith

Imagine yourself as a political force, your one voice and one vote, championing a cause or issue of concern for you or the clients whom you serve or even the profession as a whole. You call a like-minded friend, and now there are two. You e-mail others, and the numbers grow to hundreds or even thousands! As recently as 28 years ago, there was no organized lobbying effort at the state or national level for mental health counselors (MHCs). The profession was in its infancy, addressing the developmental needs of a new and emerging profession, with little awareness of the future need for effective lobbying. At that point, there was not the time, money, or organizational maturity that is needed to affect legislative changes at the state or national level. However, early on, visionary leaders within the American Mental Health Counselors Association (AMHCA) began working with the leaders of what is now the American Counseling Association (ACA) to provide lobbying and to establish a network of interested counselors to promote issues of interest to the emerging profession.

By about 1982, AMHCA retained the services of a well-known Washington lobbyist and had in place a fledgling government relations network. This network selected and trained MHCs at the grassroots level to serve as advocates and lobbyists both in their states and nationally. Within a few years, the new professionals became known and had won at least a few early legislative victories. Now both AMHCA and ACA have in place an effective network of members who are well trained in government relations and who can be called on to respond via e-mails, letters, phone calls and personal visits to legislators regarding counseling concerns at both the state and federal levels. Typically, both AMHCA and ACA have been strong advocates of licensure and credentialing of professional counselors but have directed the majority of their lobbying funds and efforts toward federal legislation. With the dream of licensure in every state a reality, perhaps now even more resources may be directed to full recognition and parity for MHCs. The issue of recognition is a far more complex one than we realized in those early years. In addition to a myriad of state and federal programs and providers, there are countless numbers of private corporate third-party payers with whom to negotiate. MHCs must continue to work toward recognition by these various payers as well as various other health maintenance groups and managed care providers (see the Chapter 10 for a complete discussion regarding insurance and reimbursement issues for Professional Counselors).

MHC RECOGNITION

In the early 1980s, MHCs scored a major victory in receiving at least partial recognition for counseling services by what was then known as the Office of Civilian Health and Medical Program for the Uniformed Services (OCHAMPUS). Yet during that same period, other attempts to include MHCs in legislation or to recognize MHCs as the "fifth core" service providers, along with psychiatrists, psychologists, clinical social workers, and psychiatric nurses, failed. These failures were attributed to a variety of causes, including the lack of universal licensure/certification of MHCs, objections from older more politically powerful professions, and a fear by legislators and others of "opening the flood gates" to new and, in their opinion, vaguely defined groups. Slowly, however, credentialed MHCs have made good progress toward recognition, facilitated perhaps by their universal success in obtaining licensure in the states.

With the onset of managed care programs over the past 10 to 15 years, recognition of the profession via state licensure became vital. Now, counselors are making rapid gains on a program-by-program basis for recognition that means reimbursement for counseling services. In the 1996 edition of this book, Weikel lamented about the lack of recognition by the "powers that be" and their refusal to extend third-party payments for services provided by counselors. Isn't it amazing what coordinated lobbying efforts and hard work can do? Although the battles have not ended, significant progress is being made!

THE LEGISLATIVE PROCESS

The legislative process is quite complex. Proposed bills are written by various groups to draft their ideas or causes into law at either the state or federal level. Before a bill is introduced into a legislative body, it must have a sponsor or several co-sponsors to have any chance of being passed by the full legislative body. Several common questions are often asked by any group attempting to introduce a new bill:

1. "What is the best strategy to guarantee successful passage of the proposed bill?"
2. "Should the bill be submitted to the House, Senate, or both?"
3. "Is there a legislative individual who can be a champion for the cause?"
4. "Is the legislative champion willing to introduce the bill as well as write letters to his or her colleagues to promote the bill?"
5. "Are there special interest group members willing to contact legislators once the bill has been introduced?"
6. "Are there lobbyists who can relate with key committee members to make sure the bill moves through committee intact and makes it to the floor for a vote?"

The development and passage of a bill is a long and complex process. Many proposed bills never make it out of committee, and fewer still become law. If a bill makes it through the committee and is approved by a majority of the legislative body, it is sent to the executive branch (e.g., governor or the president) for signature into law. Because a governor or the president must sign before it becomes law, lobbying of the executive branch is also a necessity. A few years ago, one state was popping the champagne corks celebrating counselor licensure without realizing that their governor had vetoed the bill! Passing new legislation at any level is not an easy process and demands significant amounts of time, energy, and money.

How to Lobby

Lobbying is simply an attempt to influence the outcome of proposed legislation through contacting and influencing the people responsible for the legislative process. To be a successful **non-paid** lobbyist, several important points must be taken into account:

1. **Establish a Relationship**–Before any successful lobbying can take place, an MHC must establish and nurture a relationship with his or her legislators. Usually the relationship, especially in the U.S. Congress, is

with the legislator's aides and not directly with the elected official. Establishing a relationship means making frequent contacts through letters and phone calls and keeping the legislator's office informed of your interest and willingness to maintain involvement with their office.

2. **Campaign Contribution**–Although many mental health professionals will be "put off" with the idea of donating money to get an "audience," this is frequently the fastest way to become known and get the legislators' attention. Donating to a candidate's election or re-election fund demonstrates that you are a supporter and may get you in the door before a line of others.
3. **Face to Face Contact**–Taking the time to visit legislators while they are in their home district is a key to successful input. Often while they are at their "home" offices, they are more willing to take the time to listen and exchange ideas about legislation. At home, legislators are less involved with the day-to-day politics of Washington or their state capitol. Taking the time to know your legislators before approaching with a lobbying agenda can be quite helpful and may facilitate legislative success at a later time.
4. **Long Term Relationships**–Stay in touch with legislators even during times when you have no agenda items. In this way, the member will come to know you as a concerned voter and may even seek your opinion on other matters affecting your district. Most elected officials like to hear from their constituents; therefore, staying in contact over the long term can mean a great deal to both the legislator and the MHC.
5. **Numbers Talk**–Most politicians begin to run for re-election the day after they take office, and keeping in contact with their constituents is of paramount importance to the successful ones. If they hear from 100 or 200 MHCs in their district regarding proposed legislation, they see this as an opportunity to ensure 100 to 200 votes in the next election. Numbers talk, and direct contact from the voters "back home" always gets the members attention.
6. **PACs and Lobbyists**–For a while, it seemed like Political Action Committees (PACs) ruled American politics. Then there was voter backlash, and their influence has waned, and many have gone underground. Such well-funded groups along with paid lobbyists can, however, influence the passage of legislation, but keeping a large political machine, especially a national one, "well oiled'" takes a significant financial commitment. Generally, MHCs are not "well funded" and cannot compete with many of the mega-dollar lobbying groups, but we must remember that grassroots support is vital for any successful legislation, and it is the voters back home who keep the politician in office and not any PAC or lobbying group!

7. **Grassroots Efforts**–Grassroots efforts typically involve the development of e-mail or phone trees to many members of a particular state or national association. The advent of e-mail and list servers has facilitated this once time-consuming process. At the appropriate stage of a bills movement through the process, a state or national association activates the tree and asks members to take specific action. As part of the grassroots effort, members have been taught how to write appropriate letters or make effective contact. The involvement of large numbers of members can have substantial influence on legislators when properly executed.
8. **Communicating an Issue**–When speaking to a legislator, a non-paid lobbyist has to learn to be brief and to the point. A quick phone call, brief telegram, or handwritten notes, legibly presented on your letterhead, are ways to let your lawmaker know your views. The authors do not advocate using e-mails when contacting lawmakers and prefer a brief note. Most important, when presenting your point of view, you must stress how the bill will positively affect consumers (other constituents). Keeping the MHC's clients in mind when lobbying is most helpful. As mentioned above, maintaining constant contact with the legislative aides is very important in this process. Be informed and be prepared to answer tough questions regarding the purposes and implications of the proposed legislation.
9. **Timing**–Timing is crucial to any successful legislation. When a bill is up for vote in a committee, activate the MHC support tree. When a bill passes from a committee, activate the troops; and when a bill comes up for a floor vote, pull out all the stops! Do not cease your lobbying efforts until the bill has been signed by the executive.

Recap

You most likely already are or soon will be a member of professional groups such as ACA and/or AMHCA and their state branches. They need and want you. They need your membership to add to their numbers, which helps to influence legislation; they need your membership dues to fund their efforts; and they need you to volunteer your time and energy to work on various legislative projects. Attaining full parity for MHCs is a long-term and ambitious goal. Providing equal access to all for mental health services is another. Attaining these and similar goals will require a coordinated and well-funded lobbying effort. If MHCs are to survive and prosper, they must continue to work closely with state and federal legislators, private insurers, and managed care personnel. In addition, counselors must coordinate their lobbying efforts with other mental health professionals.

The legislative battles have all been hard fought, but with each success we have moved another step closer to reaching our goals. The health care system in our country continues to be under scrutiny, and we can expect it to continue to evolve as the political climate constantly evolves. As our fellow Americans have seen repeatedly in the recent years of crises and turmoil, MHCs can effectively provide professional services and do so in a professional and cost-effective manner. It is our job to champion our cause and see that the profession prospers. As Harley M. Dirks (1996), AMHCA's first paid professional lobbyist, wrote in the first edition of this text:

> The future for MHCs growth and recognition as bona fide core providers of mental health services, and overall recognition as a significant professional group lies within the membership of the profession. Many of the doors are closed now, but the keys are there to be found. None of these doors open quickly. Persistent, steady effort is necessary to provide the means to propel the professional mental health counselor into the future. Dedicated, thoughtful leadership must continue. Counselors must take responsibility and be accountable for their professional endeavors, recognize a real challenge is ahead, and commit themselves to meeting the challenge. Recognition and professional identity was once, and still is, a goal of the other core providers. Time and monumental effort was responsible for their success, and will continue to be for the MHCs success. (p. 269)

REFERENCES

Dirks, H. M. (1986). Legislative recognition of the mental health counselor: The profession shapes its destiny. In A. J. Palmo & W .J. Weikel (Eds.), *Foundations of mental health counseling* (pp. 263–269). Springfield, IL: Charles C Thomas.

Weikel, W. J. (1996). The mental health counselor as political activist. In W. J. Weikel & A. J. Palmo (Eds.), *Foundations of mental health counseling* (2nd ed., pp. 276–282). Springfield, IL: Charles C Thomas.

Section VI

ASSESSMENT, RESEARCH, ETHICS, CURRICULUM, AND TRENDS IN MENTAL HEALTH COUNSELING

Chapter 16

THE ROLE OF ASSESSMENT IN MENTAL HEALTH COUNSELING

DEAN W. OWEN, JR.

An idea that lies at the heart of mental health counseling, in both theory and practice, is the process of individual assessment. A fundamental belief held by mental health counselors is that each client, regardless of presenting problem or circumstance, brings to counseling a unique pattern of traits, characteristics, and qualities that have evolved as a combination of genetic endowment and life experience. It can be argued that, through counseling, a client becomes more aware of and in tune with these many facets. This self-knowledge forms the basis for effective decision making and enhanced personal and social functioning.

It often falls on the mental health counselor to assist the client in the acquisition of this self-knowledge. Through the use of assessment practices, both client and counselor can gain an awareness of the unique constellation of traits, qualities, abilities, and characteristics that defines each individual as unique in the entire world. The initial phase of virtually any branch of counseling then is probably best described as one of information gathering or appraisal and provides the mental health counselor "stuff" with which to begin work. Despite the fact that counselors quite routinely gather large amounts of subjective information about their clients, many seem to view systematic and objective appraisal and testing not as an integral part of the counseling process but as an infrequently used adjunct to their work (Loesch & Vacc, 1991). Because information with, for, and about a client is gathered anyway as an integral part of the counseling process, the formal and objective collection of relevant data through the use of psychometric instruments and techniques should be a central and fundamental component of the work of a mental health counselor. Shertzer and Linden (1979) argued that a primary reason for assessment within the context of counseling is to assist in understanding an individual and, perhaps more important, to foster an individual's self-understanding. Gerald Corey (2008) in discussing the issue of assessment wrote that assessment is often seen as a prerequisite to treatment in the counseling process and that the significant issue with assessment was the importance of involving clients in the assessment process.

Before going any further, it would be helpful to define a number of basic terms that are central to any discussion of psychometrics. The first of these is the term *measurement.* Because our society tends to value science, this term has a rather precise meaning. That meaning is grounded in the concept of quantification or the process of assigning a numeric value to a trait, quality, or characteristic. To describe an individual as being "very tall" obviously implies that some sort of value judgment has been made. That value judgment can vary among individuals. In a conversation among a group of professional basketball players of the NBA, the idea of one being "very tall" might be quite different from what a group of accountants might mean if they were discussing the same topic. To describe an individual as being 79.5 inches tall would, of course, remove such subjectivity and would convey a more consistent meaning from one person to another.

The second term that must be discussed is *test.* Among the three domains of human behavior (cognitive, affective, and psychomotor), the only one of the three that can be directly observed is psychomotor. Some of the traits and qualities possessed by an individual are more or less directly observable. One's height or weight can be measured quite directly using a tape measure or scale. Even one's ability to run can be assessed by using a stopwatch as physical education teachers or coaches frequently do. But the problem becomes somewhat more difficult if the task is to measure something other than a physical characteristic or a psychomotor behavior, both of which are directly observable. Because behavior in the cognitive or affective domain is not directly observable, something else must be done to elicit some sort of psychomotor activity that can be observed. That something else is called a test. Generally, a test will represent a task or series of tasks designed to elicit a psychomotor behavior, which permits one to infer the existence of an internal cognitive or affective state. Consider for a moment that every history teacher will, at some point or another, seek to determine how much a student has learned as the result of sitting in a history class. It is obvious that there is no tape measure, no scale, and no stopwatch that can directly measure history achievement. To estimate a student's progress or achievement in the subject area, the teacher will typically create a test of some sort that will require the student to "do something." That "something" may involve reading a series of questions and selecting the correct response from among several options by marking an answer sheet. The complex series of psychomotor responses that involve picking up a pencil and carefully marking an answer sheet now provides a basis to infer something about the student's mastery of or knowledge in history. Because one cannot "see" achievement in history, the goal of a test is to elicit a response that may infer some internal cognitive or affective state. The psychomotor response that is elicited can, of course, vary from primitive responses such as circling a "T" or an "F" on an alternative response type test, or it may involve something far more complex and lengthy, as in the case of writing an extended response essay, a term paper, or even a doctoral dissertation.

Finally, the term *evaluation* may be best defined as a process of collecting as much information as is practical for the purpose of enhancing the quality and confidence of a decision. Generally, the more important the decision, the more carefully information is gathered and considered. Evaluation will usually involve some sort of interpretation and value judgment. Because mental health counselors will continually be making decisions with, for, and about their clients, it should be obvious that a careful and systematic attempt at gathering objective and valid information is essential if these decisions are to be of high quality and made with confidence.

Is evaluation necessary for decision making? The answer is not necessarily. Nearly everyone has purchased an article of clothing without trying it on and while driving home from the store has secretly wondered whether it will fit. After arriving home and trying on the article of clothing, one may find that it does, indeed, fit. Just as easily one may get home and find that the piece of clothing does not fit, and the task of having to return to the store and undo a bad decision is, at the least, inconvenient and time consuming. The entire process would have been quite different if a visit to the fitting room had occurred while in the store. By collecting a bit of information–in this case, a comparison of the internal dimensions of the garment with the external dimensions of your body–one would have the information to permit a purchase with confidence, knowing that, on arriving home, the piece of clothing would indeed fit. Can decisions be made without testing or collecting information? The answer is "of course," it is done by all of us each day, but taking the time to gather the best available information is sure to enhance both the quality and confidence of a decision.

ASSESSMENT TECHNIQUES

There are a great many techniques and procedures that can be utilized by mental health counselors, depending on their license status, to assist in the gathering of needed information with, for, and about a client. These procedures can generally be divided into two major categories.

Non-Standardized Procedures

This category of assessment techniques may be regarded as somewhat less rigorous but is absolutely essential to the work of a counselor. These procedures are idiosyncratic and may be specifically tailored to a given client or situation. Chief among the non-standardized assessment procedures is the direct observation of a client. Gibson and Mitchell (2007) identified three levels of observation:

First Level: Casual Informational Observation: The daily unstructured and usually unplanned observations that provide casual impressions. Nearly everyone engages in this type of activity. No training or instrumentation is expected or required.

Second Level: Guided Observation: Planned, directed observations for a purpose. Observation at this level is usually facilitated by simple instruments such as checklists or rating scales. This is the highest level used in most counseling programs.

Third Level: Clinical Level: Observations, often prolonged, and frequently under controlled conditions. Sophisticated techniques and instruments are utilized with training usually at a doctoral level.

Observational instruments have been utilized for many years to structure and organize the process of collecting observational information during counseling and therapy. Peterson and Nisenholtz (1987) describe a number of these instruments, including:

Checklists: A simple checklist may include whether a particular characteristic was observed. For example characteristics may include:

__1. Is Punctual; __2. Is able to carry on a sustained conversation.

Rating Scales: A rating scale is, in reality, a special form of checklist on which a rater can indicate not only the presence or absence of a characteristic but an estimation of strength, frequency, or the degree to which it is present. Frequently, a Likert-type scale is used, as is the case in the following example:

Client initiates conversation spontaneously:

__1. never __2. rarely __3. sometimes __ 4. usually __ 5. always.

Anecdotal Reports: These reports are often nothing more than subjective descriptions of a client's behavior at a specific time or place. Often case notes, completed at the conclusion of a counseling session, may include anecdotal reports that can be evaluated periodically to determine the existence of themes or patterns of behavior.

Structured Interview: The structured interview is quite literally a questionnaire that is read to a client by a counselor who carefully records the client's responses. They can be developed by the counselor or, as in many cases, may be a standard interview utilized by an agency as part of the case management system.

Questionnaires: This type of instrument is often used to collect information directly from the client, and the responses collected often form the basis for initial discussions with the client to investigate areas of concern.

Personal Essays/Journals: These instruments can be a rich source of information, which can be requested directly from the client and which can often be quite helpful in clarifying patterns of thought and behavior.

Standardized Assessment Techniques

The techniques described earlier all have a common characteristic in that they can be modified or changed to suit the client or situation. The use or administration of any of these techniques could vary from one counselor to another. The category of standardized assessment techniques differs from those above, in that they are usually developed and published by commercial test publishers, have years of development and research supporting them, and are administered and scored in strict accordance with published procedures. In this way, such a test is given and evaluated in the same fashion for each client. Nearly any test that can be administered can be categorized into one of following five general domains, all of which represent an area of interest for mental health counselors and their clients.

Achievement: These tests purport to measure what has been learned in the recent past and usually represent the change in ability as the result of formal training or life experience.

Aptitude: This is a test that purports to predict the degree to which an individual can learn and master some skill or body of information in the future. As Sax (1996) and Hills (1981) have suggested, the distinction between achievement and aptitude tests lies more in the purpose for testing than in what is tested. Both types of tests measure what has already been learned, but in the case of the aptitude test, the purpose is to predict future performance rather than to measure the effects of past learning or life experience.

Intelligence: These tests purport to measure a highly specialized and differentiated form of aptitude, and they seek to predict the extent to which an individual can succeed in school. In this sense, they are often regarded as scholastic or academic aptitude tests if for no other reason than the fact that they have been validated against measures of academic performance (Anastasi, 1996; Gregory, 2004). These tests are frequently used during initial evaluations conducted for occupational and educational counseling and in personnel selection.

Vocational Preference: This type of test is, in reality, not a test in the usual sense of the word because there is usually no "right" or "wrong" answer. These instruments usually rely on a self-report format, in which an individual is asked to indicate from among groups of activities and/or topics his or her preferences. These preferences are then later grouped and categorized into related areas, and the results generate a pattern that is assumed to be characteristic of the individual.

Personality: This group of tests purports to measure a large group of traits, preferences, and values that combine or interact to make each person a unique individual. Although each of us has a personality, each of us is unique because our particular constellation of behaviors, attitudes, beliefs, and values has been molded by a lifetime of experience. This group of tests can be further subdivided into two large categories. The first of these is a group of tests that purport to assess the degree of mental health or the existence of psychopathology. Tests of psychopathology are typically used for diagnostic purposes and typically have as their central theme a theoretical base of what constitutes a healthy or unhealthy, adaptive or maladaptive pattern of behavior. The second category represents tests that seek only to categorize the traits and patterns of normal behavior that may predispose an individual to success or happiness in particular occupations, work settings, or leisure activities. These tests are frequently used to assist clients in making decisions regarding education and work, but they may also be used in providing insight into other patterns of human interaction, such as in marriage and family counseling, for example.

ASSESSMENT FUNCTIONS IN MENTAL HEALTH COUNSELING

As mental health counselors seek to work effectively with their clients, there are those occasions where the necessary information cannot be obtained through conversation or observation, and the use of tests or some structured psychometric technique is considered desirable. These situations are usually tied to the need for the client and/or counselor to make a decision. Generally, these decisions are based on some information that can often be most objectively and efficiently collected through the use of a test or an instrument. These decisions and, therefore, reasons for testing can be categorized as follows.

Selection: Tests are frequently administered to detect differences among individuals, which may make them more or less suitable for some future activity. Tests such as the Graduate Record Exam (GRE) or the Law School Admissions Tests (LSAT) are quite well known for their use in selection. There are many other situations, however, when a mental health counselor may suggest the use of a personality or vocational preference test to assist a client with a personal selection decision regarding educational or career choices.

Placement: Tests are frequently utilized to assist in determining the best possible placement for training, treatment, or effective functioning. It should be emphasized that placement is not necessarily something that is done to a client. For many clients, placement is a personal decision often related to selecting a college major or making a career choice, for example. For such clients, the information provided through the use of psychometric techniques can be invaluable in assisting with such decisions.

Diagnosis: Tests and psychometric techniques are often employed by mental health counselors to assist in identifying specific strengths and weaknesses in a variety of areas of human performance. Although often considered in a medical sense or for the purpose of generating a *Diagnostic and Statistical Manual of Mental Disorders* (*DSM-IV-TR*) (4th ed., text revision) diagnostic label reflecting maladaptive or psychopathological behavior, this area of testing may include much more. The identification, through testing, of specific strengths or weaknesses in areas such as social function, shyness, mathematics, or reading may provide to both clients and counselors the necessary information to plan programs of remediation deemed necessary to achieve the desired counseling goal. Although third-party payers such as insurance carriers typically require a *DSM-IV-TR* diagnosis before reimbursement for services can be made, in a larger sense, mental health counselors may rely on diagnostic instruments to more effectively plan specific treatment and intervention programs.

Individual Progress: Perhaps one of the most frequent uses of tests in counseling is to assess the client's individual progress toward a stated goal. Working with a group of adolescent clients with the goal of enhancing self-esteem and self-acceptance may be facilitated by periodically assessing changes in the client's behavior. The use of psychometric instruments provides both client and counselor with objective and recordable evidence of change and progress that can be used to document rate of change and achievement or outcomes. Clearly, a counselor who sought to lead a weight control program with a group of clients would logically rely on periodic measures of body weight using a scale. Why then should it be so different to use a well-accepted, valid, and reliable measure of social skills development to assess the degree of change for a group of clients seeking to enhance their social skills?

Although there are numerous other reasons for using tests such as motivation, program evaluation, and research, the areas listed earlier provide the basic foundation for test usage among mental health counselors.

CLASSIFICATION OF ASSESSMENT INSTRUMENTS

Psychometric instruments can be classified according to a variety of categories on the basis of qualities or attributes, and an awareness of these categories is essential in the proper selection and use of assessment tools. The following classifications represent only a few of the many possible.

Group vs. Individual: Although the distinction between these categories would appear to be obvious, a bit more is usually implied through the use of these terms. Instruments designed for group administration may be used with one or more than one client at a time and usually permit administration by individuals who do not have extensive training or experience in testing. Additionally, group-administered instruments usually take the form of a paper-and-pencil test in which a client is presented a test booklet, an answer sheet, and a pencil with which to mark responses. These materials are relatively inexpensive and add to the economical nature of the group test.

However, individual tests must only be administered to one individual at a time and usually require that the administrator be highly skilled, experienced, and often specially certified for a valid and ethical administration. Because only one individual can be assessed at a time and the administrator must have much more than a general familiarity with the test administration, scoring, and interpretation, such instruments are correspondingly more expensive and time consuming to use.

Paper and Pencil vs. Performance Tests: These classifications generally refer to the means for collecting the behavior sample to be evaluated. Paper-and-pencil tests generally take the form of a prepared test booklet with a separate answer sheet on which the client marks responses. These tests have formed the backbone of group assessment because they possess a number of highly desirable characteristics. The materials–a test booklet and answer sheet–are generally quite inexpensive and permit the collection of information from potentially large numbers of individuals at the same time. Additionally, this form of testing lends itself to quick and objective scoring. Such tests generally are developed by test publishers and come with excellent supporting documentation. Administration, in most cases, requires little more than distributing materials, reading aloud a set of directions, keeping accurate track of elapsed time provided for the test, and finally the collection of the materials.

Among the limitations of this class of tests is the requirement for reading. A valid administration of a paper-and-pencil test demands that the client possess the ability to read at a certain level. Although many tests have been intentionally designed to require relatively low levels of reading ability, the practicing mental health counselor is likely to encounter far more illiterate and functionally illiterate clients than one might suppose. For this reason, such well-known paper-and-pencil tests as the Minnesota Multiphasic Personality Test (MMPI) have been adapted for use with poor or non-readers and for those with visual disabilities through the use of electronic presentations (Anastasi, 1996).

Performance tests generally elicit a behavior sample that is quite different and, in some ways, more authentic. In response to verbal instructions, the client performs a task. A common example is represented by the Goodenough-Harris Drawing Test (Harris, 1963). This instrument is frequently used to assess intellectual functioning and is administered by simply asking the client to "make a picture of a man; make the very best picture that you can." Although removing the need for reading, such tests elicit more complex behaviors, such as drawing a person, which must be evaluated by an administrator, and the results cannot be run though an optical scanning machine for grading. Such tests generally demand higher levels of training and experience and present more complicated grading and evaluation issues than does the paper-and-pencil format.

Norm vs. Criterion-Related Tests: The principle means for distinguishing between these two groups of test forms rests with the way in which a single score is evaluated. Typically, after an administration, a test is scored and a raw score is generated. This raw score generally represents the number of correct responses, or, in the case of a self-report survey, a pattern of responses is recorded. This raw score, in and of itself, has little meaning until it is compared with something. If the score is compared with the scores obtained from a large and hopefully representative sample of others in a norm group, the relative position of the raw score can be determined. It can be said, for example, that a score might represent the 89th percentile, which would be interpreted as being equal to or better than 89% of the scores from the norm group. The question such tests answer is one of relative position. Does the raw score place the individual near the top, in the middle, or near the bottom compared with others who have taken the same test?

A more recent development, which is becoming more widely utilized in a variety of tests, is the application of criterion-related scoring. In this process, the obtained score is not compared with a norm group but with a criterion score or measure. The difference is that a norm-referenced score provides an indication of relative performance within the norm group, whereas criterion-related scoring provides a measure of absolute performance. Such scoring has become increasingly popular, particularly with the publishers and users of diagnostic tests where the achievement of a particular score map be indicative or diagnostic of a particular attribute. Such scoring methods are increasingly being utilized on diagnostic tests of reading or mathematics, where scoring below a particular criterion may be indicative of a failure to achieve mastery or to demonstrate minimum competency.

Structured vs. Unstructured: When examining structured versus unstructured, the distinction is not too dichotomous. These terms are best thought of as the ends of a continuum with some tests being considered highly structured and other relatively unstructured. The basis on which the classification may be made revolves around the degree of response freedom offered to the client. A vocational preference test, like the Strong Interest Inventory, may present clients with a series of activities to which they are permitted only three options: like, indifferent, or dislike. The client is given a limited array of options from which to choose a response. Such a test is regarded as highly structured. Among the principle advantages of such a test are the fact that quick and objective scoring is possible.

At the other end of the spectrum are tests such as the Rorschach inkblot test developed by the Swiss psychiatrist Hermann Rorschach, which was first described in 1921. Quite literally, the test is composed of a standardized series of 10 cards on which are printed bilaterally symmetrical inkblots. The client is asked to tell the examiner what each of the blots could represent. Unlike a highly structured test with limited response freedom, the Rorschach elicits responses that are not limited in any fashion. Because of the virtually unlimited response freedom given to the client, scoring of such a test is neither quick nor easy and demands a high level of clinical skill and competence.

GUIDELINES AND STANDARDS FOR ASSESSMENT PRACTICES

Before delving more deeply into the topic of assessment, a few additional comments are necessary. Because assessment and the practice of testing have evolved into essential components of the counseling process, it is not surprising that this aspect of the profession has been the topic of a great deal of research and ethical and practical consideration by the professional associations that represent the profession. The American Counseling Association (ACA), the American Mental Health Counseling Association (AMHCA), and the National Career Development Association (NCDA) recognize assessment and the practice of testing as significant components of professional practice and have established standards of practice and addressed testing in their respective codes of ethics and standards (American Counseling Association, 2003, 2005; American Mental Health Counseling Association, 2010; National Career Development Association, 2007). The ACA Code of Ethics (American Counseling Association, 2005, pp. 11–13) addresses this component of professional practice in Section E with specific sections addressing 13 separate areas, including:

1. General assessment definitions and purposes;
2. Professional competence;
3. Informed consent and issues of privacy;
4. Release of assessment data to other professionals;
5. Use of assessment in the diagnosis of mental disorders;
6. Selection of assessment instruments;
7. Standards for ethical instrument administration;
8. Diversity and multicultural issues in assessment;
9. Scoring and interpretation of assessment data;
10. Security procedures for assessment materials;
11. Use of obsolete information and test results
12. Guidelines for assessment instrument construction; and
13. Forensic evaluation.

Another indication of the central importance of assessment in the counseling process is the existence of a major division of the ACA devoted to assessment: the Association for Assessment in Counseling and Education (AACE). The stated mission of the AACE is "to promote and recognize scholarship, professionalism, leadership, and excellence in the development and use of assessment and diagnostic techniques in counseling" (2008, p. 1). The ACCE, in collaboration with the ACA, produced a document titled *Responsibilities for Users of Standardized Tests, RUST* (2003). This document remains an essential defining standard for the use of standardized, counseling-related assessments instruments. This document addresses seven essential areas of responsibility, including the qualifications of test users, required technical knowledge areas, test selection procedures, test administration, test scoring, interpretation of test results, and communicating test results to clients.

THE SELECTION OF TESTS FOR USE IN COUNSELING

The process of choosing the best or correct test for a given client and a given situation will depend on a variety of factors. These include client-related factors, counselor-related factors, and test-related factors. Each of these must be weighed and balanced. If reasonable care is exercised in determining each of these factors, appropriate and useful testing information can be obtained.

Client-Related Factors: First of all, it should be emphasized that not only from an ethical standpoint but from a practical standpoint, the needs, wishes, and desires of the client should heavily influence the decision to utilize tests or other psychometric techniques. As a general rule, testing should be considered if the information needed can be obtained no other way. Obviously, if a client is bright, insightful, and possesses a large fund of personal information, testing may not be required. However, if the client and counselor both agree that additional information would be helpful in enhancing the counseling process, the idea of testing should be introduced as a relative quick and easy means of obtaining that information. The nature of the client's information deficit or interest should be the determining factor in offering the opportunity for testing. Within the counseling relationship, testing should be regarded as an offered service rather than an obligation or a requirement. In many instances, unless the client is eager, willing, and enthusiastic about the opportunity to learn about him or herself, testing will not yield useful information. If testing is considered, it should be offered as an opportunity to obtain information that cannot be easily obtained in other ways. The client's willingness to participate will depend on the degree to which the testing situation is perceived as a threat or manipulation. If the client objects, these objections should be explored, if possible, with the intent of reassuring the client of the utility of the process. Testing should be something that is done with someone rather than to someone. Unfortunately, previous experience in schools and elsewhere may make clients inherently suspicious of testing as an unwarranted intrusion or means of grading, classifying, or valuing. If clients are convinced that testing is being offered for their benefit, and that the information can be of help in addressing their counseling issues, most will not only agree but will take an active and interested part in the assessment process.

Counselor-Related Factors: One of the most important of the counselor-related factors is the counselor's competence in the field of testing. It should be emphasized that testing is a tool, and the effective application or use of any tool presumes a high degree of skill in the use of the tool. For the practicing mental health counselor, this means that not only does he or she possess a basic familiarity with the testing theory, the technical aspects of testing, and the specific instruments to be used, but that the counselor is comfortable and confident in the selection, administration, scoring, and interpretation of the instruments. Simply having completed a graduate course or two in testing does not necessarily provide the necessary clinical skills to utilize tests effectively with clients. Not only must the counselor be technically competent but equally important is the requirement to know and work within the limits of that competence. From a legal and an ethical standpoint, each counselor must recognize the limits of her or his competence and limit the scope of practice to those areas for which training, experience, and legal authority permit professional service. The laws regulating the scope of practice with regard to testing vary widely. The counselor is then guided by both ethical and legal factors in the selection and use of psychometric techniques appropriated for use with clients. The limiting factors are personal training, experience, and competence as well as legal authorization.

Test-Related Factors: The third basic group of factors that guide the selection of tests revolves around the technical qualities and limitations of the instruments. Among these technical factors are validity, reliability, and existence of appropriate and representative norms. Without a doubt the most important of these is validity because it is "the degree to which a test actually measures what it purports to measure" (Anastasi, 1982, p. 27). The counselor must have a clear idea of what it is that the test measures. An understanding of the validity of a test presumes that the counselor has a working understanding of the evidence for validity presented by the publisher of the test and others. It should be borne in mind that a standardized test is a commercial product, and claims of validity made by the publisher may at times be somewhat overstated. One of the values of using psychometric instruments that have been in use for some time is the fact that their validity will likely have been independently verified through their use in multiple research studies with a wide variety of subjects and situations. Any test to be considered for use in counseling should have considerable evidence establishing that it possesses acceptable levels of face, construct, criterion-related (including predictive and concurrent), or content validity depending on the purpose for which the test is designed.

The second major area that determines the utility of a test for a given purpose is the reliability of the test's results. Again, the counselor has an ethical obligation to ensure that instruments chosen for use with clients possess the ability to provide scores that are relatively precise and stable over time. The counselor's ability to interpret the meaning or a reliability coefficient and its associated standard error of measurement for the test as a whole as well as any component scores is essential in selecting from among related tests as well as meaningfully interpreting the results. Among the various forms of reliability with which the mental health counselor should be familiar are test-retest reliability, which measures stability over time, alternative forms reliability, which assesses the equivalence among various forms of the same instrument, and split-half reliability, which measures internal consistency (Anastasi & Urbina, 1997; Cronbach, 1990).

The final area to be considered is the currency and representativeness of the test norms. A counselor who fails to recognize the effect that age, sex, ethnic origin, cultural background, and socioeconomic status have in influencing test performance may grossly underestimate or overestimate the significance of a test score. A working knowledge of the characteristics of the normative sample and the currency of that sample is absolutely essential in deriving meaningful information from a test score.

LOCATING APPROPRIATE TESTS

The task of selecting and locating instruments appropriate for use in a mental health counseling setting may at first seem daunting, but the advent and development of the Internet with its many search engines and lightening speed have greatly simplified the task. Finding the instruments would seem to be the easier task when compared with the task of identifying the purpose or specific reason for testing. Drummond (1996) presents an excellent decision-making model that can be useful in clarifying for a counselor what dimension, trait, or attribute should be assessed in a particular situation. His description of the process includes carefully identifying what judgments or decisions have to be made along with carefully identifying what type or kind of information is needed to make a decision with, for, or about a client. Having first decided what information is needed, a counselor should then take stock of what information is already available. Once it is determined what information is still needed, the task of identifying those instruments is now relatively easy, with such large databases commonly available on the Internet. Perhaps the most imposing task of all is the objective evaluation of instruments in the attempt to select the one most appropriate for a given setting, client, or situation. A complete discussion of this evaluation process is beyond the scope of this chapter but essentially revolves around a balancing act of the three most important qualities of any instrument: validity, reliability, and, of course, practicality.

Test reviews regularly appear in the professional periodicals, including *Measurement and Evaluation in Counseling and Development,* the *Journal of Counseling Psychology,* the *Journal of Counseling and Development,* the *Journal of Mental Health Counseling,* and the *Career Development Quarterly.* Additionally, such compendiums of testing information as *Tests in Print* and the *Mental Measurements Yearbook,* both of which are published by the Buros Institute of Mental Measurements (BIMM), provide the most comprehensive source of testing related information available (Buros Institute of Mental Measurements. 2010).

COMMUNICATING TEST RESULTS

The selection and administration of psychometric instruments is only half of the practitioner's responsibility. Equally important is the ability to first interpret the results in a technically competent fashion and then to present these findings to the client in a way that is both meaningful and accurate. Because one of the primary purposes for the use of tests in counseling is to enhance the client's self-knowledge, little is gained by using a test whose results create confusion, self-doubt, or defensiveness. It should be emphasized that, for most clients, their past experience with testing has often been primarily associated with school or employment and was judgmental in nature. The testing done in counseling is quite different and seeks to assist in providing needed information that the client may need or want.

The two essentials for communicating test results in a meaningful and compassionate fashion are an awareness of the client and his or her needs or wants and the ability to organize the test results in a clear, understandable, and coherent fashion. The job of interpreting the results of a test should begin early in the counseling process when initial discussions with a client result in a joint determination of the need for additional information. The entire process of testing is obviously for the benefit of the client and not the counselor. When testing is offered as an option to the client, information should be given to describe what needed information the test results will provide. In this way, the client has a general understanding of the purpose and rationale for the test and therefore can have a pre-existing framework into which the final results will comfortably fit. A second essential in effectively communicating results is the need to organize the results so the client is not provided with what may seem to be a huge amount of quantitative data. There is virtually nothing to be gained by simply presenting a client with a basket full of numbers and then expecting her or him to first understand and then to incorporate that information into some meaningful construct. Instead, it is generally useful to return the test results and then review with a client the basic reasons that prompted the use of the test. This provides a basis for a discussion of the results in such a way that the client begins to understand what the scores mean in light of those original questions. With clients who possess a reasonable intelligence and insight, it is sometimes a wise technique to explain the meaning of the scores but to refrain from providing any interpretation or meaning to them. Instead, one may gently suggest that the client offer his or her own interpretation or meaning once the score is understood. Asking a client to offer his or her own interpretation or a score engenders a cooperative relationship and helps avoid a passive acceptance or defensive rejection of a test result on the part of the client.

A final word of caution is appropriate. It is sometimes difficult to give information without also giving advice. This is frequently much more easily said than done, especially with regard to testing. For many clients, the presentation of test results suggests that the counselor has all of the necessary information to deal with a particular problem. Clients may frequently ask the counselor's opinion or advice but are more likely to do so if they perceive that the counselor has all of the information and they have very little or what they have is of poor quality. By communicating the test results in a way that the client can understand, and by affirming the value of the client's perceptions, interpretations, and understandings, the test result can be effectively communicated to those most in need of them–the client.

ETHICAL ISSUES IN TESTING

There is little doubt that the practicing mental health counselor will be faced with a multitude of ethical and value dilemmas throughout his or her career, in both counseling-related situations and testing. Perhaps the best source of guidance in effectively confronting these ethical dilemmas is a clear and current knowledge of an appropriate code of ethics. A working knowledge of a code of ethics is essential in first recognizing the existence of a potential ethical problem and in providing options for the successful resolution of such problems.

Mental health counselors come into the field from an amazing variety of academic backgrounds, and there seems to be no single professional association that speaks for the entire profession. Perhaps the two most comprehensive statements of standards for ethical and professional conduct that address issues in testing are provided by the American Psychological Association's (2010) *Ethical Principles of Psychologists and Code of Conduct* and the American Counseling Association's (2005) *Code of Ethics and Standard of Practice.* Both of these professional associations address many of the same fundamental ethical issues associated with the use of psychometric instruments. In addition, issues of testing and assessment practice are addressed in the codes of ethics of many other professional associations that represent more specialized areas of practice, including the American Mental Health Counselors Association (2010), Association for Addiction Professionals (2010), National Rehabilitation Counseling Association (2010), National Career Development Association, (2007) and the American Association for Marriage and Family Therapy (2001). These organizations, in revising their codes of ethics, have begun to address issues that previously were largely unknown. Perhaps the best example of this is the inclusion of tenets that address the issue of computer applications in the construction, administration, scoring, and interpretation of psychometric instruments. Two of the issues that have arisen relate the comparability of computer and paper-and-pencil versions of the same instrument and the dramatically increased use of computerized interpretations of test results (Anastasi, 1996).

Another area that is again receiving increased attention in statements of ethical practice relates to ability testing, particularly with regard to the validity of many instruments in assessing cognitive development of minority individuals. The rapidly increasing numbers of immigrants from all parts of the world, but particularly from Latin American countries in recent years, has placed increased emphasis on the need for multilingual assessment instruments and testing practices to meet the needs of an increasingly diverse population. These and many other issues will continue to pose questions as the use of tests to assess human performance and characteristics collide with technology and the values of a rapidly changing society. There are a few basic components, however, that form the foundation of ethical conduct in testing, and each of these is briefly described next.

Professional Competence and Qualification: Professional conduct demands that the user of a test first be technically qualified to do so. This typically requires one or more graduate-level courses in testing to establish minimal competency. Many psychometric instruments, such as individually administered tests of intellectual development, more specialized diagnostic and projective tests of psychopathology, and neuropsychology assessment require much more specialized training, including supervised clinical internship. A second issue relates to the legal authorization to administer such specialized instruments. The licensure laws of each state are somewhat different, but nearly all states limit the scope of practice of licensed practitioners. Ethical conduct would require that not only should the practicing counselor be appropriately trained and licensed but should limit his or her practice to the use of the instruments for which qualifications have been established. An additional safeguard in this area is the increasing scrutiny that test publishers are using to determine who may purchase, and presumably use, their tests. Many test publishers now restrict the purchase of some or all of their testing products to those individuals who have established their qualifications through some mechanism.

Protection of Privacy: This area of concern has arisen particularly during the past two decades as the mechanism for information transmission and storage has undergone massive change with the increased use of computers. Practitioners are expected to obtain consent from every client before testing, and this often requires the provision of information relating to the possible storage and use of the information following the termination of counseling. The use of tests makes gathering of information with, for, and about a client relatively easy. Because it is so easy to gather this information, the ethical practitioner is conscious of potential abuse and offers testing only when it is appropriate and necessary. The unwarranted and unnecessary gathering of testing information should be regarded as a clear invasion of privacy, and when such information is gathered, it should be guarded and used in ways fully consistent with the good ethical practice. Protecting such information and releasing it only with the client's approval and when it is in the best interest of the client should be foremost in the mind of the counselor.

COMPUTER TECHNOLOGY AND PSYCHOLOGICAL ASSESSMENT

It is common to refer to computer technology as a relatively recent innovation, but the use of technology in the field of assessment has a long and distinguished history that can trace its origins to mechanical scoring machines developed in the 1920s (Moreland, 1992). Other landmarks in this history would include the construction of an analog computer for the automatic scoring and profiling of the Strong Vocational Interest Blank by Elmer Hanks in 1946 and the use of optical scanning equipment and digital computers to score and print profiles of psychological tests in the 1960s. In the 1970s, computers were used for the first time to conduct computerized adaptive testing, which permits individualized test batteries to be constructed with the fewest number of items (Weiss & Kingsbury, 1984). Throughout the 1970s and 1980s, there was a proliferation of software programs that could be run on personal computers, and many such programs were utilized in schools and counseling centers to conduct routine vocational preference and interest testing. By the 1990s, the meteoric rise in microcomputer capability, the Internet, and other networking systems made online computer assisted testing common indeed, and nationally recognized testing companies such as Educational Testing Service (ETS) made computerized administration of major college admissions tests like the Graduate Management Admission Test (GMAT) and the Graduate Record Examination (GRE) available for the first time.

Essentially, the use of computers in assessment may be found in three basic areas. The first and oldest of these is for scoring. The process of hand scoring any assessment instrument is slow and laborious, and there is always the possibility for error. Computers are exquisitely fast, never get tired, and, when properly programmed, rarely make errors. This makes them ideal for dull, repetitive, and high-volume work. The interpretation and generation of profiles based on scores is the second area in which computers aid in the assessment process. Computer-based interpretive systems for complex psychological instruments such as the Rorschach and MMPI began as early as the 1960s (Fowler, 1985; Piotrowski, 1964). This technology continues to grow, and virtually all assessment instruments available today have associated software systems to facilitate scoring and interpretation of assessment results. Many of these systems provide for the preparation of detailed interpretive profiles.

The final way in which computers are being increasingly used is in the actual administration of instruments. This is probably the newest and most advanced technology in the field of assessment. The availability of high-definition video and sound, as well as other multimedia displays, make realistic and fully interactive assessment completely possible using nothing more than a desktop computer. This "virtual reality" assessment is a relatively recent outgrowth of the incredibly popular computer game industry and permits the measurement of individuals by engaging them in a virtual reality setting and allowing them to interact with the stimuli presented.

From the use of machines to score tests near the beginning of the last century to the use of virtual reality scenarios and complex simulation and gaming theory to assess human performance, technology has been and will continue to be a tool to improve clinical and educational assessment. Despite the rapid growth and technical evolution of computer-assisted assessment and online testing, the fundamental ethical issues that underpin the practice of assessment in counseling remain unchanged, and this technology must always be regarded as a useful tool that must be wielded with care, skill, and compassion as counselors work with clients.

CONCLUSION

Of the many roles played out in mental health agencies, schools, and institutions by mental health counselors, the process of assisting clients to acquire a clear and objective view of their unique pattern of traits and abilities is likely to continue to be one of the most important. Unlike clinical psychologists or psychiatrists who often use psychometric instruments as tools to aid in the diagnosis of psychopathology, the mental health counselor's focus is often quite different. Counselors are far more likely to use psychometric instruments, rating scales, and other self-report inventories to perform initial assessment and continual monitoring of therapeutic progress throughout their work with clients. The use of such instruments to help identify areas of concern for clients and to monitor their progress during the counseling process requires that mental health counselors acquire the ability to select, administer, score, and interpret a wide variety of instruments to promote effective personal and social functioning. These instruments and the skills to use them with technical competence and compassion are nothing but tools with which to make the entire process of counseling easier, more objective, and vastly more efficient. The future of mental health counseling is sure to include advances in assessment technology and is likely to see increased use of interactive and computer-enhanced assessment models. Together with a humane, ethical, and compassionate attitude toward service to clients, these advances will do much to ensure that counseling services will become even more efficient and effective in assisting clients achieve their goals of enhanced personal and social functioning, as well as building strong and resilient individuals.

REFERENCES

American Association of Marriage and Family Therapy. (2001). *Code of ethics.* Alexandria, VA: Author.

American Counseling Association. (2003). *Standards for qualifications of test users.* Alexandria, VA: Author.

American Counseling Association. (2005). *Code of ethics and standards of practice.* Alexandria, VA: Author.

American Mental Health Counselors Association. (2010). *AMHCA code of ethics.* Alexandria, VA: Author.

American Psychological Association. (2010). *Ethical principles of psychologists and code of conduct.* Washington, DC: Author.

Anastasi, A. (1982). *Psychological testing* (5th ed.). New York: Macmillan.

Anastasi, A. (1996). *Psychological testing* (7th ed.). New York: Macmillan.

Anastasi, A., & Urbina, S. (1997). *Psychological testing* (7th ed.). Upper Saddle River, NJ: Prentice Hall.

Association for Addiction Professionals. (2010). *Code of ethics.* Alexandria, VA: Author.

Association for Assessment in Counseling and Education. (2003). *Responsibilities for users of standardized tests (RUST)* (3rd ed.). Alexandria, VA: Author.

Association for Assessment in Counseling and Education. (2008). *AACE statements of purpose.* Retrieved from http://www.theaaceonline.com

Buros Institute of Mental Measurements (2010). *18th mental measurements yearbook.* Retrieved from http://www.unl.edu/buros/

Corey, G. (2008). *Theory and practice of counseling and psychotherapy.* Belmont, CA: Wadsworth/Thompson Learning.

Cronbach, L. J. (1990). *Essentials of psychological testing* (5th ed.). New York: Harper & Row.

Drummond, R. J. (1996). *Appraisal procedures for counselors and helping professionals* (3rd ed.). Englewood Cliffs, NJ: Prentice-Hall.

Fowler, R. D. (1985). Landmarks in computer-assisted psychological testing. *Journal of Consulting and Clinical Psychology, 53,* 748–759.

Gibson, R., & Mitchell, M. (2007). *Introduction to guidance.* New York: Macmillan.

Gregory, R. J. (2004). *Psychological testing: History, principles, and applications* (4th ed.). Boston: Allyn & Bacon.

Harris, D. B. (1963). *Children's drawings as measures of intellectual maturity: A revision and extension of the Goodenough Draw-a-man test.* New York: Harcourt, Brace & World.

Hills, J. R. (1981). *Measurement and evaluation in the classroom.* Columbus, OH: Charles E. Merrill.

Loesch, L., & Vacc, N. (1991). Testing in counseling. In D. Capuzzi & D. Gross (Eds.), *Introduction to counseling* (pp. 158–180). Boston, MA: Allyn and Bacon.

Moreland, K. L. (1992). Computer-assisted psychological assessment. In M. Zeidner & R. Most (Eds.), *Psychological testing: An inside view* (pp. 343–376). Palo Alto, CA: Consulting Psychologists Press.

National Career Development Association. (2007). *Code of ethics.* Broken Arrow, OK: Author.

National Rehabilitation Counseling Association. (2010). *Code of ethics.* Manassas, VA: Author.

Peterson, J., & Nisenholtz, B. (1987). *Orientation to counseling.* Boston, MA: Allyn & Bacon.

Piotrowski, Z. A. (1964). A digital computer administration of the inkblot test data. *Psychiatric Quarterly, 38,* 1–26.

Sax, G. (1996). *Principles of educational and psychological measurement and evaluation* (4th ed.). Belmont, CA: Wadsworth.

Shertzer, B., & Linden, J. (1979). *Fundamentals of individual appraisal.* Boston, MA: Houghton Mifflin.

Weiss, D. J., & Kinsbury, G. G. (1984). Application of computerized adaptive testing to educational problems. *Journal of Educational Measurement, 21*(4), 361–375.

Chapter 17

RESEARCH IN COUNSELING

JoLynn V. Carney

People decide to become counselors for many reasons, but the majority of them revolve around the satisfaction of interaction with another individual and hopefully helping that person improve his or her quality of life (Hazler & Kottler, 2005). Relationships with others are the focus of most counselors' interests. It is also the relationship that draws clients to counseling. They have tried working out things by themselves or reading self-help guides to make themselves more knowledgeable but got nowhere with their problems. Research design, data collection, research variables, validity, and reliability are rarely topics that catch the interest of counselors in training and client interests will not cause any additional personal pressure to focus on these issues.

What is missed in this equation, which focuses on relationships, is that research is a primary ingredient in effective counseling. It is the principle portion of counselor development and their relationships with clients that promotes improvement and change rather than stagnation, rigidity, prejudice, and bias. The following case serves as a way to see the various factors involved.

> Emil was seriously injured six months ago on his job as a mill worker. The accident damaged the 35-year-old man's spinal cord, and he has lost the use of his legs and all feeling from the waist down. He has been married for 15 years with two children, ages 8 and 6 years. After three counseling sessions, Emil remains depressed with suicidal ideation, is not physically taking care of himself, and sees no real hope for a life that will satisfy him.
>
> The counselor is worried about Emil and exasperated over her inability to help him move in more positive directions. The anxieties wake her in the middle of

the night in the form of fears and a set of questions for which she doesn't have good answers.

- Am I making progress that I don't see, making no progress, or regressing with Emil?
- What should I be defining as progress for Emil? Not committing suicide? Getting back to work? Relieving his depression? Improving his family relationships? Gaining a better outlook on life?
- Is our lack of progress more about me, Emil, or a combination of the two of us?
- Is what I do or who I am wrong for Emil's recovery? Is there someone or some kind of counselor who might be better for him?
- It is so hard for me to imagine what it is exactly that a person with this kind of life disaster needs to regain hope and enthusiasm about life?

If deciding how to help clients move forward in counseling is the essence of a good counselor's work, then the anxieties surrounding why clients do not move forward in the ways we expect are the bane of the counselor's existence. The ethical and successful professional counselor uses a triangular approach to deal with this dilemma.

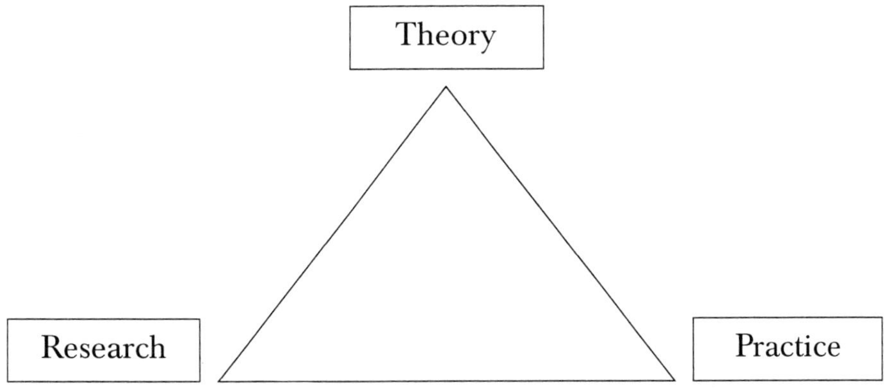

Theory is probably the starting place for counselor actions toward clients because it is the way they decide to approach the intervention. It is *research* based on some combination of scholarly study and life experience that has brought them to that theory of how they can best help others. How they apply that theory is their form of *therapy*. When counselors decide that their chosen interventions are or are not having the desired effect, they are actually doing *research* because they have evaluated the data gained from their listening to and observing clients to make decisions about how to interpret the results. Based on their *research* decision, they will likely make other decisions on what changes in their practice are necessary.

The ethical professional counselor is one who makes these decisions based on a solid understanding of the best information available, applying it in appropriate ways, and using recognized methods to evaluate the effectiveness of his or her efforts so that he or she can change in professionally expected ways. This is a professional who seeks research supported information, understands it, and then applies it appropriately. The unethical and ineffective counselor is one who does not seek or understand current available research or does not utilize recognized research designs in evaluating efforts and client outcomes. For this person, change for the betterment of clients is either non-existent or made with personal biases that can do more harm than good.

THE RELEVANCE OF RESEARCH

There has been increased emphasis on the importance for counselors to be trained in research as well as theories and methods because it is through research that counselors can evaluate the effectiveness of their clinical interventions with diverse populations (Benishek & Gordon, 1998; D'Andrea & Foster Heckman, 2008; Galluzzo, Hilldrup, Hays, & Erford, 2008; Heppner, Kivlighan, & Wampold, 2008). One way to view counseling research is that it ensures quality client care by allowing counselors to objectively examine and evaluate their practices (Bradley, Sexton, & Smith, 2005), which is at the core of the ethical issue of competency. Counselors provide clients with assurances that they are competent in their use of treatments, which offers reasonable promise of outcome success as stipulated by the code of ethics (American Counseling Association, 2005). Demands for accountability have only increased the need for counselors to document the effectiveness of their work. Counselors can work more effectively on a day-to-day basis by being competent to conduct and consume research. Being competent to conduct and consume counseling research starts with demystifying the process, terminology, and interpretation of research by understanding that it has similar steps to counseling.

It might seem on the surface that researchers and counselors speak in different languages. Researchers use such terms as *hypothesis, data, tests of significance,* whereas counselors talk about *hunches, client provided information,* and *case conceptualizations.* Yet these terms for all practical purposes hold similar meanings. Both researchers and counselors are guided by the same fundamental ethical principles: (a) nonmaleficence–do no harm, (b) beneficience–doing good for others, (c) autonomy–liberty to choose one's own course of action, (d) justice–fairness, and (e) fidelity–faithfulness, loyalty, and keeping agreements (Heppner et al., 2008; Kitchener, 1984). Counselors and researchers also take *very* similar *steps* in seeking to increase understanding of the issues and problems faced by their clients.

When clients present for treatment, counselors begin by helping clients tell their stories. They listen to the stories to *identify* the *problems* or difficulties (Step 1). From there, a collaborative *formulation* of client *goals* is constructed (Step 2) which assists in determining appropriate *interventions* (Step 3). *Implementation* of counseling interventions begins the next step (Step 4), with counselors following up by assisting clients in *evaluating* their progress (Step 5). Finally, based on an increase in client functioning, counseling sessions come to an end and *termination* occurs, where clients and counselors share a *summary interpretation* of their therapeutic work and draw *conclusions* to assist clients in the future (Step 6).

Researchers take similar steps in their process by *identifying problems* or questions to investigate (Step 1) and then *formulating* a research design that captures the goals of the investigation (Step 2). Researchers determine the method for *treatment/interventions* and identify instruments to measure outcome effectiveness (Step 3). They then *implement* the *interventions, collect data* (Step 4) and conduct data analysis to *evaluate* outcomes (Step 5). Finally, the investigators *interpret* the data and draw some *conclusions* designed to assist in implementation of knowledge gained through the research (Step 6). (Whiston, 1996).

A case can clearly be made that counselors, knowingly or not, do conduct research steps with every client they see. Any counselor who questions and observes in order to make treatment decisions based on the answers they receive is a researcher. Part of the challenge is to realize that, although there are differences in terms used, that does not make the processes totally separate. Counselors who recognize the similarity and reconcile the differences in their thinking are the ones who can provide the most effective counseling possible for their clients. The purpose of this chapter is to assist counselors in understanding different research paradigms, identify specific research designs, and provide examples of process research that have effectively enhanced clinical work.

The challenge for Emil's counselor will be to realize that the answers to her questions can only be found in the examination of previous research on these issues and her ability to ethically apply a research model to her counseling. Previous research can inform her of some pieces of information, but it will then be her task to understand the implications of that research, judge its appropriateness for Emil, apply her thoughtful decision, and evaluate the impact. There are no simple answers in the complex world of counseling, but this research process is the best way to ethically make clinical decisions.

RESEARCH WORLDVIEWS

The first step to enhancing a research knowledge base is to understand the philosophical underpinnings that guide investigators and counselors based on their views of the world and how inquiries are made to increase their understanding of that world (Heppner et al., 2008). The worldviews to be briefly discussed are positivism, post-positivism (quantitative methodology), and post-modernism or constructivism (qualitative methodology). In many ways, they define how individuals approach the assessment of others.

Positivism

Positivism in social science research follows the traditional "scientific method" as seen in the physical sciences. The underlying principle is that *truth* exists, can be observed as well as measured, and by using the scientific method of investigation, these truths can be made known. These researchers are *positive* of these truths. The researcher in this paradigm is *objective,* neither affecting or contaminating issues under study nor being affected or swayed by them.

This method used in studying phenomenon consists of well-defined steps with researchers making conjectures and predictions about occurrences, designing experiments to confirm or dispute investigators' original notions, and collecting *group, numerical data* from randomly sampled populations to see whether researchers' predictions were or were not supported. Positivistic research examines *causality* by looking to see whether variable X causes variable Y. Variable X is known as the *independent variable,* which is manipulated by researchers to cause an impact on another variable (Variable Y), such as using different counseling treatments for clients with depression. Variable Y is known as the *dependent variable* because how much of it there is "depends" on the effect of the independent variable such as a reduction in clients' depression (dependent variable) with a particular counseling therapy (independent variable) (Vogt, 2005). Positivistic research is *reductionistic and deductive* because it breaks down complex issues into simpler components that can be more easily studied and understood (Elmore & Bradley, 2001; Galluzzo et al., 2008; Heppner et al., 2008).

Post-Positivism

The positivistic approach to social sciences research has evolved into the post-positivism paradigm, which shares the "truth" perspective by attempting to discover and highlight the truth through scientific research methodology. Post-positivists differ slightly in that they do not believe that "truth" can actually be fully known. Instead, data collected from systematic investigations can only discover information about the *probability* of the investigators' conjecture (prediction based on hypothesized truths) being true. Post-positive researchers do not make absolute statements about truth. They use statistical tests to assist in corroborating their conjectures, but they assert that they cannot conclude with certainty that their thinking and investigations yield THE answer to the issue under study.

The goal of the post-positive researcher for a series of investigations is to gain closer approximations of the truth. Heppner et al. (2008) list the investigation into a link between smoking and various human diseases as an example of post-positivistic research. Here a succession of experiments using a variety of methodological designs was needed to come to the conclusion that smoking does indeed negatively impact the health of individuals. Both positivism and post-positivism fall under the category of *quantitative* research. The word *quantitative* is derived from the word *quantity,* meaning that the property of anything can be determined by numerical measurement (Elmore & Bradley, 2001).

The positivism or post-positivism approaches to Emil's issues are ones that would emphasize looking for the specific things that are needed to solve the problems. It could be seeking the specific operation that would help him function physically, finding him a new career in which other similarly handicapped individuals have found success, or applying clinical techniques found to be successful with other depressed clients. It is the search for those specific actions that we know have helped significant numbers of others overcome similar conditions.

Post-Modernism

Post-modernism has a long history in the human disciplines. These approaches have been utilized by anthropologists and sociologist for more than 100 years (Houser, 2009). Post-modernism is currently used as a broad term that encompasses paradigms such as *constructivism, critical theory,* and *feminism* (Galluzzo et al., 2008; Houser, 2009).

Constructivists hold that there is *no one truth* or reality, but instead that ideas about the world are individually constructed in the minds of individuals as they interact within their physical and social environments. Worldviews and reality are then shaped by the individual's particular culture and hold meaning for that individual, yet they do not represent absolute or universal truths.

Investigators using a constructivist approach are interested in understanding the *meaning* of an issue, not in explaining an issue, so they do not follow the objective, statistically-driven methodology of post-positivism (Heppner et al., 2008). Constructivists are *subjectively* involved with the participants of the study in contrast to the post-positivists. Investigators' values and biases are seen as valuable components of the study because participants are impacted by the investigators who enter their natural settings, and the reverse is also true as investigators are affected by research participants. This linking of investigators and participants is the vehicle by which individuals' construction of their world can be understood by the researcher through participants' personal narrative (Paisley & Reeves, 2001).

This method used to study phenomenon does not consist of making conjectures because there are no real truths to discover. Constructivists do not use random sampling procedures to identify their participants, but typically collect data from everyone whose voice might inform the investigation. Collected data are not numerical, but instead *words and phrases of individuals* that often lead investigators to interpretations that might not have been anticipated before the study began. The result is that investigators may find a need to reinterpret already acquired data or collect additional data based on their interpretations. Data analysis broadly yields verbal pictures such as written reports and data tables consisting of words not numbers (Heppner et al., 2008).

Critical theory, like constructivism, focuses on individuals' constructions of their world. Critical theorist, however, believe that social constructions are heavily influence by the people in power who have created forces that influence individuals such as social, political, economic, and so forth. Researchers who adhere to other paradigms strive to remain neutral and focus on describing and/or interpreting reality. Critical theory researchers are focused on empowering individuals, especially those whose voices might not be heard (e.g., economically disadvantaged, children, persons diagnosed with a mental illness, etc.).

Critical theorists conduct action research with the ultimate goal of confronting injustices. The research can be viewed as a first step in helping participants see that their deeply embedded beliefs, which are construed as "the truth" have been socially constructed and can be changed. Critical theory research takes on various forms, but the underlying commonality is the pressure to use research as a criticism of cultural beliefs that lead to oppression (Creswell, 2007, 2009).

Feminism, like critical theory, seeks to confront injustices. Specifically, a feminist paradigm focuses on challenging gender inequalities in the world that are rooted in traditional roles that women hold in society. Gender intersects with other forms of oppression such as age, race, economics, or orientation, that impact the way women experience their lives. Feminist theory research can have a major role in changing these social inequalities. The research can seem politically motivated, but in essence it is attempting to uncover and understand what causes and sustains oppression, thereby helping women to reject the traditional roles assigned to them by society (Creswell, 2007).

Participatory research is a hallmark of the feminism paradigm, in that participants are recognized as the experts or authorities on their own experiences. The power difference between researchers and participants is minimized, and the researchers are recognized as part of the research process. Ultimately, through social action research, the feminist paradigm is committed to working as individuals and groups toward ending all forms of oppression. The postmodernism paradigms fall under the category of *qualitative* research. Both quantitative and qualitative research methodology are explored to some extent in this chapter.

> The post-modernist trying to help Emil is not seeking answers that match large groups of people, but instead those answers that are unique to Emil based on the meaning that Emil creates for himself about his own world. The starting place is to understand Emil as a unique individual, his experience of becoming who he is, and the way he perceives and interacts with the world. From this study should emerge revised, new, and valuable questions specific to Emil's life that point to the best ways to help him, including advocating to reduce the social barriers blocking his success.

GENERAL METHODOLOGICAL ISSUES

Counselors who pose questions and set out on a quest to answer them often begin by reading current literature that addresses the issue at hand. When stepping into the scholarly literature, counselors first identify whether the research methodology in the study of interest was quantitative or qualitative. This identification assists in understanding several other methodological issues such as *laboratory versus field research,* which are related to *experimental control and generalizability.*

The broad distinction between laboratory experiments and field experiments relates to the *setting.* Experiments conducted in settings developed especially for the purpose of research are laboratory experiments, whereas studies conducted in natural or existing settings are labeled field experiments. The choice of setting is related to the investigators' ability to control as many factors (extraneous or confounding variables) as possible that could affect the outcome of the research (experimental control). The more stringent the controls in a lab atmosphere (e.g., standardizing implementation of treatment used in the counseling session; controlling temperature, lighting, and noise in the setting; etc.), the less the investigators can generalize their results to other settings, people, and/or times (generalizability). We say that *lab research* has *high internal validity* because it creates confidence in inferring that a cause-effect relationship exists among the variables under study while eliminating other explanations for the results. At the same time, laboratory research has *low external validity* because the study's results cannot be easily generalized to other people, settings, and/or times.

Field experiments, in contrast, are conducted in naturalistic settings where people actually live, work, and play. The investigators literally go to the participants, meaning there is little control over extraneous variables that might impact the results of the study. We say for this reason that *field research* has *low internal validity*. However, as you can see, an experiment that happens in a naturalistic setting has *high external validity* because the study's results can be more readily generalized to other people, settings, and/or times.

The earlier discussions on research worldviews highlights how many researchers believe that one setting is more valuable than the other and often even hotly contest each other's points of view. Can you imagine a researcher from the positivistic school willing to do field research and give up controlling the variables or investigators from the post-modernism school believing that they could conduct their study in a laboratory setting? From the perspective of mental health practitioners, field research, which is done in a realistic setting, is often seen as more applicable for answering their questions (Gladding, 2009).

The research reading that Emil's counselor will do to help her understand Emil's problem will include both laboratory and field studies. She will see that, although certain drugs or specific counseling techniques will have a specific effect on reducing levels of depression, producing chemicals in the body (laboratory studies), these results do not always reflect similar levels of decreased depressive behaviors in daily life (field studies). In fact, she will find that sometimes the mood-altering drugs or counseling techniques that increase energy levels in clients can also be related to increased levels of suicide and risky behaviors in the real world. The only way Emil's counselor will make sense out of these two types of information is to understand both of them and how to interpret the sometimes conflicting information they can produce.

MAJOR RESEARCH METHODS

The particular type of research methodology that counselors use should be guided by the type of questions they are attempting to answer, their special focus, and the resources available to support the investigation. The next sections of the chapter highlight these decisions that lead to *quantitative* research designs, including experimental, quasi-experimental, and descriptive research designs and to *qualitative* designs of ethnography, grounded theory, and case study. Quantitative and qualitative designs have unique advantages, disadvantages, and details that are beyond the scope of this chapter. For a comprehensive discussion of advantages, disadvantages, and details of various designs, consult Erford, (2008), Heppner et al. (2008), and Sheperis, Daniels, and Young (2010).

Experimental Research Designs

Between-group and within-subject designs are two quantitative experimental research designs that have a long history and tradition within social sciences research and can be thought of as "true" experimental research. Both types of designs have the following important characteristics in common.

- They use random sampling to gain subjects and random assignment to place them in different treatment groups in the study.
- They isolate and systematically manipulate an independent variable(s).
- They study cause-effect interactions.

Between-Group Designs

Several between-group designs can be explained in terms of two domains: (a) experimental groups versus control groups, and (b) pre-test versus post-test observations. *Experimental group(s)* are ones in which subjects receive a *treatment* that comes from manipulating the independent variable. *Control group(s)* are ones in which subjects receive no treatment and are used to compare the results of the "treated" subjects to the "non-treated" subjects. A *pre-test* refers to data gathered as the study begins prior to subjects being exposed to any treatment, and a *post-test* refers to data gathered from exposure to a treatment after the study is completed.

Between-group designs have names such as *post-test-only control group* and *pre-test-post-test control group.* The name post-test-only control group suggests that data on the dependent variable are collected from both the experimental and control groups after the treatment has been applied to subjects in the experimental/treatment group(s) only. Remember that even though the subjects in the control group have not received any treatment, researchers simultaneously collect data on the same measure(s) from both groups for comparison sake. Researchers using this design are interested in knowing how the treatment may have impacted the experimental/treatment group by averaging all subjects' scores and then looking at the differences in results between the experimental and control groups. These hypotheses focus on the idea that the experimental/treatment group will change in some expected way that the control group will not.

The pre-test-post-test control group design is slightly more sophisticated in that data on the dependent variable are collected on both experimental and control groups twice–before and after the treatment has been applied to the experimental group. Researchers can then compare the differences in the experimental group's average scores and the control group average scores on both the pre-test and post-test to see the change in scores more clearly. They can also use the pre-test to help identify characteristics about both groups before the study begins, such as the average level of subject depression or IQ scores.

Additionally, even more sophisticated between-group experimental designs are available for researchers to use, such as the *Solomon four-group design,* which literally combines the post-test-only control group design with the pre-test-post-test control group design. This design then has four groups–two experimental/treatment groups and two control groups. One treatment and one control group receive both a pre-test and post-test, whereas the other treatment and control group only receive the post-test. Using this design, researchers can even evaluate the impact that the pre-test might have on subjects by comparing scores across groups who did and did not receive the pre-test. The Solomon four-group design allows researchers to investigate a number of various configurations.

Factorial designs are also powerful between-group research methodology worthy of mention here. They become important when two or more independent variables are employed at the same time to see how they independently or in combination affect the dependent variable. Counselors who want to understand the effect that various therapeutic techniques have on their male versus female clients could utilize a factorial design. The independent variables in such a study are the various therapeutic techniques and the gender (male/female) of the clients.

> Reading the literature related to Emil's conditions, Emil's counselor might find a study that identified trauma victims two years after their treatments and evaluated the life satisfaction of one group that got comprehensive counseling and standard physical rehabilitation services (treatment group) and another group that only got standard physical rehabilitation (control group). The results of this post-test-only control group design might well show that there was no difference in their perceived quality of life between the two groups. Sometimes researchers, based on their clinical experience, want to check these results more closely and develop a more rigorous study that evaluates quality of life before treatment and after treatment of two groups (pre-test-post-test control group design). This study would take into account how much people had changed, thereby looking at how much the two groups had grown rather than outcomes only.

These differences are similar to evaluating counseling clients for outcomes versus change. We often choose to measure how much clients improved their quality of life rather than whether their quality of life is equal to all other clients.

Within-Subject Designs

Continuing with experimental research designs brings us to discuss within-subject designs. Within-subject designs use each participant as his or her own control, in that all participants are exposed to all treatment conditions. The major benefit of this design is that each participant acts as his/her own control thereby lessoning the amount of individual variation that would occur between different subjects using the between-group designs. Here the focus is on each individual person's change rather than the average change for a group.

The cross-over *within-subject design* is an excellent example where all subjects are

- randomly assigned, given a pre-test,
- exposed to a treatment (trt 1) of some type,
- given a post-test that examines the impact of Treatment 1 and then
- "crossed-over" to be exposed to another treatment (trt 2), and finally,
- given another post-test that examines the impact of Treatment 2.

The *Latin Square design* is an additional, uniquely sophisticated within-subject design. This design increases the number of treatments and number of groups that a researcher uses in one study. The Latin Square consists of three separate groups of subjects who are all exposed to each of three different treatments in a counterbalanced fashion with researchers collecting data between each treatment. Group 1 might receive Treatment 1 first, Treatment 2 second, and Treatment 3 last, whereas Group 2 might receive Treatment 2 first, Treatment 3 second, and Treatment 1 last, and Group 3 would receiving treatments in the order of 3, 2, and 1. This design allows researchers to investigate which treatment or sequences of treatments might have the most significant impact on the subjects.

The within-subject design is closely associated with the clinical work that Emil's counselor will do. She will not have a great number of clients like Emil, and so she will need to do a good deal of her evaluation with him based on trying things out and seeing how he responds to them. For example, will Emil be more receptive to cognitive, behavioral, or person-centered methods? The counselor may try them separately or in combination using within-subject designs to evaluate their impact on Emil. Her findings will lead her to making choices of how to approach him most effectively over time. Researchers will use a similar approach, with the difference being that they would apply these basic methods to purposely selected samples of individuals to see how the individual changes are reflected in different groups.

Quasi-Experimental Research Designs

Quasi-experimental designs differ from experimental designs in that they *lack random assignment of subjects* to various treatment and control groups. The independent variable in these designs is still manipulated, with researchers continuing to investigate the cause-effect relationship among variables under study. Quasi-experimental designs are primarily used at times when researchers cannot randomly assign subjects to various groups. In these cases, researchers will work with *intact groups,* which are already formed prior to the investigators' involvement. For example, several investigators interested in the impact of various counseling therapies on mildly, moderately, and severely depressed clients set up a research design that has three groups (two treatment groups and one control group). Can you imagine the ethical dilemma that would face these investigators if severely depressed clients were randomly assigned to the waiting-list control group that was not to receive counseling for a period of several weeks? Using intact groups as subjects such as a classroom of middle-school students is another example of research design that would lack random assignment because the researchers could not simply arrange students to fit their research design needs.

Non-randomized Pre-test-Post-test Control Group Design

A primary example of a quasi-experimental design is the *non-randomized pre-test-post-test control group design,* which is similar to the design discussed earlier in the chapter except that subjects are not randomly assigned. This lack of randomization creates a situation where the treatment comparisons are made with *non-equivalent groups* that may differ from each other in many ways. This circumstance lessens researchers' confidence that their groups are similar in characteristics before the treatment is applied. Too much variation among individuals in the various treatment and/or control groups creates a situation in which the results of the research using this design must be interpreted with caution. One way to deal with this limitation is to use a cohort research design.

Cohort Designs

Cohort designs are another example of quasi-experimental designs. Cohorts are successive groups of individuals who follow each other through an institution such as a school. Cohorts are generally assumed to be characteristically similar to each other and share a similar environment. The sixth-grade students in the local school, for example, would be expected to be similar to next year's sixth-grade students in the same school. Researchers interested in examining the effects of a new curriculum on sixth-grade students' reading abilities might decide to use a cohort design because they cannot randomly assign students to various classes for the purpose of their research. The researchers, during Year 1 of the study, would gather data from a predetermined number of sixth graders to establish a baseline of average reading abilities. The sixth-grade students' reading scores from Year 1 would then be used as the data from a control group. During Year 2 of the study, researchers would implement the new reading curriculum with the entering sixth-grade students and then collect the same data on reading abilities of these students. Finally, the investigators will compare the results from both cohort groups (Year 1 and Year 2) to examine the efficacy of the new curriculum on students' reading abilities.

Emil's counselor's review of the literature would find live-in rehabilitation programs for paraplegic injuries. Some of these programs would have specific time frames and procedures for similar injuries. In effect, these programs would also have cohort groups that enter and exit the program at the same time and do the same work there. Following groups would not be exactly matched, but they could be seen as similar in these designs.

Single-Subject Designs

Some researchers have suggested that single-subject designs can be the centerpiece of the counseling research model because they have a number of advantages for counselors, such as allowing for a more adequate description of what happens between client (individual or other unit) and counselor, as well as meeting the quality assurance goals necessary for competent practice (Brown & Trusty, 2005; Heppner et al., 2008; Sheperis & Miller, 2008). Lundervold and Belwood (2000) refer to this type of design as the "best kept secret in counseling" (p. 92).

Single-subject designs were developed to allow investigators to measure changes in target behaviors of single individuals or a unit of analysis that could be a couple, family, group, organization, and so forth (Heppner et al., 2008; Sheperis & Miller, 2008; Studer, Obermann, & Womack, 2006). The target behaviors are the dependent variables in the study, which are collected at multiple points over a period of time (McDougall & Smith, 2006). In essence, the investigators are repeatedly measuring the dependent variable(s) (target behaviors) prior to and during the application of the independent variable(s) (treatment/intervention). Single-subject (AB) designs consist of different phases of data collection which typically are defined as baseline (Phase A) and treatment/intervention (Phase B).

The AB Design

The *AB design* is typically constructed so that researchers take *multiple measurements* or observations during baseline and treatment phases. *Baseline phase (A)* refers to the time period in the study before treatment is applied in which data are collected to describe the current level of functioning. The objective is to find trends in the data that establish a subject's typical pattern of the target behavior(s). The primary purpose of this design is to detect changes in target behaviors between baseline and treatment phases. The stability of the baseline is especially important because researchers could not make a comparison to detect the actual changes in behaviors due to the treatment phase if target behaviors kept changing during baseline observations.

The intervention begins during the *treatment phase (B)* and lasts for a predetermined length of time. Results of target behavior functioning are then compared between baseline and the end of the treatment phase. There are several variations to the AB design, such as the basic *ABAB design,* also referred to as a type of *withdrawal/reversal design.* This design begins with a baseline phase (A_1), moves to the introduction of the treatment phase (B_1), withdraws or reverses the treatment essentially returning to the baseline phase (A_2), and finally reintroduces the treatment phase (B_2). The assumption behind this design is that if the B_1 (independent variable) caused the change in the target behaviors (dependent variable), then withdrawing the treatment (A_2) should have behaviors returning to similar original baseline levels. If, in fact, the behaviors do return to similar levels, reintroducing the treatment phase (B_2) should replicate the impact of the intervention on target behaviors, furthering researchers' confidence that a causal relationship exists between the independent and dependent variables. If behaviors do not revert to original baseline levels at A_2, then the investigators cannot infer a cause-effect relationship between variables because other unknown variables may have created the change (Heppner et al., 2008; Sheperis & Miller, 2008).

Single-subject design studies will be those that Emil's counselor will most closely see how to apply to her direct work with Emil. They may not have the generalizability of results that other designs offer, but they will be easily translated into how she treats Emil. She will evaluate how Emil is initially functioning (baseline), apply a treatment, evaluate how he is doing as a result of the treatment, and design the next steps in the process. It is an ongoing process that focuses all efforts on Emil as an individual.

Descriptive Designs

Descriptive designs can be used to *describe* the incidence of variables, distribution of variables, or the relationship among variables throughout a population (Heppner et al., 2008). These designs are important to counseling research because they clarify our perceptions of what the variables are, which is necessary before we begin attempting to manipulate and control variables. There are a variety of quantitative descriptive designs, such as survey or epidemiological research and ex post facto research designs.

Survey Research

Purposes for survey research are primarily to describe, explain, or explore the nature of particular variables. This type of research is widely used in the social sciences, including counseling research, where participants self-report on facts, attitudes, and even behaviors. *Descriptive survey research* provides basic information on issues, for example, the frequency of bullying in middle schools. *Explanatory survey research* tries to explain the occurrence of an issue (like bullying) by investigating such variables as students' beliefs about bullying or students' beliefs about the acceptability of bullying in their school. Finally, *exploratory survey research* is conducted when investigators would like to investigate a poorly understood issue, such as how bullies rationalize their abuse of others.

Survey research collects data using various methods, such as a questionnaires, mailed surveys, telephone interviews, or personal interviews. Data can be gained through structured or unstructured interviews. They also can be acquired from the same people over a period of time, which is known as *longitudinal research,* or from many different people all at one point in time, which is referred to as *cross-sectional research.*

There are several problematic issues with survey research. Research questions might be too unclear or vague to guide the development of appropriate items, creating surveys with irrelevant variables that reduce the validity and reliability of results. Investigators sometimes use a convenient group of subjects, for example, using college students attending a private university that leaves out all students attending public universities and is therefore not representative of all college students. Response rates can often be quite low (Gladding, 2009; Heppner et al., 2008), which raises questions about why some individuals responded while others who might give quite different answers did not. Even with these limitations, survey research has made, and will continue to make, numerous important contributions to counseling research.

Emil's counselor will find many studies in the literature that explore clients' reports of their feelings, perceptions, and beliefs. There will also be the self-report studies of counselors, doctors, family members, and others examining their actions, beliefs, and perceptions regarding the issues surrounding depression, traumatic injury, and recovery. It will never be clear in these studies why some people perceive things one way and others another, but the information does provide valuable clues to the perceptions that people have about these problems. Some of those perceptions may help the counselor better understand Emil and his situation.

Ex Post Facto Designs

Ex post facto literally translated from Latin means "after the fact." These designs use data in which the impact of one variable on another has occurred before the actual research is begun. Researchers do not manipulate an independent variable in an attempt to influence the impact on the dependent variable, but merely try to establish the relationship among the variables. For example, gender, personality types, and counseling success or failure are important variables (Heppner et al., 2008), but researchers cannot manipulate them because no researcher can simply change someone's personality type or randomly assign clients to a group that they know will have either successful or unsuccessful counseling outcomes.

Counselors interested in examining whether a relationship exists between counseling outcomes (success or failure) of their clients and the clients' personality types could use the data normally collected and housed in clients' files to answer such a question. These counselors are using an ex post facto design to inform the type of therapy they do because they are accessing data "after the fact." The data were already routinely collected and are now part of client files.

Correlational studies are one type of ex post facto design in which researchers investigate the extent to which variations in one factor are related to variations in one or more other factors. These relationships are statistically examined by a group of correlational procedures, with the most common one being the Pearson product moment correlation. This statistical procedure yields coefficient (numerical scores) ranging from +1.0 through 0 to −1.0. The coefficient specifies the degree of relationship among the variables, with stronger relationships being indicated when scores are closest to positive or negative 1.0 and weakest to no relationship among variables being indicated with scores are closest to 0. Coefficients of +1.0 indicate a perfect positive relationship, whereas scores of −1.0 indicate a perfect negative relationship.

The direction (positive or negative) of the relationship helps researchers understand the manner in which the variables are related. Brown and

Srebalus (2003) provide an example of high school grades and college achievement. A correlation of +1.0 would indicate that a student who gets straight As in high school will get straight As in college. Although a correlation of –1.0 would indicate that the student who gets straights As in high school will be a straight F student in college. As you might guess, perfect correlations or perfect relationships are rarely ever gained in research. Thus, researchers must interpret less than "perfect" correlation coefficients. Researchers do have a standardized way of determining high versus low relationships. Correlation coefficients of 0.70 are considered high, 0.30–0.69 are considered moderate, and those less than 0.30 are considered low. These cutoff points are helpful guidelines for investigators when they interpret the results of the research and helpful to counselors as they seek to understand how much confidence they should put in the results as they relate to work with clients.

> Emil may be in the middle of his experiences with depression and traumatic injury recovery, but many others have previously gone through the full experience. His counselor's attempt to understand the potential pattern for Emil's experience will look for ex post facto studies in which records of treatment were obtained. Rehabilitation services offices are one good examples of where such records would be maintained. Others would be agencies, centers, or private practitioners who deal with many similarly specialized cases. Emil's counselor would even be taking on her own research as she seeks out such sources and attempts to find correlations between the factors that seem to be attached to successful outcomes of similar cases.

Qualitative Research Designs

Qualitative research provides a different paradigm for approaching the investigation of various phenomena. Many methods and approaches are classified under the umbrella term of qualitative research or *strategies of inquiry* (Heppner et al., 2008), such as participatory action research, grounded theory, case studies, ethnography, narrative, feminist inquiry, consensual qualitative research, and critical theory, to name a few (Denzin & Lincoln, 2000). Even within these various specific strategies of inquiry (i.e., ethnography), there are multiple forms for conducting research. An alternative term used to describe qualitative research is *interpretive research* (Gay, Mills, & Airasian, 2006). Hays and Newsome (2008) provide a table briefly comparing characteristics of nine qualitative approaches. Creswell (2007) provides two succinct tables comparing characteristics of five major approaches to qualitative research. These approaches are grounded in inductive reasoning, with researchers expressing an interest in exploring a particular issue, designing a study, collecting data, and then generating written reports from the data.

This type of research is

- *sensitive to the context* in which the study is conducted,
- *nonstandardized,* and
- *dependent on the subjective experiences* of the both the investigators and participants (Choudhuri, Glauser, & Peregoy, 2004; Creswell, 2009; Gladding, 2009; Mertens, 2009).

Qualitative researchers speak in terms of trustworthiness of the data, typically using the criteria of *credibility, transferability, dependability,* and *confirmability.* One way to discuss these terms is to compare them relative to terms we have already discussed in the quantitative sections of this chapter. From that perspective, these terms could be perceived in the following ways:

- *Credibility* is approximately like internal validity, where the investigator attempts to reduce the chance of error in the study, which is a factor that can produce confusing results.
- *Transferability* can approximate a similar meaning to external validity, in that it is related to the data's ability to generalize to other populations.
- *Dependability* speaks to the reliability of the data and the importance of the findings.
- *Confirmability* parallels objectivity, where investigators are committed to developing consistent methods and procedures of study.

This commitment to methods and procedures increases a study's trustworthiness and reinforces credibility, transferability, dependability, and confirmability (Newsome, Hays, & Christensen, 2008). Morrow (2005) expands these guidelines through three additional components:

- *Social validity* proposes that treatment goals, intervention techniques, and outcomes are relevant and useful for participants who are empowered in the research process by being involved and having a sense of ownership.
- *Subjectivity and reflexivity* refer to the investigators' self-awareness and self-reflection in the research process.

The major strength of qualitative research is the ability to highlight subtle aspects of counseling that are individually focused, developmental, and experientially reported. The acceptance of qualitative research as a viable source of data increased tremendously over the past two decades as scholars and practitioners became better acquainted with the unique information it provides. Counselors will therefore find increasing numbers of qualitative research articles in relevant journals as the method to investigate a wide variety of phenomena (Berrios & Luca, 2006).

Choudhuri, Glauser, and Peregoy (2004) have published one particular article detailing guidelines for writing a qualitative manuscript in a most prestigious counseling journal–the *Journal of Counseling and Development.* Their presentation of criteria for the rigor and credibility that must be applied to these research designs is particularly valuable to those utilizing or evaluating this form of research. The following section briefly highlights a few of the most utilized approaches, including ethnographic, case study, and grounded theory from a host of possibilities. For a more detailed discussion of qualitative research, see texts such as Creswell (2007); Maxwell (2005); Rubin and Rubin (2005); and Silverman (2010).

The kind of work that Emil's counselor will do with Emil is closely associated with qualitative research. She will be seeking to understand him not only in the statistical (quantitative) ways he compares to others, but she will spend great amounts of time trying to understand his uniqueness and the stories that explain how he arrived at his current physical, social, emotional, and spiritual states. This information will be more related to the qualities of Emil rather than the quantities of things in him or his life. The counselor will also be interested in what researchers have found when they have used similar methods for exploring people with issues like those facing Emil.

Grounded Theory

Grounded theory has its roots in sociology and was conceptualized by Glaser and Strauss (1967) in *The Discovery of Grounded Theory.* Strauss and Corbin (1998) provide a structured approach for conducting grounded theory research, whereas Charmaz (2006) proposes a constructivist approach that emphasizes "diverse local worlds, multiple realities, and complexities of particular worlds, views, and actions" (Creswell, 2007, p. 65). Both approaches are recommended for readers interested in applying this type of qualitative research.

The theory emphasizes a general methodology designed to inductively form a theory from data that have been systematically gathered typically through interviews and analyzed by using extensive, direct observations in a naturalistic setting. Theories that already exist (grounded) may also be elaborated on or modified as new incoming data provide additional comparisons for the investigators to match a theory against the data. Investigators continuously make comparisons between theory and the data gathered from actual research. In other words, grounded theory is composed of continued sampling and is based on the emergent theory constantly being verified and adapted until theoretical saturation is reached and a grounded theory is articulated (Fassinger, 2005).

Grounded theory can be viewed as providing new connections between theory and real-world phenomena by

- identifying the patterns and themes recognizable within the real-life data, and
- providing the conceptual links between these themes and patterns that can increase a theory's ability to explain phenomenon.

Hays, Chang, and Dean (2004) conducted a study utilizing grounded theory to examine White counselors' views on privilege and oppression. The authors' study is a good example of how grounded theory can enhance counseling research and training. The participants included eight counselors who were diverse in age, biological sex, spiritual orientation, and sexual orientation. The participants were interviewed twice on average between 45 and 60 minutes. Findings were used to highlight implication for training counselors in the United States. An important comparison to be noted is the time difference for conducting grounded theory versus ethnography research.

Ethnography

Ethnographic research is based on the view that the "social world is an interpreted world, not a literal world" (Altheide & Johnson, 1994, p. 489). The investigation focuses on a cultural group and involves comprehensive study in the natural setting. In fact, the root word of *ethnography* is *ethnos,* which is Greek meaning "people" or "group." Ethnographers conduct investigations of collective patterns found within a cultural group (Creswell, 2007). These patterns can include values, beliefs, behaviors, and language that investigators attempt to describe and interpret. This focus on interpretation creates research where

- the relationship between what is observed (e.g., behaviors or traditions) and the larger cultural contexts is critical;
- the relationship among the observer, the observed, and the setting is an integral component of the study;
- the perspective (point of view) of the observer and the observed are both used to develop an interpretation of the results; and
- the role of the reader as a consumer of the study must also be taken into consideration (Altheide & Johnson, 1994).

Ethnographers take care to describe as accurately as possible participants' behaviors, shared worldviews, and so forth. The detailed descriptions literally use the cultural or local language as part of the text. Investigators develop their descriptions from as many sources as possible, such as interviews, observations, and documentation. The outcome from ethnography research is a *thick description* that provides an inclusive representation of the cultural group that enhances our deep understanding of an issue.

Ethnographic research has its roots and is used frequently in anthropology. This type of qualitative research can be difficult to use in counseling because of the sustained length of time the investigator stays in the field collecting data with the group under study. This intensive field involvement can often be many months, which has generally not been a viable option for those doing counseling research.

Phenomenological Research

Phenomenological research has its roots in philosophy particularly originating from the work of a German philosopher, Edmund Husserl (1859–1938), as well as psychology and education (Creswell, 2007). The function of phenomenology research is to investigate individuals' lived experiences of a phenomenon. The actual phenomenon can encompass a wide range of experiences such as bullying, grief, sexual abuse, perception of mental illness, and identity development, just to name a few that counselors might want to research. Phenomenological research provides rich descriptions of a phenomenon, and phenomenologists do not develop and test hypotheses in a manner commonly used in other research approaches.

Hays and Newsome (2008) suggest that investigators conducting phenomenology research are rather like counselors "who empathically and nonjudgmental enters into the world of clients to provide therapeutic help" (p. 177). Phenomenologists seek to understand as much as possible the perceived lived experience of their participants and then to describe those experiences as accurately as possible. Finding commonalities among the experiences shared by individuals is an important component in conducting this type of research.

The process of conducting phenomenology research is similar to other qualitative methodologies, where interviews of relative small numbers of participants are conducted. Unlike time-intensive ethnography, investigators using this approach would interview participants for an hour or so either one time or more depending on the nature of the study. Interestingly, phenomenologists refer to participants as co-researchers (Ary, Jacobs, Razavieh, & Sorensen, 2006) because they share their perspectives with the researchers, providing in-depth, rich descriptions and concrete examples of the phenomenon under study.

Case Study

You may be asking yourself what anyone can learn from an individual case study. Well, you are not alone because this has been a long-standing question. Case study research has its roots in psychology, law, political science, and medicine (Creswell, 2007). A case may be identified as an individual person (e.g., a child) or a group (e.g., a classroom of children), a program, an event, an intervention, or even a community. Consistent with our previous discussion on qualitative research, case studies focus on gaining an in-depth understanding that is derived from the meaning participants provide to the issue under study and in context of the situation.

A case study is a complex design that begins with investigators framing the study by placing boundaries around it. Before the study begins, qualitative researchers would say that investigators have defined or *bounded* the unit of analysis/case they are interested in studying (Creswell, 2007). Next steps commonly entail using multiple methods of data collection, such as interviews, observations, videotaping, and analysis of documents, surveys, and artifacts to fully explore the conceptual research questions. Most investigators agree that when conducting case studies, they do not develop the close relationship with the participants that other qualitative researchers, such as those using an ethnographic method, might espouse. The case study researcher is much more an observer who seeks to have as little influence on the content of the data as possible.

Qualitative case researchers often call for letting the case tell its own story. In fact, reading reports of case studies can vividly take the reader into the setting in great detail. A qualitative case study could be conducted, for example, on a classroom where bullying is a problem. Investigators would be interested in studying the complexities occurring in the classroom by understanding the students' reactions to each other. The investigators could quite conceivably interview the students, record (audio or video) them during their daily interactions, analyze relevant documents that the teacher holds, and even ask the students and teacher to fill out a survey instrument. The researchers would then use the qualitative information they acquired to demonstrate how bullying-related behaviors in one classroom could be relevant for understanding the larger problem of bullying in the American education system.

Consensual Qualitative Research

Consensual qualitative research is a relatively new approach to conducting qualitative studies (Heppner et al., 2008). Succinctly outlined, this form of research consists of (a) open-ended questions in semistructured data-collection techniques (typically in interviews), which allow for the collection of consistent data across individuals as well as a more in-depth examination of individual experiences; (b) several investigators who independently analyze participants' narratives throughout the data analysis process to foster multiple perspectives that leads to; (c) consensus about the meaning of the data; (d) at least one auditor to check the work of the primary team of researchers; and (e) domains, core ideas, and cross-analyses of data. For more in-depth information, see Heppner et al. (2008) and Hill, Knox, Thompson, Williams, Hess, and Ladany (2005).

CONCLUSION

We began this chapter with the theory, research, and practice triangle. Counseling theories are the underpinnings of our profession and are invaluable for us as counselors and for clients as consumers of our services. Our clinical practice can only be as good as those theories that guide us, and the key component that effectively links theory to practice is research. Research studies help us identify the connections between theory and practice by using the various research designs that exist under the two major paradigms of quantitative and qualitative research.

Researchers use these paradigms and their unique research designs to identify those ways in which counseling makes a difference in the lives of our clients. This process of research in counseling is one of continually testing our theories to provide process and outcome data from our counseling practice. These data support the credibility of the counseling profession as a whole, our individual work, and our ability to demonstrate continuous professional advancement.

If we believe the premise that research informs theory and practice, there should be countless examples in the counseling literature to support our thinking. Guess what? There are! Berrios and Lucca (2006) provide a review of contributions that qualitative methodology has made to counseling research and highlight ways in which qualitative research can continue to enhance the future of the counseling profession. Shick Tryon's (2003) edited book, *Counseling Based on Process Research: Applying What We Know,* is a detailed resource on many issues, such as the working alliance (Constantino, Castonguay, & Schut, 2002), empathy (Duan, Rose, & Kraatz, 2002), and termination (Gelso & Woodhouse, 2002). Other qualitative research provides greater understanding into the lived experiences of individuals (e.g., Hunt, Matthews, Milsom, & Lammel, 2006).

Research is relevant to our understanding of the counseling process from our first session, through the middle period of our work with clients, and onto termination. The research triangle continues to take on more and more importance for counselors as we seek to continually improve on the services we offer to our clients. The basic principles presented in this chapter should offer you the opportunity to develop a better picture yourself functioning as the counselor-researcher or the scientist-practitioner.

REFERENCES

Altheide, D. L., & Johnson, J. M. (1994). Criteria for assessing interpretive validity in qualitative research. In N. K., Denzin & Y. S. E. Lincoln (Eds.), *Handbook of qualitative research* (pp. 485-499) Thousand Oaks, CA: Sage.

American Counseling Association. (2005). *Code of ethics.* Alexandria, VA: Author.

Ary, D., Jacobs, L. C., Razavieh, A., & Sorensen, C. (2006). *Introduction to research in education* (7th ed.). Belmont, CA: Thomson Wadsworth.

Benishek, L. A., & Gordon, P. A. (1998). Bridging the gap between science and practice in the research practice: A template for counselor training. *Journal of Humanistic Education and Development, 37,* 6–20.

Berrios, R., & Lucca, N. (2006). Qualitative methodology in counseling research: Recent contributions and challenges. *Journal of Counseling and Development, 84*(2), 174–186.

Bradley, L. J., Sexton, T. L., & Smith, H. B. (2005). The American Counseling Association practice research network (ACA-PRN): A new research tool. *Journal of Counseling and Development, 83,* 488–491.

Brown, D., & Srebalus, D. J. (2003). *Introduction to the counseling profession* (3rd ed.). Boston, MA: Allyn & Bacon.

Brown, D., & Trusty, J. (2005). The ASCA national model, accountability, and establishing causal links between school counselors' activities and student outcomes: A reply to sink. *Professional School Counseling, 9,* 13–15.

Charmaz, K. (2006). *Constructing grounded theory.* London: Sage.

Choudhuri, D., Glauser, A., & Peregoy, J. (2004). Guidelines for writing a qualitative manuscript for the Journal of Counseling and Development. *Journal of Counseling and Development, 82,* 443–446.

Constantino, M. J., Castonguay, L. G., & Schut, A. J. (2002). The working alliance: A flagship for the "scientist-practitioner" model in psychotherapy. In G. Shick Tyron (Ed.), *Counseling based on process research: Applying what we know* (pp. 81–131). Boston, MA: Allyn & Bacon.

Creswell, J. W. (2007). *Qualitative inquiry and research design: Choosing among five approaches.* Thousand Oaks, CA: Sage.

Creswell, J. W. (2009). *Research design: Quantitative, qualitative, and mixed methods approaches.* Thousand Oaks, CA: Sage.

D'Andrea, M., & Foster Heckman, E. (2008). A 40-year review of multicultural counseling outcome research: Outlining a future research agenda for the multicultural counseling movement. *Journal of Counseling & Development, 86,* 356–363.

Denzin, N. K., & Lincoln, Y. S. (2000). *Handbook of qualitative research* (2nd ed.). Thousand Oaks, CA: Sage.

Duan, C, Rose, T. B., & Kraatz, R. A. (2002). Empathy. In G. Shick Tryon (Ed.), *Counseling based on process research: Applying what we know* (pp. 197–231). Boston, MA: Allyn & Bacon.

Elmore, P. B., & Bradley, R. W. (2001). Quantitative research methods. In D. C. Locke, J. E.

Myers, & E. L. Herr (Eds.), *The handbook of counseling* (pp. 481–498). Thousand Oaks, CA: Sage.

Erford, B. T. (Ed.). (2008). *Research and evaluation in counseling.* Boston, MA: Houghton Mifflin.

Fassinger, R. (2005). Paradigms, praxis, problems, and promise: Grounded theory in counseling psychology research. *Journal of Counseling Psychology, 52*(2), 156–166.

Galluzzo, G. R., Hilldrup, J., Hays, D. G., & Erford, B. T. (2008). The nature of research and inquiry. In B. T. Erford (Ed.), *Research and evaluation in counseling* (pp. 2–24). Boston, MA: Houghton Mifflin.

Gay, L. R., Mills, G. E., & Airasian, P. (2006). *Educational research: Competencies for analysis and applications* (8th ed.). Upper Saddle River, NJ: Pearson Merrill Prentice-Hall.

Gelso, C. J., & Woodhouse, S. S. (2002). The termination of psychotherapy: What research tells us about the process of ending treatment. In G. Shick Tryon (Ed.), *Counseling based on process research: Applying what we know* (pp. 344–369). Boston, MA: Allyn & Bacon.

Gladding, S. T. (2009). *Counseling: A comprehensive profession.* Upper Saddle River, NJ: Merrill.

Glasser, B., & Strauss, A. (1967). *The discovery of grounded theory.* Chicago, IL: Aldine.

Hays, D. G., Chang, C. Y., & Dean, J. K. (2004). White counselors' conceptualization of privilege and oppression: Implications for counselor training. *Counselor Education and Supervision, 43,* 242–257.

Hays, D. G., & Newsome, D. R. (2008). Qualitative research design. In B. T. Erford (Ed.), *Research and evaluation in counseling* (pp. 107–128). Boston, MA: Houghton Mifflin.

Hazler, R. J., & Kottler, J. A. (2005) *The emerging professional counselor: Student dreams to professional realities* (2nd ed.). Alexandria, VA: American Counseling Association.

Heppner, P. P., Kivlighan, D. M., Jr., & Wampold, B. E. (2008). *Research design in counseling* (3rd ed.). Belmont, CA: Thomson/Brooks Cole.

Hill, C. E., Knox, S., Thompson, B. J., Williams, E. N., Hess, S. A., & Ladany, N. (2005). Consensual qualitative research. *Journal of Counseling Psychology, 52,* 196–205.

Houser, R. (2009). *Counseling and educational research: Evaluation and application* (2nd ed.). Thousand Oaks, CA: Sage.

Hunt, B., Matthews, C., Milsom, A., & Lammel, J. A. (2006). Lesbians with physical disabilities: A qualitative study of their experiences with counseling. *Journal of Counseling and Development, 84,* 163–173.

Kitchener, K. S. (1984). Intuition, critical evaluation and ethical principles: The foundation for ethical decision in counseling psychology. *The Counseling Psychologist, 12,* 43–55.

Lundervold, D. A., & Belwood, M. F. (2000). The best kept secret in counseling: Single-case (N=1) experimental designs. *Journal of Counseling and Development, 78,* 92–102.

Maxwell, J. A. (2005). *Qualitative research design: An interactive approach* (2nd ed.). Thousand Oaks, CA: Sage.

McDougall, D., & Smith, D. (2006). Recent innovations in small-n designs for research and practice in professional school counseling. *Professional School Counseling, 9,* 392–400.

Mertens, D. M. (2009). *Research methods in education and psychology.* Thousand Oaks, CA: Sage.

Morrow, S. L. (2005). Quality and trustworthiness in qualitative research in counseling psychology. *Journal of Counseling Psychology, 52,* 250–260.

Newsome, D. R., Hays, D. G., & Christensen, T. (2008). Qualitative approaches to research. In B. T. Erford (Ed.), *Research and evaluation in counseling* (pp. 86–106). Boston, MA: Houghton Mifflin.

Paisley, P. O., & Reeves, P. M. (2001). Qualitative research in counseling. In D. C. Locke, J. E. Myers, & E. L. Herr (Eds.), *The handbook of counseling* (pp. 481–498). Thousand Oaks, CA: Sage.

Rhodes, R. H., Hill, D. E., Thompson, B. J., & Elliott, R. (1994). Client retrospective recall of resolved and unresolved misunderstanding events. *Journal of Counseling Psychology, 41,* 473–483.

Rubin, H. J., & Rubin, I. S. (2005). *Qualitative interviewing: The art of hearing data* (2nd ed.). Thousand Oaks, CA: Sage.

Sheperis, C. J., Daniels, M. H., & Young, J. S. (2010). *Counseling research: Quantitative, qualitative, and mixed methods.* Upper Saddle River, NJ: Pearson.

Sheperis, C. J., & Miller, J. D. (2008). Using single-subject research designs to document client outcomes. In B. T. Erford (Ed.), *Research and evaluation in counseling* (pp. 166–197). Boston, MA: Houghton Mifflin.

Shick Tryon, G. (Ed.). (2002). *Counseling based on process research: Applying what we know.* Boston, MA: Allyn & Bacon.

Silverman, S. (2010). *Doing qualitative research* (3rd ed.). Thousand Oaks, CA: Sage.

Strauss, A., & Corbin, J. (1998). *Basics of qualitative research: Techniques and procedures for developing grounded theory* (2nd ed.). Thousand Oaks, CA: Sage.

Studer, J. R., Oberman, A. H., & Womack, R. H. (2006). Producing evidence to show counseling effectiveness in the schools. *Professional School Counseling, 9,* 385–391.

Vogt, W. P. (2005). *Dictionary of statistics and methodology: A nontechnical guide for the social sciences* (3rd ed.). Thousand Oaks, CA: Sage.

Whiston, S. C. (1996). Accountability through action research. Research methods for practitioners. *Journal of Counseling and Development, 74,* 616–623.

Chapter 18

ETHICS IN COUNSELING

LAURA K. HARRAWOOD AND STEPHEN FEIT

INTRODUCING ETHICS

This chapter introduces the emerging mental health counselor to the concept of ethics and ethical decision making in counseling practice. We begin by first addressing the distinction between ethics and law. Counselors need to be aware of the sometimes conflicting character of the two and to recognize the complex nature of adhering to both while acting in the best interest of their client(s). Next, we provide a foundation for ethics by reviewing Kitchener's (1984) five moral principles. These moral principles provide a philosophical basis for the application of all counseling codes of ethics. This section concludes with a brief discussion going beyond Kitchener's moral principles and the complexity of application of the principles.

In the second section, a detail of the *American Counseling Associations (ACA) Code of Ethics* (American Counseling Association, 2005a) is provided, followed by a discussion of the application of Forester-Miller and Davis' (1996) ethical decision-making model. Decision-making models are the vehicle from which we operate that sets the code of ethics in motion. Through the use of an ethical decision-making model, counselors-in-training understand the importance of learning how to apply the codes as opposed to merely memorizing them.

Following the discussion on decision making, we report on the inquiries into ethical violations most often made and what occurs when ethical violations are processed. Next, we turn toward the purpose and need for informed consent. A detailed written informed consent provides the initial structure from which to operate as an ethical counselor. Finally, we conclude the chapter with information regarding our thoughts on how mental health counselors can continue to foster the development of ethical decision making and behavior throughout their career.

WHAT ARE ETHICS?

Before we begin to address the relevance of ethics in counseling, it is helpful to define what ethics are. Numerous authors have attempted to define ethics with regard to the counseling profession (e.g., Corey, Corey, & Callanan, 1998; Herlihy & Corey, 2006; Hill, 2004; Remley & Herlihy, 2001). Additionally, Merriam-Webster (2010) provided several definitions of ethics that are pertinent to this discussion. They include, but are not limited to: "the discipline dealing with what is good and bad and with moral duty and obligation" and "a set of moral principles: a theory or system of moral values" (Main Entry: Ethic). These moral values can be charged to an individual or a group and are not to be confused with *laws* that are legally bound rules enforced by a court system. Counseling ethics and the legal system sometimes contradict one another, and it is the responsibility of the counselor to understand the "cross-cultural" nature of the two and to act ethically in the best interest of their client(s) without placing themselves in the position of breaching law (Rowley & MacDonald, 2001).

THE FOUNDATION OF ETHICS

Given the prior definitions of ethics, how do you develop into an ethical counselor who is able to evaluate contextually what is considered "good and bad?" Where does the sense of "moral duty and obligation" originate? How do you develop or learn virtues? We believe the answers to these questions begin with a self-evaluation of the reasons you want to become a counselor and are grounded in who you are as a person in terms of your values. These core values in relation to the counseling profession should be in line with the values of the counseling profession that generally uphold the notion of helping clients while not causing them harm.

To assist mental health counselors to espouse to the ideals of not causing intentional harm and promoting positive change in the client, a set of moral principles have been the basis of ethics in the counseling profession. The moral principles, also referred to as principle ethics, outlined by Kitchener (1984) and informed by Beauchamp and Childress (1979) have been established as the underlying foundation of counseling ethics and ethical decision making. They are outlined below in the order in which Kitchener presented them.

Autonomy

Autonomy constitutes the individual freedom of choice and action (Kitchener, 1984). An autonomous person has the liberty to act as long as he or she does not infringe on the rights of others. In a counselor-client relationship, this means that the client has a right to make decisions about his or her treatment without undue influence from the counselor. The counselor must fully inform the client to the best of his or her ability, and as long as the client has been given as much information as possible, he or she has the right to choose his or her own course of action. Additionally, the client has this right even though the counselor may think he or she is not acting in his or her own best interest. Kitchener stated that there are two restrictions on autonomy: when the client's actions infringe on another's freedom and when the client's level of competence is in question.

Non-Maleficence

The next moral principle addressed by Kitchener (1984) is the concept of non-maleficence. Non-maleficence is the well-known decree of "do no harm." Counselors, above all else, should not engage in behaviors that will knowingly cause harm to clients. Kitchener reported that not doing harm to a client is more important than benefitting them. In other words, it is more detrimental to clients to inflict harm on them than to provide services that do not benefit them. At least the client is left unchanged instead of in a state of further deterioration. The concern with non-maleficence is what exactly constitutes harm? Clients often experience some discomfort during counseling. This discomfort, however, is qualitatively different than the discomfort a client might have as a result of engaging in a trauma-based flooding experience, for example. There are two issues relevant here. First, the clinician and the client should evaluate whether the benefits outweigh the potential harm. Second, the matter of adequate informed consent, which will be addressed later in this chapter, is crucial.

Beneficence

Beneficence implies that we are charged to contribute to the welfare and well-being of our client(s). Kitchener (1984) posited that because a profession labels itself as a "helping profession," it has agreed to not only avoid doing harm to its client(s), but it has publicly stated that its responsibility is to act for the betterment of the client. What constitutes the betterment of the client is a gray area that can be challenged, yet incompetence on the part of the counselor is another matter.

Justice

Simply put, justice constitutes fairness and equal treatment for all clients. The basis of the premise of justice is that all people are equal. For example, clients may not be treated differently because of sex, sexual orientation, race, religion, or ability to pay for services. If a counselor has standard treatment protocols and procedures, he or she must offer those services and procedures to all of his or her clients without discrimination.

Fidelity

The final moral principle that Kitchener (1984) provided is that of fidelity, which "involves questions of faithfulness, promise keeping, and loyalty" (p. 51). Counselors are expected to be honest with their clients and to fulfill obligations promised to them. Again, detailed written and verbal informed consent is how the client is made aware of the counselor's ethical obligations in the counseling relationship.

Although Kitchener's (1984) five moral principles have been established as the foundation for ethics in the counseling profession, they may not be adequate in and of themselves. Along with autonomy, beneficence, and nonmaleficence, Jennings, Sovereign, Bottorff, Pederson Mussell, and Vye (2005) identified six additional ethical values that are present in individuals they identified as "ethical master therapists." These additional qualities include (a) relational connection, (b) competence, (c) humility, (d) professional growth, (f) openness to complexity and ambiguity, and (g) self-awareness. Hill (2004) also identified *moral sensitivity* (found in empathy and social role-taking skills) and *counselor as actor in ethical dramas* (utilizing wisdom and judgment) as important aspects in acting ethically. What is clear is that acting ethically requires the mental health counselor to possess a host of moral principles and personal characteristics.

Two final thoughts regarding moral principles are in order. The first has to do with the fact that "moral principles are neither absolute nor relative, but they are always ethically relevant and can be overturned only when there are stronger ethical obligations" (Kitchener, 1984, p. 52). In other words, all aspects of the context of the ethical dilemmas must be evaluated prior to determining which moral principle takes precedence over another.

Second, ethics and ethical dilemmas are socially constructed (Guterman & Rudes, 2008) and culturally based (Frame & Williams, 2005; Henriksen & Trusty, 2005; Kitchener, 1984; Pack-Brown, Thomas, & Seymour, 2008; Sadeghi, Fischer, & House, 2003; Watson, Herlihy, & Pierce, 2006). Guterman and Rudes postulated that like the *Diagnostic and Statistical Manual of Mental Disorders* (4th ed., text revision [*DSM-IV-TR*]; American Psychiatric

Association, 2000), the *ACA Code of Ethics* (American Counseling Association, 2005a) was created from a process that included a dialog among a group of people who came to an agreement regarding what the code should entail. In other words, "ethical codes are not to be understood as objective truths but, rather, as tentative and intersubjective guidelines that have been co-created by a community of stakeholders" (Guterman & Rudes, 2008, p. 138). Henriksen and Trusty (2005) stated that more recent ACA codes of ethics¸ although more "culturally egalitarian" than previous ones, remain laden with ideologies of the dominant culture. The 2005 *ACA Code of Ethics* has a focus on multiculturalism and aspirational values, yet it is important to recognize that the code is a living document that is ever changing. With these caveats and the above moral principles in mind and before we present an ethical decision-making model, we present an outline of the content of the *ACA Code of Ethics.*

THE ETHICAL CODES

As previously described, ethics are a set of moral principles to be followed by an individual or a group of people. Mental health counselors may be bound by one or more ethical codes depending on their professional affiliations and certifications. These ethical codes may include the *ACA Code of Ethics* (American Counseling Association, 2005a), the *American Mental Health Counselor Association (AMHCA) Code of Ethics* (American Mental Health Counselor, 2010), and the *National Board for Certified Counselor's (NBCC'S) Code of Ethics* (National Board for Certified Counselor, 2005). For the purpose of this discussion, the *ACA Code of Ethics* is featured.

The *ACA Code of Ethics* (American Counseling Association, 2005a) are divided into eight sections, including: (a) The Counseling Relationship; (b) Confidentiality, Privileged Communication, and Privacy; (c) Professional Responsibility; (d) Relationships with Other Professionals; (e) Evaluation, Assessment, and Interpretation; (f) Supervision, Training, and Teaching; (g) Research and Publication; and (h) Resolving Ethical Issues. The following is a brief outline of what each code entails, along with examples of information found in each section. Students are encouraged to refer to the ACA website (http://www.counseling.org) for a complete copy of the code.

The Counseling Relationship

The first section of the *ACA Code of Ethics* (American Counseling Association, 2005a) addresses all areas of the counseling relationship with emphasis on attention to multicultural awareness. Counselors are encouraged to understand diverse backgrounds as well as examine their own cultural identities and beliefs and how they affect the counseling relationship and process. In this section, the counseling relationship is explored from its inception to termination and beyond. Procedures on informed consent are outlined as well as the prohibition of sexual relationships with clients or their family members for five years after contact and how to terminate and refer a client.

Confidentiality, Privileged Communication, and Privacy

Next, confidentiality, privileged-communication, and privacy are discussed. The cornerstone of this area is the development of trust with clients. Diversity is again addressed with an emphasis on client rights. Examples of areas covered in the section include privacy of the client's information, confidentiality and limits of confidentiality, and disclosure of client information. How to properly store and dispose of client files is also outlined here.

Professional Responsibility

Professional responsibility is the focus of the next section. Areas covered in this portion of the code include communication with the public, non-discriminatory practices, involvement in professional associations, use of evidence-based practices, and counselor self-care. Mental health counselors are to practice within the scope of their training. Additionally, they are to be "accurate, honest, and objective in reporting their professional activities and judgments to appropriate third parties" (American Counseling Association, 2005a, p. 10). Third parties may include health insurance companies and the court.

Relationships with Other Professionals

After issues of professional responsibility are addressed, relationships with other professionals are covered. Three points stand out in this section of the code. To increase the quality of care provided to their client(s), counselors should foster positive relationships with colleagues, be well informed about other professionals both inside and outside the profession, and create working relationships with clear and open communication with those individuals. Consultation services are also included in this section.

Evaluation, Assessment, and Interpretation

Next, the evaluation, assessment, and interpretation of assessments are broached with again an emphasis on the client's "personal and cultural context" (American Counseling Association, 2005a, p. 11). Counselors are to develop and utilize assessments that are relevant to the client and his or her needs. These assessments are not to be used as a stand-alone intervention but as a component of counseling. If counselors are engaging in the practice of administrating assessment instruments, they must be well trained in all aspects of administration and interpretation of the results.

Supervision, Training, and Teaching

Following the focus on evaluation, assessment, and interpretation, there is a spotlight on supervision, training, and teaching. As with counselors and the counseling relationship, supervisors and educators are to strive to develop meaningful and respectful interactions with supervisees and students that have clear professional boundaries. The supervisor has an obligation to the counselor-in-training as well as the client for whom the counselor-in-training is providing mental health services.

Research and Publication

The next section of the code promotes good practice in research and publication in counseling. Counselors are encouraged to participate in research and publication and to support others' research. They are also charged with the task of avoiding bias and respecting "diversity in designing and implementing research programs" (American Counseling Association, 2005a, p. 16). Clinicians have an ethical obligation to research participants that ensures that participants are thoroughly informed about the potential risks and benefits to participating and that they are treated fairly.

Resolving Ethical Issues

The final section of the *ACA Code of Ethics* (American Counseling Association, 2005a) solidifies counselors promise to act professionally. This includes abiding by ethical guidelines as well as the legal system. Ponton and Duba (2009) see the *ACA Code of Ethics* as the profession's public acknowledgement "to act *pro bono public*–for the good of the public" (p. 117). This section of the code clearly articulates that promise.

The preceding outline of the *ACA Code of Ethics* (American Counseling Association, 2005a) was presented to provide you with a flavor of the content of the code. What is missing from the code is how the elements of the code should be taught and implemented in the field. Therefore, we now provide an ethical decision-making model and discuss its application.

AN ETHICAL DECISION-MAKING MODEL

There are many ethical decision-making models available to review (e.g., Cottone & Claus, 2000). All of these models offer steps and suggestions to the reader as to how to decide whether a situation or proposed behavior is ethical. For example, Von Hoose and Paradise (1979) discussed a decision-making model that focused on virtue ethics and encapsulated self-awareness, knowledge of ethics, and appropriate action. Gottlieb (1993) presented a decision-making model in which power, duration of relationship, and termination expectations are important and included a decision-making tree to help direct one toward ethical behavior. The model highlighted here was written by Forester-Miller and Davis (1996). Holly Forester-Miller and Thomas Davis, writing for the American Counseling Association, outlined an ethical decision-making model that was informed by previous works (i.e., Forester-Miller & Rubinstein, 1992; Haas & Malouf, 1989; Kitchener, 1984; Sileo & Kopala, 1993; Stadler, 1986; Von Hoose & Paradise, 1979) and focused on providing the mental health professional with a seven-step framework for implementing a logical plan of action when faced with an ethical dilemma. The goal of this section of the chapter is to present one of the many models available for the student of ethics to use in his or her pursuit of appropriate ethical decision making.

The seven steps in Forester-Miller and Davis' (1996) sequence should not be viewed as the only way to make ethical decisions but rather as a model or guide to follow to help you decide whether your proposed solution or behavior would be viewed by others as appropriate in a given situation. Although some might chafe at the notion of evaluating one's ethical decisions from a third-party perspective, this is really the crux of the matter. How would a third person, perhaps a lawyer or judge, a licensing board, or the American Counseling Association Ethics Committee, see your behavior? Would they see your choices as appropriate and within ethical guidelines? Because unethical behavior usually involves two or more people, the perception and expectations of those involved become important, even more so when one party in a relationship decides that the other has acted unethically. This then becomes a major issue for the counselor regardless of how the counselor's role is defined in a particular situation.

The ethical decision-making model proposed by Forester-Miller and Davis (1996) has seven steps:

1. identify the problem,
2. apply the *ACA Code of Ethics,*
3. determine the nature and dimensions of the dilemma,
4. generate potential course of action,

5. consider potential consequences of all options and choose a course of action,
6. evaluate the selected course of action, and
7. implement course of action (p. 13).

Briefly, the scenario for using this model would be when you feel uncomfortable with an aspect of your professional relationship with a client or when a client accuses you of unethical behavior it is time to see whether a problem exists. You need to try to see the situation outside yourself. How would others view the situation? If you decide that a problem exists, the second step is to consult the *ACA Code of Ethics* (American Counseling Association, 2005a) and identify which tenets are specifically involved in the situation. If in fact you see that perhaps a code or two might be viewed by others as questioning your behavior, you in fact have the potential for an ethical problem to exist. This necessitates a full review of your behavior. This is best accomplished by entering into a clearly defined consultation relationship with another counselor who will assist you in determining the breadth and scope of the possible unethical behavior. This is followed by generating several potential solutions. There are always more than two possible solutions, and, in this case, the generation of as many courses of action as possible is most helpful. Next is the review by you and your consultant of the possible outcomes of the various solutions and ultimately the best choice for a specific course of action. This preferred action needs to be thoughtfully reviewed. How will it be looked upon by a third party, and will this action cause new issues? The last step is implementing your course of action. This can be difficult because it might include an admission on your part of unethical behavior, the consequences of which could impact you greatly.

Engaging in sound ethical decision making is an important skill for everyone, but it is critical for anyone licensed or certified because to act unethically might have severe penalties attached to it. Using a model such as Forester-Miller and Davis' (1996) can help you to avoid mistakes and be a better counselor. You can utilize this ethical decision-making model to help you aspire to the moral principles outline by Kitchener (1984) presented earlier in the chapter: autonomy, non-maleficence, beneficence, justice, and fidelity. However, despite mental health counselors' best efforts, they are occasionally charged with committing ethical violations.

COMMITTING ETHICAL VIOLATIONS

Before we take a look at what happens when an ethical violation is reported, let us review the most common inquiries into ethical behavior. Sanabria and Freeman (2008) reported on the percentage of areas of inquiry to the ACA Ethics Committee during the time between July 2002 and June 2007. The breakdown of percentage of areas of reported inquiries are as follows:

> 47% to 52% of inquiries received were about confidentiality, 24% to 32% about counseling relationships; 10% to11% about professional responsibilities; 7% to 10% about relationships with other professionals; 1% to 1.5% about assessment; 3% to 5% about supervision, training, and teaching; and 0.2% to 1% about research. (p. 250)

Clearly, counselor education programs, entities that sponsor continuing education, and the ACA Ethics Committee need to devote more resources to educating and raising awareness of counselor behavior that leads to breach of ethics, especially in the areas of confidentiality, counseling relationships, and professional responsibilities.

So what happens when a counselor's ethical behavior is in question and that alleged behavior is subsequently reported to ACA? The *ACA Policies and Procedures for Processing Complaints of Ethical Violations* (American Counseling Association, 2005b) and The Layperson's Guide to Counselor Ethics (American Counseling Association, 1996) describes how a client should file an ethics complaint. The first step is that the individual making the complaint must request in writing verification as to whether the counselor was an ACA member at the time of the reported incident or is currently a member of ACA. The ACA Ethics Committee can only investigate charges of unethical behavior by individuals who currently belong or belonged to the association at the time of the alleged incident (American Counseling Association, 2005b). Once membership has been established, the ACA Ethics Committee sends out an ethics complaint form. If one of the committee members' co-chairs, after reviewing the complaint, determines that the complaint warrants investigating by the committee, additional information, if needed, is obtained from the complainant and the ACA member charged with violating the code. The ACA member being charged has the right to request a formal face-to-face hearing or a hearing by telephone. If the Ethics Committee finds that the ACA member did indeed commit an ethical violation, the committee may impose a plan of remediation, suspend the member, or impose expulsion from ACA membership. An appeal process is outlined in the *ACA Policies and Procedures for Processing Complaints of Ethical Violations* document.

As alluded to earlier, the finding of suspension or expulsion has serious consequences to the ACA member. The committee publishes these findings in the association's monthly magazine, *Counseling Today*. They also notify state counseling boards, any relevant ACA division(s), the National Board of Certified Counselors if a member, and ACA Insurance Trust (American

Counseling Association, 2005b). As you can see, having a charge of ethical misconduct found against you by the ACA Ethics Committee has a far-reaching impact on your career as a counselor. Consequently, it is important to engage in tasks that will help you to fully inform your client(s) of sound counseling practices. One such task is providing clients with a detailed written informed consent document.

THE PURPOSE AND NEED FOR INFORMED CONSENT

A written informed consent document or professional disclosure statement is paramount to providing the client with a clear understanding of the counseling relationship. The client with adequate information about all aspect of the counseling relationship can enter into that relationship with free will. Elements of the informed consent document should address sections of the *ACA Code of Ethics* (American Counseling Association, 2005a) that pertain to the counseling relationship and the services to be provided. The components of written informed consent should include, but are not limited to, the purpose of the document, qualifications and experience of the counselor, nature of counseling and services to be provided, risks and benefits of counseling, fees and insurance reimbursement, procedures for cancellations, how client records are safeguarded, confidentiality and its limits, crisis procedures, and referral process.

Informed consent is not only a written document but the client's right to agree to accept and continue to participate in counseling services. Therefore, informed consent should be addressed not only at the beginning of the counseling relationship but throughout with information regarding termination and beyond. Continued focus on the informed consent, both in writing and verbally, will help to reduce the possibility of you being accused or charged with an ethical violation(s).

CONCLUSION

In addition to a brief look at the *ACA Code of Ethics* (American Counseling Association, 2005a), the purpose and need for informed consent, and what happens to individuals who are charged with ethical violations, this chapter foremost addressed the nature of ethics and moral principles and ethical decision making in mental health counseling. Kitchener (1986) outlined four objectives for educating students in ethics:

- sensitize students to the ethical issues in the profession and to the consequences of their own actions,
- improve students' ability to reason about ethical actions,
- develop in students the moral responsibility and ego strength to act in ethical ways, and
- teach students tolerance of ambiguity in ethical decision making (p. 308).

We do not believe that these objectives should be discarded on graduation from a counseling program. Instead, mental health counselors should develop an action plan on how to continue to foster the development of ethical decision making and behavior throughout their careers.

There are a number of post-graduation tasks in which counselors can engage to help them continue to develop good ethical practices. First, counselors should attend continuing education seminars on the current trends in ethics. Many state licensing boards now mandate that counselors attend a certain number of continuing education units per year on ethics. Second, counselors should follow sound informed consent practices and maintain formal plans for supervision (Cobia & Boes, 2000). In addition, Gottlieb (2006) outlined a step-by-step plan with recommendations on how to seek and provide peer ethics consultation. Third, counselors can access such reading as *The ACA Ethical Standards Casebook* (Herlihy & Corey, 2006) and Ethics Desk Reference for Counselors (Barnett & Johnson, 2010). The fourth and final point to be made here is that clinicians should continue to foster self-awareness in themselves and their practice that includes continued reflection on what it means to be a mental health counselor.

CASE STUDY

You are a mental health professional in private practice. You have been providing individual counseling services to Jane, a 42-year-old married female, for nearly two months. Your counseling sessions have addressed issues of child sexual, mental, and physical abuse. Jane also talked about having trouble with authority figures (i.e., parents, older brother, and her priest), in that it is difficult for her to not be overly influenced by them. She reported often following their suggestions even though she felt uncomfortable. During Jane's seventh counseling session, she brings to your attention that her past counselor submitted insurance claims to her insurance company for sessions that she did not attend. Jane brings some documents out of her purse while talking and then quickly places them back in her purse. You think to yourself that here is yet another authority figure who Jane cannot stand up to, and the actions of her previous counselor could constitute insurance fraud. You attempt to engage in conversation with Jane about the previous counselor's behavior. Jane states that she in no way wants to do anything about the previous counselor's actions, stating she could never stand up to her and fears that she will get in trouble from the insurance company and even lose her coverage. Jane is adamant about not doing anything about what happened and begs you to do the same.

Consider the following:

1. Which principle ethics described earlier in this chapter takes precedence in this scenario?
2. Which ethical codes found in the *ACA Code of Ethics* (American Counseling Association, 2005a) are pertinent to this dilemma?
3. How would you apply Forester-Miller and Davis' (1996) ethical decision-making model to this scenario?

REFERENCES

American Counseling Association. (2005a). *ACA code of ethics.* Alexandria: VA: Author.

American Counseling Association. (2005b). *ACA policies and procedures for processing complaints of ethical violations.* Retrieved from http://www.counseling.org/Resources/CodeOfEthics/TP/Home/CT2.aspx

American Counseling Association. (1999). *The laypersons' guide to counselor ethics.* Retrieved from http://www.counseling.org/Resources/CodeOfEthics/TP/Home/CT2.aspx

American Mental Health Counselor Association. (2010). *American mental health counselor association code of ethics.* Retrieved from https://www.amhca.org/assets/content/AMHCACodeOfEthics2010Final.pdf

American Psychiatric Association. (2000). *Diagnostic and statistical manual of mental disorders* (4th ed., text revision). Washington, DC: Author.

Barnett, J. E., & Johnson, W. B. (2010). *Ethics desk reference for counselors.* Alexandria, VA: American Counseling Association.

Beauchamp, T. L., & Childress, J. F. (1979). *Principles of biomedical ethics.* Oxford: Oxford University Press.

Cobia, D. C., & Boes, S. R. (2000). Professional disclosure statements and formal plans for supervision: Two strategies for minimizing the risk of ethical conflicts in post-master's supervision. *Journal of Counseling & Development, 78,* 293–293.

Corey, G., Corey, M. S., & Callanan, P. (1998). *Issues and ethics in the helping professions.* Pacific Grove, CA: Brooks/Cole.

Cottone, R. R., & Claus, R. E. (2000). Ethical decision-making models: A review of the literature. *Journal of Counseling & Development, 78,* 275–283.

Forester-Miller, H., & Davis, T. (1996). *A practitioner's guide to ethical decision making.* Retrieved from http://www.counseling.org/Resources/CodeOfEthics/TP/Home/CT2.aspx

Forester-Miller, H., & Rubinstein, R. L. (1992), Group counseling: Ethics and professional issues. In D. Capuzzi & D. R. Gross (Eds.), *Introduction to group counseling* (pp. 307–323). Denver, CO: Love Publishing.

Frame, M. W., & Williams, C. B. (2005). A model of ethical decision-making from a multicultural perspective. *Counseling and Values, 49,* 165–1179.

Gottlieb, M. C. (1993). Avoiding exploitive dual relationships: A decision-making model. *Psychotherapy, 30*(1), 41–48.

Gottlieb, M., C. (2006). A template for peer ethics consultation. *Ethics & Behavior, 16*(2), 151–162.

Guterman, J. T., & Rudes, J. (2008). Social construction and ethics: Implications for counseling. *Counseling and Values, 52,* 136–144.

Haas, L. J., & Malouf, J. L. (1989). *Keeping up the good work: A practitioner's guide to mental health ethics.* Sarasota, FL: Professional Resource Exchange.

Henriksen, R. C., & Trusty, J. (2005). Ethics and values as major factors related to multicultural aspects of counselor preparation. *Counseling and Values, 49,* 180–192.

Herlihy, B., & Corey, G. (2006). *The ACA ethical standards casebook.* Alexandria, VA: American Counseling Association.

Hill, A. L. (2004). Ethical analysis in counseling: A case for narrative ethics, moral visions, and virtue ethics. *Counseling and Values, 48,* 131–148.

Jennings, L., Sovereign, A., Bottorff, N., Pederson Mussell, M., & Vye, C. (2005). Nine ethical values of master therapists. *Journal of Mental Health Counseling, 27*(1), 32–47.

Kitchener, K. S. (1984). Intuition, critical evaluation and ethical principles: The foundation for ethical decisions in counseling psychology. *The Counseling Psychologist,* 12(3), 43–55.

Kitchener, K. S. (1986). Teaching applied ethics in counselor education: An integration of psychological processes and philosophical analysis. *Journal of Counseling and Development, 64,* 306–310.

Merriam-Webster. (2010). *Ethics.* Retrieved from http://www.merriam-webster.com/dictionary/ethics

National Board for Certified Counselors. (2005). *NBCC's code of ethics.* Retrieved from http://www.nbcc.org/AssetManagerFiles/ethics/nbcc-codeofethics.pdf

Pack-Brown, S. P., Thomas, T. L., & Seymour, J. M. (2008). Infusing professional ethics into counselor education programs: A multicultural/social justice perspective. *Journal of Counseling & Development, 86,* 296–302.

Ponton, R. F., & Duba, J. D. (2009). The ACA code of ethics: Articulating counseling's professional covenant. *Journal of Counseling & Development, 87,* 117–121.

Remley, T. P., & Herlihy, B. (2001). *Ethical, legal, and professional issues in counseling.* Upper Saddle River, NJ: Merrill Prentice-Hall.

Rowley, W. J., & MacDonald, D. (2001). Counseling and the law: A cross-cultural perspective. *Journal of Counseling & Development, 79,* 422–429.

Sadeghi, M., Fischer, J. M., & House, S. G. (2003). Ethical dilemmas in multicultural counseling. *Multicultural Counseling and Development, 31,* 179–191.

Sanabria, S., & Freeman, L. T. (2008). Report of the ACA ethics committee: 2006–2007. *Journal of Counseling & Development, 86,* 249–252.

Sileo, F., & Kopala, M. (1993). An A-B-C-D-E worksheet for promoting beneficence when considering ethical issues. *Counseling and Values, 37,* 89–95.

Stadler, H. A. (1986). Making hard choices: Clarifying controversial ethical issues. *Counseling & Human Development, 19,* 1–10.

Von Hoose, W. H., & Paradise, L. V. (1979). *Ethics in counseling and psychotherapy: Perspectives in issues and decision-making.* Cranston, RI: Carroll Press.

Watson, Z. E. P., Herlihy, B. R., & Pierce, L. A. (2006). Forging the link between multicultural competence and ethical counseling practice: A historical perspective. *Counseling and Values, 50,* 99–107.

Chapter 19

MENTAL HEALTH COUNSELOR PREPARATION

CASEY A. BARRIO MINTON

INTRODUCTION

In late 2009, Governor Arnold Schwarzenegger signed California Senate Bill 788 into law, making California the 50th state to approve legislation allowing for independent practice of Professional Counselors. Today, you might be a Licensed Professional Counselor (LPC) in Alabama, Alaska, Arizona, Arkansas (or 20 other states); a Licensed Professional Clinical Counselor (LPCC) in California or Kentucky; a Licensed Mental Health Counselor (LMHC) in New York or Washington; or an LCPC, LCMHC, LPCMH, LIMHP, LMHP, LCMHC, or LPC-MHSP elsewhere (Lum, 2010). In addition to unique naming, each state determines the "Three Es": **e**ducational, **e**xperiential, and **e**xamination requirements for counselor licensure.

States are fairly well divided between whether they require 48 or 60 graduate semester hours in counseling or a related field for licensure, and some states require different educational experiences for different "tiers" of counselors (Lum, 2010). As of 2009, 22 states require completion of one's degree in a program that is either accredited by the Council for Accreditation of Counseling and Related Educational Programs (CACREP) or "equivalent" to CACREP. Some states also require completion of additional specialty coursework in areas such as substance abuse, human sexuality, diagnosis, or psychopharmacology. Although examinations are determined by the state, 42 states require the National Counselor Examination (NCE) and/or the National Clinical Mental Health Counselor Examination (NCMHCE) for licensure, both standardized examinations offered by the National Board for Certified Counselors (NBCC). CACREP, the NCE, and the NCMHCE are key players in licensure, and thus preparation, of Mental Health Counselors (MHCs). Thus, we review educational requirements for each before focusing on emerging trends in MHC preparation.

CACREP

As the counseling profession developed in the 1960s and 1970s, counselor educators began coming together to establish standards for counselor preparation. As a result, CACREP was founded in 1981. Its mission is "to promote the professional competence of counseling and related practitioners through the development of preparation standards; the encouragement of excellence in program development; and the accreditation of professional preparation programs" (Council for the Accreditation of Counseling and Related Educational Programs, 2009, p. 20). This mission is accomplished through systematic development of standards regarding MHC learning environment, curriculum, and field experiences. To be accredited, programs must also engage in rigorous self-study processes, undergo external peer review, and demonstrate "continuous systematic program evaluation" for quality assurance purposes.

Until 2009, CACREP accredited both 48-hour Community Counseling programs and 60-hour MHC programs. In 2009, CACREP merged the two programs into Clinical Mental Health Counseling, a 60-credit-hour program that includes core coursework and experiences related to (a) professional orientation and ethical practice, (b) social and cultural diversity, (c) human growth and development, (d) career development, (e) helping relationships, (f) group work, (g) assessment, and (h) research and program evaluation. In addition, students complete at least 100 hours of practicum and 600 hours of internship in closely supervised counseling settings and demonstrate attainment of knowledge, skills, and practices required for success as an MHC in six main areas: (a) foundations; (b) counseling, prevention, and intervention; (c) diversity and advocacy; (d) assessment; (e) research and evaluation; and (f) diagnosis. You can review *2009 CACREP Standards* and identify accredited programs by visiting www.cacrep.org.

NBCC

Established in 1982, the NBCC "is the nation's premier professional certification board devoted to credentialing counselors who meet standards for the general and specialty practices of professional counseling" (National Board for Certified Counselors, 2010). NBCC is perhaps best known for promoting counseling as a profession and developing a series of standardized examinations to certify counselors nationally. In particular, the National Counselor Examination (NCE) is a multiple-choice examination to "assess knowledge, skills, and abilities viewed as important for providing effective counseling services" (National Board for Certified Counselors, 2010) and is required for licensure in many states. The content areas covered on the NCE mirror the eight core areas required by CACREP, and the examination encompasses five work behaviors required of professional counselors: (a) fundamentals of counseling, (b) assessment and career counseling, (c) group counseling, (d) programmatic and clinical intervention, and (e) professional practice issues.

In contrast to the NCE, the NCMHCE is an applied examination in which test takers respond to a series of simulated cases that assess clinical problem-solving ability, including identifying, analyzing, diagnosing, and treating clinical issues (National Board for Certified Counselors, 2010). Thus, the focus of the applied examination is on skills best captured within the skills and practices requirements of students who pursue a CACREP-accredited program in Clinical Mental Health Counseling. Altogether, 42 states require a passing score on the NCE and/or NCMHCE as part of the licensure process.

Although only mentioned in licensure requirements for three states, NBCC also offers the Certified Clinical Mental Health Counselor (CCMHC) credential. The CCMHC requires successful attainment of the NCC, 60 credit hours of coursework including abnormal psychology and psychopathology, additional clinical experiences, completion of the Examination of Clinical Counseling Practice (ECCP) or NCMHCE, and submission of a recorded clinical counseling session. Individuals who have completed fewer than 60 hours of coursework and have completed coursework in all required areas may apply additional coursework and experience toward the requirements (National Board for Certified Counselors, 2010).

CACREP, NBCC, AND MHC PREPARATION

As CACREP approached its 20th birthday, Schmidt (1999) conducted a review of articles and studies regarding CACREP and CACREP-accredited programs. He concluded that most published reviews and discussions regarding CACREP were favorable; however, there was no evidence that counselors from CACREP-accredited programs were more competent or marketable than those from non-accredited programs. Although Adams

(2006) found that test takers from CACREP-accredited programs scored higher on the NCE than those from non-accredited programs, we have not made much progress regarding research in this area over the last decade. Further, Herrick and Barlieb (2006) noted that accreditation is a worthy goal but warned that external factors may prohibit some high-quality programs from seeking accreditation. Thus, accreditation alone cannot be used as an indicator of quality preparation. Nonetheless, accreditation standards reflect the pulse of the profession.

The most recent CACREP *Standards* (2009) include significant shifts that reflect necessary changes and innovations for preparing MHCs. In particular, new core and specialty standards related to Clinical Mental Health Counseling include enhanced attention to diversity and advocacy counseling; standards for preparing for and responding to crises, disasters, and trauma; increased integration of wellness, optimal development, and resilience; and enhanced attention to accountability and consumption of research. In the remainder of the chapter, we explore how changes in the CACREP *Standards* reflect necessary innovations in MHC preparation.

MULTICULTURALISM, DIVERSITY, AND ADVOCACY

Our world is changing. More than 50% of children will be "minorities" by 2023, and "minorities" will comprise a majority of all U.S. residents by 2042 (U.S. Census Bureau, 2008). By 2050, the proportion of U.S. residents who are Hispanic or Asian will double (from 15% to 30% and 5% to 9%, respectively), and the proportion of those identifying as two or more races will more than triple. Meanwhile, the percentage of U.S. residents who identify as Black will remain steady (14% to 15%), and the percentage who identify as White alone will decrease from 66% to 46%. In addition, the number of U.S. residents who are 65 and older will more than double by 2050.

Of course, elements of difference are not always as visible as race, ethnicity, gender, or age. Our physical abilities, sexual/affectional orientation, religious/spiritual beliefs, and socioeconomic status impact the ways in which we experience and are experienced by the world in profound ways (Johnson, 2006). In 2005, 54.4 million (18.7%) people in the United States had a disability: 11.9% had ambulatory difficulties; 7.0% had difficulty in cognitive, mental, or emotional functioning; and 6.4% had limitations in seeing, hearing, or speaking (Brault, 2008). Although stigma, social climate, and lack of inclusion in Census data make it nearly impossible to estimate how many people identify as gay, lesbian, bisexual, or questioning, widely publicized debates regarding rights to marriage and adoption and consistent evidence of harassment, discrimination, and hate crimes make attention to issues of sexual diversity critical for counselors. Similarly, the United States is a decidedly Christian and spiritual nation, with 76% of American adults identifying as Christian, 70% believing in a personal God, and 12% believing in a higher power (Kosmin & Keysar, 2009). Understanding issues of spirituality and religion will be important to many in the United States, especially the small minority of individuals who are Jewish (1.2%), agnostic (0.9%), atheist (0.7%), Muslim (0.6%), and adhere to other religions (2.1%). Finally, 13.2% of all U.S. residents and 19.0% of children lived in poverty in 2008, with poverty rates among Black and Hispanic households nearly double that of the national average and poverty rates for female-headed single-parent households (DeNavas-Walt, Proctor, & Smith, 2009) and individuals with severe disabilities (Brault) at more than double. Clearly, multicultural competencies will be vital to your success as a MHC.

CURRICULAR STANDARDS

Programs consistent with CACREP *Standards* include "studies that provide an understanding of the cultural context of relationships, issues, and trends in a multicultural society" (2009, p. 90). More specifically, these curricula include

> a. multicultural and pluralistic trends, including characteristics and concerns within and among diverse groups nationally and internationally;
> b. attitudes, beliefs, understandings, and acculturative experiences, including specific experiential learning activities designed to foster students' understanding of self and culturally diverse clients;
> c. theories of multicultural counseling, identity development, and social justice;
> d. individual, couple, family, group, and community strategies for working with and advocating for diverse populations, including multicultural competencies;
> e. counselors' roles in developing cultural self-awareness, promoting cultural social justice, advocacy and conflict resolution, and other culturally supported behaviors that promote optimal wellness and growth of the human spirit, mind, or body; and
> f. counselors' roles in eliminating biases, prejudices, and processes of intentional and unintentional oppression and discrimination. (pp. 90–91)

The 2009 CACREP *Standards* require that students understand how providing a wide a range of services can "promote mental health in a multicultural society" (p. 110) and understand current literature about counseling specific diverse populations. New MHCs must be able to conceptualize how living in a multicultural society affects clients in a way that goes beyond simple understanding of cultural characteristics and beliefs to an understanding of "the effects of racism, discrimination, sexism, power, privilege, and oppression" on counselors and clients alike (p. 111). The curriculum must include attention to "advocacy processes needed to address institutional and social barriers" (p. 90), and MHCs must be able to advocate for clients on local, state, and national levels. Perhaps most important, preparation programs must be able to demonstrate how MHCs apply multicultural counseling competencies across counseling and related tasks, modify counseling interventions to make them culturally sensitive, and advocate for resources and policies that are responsive to their clients' needs.

COMPETENCY STATEMENTS

Known as the fourth force in counseling (behind psychoanalysis, behaviorism, and humanism), the multicultural counseling movement began along with the civil rights movement and has been in development for more than 40 years (Arredondo, Tovar-Blank, & Parham, 2008). As you may have learned in Chapter 6, counselor educators have many resources to prepare MHCs to be culturally skilled. In particular, the multicultural counseling competencies (Sue, Arredondo, & McDavis, 1992) specify the ways in which successful counselors develop knowledge, awareness, and skills related to our own worldviews (including our biases and assumptions), clients' worldviews, and culturally appropriate interventions. Arredondo et al. (1996) also provided MHCs and counselor educators additional resources when they operationalized the multicultural counseling competencies. These competencies are endorsed by the American Counseling Association (ACA), incorporated throughout the ACA's *Code of Ethics* (2005), and required by the CACREP *Standards* (2009).

Counselor educators may draw from a number of other more specific competency documents when helping MHCs to develop knowledge, skill, and awareness. For example, Logan and Barret (2005) worked with leaders of the Association for Lesbian, Gay, and Bisexual Issues in Counseling (now ALGBTIC) to present a series of competencies for working with sexual minority clients that follow the CACREP core areas. They urged counselor educators to integrate attention to sexual orientation throughout the curriculum. The Association for Spiritual, Ethical, and Religious Values in Counseling (2009) identified 14 competencies for addressing spiritual and religious values in counseling within six areas: culture and worldview, counselor self-awareness, human and spiritual development, communication, assessment, and diagnosis and treatment. Counselor educators may use these competencies to help MHCs support clients in spiritual growth and coping.

Recently, researchers have discovered strong evidence connecting social injustice to mental health issues, meaning that "counselors must adjust their roles and responsibilities to include activities that foster a socially just world" (Chang, 2010, p. 1). Social justice counseling "represents a unique and multifaceted approach to mental health care in which counselors strive to promote human development and the common good by addressing issues related to both individual and distributed justice" (Crethar, Rivera, & Nash, 2008, p. 270). Accordingly, some counselors are beginning to call social justice counseling the "fifth force" of counseling. Counselor educators may use the ACA advocacy competencies (Lewis, Arnold, House, & Toporek, 2002) to help MHCs develop the skills to influence necessary changes to environments and help clients develop a sense of personal power (Toporek, Lewis, & Crethar, 2009). The advocacy competencies involve either "acting with" or "acting on behalf" and take place at the client, community, or public level. Thus, the competencies include a total of six domains: client/student empowerment, client/student advocacy, community collaboration, systems advocacy, public information, and social/political advocacy.

Crethar et al. (2008) provided a history of attention to social-environmental changes in counseling and suggested that multicultural, feminist, and social justice counseling paradigms have common threads that united them: Among other things, all address concepts of privilege and unintentional injustice and focus on empowerment and advocacy processes. Further, multicultural and social justice are ethical issues because we may cause unintentional harm when we use culturally biased theories and interventions with diverse clients (Pack-Brown, Thomas, & Seymour, 2008). Thus, MHC preparation programs must provide opportunities for multicultural self-exploration and awareness, development of conceptualization skills inclusive of social justice and multiculturalism, and building of culturally appropriate intervention skills. In the following section, we examine some challenges and resources that counselor educators may use to help MHCs develop multicultural and social justice advocacy competencies.

Curricular Innovation

Despite the fact that most people will whole-heartedly endorse the concept of equality, justice, and a culturally embracing world, the journey toward multicultural counseling competency is difficult. Many of us have been taught to fear or pretend not to see differences, culture, or privilege. We might not understand what culture is, and we might even think that culture is simply something other people have. Perhaps most important, we might not grasp the degree to which our cultural identities and experiences, including privilege, influence our lives (Arredondo et al., 2008). You are not alone if simply reading this paragraph leaves you feeling defensive, anxious, or angry. Johnson (2006) says, "We can't talk about it if we can't use the words" (p. 9) and he argues that we need to get past negative emotional reactions to words such as *privilege, racism,* and *oppression* to have honest and open conversations about cultural issues and social problems. Although necessary, these "difficult dialogues" upset our status quo and may lead us to develop creative strategies for managing emotional responses without truly exploring the meaning of the response (Watt et al., 2009).

Counselor educators have conducted a number of studies regarding the characteristics and experiences needed to develop multicultural counseling competencies. Although most counseling programs offer one or two courses specific to multicultural issues, programs are now working to move multicultural counselor education from periphery to core so that multiculturalism permeates the curriculum just as cultural issues permeate our lives (Stadler, Suh, Cobia, Middleton, & Carney, 2006). This movement is consistent with findings by Dickson and Jepsen (2007) that integration of multicultural issues throughout programs, in supervision, and in recruitment efforts lead to stronger multicultural competencies in counseling students. Similarly, Vereen, Hill, and McNeal (2008) studied curricular, practical, and experiential exercises related to multicultural counseling and found that seeing more non-White clients and participating in clinical supervision regarding multicultural issues predicted higher levels of multicultural competence. It seems as if being in environments where multicultural issues are encountered and lived is key for developing multicultural competencies.

Counselor educators rely on a variety of instructional methods when fostering multicultural competencies: traditional strategies (e.g., lectures, readings), exposure strategies (e.g., affective experiences, connections to minority group members), and participatory strategies (e.g., active participation, introspection, and experiencing) (Dickson & Jepsen, 2007). Many experts recommend a multifaceted approach to counselor education, and Council for the Accreditation of Counseling and Related Educational Programs (2009) requires that programs include experiential exercises to help students develop multicultural awareness of self and others. These exercises may include things such as journaling, growth groups, role plays, service learning activities, investigation of one's own cultural heritage, and guided imagery exercises. You might be asked to watch specialized instructional videos of others exploring their cultural experiences (e.g., *The Color of Fear*), reflect on intense popular cultural videos such as *Crash* or *Boys Don't Cry,* interview others about their cultural experiences, put yourself in culturally unfamiliar situations, or take some sort of social action.

Research regarding the effectiveness of participatory strategies for developing multicultural competence is promising. In one study, students who engaged in personal growth groups as part of multicultural course requirements made greater gains in ethnic identity development than those who did not (Rowell & Benshoff, 2008). Similarly, students who participated in a specialized role-play experience that helped them to understand cultural perspectives showed positive, sustained increases in multicultural counseling competency compared with when they simply participated in traditional classroom strategies (Seto, Young, Becker, & Kiselica, 2006).

As counselor education continues to develop, we must continue asking difficult questions. What instructional exercises are most effective for developing cultural self-awareness and sensitivity? Does participation in these exercises result in changes in counselor behaviors? Do these changes result in better, more effective services for clients? Do these changes result in healthier communities overall? As the amount of information available to us grows, how do we decide what to include or exclude?

CRISIS, DISASTER, AND TRAUMA

If you are interested in becoming a MHC, you are probably well aware of the potential impact of crisis, disaster, and trauma on our lives. You have likely experienced at least one crisis in your personal life, and your healing process may have inspired you to become an MHC. Over the past decade, many of us have followed crises and disasters as they unfolded on television and the Internet. You may remember watching students and teachers flee Columbine High School after two students killed 13 and wounded 21 before taking their own lives. You likely know exactly where you were when the World Trade Center and Pentagon were attacked by terrorists on September 11, 2001. Perhaps you watched as stranded survivors of 2005 Hurricane Katrina pled for help from the Superdome Convention Center and along rooftops and frantically searched to reunite with loved ones. You may have participated in discussions about mental health care for college students following the 2007 Virginia Tech Massacre, in which a student who had a history of mental illness killed 32 and wounded many others before taking his own life. Images of the 2010 earthquake in Haiti that killed (at last count) nearly one quarter of a million, injured many more, and left still more homeless (CBS/AP, 2010) are likely still fresh in your mind. In some of these tragedies, the public questioned whether counselors could have prevented such heartache; in nearly all of them, the public looked to MHCs for answers, leadership, and support.

Although we are well aware of large-scale traumatic events and disasters, local crises are also a part of our everyday experiences. We see accounts of the devastating car accident, house fire, or bullying incident on the daily news, and we may relive traumatic events caught on video or via Internet services. Unfortunately, many in the United States may be vulnerable to crisis. A national study of high school students indicated that 18.0% of students had carried a weapon on a least one day during the previous month, and 10.5% of students had driven while under the influence of alcohol in the past month (Eaton et al., 2008). In the past year, 28.5% "had felt so sad or hopeless almost every day for 2 weeks in a row that they stopped doing some usual activities," 14.5% had seriously considered suicide, and 6.9% had attempted suicide (p. 9). Similarly, adults reported an average of 3.4 mentally unhealthy days per month, and 10.3% reported frequent (14+ days per month) mental distress (Centers for Disease Control, 2010). Among adults, 17.6% of women and 3.0% of men had been victims of completed or attempted rape, and 22.1% of women and 7.4% of men experienced intimate partner violence. Clearly, counselors must be prepared to respond to crises, disasters, and traumatic events that affect individuals, families, and communities.

CURRICULAR STANDARDS

The 2001 CACREP *Standards* included only one mention of crisis intervention and did not specifically mention crisis, disaster, trauma-causing events, or the need for suicide assessment and management skills. Perhaps because of the well-publicized crises and disasters outlined above, the 2009 CACREP *Standards* require curricular experiences that help MHCs understand the "effects of crises, disasters, and other trauma-causing events on persons of all ages" (p. 91), "crisis intervention and suicide prevention models, including the use of psychological first aid strategies" (p. 92), and "counselors' roles and responsibilities as members of an interdisciplinary emergency management response team during a local, regional, or national crisis, disaster or other trauma-causing event" (p. 90). MHCs must demonstrate that they understand the impact of crisis, disasters, and other trauma-causing events, the operation of an emergency management system, principles of crisis intervention, and appropriate use of diagnosis during a crisis, disaster, or other trauma-causing event. Further, MHCs must be able to assess and manage suicide risk and differentiate "between diagnosis and developmentally appropriate reactions during crises, disasters, and other trauma-causing events" (p. 114).

CURRICULAR INNOVATION

These new standards reflect the need for an important change in MHC preparation. Although few published studies have included MHCs, studies of school counselors have indicated that most do not feel prepared to address crises (Allen et al., 2002; Wachter, 2006). More recently, Wachter Morris and Barrio Minton (2010) surveyed a national sample of new professional counselors and found that participants engaged in fewer than two class periods of preparation for crisis during their master's programs, and more than one third (36.3%) of participants had no training in crisis preparation! Participants noted that they received no or minimal preparation for most crisis-related topics, with nearly three quarters of counselors receiving "no" or "minimal" preparation related to crisis theory and disaster. New counselors reported the best preparation for ethical issues and suicide assessment, but less than half rated their preparation as "good" or "excellent." Despite this lack of attention, 86.5% of new counselors used basic crisis intervention skills and 82.9% worked with a suicidal client at least once during their field experiences; most participants reported frequent use of crisis intervention skills. The new counselors reported the least amount of confidence in their skills for responding to community-level disasters, administering psychological first aid, and participating on an interdisciplinary crisis team. These findings are consistent with reports that only about one half of CACREP-accredited master's programs even offered courses in crisis intervention; when offered, the crisis courses rarely addressed developmental impact of crisis and disaster or addressed disaster (Barrio Minton & Pease-Carter, in press).

In the coming years, curricular innovations in MHC preparation will include sustained attention to the impacts of crisis, disaster, and trauma; crisis intervention skills; and skills for supervising counselors who respond to crises, disaster, and trauma. Many counselor educators will need to seek continuing education to develop knowledge and skills needed to prepare new MHCs in these areas. MHCs and educators alike may organize activities according to the "preparation, action, recovery" framework presented by McAdams and Keener (2008). In particular, McAdams and Keener suggest that pre-crisis preparation includes acquiring accurate information, assessing client risk, learning and practicing crisis procedures, and clarifying personal-professional perspectives. During the pre-crisis phase, counselors must be aware of their own limits, limits of the counseling process, influence of personal bias, and need for professional support. During a crisis, the counselor's primary priority is to ensure safety. To do this, counselors may shift priorities to address the crisis and should work to adhere to protocol while maintaining flexibility. During a crisis, counselors must be aware of professional territoriality, the potential for intellectual-emotional fusion, their performance anxiety, and their potential for tunnel vision. During the post-crisis recovery phase, counselors triage, address loss, facilitate reinvestment, and promote change. We must be aware of inclinations to return to pre-crisis functioning too quickly, understand the potential of clients to deny the significance of the crisis, manage fears of intrusion with clients' need for connection, and attend to our own self-care. Be sure to read Chapters 13 and 14 carefully to learn more about MHC skills for responding to crisis and trauma.

Perhaps the largest area of curricular change will be on incorporation of Psychological First Aid (PFA) and understanding of disaster mental health needs into the counseling curriculum. PFA is an evidence-based approach for helping individuals and groups to respond to disaster, and it works by helping survivors maximize variables associated with positive recovery from disaster: social support, access to resources, and coping skills (Brymer et al., 2006). Within this interdisciplinary approach, the PFA practitioner engages in core actions such as engaging with survivors, assessing for safety and comfort, providing stabilization, and gathering information regarding needs and concerns. Then the PFA practitioner connects the survivor with practical assistance, social supports, or information on coping. Thankfully, many counselors and counselor educators seek training and resources from services such as SAMHSA's Disaster Technical Assistance Center (http://mentalhealth.samhsa.gov/dtac/default.asp), the National Center for PTSD (www.ptsd.va.gov), and the American Red Cross (www.redcross.org).

Curricular innovations will also include attention to provision of supervision and support related to crisis, disaster, and trauma. In recognition of the reality that few school counselors participate in post-graduate supervision, Wachter, Barrio Minton, and Clemens (2008) proposed P-SAEF, a peer supervision model in which school counselors help each other to prepare and respond to crises. P-SAEF stands for preparation and training, safety of client, affective support, evaluation and feedback, and follow-up planning. MHCs might adopt this model as a way of facilitating necessary continuing education and support related to crisis. In recognition of the pervasiveness of crisis, Sommer (2008) warned that many counselors are at risk for vicarious traumatization, a process wherein the counselor begins to experience similar physical and emotional symptoms as the client. Trauma-sensitive supervision helps counselors to engage in self-care and may include strategies such as guided imagery, breathwork, and reflective reading.

In the coming years, counselor educators will begin to address many important questions related to crisis, disaster, and trauma. Have we addressed these areas sufficiently in our curriculum? Do MHCs have the skills to respond to the daily crises (e.g., abuse, assault, suicide) *and* the large-scale disasters they encounter? What methods are most effective for teaching crisis-specific skills? Do MHCs who engage in preparation activities perform more effectively when faced with client crises?

WELLNESS AND OPTIMAL DEVELOPMENT

If you have made it this far in the textbook, you are likely quite dedicated to becoming an MHC. Hopefully, you decided to become a MHC because you believe in the power of a holistic approach to human growth, development, and wellness. Consider for a moment this 1989 resolution of the American Association for Counseling and Development (now ACA) that lead Myers and Sweeney (2008) to proclaim that wellness is "*the* paradigm for counseling" (p. 482):

> WHEREAS, optimum physical, intellectual, social, occupational, emotional, and spiritual development are worthy goals for all individuals within our society; and
> WHEREAS, research in virtually every discipline concerned with human development supports the benefits of wellness for both longevity and quality of life over the life span; and
> WHEREAS, the AACD [ACA] membership subscribe to values which promote optimum health and wellness;
> THEREFORE BE IT RESOLVED that the Governing Council of AACD [ACA] declare a position for the profession as advocates for policies and programs in all segments of our society which promote and support optimum health and wellness; and
> BE IT FURTHER RESOLVED that AACD [ACA] support the counseling professions' position as an advocate toward a goal of optimum health and wellness within our society.

This dedication to wellness is reflected in the *ACA Code of Ethics* (2005) Section C, which says that "counselors engage in self-care activities to maintain and promote their emotional, physical, mental, and spiritual well-being to best meet their professional responsibilities" (p. 9) and further specify expectations for monitoring effectiveness and impairment.

Wellness is defined as "a way of life oriented toward optimal health and well-being in which body, mind, and spirit are integrated by the individual to live more fully within the human and natural community" (Myers, Sweeney, & Witmer, 2000, p. 251). Hopefully, you are well aware of how these aspects influence our overall physical and emotional well-being. Unfortunately, the United States is quite the unhealthy country. Only 61% of adults reported excellent or very good health, only 26% engaged in vigorous activity three or more times per week, 59% *never* engaged in 10 minutes or more of vigorous leisure-time activity, 35% were overweight, and 27% were obese (Pleis, Lucas, & Ward, 2009). In addition to the experiences noted in the previous section, 12% experienced sadness, 17% experienced nervousness, and 19% experienced restlessness for all, most, or some of the month prior to the study. In each case, wellness indicators were worse for non-Hispanic Whites, individuals with lower levels of education, and people who lived in poverty.

Sadly, youth experience similar wellness threats as adults. In addition to the emotional and social concerns we reviewed in the last section, only 21.4% met FDA recommendations for five or more fruits and vegetables daily, and just 34.75% met guidelines for an hour of exercise daily (Eaton et al., 2008). One quarter did not engage in any physical activity, 24.9% played non-school-related video or computer games for three or more hours each school day, and 35.4% watched three or more hours of television on an average school day. Although 15.8% were overweight and 13.0% were obese, 45.2% were trying to lose weight; many fasted for 24 hours (11.8%), took diet pills (5.9%), or engaged in purging (4.3%) in the last month to lose weight or keep from gaining weight.

Curricular Standards

Although the 2001 CACREP *Standards* did not include any mention of wellness or optimal development outside of genontological counseling areas, 2009 *Standards* include greater integration of these concepts. In particular, CACREP-accredited programs must include coverage of theories and models of resilience, "theories for facilitating optimal development and wellness over the lifespan" (p. 91), "an orientation to wellness and prevention as desired counseling goals" (p. 92), and self-care strategies for counselors. Clinical mental health counselor candidates must show an ability to promote "optimal human development, wellness, and mental health through prevention, education, and advocacy activities" (p. 111).

Curricular Innovation

Age-old wisdom in our profession says, "Counselor, Heal Thyself" and advises us not to ask of clients that which we ourselves do not do. Lawson, Venart, Hazler, and Kottler (2007) captured the importance of wellness when they advocated for a "culture of counselor wellness," explaining,

> counseling is a profession in which the person of the counselor serves as the instrument for the work that we do. As counselors, we are taught to see the world through our client's eyes, to experience our clients' feelings through

> empathy, and to connect to our client's pain when they are vulnerable. The level of connection, commitment, and caring are among the greatest strengths that we counselors bring to the work that we do, and they are also among the characteristics that make us most vulnerable. (p. 5)

Counselor wellness and self-care is so important that the ACA established a task force to address issues of wellness and impairment within our ranks, and many counselors have investigated the usefulness of promoting wellness and self-care for counselors and, in turn, reducing burnout, impairment, and vicarious traumatization. Research regarding counseling students indicates that students have equivalent or slightly higher levels of holistic wellness compared with norm groups (Myers, Mobley, & Booth, 2003; Roach & Young, 2007). Given the poor state of physical and mental wellness in the United States, Myers and colleagues warned that average may be dangerous. Certainly, we should be more well than the clients we serve, and our curricular experiences should help us attain that level of wellness. If that were the case, we would expect counseling students to become more well over time. Roach and Young found no differences in a cross-section of counseling students at the beginning, middle, and end of their programs; even students who had taken entire courses on wellness were only slightly more well than those who did not. As a result, the authors questioned whether "counselor education has retreated from its founders' ideas that personal wellness is crucial (Rogers, 1961)and that counselor education is now more focused on content over personal development" (p. 40).

There are a number of reasons that counseling students may not be more well. If you chose to read this chapter rather than sleep, eat a nutritious meal, meditate, exercise, or engage in healthy humor with a loved one, perhaps the rigors of your training make attending to other areas of wellness more difficult. Perhaps you, like many counselors, focus so much on others that it is hard to find time for self. If so, you are not alone. Cummins, Massey, and Jones (2007) identified many ways in which counselors may be vulnerable to distress and provided strategies for promoting and maintaining counselor wellness. They suggested that counselors use wellness assessments to develop personal and professional wellness plans. Yager and Tovar-Blank (2007) went further to suggest ten strategies for promoting student wellness during counselor training:

1. Introduce wellness directly
2. Associate the self-growth, self-awareness emphasis of counselor education with wellness
3. Model wellness for counseling students
4. Communicate that perfection is not the goal of wellness

5. Present wellness as a lifestyle choice for counselors
6. Encourage personal counseling as a support
7. Review the perspectives on wellness in the ACA Code of Ethics
8. Promote a wellness philosophy in all courses
9. Develop innovative ways to reinforce students' attention to wellness
10. Expose counseling students to a positive humanistic view of human nature (pp. 143–152)

Counselor educators may use these strategies in efforts to meet the 2009 CACREP *Standards* regarding wellness and self-care.

As counselor educators develop curriculum to help MHCs maximize holistic wellness and self-care while learning skills to help clients to do the same, they may pull from exciting new research that highlights the impact of such activities on counselors. For example, counseling self-efficacy is predicted by a counselor's ability to be mindful, empathic, and in control of his or her attention in session (Greason & Cashwell, 2009); thus, counselor educators might incorporate mindfulness strategies (which have a host of other wellness benefits) into counselor preparation. Schure, Christopher, and Christopher (2008) did just that when they used yoga, meditation, and qigong to teach mindfulness and mind-body medicine to counseling students. At the end of the course, students reported physical, emotional, attitudinal, spiritual, and interpersonal changes that were reflective of greater levels of holistic wellness. Students also reported that they were more comfortable with silence, more attentive to the counseling process, and understood counseling in a more holistic nature. In addition, these practices helped students understand how they might move toward incorporation of holistic wellness principles in session with clients.

In the coming years, counselor educators will need to continue addressing the issue of wellness and optimal functioning in MHC preparation. Have we addressed these areas sufficiently in our curriculum? Have MHCs attained the levels of wellness needed to promote optimal growth in clients? What methods for teaching about wellness are most effective? How can we manage attention to wellness with growing demands for coverage regarding other content areas such as crisis and trauma, psychopharmacology, diagnosis, and understanding of evidence-based treatments? Are MHCs who are more well more effective as counselors?

ACCOUNTABILITY AND RESEARCH

In 2006, mental disorders and trauma-related disorders ranked behind heart conditions and cancer as the most expensive medical conditions in the

United States (Soni, 2009). Even after adjusting for inflation, costs of these services increased the most: from $35.2 billion to $57.5 billion for mental disorders and from $46.2 billion to $58.1 billion for trauma-related disorders; the number of people reporting spending on mental disorders nearly doubled (from 19.3 to 36.2 million). This is reflective of trends in the 1980s that led costs of care to skyrocket (Davis & Meier, 2001) and managed care to be born.

In this era of accountability, it is no longer sufficient for schools, agencies, government entities, or counselor preparation programs to request funding or accreditation on the sole basis of service provision: We have to show that what we are doing works. In practice, this means that mental health services are becoming more focused, brief, supportive and coping-oriented, and focused on medication and compliance (Davis & Meier, 2001) rather than focused on optimal growth and wellness. Davis and Meier point out both positives and negatives of this shift. On the one hand, more people may access mental health care, more outpatient options are available, care is standardized to some degree, and clinicians are held to higher standards for documenting services and measuring outcomes. On the other hand, requirements increase administrative overhead, may impact the therapeutic alliance and treatment planning, and reduce provider autonomy. Certainly, brief and symptom-oriented approaches to counseling run counter to the benefits of holistic wellness we just discussed–even though we know that attention to holistic wellness could prevent costly medical and mental health concerns in the future.

The *ACA Code of Ethics* (2005) reflects the need for accountability quite clearly. Ethical standard A.1.c. requires counselors to develop "integrated counseling plans that offer reasonable promise of success" (p. 4). Section C says that "counselors have a responsibility to the public to engage in counseling practices that are based on rigorous research methodologies" (p. 9). Section C goes on to specify that counselors operate within their boundaries of competence, monitor their effectiveness, and use approaches that are "grounded in theory and/or have an empirical or scientific foundation" (pp. 10–11).

Curricular Standards

CACREP core curricular standards related to research and program evaluation have changed relatively little between 2001 and 2009. MHC preparation programs must still provide coverage of "the importance of research in advancing the counseling profession" (p. 94); specific research and statistical methods; strategies for needs assessment, program evaluation, and program modification; and strategies for interpreting and reporting research and program evaluation studies. Today, however, programs must also help students understand how to use "research to inform evidence-based practice" (p. 94). MHC students must demonstrate an understanding of current literature regarding specific "theories, approaches, strategies, and techniques shown to be effective when working with specific populations of clients with mental and emotional disorders" (p. 111). In response to accountability expectations, MHC students must know "evidence-based treatments and basic strategies for evaluating counseling outcomes" (p. 113), apply research findings to counseling practice, develop measureable outcomes, and analyze and use data "to increase the effectiveness of clinical mental health counseling interventions and programs" (p. 113).

Curricular Innovations

The American Psychological Association (APA) has been quite active in developing standards and recommendations for identifying Empirically Supported Therapies (ESTs) and Evidence-Based Best Practices (EBBPs). A 1995 task force categorized treatments into three areas: well established, probably efficacious, and experimental (Chambless & Ollendick, 2001). Well-established treatments were established via at least two rigorous between-group design experiments, superior to pill or placebo, at least equivalent to already established treatments; conducted with treatment manuals; specified characteristics or samples; and investigated by at least two different researchers. Probably efficacious treatments had somewhat relaxed standards but still required experimental design and the use of treatment manuals. In both cases, the task force made some provisions for consideration of a large series of single-case design experiments. In 2005, an APA task force on EBBPs broadened guidelines to efforts to be more consistent with the realities of practice (APA Presidential Task Force, 2006). In particular, the task force defined EBBP as "the integration of the best available research with clinical expertise in the context of patient characteristics, culture, and preferences" (p. 273). They also recognized that multiple research designs contribute to knowledge base regarding practice and endorsed more than just experimental designs as valuable to practitioners. Today, the evidence-based movement is reflected in our accreditation and ethical standards and the development of resources such as SAMHSAs National Registry of Evidence Based Programs and Practices (www.nrepp.samhsa.gov).

Huber and Savage (2009) proposed that counselor educators promote research as a core value in counselor education by helping practitioners to learn how to conduct action research. Within action research, practitioners identify specific, practical issues on which they collect data, analyze and interpret data, and create action plans. Huber and Savage identified N = 1, single-case methodology, and qualitative methodology as especially practitioner-friendly and valuable. Similarly, Ray, Barrio Minton, Schottelkorb, and Brown (in press) offered suggestions for how counselor educators can help master's and doctoral students use single-case design in child counseling research. In the coming years, MHC preparation should include greater attention to practice-based evaluation so that MHCs have the tools they need to advocate for their own services. Be sure to review Chapter 7 carefully for more information regarding MHC and research.

In the coming years, counselor educators can further help MHCs develop accountability era survival skills in understanding processes, functions, and advocacy skills necessary for work with managed care (see Anderson, 2000), government, and nonprofit funding systems. Counselor educators may need to attend more directly to incorporating evidence-based practices into the curriculum so that counselors have the skills needed to provide ethical services within their scope of practice. In a similar vein, counselor educators can continue to integrate curricular attention to critical skills for working with managed care, including diagnosis, psychopharmacology, interdisciplinary skills, treatment planning, outcome-based assessment, and advocacy. Attention to specific ethical considerations related to working with managed care will also be critical (Braun & Cox, 2005; Daniels, 2001).

Given that MHCs often work in governmental and non-profit organizations that also have their own set of accountability expectations, counselor educators may also need to attend to grant-writing and program development skills. The logic model may be especially helpful for designing intentional, effective, and evidence-based programs (Kettner, Moroney, & Martin, 2008). Educators may also teach Calley's (2009) model, a 12-step model for comprehensive program development that takes MHCs from problem identification to program design to evaluation and budgeting.

Finally, accountability is at the forefront of higher education, and counselor educators will need to attend to accountability practices within their own programs. CACREP's 2009 requirement that counselor education programs document evidence of student learning outcomes mirrors expectations for MHCs to document success with clients. In the coming years, counselor educators will continue to conduct research regarding what works in MHC preparation. Whether evaluating the effectiveness of teaching and supervision methods, predicting success for admissions purposes, or identifying the impact of personal growth experiences and wellness on counselor performance, accountability in counseling and counselor education is here to stay.

CONCLUSION

Our world, the world of counseling, and the world of counselor education are experiencing rapid changes. Counselors are now licensed in all 50 states, Washington DC, and Puerto Rico. Although states set unique expectations for counselor education, examination, and experience, most states look to CACREP and NBCC for leadership related to MHC preparation. As we have discussed in this chapter, the 2009 CACREP *Standards* reflect the need for continued and enhanced attention to multiculturalism, diversity, and advocacy; crisis, disaster, and trauma; wellness and optimal development; and accountability.

REFERENCES

Adams, S. A. (2006). Does CACREP accreditation make a difference? A look at NCE results and answers. *Journal of Professional Counseling, 33,* 60–76.

Allen, M., Burt, K., Bryan, E., Carter, D., Orsi, R., & Durkan, L. (2002). School counselors' preparation for and participation in crisis intervention. *Professional School Counseling, 6,* 96–102.

American Counseling Association. (2005). *ACA code of ethics.* Retrieved from www.counseling .org/ethics

Anderson, C. E. (2000). Dealing constructively with managed care: Suggestions from an insider. *Journal of Mental Health Counseling, 22,* 343–353.

APA Presidential Task Force of Evidence-Based Practice. (2006). Evidence-based practice in psychology. *American Psychologist, 61,* 271–285.

Arredondo, P., Toporek, R., Brown, S. P., Sanchez, J., Locke, D. C., Sanchez, J., & Stadler, H. (1996). Operationalization of the multicultural counseling competencies. *Journal of Multicultural Counseling & Development, 24,* 42–78.

Arredondo, P., Tovar-Blank, Z. G., & Parham, T. A. (2008). Challenges and promises of becoming a culturally competent counselor in a sociopolitical era of change and empowerment. *Journal of Counseling & Development, 86,* 261–268.

Association for Spiritual, Ethical, and Religious Values in Counseling. (2009). *Competencies for addressing spiritual and religious values in counseling.* Retrieved from www.aservic.org/competncies.html

Barrio Minton, C. A., & Pease-Carter, C. (in press). The status of crisis preparation in counselor education: A national study and content analysis. *Journal of Professional Counseling.*

Brault, M. W. (2008). Americans with disabilities: 2005. *Current Population Reports.* Retrieved from http://www.census.gov/prod/2008pubs/p70-117.pdf

Braun, S. A., & Cox, J. A. (2005). Managed mental health care: Intentional misdiagnosis of mental disorders. *Journal of Counseling & Development, 83,* 425–433.

Brymer, M., Jacobs, A., Layne, C., Pynoos, R., Ruzek, J., Steinberg, A., Vernberg, E., & Watson, P. (2006). *Psychological first aid: Field operations guide* (2nd ed.). National Child Traumatic Stress Network and National Center for PTSD.

Calley, N. G. (2009). Comprehensive program development in mental health counseling: Design, implementation, and evaluation. *Journal of Mental Health Counseling,* 31, 9–21.

CBS/AP. (2010, February 9). Haiti raises death toll to 230,000. *CBS News.* Retrieved from www.cbsnews.com/stories/2010/02/09/world/main6191626.shtml

Centers for Disease Control. (2010). *Behavioral risk factor surveillance system.* Retrieved from www.cdc.gov/brfss

Chambless, D. L., & Ollendick, T. H. (2001). Empirically supported psychological interventions: Controversies and evidence. *Annual Review of Psychology, 52,* 685–716.

Chang, C. (2010, Spring). Social justice: The heart of *Chi Sigma Iota. Exemplar, 25*(1), 1–2.

Council for the Accreditation of Counseling and Related Educational Programs. (2001). *2001 Standards.* Retrieved from http://www.cacrep.org

Council for the Accreditation of Counseling and Related Educational Programs. (2009). *CACREP accreditation manual: 2009 standards.* Alexandria, VA: Author.

Crethar, H. C., Rivera, E. T., & Nash, S. (2008). In search of common threads: Linking multicultural, feminist, and social justice counseling paradigms. *Journal of Counseling & Development, 86,* 269–278.

Cummins, P. N., Massey, L., & Jones, A. (2007). Keeping ourselves well: Strategies for promoting and maintaining counselor wellness. *Journal of Humanistic Counseling, Education and Development, 46,* 35–49.

Daniels, J. A. (2001). Managed care, ethics, and counseling. *Journal of Counseling & Development,* 79, 119–122.

Davis, S. R., & Meier, S. T. (2001). *The elements of managed care: A guide for helping professionals.* Belmont, CA: Wadsworth.

DeNavas-Walt, C., Proctor, B. D., & Smith, J. C. (2009). Income, poverty, and health insurance coverage in the United States: 2008 (U.S. Census Publication No P60-236(RV)). *Current Population Reports.* Retrieved from http://www.census.gov/prod/2009pubs/p60-236.pdf

Dickson, G. L., & Jepson, D. A. (2007). Multicultural training experiences as predictors of multicultural competencies: Students' perceptions. *Journal of Counseling & Development, 47,* 76–96.

Eaton, D. K., Kann, L., Kinchen, S., Shanklin, S., Ross, J., Hawkins, J., & Weschler, H. (2008). Youth risk behavior surveillance–United States, 2007. *Surveillance Summaries MMWR, 57.* SS-04. Retrieved from www.cdc.gov/mmwr/pdf/ss/ss5704.pdf

Greason , P. B., & Cashwell, C. S. (2009). Mindfulness and counseling self-efficacy: The mediating role of attention and empathy. *Counselor Education & Supervision, 49,* 2–19.

Herrick, M., & Barlieb, D. (2006). Curriculum innovation in the education and training of mental health counselors. In A. J. Palmo, W. J. Weikel, & D. P. Borsos (Eds.), *Foundations of mental health counseling* (3rd ed., pp. 369–386). Springfield, IL: Charles C Thomas.

Huber, C. H., & Savage, T. A. (2009). Promoting research as core value in master's-level counselor education. *Counselor Education & Supervision, 48,* 167–178.

Johnson, A. G. (2006). *Privilege, power, and difference* (2nd ed.). New York: McGraw Hill.

Kettner, P. M., Moroney, R. M., & Martin, L. L. (2008). *Designing and managing programs: An effectiveness-based approach* (3rd ed.).Thousand Oaks, CA: Sage.

Kosmin, B. A., & Keysar, A. (2009). *American religious identification survey [ARIS 2008) summary report.* Retrieved from http://www.americanreligionsurvey-aris.org/reports/ARIS_Report_2008.pdf

Lawson, G., Venart, E., Hazler, R. J., & Kottler, J. A. (2007). Toward a culture of counselor wellness. *Journal of Humanistic Counseling, Education and Development, 46,* 5–19.

Lewis, J. A., Arnold, M. S., House, R., & Toporek, R. L. (2002). *ACA advocacy competencies.* Retrieved from American Counseling Association website: http://www.counseling.org/Publications/

Logan, C. R., & Barret, R. (2005). Counseling competencies for sexual minority clients. *Journal of LGBT Issues in Counseling, 1,* 3–22.

Lum, C. (2010). *Licensure requirements for professional counselors–2010.* Retrieved from www.counseling.org

McAdams, C. R., & Keener, H. J. (2008). Preparation, action, recovery: A conceptual framework for counselor preparation and response in client crises. *Journal of Counseling & Development, 86,* 388–398.

Myers, J. E., Mobley, A. K., & Booth, C. S. (2003). Wellness of counseling students: Practicing what we preach. *Counselor Education & Supervision, 42,* 264–274.

Myers, J. E., & Sweeney, T. J. (2008). Wellness counseling: The evidence base for practice. *Journal of Counseling & Development, 86,* 482–493.

Myers, J. E., Sweeney, T. J., & Witmer, J. M. (2000). The wheel of wellness counseling for wellness: A holistic model for treatment planning. *Journal of Counseling & Development, 78,* 251–266.

National Board for Certified Counselors. (2010). *Certifications.* Retrieved from www.nbcc.org

Pack-Brown, S. P., Thomas, T. L., & Seymour, J. M. (2008). Infusing professional ethics into counselor education programs: A multicultural/social justice perspective. *Journal of Counseling & Development, 86,* 296–302.

Pleis, J. R., Lucas, J. W., & Ward, B. W. (2009). *Summary health statistics for* U.S. adults: National health interview survey, 2008 (DHHS Publication No PHS 2010-1570). *Vital and Health Statistics, 10*(242). Retrieved from http://www.cdc.gov/nchs/data/series/sr_10/sr10_242.pdf

Ray, D. C., Barrio Minton, C. A., Schottelkorb, A. A., & Brown, A. G. (in press). Single-case design in child counseling research: Implications for counselor education. *Counselor Education & Supervision.*

Roach, L. F., & Young, M. E. (2007). Do counselor education programs promote wellness in their students? *Counselor Education & Supervision, 47,* 29–45.

Rowell, P. C., & Benshoff, J. M. (2008). Using personal growth groups in multicultural counseling courses to foster students' ethnic identity development. *Counselor Education & Supervision, 48,* 2–15.

Schmidt, J. J. (1999). Two decades of CACREP and what do we know? *Counselor Education & Supervision, 39,* 34–46.

Schure, M. B., Christopher, J., & Christopher, S. (2008). Mind-body medicine and the art of self-care: Teaching mindfulness to counseling students through yoga, meditation, and Qigong. *Journal of Counseling & Development, 86,* 47–56.

Seto, A., Young, S., Becker, K. W., & Kiselica, M. S. (2006). Application of the triad training model in a multicultural counseling course. *Counselor Education & Supervision, 45,* 304–318.

Sommer, C. A. (2008). Vicarious traumatization, trauma-sensitive supervision, and counselor preparation. *Counselor Education & Supervision, 48,* 61–71.

Soni, A. (2009, July). *The five most costly conditions, 1996 and 2006: Estimates for the U.S. civilian noninstitutionalized population* (Statistical brief #248). Retrieved from http://www.meps.ahrq.gov/mepsweb/data_files/publications/st248/stat248.pdf

Stadler, H. A., Suh, S., Cobia, D. C., Middleton, R. A., & Carney, J. S. (2006). Reimagining counselor education with diversity as a core value. *Journal of Counseling & Development, 45,* 193–206.

Sue, D. W., Arredondo, P., & McDavis, R. J. (1992). Multicultural counseling competencies and standards: A call to the profession. *Journal of Counseling & Development, 70,* 477–483.

Toporek, R. L., Lewis, J. A., & Crethar, H. C. (2009). Promoting systemic change through the ACA advocacy competencies. *Journal of Counseling & Development, 87,* 260–268.

U.S. Census Bureau. (2008). *2008 national population projections.* Retrieved from http://www

.census.gov/population/www/projections/2008projections.html

Vereen, L. G., Hill, N. R., & McNeal, D. T. (2008). Perceptions of multicultural counseling competency: Integration of the curricular and the practical. *Journal of Mental Health Counseling, 30,* 226–236.

Wachter, C. A. (2006). *Crisis in the schools: Crisis, crisis intervention training, and school counselor burnout.* Unpublished doctoral dissertation, the University of North Carolina at Greensboro, Greensboro, NC.

Wachter, C. A., Barrio Minton, C. A., & Clemmons, E. V. (2008). Crisis-specific peer supervision of school counselors: The *P-SAEF* model. *Journal of Professional Counseling: Practice, Theory, and Research, 36,* 13–24.

Wachter Morris, C. A., & Barrio Minton, C. A. (2010). *Crisis in the curriculum? Crisis preparation, experiences, and self-efficacy of new professional counselors.* Manuscript submitted for publication.

Watt, S. K., Curtis, G. C., Drummond, J., Kellogg, A. H., Lozano, A., Nicoli, G. T., & Rosas, M. (2009). Privileged identity exploration: Examining counselor trainees' reactions to difficult dialogues. *Counselor Education & Supervision, 49,* 86–105.

Yager, G. G., & Tovar-Blank, Z. G. (2007). Wellness and counselor education. *Journal of Humanistic Counseling, Education and Development, 46,* 143–153.

Chapter 20

TECHNOLOGY AND MENTAL HEALTH COUNSELING

RUSSELL A. SABELLA AND J. MICHAEL TYLER

The march of human progress has been marked by milestones in science and technology. Gutenberg's creation of moveable type in the 15th century laid the foundation for universal literacy. Watts' invention of the steam engine in the 18th century launched the Industrial Revolution. The inventiveness of Bell and Marconi in the 19th and 20th centuries–creating the telephone and radio–helped bring a global village into being. The United States and the world are now well into the midst of an economic and social revolution every bit as sweeping as any that has gone before: Computers and information technologies have transformed nearly every aspect of American life. Technology has changed the way Americans work and play, increasing productivity, and creating entirely new ways of doing things. Every major U.S. industry, either directly or indirectly, relies on technology and global networks to do its work.

The 1990s were a particularly exciting and energizing period in this realm. Technology, fueled by rapid advancements in microprocessor design as well as the development of the World Wide Web, impacted every aspect of life in our country. Virtually no industry was left untouched and no profession left unaltered by these changes. In the counseling field, practitioners were left with new ways to meet and interact with clients, changes in how we managed our offices, and alterations in how we received training, updated research, and prepared for the future. We developed new words and new concepts, and we began to think about what we did in new ways because of these changes. Like most people, counselors are also awed by the ways that technology can assist us in achieving more than we could achieve without it. We are surrounded by "smarter" machines, from our automobiles that can anticipate and assist in preventing a crash to our kitchen toaster that "knows" when your pastry is hot enough. Equipment inside our homes, including computers, televisions, stereos, and other appliances, are increasingly being networked and can be operated onsite or remotely using the Internet or even a smart phone. The 1990s witnessed the spawning of new technology-related careers and made others extinct. Some of these new careers were not even envisioned 10 years ago by most Americans (Tyler & Sabella, 2004).

One would be hard pressed to find any aspect of our modern lives that is not being affected by the rapidly expanding enterprise of computer-related technology (CRT). Lindsay (1988; cited in Hayden, Poynton, & Sabella, 2008) wrote, "Computer technology has revolutionized many aspects of our society and is without a doubt the most significant innovation of the century." It is, therefore, inevitable that computer technology is changing the mental health professions as well. As Sampson, Kolodinsky, and Greeno (1997) point out, "During the past 30 years, computer applications have become an increasingly common resource used in the delivery of counseling services" (p. 203; cited in Cabaniss, 2002). The future holds only more changes and developments that promise to create new opportunities (and challenges) for how we work, live, and play. Whether we like it or not, information technologies are now essential tools for manipulating ideas and images and for communicating effectively with others–all central components of a counselor's job (Sabella, 1998).

With all that changed and the lasting impact those changes have had, some things did not change. The expectation (or perhaps hope) of a typical 40-hour workweek remains. The need to focus our time and energy on meeting the social, emotional, and developmental needs of our clients has not changed. The expectation that counseling professionals remain current in the body of knowledge that comprises their field remains. The daily stresses and overcommitments that mark the identity of many professionals have been left unaltered. Add to these the need to know, understand, and interact competently with a wide range of new technologies, and the dark side of these technological changes becomes more obvious. However, as these technologies develop, they become easier and more user-friendly. Many technologies promote time savings, and others promise greater efficiency in our efforts.

In this chapter, we overview the nature of counselor technological literacy and specific areas of implementation in mental health counseling.

Technological Literacy

Imagine the frustration of suddenly living in a new country where you cannot effectively and efficiently communicate or interact with others, you are not able to decipher road signs, and you cannot navigate basic living tasks because you are unfamiliar with the country's language and customs. Children watch you in amazement and find it difficult to believe that you live in such a place without these basic capabilities. Increasingly in the United States, this might be the experience of counselors who do not have a basic level of technological literacy. Some people still take refuge by being able to live their lives in a relatively low-tech manner, although this lifestyle is becoming more difficult every day. Americans understand the rapid progress in the development and integration of technology through everyday experience and have thus embraced technological literacy as the "new basic" for today's world, along with reading, writing, and arithmetic.

Today's children find it difficult to imagine a life as we lived it not so long ago–without blue-ray discs, laptop computers, and palm-sized gadgets such as smart phones, mp3 players, and e-book readers. Social interaction is based on virtual connections through Facebook, and communication is done in a series of tweets and IMs. Future counselors, now in grade school and even college, will not hesitate to integrate high-tech tools in their work. They will merely continue along an already well-established path of learning to use and apply new technologies as they become available, probably assisted by the technologies themselves. The majority of today's counselors grew up learning and practicing counseling in a different environment. We used index cards instead of spreadsheets, typewriters instead of word processors, reference books instead of online journals and the web, and overheads in lieu of multimedia presentations, and we waited until class to communicate with the professor and our classmates instead of sending e-mails or conversing in chat rooms (Tyler & Sabella, 2004).

Many of today's counselors acknowledge the usefulness of technology and the need for keeping up with the rapidly changing times yet remain frozen in the fear generated by an unknown frontier. "I feel intimidated by computers" has been a common comment by counselors, who, even after training, sometimes revert to more traditional procedures. The customary statements, "My clients know more about technology than I do" and "I'm not a technical person," suggest that, although counselors may be interested or even intrigued, they frequently feel awkward and uneasy with computers and their operations (Myrick & Sabella, 1995). Our experience is that once such counselors are exposed to and begin to truly learn how to use technology in their work, they quickly become excited and adept. Many of our older students who are forced to learn high-tech tools in our classes often comment on the many kudos they receive from their own children who perceive their moms or dads to be "more with it." Their more highly technologically literate friends and partners share in their delight and also get excited about new shared interests. The students bask in the pride they take in working with contemporary tools.

What Exactly is Technological Literacy?

Many people have written on the subject of technological literacy. Hayden (1989), after a literature review, takes the position that technological literacy is having knowledge and abilities to select and apply appropriate technologies in a given context. Although not revealing the source of his thoughts, Steffens (1986) claims that technological literacy involves knowledge and comprehension of technology and its uses; skills, including tool skills as well as evaluation skills; and attitudes about new technologies and their application. This insight is similar to that of Owen and Heywood (1986), who say there are three components to technological literacy: the technology of making things, the technology of organization, and the technology of using information. Applying a Delphi technique to opinions expressed by experts, Croft (1991) evolved a panel of characteristics of a technologically literate student: abilities to make decisions about technology; possession of basic literacy skills required to solve technology problems; ability to make wise decisions about uses of technology; ability to apply knowledge, tools, and skills for the benefit of society; and ability to describe the basic technology systems of society (Waetjen, 1993).

A theme among various attempts to define technological literacy is that technology has evolved to become a powerful medium–not only a set of high-tech tools. If technology functioned merely as a set of tools, as the pervasive mechanical, user-in-control view of technology holds, the problem of advancing technological literacy would not be so challenging. A few more required courses or conference training sessions, and more specialists to teach them, could simply be added. But technology has become more than a set of devices to be picked up and used when a person decides he or she needs them. It has become a required medium that mediates experience in most aspects of people's lives (Fanning, 1994). Broadly speaking, technological literacy, then, can be described as the intellectual processes, abilities, and dispositions needed for individuals to understand the link among technology, themselves, and society in general. Technological literacy is concerned with developing one's awareness of how technology is related to the broader social system and how technological systems cannot be fully separated from the political, cultural, and economic frameworks that shape them (Saskatchewan Education, 2002).

Some of the professional literature in the area of counseling technology focuses on technological (or sometimes referred to as technical) *competencies* and other times on technological *literacy*. What is the difference? Competencies are what school counselors are able to demonstrate or *do* with technology, such as "insert a table into a document" or "compute a correlation between two variables using Microsoft Excel™." Bandura (1986) calls these "subskills." In other words, competencies are skills that can be observed and measured and are part of an individual's overall ability to perform a task (Sabella, Poynton, & Isaacs, 2010).

Comparatively, technological literacy is far more than the knowledge one has about the appropriate use of available technological tools and processes. Technologically literate citizens employ systems-oriented thinking as they interact with the technological world, cognizant of how such interaction affects individuals, our society, and the environment. Technological literacy is the knowledge of when using technology is advisable and efficient in day-to-day counseling situations. Citizens of all ages benefit from technological literacy, whether it is obtained through formal or informal educational environments (International Technology Education Association, 2007; Poynton, 2005). Thus, technological literacy is the ability to understand and evaluate technology. It complements technological competency, which is the ability to create, repair, or operate specific technologies, commonly computers (NationMaster, 2008).

Specialized technological competencies or skills do not guarantee technological literacy or efficacy. Counselors who know every operational detail of a Client Information System, for instance, or who can troubleshoot a software glitch in a personal computer may not have a sense of the risks, benefits, and trade-offs associated with technological developments generally and may be poorly prepared to make choices about other technologies that affect their work or lives. Furthermore, one may have skills and an understanding of the broader implications of technologies but may not connect the skill with the specific use for a specific project (e.g., creating and disseminating an Accountability Results Report).

These definitions, together with one provided by the International Technology Education Association (2007) have provided the foundation for our definition of counselor technological literacy (Tyler & Sabella, 2004): "The intellectual processes, abilities and dispositions needed for counselors to understand the link among technology, themselves, their clients, and a diverse society so that they may extend human abilities to satisfy human needs and wants for themselves and others" (p. 22). This means that counselors who have adequate levels of technological literacy are able to:

- understand the nature and role of technology, in both their personal and professional lives;
- understand how technological systems are designed, used, and controlled;
- value the benefits and assess the risks associated with technology;
- respond rationally to ethical dilemmas caused by technology;

- assess the effectiveness of technological solutions;
- feel comfortable learning about and using systems and tools of technology in the home, in leisure activities, and in the workplace; and
- critically examine and question technological progress and innovation.

Counselor Technological Competencies

Previous efforts to establish some standards of minimum levels of technological competencies for all counselors have been available for some time. In 1999, the Association for Counselor Education and Supervision (ACES) developed the *Technical Competencies for Counselor Education Students: Recommended Guidelines for Program Development.* The competencies included a list of 12 general areas of technological competencies that students should have at the completion of a counselor education program:

1. Be able to use productivity software to develop web pages, group presentations, letters, and reports.
2. Be able to use such audiovisual equipment as video recorders, audio recorders, projection equipment, video conferencing equipment, and playback units.
3. Be able to use computerized statistical packages.
4. Be able to use computerized testing, diagnostic, and career decision-making programs with clients.
5. Be able to use e-mail.
6. Be able to help clients search for various types of counseling-related information via the Internet, including information about careers, employment opportunities, educational and training opportunities, financial assistance/scholarships, treatment procedures, and social and personal information.
7. Be able to subscribe, participate in, and sign off counseling-related listserv.
8. Be able to access and use counseling related CD-ROM databases.
9. Be knowledgeable of the legal and ethical codes that relate to counseling services via the Internet.
10. Be knowledgeable of the strengths and weaknesses of counseling services provided via the Internet.
11. Be able to use the Internet for finding and using continuing education opportunities in counseling.
12. Be able to evaluate the quality of Internet information.

The document did provide an important beginning set of guidelines for counselor training, although it still left some counselor educators with questions such as, "Exactly which technical skills in each area are most important, what do they look like, and how do we measure proficiency?" In response,

Tyler and Sabella (2004) wrote a book titled *Counseling in the 21st Century: Using Technology to Improve Practice,* which uses the ACES competencies as a framework and provides extensive examples and resources for use in each competency area.

In 2007, ACES updated the technical competencies, which significantly expanded the original guidelines by (a) consolidating the competencies to 11 instead of 12; (b) addressing master's-level versus doctoral-level technical competencies; (c) providing a rationale for each competency; and (d) and including examples of each technical competency at different levels, including basic knowledge, basic competence, and integrated competence.

Basic knowledge focuses on the graduate's ability to recognize and be informed regarding technology as it applies to the counseling profession. Basic competence refers to technology skills that are essential for current master's graduates entering counseling practice. ACES suggests that all master's graduates demonstrate basic competence across each of the 11 technology competencies. The integrated competence level, although beyond the current reach of many counselor education and training programs, suggests an advanced level of ability in technology that only some graduates will acquire or possess (Association for Counselor Education and Supervision, 2007).

New Technologies Mean New Opportunities

Indeed, new technologies can create challenges to which we must learn to appropriately respond. However, throughout these challenges exists a wave of new opportunities for the professional as well as our clients. Understanding these new opportunities and exploiting them may help decrease some of the unintended and negative consequences introduced by technology. For instance, the World Wide Web–the most popular and powerful part of the Internet–is an example of technology that at one time was seen as only a store of information. Today, the Web is a medium for communication, collaboration, data and file warehouses, and much more. What once required different software applications or procedures for e-mail, chat rooms, sharing files, and so on can now be done with only a browser and a connection to the Web. As you think about the potential of various technologies and the Web in particular in your work, you might use the following schema to help conceptualize the range of available technologies (Sabella, 2003).

1. **Information/resource:** In the form of words, graphics, video, and even three-dimensional virtual environments, the Web remains a dynamic and rapidly growing library of information and knowledge.

2. **Communication/collaboration:** Chat rooms, discussion boards, instant messaging, blogs, listservs, virtual offices, video conferencing, electronic meetings, e-mail–the Web is now a place where people connect, collaborate, exchange information, and make shared decisions.
3. **Interactive tools:** The maturing of web-based programming has launched a new and an unforeseen level of available tools. Interactive tools on the Web can help counselors build and create anything ranging from a personalized business card to a set of personalized website links. In addition, interactive tools help counselors to process data, convert text to speech, create a graph, manage payment and billing, or even determine the interactive effects of popular prescription drugs, to name a very few.
4. **Delivery of services:** Most controversial yet growing in popularity is how counselors use the Web to meet with clients and deliver counseling services in an online or "virtual" environment.

In fact, many technology-assisted tasks or endeavors are actually a combination of two or more of these types of areas. We now turn our attention to several examples.

Information and Resources

One of the most direct and significant changes that technology has brought to the lives of most individuals is the ability to access a previously unimagined amount of information about every topic under the sun. In fact, sharing information and resources is really what the Internet was designed to do and today remains its specialty. This vast network allows people to share not only text and links but a dizzying array of multimedia that includes video, audio, charts, links, and more. Anyone with a Web-enabled device or computer can contribute to the universe of knowledge. The shift from institution-generated knowledge to individually generated knowledge has proliferated to the degree that we now consider the Web to have entered its first major upgrade–Web 2.0.

Web 2.0 is a Web developed by you and me. In the Web 2.0 world, companies provide the "microphone" and we do the "talking." In fact, you may recall that *Time Magazine's* Person of the Year in 2006 was You. Lev Grossman of Time Magazine wrote, "The new Web is a very different thing. It's a tool for bringing together the small contributions of millions of people and making them matter" (Sabella, 2008). Wikipedia describes Web 2.0 as:

> Web 2.0 is a term describing changing trends in the use of World Wide Web technology and web design that aim to enhance creativity, information sharing, and collaboration among users. These concepts have led to the development and evolution of web-based communities and hosted services, such as

> social-networking sites, video sharing sites, wikis, blogs, and folksonomies. The term became notable after the first O'Reilly Media Web 2.0 conference in 2004. Although the term suggests a new version of the World Wide Web, it does not refer to an update to any technical specifications, but to changes in the ways software developers and end-users utilize the Web. (Web 2.0, 2008)

But not all available information is of high quality or even useful. Like so much in technology, this creates challenge as well as opportunity. The challenge lies in helping clients sort through the available information to find that which is of high quality and targets their particular needs. Many clients, although technologically capable, may not have the skills necessary to evaluate a site or the information provided. Lacking any sort of review or oversight, anyone can put any information they choose on the Web. With basic technology skills, a site can be created that looks quite polished. Without adequate knowledge and skills to evaluate sites, clients may be drawn to sites that appear professional and are easy to understand, rather than sites that contain accurate and current information that may be slightly more difficult to understand and navigate (Tyler & Sabella, 2004).

As professionals with a particular body of expertise, we have the capacity to help clients in two ways. First, clients can be provided with information that will assist them in evaluating information that they are obtaining, whether from the Web, books, friends, or even counselors! One way to implement this intervention is to work with others within your agency or organization to create a pamphlet with tips and approaches to evaluating information (e.g., visit http://www.schoolcounselor.com/website-evaluation.htm). Second, a more active approach may be helpful. By knowing the particular client population with whom you work, the mental health counselor may be the best person to evaluate specific types of information for clients to review. By spending time evaluating sites on the Internet in collaboration with colleagues, schools and agencies can then create lists of websites to provide to clients on various topics. In mental health settings, lists of websites focused on a particular diagnosis or problem areas such as depression, chronic medical concerns, or grief/bereavement may be helpful. No matter what the focus, counselors should never recommend a site that they have not personally visited and thoroughly evaluated. Sites that may initially appear appropriate may have less appropriate content buried within. Never provide a recommendation to a client of which you do not have clear and current personal knowledge.

Recommending to clients information that is created and disseminated by others can be helpful but may not be as useful as information created locally by professionals. Technology makes it easy for anyone to create content (see e.g., http://bit.ly/a9lvIs, http://www.successful-therapist.com/, or http://www.therapysites.com/). For example, rather than referring clients to other websites about depression, local agencies may consider setting up a team to work in conjunction with psychiatrists, psychologists, social workers, and counselors to create a rich and locally maintained website. Such a site would include information about a variety of local resources, including counseling help, support programs, financial assistance, and emergency access.

Consultation, Collaboration, and Shared Decision Making

Collaboration is a process by which people work together on an intellectual, academic, or practical endeavor. In essence, they "co-labor" toward a common mission or goal. In the past, the process of collaboration occurred in person, by letter, fax, or on the telephone. Today's high-tech collaboration connects individuals over an electronic network (e.g., Internet, intranet, cellular network, closed circuit television) using tools that are becoming increasingly cheap, powerful, and more easily accessible. Working over an electronic medium allows collaborators to communicate and work together anytime, from anywhere, and from virtually any place. People from different parts of a building, school district, state, country, or continent can exchange information and, together as a team, develop documents, ponder ideas, discuss issues, reflect on their own practices, make decisions, or collate data. Collaborators can now work from geographically distinct locations and accomplish just about anything that they at one time could only do if they were actually together in the same room. The limitations of space, pace, and time are dissolved with anytime, anywhere, on-demand work spaces and high-tech tools designed to help us synergize our talents and passions (Sabella, 2010).

Overcoming Limitations of Space (or Distance)

The potential to collaborate with others from all over the world provides a body of resources and professional colleagues that counselors may not otherwise have access to, especially within their own offices. Collaborating on a global scale can also provide counselors with a sense of belonging, a sense of identity within a larger community. Using high-tech tools to collaborate, counselors can actively and interactively explore innovative ideas and share best practices. With electronic collaboration, the adage "Two heads are better than one" could just as well be "Two thousand heads are better than one." One person's provocative question can lead to many creative, exciting solutions. By sharing what they know with others, participants advance their own knowledge and the collaborative community's knowledge.

Overcoming Limitations of Pace (or Efficiency)

During a typical work day, most counselors are pressed for time and lack opportunities to stop and reflect on their work experiences or move beyond on-the-fly brainstorming that often happens by chance in the hallway (Finkelstein, 2009). The asynchronous nature of electronic collaboration allows participants to contribute to the conversation when it's convenient and to reflect on what others have said before responding. In addition, having to articulate in writing professional struggles and suggestions forces writers to take time to be thoughtful and reflect carefully about new ideas and pathways (Koufman-Frederick, Lillie, Pattison-Gordon, Watt, & Carter, 1999).

Overcoming Limitations of Time

Most counselors are accustomed to short-term professional development seminars and workshops that provide finite information. Similarly, traditional collaboration occurs mostly during defined and time-limited meetings convenient to all parties involved. Electronic collaboration allows for a *sustained* effort, where participants can propose, try out, refine, and shape ideas using a combination of live and electronic media or venues. For instance, together, counselors in any setting or among settings could attend an online seminar (better known as a webinar) about changes made in the *Diagnostic Statistical Manual of Mental Disorders,* 5th edition (*DSM-5*). They can then interact over a follow up discussion board, where participants share how they have demonstrated what they learned at their own offices. As they continue, they may identify other counselors to work more closely with and schedule a video conference to partner and collaborate further.

Collaborating electronically can take many different forms. Some of the more common activities include the following (Koufman-Frederick et. al, 1999):

- *Discussion groups* are focused around a topic or a specific activity, goal, or project. Some groups are open ended and unmoderated, allowing users to solicit information from each other. Other, more structured groups may use a moderator to guide the discussion by filtering and posing questions and/or making comments, suggestions, and connections. (p. 1)
- *Data-collection and organization* activities use databases and search engines to organize and retrieve data. Users contribute data individually to a shared database and retrieve data from it as needed. Data can be in the form of references (such as pointers to related work and websites), information (such as best practices), curriculum projects, research

papers, and contact information for colleagues. (p. 2)

- Some projects involve *sharing documents*–from simply displaying them to having several people work on them simultaneously. Collaborators can display documents online and discuss the contents via e-mail, video conference, or chat. They can use annotation systems to comment on shared documents and editing tools to co-edit documents online. (p. 2)
- *Synchronous communication activities,* such as instant messaging and video conferencing–differ from the other types of activities in that they happen in real time over a short period. In text-based "chat" environments, participants see what the other person is typing on the screen in real time. Video conferencing is like a telephone conference call, yet with video and sometimes more (e.g., file sharing, chat, recording). These technologies allow users to discuss ideas, debate problems, and share information electronically when face-to-face interaction is desired but not possible. (p. 2)
- Educators participate in *online courses or workshops* to learn something new. They are like traditional courses and workshops but without face-to-face meetings. The electronic component allows people to participate whenever and from wherever they want. Such activities involve an instructor who distributes assignments, guides the conversation, and responds to participants' questions. The material for discussion, as well as the discussions themselves, can take place via a discussion group or through an integrated distance learning tool. An added benefit is that participants learn about using an electronic medium. (p. 2)

Several free collaboration tools available on the Web now exist. Examples of these include the following (Sabella, 2010):

- *DimDim.* An online application sharing and webinar delivery system. Users can start or join meetings with just a few clicks. http://bit.ly/bioQAp
- *Elluminate.* Elluminate is a learning platform that allows users to come together and interact through online meetings. Technologies used in Elluminate include video, voice, text messaging, and virtual whiteboards. http://www.elluminate.com/
- *GoToMeeting.* GoToMeeting is an online meeting service that enables individuals and organizations to easily, securely and cost-effectively collaborate, present information, and demonstrate products online. http://www.gotomeeting.com
- *Mikogo.* Mikogo is a cross-platform desktop sharing tool, ideal for web conferencing, online meetings, or remote support. http://www.mikogo.com/

- *ooVoo.* Similar to Skype, ooVoo allows for video/audio conferencing, file transfer, and instant messaging. http://www.oovoo.com/
- *Skype.* Skype is free software that allows one to video/audio conference with others and includes instant messaging and file transfer. http://www.skype.com
- *Webex.* WebEx delivers a suite of on-demand collaborative applications. http://www.webex.com/
- *Windows Meeting Space.* This enables face-to-face collaboration among small groups of Windows Vista users–virtually anytime, anywhere. Useful for both business and personal purposes, this tool enables you to share work on computer-based projects with other people more easily and comfortably. Windows Meeting Space uses peer-to-peer technology and automatically sets up an ad hoc network if it can't find an existing network. Windows Meeting Space is on the Start menu under All Programs. http://bit.ly/9Ls82w
- *Vyew.* With Vyew you can give a presentation to 100 people online or post a document you've been working on for review by your colleagues at their convenience. http://vyew.com/
- *Yugma.* Yugma is a web conferencing service that allows users to host or attend online meetings on Windows, Mac, or Linux computers. http://www.yugma.com/

Delivery of Services

When you think of conducting counseling with your clients, you probably envision yourself doing this in your office, an agency, in their home, or perhaps even on a "walk and talk." However, with increasing probability, you may also have a mental image of a counselor who sits in front of the computer and conducts counseling over the Internet. Web counseling is the process of providing counseling services via the Internet. This may be done by connecting with your client via e-mail, chat rooms, instant messenger, Internet video conferencing, or a virtual environment (e.g., Second Life). The practice of Web counseling, also referred to as cybercounseling, cybertherapy, e-therapy, e-counseling, and online counseling, to name a few. It began slowly but is rapidly finding popularity among both counselors and clients (e.g., Goss & Anthony, 2009; Murphy, McFadden, & Mitchell, 2008; Pollock, 2006; Tyler & Sabella, 2004). Among counseling professionals, Web counseling has created a debate about the utility and effectiveness of this new medium and whether "cybercounseling" even really exists. Moreover, those involved in traditional ethical and legal issues in counseling are wondering how such matters relate to the Internet environment (e.g., Phillips, 2008).

What is Web Counseling?

Meeting and interacting with each other online has become an everyday experience for many people nowadays. Activities such as communication, shopping, and even learning, which have been traditionally conducted via face-to-face meetings, have acquired new parameters in the virtual world. Counseling services are another candidate with promising potential (Anthony & Nagel, 2010; Wong, & Law, 2002). Although some authors have attempted to demonstrate that online counseling can be an extension of traditional face-to-face services (e.g., Tyler & Guth, 2003), a common working definition of Web counseling has not yet materialized among practitioners and researchers. In fact, it seems as if a continuum of beliefs about the nature of cybercounseling exists, ranging from a belief that it does not actually exist to a belief that it is proliferating and thriving. Some counselors would say that defining the nature and practice of Web counseling is futile and misleading. Counselors and others in this camp believe that Web counseling is a term that leads people to erroneously believe that the work of professional counselors can effectively and appropriately be conducted in an electronic or "virtual" environment, such as over the Internet. They argue that, although noteworthy attempts are currently in progress (e.g., see Ookita & Tokuda, 2001), empirically supported counseling theories and techniques have not yet been adequately tested in the virtual environment. Thus, we cannot confidently assume current approaches have the same effect or, even worse, do not have unanticipated negative effects for online clients. This group further argues that these online services cannot be considered counseling unless and until they can be demonstrated to be effective. Similarly, an important question has remained unanswered: Is counseling in cyberspace so different from traditional face-to-face counseling that it requires special training and certification?

Some counselors wonder whether the therapeutic alliance can reliably be established without ever working with the client in person. Even if the counseling relationship could be developed in cyberspace, they wonder whether the online personality with whom you are working is the same as the "real-world" personality of the client. Finally, it is unknown whether potential growth or progress made during online sessions will generalize to life in the real world as we would expect to happen in face-to-face counseling. Counselors who view cybercounseling as more of a potential than an existing counseling modality may be optimistic about how developing technology can help counselors do their work in alternative environments and media. However, for now, they caution us that traditional or face-to-face counseling is not well understood by the general public, notwithstanding its much longer history and exposure via public relations, and that discussing Web counseling as if it exists stands to confuse the practice of counseling even more. This group wants the public to understand the difference between the special relationship a counselor and client share, as compared with the relationships established in other related helping activities such as advising, mentoring, coaching, and teaching. These counselors argue that "cybercounselors" who believe they are counseling in cyberspace are more accurately providing cyberadvice, cybercoaching, cybermentoring, and distance learning. Although each of these is important and valuable, none is an adequate substitute for professional counseling.

Other counselors have adopted a more "middle-of-the-road" belief about cybercounseling. They espouse that cybercounseling is not counseling per se but an effective means to supplement live counseling sessions. They believe that technology has not yet developed tools to effectively create an environment that can substitute for a live setting, although tools do exist to help counselors (and clients) be more effective and efficient in meeting their goals. Such counselors may indeed call themselves cybercounselors or e-therapists, for instance, but only insofar as it describes their use of computer and Internet technologies as part of their face-to-face work with clients. These counselors affirm the role that technology plays throughout the process of counseling, including collaboration and communication, and they continue to explore how such tools can enhance the probability of successful live interaction.

On the other side of the continuum reside counselors and researchers who view the Web as a new delivery and management system for doing the work of professional counseling. These cybercounselors celebrate the latest tools provided by computers and networking technologies as providing the means to work with clients whom, without these tools, they could never connect. With some adaptations, they posit that they can effectively use their counseling knowledge and skills to provide counseling services in cyberspace.

We suspect that where you lie on the continuum is influenced by your approach and beliefs about the counseling process, your level of technological literacy, and your comfort with the unknown. For instance, we believe that a psychodynamic therapist might view cybercounseling differently than a solution-focused brief therapist. How does the emphasis on a client's past relationships as guided by your approach affect your perception of the conduciveness of the Internet to appropriately conduct counseling? How important are the dynamics of transference and countertransference in your work and how might this play a part in the usefulness of the Internet in conducting counseling? Once a counselor determines that his or her style of counseling can be supported by electronic media, how does his or her (and the clients') competency in using these tools help or hinder the process? A counselor's perception concerning the level of risk introduced by conducting counseling in cyberspace would probably also influence his or her belief about the utility of cybercounseling. Indeed, no matter where on the continuum of beliefs you are, research and training about the nature and practice of conducting cybercounseling promises to continue to change how we approach and engage in cybercounseling (Jones & Stokes, 2009; Tyler & Sabella, 2004).

To more fully understand these services, it may be beneficial to explore a few of them in more depth. One such service is http://TherapyOnLine.ca. This Canadian-based service attempts to provide counseling by exchanging e-mail with clients. Clients are asked to write an e-mail to their counselor about their concerns, and the counselor then responds (this is similar to the procedures of another Web-based therapy service found at http://www.deeannamerznagel.com/id70.html). Because the client controls the flow of e-mail, "sessions" may occur as often or seldom as the client chooses. Another online service, http://ReadyMinds.com, focuses on career counseling. ReadyMinds uses a highly structured approach that begins with an online assessment, including both open-ended questions and the completion of the Self-Directed Search (SDS). This is followed by 2 hours of counseling provided over the telephone, and then the client receives a written report. Along the way, clients also engage in other exploration activities and career research. This model, because of its focus on the specific topic of career exploration, takes a more structured approach than TherapyOnLine.ca.

Although controversial, these services seem to be meeting a counseling need, and it is anticipated that Web-based or Web-enhanced counseling services will continue to grow in the coming years. As the profession of counseling better understands and learns how to use the Internet to support services, it is likely that online counseling will become increasingly routine and accepted.

Potential advantages of Web Counseling

- *Delivery of counseling services:* Walz (1996) noted that the information highway "allows counselors to overcome problems of distance and time to offer opportunities for networking and interacting not otherwise available" (p. 417). In addition, counseling over the Net may be a useful medium for those with physical disabilities whom may find even a short distance a significant obstacle. For others whom are reticent to meet with a counselor and/or self-disclose, the Net may prove to be an interactive lubricant that may foster the counseling process. Similarly, Lee (2000) wrote that Web counseling affords clients with a choice in therapeutic setting. For example, those who are economically disadvantaged can use computers in public libraries, churches, or schools to interact with counselors at other locations. The immigrant, rather than meeting in the potentially alienating or intimidating confines of the professional office, can engage in a counseling session in more familiar surroundings. Furthermore, distance counseling via computer technology opens up new opportunities for those who have been marginalized due to socioeconomic circumstances. Manhal-Baugus (2000) and Fenichel et al. (2002) also point out the benefit of affordability, because online therapy is typically less expensive than traditional formats.

- *Delivery of information resources:* The Internet is a convenient and quick way to deliver important information. In cybercounseling, information might be in the form of a homework assignment between sessions or bibliocounseling. Also, electronic file transfer of client records, including intake data, case notes (Casey, Bloom, & Moan, 1994), assessment reports, and selected key audio and video recordings of client sessions, could be used as preparation for individual supervision, group supervision, case conferences, and research (Sampson et al., 1997).
- *Assessment and evaluation:* Access to a wide variety of assessment, instructional, and information resources, in formats appropriate in a wide variety of ethnic, gender, and age contexts (Sampson, 1990; Sampson & Krumboltz, 1991), could be accomplished online.
- *Communications:* Especially via e-mail, counselors and clients can exchange messages throughout the counseling process. Messages may inform both counselor and client of pertinent changes or progress. E-mail can provide an excellent forum for answering simple questions, providing social support, or scheduling actual or virtual meeting times.
- *Marriage and family counseling:* If face-to-face interaction is not possible on a regular basis, marriage counseling might be delivered via video conferencing, in which each couple and the counselor (or counselors) are in different geographic locations. After independent use of multimedia-based computer-assisted instruction on communication skills, spouses could use video conferencing to complete assigned homework (e.g., communication exercises) (Sampson et al., 1997).
- *Supervision:* Anecdotal evidence has shown that e-mail is an enhancing tool in the process of counselor supervision and consultation. It provides an immediate and ongoing channel of communication between and among as many people as chosen (Coursol & Woitte, 1998; Myrick & Sabella, 1995; Scherl & Haley, 2000).

Potential Disadvantages of Web Counseling

The evolution of the Internet offers many future possibilities and potential problems in the delivery of counseling services. Although some research efforts exist in the area of technology in counseling (e.g., see the *Journal of Technology in Counseling* at http://jtc.colstate.edu), we need to continually strive to identify the salient interpersonal processes unique to therapeutic relationships. The following is a beginning list of potential advantages and disadvantages of Web counseling according to individuals who have investigated, observed, or participated in it (Sabella, 2003):

- *Confidentiality:* Although encryption and security methods have become highly sophisticated, unauthorized access to online communications remains a possibility without attention to security measures. Counselors who practice online must ethically and legally protect their clients, their profession, and themselves by using all known and reasonable security measures.
- *Computer competency:* Both the counselor and client must be adequately computer literate for the computer/network environment to be a viable interactive medium. From typing skills to electronic data transfer to navigating online tools, both the counselor and client must be able to effectively harness the power and function of both hardware and software. Similar to face-to-face counseling, counselors must not attempt to perform services outside the limitations of their technological competence.
- *Location-specific factors:* A potential lack of appreciation on the part of geographically remote counselors of location-specific conditions, events, and cultural issues that affect clients may limit counselor credibility or lead to inappropriate counseling interventions. For example, a geographically remote counselor may be unaware of traumatic recent local events that are exacerbating a client's reaction to work and family stressors. It may also be possible that differences in local or regional cultural norms between the client's and counselor's community could lead a counselor to misinterpret the thoughts, feelings, or behavior of the client. Counselors need to prepare for counseling a client in a remote location by becoming familiar with recent local events and local cultural norms. If a counselor encounters an unanticipated reaction on the part of the client, the counselor needs to proceed slowly, clarifying client perceptions of his or her thoughts, feelings, and behavior (Sampson et al., 1997).
- *Equity:* Does the cost of online access introduce yet another obstacle for obtaining counseling? Does cybercounseling further alienate potential clients whom might have the greatest need for counseling? Even when given online access, could a client competently engage in cybercounseling without possibly having ever had a computer experience? Web counseling may exacerbate equity issues already confronting live counseling.

- *Credentialing:* How will certification and licensure laws apply to the Internet as state and national borders are crossed electronically? Will counselors be required to be credentialed in all states and countries where clients are located? Could cybercounseling actually be the impetus for a national credential recognized by all states? Will we need to move toward global credentialing? Who will monitor service complaints out of state or internationally?
- *High tech vs. high touch:* How can counselors foster the development of trust, caring, and genuineness while working with clients in cyberspace? Online video-based interaction is now a reality, although how does verbal, non-verbal, and extra-verbal communication compare to live counseling? Does online video communication help us to communicate and facilitate the counseling process in a way that is similar, different, or the same as live counseling? Further, Lago (1996) poses a key question: "Do the existing theories of psychotherapy continue to apply, or do we need a new theory of e-mail therapy?" (p. 289). He then takes Rogers' (1957) work on the necessary and sufficient conditions for therapeutic change as his starting point and lists the computer-mediated therapist competencies as: the ability to establish contact, the ability to establish relationship, the ability to communicate accurately with minimal loss or distortion, the ability to demonstrate understanding and frame empathic responses, and the capacity and resources to provide appropriate and supportive information. This proposal begs the question of whether such relationship conditions as outlined by Rogers can be successfully transmitted and received via contemporary computer-mediated telecommunications media.
- *Impersonation:* A famous cartoon circulated over the Net depicts a dog sitting in front of a computer. The caption says, "The nice thing about the Internet is that nobody knows you're a dog." Experienced Internet users can relate to the humor in this cartoon because they know that there are many people who hide behind the Internet's veil of anonymity to communicate messages they ordinarily would not communicate in real life. Messages that convey unpopular sentiments and would ordinarily be met with castigation are more easily proliferated when one's identity is perceived to be hidden. Others rely on anonymity provided by technology to play out fantasies or practical jokes. Who is your cyberclient, really? Does your client depict him or herself as an adult while he or she is actually a minor? Has the client disguised his or her gender, race, or other personal distinctions that may threaten the validity or integrity of your efforts.

- *Ethics:* How do current ethical statements for counselors apply or adapt to situations encountered online? For the most part, counselors can make the leap into cyberspace and use current ethical guidelines to conduct themselves in an ethical fashion. However, problems exist. The future will inevitably see a change in what it means to be ethical as we learn the exact nature of counseling online.

SUMMARY

No counseling professional is immune from the significant impact technology has made on how we practice, communicate, manage, and measure the outcomes of our work. Technology is changing the way we all work regardless of our own desire to implement specific changes in our personal approach. High-tech tools of the new millennium are providing new methods for how we train, conduct research, manage our practices, interact with others, and overall promote individual and systemic changes in the mental health field.

In addition, technology is also changing the types of counseling issues presented by our clients within the various environments in which they live and work (e.g., family, peer). For example, counselors are now working with clients whom are experiencing new high-tech counseling issues, including various forms of Internet addictions (e.g., online shopping, gambling, auctioning, video gaming, and pornography), marital discourse (e.g., online affairs), and behavioral problems (e.g., cyberbullying, stalking, and hate websites).

The message is clear: Opting out of technological literacy and implementation in today's high-tech world reduces effectiveness and efficiency while increasing the risk of engaging in the unethical behavior of practicing with less than minimal competency. However, counselors who march along with the progress of high-tech tools and electronic media stand to enjoy the benefits and temper the potential dangers that prevail. Technological literacy and implementation is not merely a response to a problem but an important and life-long part of professional development and training. For better or worse, the availability of various technologies and how we apply them in mental health will continue to change. Changes will be pleasant or unpleasant, in large part determined by our technical competency, our ability to adapt to change, and, most important, our ability to harness technology in ways that promote our goals of helping clients.

REFERENCES

Association for Counselor Education and Supervision Technology Interest Network. (1999). *Technical competencies for counselor education students: Recommended guidelines for program development.* Available at http://www.acesonline.net/

Association for Counselor Education and Supervision. (2007). *Technical competencies for counselor education: Recommended guidelines for program development.* Available at http://www.aces online.net/

Anthony, K., & Nagel, D. (2010). *Therapy online: A practical guide.* Basingstoke: Palgrave Macmillan.

Bandura, A. (1986). *Social foundations of thought and action: A social cognitive theory.* Englewood Cliffs, NJ: Prentice-Hall.

Cabannis, K. (2002). Computer-related technology use by counselors in the new millennium: A delphi study. *Journal of Technology in Counseling, 2*(2). Retrieved February 5, 2003, from http://jtc.colstate.edu/vol2_2/cabaniss/cabaniss.htm

Casey, J. A., Bloom, J. W., & Moan, E. R. (1994). Use of technology in counselor supervision. In L. D. Borders (Ed.), *Counseling supervision.* Greensboro: University of North Carolina, ERIC Clearinghouse on Counseling and Student Services. (ERIC Document Reproduction Service No. ED372357)

Coursol, D. H., & Woitte, S. (1998). *Cybersupervision: Strategies for improving the internship experience.* Paper presented at the annual meeting of the North Central Association of Counselor Educators and Supervisors, Kansas City, MO.

Croft, V. (1991). *Technological literacy: Refined for the profession, applications for the classroom.* Unpublished paper presented at the 1991 annual conference of the International Technology Education Association. Quoted in "Technological literacy re-considered" by W. B. Waetjen, *Journal of Technology Education, 4*(2), 1993. Available at http://scholar .lib.vt.edu/ejournals/JTE/v4n2/pdf/waetjen.pdf

Fanning, J. M. (1994). Integrating academics and technology: Uncovering staff development needs. In J. Willis, B. Robin, & D. A. Willis (Eds.), *Technology and teacher education annual, 1994* (pp. 331–334). Washington, DC: Association for the Advancement of Computing in Education.

Fenichel, M., Suler, J., Barak, A., Zelvin, E., Jones, G., Munro, K., Meunier, V., & Walker-Schmucker, W. (2002). Myths and realities of online clinical work. *CyberPsychology and Behavior, 5,* 481–497.

Finkelstein, D. (2009). *A closer look at the principal-counselor relationship: A survey of principals and counselors.* New York: The College Board. Available at http://professionals.collegeboard .com/profdownload/a-closer-look.pdf

Goss, S., & Anthony, K. (2009). Developments in the use of technology in counselling and psychotherapy. *British Journal of Guidance & Counselling, 37*(3), 223–230.

Hayden, M. (1989). What is technological literacy? *Bulletin of Science, Technology and Society, 119,* 220–233.

Hayden, L., Poynton, T. A., & Sabella, R. A. (2008). School counselors' use of technology within the ASCA National Model's delivery system. *Journal of Technology in Counseling, 5*(1). Available at http://jtc.colstate.edu/Vol5_1/Index.htm

International Technology Education Association. (2007). *Standards for technological literacy: Content for the study of technology* (3rd ed.). International Technology Education Association. Retrieved May 6, 2010, from http://www.iteaconnect.org/TAA/PDFs/xstnd.pdf

Jones, G., & Stokes, A. (2009). *Online counselling: A handbook for practitioners.* London, UK: Palgrave Macmillan.

Koufman-Frederick, A., Lillie, M., Pattison-Gordon, L., Watt, D. L., & Carter, R. (1999). *Electronic collaboration: A practical guide for educators.* Providence, RI: The LAB at Brown University. [Online]. Available at http://www.alliance.brown.edu/pubs/collab/elec-collab.pdf

Lago, C. (1996). Computer therapeutics. *Counselling, 7,* 287–289.

Lee, C. C. (2000). Cybercounseling and empowerment: Bridging the digital divide. In J. W. Bloom & G. Walz. (Eds.), *Cybercounseling and cyberlearning: Strategies and resources for the millennium* (pp. 85–95). Alexandria, VA: American Counseling Association.

Lindsay, G. (1988). Techniques and technology–Strengthening the counseling profession via computer use: Responding to the issues. *The School Counselor, 35,* 325–330.

Manhal-Baugus, M. (2000). *E-therapy: Practical, ethical, and legal issues.* Retrieved March, 25, 2006, from http://cybercounsel.uncg.edu/articals/etherapy.htm

Murphy, L., MacFadden, R., & Mitchell, D. (2008). Cybercounseling online: The development of a university-based training program for e-mail counseling. *Journal of Technology in Human Services, 26*(2-4), 447–469.

Myrick, R. D., & Sabella, R. A. (1995). Cyberspace: New place for counselor supervision. *Elementary School Guidance & Counseling, 30*(1), 35–44.

NationMaster. (2008). *Technological literacy.* Retrieved January 4, 2009, from http://www.nationmaster.com/encyclopedia/Technological-literacy

Ookita, S., & Tokuda, H. (2001). Virtual therapeutic environment with user projective agents. *CyberPsychology & Behavior, 4*(1), 155–167.

Owen, S., & Heywood, J. (1988). Transition technology in Ireland. *International Journal of Research in Design and Technology Education, 1*(1), 21–32

Phillips, A. (2008). *Asperger's therapy hits Second Life: Experts express concern about applying online actions to real life.* Available at http://abcnews.go.com/Technology/OnCall/story?id=4133184&page=1

Pollock, S. (2006). Internet counseling and its feasibility for marriage and family counseling. *Family Journal, 14*(1), 65–70.

Poynton, T. A. (2005). Computer literacy across the lifespan: A review with implications for educators. *Computers in Human Behavior, 21*(12), 861–872.

Rogers, C. R. (1957). The necessary and sufficient conditions of therapeutic personality change. *Journal of Consulting Psychology, 21,* 95–103.

Sabella, R. A. (1998). Practical technology applications for peer helper programs and training. *Peer Facilitator Quarterly, 15*(2), 4–13.

Sabella, R. A. (2003). *SchoolCounselor.com: A friendly and practical guide to the world wide web* (2nd ed.). Minneapolis, MN: Educational Media Corporation.

Sabella, R. A. (2008). *GuardingKids.com: A practical guide to keeping kids out of high-tech trouble.* Minneapolis, MN: Educational Media Corporation.

Sabella, R. A. (2010). *Technology tools for facilitating school counselor and school administrator collaboration.* Unpublished manuscript.

Sabella, R. A., Poynton, T. A., & Isaacs, M. L. (2010). School counselors perceived importance of counseling technology competencies. *Computers in Human Behavior, 26*(4), 609–617.

Sampson, J. P., Jr. (1990). Computer-assisted testing and the goals of counseling psychology. *The Counseling Psychologist, 18,* 227–239.

Sampson, J. P., Jr., Kolodinsky, R. W., & Greeno, B. P. (1997). Counseling on the information highway: Future possibilities and potential problems. *Journal of Counseling and Development, 75*(3), 203–213.

Sampson, J. P., Jr., & Krumboltz, J. D. (1991). Computer-assisted instruction: A missing link in counseling. *Journal of Counseling & Development, 69,* 395–397.

Saskatchewan Education. (2002). *Understanding the common essential learnings: A handbook for teachers.* Regina, SK: Author.

Scherl, C. R., & Haley, J. (2000). Computer monitor supervision: A clinical note. *The American Journal of Family Therapy, 28,* 275–282.

Steffens, H. (1986). Issues in the preparation of teachers for teaching robotics in schools. In J. Heywood & P. Matthews (Eds.), *Technology, society and the school curriculum.* Manchester, England: Roundthorn Publishing.

Tyler, J. M., & Guth, L. J. (2003). *Understanding online counseling services through a review of definitions and elements necessary for change.* Available at http://bit.ly/bWtNWT

Tyler, J. M., & Sabella, R. A. (2004). *Using technology to improve counseling practice: A primer for the 21st century.* Alexandria, VA: American Counseling Association.

Waetjen, W. B. (1993). Technological literacy reconsidered. *Journal of Technology Education. 4*(2). Retrieved May 6, 2010, from http://scholar.lib.vt.edu/ejournals/JTE/v4n2/waetjen .jte-v4n2.html

Walz, G. R. (1996). Using the I-Way for career development. In R. Feller & G. Walz (Eds.), *Optimizing life transitions in turbulent times: Exploring work, learning and careers* (pp. 415–427). Greensboro: University of North Carolina, ERIC Clearinghouse on Counseling and Student Services.

Web 2.0. (2008, September 1). In Wikipedia, The Free Encyclopedia. Retrieved September 1, 2008, from http://en.wikipedia.org/w/index.php?title=Web_2.0&oldid=235590596

Winfeld, L. (2004). Web conferencing made simple. *Communications News, 41*(6), p. 14–16.

Wong, Y., & Law, C. (2002). *Online counseling for the youth in Hong Kong: A synchronized approach.* Retrieved June 21, 2002, from http://www2.uta.edu/cussn/husita/proposals/wong.htm

Chapter 21

THE FUTURE OF PROFESSIONAL COUNSELING

ARTIS J. PALMO, WILLIAM J. WEIKEL, AND DAVID P. BORSOS

Predicting the future of any profession is obviously fraught with danger. The best prognosticators often err and end up wiping symbolic egg from their reddened faces. Forty years ago, we were encouraged to learn the German language because we would need to know the language to advance in our careers. Germany had all of the best scientists, including the founders of counseling and psychotherapy, such as Freud, Adler, and Jung. The German language would be the international language of all sciences. Another foolproof prediction gets fooled. It seems that with each passing decade, we are bombarded with predictions that do not come to fruition. The Cold War produced numerous frightful predictions about the future and whether we would survive the threats of the Eastern Bloc countries. Obviously, many of those predictions proved to be wrong.

Predicting or anticipating the direction of the counseling profession may be as foolhardy as attempting to predict the behaviors of the world's powers. Yet based on the recent trends and phenomenal growth of the profession, we can make some predictions about the profession's future direction. We have characterized the types of changes, demands, and expectations of the future into three categories: (a) factors and forces the professional counselor will face for sure in the future, (b) factors and forces *most likely* to be faced in the future, and (c). factors and forces to be faced that are a little more *up in the air.*

21ST CENTURY SOCIETAL ATTITUDES

One of the more important factors in the growth of the profession of counseling has been the steady evolution of the acceptance of and need for counseling by society in general. Just 35 years ago, people rarely talked of attending counseling/psychotherapy sessions. Going to psychotherapy was seen as a personal weakness or sign of being "crazy" or unstable. In fact, the original edition of this text noted that one of the major selling points for the profession of counseling was the name itself (Palmo, 1986). Surveys showed that the general population was much more comfortable with the term *counseling* compared with terms such as *psychotherapy* or *psychological assessment.*

In fact, in1972, the Democratic Vice-Presidential candidate, Senator Thomas Eagleton, was pressured to quit the ticket once it was discovered that he had been treated for depression. Contrast this with the Democratic presidential ticket of 1992 comprised of Bill Clinton and Al Gore. Both men spoke openly of their experiences with counseling to assist them in handling various family dysfunction and losses. No one across America even blinked. It became common knowledge that Clinton was raised by an alcoholic, abusive stepfather and that Gore suffered through the agonies of his son being hit by a car and a sister who died an early death from lung cancer. Tipper Gore, the vice-president's wife, has a master's degree in counseling and became a vocal and open advocate for many mental health and counseling issues. In fact, the open discussion of these topics was often seen as a strength by the public, rather than a weakness, because both men seemed more human and in touch with the issues of the "common man."

The *societal acceptance* and *encouragement of counseling* is now so common and ubiquitous that we barely notice its societal manifestations. Public figures talk openly of their mental health problems and their treatments. Talk show host Oprah Winfrey spoke openly of her counseling and its benefits and then launched the career of psychologist, Dr. Phil McGraw, into the living rooms and bookstores across America. Tiger Woods sought treatment for sexual addiction in an attempt to save his marriage. Many other well-known people have spoken openly of their mental health struggles, thus increasing the normalization of counseling for everyone in society in need of help. This list includes people such as Roseann Barr, Patty Duke-Austin, and Mike Wallace of "60 Minutes" fame. The hard rock band, Metallica, even released a documentary about the use of group counseling in an attempt to keep the band together and to assist in the resolution of problems that erupted among band members.

Popular culture has helped normalize the use of mental health counseling in many other ways. Think of Mafia don, Tony Soprano, going to therapy on the HBO series, *The Sopranos.* Movies such as *What About Bob?, Patch Adams,* and *The Prince of Tides* portray different counseling experiences as an acceptable part of life. Every bookstore has an ever-expanding shelf line of *self-help,* counseling, and psychotherapy books dealing with topics as diverse as addictions, bi-polar disorder, phobia, and marriage counseling. The Public Broadcasting System (PBS) often shows a series on counseling alcoholics and their families given by John Bradshaw.

As society has become more aware of the various mental health issues that can interfere with people's lives, it has accepted the counseling profession as a necessary and integral part of the array of basic health care services. This acceptance and open acknowledgment of counseling has led to the expansion of services and counseling programming around the country, leading us to believe that there will be continued growth of the profession in the future. With this thought in mind, let us take a look at what the future holds for the Professional Counselor.

Factors and Forces the Professional Counselor Will Face *for Sure* in the Future

Societal Effect of Divorce/Remarriage

This particular topic is listed first because the societal impact of divorce and remarriage has touched all aspects of life. The Professional Counselor will need to be familiar with the treatment and research literature on the impact of divorce on adults and children. There is no aspect of society that is not influenced by the fallout of the breakdown of marital and family relationships. No matter what specialty to which the counseling student aspires, his or her work will be touched by the impact of the changes in the marital and family structure in today's society.

For example, while working with a very agitated, tearful gentleman of age 86 who resided in an assisted living facility, it was determined that his present emotional state was related to some sad and traumatic memories of his first marriage and divorce. Although his three adult children never knew he was married to someone other than their mother, the counselor learned that he remained saddened by the events and decisions leading to his first marriage. The point being, no matter what area of expertise you develop in the field of counseling, you will need to be familiar with the impact and changes that arise for the individual and family as a result of marriage, divorce, and remarriage. This discussion provides a lead-in to the next section.

Need for a Working Understanding of Family Structures

Alfred Adler would be pulling his hair out trying to understand the modern-day family constellation. In the authors' day, we simply had older and younger brothers and sisters–not true in today's world. One of the first steps in the counseling process for the counselor working with children, the elderly, or anybody is determining the family patterns of the individual early as well as later in life. The first step is understanding that there are an infinite number of potential family structures in today's society; but more important, it is critical to understand that the impact of the changing family structures leaves an indelible mark on the individual.

So whether you are doing career counseling or play therapy, you will need to know how to account for brothers and sisters, stepbrothers and stepsisters, as well as half brothers and half sisters! In practice, we have seen the adult child of divorce be devastated by the impact of the divorced father abandoning his own children for the stepchildren or neglecting his older children for the new baby he has had with the second wife. The point being, as you progress in the profession, you will have to understand the psychological research and treatment methods for working with those impacted by divorce and changing family structures.

We would be remiss to not mention the family structures involving gay and lesbian individuals and couples. Those professionals actively involved in the treatment of couples and families have been faced with new challenges. Because society has generally become more accepting of gay and lesbian couples, counselors will need to have an understanding of the effects of such changes on the family structure. Whether it is the adolescent attempting to deal with the information that his parents are divorcing because one parent is gay or a preteen attempting to come to terms with the issues of being adopted into a family with gay parents, it is clear that society and family structures are changing.

Understanding the Courts and Legal System

Fortunately or unfortunately, counseling has been integrated into various parts of society where it has barely or rarely existed until recently. The court system routinely refers defendants for assessment and treatment as part of the sentencing process or simply in an attempt to resolve a problem through counseling/mediation rather than through a trial. Problems relating to issues such as drug and alcohol abuse, spousal or child abuse, divorce, aggression, impulsivity, delinquency, or gambling are seen as counseling as well as legal issues. Counseling those convicted of crimes is accepted by society as being as important as simply punishing them with incarceration or fines. In addition, many counseling interventions and programs exist to aid the victims of crimes. It is relatively easy to predict a larger and larger role for counseling professionals within the court system because of more concerted efforts by the government to rehabilitate defendants rather than simply put them behind bars. Once again, regardless of the specialty developed by the counseling professional, he or she will have to be familiar with the workings of the court and the laws affecting those utilizing the court system. Professional Counselors will be unable to avoid the impact of the legal system on their practice.

Impact of Trauma and PTSD on Clients

As noted throughout the book, the impact of trauma on an individual is devastating and leaves long-lasting emotional scars. Whether the individual has suffered childhood sexual abuse (Hernandez et al., 2009), family violence (Ben-Poriat & Itzhaky, 2009), or post-traumatic stress disorder (PTSD) (Mueser, Rosenberg, & Rosenberg, (2009), the effect on the individual's psyche can be lifelong. Working with a family who lost a seven-year-old child in an auto accident is an appropriate example. The mother who was driving the car when the child was killed was haunted by guilt for not being more careful in her driving (the accident was not her fault), depressed by the loss of her oldest child, and angry at the driver of the other vehicle. The father, who was not in the car, suffered guilt for not being there when his daughter was needed, devastation at the horrific death of his daughter, and worry about their other daughter who survived. The surviving daughter, only five years old, was in disbelief that her sister was gone and never returning.

This example reflects the long-term effects of trauma and tragedy in the lives of individuals. This couple went on to have two more children in an attempt to solidify their family and hopefully fill in the space left by the death of the first child. The point of note is that when one of the two younger daughters presents for counseling, it will be important to know her family history to appropriately treat her. Even though she was not around when her sister died, that family trauma directly affects her emotional status because she has lived her life with three others who were never the same after the accident. The Professional Counselor has to be familiar with the effects of trauma in order to appropriately treat those individuals seeking services (see Section IV).

It is apparent that today's world is forever changing and more dangerous than ever. As noted in Section IV, terrorism, disasters, and trauma have become major worries and a reality for most Americans. More and more of Professional Counselors' training will include the handling of stress reactions and fears because of the traumas of people's daily lives. The general public has developed a greater awareness of the effects of traumatic situations on the daily functioning of individuals. Sexual abuse and assaults, emotional abuse, threats of terrorism, and other similar problems have led to a situation where more and more professional assistance is needed to help those in trouble. The ripple effects of 9/11 on the general population were overwhelming. In the future, there will be an even greater need for trained counselors who are effective with PTSD types of diagnoses.

Schools

Public and private schools routinely integrate counseling into their student services above and beyond the services of the school counselor. Guidance counselors have existed for many years to help with academic or college issues. However, schools have increasingly expanded services to include mental health counseling for students and their families. Many schools have brought Professional Counselors into their buildings to treat students. The counselors lead groups, offer individual counseling to students, consult with the teaching staff, and consult/counsel with parents. They treat such problems as teenage pregnancies, child abuse, runaways, depression, suicidal ideation, substance abuse, self-esteem issues, and much more.

It is apparent that the Professional Counselor's role within the school system will continue to expand over the next decade. There will be more attention given to those students who are not functioning in school or the community. Working with school-age children and adolescents will be an ever-expanding and reliable source of opportunity for the effective Professional Counselor.

Expansion of Treatments for Children and Adolescents

In addition to schools, Professional Counselors have taken a more active role in the administration and treatment of individuals and families through resources in the community. The teenager who has become too much of a problem in school is often placed in a program operated by the local government or conglomeration of schools for the treatment of the difficult child. Adult schizophrenics who no longer have the support of their family will utilize community resources to survive and improve. The various community agencies and programs have become major resources for employment for the Professional Counselor. Community-operated treatment programs will significantly expand over the next 10 years, providing a valuable professional opportunity for counselors. This includes the growing use of the "recovery model" for the chronically mentally ill rather than the recent maintenance models of treatment.

Need for Working Knowledge of Substance Abuse/Addiction Treatment

When looking into the future of professional counseling, nothing is more imposing that the need for well-trained and competent counselors who can identify, treat, and/or refer those individuals suffering from addictions (Laudet & White, 2010). EVERY Professional Counselor will deal with addictions in one form or another no matter where they practice their trade. The Professional Counselor providing services for children may think, "Well, I am safe from dealing with addiction," but they are wrong! Children at very young ages can be addicted to computer games, sometimes drugs, and other self-abusive behaviors. More important, the parents of the children served may have a major substance use disorder. No professional will escape the impact of addictions, and it is clear that the upcoming decade will experience an ever-increasing demand for counselors who can handle the problem.

It is quite apparent that there will continue to be a critical need for counselors to serve the field of addictions in both inpatient and outpatient programs. It would behoove the new graduate student in counseling to enroll in as many formal and informal training seminars as possible that deal with treatment for addictions. Substance abuse is a serious problem for many Americans and will continue to be a problem in the foreseeable future. Professional Counselors will have more and more opportunities in this area.

In addition to substance abuse, professional counseling will grow to include more and more work with other addictions, such as gambling, pornography, computer games, chat rooms, overeating, and a plethora of other concerns. Professional Counselors will need to have as much training as possible in the area of addictions because of the overwhelming number of serious problems that exists in society today. Addictions will be a major growth area for Professional Counselors.

Business

Although the human resources personnel have been the source for counseling and referral within the business world, there has been more and more use of counseling services and coaching. Rather than simply terminate employees, more and more companies have established services through Employee Assistance Programs (EAPs) to assist in identifying, assessing, referring, and treating employees who are problematic at work due to mental health issues, stress, or other life concern. The list of concerns handled by the EAPs has grown from addictions to include marital stress, problem children, gambling, chronic lateness, explosive behaviors at work, and many others.

Diversity and Social Concerns

It is clear that society will continue to shift and change throughout the foreseeable future. As noted in various chapters in the book, being able to accept cultural changes and shifts, alternate lifestyles, gay marriage, and a myriad of other changes is paramount for the Professional Counselor. Professional personal belief systems will be tested on a daily basis! All of us will have to examine and re-examine our values to determine our ability to treat individuals, families, and groups who are "different" from us–this will be the true test of Professional Counselors in the upcoming years.

Clearly, examples from business and education reflect the enormous shift in societal attitudes regarding the use of mental health counseling in a variety of non-traditional settings with groups of non-traditional clients. Not only is counseling seen as important, but institutions are putting time, personnel, and money into improving the lives of students, employees, and their families regardless of their personal situations or beliefs. Mental health as a profession will take greater strides to be inclusive and reduce the barriers that inhibit the progress and growth of any individual (Barnett, 2009b).

Psychopharmacology

There are two parts to the discussion about psychopharmacology. First, every mental health professional will need to educate themselves regarding the ever-increasing use of medications in the treatment of mental health problems. No matter what the setting, each professional needs to have an understanding of the effects of the many medications in use today to treat depression, anxiety, attention deficit, panic, and a myriad of diagnoses.

Second, there will be a continuing trend toward more and more of the distribution of drugs through the family practice physician. Because there is an overall shortage of availability of psychiatrists, especially in rural areas, more and more pressure to prescribe psychotropic medications falls in the lap of the family physician. The success of psychologists in gaining prescriptive authority in New Mexico and Lousianna (Fox, DeLeon, Newman, Sammons, Dunivin, & Baker, 2009) is an indication of the problem that exists in providing effective psychiatric care in some areas. Counselors will have a more important role in advising the family physician about the mental health needs of their patients, which will require more expertise in the use of medications.

Acceptance and Tolerance of Technology

Whether we like it or not, electronically mediated communications among individuals and groups is here to stay. Koocher (2009), discussing electronically mediated mental health, reports that video conferencing and distance learning modalities are already being used in mental health research and treatment, and it is highly likely that it will expand over the upcoming years. Garb (2009) writes about the use of computer administrated instruments to assist in "screening and diagnosis of mental disorders and . . . identification of treatment problems and monitoring of the course of psychotherapy" (p. 141). Imagine, *monitoring the course of psychotherapy!*

In addition to these uses, there are other important ways that technology will become a part of the practice of counseling. For example, managing the day-to-day activities of an office would be next to impossible without technology. From scheduling clients, to collecting money, to maintaining records, technology is a major facet of the counseling world. There are concerns about the use of technology in counseling because of privacy concerns (Richards, 2009), but new and veteran counselors will have to improve their technology expertise to effectively manage their practice as well as provide the best services for clients.

Factors and Forces the Professional Counselor Will Face *Most Likely* in the Future

Expanding Specialization

Counseling opportunities have grown and will continue to do so in certain specialty areas. With the extensive list of problems being faced by individuals, families, and groups, the potential areas for growth for the Professional Counselor are quite numerous. In addition to the issues surrounding everyone in society, there are other areas of change that will have a significant effect on the growth of the profession.

Gerontology. As noted in Chapter 5, there will be a major shift in the U.S. population over the next two decades, leading to more people being retired and living to be quite old. The need for counselors with geriatric training will be overwhelming, but as Drs. Myers and Shannonhouse notes in their chapter, the enrollment of students in geriatric programs has been miniscule. This one area will expand 10 times over the next decade or two, leaving many challenging and exciting opportunities for the Professional Counselor. Geriatrics can be a rewarding field, and the need will be great in the near future. As a major aspect of the gerontology, the growth of hospice treatment facilities will expand, and the need for hospice mental health professionals will also expand.

PTSD Counseling. As noted in the earlier section of this chapter, professional counseling will play a larger role in treating trauma victims. With the extended war over the previous decade, the need for mental health professionals to work with military personnel and related staff will be tremendous. In fact, the Army is actively recruiting mental health professionals through the Wounded Warrior Program.

Coaching. The most recent trend has been the use of professional coaches to assist with daily living. Business professionals seek assistance with everyday planning and organization, utilizing coaches for advice and direct suggestions. Coaching has managed to circumvent the insurance dilemma, thereby leaving the counselor/coach free of many practice restrictions. Coaches not only deal with business professionals but also are available to assist the individual in daily decisions, whether it be a housewife or an individual looking for assistance with managing his or her daily life. Coaching appears to be an area of growth and related to the training of the Professional Counselor.

Related Areas of Change

Parity: Increases in Counselor Fees and Rates. Parity means having mental health services and coverage on an equal basis with other health care services and coverage. Recent legislation has created parity for mental health, meaning that insurance companies have to recognize that mental health issues are equally important in the overall health of the individual (Clay, 2008; Glied & Frank, 2008; Koyanagi, 2009; Patel & Wells, 2009; Trevedi, Swaminathan, & Mor, 2008).

Although there are both pros and cons to the situation, it remains clear that the master's-level Professional Counselors are "cheaper" than doctoral-level psychologists. The insurance industry has now learned that they can circumvent the costs of psychologists by choosing social workers or counselors for their panels. Professional Counselors will find that the insurance industry will be pursuing them to provide services primarily because they are affordable and not because they have exceptional training. The good news for counselors is that they are in demand and will continue to be in demand, but the bad news is that they will provide services at cheaper levels.

Health Care. It is apparent from the rapid changes happening in the field that Professional Counselors will find that they have a broader array of settings available for employment. For example, more and more nursing homes, assisted living facilities, and hospitals are employing counselors to work with clients and staff. The ever-expanding role of mental health services in health care (Johnson & Radcliffe, 2008) has arisen because of the evidence that good health and good mental health are inextricably connected. In the new role, counselors are not only asked to counsel but are asked to consult with staff about issues related to better serving clients. The new roles for counselors are psycho-educational in nature and call for them to be effective in educating the constituents about the need for taking care of their emotional selves in order to have a full and complete life. Another aspect of the growing opportunities in health care is the expanding field of grief counseling.

Treatment of the Chronically Mentally Ill. With the changes in the views of society regarding the treatment of the chronically mental ill, no longer warehousing the patients has provided a wide variety of professional positions in the community. Serving the chronically mentally ill in special schools, treatment facilities, group homes, and a wide variety of community placements will provide a plethora of work opportunities for counselors over the next decade.

Forensics: Expanding Field of Interest. The expanding field of forensics that has grown beyond the criminal field will provide many opportunities for counselors in the foreseeable future. Barnett (2009a) was an editor for a series of brief exposes regarding forensics in family law. The various authors stated that the use of mental health professionals to provide mediation, parent training, child counseling, and other services through domestic relations will be expanding. The professionals who choose this direction for their future will need special training and specific skills to deal with the many aspects of issues related to divorce. The major concern with this area of treatment and assessment is that it is filled with potential ethical and legal problems for the professional. A Professional Counselor has to be aware of the potential "potholes in the road" when they choose to develop a career involving child custody and divorce.

Factors and Forces the Professional Counselor Where the *Jury Is Still Out*

Evidence-Based Practice (EBP)

Hunsley (2007) provides a comprehensive definition of EBP, stating that it "involves the integration of information drawn from systematically collected data, clinical expertise, and patient preferences when considering service options for patients" (p. 113). There are numerous discussions regarding EBP in the literature, reporting that it is effective in directing treatment (Bobbitt, 2006) and determining therapy effectiveness, on the one hand, and a conflicting view about the intrusion of EBP into the therapeutic environment, on the other hand (Goodheart, 2004). Regardless, EBP will more than likely be a part of the mental health care discussions into the foreseeable future. It would behoove the Professional Counselor to investigate and study this important area because EBP will be a major aspect of the impetus to have "hard" data regarding client improvement that is being pushed by managed care and insurance companies.

Counseling Without Walls

There has been more and more discussion among our colleagues about the use of technology to be able to offer counseling services to clients who are at home or unable to come to the counselor's office. Early in our careers, during client emergencies, we often did phone sessions to attempt to alleviate whatever crises were presented. However, with e-mail, texting, Facebook, and other electronic communication systems, the ability to work with clients through other media is possible. Those early phone sessions were generally not covered by insurance, so the client had to pay out of pocket or the counselor just accepted that phone consults/counseling were a part of their responsibility.

Regardless of whether you accept the use of electronic communications, there will be more and more counseling done without walls. There are numerous potential problems with the "office without walls," such as privacy issues and confidentiality, data to support the effectiveness of the methods used, reinforcing those clients with social anxiety but allowing them to remain at home, and the lack of rules for doing such counseling. There is a lot to consider with the expansion of counseling in the electronic age. New counseling professionals will need to clarify their position on the issue and be able to support their stance to other professionals.

Self-Help Books and Materials

According to Redding, Herbert, Forman, and Gaudiano (2008), "Self-help books for psychological disorders have become increasingly popular, yet there is surprisingly little research on their scientific status or overall utility" (p. 537). However, the use of books, tapes, and videos in counseling continues to be one of the major adjuncts in the counselor's toolbox. This area of self-help will continue to grow even though there are little data to support the effectiveness other than self-reports from clients who tell their counselor whether they thought the book or video was helpful. Dr. Phil has made counseling popular and the process appears simple; however, the process is not simple and more than likely cannot be effectively condensed into a book or a TV episode. It is likely that the self-help movement will continue to grow and expand because of the previously mentioned growth of the media and electronics field.

Alternative Types of Counseling

Over the years, numerous variations in the counseling process have been proposed and utilized. The literature is replete with various titles of new and/or exciting methods that are being used, such as Mindfulness (Carmody,

Baer, Lykins, & Olendzki, 2009; Greason & Cashwell, 2009; McCown & Reible, 2010), Eye Movement Desensitization and Reprocessing (Cook, Biyanova, & Coyne, 2009), Motivational Interviewing (Slagle & Gray, 2007); Spirituality (Miller & Thoresen, 2003), and so on. The important points to consider are that (a) there will continue to be an accumulation of various techniques/methods of counseling that claim to offer relief for clients, (b) two, every one of the new approaches advertised will have to be carefully assessed by each of us.

One Final Note

Our careers that began in the late 1960s are winding down as your career as a graduate student is preparing to take off. We have had a ride that was sometimes bumpy, but always exciting, and we invite you to strap in and get ready for a ride that will be sure to enthrall and perhaps land you in some exciting places!

REFERENCES

Barnett, J. E. (2009a). Ethical and professional considerations in the divorce and child custody cases. *Professional Psychology: Research and Practice, 40,* 539–549.

Barnett, J. E. (2009b). Psychologists, APA, and diversity: Too close for comfort? *Independent Practitioner, 29,* 68–71.

Ben-Porat, A., & Itzhaky, H. (2009). Implications of treating family violence for the therapist: Secondary traumatization, vicarious traumatization, and growth. *Journal of Family Violence, 24,* 507–515.

Bobbitt, B. L. (2006). The importance of professional psychology: A view from managed care. *Professional Psychology: Research and Practice, 37,* 590–597.

Carmody, J., Baer, R. A., Lykins, L. B., & Olendzki, N. (2009). An empirical study of the mechanisms of mindfulness in a mindfulness-based stress reduction program. *Journal of Clinical Psychology, 65,* 613–626.

Clay, R. A. (2008). Parity: What does the law mean? *Substance Abuse and Mental Health Services Administration, 16,* 1–4.

Cook, J. M., Biyanova, T., & Coyne, J. C. (2009). Comparative case study of diffusion of Eye Movement Desensitization and Reprocessing in two clinical settings: Empirically supported treatment status is not enough. *Professional Psychology: Research and Practice, 40,* 518–524.

Fox, R. E., DeLeon, P. H., Newman, R., Sammons, M. T., Dunivin, D. L., & Baker, D. C. (2009). Prescriptive authority and psychology: A status report. *American Psychologist, 64,* 257–268.

Garb, H. N. (2009). Computer interviews and rating scales. *Independent Practitioner, 29,* 141–144.

Glied, S. A., & Frank, R. G. (2008). Shuffling toward parity: Bringing mental health care under the umbrella. *New England Journal of Medicine, 359,* 113–115.

Goodheart, C. (2004). Evidence-based practice and the endeavor of psychotherapy. *Independent Practitioner, 24,* 6–10.

Greason, P. B., & Cashwell, C. S. (2009). Mindfulness and counseling self-efficacy: The mediating role of attention and empathy. *Counselor Education and Supervision, 49,* 2–19.

Hernandez, A., Ruble, C., Rockmore, L., McKay, M., Messam, T., Harris, M., & Hope, S. (2009). An integrated approach to treating non-offending parents affected by sexual abuse. *Social Work in Mental Health, 7,* 533–555.

Hunsley, J. (2007). Addressing key challenges in evidenced-based practice in psychology. *Professional Psychology: Research and Practice, 37,* 590–597.

Johnson, N. G., & Radcliffe, A. M. (2008). The increasing role of psychology health research and interventions and a vision for the future. *Professional Psychology: Research and Practice, 38,* 113–121.

Koocher, G. P. (2009). Any minute now but not far away: Electronically mediated mental health. *Clinical Psychology: Science and Practice, 16,* 339–342.

Koyanagi, C. (2009). Can we learn from history? Mental health care reform, revisited. *Psychiatric Services, 60,* 17–20.

Laudet, A. B., & White, W. (2010). What are your priorities right now? Identifying service needs across recovery stages to inform service development. *Journal of Substance Abuse Treatment, 38,* 51–59.

McCown, D., & Reibel, D. (2010). Mindfulness and mindfulness-based reduction. In D. A. Monti & B. D. Beitman (Eds.), *Integrative psychiatry* (pp. 289–338). New York: Oxford University Press.

Miller, W. R., & Thoresen, C. E. (2003). Spirituality, religion, and health: An emerging research field. *American Psychologist, 58,* 24–35.

Mueser, K. T., Rosenberg, S. D., & Rosenberg, H. J. (2009). *Treatment of posttraumatic stress disorder in special populations: A cognitive restructuring program.* Washington, DC: American Psychological Association.

Palmo, A. J. (1986). Professional identity of the mental health counselor. In A. J. Palmo & W. J. Weikel (Eds.), *Foundations of mental health counseling* (pp. 39–56). Springfield, IL: Charles C Thomas.

Patel, K., & Wells, K. (2009). Applying health care reform principles to mental health and substance abuse services. *Journal of the American Medical Association, 302,* 1463–1464.

Redding, R. E., Herbert, J. D., Forman, E. M., & Gaudiano, B. A. (2008). Popular self-help books for anxiety, depression, and trauma: How scientifically grounded and useful are they? *Professional Psychology: Research and Practice, 39,* 537–545.

Richards, M. M. (2009). Electronic medical records: Confidentiality issues in the time of HIPAA. *Professional Psychology: Research and Practice, 40,* 550–556.

Slagle, D. M., & Gray, M. J. (2007). The utility of motivational interviewing as an adjunct to exposure therapy in the treatment of anxiety disorders. *Professional Psychology: Research and Practice, 38,* 329–337.

Trivedi, A. N., Swaminathan, S., & Mor, V. (2008). Insurance parity and the use of outpatient mental health care following a psychiatric hospitalization. *Journal of the American Medical Association, 300,* 2879–2885.

ACRONYMS

Most professions have long lists of acronyms that are used by the members of those groups. Here are some of the most commonly used acronyms in the counseling profession and what they stand for. A few are no longer current, yet often appear in the literature.

AA–Alcoholics Anonymous
AoA–Administration on Aging
AACE–Association for Assessment in Counseling and Education
AADA–Association for Adult Development and Aging
AAGP–American Association for Geriatric Psychiatry
AAMFT–American Association for Marriage and Family Therapy
AASCB–American Association of State Counseling Boards
ACA–American Counseling Association
ACC–Association for Creativity in Counseling
ACCA–American College Counseling Association
ACEG–Association for Counselors and Educators in Government
ACES–Association for Counselor Education and Supervision
ADAMHA–Alcohol, Drug Abuse, and Mental Health Administration
ALC–Associate Licensed Counselor
ALGBTIC–Association for Lesbian, Gay, Bisexual, and Transgender Issues in Counseling
ALPC–Associate Licensed Professional Counselor
AMCD–Association for Multicultural Counseling and Development
AMHCA–American Mental Health Counselors Association
APA–American Psychiatric Association
APA–American Psychological Association
APGA–American Personnel and Guidance Association
ARCA–American Rehabilitation Counseling Association
ASCA–American School Counselor Association
ASERVIC–Association for Spiritual, Ethical, and Religious Values in Counseling

ASGW–Association for Specialists in Group Work
BLS–Bureau of Labor Statistics
BSFT–Brief Solution Focused Therapy
CACREP–Council on the Accreditation of Counseling and Related Educational Programs
C-AHEAD–Counseling Association for Humanistic Education and Development
CBM–Cognitive Behavior Modification
CCA–Canadian Counseling Association
CCMHC–Certified Clinical Mental Health Counselor
CPC–Certified Professional Counselor
CRC–Certified Rehabilitation Counselor
CSA–Child Sexual Abuse
CSJ–Counselors for Social Justice
DHHS–Department of Health and Human Services
DOT–Dictionary of Occupational Titles
DSM-IV–Diagnostic and Statistical Manual of Mental Disorders
DSM-V–Fifth Edition in press (2010)
ESEA–Elementary and Secondary Education Act
EBP–Evidenced-Based Practice
EBPP–Evidenced-Based Practice in Psychology
EMDR–Eye Movement Desensitization and Reprogramming
FEHBP–Federal Employees Health Benefits Program
GED–General Education Development Testing
GRE–Graduate Record Examination
HHS–Health and Human Services or DHHS (Department of)
HIPAA–Health Insurance Portability and Accountability Act
HMO–Health Maintenance Organization
IAAOC–International Association of Addictions and Offender Counselors
IAMFC–International Association of Marriage and Family Counselors
IP- Indemnity Plan
JCD–*Journal of Counseling and Development*
JMHC–*Journal of Mental Health Counseling*
LAC–Licensed Associate Counselor
LACMH–Licensed Associate Counselor of Mental Health
LAPC–Licensed Associate Professional Counselor
LCPC–Licensed Clinical Professional Counselor
LCSW–Licensed Clinical Social Worker
LIMHP–Licensed Interim Mental Health Professional
LMHC–Licensed Mental Health Counselor
LMHCA–Licensed Mental Health Counselor Associate

LMHP–Licensed Mental Health Professional
LPC–Licensed Professional Counselor
LPCC–Licensed Professional Clinical Counselor
LPCMH–Licensed Professional Counselor of Mental Health
LVI–Life Values Inventory
MAC–Masters Addiction Counselor
MBTI–Myers-Briggs Type Indicator
MCO–Managed Care Organization
MMPI–Minnesota Multiphasic Personality Inventory
NACCMHC–National Academy of Certified Clinical Mental Health Counselors (Now a part of NBCC)
NBCC–National Board for Certified Counselors
NCC–National Certified Counselor
NCCBH–National Council of Community Behavioral Healthcare
NCCC–National Certified Career Counselor
NCDA–National Career Development Association
NCE–National Certification Examination
NCGC–National Certified Gerontological Counselor
NCMHCE–National Clinical Mental Health Counselor Examination
NCSC–National Certified School Counselor
NDEA–National Defense Education Act
NECA–National Employment Counseling Association
NIMH–National Institute of Mental Health
NLP–Neuro Linguistic Programming
NVGA–National Vocational Guidance Association
OCHAMPUS–Office of Civilian Health and Medical Programs for the Uniformed Services (see TRICARE)
OOH–Occupational Outlook Handbook
PC–Professional Counselor
PFA–Protection from Abuse
PFA–Psychological First Aid
PLMHC–Provisional Licensed Mental Health Counselor
PLPC–Provisional Licensed Professional Counselor
PPO–Preferred Provider Organization
PRN–Practice Research Network
PTSD–Post-Traumatic Stress Disorder
REBT–Rational Emotive Behavioral Therapy
RBT–Rational Behavioral Therapy
RMHCI–Registered Mental Health Counseling Intern
SASSI–Substance Abuse Subtle Screening Inventory
SCII–Strong Campbell Interest Inventory

TRICARE–(replaced OCHAMPUS) Health Care for Military and Families
VA–Veteran's Administration

AUTHOR INDEX

C

D

H

I

J

M

Q

R

T

Y

Z

SUBJECT INDEX

B

C

R

V